Churchill's Indian Summer

To my parents,
Arthur and Marjorie Seldon

Churchill's Indian Summer

The Conservative Government, 1951–55

Anthony Seldon

HODDER AND STOUGHTON
LONDON SYDNEY AUCKLAND TORONTO

British Library Cataloguing in Publication Data

Seldon, Anthony
    Churchill's Indian summer.
    1. Great Britain – Constitutional history
    2. Great Britain – Politics and government –
    1945–
    I. Title
    354.41′0009   JN234

    ISBN 0-340-25456-4

Contents

Illustrations

Acknowledgments

1 Popperfoto
2 Universal Pictorial Press
3 BBC Hulton Picture Library
4 *Punch*

ix

A Note on Sources, Nomenclature and Terminology

The historian of post-war British history faces a formidable range of material for research. Not only the standard sources – Hansard, articles and books, but also, to a far greater extent than for earlier periods, he has access to interesting material and comment in newspapers, periodicals and lectures, and an ever-expanding amount of oral history (interview) evidence. An attempt has been made in the Bibliography to clarify these sources and to group published works into sections corresponding to the relevant chapters.

I chose to focus on two primary sources: private papers and diaries, where I was able to uncover much that was new, and interviews. No fact has been mentioned in the book unless it could be based on reliable evidence from more than one source. This was particularly the case with oral evidence, where, owing to the fallibility of memory, facts were cross-checked with written sources wherever this was possible. The aim has always been to disclose evidence for an opinion or statement of fact. Some people gave me access to private papers in their possession, however, but did not always wish me to disclose their names: accordingly reference is made just to *Private Papers* in the Notes. The only occasion where precise sources have not been given to support an important or controversial point is where statements were based on an interview and where either the interviewee or I felt it inappropriate to disclose his name. In such cases there is usually reference in the Notes made to *Private Information*.

A wider variety of secondary sources was employed. To eliminate the need of littering the notes with confusing *ibids* and *op cits*, the books and articles consulted were numbered (*1*) to (*300*). At an instant one can thus see the author's name, and those who seek further details can look up the number in the Bibliography. Although all the well-informed newspapers and periodicals of the day were consulted, for the sake of space I concentrated on just one daily, *The Times*, and three weeklies, *The Economist*, the *Observer* and the *Sunday Times*. The views expressed in them were usually sensible, and, relying substantially on just these four, especially *The Times*, had the great merit of providing comment from consistent view-points.

All references throughout the book were checked back to the source except. to my regret. unpublished material in the United States libraries. To avoid further cluttering of the Notes with a surfeit of information. precise references to volume and column numbers of Parliamentary debates are confined to those cases where direct quotation is made.

The most frequently cited reference in the Notes is Lord Moran's book on Churchill. It was found to be a remarkably accurate document in its reporting of fact. though Moran's own judgment was not always reliable. Not only does he give an exaggerated view of Churchill's poor state of health during 1951–5. inevitable perhaps as he tended only to see Churchill when the latter was ill. but he tends also on occasion to be over-credulous about what he was told or heard. He thus, for example. over-plays the significance of Harold Macmillan's part in inducing Churchill to retire. and accepts uncritically what Eden told him on the flight to the Bermuda Conference on 2nd December. 1953. that he wanted to give up the Foreign Office in favour of a domestic Department, but the move was blocked by Churchill. This is only a partial truth.

Moran records how he would write out notes immediately after leaving Churchill or one of his entourage. and says that these notes are reproduced exactly in the book. Yet many felt they had been misrepresented. Either they did not hold the views that Moran attributes to them or those views only represent a part of what they felt. After seeing Churchill. Moran would often call at the Private Office where he would pick up more news; the secretaries would listen to him with one ear and chat whilst continuing with their work. A valid criticism of Moran is indeed his tendency to give off-the-cuff remarks the status of considered judgments. The diary is thus an imperfect record. while at the same time being a minor work of art and an invaluable source for the period.

The policy on nomenclature is as follows. When an individual is first mentioned in any Chapter Part. his full name is given: thereafter only his surname usually appears. If he received a knighthood or was created a peer at any time up until the end of 1955. he appears with his new title (apart from some cases where given a title on leaving Government). A man ennobled or made a knight in 1956 or thereafter appears with his earlier rank or title. The exceptions are Winston Churchill and Anthony Eden. knighted respectively in 1953 and 1954 with the K.G.. who appear without their titles. R. A. Butler appears in his first mention in each section with the prefix 'Rab', the name by which he is widely known.

British Government has a complex array of different titles: an outline of the major terms to be found in the book may therefore be useful.[1] The explanation for the often confusing plethora of names and titles lies in the historical development of British Government. The position as it existed in the early 1950s is described below: much has since changed.

The older Departments (interchangeable in this book with 'Ministries') tended to be headed by a Secretary of State: thus the Home Office and Foreign Office. which have existed continuously since 1782. and the War Office since 1794, were headed by a Secretary of State. as were the Colonial Office (1854). Air Ministry (1917). Scottish Office (1926). and Commonwealth Relations Office (initially Dominions Office) from 1925. The title of 'Ministry'. headed by a Minister. first came into being in 1915 with the wartime Ministry of Munitions. and since the Ministry of Health was formed in 1919 this was the common term for all Departments not created (like the Commonwealth Relations Office) by the subdivision of an existing Department. Within Government Departments existed sub-groupings, known as divisions. departments or branches.

It is hard to say of what the Administration consisted. There were thousands of bodies. exercising legal powers delegated by the Queen or conferred by Parliament. In the Appendices of this book can be found a list of those Government Departments directly under the control of a Minister (Appendix II). and a limited selection of officers of the major non-ministerial bodies. nationalised industries. public authorities. boards and commissions (Appendix VI). The degree of autonomy of these bodies varied widely: the Boards of Inland Revenue and of Customs were so much under Treasury control they could almost be regarded as a part of that Department; the British Broadcasting Corporation. on the other hand. had so much independence that one could regard it almost as a private institution.

The political head of the older Departments was usually called a Secretary of State. and a Minister headed the newer Ministries. Junior Ministers were on two levels: the senior. named Minister of State. and below him Parliamentary Under-Secretaries (of State), the usual term in the older Departments. and Parliamentary Secretaries in Ministries. Ministers in the Treasury. the Service Departments. the Board of Trade and the Post Office had more specialised names. Further details of Ministers, including older non-departmental offices such as the Lord President and Lord Privy Seal, can be found in Chapter 3 Part 3.

The top ranking civil servant or official in the older Departments was normally known as the Permanent Under-Secretary (of State). in a Department. or just plain Permanent Secretary in the younger Ministries.[2] There was only one per Department. but there could be up to three or four at the number two level, Deputy Under-Secretary (of

State) or Deputy Secretary accordingly. The third rank, known as Assistant Under-Secretaries (of State) or Under-Secretaries varied in number from two (Defence) to fifteen plus (Supply).[3] The Treasury, the Board of Trade and the Scottish Office had a body of three at second rank known as Second Secretaries (plain Secretaries at the Scottish Office). At the Treasury they were graded as Permanent Secretaries, at Trade and the Scottish Office as Deputy Secretaries. (The Treasury, because of its key position, also had about eight 'Third Secretaries', graded at Deputy Secretary rank.)

The senior secretary to the Secretary of State or Minister was known as the Principal Private Secretary or Private Secretary, depending on the Department. There was normally just one apart from Number Ten where Churchill had, as an exceptional arrangement, two Principal Private Secretaries. The second level of secretaries to Ministers were known as either Private Secretary (as to the Prime Minister or Chancellor of the Exchequer), or, the more usual, Assistant Private Secretary. These Civil Service secretaries are not to be confused with the Parliamentary Private Secretaries, unpaid political appointments by Ministers from amongst their supporters in Parliament.

Abbreviations

A.E.C.   Association of Education Committees
A.E.I.   Associated Electrical Industries
A.G.   Attorney-General
A.P.S.R.   *American Political Science Review* (see Bibliography)
A.S.L.E.F.   Associated Society of Locomotive Engineers and Firemen
B.A.O.R.   British Army on the Rhine
B.B.C.   British Broadcasting Corporation
B.E.A.   British European Airways
B.E.C.   British Employers Confederation
B.J.S.   *British Journal of Sociology* (see Bibliography)
B.L.E.S.M.A.   British Limbless Ex-Servicemen's Association
B.M.A.   British Medical Association
B.O.A.C.   British Overseas Airways Corporation
B.O.A.P.A.H.   British Oral Archive of Political and Administrative History
   (see Bibliography)
B.R.S.   British Road Services
C.A.S.   Chief of Air Staff
C.B.I.   Confederation of British Industries
CENTO   Central Treaty Organisation
C.D.C.   Colonial Development Corporation
C.H.   Companion of Honour
C.I.A.   Central Intelligence Agency
C.I.D.   Committee of Imperial Defence
C.I.G.S.   Chief of the Imperial General Staff
C.-in-C.   Commander-in-Chief
C.J.E.P.S.   *Canadian Journal of Economic and Political Science* (see
   Bibliography)
C.N.S.   Chief of Naval Staff
C.R.D.   Conservative Research Department
C.R.O.   Commonwealth Relations Office
D.B.Y.   *Day Before Yesterday* (see Bibliography)
D.E.S.   Department of Education and Science
D.T.I.   Department of Trade and Industry
E.D.C.   European Defence Community
E.I.S.   Educational Institute of Scotland
E.P.L./T.   Excess Profits Levy/Tax

E.P.U.   European Payments Union
F.A.   *Foreign Affairs* (see Bibliography)
F.B.I.   Federation of British Industries
F.R.S.   Fellow of the Royal Society
G.A.T.T.   General Agreement on Tariffs and Trade
G.C.E.   General Certificate of Education
G.D.P.   Gross Domestic Product
G.O.C.   General Officer Commanding
G.P.   General Practitioner
I.A.   *International Affairs* (see Bibliography)
I.C.I.   Imperial Chemical Industries
I.L.O.   International Labour Organisation
I.M.C.O.   Inter-governmental Maritime Consultative Organisation
I.M.F.   International Monetary Fund
I.S.H.R.A.   Iron and Steel Holding and Realisation Agency
I.T.A.   Independent Television Authority
J. of P.   *Journal of Politics* (see Bibliography)
J.R.U.S.I.   *Journal of the Royal United Services Institution* (see Bibliography)
K.C.V.O.   Knight Commander of the Royal Victorian Order
K.G.   Knight of the Order of the Garter
L.E.A.   Local Education Authority
M.A.P.   Ministry of Aircraft Production
M.E.L.F.   Middle East Land Forces
N.A.C.T.S.T.   National Advisory Council on the Training and Supply of
   Teachers
NATO   North Atlantic Treaty Organisation
N.C.B.   National Coal Board
N.F.U.   National Farmers' Union
N.J.A.C.   National Joint Advisory Council
N.H.S.   National Health Service
N.U.M.   National Union of Mineworkers
N.U.T.   National Union of Teachers
O.E.E.C.   Organisation for European Economic Co-operation
Parl. Aff.   *Parliamentary Affairs* (see Bibliography)
P.E.P.   Political and Economic Planning
P.M.G.   Postmaster-General
P.P.S.   Parliamentary Private Secretary
P.Q.   *Political Quarterly* (see Bibliography)
P.S.   *Political Studies* (see Bibliography)
Pub. Admin.   *Public Administration* (see Bibliography)
P.U.S.   Permanent Under-Secretary
R.A.   Royal Assent
R.A.F.   Royal Air Force
S.A.C.E.U.R.   Supreme Allied Commander, Europe
S.A.S.   Special Air Service
S.E.A.T.O.   South-East Asia Treaty Organisation

S.O.E.   Special Operations Executive
S.S.T.A.   Scottish Secondary Teachers' Association
T.M.A.C.   Treasury Ministerial Advisory Committee
T.U.C.   Trades Union Congress
U.G.C.   University Grants Committee
U.N.   United Nations
UNESCO   United Nations Educational, Scientific and Cultural Organisation
W.E.U.   Western European Union

Introduction

This book does not claim to be a definitive study of the years 1951–5: far from it. The intention has been to provide, within a manageable length, a survey of the main issues and personalities of British history during one particular Administration, and an account of the way the Government machine then functioned. In so doing tentative themes and conclusions are advanced. If the contents prove of some interest to the general reader, and also define the territory a little more clearly for the specialised historian on the eve of the release of the Government's records at the Public Record Office, then my purpose in writing the book will have been achieved.

The record of the Churchill Government was seen at the time, and well into the 1960s, as being one of unusual success, especially in contrast to the work of Governments in the depressed 1930s and the years of austerity under the Attlee Governments of 1945–51. But from the middle of the 1960s onwards, with increasing anxieties about unemployment and stagnation, the 1950s came to be seen as a period of wasted opportunities, of failed leadership. The feeling was that Britain had lagged behind, entertaining out-dated illusions of world grandeur, whilst at the same time being overtaken economically by the rest of the industrialised nations. This view is to some extent still the prevalent one today. The former, however, presents too rosy a picture, the latter is based on an unreasonable assumption about the ability of Government to probe into and affect maladies with deep-rooted causes. The time is thus ripe for a more balanced consideration of the Government during the early 1950s.

The most controversial element in the book is likely to prove the reassessment of Churchill's contribution as a peacetime premier. The title *Churchill's Indian Summer* is not intended to be sensational, but it is meant to be combative. I do not suggest that he was as fit or as brilliant as he had been during the war. He clearly was not. The characteristic of an Indian Summer is that the temperature is cooler than at the height of the season: indeed, a feature one would expect of a man a month off his seventy-seventh birthday on his return to Number Ten.

Yet despite his failing powers, he was, I believe, right to remain in

1

office. at least until his major stroke in the summer of 1953, and a good case can be made for his retention of power until the autumn of 1954. Only in his last six months in office was he not fully up to the task.

The book. though. is about far more than Churchill's own perform-ance. Indeed. only ten per cent is concerned directly with Churchill. The general approach is not chronological but thematic. This seemed the best method for a number of reasons. So much happened in individual Ministries independently of other Departments and of co-ordination at the centre that a Department-by-Department approach appeared the most advantageous. Those sections that are chronologically based, Chapter 2 Parts 2 and 3, Chapter 5 Part 2, Chapter 8 Part 6 and Chapter 10 Part 2. all focus on the examination of one issue. But a chronological approach throughout would have given a misleading impression of the way that policy was conducted. which was often not in a logical seam directed from the centre. It also would not have been possible to discuss Ministers and civil servants individually, and their relationships, in so much detail. Neither would it have been possible to discuss the way the Government machine as a whole, as well as individual Departments. worked in the early 1950s. This is an important exercise because of the way the machine adapted and changed so swiftly in the early years after the war. One necessary consequence of the thematic approach is that it was felt necessary to repeat at certain points information that occurs in other sections.

There was initially some suspicion amongst those to whom I talked about my reasons for seeking details of individuals. But the fact is that for most of those discussed in the following pages, and this is particularly true of civil servants, little information ever becomes generally avail-able; a few lines in obituary columns perhaps, but little more. A problem for historians of the inter-war years is that little is known about certain key figures, especially officials. I therefore determined to tap memories of figures from the early 1950s so that I could paint brief portraits of officials and Ministers, to prove of interest to both general reader and scholar.

To this end I wrote to almost all surviving Ministers, Permanent and Deputy Secretaries, Chiefs of Staff, Principal Private Secretaries and other prominent politicians and officials. Well over two hundred in-terviews were thereby conducted, the response being always friendly and invariably positive. 'Oral history' is a rapidly expanding field of historical research in this country, and rightly so, for properly conducted and used it can fill in much of the necessary flesh which the bare documents do not provide. There are of course many hazards with the technique. not the least being the fallibility of memory and the risk of being over-influenced by the evidence of particular witnesses. These shortcomings cannot be denied, but they can be countered to a large extent by width of interviewing and cross-checking of evidence. Lord Greenhill of Harrow (a former Permanent Under-Secretary of State of the Foreign and Commonwealth Office) has written in a letter to *The Times* on 7th May, 1977:

> I think all my colleagues would agree that it will be in the future quite impossible for anybody to unravel with any accuracy from the archives the detailed history of events. The sheer volume of documents, the inevitable decline in the standards of filing, the mass of unrecorded telephone conversations, all contribute to the fact that the course of events can no longer be followed from the original documents, and individual documents of special interest may well be overlooked.

Working on the frontiers of the thirty-year rule, and such a long time after the events, not only helped people interviewed to see events more objectively, but also allowed for a greater frankness. Not that I sought to seek out controversial or sensational information. I did not. I have steered clear of the trend towards 'frank revelations' seen in some present-day memoirs and other published works, often justified on the dubious grounds of being in the interests of 'open government'.

This book is already quite long enough: to prevent it being even longer, I do not write at any length about topics already discussed elsewhere, but instead refer the reader to further literature on the subject. Thus I deal only briefly with the following: the creation of the Atomic Energy Authority; the establishment of independent television, and the Select Committee on the Nationalised Industries; Crichel Down; the history of industrial disputes; the Labour and Liberal Parties during 1951–5; and finally the details of economic, defence, colonial and foreign policy. In foreign affairs I have concentrated on only two aspects – the special relationship with the United States and the proposal for a summit meeting with the Soviet Union – for the reason given above and because Churchill's influence was of prime importance in these two areas.

I have endeavoured as far as possible, by having different sections read over by fifty expert pairs of eyes, and by meticulous checking of facts, to remove all errors and unjust comments on individuals. I fear that mistakes may still remain and for these I offer my profound apologies.

ANTHONY SELDON
London, June 1981

3

Chapter 1   The Post-War Inheritance

Part 1   The Road to 1951[1]

By mid-afternoon of Friday, 26th October, 1951, it had become clear to Clement Attlee and his advisers that Labour had lost the Election. At 5 p.m. that evening he drove to Buckingham Palace to tender his own and his Government's resignation to the King, George VI,[2] then a sick man (he had only fifteen more weeks to live). Attlee, himself, was tired: he had been Prime Minister for nearly six and a half years, and had seen the country through the difficult recovery period after the terrible drain of the war years on Britain's resources. An hour later another vehicle drove through the gates of the Palace, this time bearing a man a month off his seventy-seventh birthday, who the King for the third time within twelve years[3] asked to form a Government.[4] The meeting over, Winston Churchill, huddled in the back seat of the car, drove out through the cheering crowds once again to govern the country.

Labour had initially come to power in the landslide Election of July 1945, winning 393 seats to the Conservatives' 213. Attlee, Leader of the Parliamentary Party since 1935, headed a Government in a position of considerable power, whereas neither of the two previous Labour Administrations to hold office, in 1924 and 1929–31, had had a majority in the House of Commons. *The Times*, the day after the results were declared, opened its editorial with these words: 'The sweeping and unexpected victory of the Labour Party at the polls gives them not only a clear majority in the new House of Commons, which they have never enjoyed before, but a sufficient margin to justify them in looking forward to several years of secure authority.'[5] A new era had begun.

The two Labour Governments of the next six and a half years were the most reforming Administrations of the century. Yet it should be remembered that the ground for these innovations had been prepared by the work of preceding Governments, in particular the War Coalition of 1940–5. Surprising though it may seem today, the public were fully prepared for, and indeed welcomed, many of the reforms. Thus Labour's policies received little resistance in the country, and a surprising degree of acquiescence by the Conservatives in Parliament. It also helps us to explain why the Conservative Governments after 1951 reversed so few of Labour's reforms.

Attlee had a further advantage over the two pre-war Labour Administrations: he led a body of men who, during the War Coalition Government of 1940–5, had become experienced in the art of government and in the administration of departments of state. Attlee displayed high intelligence in the deployment of these subordinates. Ernest Bevin, former union leader and wartime Minister of Labour, went to the Foreign Office (1945–51). Herbert Morrison, one of the most talented Party organisers of the century, who had proved himself as Home Secretary and Minister for Home Security in the Coalition Government, moved up to Lord President of the Council (1945–51), responsible for co-ordinating home affairs, economic planning and development. Hugh Dalton, President of the Board of Trade, 1942–5, became Chancellor of the Exchequer (1945–7). Sir Stafford Cripps, who had briefly been Lord Privy Seal and Leader of the Commons in 1942, went to the Board of Trade (1945–7). Another left-winger in the Party, Aneurin Bevan, was appointed Minister of Health (1945–51), then responsible also for housing and local government.

Yet the Labour Government, despite the presence of left-wingers in high-ranking jobs, did not become nearly as doctrinaire as Conservatives had forecast, in particular Churchill in his over-blown statements during the 1945 Election campaign, when he might well have done much damage to his own and his Party's interests by implying that if Labour were elected, Britain would be in danger of becoming a police state. Partly it was constrained from pursuing more radical and expensive policies by continuous economic difficulties at home and by external sanctions, such as the need to avoid upheavals that would have damaged Britain's exports, weakened confidence in sterling or alienated American generosity in providing aid. Most of the senior men in the Cabinet were pragmatists: Attlee, Bevin, Morrison, Chuter Ede, the Home Secretary (1945–51), Tom Williams, Agriculture Minister (1945–51) and A. V. Alexander, the Minister of Defence (1946–50). Even those on the left such as Cripps, Bevan and Shinwell, the Minister of Fuel and Power (1945–7), though passionate in their desire to re-order society in a more egalitarian manner, were determined at all times to act constitutionally. The Government, moreover, was always concerned to work closely alongside business as well as with labour.[6]

Ministers were gratified by the co-operation they received from their civil servants after an initial period of suspicion which Labour Ministers in particular have been prone to feel on first arriving in office. Labour had the benefit of advice from several powerful Permanent Secretaries, among them Sir Alexander Cadogan at the Foreign Office (1938–46), Sir Alexander Maxwell at the Home Office (1938–48), Sir Godfrey Ince at Labour (1944–56) and Sir Thomas Phillips at National Insurance (1944–9). The Government was further able to draw on the services of two men, newly promoted to their jobs and, surely, the most distinguished officials of the post-war world, who without doubt had a crucial, stabilising effect on the Government: Sir Edward Bridges, the Head of the Civil Service (1945–56), and Sir Norman Brook, who followed Bridges as Secretary of the Cabinet (1947–62). Here then were some of the individuals who ensured continuity between the War Coalition and the Labour Government.

The *Spectator* noted at the time of the 1951 General Election that: 'Foreign affairs have been kept reasonably well out of the Party controversies since 1945';[7] indeed it was in domestic affairs that the most bitter strife came, as well as Labour's most immediate problems. During the war Britain had lost as much as a quarter of her national wealth – approximately £7,000m. The economy had been up-ended to produce the maximum war effort: two-thirds of her export trade was lost, over a quarter of her merchant shipping, and after the conclusion of hostilities nine million able workers were still actively involved in war-related activities; damage to housing by bombs and rockets was assessed at about £1,500m., the national debt had tripled while the country's standards of living had fallen heavily; the cost of Britain's war effort for four years exceeded her national income by fifty per cent.[8]

Yet in the teeth of this legacy Labour came to power in 1945 committed to a policy of either planning or restructuring the whole economy. All its ideas on economic policy were founded on a determination to remedy the social miseries that had been so prevalent in the interwar years. With such a large majority Labour could introduce radically new economic policies, unlike the minority Governments of 1924 and 1929–31. Yet here, as elsewhere, the Government failed to realise its hopes, partly due to unrealistically ambitious aims, bad luck and a succession of unfortunate economic factors. The first of these came within four weeks of the Labour victory when President Truman, following the unexpectedly swift termination of the war against Japan, abruptly ended Lend-Lease, the system of wartime economic aid in operation since 1941. The economist, John Maynard Keynes, was dispatched by Attlee to Washington, but failed to persuade the Americans to part with as much money as the Government felt it needed. By July 1947 the loan which had been secured all but ran out, and a convertibility crisis ensued and a major redirection of economic policy. But fortunately for Britain, as well as other countries in Europe, who also benefited, further financial help came in the form of aid, initiated by the U.S. Secretary of State, George Marshall (1947–9), who had become convinced of the need to extend further financial assistance to Europe. 'Marshall Aid', as it became known, was to play a major part in assisting European recovery throughout the following two years, and it was generally agreed that without it Britain would have suffered both severe unemployment and a considerably reduced standard of living. As the *Spectator* put it: 'Without America's military aid we could not have survived the war: without her financial aid we could not have survived the peace.'[9]

This persistent economic weakness dogged the work of Hugh Dalton, the first of Labour's three Chancellors. His policy at the Treasury was dominated by the twin plans of demobilisation and reconversion after the war dislocations.[10] After leaking the details of his autumn Budget of 1947 to a London evening newspaper, he was replaced by Sir Stafford Cripps, the first fully Keynesian Chancellor. According to the economics commentator Samuel Brittan: 'During his reign the idea of planning through the Budget first became established.'[11] Yet as Cripps' Economic Adviser Sir Robert Hall was later to comment: 'I don't think there was much planning in the socialist sense of the word under Cripps. [Sir Edwin] Plowden was the Chief Planning Officer and Cripps thought Plowden would plan the economy for him, but I don't think they ever had the time to do it.'[12] Moreover, for all his socialist inclinations, Cripps was as dependent as Dalton upon the advice of his Treasury civil servants. In one matter, though, he ignored the advice of his officials – the devaluation of the pound to $2.80 in September 1949, a cut of thirty per cent. This decision cast a shadow over Cripps' performance as Chancellor and he was fortunate to retire from office before the economic problems brought on by the Korean war and the 1950 economic boom had time to strike home.[13]

Cripps' successor, Hugh Gaitskell, had as good a grasp of economics as any post-war Chancellor, but he was unfortunate to have held the job at a very difficult time. The outbreak of the Korean war in 1950 forced the Government to adopt a three-year defence programme, initially of £3,400m., later upgraded to £4,700m. over the same time period. Gaitskell's one Budget, in April 1951, was dominated by the need to deal with the complex repercussions of the war. Labour's lingering hopes of introducing a socialist economy were thus finally pole-axed.

These internal and external crises explain why, in Brittan's words, 'It is a myth to suppose that the Labour Government of 1945–51 engaged in detailed long-term planning of the country's production,'[14] and why, of the economic policy of the Conservatives after October 1951, another commentator could write: '. . . policy showed no abrupt break.'[15]

In certain areas, Labour even moved away from the planned economy. As 1950 approached, the year when a General Election would have to be held, the Government, with an eye on the electorate, decided that it must rid the country of rationing and controls, a legacy from the war. Harold Wilson, President of the Board of Trade (1947–51), and other Ministers set about the task with ardour; potato rationing was ended in the spring of 1948, with bread following in July and jam in December.[16] In March 1949 the Board of Trade announced the removal of nearly a million licences, which led to the abolition of all clothes and textile rationing. By this 'bonfire of controls' Labour prepared much of the groundwork for the Conservatives' final abolition of rationing and most controls during 1951–5. In two other areas within the Board of Trade's jurisdiction, however, the Labour Government seemed set to make fresh departures. Labour had always been more concerned about unemployment, and from 1945 pursued a vigorous regional policy of controls and incentives which ensured that about half of new building in 1945–7 was concentrated in the areas of traditionally high unemployment. But after the return to office of the Conservatives in 1951, interest in regional policy lapsed due not so much to doctrinal differences as to full employment, which pre-empted the need for a radical policy for 'development areas'. With Labour's suspicion of capitalism, a far more rigorous policy might have been expected against monopolies, but the Monopolies and Restrictive Practices Act of 1948 was passed without a division and followed, with surprising similarity, the arrangements suggested in the Conservatives' 1947 statement, the 'Industrial Charter'.

Nationalisation was by no means an ideology first introduced by the Labour Government after 1945, as popular myth is apt to claim. Public ownership in varying degrees had been established since long before: the Port of London Authority (1909), the Central Electricity Board (1926), the British Broadcasting Corporation, granted its first charter as a public corporation the same year, the London Passenger Transport Board, established in 1933, British Overseas Airways Corporation (B.O.A.C.) (1939) and the North of Scotland Hydro-Electricity Board (1943) – all indicated the direction in which Government thinking on public services was moving. The war, which gave Government wide experience in running industry, accelerated the tendency for the state to become involved in peacetime. The Labour Government's nationalisation programme during 1945–51 – not significantly increased until after 1975 – was the logical outcome. The need for drastic reorganisation in the coal mines, with their exceptionally poor record on labour relations as well as the many badly-run and uneconomic pits, had been recognised by the Reid Report of 1944, as well as by the Conservative Party. Coal royalties had already been nationalised in 1938, and when on 1st January, 1947, the industry as a whole came under state ownership, Conservative resistance was far less than had been initially expected. The case for nationalisation in Britain's other two fuel industries, gas and electricity, was also indisputable: neither was sufficiently well organised to undertake co-ordinated modernisation and expansion programmes. Not that this obviated Conservative criticism of the Government's fuel policy, which came to a head in March 1947. That year, one of the severest winters on record precipitated a fuel crisis: a censure motion was moved by Churchill, who argued that Britain's economic difficulties were being exacerbated by Labour's doctrinaire nationalisation plans.[17] Public ownership was also extended further over transport: British European Airways and British South American Airways were established (the latter being merged with B.O.A.C. in 1949), but more far-reaching was the British Transport Commission, a cumbersome body, set up in 1947 to create a 'properly integrated system of public inland transport and port facilities', an ambitious plan which fell victim to vested interest and bureaucratic ineptitude. Railways, which needed vast capital investment to make good the ravages of war, canals and the road-haulage industry were all nationalised, to be administered by six executive boards. The Bank of England had already passed out of private ownership in 1946, but this was largely a symbolic act, and did not, according to Churchill in the House, raise any matter of principle.[18] The most hard-hitting debate came on the Iron and Steel Bill:[19] Attlee and Morrison had been against pressing ahead with full nationalisation, but were overridden by left-wingers in the Cabinet such as Bevan as well as by Labour's more radical backbenchers.

The Bill to nationalise the industry received the Royal Assent in November 1949. Conscious that the Conservatives might use their majority in the House of Lords to reject the Iron and Steel Bill, the Government had passed a Parliament Act in 1949, which effectively halved to one year the time by which the Lords could delay legislation. Vesting date for nationalisation, with further delay being caused by the General Election of February 1950, was not until February 1951.

Labour's programme of nationalisation cannot thus be regarded as revolutionary. Not merely was it the culmination of a long trend, but the form which nationalisation took, the public corporation, had several precedents. The Conservatives, too, saw the need for much of the Labour programme, only denationalising two industries after 1951, steel and road haulage (the only ones for which they thought private offers might be forthcoming), and even then the industries were by no means completely returned to private enterprise.

For the unions the crucial pronouncement on post-war policy had been the White Paper 'Employment Policy', published in May 1944, which committed post-war Governments to the primary objective of maintaining a high and stable level of employment, influencing demand to achieve this. Yet, in spite of the Attlee Government's extension of public ownership and other measures which met union objectives of the 1930s and earlier, as well as the close bond that existed between many senior union leaders and the Government, relations were not always easy.[20] Strange, too, that to follow Bevin as Minister of Labour, Attlee appointed the colourless figure, by contrast, of George Isaacs (1945–51). Inflation and balance of payments difficulties caused severe Government-union strains, the dominant problem throughout being how to reconcile a policy of wage restraint with free collective bargaining. The wartime Order 1305, which limited the right to strike and made provision for compulsory arbitration, was continued after 1945. But the number of unofficial strikes, in breach of the Order, rose dramatically. The five unofficial dock strikes between 1945 and 1950 were particularly damaging to the economy, and in three of these the Government used its emergency powers to bring in troops.[21]

Agricultural policy had never been one of Labour's main strengths, since the vast majority of its M.P.s were drawn from urban seats. Fears and unrest amongst the farmers, which had been prevalent before 1939, had, however, to a large extent been allayed both by the War Coalition Government's promises that a well-balanced agricultural industry would be maintained after the war, and by the recovery during the war of demand for farm produce following the agricultural slump of the 1920s and early 1930s. Labour was fortunate to have had as their Minister Tom Williams, who was trusted by the farmers. Their lingering doubts were finally dispelled by the Agriculture Act of 1947, with its guaranteed prices system, which offset competition from abroad. This helped ensure that agriculture was to become one of the most efficient British industries: gone for ever the slough of the pre-war years.

Of all the achievements of the Attlee Government, Labour perhaps felt proudest of its social policy. Yet here again one finds that much of the groundwork of Labour's establishment of the welfare state had been laid by the War Coalition Government of 1940–5. The Labour Government introduced an Industrial Injuries Act designed to take over from the former system of workmen's compensation, and this was followed by the seminal National Insurance Act of 1946, which relied heavily on

William Beveridge's Report *Social Insurance and Allied Services* of November 1942. This had recommended public protection for all 'from the cradle to the grave'. The 1946 Act brought the whole nation, for the first time, into a comprehensive benefit system covering unemployment, sickness, maternity, guardianship, retirement and death. By Clause 12 of the Act, the basic condition was spelled out that claimants must have paid a minimum number of contributions during the year before benefits were to be awarded. Although the Conservatives were unhappy about aspects of the Bill, such as the proposal that the self-employed should have to wait twenty-four days before becoming eligible for benefits, an item that was eventually dropped, they did not oppose its Second or Third Readings. The unpopular legacy from pre-war days, the means test, was not, however, eliminated altogether: the 1948 National Assistance Act established a Board whose regional officers administered tests for those in particular need who lacked sufficient minimum income from other sources. Beveridge had hoped that in time national assistance would be confined to exceptional cases as the bulk of the population became entitled to full national insurance benefits. But this was not to be: the choice of low flat-rate contributions for insurance benefits, coupled with the Exchequer's determination to limit its own contribution, and also the effects of inflation and steadily rising numbers eligible for benefits, meant that national assistance was needed extensively to support other forms of benefits.

Only Labour's policy towards the health services, of the four main aspects of its social policy, aroused serious, sustained opposition from the Conservatives. This was not surprising, since it was the one area of welfare policy that departed most dramatically from precedent. A White Paper of February 1944 had agreed with Beveridge's plea for a universal service which made no distinction between rich and poor, but after 1945 the Conservatives felt unable to endorse Labour's specific plans. The Government also faced a passionate denouncement of the proposed service from the British Medical Association, which feared deeply that the independence of the profession would be eroded and the personal relationship of doctor and patient destroyed. It also hotly opposed Bevan's decision to nationalise the entire hospital service to ensure a balanced distribution of specialist knowledge and services throughout the country. Administrative responsibility for the 388 hospitals within the system was therefore transferred to new regional hospital boards. On the general practitioner front, Bevan believed that doctors should have a basic salary, plus fees according to the number of their national health patients, and he also came to see that there would have to be scope for private practice – rather than the more radical solution canvassed by left-wingers for a fully salaried health service. The main finance for the service was to come from central government, with only one-twentieth of the N.H.S. to be paid direct from national insurance contributions. The National Health Service Act embodying these plans received the Royal Assent in November 1946. The proposals were highly popular with the public and gradually over the months until the scheme came into operation in July 1948 the harsh opposition of the doctors began to soften; in the end 20,000 general practitioners – 90% of the total – felt able to participate from the start.

Housing, arousing less controversy, provided Labour with its most pressing domestic problem. Much property had been destroyed or damaged by enemy action during the war, and still more buildings had been allowed to fall into disrepair. Demand for homes was further intensified by the spate of post-war marriages and births. Bevan was dogged by the dearth of skilled building labour and lack of materials, which were also being cagerly sought by those wanting to erect schools, factories and hospitals. Fearing that if private builders were given too much freedom this would produce an inflationary scramble for scarce materials, Bevan chose to work mainly through the 1,700 local authorities, providing them with generous subsidies and other direct aid. As a result an average of well over 200,000 new houses per year were built between 1945 and 1951, with a commendable emphasis not just on quantity, but also on quality. The Conservatives, however, claimed that houses could be built more quickly if they were in power and if private builders were given freer rein. Less was done, however, to improve damaged housing, a problem bequeathed to Harold Macmillan, the Conservatives' Housing Minister. Town and country planning under Labour was the responsibility of another Minister, Lewis Silkin. A major new initiative, which owed much to civil servants, was the New Towns Act of 1946, which attempted through the creation of fourteen new towns to relieve pressure in London and some other major cities. The Town and Country Planning Act of 1947 was vigorously opposed by the Conservatives on its Second Reading that January. The Act made major changes to planning law and also introduced a controversial development charge on any increase in land values brought about by development and projected development. But it was a complex and unsatisfactory piece of legislation which had to be considerably modified by the Churchill Government six years later.

The final aspect of social policy, education, was the least controversial. The Education Act of 1944, commonly associated with the then Minister of Education, Rab Butler, had made provision for secondary education for all, and had been happily accepted by the Labour Party.

13

When in power their two Ministers, Ellen Wilkinson (1945–7) and George Tomlinson (1947–51), decided neither to press ahead with a universal comprehensive system nor to abolish private schools, as left-wingers in the Party demanded. Out of necessity their twin priorities became the provision of adequate school buildings and the increase in numbers of school-teachers. There was little in this programme to which the Opposition could take serious exception.

Labour politicians had gained considerable experience during the War Coalition of serving in Ministries concerned with domestic policy: yet the Conservatives had all but monopolised defence, the Commonwealth and Empire, and foreign affairs.[22] With so little previous experience of coalition government to guide the new Government, major departures from precedent might reasonably have been expected. Yet congruity of policy was to be even more marked in these areas than in home policy.

Labour in power after 1945 abandoned its pacifist stance of pre-war days. The Government indeed showed itself to be quite unmoved by those of its supporters who demanded unilateral disarmament. Although it was intent on cutting overseas commitments, this only took place gradually, and two years after the end of the war there were still half a million British servicemen stationed abroad. Numbers were cut in the next three years, but had to be increased drastically after the outbreak of the Korean war. By a Cabinet decision taken in January 1951 the expenditure on defence was doubled from that envisaged at the beginning of 1950. As this proved a severe strain on the economy and, as the threat of war receded during 1951–2, one witnessed the seemingly paradoxical position of a Conservative Administration cutting back on a defence programme inaugurated by Labour. Not that the Services were strengthened significantly by Labour's rearmament programme: debates in Parliament in March 1952 revealed that Britain's defences were in some respects weaker then than they had been during the Battle of Britain in 1940. Britain was also set on the path of having its own independent nuclear deterrent by the Attlee Government's secret decision in 1946 to build a British atomic bomb. Fortunately for the Party leadership, this was too new a development for Labour's left-wing to have formed a hardened attitude.

Another precedent was set by the establishment in 1947 of a Ministry of Defence to co-ordinate defence plans: after this initial step it was only a matter of time before the three Service Departments came together under a single unified Ministry, although this was to take seventeen years. This development owed much to the contributions of officials, as indeed did defence policy generally. As the first Defence Minister,

Attlee appointed A. V. Alexander, one of the few Labour Ministers to have served in Defence during the war, which he did as First Lord of the Admiralty (1940–5), a position he kept until his new appointment. Although Alexander was not particularly forceful or influential, many of the Chiefs of Staff were – Lord Montgomery of Alamein (Chief of the Imperial General Staff, C.I.G.S., 1946–8), Sir William Slim (C.I.G.S., 1948–52), and Lord Tedder (Chief of Air Staff, 1946–50). But in this area one Labour Minister who made a conspicuous impact was Emanuel Shinwell (Secretary for War, 1947–50, and Minister of Defence, 1950–1), and it was to him that Churchill paid a conspicuous compliment in the first defence debate in the House after the 1951 Election. Churchill in his opening remarks acknowledged the broad agreement on defence subjects: 'Let me, first of all, make my acknowledgments to the late Government for several most important decisions about our defence policy which they took during their six years of office and which form the foundation on which we stand today.'[23]

If defence was regarded as a specialist Conservative preserve, how much more so the Commonwealth and colonial territories with which so many leading Tories had intimate family, financial or emotional connections. Yet here again there was no major about-turn on policy.

Before the war, the Conservative Party had prided itself on being the Party of the Empire, and Labour had taken its stand against any form of imperialism. How would the new Government after 1945 react? No one was exactly sure. Attlee became responsible for the transfer of power in the Indian subcontinent; both India and Pakistan received independence in 1947, with Burma following in 1948. The pace and manner of these moves were hotly argued against at the time by the Conservatives, and in particular by Churchill: 'It is with deep grief that I watch the clattering down of the British Empire . . . Many have defended Britain against her foes. None can defend her against herself.'[24] But the Labour Party gave whole-hearted support to the new concept of the Commonwealth[25] as an association of equal or near equal states joined together for their mutual benefit. If member countries wished to join in defence pacts with non-Commonwealth countries, this was quite acceptable to Labour, as in the so-called A.N.Z.U.S. Pact of 1951, which the Conservatives (and Churchill in particular) had far more difficulty in accepting.

Labour seemed anxious, however, to preserve a bipartisan approach. 'In these Commonwealth matters,' declared Herbert Morrison in April 1949, 'the more we can march together in this House, the better it is for everybody.'[26] Labour's most effective Commonwealth Secretary of the three who served in that capacity under Attlee,[27] Patrick Gordon Walker (1950–1), cared deeply for his subject, and held strongly to the view that the Commonwealth was an association of peoples rather than an alliance of Governments.[28]

Anxieties were increasingly aired about how the Conservatives after 1951 would treat the Commonwealth. Would they resist the trend, initiated by the case of India, following the Commonwealth Prime Ministers' meeting of April 1949, of Commonwealth membership being granted to a republic, to those who did not recognise the sovereignty of the British Crown?[29] Would they even try to resurrect the Commonwealth as a vital political, military and economic unit? But in the event the Conservatives went further than anyone would have predicted in 1951 in following Labour's course, in particular by abandoning their long attachment to Empire trade.

At the Colonial Office, George Hall (Colonial Secretary, 1945–6), in his first peacetime statement on colonial policy since the Election, declared that: 'It is our policy to develop the colonies and all their resources so as to enable their people speedily and substantially to improve their economic and social conditions, and, as soon as may be practicable, to attain responsible self-government.'[30] Hall went on to thank his Conservative predecessor, Oliver Stanley (1942–5), for laying the foundations, and Stanley welcomed implicitly the bipartisan basis of Hall's statement.[31] These aims were re-stated by the Conservative Colonial Secretary, Oliver Lyttelton, within three weeks of assuming office in 1951: 'I should like to make it plain at the outset that His Majesty's Government intend no change in these aims.'[32] However, Labour after 1945 possessed no well-developed programme or philosophy for either political or economic development, and their policy was essentially pragmatic, often suffering from lack of sufficient forethought. Two important territories reached independence: Ceylon, long regarded as the most 'mature' of the Colonial Office's charges, and mandated Palestine, most of which a few months later became independent Israel. Developments in two further states were of key importance, and in both cases Ministers were to a large extent guided by their civil servants: in the Gold Coast, the Watson Commission, reporting after the 1948 riots, helped set the Gold Coast on the path to becoming the first self-governing British colony in the continent. In Central Africa, talks were initiated and plans made for a federation of the three British colonies, Northern and Southern Rhodesia and Nyasaland. The Conservatives after 1951 continued along the same lines, although, in the latter case, this was to accelerate the eventual breakdown of bipartisan policy.

*

Labour had maintained during the 1945 Election campaign that it would be better placed than the Conservatives to talk to the Soviet Union on its own terms. The Tories for their part claimed, as they were to do throughout 1945–51, that they were uniquely placed to foster the 'special relationship' with the United States in the crucial phase of post-war recovery. Moreover, Labour had a strong pacifist tradition. All was set for a major show-down. Yet it transpired after 1945 that Labour was no more successful at dealing with the Soviet Union than the Conservatives were after 1951 in harmonising with the United States. Eden, who had served as Foreign Secretary throughout the last four and a half years of the war, admired Bevin and both men frequently engaged in private consultations. Not only was the Opposition able to maintain general support for the Government's foreign policy, but it also supported the Marshall Aid programme and respected the Government's request not to press for a debate on the international situation at the time of the Berlin blockade. On the other hand, it attacked the Government strongly for its Middle East policy, in particular towards Palestine,[33] and was critical of Labour's hesitant approach to European Union.[34]

According to the historian, Joseph Frankel, Labour's foreign policy was governed by three main factors.[35] First, a determination to maintain continuity with wartime foreign affairs policy, where both Bevin and Eden testified to the fundamental agreement of both parties.[36] This trend continued after 1951: following Eden's first major foreign policy statement in the House, Herbert Morrison, who had been Foreign Secretary from March to October 1951 after Bevin's resignation due to ill health, said: 'As far as I can see, the policy which we pursued is substantially being carried on.'[37] The second aim was to pursue a 'socialist' foreign policy as advocated at the 1945 Labour Party Conference. Here the main plank was close alignment with the Soviet Union; but the unrealistic nature of this stance quickly dawned on Labour Ministers. Finally, there was Bevin's own personality and views. Left a freer hand by Attlee than possibly any other Foreign Secretary by his Prime Minister since the war, Bevin nevertheless reached similar conclusions to his Foreign Office advisers, despite their vastly different backgrounds and experience. The two main aspects of his policy were the stressing of relations with the Super Powers and a corresponding neglect of matters elsewhere, particularly in Europe.

Europe might indeed have provided the Conservatives with a chance for a fresh initiative after 1951. Ardent Europeans certainly had high hopes, engendered by the encouraging noises made by senior Conservatives in Opposition on the subject of closer ties with Europe. Yet these hopes were soon to be dashed as the Conservatives showed themselves after 1951 to be no more pro-Europe than Labour. Other Labour initiatives were followed as well by the Conservatives after 1951: phased withdrawal from large overseas bases, entry into defence pacts (S.E.A.T.O. and CENTO followed NATO), a negotiated rather than a military solution to the problems in Persia, recognition of Communist China – in the teeth of United States pressure to do otherwise – and military support for the war in Korea.

In the Chapters that follow, which describe the Conservatives' policy in the various Departments, one can see in detail the extent to which they adhered to the direction indicated by Labour during 1945–51.[38] The truth of this underlying continuity in most areas was distorted by the Party's propaganda, which needed to stress the points of difference: yet the fact remains that during the early 1950s the post-war consensus was, quietly and unobtrusively, being consolidated.

Part 2   The 1951 Election Issues[1]

The 1951 General Election campaign was one of the more stormy in the post-war period, reflecting in part the mounting antipathy between the main Parties since the previous Election in February 1950, following a Parliament where there had been widespread agreement in many areas. 'Mr. Attlee's Government, with its slender majority, has survived longer than anyone expected in February 1950,' declared a leader in *The Times*, the day after the Election was announced in September 1951, 'but a price has had to be paid. Uncertainty in the country and frustration at Westminster have been the predominant features of the past eighteen months.'[2] The main underlying points of disagreement were Conservative criticism about the rise in the cost of living under Labour, and Labour's own claim that they were the Party of peace. Less significant were the twin issues of full employment and housing. State ownership, however, played little part in the campaign, surprisingly in view of the row over the nationalisation of iron and steel, the main source of domestic controversy in the 1950 Parliament, and the pledges on nationalisation in the Party Manifestoes.

During the course of the campaign, one of the least prominent issues in terms of time, but perhaps the most significant for its long-term influence, was trade union legislation. Here Sir David Maxwell Fyfe, thought likely to be the Conservative Minister of Labour, uttered an uncharacteristically incautious remark during the campaign. In a radio broadcast on 20th September, he repeated a long-standing Conservative pledge that the Party would not take any legislative action on trade unions, adding the ominous appendage *without prior union agreement*. Uproar ensued: what exactly did the Conservatives have in mind, demanded the unions? What would happen, moreover, if that 'prior agreement' could not be reached? Labour sensed the Party capital to be gained and pounced sharply, led by Patrick Gordon Walker and Herbert Morrison. Churchill took command for the Conservatives, now in retreat, and on several occasions entered the fray in an attempt to defuse the issue. It soon blew over, but it had four probable outcomes: it may have discouraged trade unionists from voting Conservative, helping to explain why the Conservatives received a smaller majority in the Election than anticipated; it stiffened Churchill's resolve to avoid trouble with the unions at all costs; it put an end to Maxwell Fyfe's hopes of becoming Minister of Labour, the appointment going instead to a man thought likely to be 'soft' (Sir Walter Monckton, formerly Edward VIII's counsel); finally, it forced the Conservatives to withdraw their active opposition to 'contracting out' and the closed shop.

The question of the cost of living was a more protracted point of disagreement. Indeed, the Conservatives thought that this was the issue on which the Election could be won. Their Party propaganda set out to show how the increase in the cost of living stemmed from Labour's devaluation of sterling in September 1949 rather than from factors connected with the Korean war, as Labour maintained. Television, used for party political broadcasts for the first time,[3] provided the forum, each party being offered one fifteen-minute slot by the B.B.C. For the Conservatives Anthony Eden produced a graph illustrating their point. Christopher Mayhew,[4] who with Sir Hartley Shawcross,[5] presented the programme for Labour, produced further tables which showed convincingly that the Conservative chart had been inaccurately drawn to support their argument. 'Crippen,' Mayhew concluded, 'was the first criminal to be caught by wireless; the Conservative Central Office are the first criminals to be caught by television.' The press eagerly picked up the argument, and Labour appeared to have got the better of the case.

Ever since Aneurin Bevan had resigned from his Cabinet post as Minister of Labour in April 1951, tensions in the Party increased between left and right. The Conservatives sought to make capital out of the issue, although, interestingly enough, not as much as they might have done. They did this both by stating or implying that Bevan was a communist sympathiser and also by exposing the internal differences within the Party whereby Bevan and a sizeable minority of his supporters disagreed with the party leadership on a number of major policy issues, notably rearmament. These differences within the Labour Party

were to continue long after the Election was over, and did them protracted electoral harm. The Conservatives no longer had to expose these
divisions to the public gaze; they were there for all to see.

One overseas issue, Persia, had caused concern since earlier in 1951:
three weeks before polling day trouble there flared up sharply.
The Persian Government, headed by Prime Minister Dr. Mossadeq,
nationalised the Anglo-Iranian Oil Company. Abortive international
discussions followed, and by the beginning of October the internal
position deteriorated to such an extent that Attlee ordered the remaining British technicians to leave Abadan, the evacuation taking place on
3rd October. Until then, partisan disagreement on the Persian situation had been kept within limits, but the evacuation unleashed a
welter of criticism and counter-criticism which for the week it lasted
obscured almost every other issue in the campaign. The main reason
for the issue receding in importance was developments in another
Middle East country, which ironically helped restore a bipartisan
approach and dispel the belief that the Labour Government was not
prepared to stand up to a challenge to British authority. The Egyptian
Government on 8th October denounced the 1936 Treaty defining British
rights in the Suez Canal Zone, and proclaimed King Farouk King of the
Sudan. The Labour Government announced it was standing firm on its
rights, a position which Conservative leaders applauded. Labour also
posed the succinct but highly effective question, 'Would the Conservatives have gone to war over Persia?' Labour argued that war would
indeed have been inevitable if they had not pulled out the technicians.
The Conservatives for their part were not able to dispel the impression
that their own handling of the Persian situation would have led to
hostilities.

David Butler, in his history of the Election, wrote: 'It seems not
impossible that this Election will go down to posterity as the "warmonger" Election.'[6] The issue at stake was encapsulated and publicised
by the *Daily Mirror*'s refrain: 'Whose Finger on the Trigger?', which it
had carried in the late summer and which it repeated in its first editorial
of the Election. On 25th October, polling day, it returned to the theme:
above what appeared to be a 'cowboy' six-shooter, it posed the question
'Whose finger?', and, beneath the barrel: 'Today *YOUR* finger is on the
trigger.'[7] The theme appeared in muted form in the Labour Manifesto,
which stressed as its first aim preservation of peace in the world, and the
motif that Labour was the Party of peace was formally launched at their
Party Conference held in Scarborough between 1st and 3rd October. As
Morrison, the Foreign Secretary, put it: 'I do not accuse the average
Conservative of being a warmonger . . . But it is their temperament; it is

20

the background of their mental outlook – the old imperialist outlook
. . . Therefore if the country wants peace it had better vote for the
people who can most surely be relied upon to preserve peace . . .'[8] This
was tame compared with the manner in which many put the message
across in the following three weeks. The Conservatives hotly disputed
the claim, from a straight denial in their expanded Manifesto, 'Britain
Strong and Free', to a further powerful refutation in Churchill's final
speech at Plymouth – 'a cruel and ungrateful accusation'. But as David
Butler makes clear, the Conservatives probably did themselves more
harm than good by being so quick in their denial that they were war-
mongers. In taking an unjust accusation so seriously they made, in his
words, a 'basic tactical error'.[9]

The episode had one incalculable effect, probably of the highest
significance. It stiffened Churchill's resolve to do all in his power to
expose Labour's charge as an utter travesty. Once back in office his
search for a high-level meeting with the Soviet Union became one of his
greatest priorities, and was one of the principal reasons why for so long
he clung on to power.

Part 3   The Inheritance: October 1951

'The gravity of the crisis we are facing needs no demonstration,' proclaimed the *Spectator* following polling day in 1951.[1] Nor was that
usually sober journal alone in airing the view that few Governments had
ever come to power faced by such formidable problems.

Economic and financial instability was the most vexing and pressing of
Britain's difficulties. As Harry Crookshank, the Conservatives' Leader
of the House, said, three weeks after the Election: 'Finance, of course,
at the moment overshadows everything. We are in a desperately serious
position.'[2] He was not exaggerating. At the beginning of July 1951 it had
been estimated that there would be a dollar deficit for 1951–2 of $500m.
and a United Kingdom overall balance of payments deficit, including
stockpiling, of £375m. Only two months later the former had risen to an
incredible $1,200m.[3] Within hours of becoming Prime Minister,
Churchill was presented at his London house in Hyde Park Gate with a
Treasury Report, brought personally to him by the two most senior civil
servants, Sir Edward Bridges and Sir Norman Brook.[4] Churchill at once
sent a copy to Clement Attlee so that he might be under no illusions over
the Government's starting-point. As Churchill told the House ten days
later:

It was certainly scratch. In overseas payments we are in a deficit crisis worse than 1949, and in many ways worse than even 1947. Confidence in sterling is impaired. In the present half-year, we are running into an external deficit at the rate of £700m. a year compared with an annual rate of surplus of about £350m. in the same period a year ago. That means a deterioration of more than £1,000m. a year. The latest estimates show that in 1952, on present trends and policies and without making any allowance for further speculative losses, the United Kingdom would have a deficit on its general balance of overseas payments of between £500m. and £600m., and the loss to the central gold and dollar reserves in the transactions of the sterling area as a whole with the rest of the world might be appreciably more.[5]

According to Rab Butler, the new Chancellor, his officials visualised 'a collapse greater than had been foretold in 1931'.[6] Indeed, the Treasury feared that Britain was 'heading for early bankruptcy unless immediate remedies were employed'.[7] This news was undoubtedly a shock to the new Government, as the full gravity of the economic situation had not unnaturally been minimised by Labour Ministers during the course of the Election campaign. The *Observer* was severe in its strictures: 'Chief responsibility for their misleading reticence must attach to Labour, for Labour Ministers were aware of facts which have become more fully accessible to their Conservative successors only within the last week.'[8] Comparison with the country's position in the worst days of the war did not seem far-fetched. In the words of *The Times*: 'The supreme test of Mr. Churchill and his chosen colleagues, many of them his aides in the wartime enterprise, is to prove that they really have a policy for 1951 as they had for 1940.'[9]

Election pledges were, as a result, hard to keep, not least in the social services which were, according to the *Sunday Times*, in 'a muddle'.[10] A shortage of money had already begun to hamper Labour's welfare plans in its last year in power. To pay for the Korean rearmament, Hugh Gaitskell, in his Budget of April 1951, had felt it necessary to charge adult patients under the N.H.S. half the cost of their dentures and spectacles. This led to the resignation of Aneurin Bevan, who had been Minister of Labour only since January, Harold Wilson[11] as President of the Board of Trade and John Freeman[12] as Parliamentary Secretary at the Ministry of Supply. As a leader in *The Times* neatly put it: 'The years 1950–1 will go down to history as the years in which a Labour Government . . . concluded that Britain could not enjoy social security without national security.'[13]

The problem was caused essentially by the attempt, with few more resources than in 1938, to provide for a million more young children as well as nearly two million more elderly men and women drawing pensions without a means test. After 1945 Labour had initially attempted to disregard the view of the Beveridge Report that subsistence pensions for all old people must be ruled out for at least twenty years on grounds of expense, but they soon came to realise the impossibility of realising their hopes. As swollen numbers of school children began to pass through the schools – the post-war 'bulge' – Britain faced the prospect of having to pay for the welfare state at a time of falling living standards. The Conservatives came to power when the high hopes of just a few years before of a universal and free welfare service appeared about to be dashed.

In the Commonwealth and colonies, the new Government was faced by two urgent problems. A comparatively minor matter had come before Labour's Commonwealth Secretary, Patrick Gordon Walker, but it nevertheless was to occupy the attention of his Department for a long period and to earn it more criticism than any other single matter in the early post-war years.[14] Within a week of assuming office in March 1950 Gordon Walker banished the heir to the chieftainship of the Bamangwato tribe of Bechuanaland after unrest in Southern Africa caused by his marriage to a white Englishwoman, Ruth Williams, in 1948.[15] This produced a rumpus in the House and criticism in the press, the more so because Gordon Walker also felt it necessary, while the chieftainship was in abeyance, to exile the regent, his uncle, Tchekedi Khama. The Conservatives, having called for the immediate termination of Tchekedi's banishment, found that the Election bequeathed the problem to them to solve. Labour had 'left a legacy of trouble' in the area according to *The Times*,[16] and the *Observer* commented in a leader that as a result of their policy in this and other colonial territories, there was an urgent need for the new Government to improve on Labour's handling of African questions. Indeed, added the article, Africa had become a 'cockpit of inter-racial conflict'.[17]

In Malaya there had been an escalation in communist terrorism culminating in the assassination on 6th October of Sir Henry Gurney, the British High Commissioner, news of which broke in the midst of the Election campaign. October saw as much tension and violence as during any previous month. All were agreed that drastic action was needed: 'If public confidence is to be restored a new outlook, new plans . . . a new organisation, and it may be new tactics also, are needed in Malaya.'[18]

A further underlying but largely hidden crisis lay buried in the very structure of the Commonwealth. Already India had entered the Commonwealth as a republic. What ties would hold the member countries together if not allegiance to a common Crown? Traditionally, Britain's bipartisan policy had been to encourage dependencies to develop into self-governing and independent states 'within the Commonwealth'. This policy had gone unchallenged until the South African Prime Minister Dr. Malan insisted in 1951 on the right of all Commonwealth countries to be consulted before new members were admitted. But, as Colin Legum wrote in the *Observer*, 'The implications of Dr. Malan's demand left no doubt as to what he had in mind since it was made with reference to the Gold Coast,'[19] then moving swiftly towards independence. The Conservatives were thus faced with the imminent prospect of the break-up or at least radical change to the Commonwealth.

In his first full statement in the House on foreign affairs, on 19th November, 1951, Eden spoke of the 'grim reality' of several problems confronting Britain. 'The outlook is admittedly grave. It is even danger-ous.' Although he continued, with characteristic reassurance, to state 'It is by no means desperate.'[20] Churchill echoed Eden's last sentiment when he reflected: 'Looking back over the last few years, I cannot feel that the danger of a third world war is so great now as it was at the time of the Berlin Air Lift crisis in 1948,'[21] the military position of the West having greatly improved over the previous twelve months.

In Eden's view the 'forbidding chasm that separates East and West' was 'the cardinal issue in international affairs'. He also deplored the fact that there was 'virtually no diplomatic contact between East and West'.[22] This was itself a startling observation after six and a half years of Labour Governments which initially boasted of their ability to talk frankly with the Soviet Union.

The outbreak of hostilities in Korea in June 1950 led to an immedi-ate intensification of the cold war. The United Nations' forces swept forward in October but could not end hostilities, and the war escalated after the intervention of the Chinese. Alarm at demands voiced in the United States for drastic action against the Chinese was one main reason which led Attlee to fly to Washington at the end of November for urgent consultations with President Truman. Events however stabilised and in July 1951 protracted armistice negotiations began at Panmunjom. But further blows to British interests had occurred in Persia and Egypt,[23] the latter escalating seriously during the Election campaign. The Conserva-tives came to power in 1951 when British interests were under attack in Europe (with the continued threat of invasion by the Soviet Union), and in the Middle and Far East, at the very time when her ability to pay for overseas commitments was under severe strain. Could Britain afford to maintain its position as a Super Power in 1951, or would it have to drastically reduce its commitments? Few could see the Conservatives. especially with Churchill at the helm, being willing to allow Britain to become a second-rate nation in international affairs.

What policies did the Conservatives offer to the electorate for administrating this bewildering inheritance?

The 1951 Manifesto outlined a number of general principles as well as specific policy proposals. It bore the distinctive mark of Churchill's own writing and philosophy: 'The prime need is for a stable Government with several years before it, during which time national interests must be faithfully held far above party feuds or tactics.'[24]

The common promise appeared that, 'A Conservative Government will cut out all unnecessary Government expenditure, simplify the administrative machine, and prune waste and extravagance in every department.' Freedom of the individual and incentives were stressed, as was sound finance. The Manifesto pledged the maintenance of Imperial Preference and a place for 'the Empire producer in the home market', second only to 'the home producer'. Progress would be made towards a 'united Europe', a statement open to wide interpretation. The heavy rearmament programme of the socialists was to be supported with an excess profits tax on company profits to trap those industrialists benefiting excessively from the rearmament boom.

This determination not to revert to an out-and-out capitalist society was extended on other fronts. Tax revision on commercial and industrial profit was promised, restrictive practices were to be minimised and the Monopolies Commission greatly strengthened. Iron and steel, and road haulage were to be denationalised, but that was all: coal and rail were only to be reorganised and decentralised. All remaining nationalised industries were to be brought under the jurisdiction of the Monopolies Commission, and their activities overseen by 'strict Parliamentary review'. The 'Workers' Charter', which had appeared during the period of Opposition, was to be brought into being as early as possible after talks with employers and unions, and where practicable the same principles would be extended to agriculture. The system of guaranteed agricultural prices and markets would be maintained. The fishing industry was to have protection from unrestricted foreign dumping, and efforts were to be made to secure international agreement to prevent over-fishing. Food subsidies were not to be altered radically for the present, but the longer term aim was to move from universal to selective benefits for the needy.

Housing was regarded as the priority in the field of social policy, and overall second only to national defence: the target was to be 300,000 houses a year, with emphasis on private ownership. Town planning and development charges were to be overhauled. But there were no detailed pledges for education, health or pensions, other than a general commitment to providing a better service.

Various administrative changes were advocated. 'Orders and rules' were to be reduced, and existing regulations kept under more rigorous Parliamentary scrutiny. An all-Party conference was to be called to consider proposals for the reform of the House of Lords. University constituencies which had been disenfranchised contrary to the agreement reached by all three Parties during the war were to be restored. Scotland was to have greater control over her own affairs, and a Cabinet Minister was to be appointed charged with the care of Welsh affairs. In a singularly banal phrase, 'confidence and responsibility' were to be restored to local government.

Several ideas expressed in the Manifesto were developed in detail in a further statement of Conservative policy, 'Britain Strong and Free', published five days later. The three main 'heads' of policy were described as an effective defence programme, safeguards for the traditional way of life, and the maintenance of full employment and improvement in living standards.

In non-domestic objectives, the document was more precise than the Manifesto. The Conservatives would do their best to make the United Nations an effective instrument, but the surest hope of peace lay in close association with the Commonwealth and the United States. An organisation on the lines of the wartime Combined Chiefs of Staff was suggested, a proposal that aroused considerable apprehension in the White House. The threat to Western Europe would best be met by organising a European force containing contingents from the countries to be defended. For home defence, the formation of a Home Guard cadre was proposed. Proposals for Commonwealth defence included the establishment of an advisory Commonwealth Defence Council, a combined staff, and standardisation of equipment, organisation and training. A permanent civil liaison staff was suggested to improve Commonwealth cooperation in other spheres, and an Empire economic conference was to be called as a matter of urgency.

'Britain Strong and Free' had less fresh material to add on the domestic side. Major reforms for local government were proposed, among them being legislation to re-allocate functions, the creation of a new Boundary Commission, and an overhaul of methods of raising local revenue. Proposals for social policy were expanded. The Rent Restriction Acts were to be reviewed, and on the health services side, the system of charges was to be re-examined to establish 'proper' priorities, over-centralisation in hospital services was to be reduced, doctors were to be given greater freedom from paper-work, and a system of priorities was to be established for dental treatment. But still no precise pledges on education appeared, a strange omission in view of the pressure on school buildings and the shortage of teachers. Pensions received more specific treatment: the whole position of pensioners was to be reviewed to see that the most pressing needs were met first.

Considering the bitterness of Party strife since the war, and in particular during the year and a half following the 1950 Election, the Conservatives' two policy statements were surprisingly undoctrinaire. The following Chapters examine the extent to which these pledges were executed and, in the Epilogues, the position that the Churchill Government left to *its* successor in the spring of 1955.

Chapter 2 Prime Minister and Government I

Part 1 The Prime Minister

After his defeat in the General Election of 1945, Winston Churchill was determined to be re-elected as Prime Minister. Throughout the long period in Opposition, he had taken little interest in details, nor did he after 26th October, 1951 when the Conservatives returned to power. Instead he had broad ideas which he strove to implement on three fronts: personnel, machinery of government and policy.

The selection of senior Ministers for the Government bore Churchill's distinctive stamp. Not just responsible for its balance in Cabinet being weighted in favour of moderate rather than doctrinaire Conservatives, he also favoured the appointment of non-specialist Ministers to a number of Departments. 'Mr. Churchill has shaped [the Government] in his own way . . . The Prime Minister does not rate specialist knowledge necessarily high' was how the *Spectator* on 9th November described his appointments. Further, he adapted uneasily to new faces, wanting around him only men whom he knew and trusted. He thus persuaded five men who had either not been in politics or who had not been particularly active politically between 1945–51 to join the Cabinet: Lord Cherwell,[1] Lord Ismay,[2] Lord Leathers,[3] Sir Walter Monckton,[4] and, from March 1952, Lord Alexander of Tunis.[5] But some others he also knew well turned him down: Sir John Anderson,[6] Lord Asquith of Bishopstone,[7] Brendan Bracken[8] and Lord Portal.[9] He further insisted on rearrangements to the Prime Minister's Private Office.

David Pitblado had only three months previously been appointed Principal Private Secretary to Clement Attlee. Churchill did not know him, and consequently wanted to reappoint Leslie Rowan, who had been Private Secretary, 1941–5 and Principal Private Secretary to the Prime Minister, 1945–7. Sir Edward Bridges, the Head of the Civil Service,[10] told him flatly that this was impossible: Rowan, Head of the Overseas Finance Division at the Treasury since earlier in the year, held too senior a position. Churchill's thoughts then turned to a young man whom he had much liked in the Private Office during the war, John Colville. Although told that he was far too junior,[11] Churchill persisted,

28

and Colville, having refused a proposal that he should replace Pitblado, was made Joint Principal Private Secretary alongside him.[12]

For the first four months of the Government, Churchill was also Minister of Defence. He found the incumbent Chief Staff Officer, his chief defence aide, Sir Kenneth McLean, unsympathetic, not due to any lack of quality but because, as with Pitblado, he did not know him. After some fuss,[13] Sir Ian Jacob, who had been Military Assistant Secretary of the War Cabinet, was brought in to replace McLean.

One further rearrangement of official personnel was the most significant of all. Churchill reversed a decision, announced shortly before the General Election, to appoint Sir Thomas Padmore as Secretary to the Cabinet in succession to Sir Norman Brook, a man with whom he had built up an intimate relationship during the war.[14] After much discussion, it was arranged that Padmore should return to the Treasury, with increased status, and Brook should continue as Cabinet Secretary.[15]

As he particularly wanted a small Cabinet, Churchill decided to appoint three co-ordinating Ministers,[16] hoping, as a result, that this would cut down on the need for Cabinet and official Committees, which he distrusted, especially when peopled exclusively by civil servants.[17] He foresaw major reorganisations on the economic front, and tried to appoint Ministers to co-ordinate nationalised industries and production, and to implement a number of measures designed to curb the power of the Treasury, which he considered excessive.[18] But his attempts to reorganise the machinery of government were largely abortive, and within two years the traditional pattern of the Civil Service had reasserted itself.[19]

Churchill's main interest in policy lay in foreign affairs, followed by defence, but he was not without broad aims on the domestic side. Determined to build a relationship of trust with the trade unions, he gave precise instructions to the Minister of Labour to avoid conflict at all cost, even intervening personally on a number of occasions to ensure that his policy was carried out.[20] The Cabinet, however, was not always found in favour; some members felt Churchill was going too far to woo the unions. The Leader of the House, Harry Crookshank, a not uncommon critic of the Prime Minister, noted in his diary in October 1952 how at a party at Number Ten there were 'eyebrows raised' because Churchill had invited three trade union leaders.[21] Anxious that road transport be denationalised as he considered state control an infringement of the liberty of the individual, he drove the Minister hard to speed up the process. Similarly, he wanted to push ahead with derationing and de-control, to abolish all unnecessary restrictions on the individual, such as identity cards. Shortly after the Election, Churchill told Colville his policy was 'houses, red meat and not getting scuppered'.[22] Churchill felt deep concern for the condition and quality of life of the 'ordinary man'. He therefore supported the Minister of Housing against the Treasury in his effort to speed up new home-building, and sought ways that meat production could be increased. Even the continued widespread existence of bomb sites concerned him: he wanted people to be able to forget about war and enjoy the fruits of peace.

Details, however, bored him. He continued his wartime 'searchlight technique' of focusing his attention on particular policy matters, but the beam was dimmer and moved at a slower tempo. Though he spent hours closeted with the Chancellor, he had increasingly little to contribute to discussions on the Budget or other aspects of Treasury policy. Highly selective in the areas that interested him, he contributed little to social policy apart from the support for the house-building programme. Similarly the nationalised and private industries, trade policy, and the work of Departments such as the Home Office, Scottish Office and Post Office continued untroubled by more than his minimal interest or interference. Even one of the most important items of domestic legislation during 1951–5, the setting up of independent television, he regarded as rather a distraction.

Churchill was, however, concerned to foster the relationship with the Commonwealth, particularly with its older partners, and shone during the two meetings in London of the Commonwealth Prime Ministers. Yet he contributed little of practical value to Commonwealth or colonial affairs. Defence policy was another matter. He had been Minister of Defence throughout the war and had a long and abiding interest in defence topics, having also served as Minister responsible for each individual Service, and as Minister responsible for their supply.[23] He initially appointed himself Minister of Defence in 1951, and despite giving up the post after four months he deliberately appointed a new Minister, Lord Alexander of Tunis, who would not object to his continued interference. He initiated a major review, the 'Global Strategy Paper' of 1952, which decisively altered British defence thinking. He chaired the key Cabinet Defence Committee throughout, but once again when it came to detail – unlike during the Second World War – he contributed little.

Foreign affairs were Churchill's main interest. Above all he sought to encourage the 'special relationship' with the United States, and reduce world tension by arranging a summit meeting between the Heads of Government of the United Kingdom, the United States, the Soviet Union, and possibly also, France. Privately, he also coveted the Nobel Peace Prize. His nurturing of the relationship with the United States met with some success, and as one of his first tasks when back in office he visited President Truman in January 1952. Only when the last hopes of his proposed summit meeting faded early in 1955, did he decide to retire.

Churchill was always very much his own man, relying less than any other post-war Prime Minister on the advice of others, either inside or outside the Government. Ironically, there was some criticism that he surrounded himself with 'cronies',[24] but this tended to be for companionship rather than advice. Brendan Bracken, a close friend for almost thirty years, resigned his seat in February 1952, having decided he found politics and politicians no longer sufficiently stimulating, but he continued to be a close observer and commentator from the wings. Though he accepted a viscountcy, he seldom went to the House of Lords; 'the morgue', he called it. His influence on Churchill, once considerable, gradually receded over the following months: Churchill seldom went to Bracken's Lord North Street home (in Westminster) and the latter visited Number Ten only infrequently, although they would meet at the 'Other Club', the dining club formed by Churchill and F. E. Smith in 1911, which continued to meet at regular intervals.[25] Certainly he urged Churchill to rationalise some Government Departments,[26] and offered him advice on appointments,[27] but these interventions were not particularly significant.[28]

Yet Bracken and another old friend, Lord Beaverbrook, were, if temporarily, much in evidence after Churchill's stroke in June 1953. Until then, Beaverbrook was an infrequent visitor to Number Ten or Chartwell, and had little success in his attempts to influence policy.[29] Both had great affection for Churchill and were deeply upset by the news of his illness: they were amongst the very few close friends who regretted his retirement in April 1955.[30] Yet Churchill had, since the end of the war, become increasingly distrustful of Beaverbrook's political advice,[31] and during his last Administration listened more carefully to Lord Camrose, proprietor of the *Daily Telegraph*.[32] It is, however, a feature of this period that Churchill not only listened less closely to press friends than he had done during the war, but also that their influence steadily declined throughout his last premiership.[33]

Churchill remained close to three older friends in particular: Violet Bonham Carter, who would join the family for occasional weekends, Lady Lytton, formerly Pamela Plowden, his first love and a friend of Lady Churchill too, and Bernard Baruch, the American financier and elder statesman, with whom Churchill stayed in New York in January 1953, and maintained an irregular correspondence. Weekends and holidays were often spent in the company of his family: there were far fewer 'political' and other friends than had been the case in the war. Lady

31

Churchill, the only person who never bored her husband and was never overawed by him in any way, had a considerable influence.[34]

Churchill's relationship with his doctor, Lord Moran, is of key significance. Not only does Moran himself claim to have had a decisive influence on the Prime Minister's plans, but he also wrote a diary which will remain a major source on this period.[35] Churchill's doctor since late 1941, he was an ambitious man, a former President of the Royal College of Physicians, 1941–50, who even asked to be made Minister of Health early on in the Administration.[36]

Without doubt Moran was a tireless and loyal friend to Churchill, endlessly prepared to put himself out to accommodate the eccentricities of his patient, of whom he had an excellent understanding.[37] Churchill for his part always treated him in a polite and friendly fashion, but he never regarded Moran as an intimate, nor is there any evidence that on matters of major importance, he let himself be influenced by him,[38] even though Moran believed he was decisive in encouraging Churchill to continue as Prime Minister. Moran took the view that it was his duty, as Churchill's doctor, to encourage him to remain in office, even though for at least the last year of Churchill's premiership, he judged him unfit for the task. In his preface to the diaries he wrote: 'I was, I think, alone in urging him to hang on . . . It was my job as his doctor to postpone [the day of his retirement] as long as I could.'[39] Churchill took Moran on three of his four official transatlantic trips,[40] not just because it was a comfort to have his doctor on call, but also, one feels, because Moran would have been hurt not to have been included. Churchill's style of tossing ideas around with his companions, often to test their effect, mistakenly inclined Moran to give these half-formed thoughts and suggestions the status of hard fact.

After Moran had seen Churchill he would often drop in on the Private Office. The two Joint Principal Private Secretaries, Colville and Pitblado, were meant to look after the foreign and home sides respectively, but in practice there was no such clear-cut division.[41] Churchill grew to like and value Pitblado, an exceptionally able official, though he never became as close to him as he did to Colville,[42] a man of initiative and wit.[43] As he was widely known to be in Churchill's confidence, Ministers would talk to Colville as a preliminary to approaching the Prime Minister, and Colville would often discuss with Ministers what Churchill thought or had in mind.

Colville and Pitblado both worked in an office which led out of the Cabinet room at Number Ten. In a further room beyond were the Private Secretaries, initially three, but after Colville's arrival reduced to two. E. G. Cass held the job until 1952 and was succeeded by P. G.

Oates until 1954; they were broadly responsible for home affairs and Parliamentary Questions. Churchill liked both men but never found their company as congenial as that of the Private Secretaries on the foreign side, David Hunt,[44] who was succeeded in October 1952 by Anthony Montague Browne, Colville's own suggestion from the Foreign Office as a man Churchill was likely to find sympathetic.[45] It was an inspired choice, and Montague Browne remained as Private Secretary to Churchill from his retirement in 1955 until his death in January 1965.[46]

Churchill initially did not appoint a Parliamentary Private Secretary. During the years in Opposition Lord John Hope had been asked, but declined,[47] and after the General Election, Douglas Dodds-Parker was similarly approached but to no avail.[48] Churchill, somewhat anxious to avoid a further rebuff from another young man, decided after the Election to appoint his son-in-law Christopher Soames,[49] but, on the advice of his wife, who was wary of the charges of nepotism her husband had endured in the past, he agreed not to make the appointment public. After some months it became clear to all that Soames was proving a most valuable aide; thus in February 1953 Churchill decided to make his appointment official. Soames 'managed' Churchill very well, keeping him in good temper but not minding when he lost it. He also kept him in touch with backbench opinion and the Party at large, throwing himself into the job with enormous energy far beyond the demands of the office. He was available whenever Churchill needed him and, like Colville, spent much time with the old man, his youth and enthusiasm bringing him solace.[50]

Assessing precisely the influence of Colville and Soames is difficult. Moran remarked, 'The manner in which anything is presented to Winston before he has made up his mind – that is the crucial point – and the time chosen to bring it forward surely plays a part in shaping things. It would be easy, I think, to underrate the part [secretaries] have played in the shaping of events.'[51] As Churchill was absorbed increasingly by foreign affairs, those close to him were able to bring more influence to bear on domestic policy matters, although it must be said that neither Colville nor Soames imposed their own judgment in affairs of state.

Churchill's health and performance undoubtedly deteriorated from 1951 to 1955, but even in the last months he was far from 'ga-ga', or incapable of performing his job. It is a feature of an Indian Summer that the autumn temperature is more subdued, and that the atmosphere has a hazy or even smoky appearance. His staff who had worked with him during the war found him generally less effective after 1951,[52] but eye-witnesses disagree as to how much and by what stages his faculties actually declined. During the period in Opposition he had suffered two strokes[53] and once in power suffered two more, a minor arterial spasm in February 1952 and a major stroke in June 1953.[54] Some found him equally alert after the 1953 stroke as before, others saw a major decline. Naturally, he had both good and bad days, so witnesses who saw him irregularly are likely to give a misleading picture. The most reliable overall view is given by the man whose relationship with Churchill was the most important during 1951–5, Sir Norman Brook.[55] Not only was Brook a man of great integrity, whose judgment Churchill's successors as Prime Minister, Anthony Eden and Harold Macmillan, came to value highly, but also Brook was one of the very few who encountered Churchill almost daily throughout his last period at Number Ten.

Brook saw three distinct periods, from October 1951 to his June 1953 stroke, from June 1953 until late 1954, and from then until his retirement in April 1955. In the first, he was less energetic than in the war, the pace of his work was slower, he was less absorbed by peacetime problems, and he found speeches more of a burden, but his performance did not fall far short of his own expectations; he could rise to the big occasion, had the full support of his Party, and dominated his colleagues in Cabinet. Initially in the second period Churchill was concerned to preserve his life and thereafter to remain in office.[56] Until late 1954 his confidence and energy were reduced, and he was less masterful with his Cabinet colleagues, but still managed to hold his own with the work.[57] From late 1954 onwards, however, he lacked the physical and mental energy to give to papers and people the full attention they deserved.[58] Only in his last six months in office was his unfitness for the task beyond doubt.[59]

Churchill was undoubtedly less happy as a peacetime Premier than he had been in tackling the problems of war. In particular he found economic problems baffling and bemoaned the loss of co-operation that had existed during the War Coalition.[60] As he was to say later to the American President, Eisenhower: 'In the last twenty-five years of peace and war, things have gotten [sic] ten or fifteen times more complicated. The problems I have now to face are much greater in numbers and complexity than they used to be.'[61] When he took over the Foreign Office temporarily in the late spring of 1953, he even found the details of diplomatic affairs difficult and irksome.

Churchill never felt entirely happy as Leader of the Conservative Party, and at times became upset at the inevitable quarrels with his former wartime colleagues, now on the Opposition benches. At one point during 1952 he was saying that he thought the country in such a bad state economically that a new Coalition Government was desirable.[62] In his Party political broadcast just before Christmas of 1951, Churchill said that on social services, foreign affairs and defence, nine-tenths of the people agree on nine-tenths of what has been and will be done.[63] Certainly he shared some Tory attitudes: belief in the Empire, for instance, the need for good defence provisions and the liberty of the individual, but he never completely identified himself with the Conservative Party. He told Eisenhower: 'Many men in the Labour Party are very careful not to go too far. Our Labour Party is very sensible. Attlee and Morrison have a very great deal of courage and have come forward in favour of Germany's rearmament.'[64] At times it even appeared that his great mission during his last premiership, his hope of top-level talks between the Super Powers, was more popular with the Opposition than with his own Party.

Despite his declining powers, he insisted on one point: the language of his major speeches remained his own: he would often scribble over drafts submitted by the relevant Government or Party officials.[65] His last two major speeches as Prime Minister, on foreign affairs and defence in March 1955,[66] were entirely his own work, evidence to show that even at the end he could still rise magnificently to the big occasion.

Churchill's achievement was the least significant in the first of the three main ways that a Prime Minister makes his impact on public affairs: as a co-ordinator of administration and policy.[67] The Government machine, after some initial grinding, adapted itself well to Churchill's unusual style after the clockwork efficiency of Attlee. But *The Economist*, in a valedictory article on 9th April, 1955, told of complaints that he paid insufficient time to domestic problems, that in defence affairs he preferred his personal predilections to the carefully considered policies of the expert advisers, and that his wishes on the foreign policy front were often at variance with those of the Foreign Secretary, the Foreign Office and Britain's principal allies. This criticism, however, fails to account for or give sufficient credit to Churchill for his own peculiar working methods. Once he had appointed a Minister, with few exceptions, mainly Anthony Eden at the Foreign Office, John Maclay at Transport and Harold Macmillan at Defence, he allowed them a free hand, in marked contrast to many of his successors who attempted to over-centralise and over-interfere. He was also impartial, and backed a Minister if he felt it necessary, regardless of his personal feelings about him. His presence provided a stable environment in which Ministers were free, untroubled by rivalries, to carry out the pledges of the Party Manifesto and administer their own Departments.

Churchill should also be given credit for the way in which, as a man in his late seventies, he adapted himself to the post-war world, and moved with the times even in areas for which he had no great personal enthusiasm. He willingly acquiesced in development of the welfare state, progress towards independence in the colonies and the prospect that the old Dominions of the Commonwealth would be swamped by new members. More than many, he saw the need for a rearmed Germany. The withdrawal from the Sudan and the Suez base caused him considerably more distress, but in the end he did not allow sentiment to get the better of him.

he was given credit for at the time. Critics belittled his role, as he played little part in the rethinking of Conservative policy during 1945–51, instigated chiefly by Rab Butler, or the restructuring of the Party's organisation, where Sir David Maxwell Fyfe and Lord Woolton were mainly responsible. Others felt he lacked the common touch, or that they needed a Leader who performed well on television, then just beginning to become a force. But Churchill's presence gave the Party an exalted and non-partisan Leader, who provided a broad and protective umbrella under which the Party could adapt itself to the problems of being in power.[68] By his choice of Ministers in 1951 and his continual moderating influence, Churchill personally ensured that the representatives of empirical and pragmatic Conservatism commanded the senior posts in the Party, a position they were to hold until the departure of Edward Heath as Leader in 1975.

His major success, however, came as the nation's leader. Here lay his greatness, in which he rises far above any other post-war Prime Minister. The job is not just to be the head of an efficient machine, as Attlee and Macmillan frequently became. Nor is it merely to ensure the survival of, and to foster the interests of his own Party, an end with which Harold Wilson and James Callaghan were all too often preoccupied. The Prime Minister has a larger responsibility, to lead, inspire and unite his countrymen. Churchill had a spiritual nature, of which he had little understanding, and which could on occasion be smothered as he strove to snatch at the vainglory of the hour. But he did not always allow himself to be cheated in this way; during 1951–5 his spirit could still flow out, unhampered by considerations of personal gain.

Few Prime Ministers would have insisted that his own and his Ministers' salaries should be reduced during the period of rearmament and economic stringency (Ministers by £1,000 to £4,000 and his own by £3,000 to £7,000), or pleaded in his first major speech as Prime Minister in the House of Commons (on 6th November) for the end of sterile Party strife and doctrinaire policy-making.[69]

Two years later, in November 1953, he pleaded again for limitations on the extent to which Party strife intruded into the scrutiny of national problems: 'It is really not possible to assume that one of these . . . masses of voters possess all the virtues and all the wisdom and the other lot are dupes or fools . . .'[70] 'Chips' Channon[71] commented in his diary: 'It was an Olympian spectacle. A supreme performance which we shall never see again from him or anyone else. In eighteen years in this honourable House I have never heard anything like it . . .'[72] A unifying force in Parliament, he helped to prevent the emergence of personal antipathies between the Parties and elevated the entire ambience in which politics were conducted. To an extent he was regarded as above Party politics, which accounts for Labour forgiving his occasional blunders, in particular the lack of judgment he displayed in the debate on the hydrogen bomb in April 1954[73] and his sensational error in mentioning at a trivial speech in Woodford in November 1954 a telegram he believed (in fact incorrectly) he had sent Montgomery at the end of the war urging him to stack German arms so they could be issued to German soldiers if the Soviet advance continued.[74]

None could match his vision (or, indeed his oratory and power to move), as can be seen by his thoughts on three key issues facing the post-war world. He was one of the first to foresee the way in which individual liberty would be eroded in totalitarian and the so-called free countries in the West. On relations with the Soviet Union he believed more could be gained through friendship than enmity:

> If there is not at the summit of the nations the will to win the greatest prize and the greatest honour ever offered to mankind, doom-laden responsibility will fall upon those who now possess the power to decide. At the worst the participants in the meeting would have established more intimate contacts. At the best we might have a generation of peace.[75]

He fostered and popularised the development in strategic thought heralded by the coming of atomic and nuclear weapons:

> Unless a trustworthy and universal agreement upon disarmament, conventional and nuclear alike, can be reached . . . there is only one sane policy for the free world in the next few years. That is what we call defence through deterrents [which] may at any time become the parents of disarmament . . . it may well be that we shall by a process of sublime irony have reached a stage in this story where safety will be the sturdy child of terror, and survival the twin brother of annihilation.[76]

Paradoxically, however, his success in the role of the nation's leader was also the area of his main failure. For Churchill after the war possessed only the strength to sense the direction, but not to follow through policy. With Europe, he had given a mighty clarion call for greater unity in Opposition. But once in office he lacked the energy to translate his thoughts into precise proposals and the determination which would have been needed to force them on Eden and the Foreign Office. Further, he did not envisage the tight-knit federation nor the extent of British commitment favoured by his supporters on this issue. So, too, with his enthusiasm for summits. He was fully awake to the danger from the Soviet Union, especially after the advent of nuclear weapons, and the need to maintain vigilant defence. Yet at the same time he anticipated the utter futility of the Cold War, in material and moral terms, and the consequent need to seek an accord, a partial opening of the Iron Curtains of distrust, but from a position of strength. He saw in the death of Stalin a unique opportunity for pushing ahead with his ideas, but he lacked the ability to convince his colleagues (or indeed the Eisenhower Administration in America), and ultimately the physical fitness to see his hopes realised.

Part 2 The Succession

Within nine months of the Conservatives' return to power in October 1951, four senior members of the Cabinet met privately at Harry Crookshank's Pont Street mansion in Knightsbridge to discuss how the Prime Minister, Winston Churchill, might be induced to retire. Four years before the same house had been the scene of another clandestine meeting of a group of Churchill's senior colleagues, to discuss the same question. One of their number, James Stuart, described the event:

> [The house] was thought to be a discreet place as it was desirable to avoid the attention of the press. I can think of nowhere better suited to such a purpose. As you entered through the heavily leaded glass door – the glass was of colours calculated to obscure all light – the catacomb-like gloom was relieved only by one small weak electric bulb, like the light on the tabernacle 'dimly burning'. . . . We gathered in an upstairs drawing-room decorated with screens, Eastern *objets d'art*, and uncomfortable Victorian furniture. It was all very serious and intense. . . .[1]

It is not as if the Conservatives were without an heir apparent. From the middle of the Second World War at least there had been little doubt that

Anthony Eden would succeed Churchill as Party Leader; only the timing remained in doubt.[2] Why then was Churchill so intransigent when the moment of decision came?

Throughout the six years of Opposition he had longed to be returned as Prime Minister by the vote of the people.[3] He had never won an Election as Party Leader, but had lost two, in 1945 and 1950, the former disastrously.[4] Yet he continued in politics, despite his wife's view that he should have retired in 1945.[5] Even his eventual Election success was tinged with mild disappointment at the Conservative majority of only seventeen.

Privately there were those who shared Lady Churchill's view. Influential Conservatives had reservations about his age and his lack of familiarity with modern trends and the Party's younger men but in 1951 these thoughts were not aired openly. A confidential poll, conducted in August 1949, however, found that if Churchill were to resign as Party Leader the total Conservative vote was unlikely to be affected.[6]

Initially he intended to stay just one year, or so he told his intimate friends,[7] and had certain limited but specific objectives.[8] But after George VI's death in February 1952 he was provided with an excuse for staying on; how could he possibly retire before seeing the young Queen crowned the following year?[9] Even a major breakdown in his health, when he suffered an arterial spasm a few days after the death of the King did not affect this determination to remain in office.

While Churchill dug in his toes, Eden worried. Even though Churchill always made a point in public of treating him as the next Conservative Leader, Eden still felt that he might be passed over. After 1951, he was conscious that the coverage Rab Butler was receiving as Chancellor of the Exchequer might eclipse his own work at the Foreign Office, which was less in the public eye than during the war.[10] Indeed, within a few months of the Election, the *Spectator* was reporting that Butler was being seen as the next Tory Prime Minister, 'if, for any unhappy reason, Mr. Eden fell out'.[11]

To help ward off the possibility of any rivals Eden decided to seek from Churchill the title of Deputy Prime Minister in the new Government,[12] arguing that this was the position held *de facto* by Clement Attlee in the war and by Herbert Morrison in the recent Labour Administration.[13] But Sir Norman Brook, the Cabinet Secretary, did not like the proposal[14] and neither did the King's Private Secretary, Sir Alan Lascelles,[15] who on George VI's own instructions, advised Churchill against such an appointment, even though there had been unofficial usage of the title for eleven years. He argued that it was an infringement of the King's prerogative to name a man Deputy Prime Minister,[16] as it suggested the King might not be free to choose Churchill's successor.

Yet despite the King's wishes, Eden adopted the title unofficially[17] and within a few months Churchill reaffirmed that he wished to formalise the appointment.[18] But several senior members of the Cabinet dissented, notably James Stuart[19] and Harold Macmillan,[20] and the notion was dropped. Churchill's support for Eden can now be seen as Machiavellian. He could couple the formal appointment of Eden as Deputy Prime Minister with a Cabinet reshuffle that would enable him to remain at the helm a year or two longer. Churchill envisaged Eden leaving the Foreign Office to take on the leadership of the House[21] and the co-ordination of home policy, as well as becoming Lord President and hence Chairman of the key Lord President's (Cabinet) Committee. His desire to remain in office apart, Churchill also thought, quite genuinely, that it would be desirable for his heir apparent to gain experience outside the Foreign Office.[22] On more than one occasion Churchill said that it had been a 'black mark' against his wartime contemporary, President Roosevelt, that he had not kept his successor, Harry Truman, completely *au courant* with political developments when it became clear his physical condition was failing.[23] But Eden was in a quandary: if he became home co-ordinator and failed then he would be discredited, and yet if he was a success Churchill would say that the new arrangement was working so well that there would be no point in making the change.[24] There was also the international situation to be considered: in the spring of 1952, Eden was reluctant to make any change until the Egyptian and European defence positions had been settled.[25] By June the issue of Eden's job was being aired in public: *The Economist*[26] said the Government might function more smoothly were Churchill to agree to limit his responsibilities and Eden give up the Foreign Office to become Deputy Prime Minister in fact as well as in name, taking over responsibility for domestic affairs.[27]

June was also the month of that first secret meeting of Churchill's Ministers in which they discussed how he might be persuaded to retire. But first let us consider further Eden's position as far as the Party, the House of Commons and the country were concerned. If Churchill had resigned within a year of taking office few would have questioned Eden's suitability as his successor. But the longer Churchill held out the more were doubts about Eden expressed.

Eden's health had never been strong. In the early summer of 1953 he underwent three major abdominal operations (the last in the United States).[28] Churchill leapt at the fresh opportunity this provided for a change in Eden's role, suggesting yet again that on his return to work he

40

should become Lord President, Leader of the House and principal speaker on foreign affairs.[29] At first Eden seriously considered this, not least as he again doubted his strength to continue in the arduous role of Foreign Secretary. But by the end of September, on his return to London, the lure of important speeches on the Egyptian and Persian positions renewed his enthusiasm for the Foreign Office.[30] Churchill let the matter rest, but in the late summer of 1954 he enquired once more whether Eden could be induced to leave the Foreign Office to devote himself to domestic affairs.[31] Eden, in the midst of delicate negotiations on the future of European defence and seeing in Churchill's suggestion a clear pretext for procrastination, declined.[32]

In the Cabinet, Churchill was not alone in wishing to see Eden broaden his horizons: Lord Swinton[33] and Stuart[34] were among those who felt that Eden's narrow domestic experience would prove a severe handicap. Many others – including Butler, Lord Cherwell, Oliver Lyttelton, Macmillan and Lord Woolton – also had anxieties about how well he would stand up to being Prime Minister, but they were also keen for Churchill to retire, and it was so widely accepted that Eden would be the successor, that they saw little advantage in canvassing their doubts.

Doubts, however, were growing. In the country as well as in his Party as a whole, Eden's standing for a would-be Prime Minister was generally high, but in the upper levels of the Party many queried his suitability.[35] The anxieties centred on his vanity and 'prima donna' affectation, as well as his limited experience and knowledge of domestic politics, even though Eden had in fact gone out of his way to take a wide interest in domestic affairs during the latter part of the Labour Government. In particular, he did not inspire universal confidence amongst his own Party in Parliament, and this disenchantment fluctuated widely during the years 1951–5,[36] though his diplomatic achievements in 1954, in particular over the problem of European defence and the war in Indo-China, greatly enhanced his reputation.[37] Despite these reservations, one should not underestimate the strength of his hold on the House of Commons and the country until the Suez crisis in 1956.

Yet in Parliament even those more interested in foreign than domestic issues increasingly had fault to find. Eden's coolness towards the various plans for British inclusion in a more integrated European community, in marked contrast some felt to his attitude during the war when he had been distinctly pro-Europe, damaged his reputation with a number of influential colleagues, including Sir David Maxwell Fyfe, Macmillan, Sir David Eccles and Duncan Sandys, as well as other Conservatives on the backbenches such as Julian Amery and Sir Robert Boothby.[38] Eden's standing with backbenchers, especially the activists on the influential Foreign Affairs Committee, was further eroded by his forward-looking ideas on independence for the Sudan and withdrawal from the large military bases in Egypt. This provoked the most serious backbench revolt during the Government; throughout 1953–4 about thirty to forty M.P.s, known as the 'Suez Group', opposed the Government's proposal to evacuate the military base on the Canal. The group contained many influential backbenchers, both old faces and new, among them Amery, Angus Maude and Enoch Powell.[39] Nor throughout 1951–5 was he able to build up a body of support amongst those men primarily interested in economic and social issues.[40] It was not just Eden's attitudes on matters of policy that aggravated Conservatives. Some (including key men in the Cabinet),[41] out of intense loyalty to Churchill, felt some antipathy towards Eden just because he was the heir, and were not subdued in expressing their feelings. It is quite possible that had the Government majority in the House during 1951–5 been greater and thus its position safer, these feelings would have come out more into the open.[42]

Churchill, too, certainly had doubts about Eden's qualifications as his successor, and again it was the lack of domestic experience that fuelled this concern,[43] a feeling shared by many in Churchill's close family and entourage. Eden, undoubtedly, knew what was said in Number Ten.

Yet underlying Churchill's thoughts was the feeling that he simply did not want to give up,[44] hence his decision to stay on so long as Prime Minister. Some of the other factors he produced have an air of 'motive hunting'[45] about them. It is not clear who among Churchill's senior colleagues first suggested that it was time he retired. Suspicion must rest on Harry Crookshank, the Leader of the House and Lord Privy Seal, at whose house the meeting of the four highly-placed Conservatives took place on 16th June, 1952.[46] Be that as it may, Crookshank and his guests, Lord Salisbury, the Commonwealth Secretary, Stuart, the Scottish Secretary, and Patrick Buchan-Hepburn, the Chief Whip, decided to take the first definite step since the Election to put pressure on Churchill: if he would not give up immediately, he must, at least, publicly set a date.[47] Moreover, Churchill's popularity as a Prime Minister with the nation at large had been steadily falling since the Election in the previous October. By May 1952, only fifty-one per cent of those interviewed in a Gallup survey said they were satisfied with his performance.[48]

Six days after the meeting most newspapers carried a rumour that Churchill was going, and on the following evening, 23rd June, Buchan-Hepburn had the unenviable task of passing on to the Prime Minister his colleagues' views.[49] He received a cold response, and the event did little to improve their relationship.[50] With Churchill unreceptive, there was little that those unhappy about the leadership could do other than bide their time. The moment had not yet come for a show of force.

Whatever Churchill's outward response, from now on the question of retirement was to remain ever present in his mind. But his views chopped and changed: in September 1952 he was undecided when to go;[51] in November he told his niece, Clarissa, who had become Eden's second wife the previous month, that he was merely looking for the opportunity, but Eden must first let him visit the United States.[52] Eden despite his impatience to inherit took the position reasonably well at this stage, but Salisbury urged him to confront Churchill and discover his intentions, and if he received an unsatisfactory reply then a group of senior Ministers (minus Eden) should sit down to consider what action to take.[53] By early 1953, Eden's attitude was hardening: with Crookshank he decided that the time was coming for a 'show-down'.[54] Eden had spent a weekend before Christmas at Chequers and had pressed Churchill for a date, but all he got was indecision.[55] By February he became so depressed by criticism of his foreign policy, especially in the Middle East, as well as by Churchill's procrastination, that he seriously considered resigning.[56]

At this point Churchill's resistance might have weakened, if it had not been for a major world event which made him all the more determined to remain. On 5th March, 1953, Stalin died after nearly thirty years as the Soviet dictator. News from the United States of the shattering power of the newly developed hydrogen bomb[57] reinforced his views on the implications of Stalin's death and encouraged him to work towards an accord between East and West, thus alleviating the possibility of war.[58] Besides, talk of Churchill's retirement was temporarily shelved when Eden was forced to give up his Foreign Office duties at the end of March to have an operation; a series of abdominal operations dictated his absence for six months. The young Queen, Elizabeth the Second, was accordingly crowned on 2nd June with few thoughts of a change of guard at Downing Street.

But this general acquiescence in Churchill's continued leadership was not to last. Three weeks after the Coronation speculation about Churchill's retirement was revived following his stroke on Tuesday 23rd June, 1953. Despite attempts to play down the severe nature of the illness news gradually leaked out to his colleagues.[59] Had Churchill died then there was a plan to make Salisbury acting Prime Minister until Eden, still in the United States recovering from the third of his operations, was restored to health.[60] Had Eden been fit he would have presided at the Cabinet (as, in the event, Butler did). Not that Churchill ever ceased to act formally as Prime Minister: his powers of recovery were remarkable; within ten days or so after his stroke he had begun to deal with official papers.

Simultaneously, his thoughts turned towards the future. He set himself at first the target of remaining until the autumn when Eden would have recovered sufficiently to take over.[61] But as Churchill's strength returned he once again became less anxious to commit himself: he would see how well his speech went at the Conservative Party Conference to be held at Margate in October.[62] To Eden, who returned to London on 26th July from the United States following an operation in Boston in June,[63] went the message that Churchill hoped he would not be over-anxious in pressing his case. In fact Eden's return to England was precipitated by a disturbing letter from Macmillan, full of news of the unsettled position in the Party due to Churchill's illness. Now, encouraged by Salisbury, he was disinclined to be lenient, but on seeing Churchill at Chequers at the beginning of August, he again backed down, not even bringing up the question.[64]

In early August, Churchill first began to mention a new date for the handover – the Queen's return from her tour of Australia in May or June 1954. At the same time he also began to work increasingly towards a meeting with the Russians after preliminary discussions with President Eisenhower (who had succeeded Truman as American President in January 1953[65]) and in these plans he saw his main justification for holding on just a little longer.[66]

His new-found vigour began to unsettle his more disgruntled colleagues,[67] who had thought the stroke would probably finish his political career.[68] Discussion continued throughout the summer recess with Salisbury, the acting Foreign Secretary, at the helm and Butler as first mate.[69] Salisbury's ploy was to write to Churchill in September saying he was worried about the age of the Cabinet and the absence of space for younger men; if it would help he was prepared to resign.[70] Although clearly intended to stimulate Churchill's own decision to retire, he was not to be moved.

Salisbury would not let the subject drop. He talked the matter over with Woolton, who agreed that Churchill should go, a view now shared by most of the Cabinet: even the unassuming Lord Alexander of Tunis thought Churchill had had his day.[71] Meanwhile Brook,[72] John Colville and Christopher Soames, Churchill's most loyal associates, felt he should carry on if he wished, and did little at this stage to discourage him.

Churchill and Eden met on 1st October on their return from their recuperative holidays, having seen very little of each other over the previous six months.[73] Although Churchill told Eden he would quit if he was unable to do his duty, he gave no clear idea of his future plans and Eden, still far from fit on his return to London, did not feel inclined to challenge his master. After the meeting, Eden invited Butler, Sir Walter Monckton and Salisbury for talks on what course to take, but all were baffled,[74] all the more so at the success of Churchill's Margate speech to the Conservative Party Conference on 10th October, a triumphant exhibition of his courage and determination. Returning to the town for the first time since 1940 in the height of the Battle of Britain, he told delegates that he would stay on for the time being, and in the speech expanded on his major theme of personal talks with leading figures in the East and West. The vote of thanks was given by a young Conservative Whip, Edward Heath, whose praise for Churchill and the 'magnificent speech' suggested more than pure form: 'Every one of us here today knows that the sum of [the Government's achievements] is due to his vision, to his inspiration and to his leadership throughout the past two years.'[75] With the speech behind him, and with growing confidence that he was still up to the task,[76] Churchill put all his energies into pursuing his proposal for summit talks. This was all very well, but Buchan-Hepburn was deeply concerned that he could not engage Churchill's interest in domestic affairs and that this created problems for other Ministers.[77] Nonetheless, Churchill's critics in the Cabinet and in the Party were temporarily silenced, and for a few months there was less evidence of rumours and discussions about his retirement[78] than there had been for fifteen months. The Queen left for her six-month Commonwealth tour at the end of November, and Churchill reaffirmed his intention of retiring in May or June[79] – or at least reconsidering the matter as that time approached.

Regardless of his disappointment at Eisenhower's lack of interest in the summit proposal at the Bermuda Conference of December 1953[80] Churchill hung on throughout the winter and early spring of 1954. He dreaded giving up and being out of it, feeling that his own unique experience should continue to be available for the benefit of the country.[81]

Churchill was seeing less of his Cabinet colleagues on an informal level, and had almost abandoned social contacts with Eden. Butler was an exception, the only person, according to Woolton, to whom he now talked.[82] At dinner on 11th March, 1954, Churchill told him he was just looking for a good opportunity to go. To Butler it seemed that Churchill's one political interest was high-level meetings with the Russians.[83] Not surprisingly, the Cabinet was again becoming restless with some of the senior members, in particular Eden, Salisbury, Butler and Woolton,

45

feeling increasing lack of direction in economic policy and home affairs generally at a time when a comprehensive new programme was needed.[84] Churchill, however, had declared he would not lead the Party in another Election, but that was all.[85] In his own mind the idea was still firmly fixed that he would retire at the end of June – or possibly July when the Parliamentary Session finished, thereby allowing certain Ministers to see through their Bills before the changeover[86] – but this was either not communicated to his colleagues or, if it was, they did not think he would stick to his word.

The debate in the House on the hydrogen bomb on 5th April,[87] described by Woolton as 'the most distressing thing I had ever seen in the House',[88] displayed Churchill's lack of judgment, in his biting attack on Clement Attlee and Herbert Morrison after the Labour Leader had gone out of his way to make a conciliatory and constructive speech. He was quite unable to deal with the uproar which fuelled the unrest in the Cabinet and also in the Party.[89] The next day Woolton dined alone with Eden. They were alarmed not the least by Churchill's decline in popularity with the electorate. The previous October, 56% of those interviewed in a Gallup survey said they were satisfied with him as Prime Minister. By April 1954 this had fallen to 48%.[90] Eden told Woolton about the circuitous route by which Churchill's intention to retire before the autumn had been transmitted to him (illustrating the distance that had come between the two men). Churchill told his friend, Henry Luce (the U.S. publisher and editor); Luce told Winthrop Aldrich (U.S. Ambassador in London), who then told Eden.[91] Both he and Woolton felt Churchill should go, Eden arguing that the coming Whitsun would be the right time, Whit Monday that year falling on 7th June, and discussed possible dates for the dissolution.[92] A week later, on 13th April, Churchill, at his own instigation, called a meeting of senior Cabinet Ministers to discuss Election dates. There Churchill announced boldly that he hoped their discussions would have nothing to do with his own plans, and that he was most anxious to have a fourth year in office.[93] This confirmed his colleagues' worst suspicions, but what could they do? The following day, Salisbury told Woolton that after the meeting the day before Eden said he could not stand it much longer and was at the end of his tether. Woolton and Salisbury were particularly suspicious that Churchill should have started telling them what Gladstone had done at the age of eighty-two – how, when a large number were trying to get rid of him, he went to Mentmore[94] and had no Cabinets for six weeks and everyone thought he was finished, but then he returned and again began to take charge of affairs.[95]

Throughout the rest of April and May an uneasy calm enveloped the issue as Churchill gave no further indication of his intentions.[96] Lady Violet Bonham Carter who stayed at Chartwell for a weekend in May, later wrote to the eminent classicist Gilbert Murray,[97] on 6th July, 1954:

> He was going through a Valley of Decision, or rather of indecision, about the time when he should relinquish power and I felt that he was in great agony of mind. I urged him, rightly or wrongly, to stay on. He said to me: 'You know you and Beaverbrook are the only two people who really want me to stay.' (If this is true I think it is the first time I have ever held the same opinion as Beaverbrook about anything!)[98]

Meanwhile from 9th May Eden was fully engaged at the Geneva Conference, where he was acting as co-Chairman, and as long as he was there an imminent changeover was out of the question,[99] a possible reason why Churchill told Eden early in June that he meant to retire at the end of July.[100] In April, however, Churchill had resumed his theme of arranging a summit, and became more determined than ever not to give up. 'I shall not relinquish office until I meet Malenkov,'[101] (Stalin's main successor) he announced. The prospect of such a meeting made him more than ever determined not to hand over to accommodate the wishes of his colleagues.[102] At the end of April he had proposed a meeting with Eisenhower as an essential preliminary to high-level meetings with the Russians, although neither the Cabinet (including Eden) nor Eisenhower[103] were keen. Nevertheless it was arranged for the last week in June. As a result, with the date of his departure for the United States approaching, Churchill felt increasingly that he could not possibly now retire in July, as this would put him in a weak position when bargaining with the President. He was clear in his own mind that the present state of international relations made resignation impossible.[104] Instead he would retire at the end of September,[105] and on 11th June he wrote accordingly to Eden.[106] He even began to talk freely of this as the date he would relinquish power,[107] to the extent of naming a specific day, 18th September.[108]

The question of summit meetings proved a flash point, which allowed the disquiet many in the Cabinet felt about his continuation in office to flare up into a full-scale row in June and July. Ministers felt that Churchill had acted over their heads in inviting the Soviets to the conference table, and threats of resignation were voiced, notably from Salisbury and Crookshank, and even in the heat of the moment Churchill himself.[109] The lack of trust and mutual recrimination over an issue of foreign affairs illustrated the extent to which the gulf had grown between Churchill and his colleagues.

The episode spurred Butler, Buchan-Hepburn, Macmillan and Salisbury to reconsider their tactics, and from their discussions emerged a new policy, to ask one of their number, Macmillan, to approach Lady Churchill to seek her support in trying to persuade her husband to retire. Ferocious in her condemnation of anyone who was disloyal to her husband, she had, nevertheless, felt increasingly over the months that he should at last give up.[110] Macmillan accordingly saw Lady Churchill on 16th July,[111] informing her that in the view of several senior colleagues Churchill should retire. She told her husband, who that day sent for Macmillan. He was in an expansive mood, saying that he had a continuing part to play in the conduct of world affairs, but if the Party were determined to get rid of him, they were at liberty to try.

Lyttelton retired as Colonial Secretary on 28th July, an event he had intended should coincide with the resignation of his beloved chief.[112] Meanwhile, the Cabinet feeling on the subject was increasingly sharp and bad tempered.[113] But his discontented colleagues were in a quandary, and Churchill knew it: they were afraid he might tell the country that he had not been allowed to continue in office, thus splitting the Party and losing the next Election. Throughout the first half of August Churchill, too, had a problem; yet again he had changed his mind and was bracing himself to tell Eden and the Cabinet that he did not, after all, wish to go in September. Although he had his doubts about continuing, now as always,[114] he simply could not bring himself to give up. This was the factor at the root of his decision to stay as Prime Minister, even if once again he justified his decision by saying that only his personal reputation could help ameliorate the uncertain international position,[115] and he also began to produce the largely spurious argument that 'fag-end' Governments were never successful.[116] He even began to voice a lack of confidence in Eden as his successor. But one should be clear that these were only justifications for his action, not the cause.

Churchill was emboldened in his resolve to remain following a lunch on 17th August with Woolton. It appears that as a result of a genuine misunderstanding, he took Woolton to be saying that he should stay on as Prime Minister.[117] The following day he boldly announced: 'I've made up my mind. I shan't go. At any rate till Christmas.'[118] Next he squared the position with those colleagues he regarded as being sympathetic. He invited Macmillan, at this stage a firm favourite, to lunch at Chartwell on 24th August and outlined his intentions. Macmillan argued, but Churchill took little notice: he was not to be deflected at this stage.[119] Butler had also been talking to Churchill and wrote to let Eden know on 16th

August of Churchill's renewed procrastination (the date of Butler's letter to Eden suggests that Churchill had decided to stay on before the Woolton meeting),[120] and two days later sent an equivocal letter to Churchill,[121] the underlying message of which was similarly brushed aside. Churchill wrote to Eden to inform him of his change of plan, again offering to make him Deputy Prime Minister, Leader of the House and give him responsibility for the 'home front'.[122] They saw each other at the end of the month, and in a reasonably calm exchange[123] Eden accepted Churchill's new plan but declined the offer of new jobs. Churchill, with his mind clearer about his intentions, and happy about the position in the Cabinet,[124] relaxed. He wrote to Bernard Baruch:

> You will, I am sure, be glad to hear that I am not thinking of retirement at the present time. I feel earnestly I still have something to contribute to the cause of 'Peace through Strength' . . . I have seemed to gather vigour as this year has progressed . . . My mind is continually oppressed by the thermonuclear problem, though I still believe it is more likely to bring war to an end than mankind.[125]

The Cabinet certainly did not like the most recent news of Churchill's plans, but were compelled for the time being to accept them.[126] Crookshank had a long talk with Macmillan at dinner on 8th September. Macmillan filled him in on Churchill's plans. Crookshank wrote in his diary 'Winston is trying to double cross Anthony and says instead of retiring mid-September he is going on indefinitely. This raised . . . whether some . . . us [sic] should resign and break up the Government. Very difficult . . .'[127]

Churchill had a quietish, more settled month in September, spending much of the time at Chartwell. He was no longer so preoccupied by the international situation and prospect of summit meetings, rather more by the long-awaited reshuffle of his Government.[128] The pressure was also off because throughout much of the month Eden was fully occupied with European affairs, and his happiness with his diplomatic successes made him less eager to press Churchill. Macmillan wrote to the Prime Minister on 2nd October asking for full consideration to be given to Eden's position, but this was brushed aside.[129] There was a vague idea in the air that Churchill might resign on his eightieth birthday on 30th November (although there is no evidence that Churchill ever seriously considered this),[130] and his colleagues had to content themselves with that.

By the autumn of 1954, however, the Party at large was becoming increasingly restless for definite news about Churchill's retirement. Speculation in the press had been almost continuous since news broke of his illness in the summer of 1953: the uncertainty had continued for too long. These feelings came to the fore at the Party Conference at Blackpool. Yet instead of giving delegates some indication of when he might retire, he delivered the Party Leader's speech on 9th October which was considered to be of great range and power.[131] It was to his surprise and chagrin then that Soames, who was keeping Churchill in touch with the views of the Party in and out of the House, reported that they now felt the time had come for him to go.[132] It is uncertain how much he took this piece of news to heart, but it does not appear to have deflected him from his determination to stay on.

For the next few weeks, until Christmas, there were other preoccupations. Major changes in the Government, announced on 18th October, encouraged the feeling that a change at Number Ten was unlikely, at least for the present. In particular, Macmillan, widely regarded as Eden's most likely successor at the Foreign Office, had just been appointed Minister of Defence.[133] Churchill discussed retirement with Macmillan at dinner on 1st November,[134] but he was reluctant to raise the question with Cabinet colleagues. A further flutter of speculation that there might be a change at Number Ten by the end of the year was provoked by some of the closing words of his birthday speech on 30th November at Westminster Hall: 'I am nearing the end of my journey: I hope I shall still have some service to render.'[135] But change there was not to be. It was felt in some quarters that talk of retirement would have been ungracious in the run-up to and aftermath of his birthday celebrations. Meanwhile confidence was beginning to return to the Party with more favourable opinion polls and by-election results.[136] Above all there was the feeling in both the Cabinet and the Party as a whole of absolute stalemate: they did not see any way of forcing Churchill out without risk of splitting the Party.

The Cabinet on 15th December was, according to available evidence, the first for some weeks where the question of Churchill's retirement was again aired, by now utterly inseparable from the timing of the next General Election. A sheet of Prime Minister's writing paper was circulated at that Cabinet between Woolton, Eden and Salisbury, on which they wrote comments: that a meeting between them should be arranged before long to discuss the problem of Churchill's retirement.[137] A week later a meeting took place at Number Ten with seven senior Cabinet Ministers and Churchill in attendance,[138] ostensibly to discuss Election dates, and it seems unlikely that there had been prior talks between the seven to agree on a common approach, particularly since Butler, much preoccupied with the illness and eventual death of his wife on 9th December, appeared at odds with his colleagues.[139] Churchill meanwhile had told the Duke of Edinburgh the previous night that he intended to go in June or July 1955, and stuck to this view at the meeting.[140] Eden said this would be unacceptable because it would give him insufficient time to prepare for an autumn General Election. There was a long pause before Churchill burst out:

> I know you are trying to get rid of me and it is up to me to go to the Queen and hand her my resignation and yours – but I won't do it. But if you feel strongly about it you can force my hand by a sufficiently large number of Ministers handing in their resignations, in which case an Election will be inevitable; but if this happens I shall not be in favour of it and I shall tell the country so.

June or July therefore appeared to be the earliest date he would retire of his own volition. This stunned his audience, and Eden and Macmillan made ineffective ripostes before the meeting broke up.[141] A Cabinet meeting followed in the late afternoon then an inconclusive secret meeting at Number Eleven of Butler, Macmillan, Crookshank and Stuart,[142] who went their separate ways for the Christmas break with a sense of great uncertainty about the future.

Crookshank's Pont Street home once again became the meeting-place of the malcontents. Salisbury, Butler, Macmillan, Stuart and Monckton were there on 28th December, but no firm strategy was agreed or decisions reached.[143] Three weeks later the same group, minus Stuart and Monckton, met 'to discuss the same old topic of getting rid of Winston'.[144] Their anxieties, however, were out of place – Churchill, at the same time, and of his own free will, had made up his mind at last: he would go before July. As Brendan Bracken wrote to Beaverbrook: 'Our friend, under no pressure from Cl Eden [?Clarissa] or other Ministers [sic], intends to depart before July . . . I am certain that he will not change his mind. All his plans are made and when he leaves No. 10 [John] Colville will resign from the Civil Service . . .'[145]

What was the crucial factor that prompted Churchill's final decision to go? Certainly not any dramatic decline in his health in January, nor the promptings of his colleagues,[146] but rather the eventual realisation that his proposal for a summit meeting would simply come to nothing.[147] This realisation broke his will to continue and overcame his fear of giving up. At the beginning of February he decided the first week in April would be the most suitable time to go,[148] though the actual day remained uncertain until the end of the month when he settled on 5th April.[149] It is unclear exactly how and when this news was transmitted to Eden and the Cabinet.[150] Churchill's reluctance to make the news public and to be

51

precise about dates was in part due to his feeling that if a Prime Minister announces in advance he is to retire – as Stanley Baldwin had done before the war – he loses influence.[151]

Churchill was mildly tempted once again to reverse his decision, particularly during the minor financial difficulties in February 1955.[152] He felt his experience was indispensable in a crisis, although – despite what might appear as evidence to the contrary – he had also long been aware of the frustration and difficulty his procrastination had been causing for his successor, a fact that caused him some inner conflict. Indeed, sympathy for Eden's position was largely responsible for his resolution not to reverse his decision to go in early April.[153]

This resolution was, however, severely tested by an episode, the knowledge of which has remained a closely-guarded secret.[154] Churchill threatened to make an eleventh hour *volte-face* in mid-March after Eisenhower announced, without prior warning, that there should be a great celebration of the tenth anniversary of V.E. day on 8th May, indicating that he would be willing to come to Europe if invited. The aim would have been a meeting in Paris to exchange the notes of ratification on the Paris Agreement on European security, in an attempt to encourage the French agreement to the document. Eisenhower also proposed that the German Chancellor, Konrad Adenauer,[155] should be invited to the meeting, and that it should immediately be followed by a discussion between the Foreign Secretaries of the United States, France, Britain and Russia on ways to eliminate the possibilities of war. This news was conveyed in a telegram from John Foster Dulles,[156] the American Secretary of State, received over the weekend of 12th–13th March.

On Monday morning, 14th March, Eden, Salisbury, Butler, Crookshank and Macmillan met at the Foreign Office and expressed concern lest Churchill saw in this proposal an opportunity for yet another eleventh-hour switch.[157] At the Cabinet that followed Churchill, naturally, was keen to invite Eisenhower: he had always wanted Eisenhower to visit Britain, and he had already made private enquiries into the possibility of his staying at Buckingham Palace. The question of the General Election was raised as a way of making Churchill see that at this late hour he could not possibly delay the handover. Woolton suggested a postponement of Eisenhower's proposed visit. Churchill did not like the way the conversation was going: neither did Eden, who, under great strain, asked Churchill if their 'private agreement' on the date of retirement was still standing. Churchill replied that it was his own business when he should retire, and anyone who disliked it could resign. At this tense moment, the meeting was adjourned.[158]

That evening Aldrich,[159] the American Ambassador, was secretly informed by Churchill's colleagues of the impending General Election, and was apparently asked if the President would delay his proposed visit until June. In this daring move probably some or all of the following, Salisbury, Butler, Crookshank, Woolton and Macmillan, were involved, though none mentions it in his respective diary or memoirs.[160] At Cabinet next day, 15th March, Churchill's colleagues talked him out of staying on, thereby making any involvement of Aldrich unnecessary. They managed to convince Churchill that the real talking at the proposed meeting in Paris would be carried out by Foreign Secretaries, and that Eisenhower did not intend that Heads of State should themselves take part in the actual discussions. Churchill appeared to yield quite easily, all the fight having gone out of him.[161]

This was the last serious attempt Churchill made to overcome the inevitable. Even some last-minute wobbling, temporary loss of nerve as he gazed onward into the abyss before him, did not last for long. According to Woolton, Butler remarked: 'We've got the fish on the hook but he hasn't been gaffed yet.'[162] The last few days were difficult for Churchill, and he displayed, untypically, signs of bitterness towards his colleagues. Press speculation and comment in the last two weeks before the handover were, however, kept to a minimum, as the result of a strike of national newspapers from 25th March, although *The Times* four days before had included a story of growing expectation that Churchill would go in the next three weeks. The *Manchester Guardian* alone of the major newspapers was printed.[163]

To coincide with Churchill's departure a dinner was held at Number Ten on 4th April in honour of the Queen, to which many senior political figures from the present and the past were invited, although not Crookshank and Woolton,[164] evidence of the growing rift that had come between Churchill and some of his senior colleagues during his last years in power. Churchill's last Cabinet took place at noon on 5th April: a small amount of Foreign Office business about China, but the time was mostly taken up with valedictory speeches from Churchill and Eden. Churchill himself looked drawn and weary, although still in high spirits about the previous night's dinner.[165] He was most insistent that, in accordance with Royal Prerogative, there should be a full day's delay before Eden was formally installed as Prime Minister.

Eden had been sorely tried during more than two years of delays, but behaved remarkably well, particularly under the extremely difficult circumstances.[166] Indeed it is remarkable that tempers were kept so restrained throughout the long period of indecision.[167] There was a marked absence of jockeying for position or acting for the sake of personal gain. The unrest that existed centred on Salisbury, Butler,

Woolton, Crookshank, Macmillan and Buchan-Hepburn, but they could not be described as plotters;[168] rather they witnessed Churchill's declining powers, saw that the changeover would be inevitable before long, and were concerned to see how this could be brought about most equably.

Part 3   Government Policy and the Media

Conservative memories of the defeat at the polls in 1945 were by no means entirely purged by the Party's victory of October 1951. Not only did they win fewer seats than popularly predicted (321 out of 625, giving a majority of seventeen), but the Conservative vote was actually smaller than Labour's.[1] Lack of confidence, which continued and even grew for some months after the Election, was experienced at all levels from Party workers to Cabinet Ministers.[2] The Prime Minister, it was widely felt, was losing his grip,[3] the leadership in the House was considered unsatisfactory, especially the Leader of the House, Harry Crookshank, who made an unconfident start,[4] and the seven-week break over the first Christmas was regarded as excessive.[5] Disquiet was further fired by disasters in the local elections in the spring of 1952, when the Conservatives and Independents with Conservative support gained 54 and lost 559 seats,[6] the Government faring particularly badly in the cotton areas and on the London County Council.

The Government's unhappy position was exacerbated by the widespread feeling that it had mishandled the issue of rail and bus fares in April,[7] where the increases were felt to have broken Election pledges. Conservative backbenchers were critical of the slow progress towards denationalisation of iron and steel and road haulage,[8] as well as the fulfilment of other election pledges. The legislation that was enacted was regarded by most as superfluous, in particular the Home Guard Act of 1951, for which the Conservatives pressed strongly in Opposition.[9] Some members even felt that the Government was Churchill's rather than the Conservative Party's. The Gallup polls for the first ten months of 1952 showed a Labour lead ranging from $3\frac{1}{2}\%$ to 10%.[10] By-election swings went against the Government in six out of nine results during the year, including 7.5% against them at Dundee East in July 1952. *The Times* had even gone so far as to suggest in April: 'It is possible that there is evidence here of a permanent shift in political power – the result of the granting of universal suffrage.'[11]

When the House broke up for its Whitsun break at the end of May a mood of despondency pervaded Conservative members. According to Hugh Massingham in the *Observer*: 'Mr. Churchill is the chief target of his rank and file,'[12] a position unlikely to come to a head because 'some M.P.s are by no means certain that Mr. Eden would be an improvement'.[13] At the end of June Churchill managed to head off some unrest by an appearance before the 1922 Committee, long overdue in the eyes of many backbenchers who felt they were not seeing enough of their Prime Minister.[14] Churchill reassured members on three points: Eden was to remain as Foreign Secretary; the Government would not waver from its intention to press ahead with denationalisation and stabilise the cost of living; and finally – he had no immediate intention of retiring. This last point disposed of the unease many felt about the damage inflicted due to uncertainty about his future.[15] Yet discontent remained when Parliament adjourned for the 1952 summer recess.[16] The *Observer* expressed the feeling of many: 'Disappointment with the performance of the Conservative Government in its first Parliamentary year is widespread.'[17]

The summer break, however, put fresh hope into Conservative hearts, and a new mood of optimism prevailed at the Party Conference in October.[18] As the country's economic fortunes improved, public opinion polls began to turn in the Government's favour.[19] When M.P.s assembled at Westminster after the summer recess they were, according to the *Sunday Times*, 'in good heart. [The Conservative Party] seems to have thrown off much of the doldrums that afflicted it earlier in the year'.[20] But the Government was still far from being in a position of strength. It did not fare well in the tough and often bitter session at the end of the year.[21] Attlee, with some justification, criticised the Government by saying that despite their long period in Opposition, the Conservatives had not organised themselves or put in sufficient work to allow them to pass through in their first year the Transport, Steel and Monopolies Bills, but instead had concentrated on minor items such as the Licensed Premises in New Towns Act.[22]

By March 1953, Gallup put the Conservatives in the lead, but the fickleness of the electorate was shown at two by-elections. In Stoke-on-Trent North at the end of the month there was a swing against the Government of 4.1%,[23] but in May confidence was restored dramatically at Sunderland South, a highly marginal constituency, where, with a swing to the Government of 2.4%, they managed to capture the seat from Labour.[24]

The Coronation of Queen Elizabeth in June, with talk of a new 'Elizabethan age', contributed much to the impression of contentment, although this was to wane slightly as the summer wore on[25] and the ill health of Churchill and Anthony Eden continued to prevent their return to active duty. As Hugh Massingham wrote in the *Observer*: 'To put the point briefly: the Central Office must produce either Sir Winston or Mr. Eden [at the October conference]. If neither of them turns up, their absence will give rise to a great deal of speculation and uneasiness about the future.'[26] In the event, however, the conference held that year at Margate dispelled the anxious feeling in the Party. Churchill and Eden both spoke with vigour, Macmillan was able to announce that the magical 300,000 annual house-building target was within hailing distance, and Lloyd-George that the present ration books would be the last.[27] Yet no sooner did the Party look secure than a feeling began to be aired in the press that autumn that the Government did not know what to do next. In fact the Cabinet had decided in August not to offer a policy statement for the Party Conference;[28] for like Labour by 1951, the greater part of their programme had been completed. In only two years they had, despite a slow start, denationalised iron, steel and road haulage and removed the bulk of rationing and the major excesses of socialism.[29] And again like Labour, they were in a dilemma about the policies they were next to advocate.

These doubts had largely disappeared by 1954, the year which was the Government's high point: food ration books finally disappeared and building licences were abolished. The early summer was a restless time for the Party, with a furore in the House over the level of M.P.s' salaries,[30] and a 'malaise and fretfulness' amongst the rank and file at the lack of promotion prospects.[31] But by October the way the Government dealt with the London dock strike showed a confidence and strength too often lacking previously, a position further consolidated by Eden's notable diplomatic successes that summer and autumn. Anxiety about Churchill's future remained the one cloud looming on the horizon.[32]

The work of the Conservative Research Department during the period in Opposition,[33] which owed much to the foresight and intellect of Butler, his principal lieutenants, Iain Macleod, Reginald Maudling, Enoch Powell, and its Director, David Clarke,[34] was of enormous importance at the time. The policies, the majority of which were widely based, providing a broad philosophical framework rather than a precise programme for the next Parliament, enabled the Conservatives to resist the Labour criticism that they had no constructive policies. The 're-formulation of Conservative philosophy' was, in fact, unoriginal in terms of pure policy, but successful as Party strategy.[35]

It is striking just how little impact the work of the Research Department between 1945–51, embodied in the Charters and other publications, actually had on the legislative programme of the Government from 1951 to 1955. This work played a major role in ensuring that the

Party adjusted to post-war truths: the welfare state, the mixed economy and full employment. The Charters helped change the public's view of the Conservative Party, from a *laissez-faire* imperialist organisation to a more interventionist forward-looking one.[36] The Research Department's work was thus of most importance in creating a climate and changing attitudes.[37] The 'Industrial Charter' of May 1947,[38] the first and the major Charter, was concerned with 'the future structure of British industry'.[39] It was notable mainly for its broad acceptance of Labour's nationalisation proposals, a wider measure of planning than had hitherto been thought desirable by the Conservatives,[40] and the commitment to the financial burdens of the welfare state. But little came of its practical proposals for reorganisation and decentralisation of the nationalised industries.[41] Even less came of the 'Workers' Charter', as the final section of the 'Industrial Charter' was known. Sir Walter Monckton, who had not been a member of the Industrial Charter Committee, was appointed Minister of Labour in 1951 and did not implement any of the Charter's far-seeing proposals, such as contracts of service, or 'equal pay' for 'equal work'.[42]

The other documents were secondary. The 'Agricultural Charter', published in June 1948, had largely been forgotten when over three years later the Minister, Sir Thomas Dugdale, arrived at the Ministry of Agriculture. 'A True Balance', published in February 1949, was a document of some foresight in its attempt to examine the position of women and their affairs, but was almost too far ahead of its time. 'Imperial Policy', of June 1949, the first post-war Party statement on overseas affairs, was soon passed over as the Conservatives once in power grappled with the realities of foreign and imperial problems. 'Conservative Policy for Wales and Monmouthshire' and 'Scottish Control of Scottish Affairs', however, both had some effect in alerting the Party to the demands for more recognition of the separate identities of Wales and Scotland.[43]

The Research Department after 1951, ably headed by the new Director, Michael Fraser,[44] with a gifted team, notably Peter Goldman,[45] had a changed role from one of exploring policy options to becoming almost a high-flown adjunct of the publicity machine.[46] The Conservative Political Centre played a prominent part during the years in Opposition in encouraging ideas from the constituencies, but had a different role after 1951 when receptivity amongst the Party leadership to ideas 'from below' was greatly reduced.[47]

The One Nation Group was formed in 1950 by young Conservative M.P.s principally interested in progressive social legislation, among them Cuthbert Alport, Robert Carr, Macleod, Angus Maude and

Powell – 'perhaps the ablest backbencher on either side of the House' – according to Massingham.[48] The group may have had some influence on opinion in the country in these early years, but it had virtually none on policy.[49] With a small majority, backbenchers were concerned not to press their differences of opinion to the point where a defeat for the Government might have been risked. Their influence on policy was correspondingly diminished. The 1922 Committee was firmly led by Derek Walker-Smith,[50] but only rarely did either this body or the individual backbench Party Committees ever cause Ministers to alter departmental policy. In the main, their advice was listened to politely, then ignored.[51] Backbenchers did, however, score some notable victories, especially in 1953–4, causing the Government to speed up and even to alter policies, as over commercial television,[52] Members' pay,[53] the abandonment of a Bill by Peter Thorneycroft on development councils, and pressure that led directly to the resignation of Sir Thomas Dugdale as Minister of Agriculture.[54] But these pockets of rebellion tended to be from *ad hoc* formations rather than based on organised homogeneous groups, and little attempt was made by backbenchers to gang up into a unified pressure body.[55] As a result Patrick Buchan-Hepburn (Conservative Chief Whip, 1948–55) and his team had a relatively easy time, which was the more remarkable considering the great changes the Party had had to digest since the last peacetime Conservative Governments.[56] Buchan-Hepburn was a sound if unspectacular Chief Whip, lacking the charm of James Stuart (1941–8) or the brilliance and tactical grasp of Edward Heath (1955–9). Buchan-Hepburn's standing reached a low point in mid-1952; at that time 'A Student of Politics' in the *Sunday Times* noted that he '. . . has his critics – and not least among his own backbenchers. He can at times be much less pleasant than his appearance [suggests] . . . even the strictest disciplinarian can earn respect, if not popularity; but excess of dignity is not normally considered the road to either.'[57] Hugh Massingham in the *Observer* went further, and said the backbenchers blamed Buchan-Hepburn equally with Churchill for the Government's problems: Buchan-Hepburn, he wrote: 'believes in fighting wars according to the drill book', his good looks and clothes earning him the name of 'the ageing peacock'.[58]

The three Party Conferences during the life of the Government[59] posed, like the backbenchers, little threat to the Government, nor were they responsible for new initiatives (as had occurred at the 1950 Blackpool Conference with the housing target).[60] As ever Conservative Party Conferences were different from those of Labour, being, in effect, rallies of local party organisations, and though policy was discussed and criticisms made, the party platform was not bound by decisions. A leader in the *Sunday Times* after the 1953 Conference noted, however, that conferences have 'lately played a very significant and constructive part'.[61]

Not that the Government always had its own way: it failed to implement two constitutional proposals, both of which were unpopular with the Labour Party. At both the 1950 and 1951 General Elections, the Conservatives, encouraged by Lord Salisbury, pledged themselves to reopen negotiations on House of Lords reform. In May 1952 Churchill announced in the House the Government's intention to set up an all-Party Conference when circumstances permitted,[62] and on 3rd February, 1953, Churchill wrote to the Liberal and Labour Leaders. Clement Davies wrote back saying the Liberal Party welcomed the invitation,[63] but Attlee refused to join in talks, because of the gulf in views displayed in the 1948 talks.[64] The matter was not, however, left there. A Cabinet Committee was set up that spring under Salisbury's chairmanship to consider the question, but little progress was made. Lord Simon[65] tried to get the Government to support his Life Peers' Bill,[66] but this particular scheme found little favour with them. In early 1955 both Salisbury in the Lords[67] and Churchill in the Commons[68] once more aired the question, but in a debate in the Lords in March, Lord Jowitt said Labour was still not ready to join in an all-Party Conference.[69] Yet this did not quench the Government's enthusiasm for examining reform: as Salisbury said, 'If we cannot get the co-operation of the Labour Party we shall have to go on without them.'[70] Overall, 1951–5 was not the happiest period for the House of Lords: the standard of debate was often low, and some members of the Lower House were distinctly unimpressed.[71]

The question of the twelve University seats, abolished in 1948, was discussed anew.[72] But a meeting, in February 1953, of the Vice-Chancellors of Oxford and Cambridge and certain heads of Colleges declared unanimously against their restoration,[73] and in October Churchill announced that the Government was of the same view.[74] One item not included in the 1951 Manifesto was a reiteration of Churchill's March 1950 suggestion for a House of Commons Enquiry into electoral reform,[75] a proposal he must have regretted when in power. He received a Liberal Party deputation on the subject in February 1953, and another from the all-Party Committee seeking a Royal Commission. But Churchill was unenthusiastic, as was the Cabinet.[76]

A major reason for the dissatisfaction with the Government's performance during 1952 emanated from Churchill's attitude to the press and to publicity. Churchill inherited the publicity system built up by Clement Attlee. Francis Williams,[77] a Labour man and confidant of Attlee. had held the job of Public Relations Adviser to the Prime Minister. and lobby relations had been left to Herbert Morrison,[78] who enjoyed the company of political journalists. Williams was succeeded first by Philip Jordan and then by R. K. Bacon, a Civil Service appointee.[79] Churchill, however, decided to sever all links with the press, and Bacon soon returned to the Treasury, having had a fairly rough time. Churchill felt that the Prime Minister should make his pronouncements in the House of Commons rather than to journalists.

During that first autumn and winter, Ministers were strongly discouraged from seeing the press, although, unknown to the Prime Minister. a few disobeyed, notably Rab Butler and Lord Swinton. Dissatisfaction with the poor flow of information was soon apparent: this, however, was directed against Government rather than Party,[80] where the machine had been greatly improved as a result of a Liaison Committee set up in December 1951 under the chairmanship of Swinton.[81] The dissatisfaction came from a number of quarters: Fleet Street proprietors and editors as well as political correspondents were increasingly agitated about the absence of contact with Number Ten or the Government; with little exchange of information, morale amongst public relations men in the Government Departments was poor; the 1922 Committee was dissatisfied about the way the Government had failed to make political capital from the state of the nation as bequeathed by Labour in October 1951 – as well as by the failure to make sufficiently concrete plans in Opposition;[82] finally, Ministers themselves felt the Government was increasingly giving the impression of being rudderless.[83]

The opposition came to a head in March and April 1952. Unrest had deteriorated so much that after a series of talks[84] Butler and Swinton were able to prevail on Churchill to rethink his attitude to press contacts, on the basis that these would not take place in Number Ten itself, and that the Press Secretary, or Public Relations Adviser, would be on Swinton's personal staff. As a result of their efforts T. Fife Clark,[85] after a long interview with Churchill on 26th May, was appointed 'Adviser on Government Public Relations',[86] situated not inside Number Ten but next door in the old Treasury. Clark was to advise and assist Swinton, who Churchill decided was to guide and co-ordinate Government publicity.[87] in addition to his responsibilities for co-ordination of Party publicity as Chairman of the Liaison Committee.

The Parliamentary Lobby system was thus restored. The main source of political news came from these off-the-record Lobby meetings, consisting both of formal gatherings and *ad hoc* talks between correspondents and individual Ministers, a system that had become consolidated during the war. Downing Street was responsible for two formal briefings each weekday for the Lobby Correspondents:[88] at 11.30 a.m. in the old Treasury (Churchill remained adamant that he would not have a Press Office in Number Ten), but this was usually thinly attended, being mainly of interest to the provincial and London evening papers,[89] and at 4.00 p.m. in the House of Commons, when a fuller meeting was held at which would be present some of the Lobby Correspondents from the daily papers.[90] The other main briefings were given on Thursday afternoons by Harry Crookshank as Leader of the House, who the Lobby men felt handled the job well,[91] by Clement Attlee as Leader of the Opposition, and by Swinton himself, usually on Wednesday afternoons. Opinions about the value of Swinton's meetings differ markedly: some Lobby Correspondents recall him as garrulous yet uncommunicative, completely absorbed in his own subject, be it as Minister of Materials or as Commonwealth Secretary, uttering with great earnestness a remark such as, 'Zinc's been very difficult.'[92] Others felt that, like Fife Clark, Swinton played a vital role in holding together the Government's publicity and repairing the damage caused by Churchill's neglect of the press.[93] The regular morning and afternoon meetings were taken by Clark or his deputy, whose main sources of information of Government plans and action were Swinton and Butler – and also Churchill who within a week of the restoration of normal Lobby relations was agreeing to talk to Clark.[94] In addition, at departmental level, through a letter sent by Butler in mid-June and Swinton's personal influence, Ministers were encouraged to give their own Lobby Conferences, and to give full rein to their Chief Information Officers.[95] Occasionally, perhaps once a fortnight, a Minister would come and give an off-the-record address to the Lobby. 'Leaks' of Government classified information were a comparative rarity in the early 1950s: it just would not have occurred to most Ministers to leak facts to advance their political cause. Conservative Ministers were always less likely to leak information to the press than their Labour counterparts, though by 1962, towards the end of the Macmillan Government, when William Deedes became responsible for Government publicity, leaks had become widespread.[96]

By the end of 1952, an efficient publicity machine was in action: Clark was doing a brilliant job on Government publicity, especially considering the obstacles under which he had had to labour. George Christ,[97] the Parliamentary Liaison Officer, located in the House of Commons, managed Parliamentary briefings, and Gerald O'Brien, like Christ a Party man, was Chief Press Officer, situated in Central Office, and dealt with

Party briefings. O'Brien worked under Mark Chapman Walker, the forceful but unorthodox Conservative Party Chief Publicity Officer from 1949 until his departure in November 1955, who played such a prominent part in converting the Government to support for commercial television.

Throughout the 1950s, Lobby Correspondents were becoming steadily more reliable and penetrating in what they wrote. Chief among them on London's daily newspapers was Wilfrid Sendall, Political Correspondent of the *Daily Telegraph*, although he seldom wrote reflective articles. By 1956 he had decided he would like to be free of the hammering routine life of a Lobby man and to the surprise of many of his colleagues accepted a job that offered more variety, writing the 'Crossbencher' column in the Beaverbrook *Sunday Express*.[98] The *Daily Telegraph*, described in 1952 by David Butler as the 'most nearly "official" Conservative daily',[99] was the only one of the four serious London dailies to have a circulation of over a million,[100] and to be in serious competition with the more popular Conservative papers, the *Daily Mail* and *Daily Express*. The paper remained unfailingly loyal to Churchill at a time, particularly during 1954, when formerly friendly papers such as *The Times* were turning against him.[101] Considerable subdued criticism of Churchill was aired in both Westminster and Fleet Street when the October 1954 Cabinet changes were announced, signifying that he had no immediate intention of retiring. Yet a leader in the *Daily Telegraph* declared, 'Sir Winston Churchill, like some indestructible oak, still towers over all.'[102]

The Times had supported Labour in the 1945 General Election, but then slowly found its way back into the Conservative camp, cautiously in the 1950 Election, far more explicitly in 1951, a trend that continued after Sir William Haley became Editor in September 1952. Max Mason, who had been Political Correspondent since 1938, was a confidant of Ministers, but handicapped by a ponderous manner. He had become so accustomed to writing briefly that when Haley sought longer articles once restrictions had been lifted on the availability of newsprint, restrictions which had so drastically curtailed news coverage, not least during the 1951 Election, he was unable to adapt his style. In October 1957 he was replaced by David Wood, a younger man who wrote the far more lively and enterprising pieces which changed circumstances demanded.

The *Manchester Guardian* abandoned its traditional Liberal stance in 1951, having been sharply critical of Labour, and expressed the clear conviction that a Conservative Government was now required, coming to the same conclusion again in 1955. Francis Boyd was the long-serving Political Correspondent (1945–72), hard-working and shrewd, and possessing invaluable contacts, particularly with the Opposition Front Bench.[103] The Parliamentary Correspondent between 1929 and 1958, Harry Boardman,[104] described by James Margach as the only working journalist whose judgment Churchill valued,[105] wrote in a highly appreciative fashion about Churchill's Parliamentary performances. When a report implying criticism of the Prime Minister appeared in the *Manchester Guardian*'s headline on 23rd March, 1955, Churchill solemnly commented: '. . . this was not their Parliamentary Correspondent, he is very sound; it was their Lobby Correspondent.'[106] So delighted had Churchill been with Boardman's articles that he offered him a knighthood, which the latter politely declined.[107] On the *Financial Times* Paul Einzig[108] was a brilliant economist and prolific author, although his flair never perhaps communicated itself as well in his political reporting. He had, however, one notable scoop: by examining the form of the 1929 General Election he predicted correctly that polling day in 1955 would fall on 26th May.[109]

The *Daily Express* voiced Lord Beaverbrook's very independent support for Churchill and the Conservatives. It was passionate in its advocacy of Empire trade, and criticised British commitment of armed forces to Europe.[110] 'Eden's pledge' of troops, thundered the paper, was 'perilous' and might even prove 'deadly . . . Mr. Eden has separated Britain, in legal and moral obligation, from the Dominions.'[111] Derek Marks[112] was Political Correspondent and benefited from the paper's good contacts with backbenchers, particularly from the 'imperial' right wing. He was slowly beginning to learn what was said behind closed doors in the deliberations of the 1922 Committee, which he later developed into a fine art, to the embarrassment of the Macmillan Government.[113] Marks benefited from a number of hot leads direct from Beaverbrook, learned from his dealings in high places. Einzig at the *Financial Times* had no such joy, however, from his proprietor, Brendan Bracken, who did not believe it right to disclose such information to his own newspaper.[114] The principal Conservative rival in this category, the *Daily Mail*, was both more orthodox in its support of the Conservative Party, and also more hard hitting than the *Express*. Geoffrey Wakeford was Lobby Correspondent for most of the period, an affable man but apt to chance his arm, sometimes rather wildly. His classic error, at the time much commented upon, was his suggestion after the East Coast floods on the last night of January 1953 that a vast 'Churchill Wall' was to be built along the East Coast of Britain.[115] Wakeford was followed by Henry Fairlie, who quickly made his mark, being described by David Butler in 1955 as 'one of the liveliest and most outspoken of political commentators'.[116] The *News Chronicle* was fortunate to have two of the best Political Correspondents in Fleet Street, both of whom subsequently went into television, Geoffrey Cox,[117] who in April 1951 had been the first to predict the resignation of Ernest Bevin from the Attlee Government,[118] and from 1955, Ian Trethowan,[119] renowned for his felicitous pen. The paper was traditionally regarded as being the organ of radical Liberalism, but in fact nearly all the staff were Labour supporters. Aneurin Bevan, however, felt decidedly antipathetic to it, and editorially it tended to support the Attlee–Gaitskell wing of the Party.

The Labour side was better represented amongst the three more popular dailies. On the *Daily Herald*, the official Labour paper, Leslie Hunter, their Political Correspondent, strongly supported the official Party leadership rather than the Bevanites,[120] and benefited from being given the inner angle on many stories direct from the Party. The *Daily Mirror*, with the largest circulation, was both more important and less official. Bill Grieg, their political man, was more of a heavyweight writer than Hunter, but possessed, like him, a very good contact in Herbert Morrison, and was close to all sections of the Party. Grieg himself wrote well-informed short pieces and was a milder man than might have been thought by his newspaper's missionary campaigns such as the 'Whose Finger on the Trigger?' refrain of 1951. The *Daily Mirror*, almost alone until *Punch* came under the editorship of Malcolm Muggeridge in 1953,[121] was the main voice calling for Churchill's resignation on grounds of failed health. The Conservative *Daily Sketch* rather took over from the *Daily Mirror* in 1955, and was the only newspaper to attempt a sensational scare during the Election, a far-flung effort that backfired, in which it gave details of a plot to substitute Aneurin Bevan for Attlee if Labour won the Election.[122] Their Political Correspondent was Guy Eden, who, with over twenty-five years' experience, could justifiably be called the architect of the mid-century Lobby,[123] having played a major part in its becoming institutionalised. Rather limited as a commentator on politics, his main strength lay in his ability as a news-gatherer: indeed, one Lobby journalist said Eden was one of the two Political Correspondents in Fleet Street whom he had constantly to keep his eye on, the other being Wilfrid Sendall.[124] Eden had achieved scoops in the 1930s by predicting the resignations both of Oswald Mosley in 1930 and Anthony Eden in 1938; and he (along with Randolph Churchill[125] in the *Evening Standard*) correctly. surmised, unlike the rest of Fleet Street, that Macmillan rather than Butler would succeed Eden in January 1957. The remaining daily was the Communist *Daily Worker*, the forerunner of the *Morning Star*, whose Political Correspondent, Peter Zinkin, turned out uncritical pieces faithful to his paper's beliefs. Ministers were more careful if they knew Zinkin was present at Lobby meetings, although unlike many journalists of his persuasion he took trouble to respect confidences given to him.[126]

The three London evening papers carried an influence out of all proportion to their weight, largely because they were published when politicians were gathering together at Westminster. But they also possessed greater importance because they then contained far more news, and the later editions frequently led on the news from Question Time in the House or from information gleaned from the morning Lobby briefings, when spokesmen often went out of their way to give them interesting leads.[127] The papers' Lobby Correspondents essentially saw their job as fast news-gatherers who did not have to discuss politics at any length. Their treatment therefore seldom rose above the superficial, although Bill Alison of the *Evening Standard* and his successor, George Hutchinson (1953–60), were exceptions. Hutchinson had good contacts with several Conservatives, whose sympathies were later confirmed by his appointment as Director of Conservative Party publicity.[128] John Carvel of the *Star*, to whom Hugh Dalton had leaked the details of his Budget in 1947 in the infamous episode that led to Dalton's resignation, was succeeded in the early 1950s by his son Robert, who, following the demise of the *Star* in 1960, moved over to the *Evening Standard*, supplanting Hutchinson.

On two major items during 1951–5 – Churchill's stroke in 1953, and hard fact (as opposed to gossip) about his retirement plans – surprisingly little appeared in the media. On both of these, two prominent Lobby Correspondents from provincial newspapers achieved minor scoops, although neither was followed up significantly by Fleet Street, in the latter case because of the March–April 1955 newspaper strike. Trevor Lloyd-Hughes,[129] Political Correspondent of the *Liverpool Daily Post*, had been standing in the Members' Lobby in the House of Commons early on the evening of 8th July, 1953, when a Conservative M.P., an old and trusted friend, walked by. Without stopping, the M.P. whispered to Lloyd-Hughes: 'Churchill's had a stroke: he's going to retire.' If true, this would obviously be a prime political story, but hard confirmation could not be obtained. Lloyd-Hughes discussed it with his Editor, Ian Hosie, who advised either carrying nothing, or giving the story maximum full-page treatment, leaving the decision to his Political Correspondent. Later that evening, after careful consideration of such points as had been established (with the help of Douglas Haig of the *Birmingham Post*, who co-operated closely with Lloyd-Hughes in the daily hunt for political news), he telephoned his Editor in Liverpool to advise the go-ahead. The story, incorporating some 'escape clauses' (such as Churchill changing his mind, and the possibility of an immediate official denial), duly appeared on 9th July under the headline 'Churchill Planning to Retire'.[130] Yet this was not picked up by the national press: the *Daily Mirror* on 17th August, 1953, complained that the *New York Herald Tribune* stated that Churchill had a stroke in the last week of June 1953, but that the British people had not been given the facts about their leader's health. Churchill commented wryly: 'It's rubbish, of course, but it won't help at Margate.'[131] How the world's press came freely to discuss Churchill's stroke while information about it hardly appeared at all in British newspapers remains something of a mystery: the historian John Grigg asserts that two of the leading proprietors, Bracken of the *Financial Times* and Camrose of the *Daily Telegraph*, recommended suppression in their respective newspapers, but a more widespread factor was the wartime instinct to stand by the Leader in times of crisis, and reluctance to print such a sensational story about a stroke without hard corroboration.[132]

Harry Boyne,[133] Political Correspondent of the *Glasgow Herald* (1950–6), recorded the other scoop, concerning Churchill's retirement plans. In retrospect, he regarded this as his best exclusive story in the Lobby.[134] Boyne heard that Clarissa Eden had a day or two before been shown around Number Ten by Churchill. He was quick to deduce the significance: 'There are some people at Westminster who will not be surprised if Sir Winston Churchill has ceased to be Prime Minister by the time he arrives in Sicily for his long-overdue holiday,'[135] was how he opened 'London Correspondence' on 6th March, correctly predicting the retirement to follow the dinner party for the Queen at Number Ten on 4th April.

Most newspapers at that time had only one correspondent entitled to belong in the Lobby; numbers began to grow dramatically only in the following decade. In consequence there was a strenuous cut and thrust between rival journalists, excessively hard work, and the development of several small packs working together, hunting for information. The combination of Lloyd-Hughes and Douglas Haig has already been mentioned,[136] and they would also team up with Wilfrid Sendall. Sendall would in addition work in combination with Paul Einzig;[137] and Bill Alison, of the *Evening Standard*, worked with James Margach in his capacity as a correspondent for Scottish evening newspapers.[138] Another combination existed between the two main Liberal dailies, Francis Boyd of the *Manchester Guardian* and Geoffrey Cox of the *News Chronicle*.[139] Political Correspondents from the *Daily Express*, *The Times* and the *Daily Herald* always worked alone.

Accurate political reporting and commentary was by no means restricted to membership of the Lobby. The Sunday newspapers were allowed into the Lobby on a one-day-a-week basis, a position which endured until after the birth of the *Sunday Telegraph* in 1961, whose pressure led to full Lobby status. During the early 1950s their Political Correspondents would tend to write more general reflective pieces, and would not become involved in the routine work of explaining Bills and White Papers. Two of the Sunday papers provided the best political commentary to be found then in Fleet Street – that written by Hugh Massingham, who contributed a regular 'political notebook' in the politically neutral *Observer*, and by James Margach,[140] who wrote an occasional column (perhaps one in three) in the *Sunday Times* under the name 'A Student of Politics'.[141] Charles Gayton was the *de facto* Political Correspondent of the orthodox Conservative *Sunday Times*, but from the beginning of the decade was increasingly absent through ill health, and Margach, like Boyne a representative of the older generation of gentlemanly Scots professionals, wrote the column in his place.[142]

Margach was close to several Cabinet Ministers, including Butler[143] and Swinton,[144] and had a reputation for utter discretion. Indeed, he often knew more than any other journalist about the state of play in the Conservative Party, but tended to write less fully than many who knew much less. His articles would thus reflect the establishment point of view; indeed, on one occasion he was given information about an awkward constitutional issue by Number Ten, and wrote it up precisely as the Government desired.[145] Despite this, his pieces were the most subtle and incisive in Fleet Street. Though not as skilful or as amusing a writer as Massingham, Margach was nevertheless more penetrating, had better contacts on the Conservative side, and covered a broader range of subjects. Massingham, who served as the *Observer*'s Political Correspondent from just after the war until 1961, was the more irreverent and could be mercilessly witty about certain individuals, such as Lord Woolton, even on occasion sacrificing accuracy for humour. He had the benefit over Margach in the early 1950s of writing a column every week. The most widely read political writer in the Sunday papers, his reputation was made by uncannily accurate recording of disagreements within the Labour Government of 1945–51, in particular over debates on steel nationalisation in its last years in power. George Strauss and Lady Cripps had been particularly informative sources for Massingham during that period, and during their time in Opposition after 1951 Richard Crossman and George Wigg would feed him many leads. Years later, Margach paid his old rival a generous compliment: 'It is still universally agreed that Hugh Massingham of the *Observer* was the most scintillating of all political writers.'[146]

The weekly journals were the final major source of political news. The

Spectator was the least influential of the three main political weeklies, but steadily increased in importance under the editorship of Ian Gilmour[147] (1954–9). The *New Statesman and Nation*, still edited by Kingsley Martin (1931–61), was the principal commentator on the left, but had much less of value to contribute on the Conservative Government. *The Economist*[148] was then the outstanding journal, having a large number of highly able staff writing authoritatively not just on economic, but also on political, defence and Commonwealth affairs.

The disadvantage experienced by the weeklies – both newspapers and journals – at being excluded from regular Lobby meetings was steadily lessened during these years as the value of the briefings declined after the entry of the provincial evening newspapers at the end of the previous decade. 'Post-war growth has greatly weakened the Lobby's potential,' wrote Ian Waller[149] in the mid-1960s. 'The extent to which politicians are willing to talk frankly at a meeting must diminish with the size of the audience.'[150] The atmosphere had indeed changed dramatically after the entry of the provincial papers; formerly meetings would often consist of just a dozen or so journalists sitting around a table; almost overnight, according to Wilfrid Sendall, the meetings became larger formal gatherings. The style of Herbert Morrison during 1945–51, with his highly calculated indiscretions, or Rab Butler for the Opposition, with his more artistic approach to leaks, all of which required active following up by the Fleet Street correspondents, was not of so much value to men from evening and provincial papers. What they wanted far more was crisp explicit statements; the Lobby meetings then became less informative and more straight question and answer sessions for the record.[151] Not that by any means the formal Lobby meetings ceased to be a valuable exercise: the continued large attendance testified to their importance.

How then could the Lobby Correspondents obtain exclusive and penetrating stories if not from the official meetings? Increasingly they relied on informal off-the-record chats with politicians. Yet the problem was that senior Cabinet figures, after the return of the Conservatives in 1951, and the Prime Minister in particular, were simply not at home hobnobbing in corridors or bars with journalists, however senior they might be or however influential the newspaper they represented.[152] Labour Ministers in their efforts to extend the role of the state were anxious to carry the press with them at every stage. Ministers in the Churchill Government, often reared in politics in the interwar days, or even outside politics altogether, were of a different breed; they were not as concerned to sell their policies to the Lobby as were those in the Labour Party, not even seeing this a major part of their role. Instead they preferred to rely on announcements made in Parliament backed up by the old tactic of going into the country at the weekend to make speeches.[153]

This is one reason why the press failed to provide details of many of the most politically sensitive issues during 1951–5, such as Churchill's health and retirement plans and the struggles to induce him to retire, or those most disputed in Cabinet such as the denationalisation of steel, the future of commercial television, or policy towards a summit meeting with the Soviet Union.[154] Where the press did excel was in the reporting of internal Party disagreements: as a leader in the *Observer* commented, 'The real policy discussions no longer take place on the floor of the House but at Party meetings.'[155] Political Correspondents found few Cabinet Ministers approachable: Butler would talk on a limited field, and then far less readily than before the 1951 Election; Swinton was found to be surprisingly open to several correspondents in his semi-articulate style in the manner of Lord Home; James Stuart would talk to Hugh McMichael of the *Scotsman* and Harry Boyne of the *Glasgow Herald*: he would not exactly 'leak' information, but helped provide those Scottish Political Correspondents with a view or perspective on events.[156] Non-Cabinet Ministers such as Iain Macleod, Ernest Marples – particularly about his boss, Macmillan – and Harold Watkinson were found to be the most fruitful source of information. Not that they could furnish the press with news about the Prime Minister, as they were all excluded from the 'inner circle'. But Christopher Soames was found to be an unexpectedly frank source about the Premier, and Randolph Churchill was always a tremendous publicist for his father. Few items of gossip about Churchill or other high-level matters failed to reach the ears of Sir Robert Boothby – 'probably the most popular member' of the House of Commons according to 'Pendennis' in the *Observer*.[157] Boothby would talk frankly not just to journalists but to Labour's inveterate diary keepers, Richard Crossman and Hugh Dalton. Violet Bonham Carter would pass on odd bits of information to the *Manchester Guardian* about the Prime Minister out of loyalty to the newspaper's traditionally Liberal stance.[158] The major media access to Churchill was, however, reserved for the newspaper proprietors, Lords Beaverbrook, Bracken, Camrose and Kemsley, often far from frank in the information they passed on.

Part 4   General Elections

1951 General Election

Clement Attlee had no need to call an Election for 25th October, 1951, and it came as a surprise to his colleagues,[1] many of whom were critical of the timing.[2] But Attlee, unused to governing with a small majority (only five following the February 1950 Election compared with 146 after July 1945), was tired, as were many of those who had served with him continuously since the formation of the Coalition Government in 1940.[3] The Conservatives were not unprepared, having for eighteen months anticipated and attempted to provoke an early Election. By the spring of 1951, unsure whether the Election would be that year or not, Rab Butler decided that a policy statement should be prepared for the Party Conference to approve in the autumn.[4] Attlee's announcement of the General Election on 19th September prevented the Party Conferences going ahead, but the Conservative policy document, 'Britain Strong and Free', was, nevertheless, published on 3rd October.

This document had many similarities with two earlier documents: the policy statement, 'The Right Road for Britain', 1949, and the 1950 Election Manifesto, 'This is The Road'. Due to the shift in mood in the intervening year it was far more forcefully libertarian with much less emphasis on planning.[5] David Clarke (Director of the Conservative Research Department, 1945–51),[6] also responsible for the title,[7] wrote the first draft.

Later in the summer, Butler brought Selwyn Lloyd in to the Conservative Research Department to add polish to the document,[8] and he attended regularly for a few weeks.[9] Under him was a committee consisting of officials from the Research Department, and also Antony Head[10] who helped on the defence side, and Anthony Nutting[11] on the overseas. The final draft was written by Peter Goldman,[12] who produced a far better written document than his two predecessors. The 'inner core' group under Anthony Eden's chairmanship then met to approve the document,[13] which differed on only two substantial points from the earlier drafts.[14] Firstly, it aimed at a building target of 300,000 houses annually,[15] and secondly to introduce an excess profits tax,[16] as long as rearmament continued. Churchill insisted upon the latter,[17] no doubt recalling the experience of his Coalition Government which had introduced a one hundred per cent excess profits tax in 1940,[18] and Butler and the Research Department had reluctantly to accept.[19] Last minute changes meant that the presses had to be stopped twice during printing;

70

once to insert the passage about the profits tax,[20] and the second time to add passages to make it appear to be a General Election statement.

Meanwhile, five days before this 10,000 word statement appeared, the Election Manifesto was hurriedly published on 28th September, the publication date being brought forward two days after news of the excess profits tax appeared in the London evening newspaper, the *Star*.[21] This 3,000 word leaflet was in the form of a personal statement from the Party Leader,[22] and if many of the ideas were not Churchill's own, the writing certainly was. It contained the substance of 'Britain Strong and Free', which was regarded as an amplification of the Manifesto. Churchill had invited some leading colleagues to lunch on 20th September to discuss the Election strategy.[23] The full shadow Cabinet spent all day discussing the contents of the Manifesto at his home, 28, Hyde Park Gate, on 22nd September and approved it at a shorter meeting on 25th September.[24]

The Conservatives won the Election with an overall majority of seventeen.[25] It was believed in Conservative circles at the time that the *Daily Mirror*'s last minute anti-Churchill warmongering scare spread, over the Election campaign period, may well have worked to Labour's advantage:[26] if this was so it would have been one of the very rare examples of a newspaper campaign exercising any major electoral effect. The Party undoubtedly felt disappointed at the size of the majority,[27] since polls had led them to expect one of around fifty.[28] The swing to the Conservatives was only 1.1%, and they won with a quarter of a million fewer votes than Labour's record 13,949,000. The Conservatives with 321 seats had a net gain of twenty-three over 1950, Labour with 295 a net loss of twenty. Yet despite the slender majority, Labour were unable to inflict anything like the suffering on the Government that they themselves had endured during 1950–1: at worst they posed a minor inconvenience.

Relations with the Liberal Party were a matter of some uncertainty. Churchill had been keen to forge closer links,[29] but Lord Woolton, the Party Chairman, was less enthusiastic.[30] After much discussion, only two agreements were made in 1951, at Bolton[31] and Huddersfield,[32] strongly against the advice of the local Conservative Associations,[33] though they undoubtedly operated to the disadvantage of Labour. Churchill also supported Lady Violet Bonham Carter's unsuccessful stand at Colne Valley, where no Conservative candidate stood, and where Churchill's intervention caused considerable furore in the Liberal Party.[34] In the event, it was the Liberals' least successful General Election of the century. They put up 109 candidates; their share of the total vote was 2.5%, and they won just six seats.[35] After the Election,

71

Churchill offered Clement Davies, the Liberal Leader, the Ministry of Education, which would, in effect have meant a Conservative–Liberal Coalition, but to Davies' regret his colleagues could not approve the plan, although they did promise to support the Government on all measures which were in 'the interests of the country as a whole'.[36]

The 'National' Liberals[37] had been firmly integrated into the Conservative Party as a result of the Woolton–Teviot agreement of May 1947, which provided for the establishment of joint Conservative and Liberal Associations in certain constituencies. Eighteen of their members won seats in 1951, and a number, including their chairman, John Maclay, were given jobs. Their Chief Whip, Sir Herbert Butcher, was appointed Government Deputy Chief Whip and given responsibility for liaison with Clement Davies' Liberals in the House. They met regularly as a group, on Wednesday evenings, throughout 1951–5 when the House was sitting, but, not surprisingly, never as a whole voted against the Government.[38] As the decade wore on the group gradually faded away.

1955 General Election

The question of the timing of the next General Election was inextricably bound up with the timing of Churchill's retirement as Prime Minister, an issue that, as we have seen, arose within months of his taking office. Soon after Parliament assembled in November 1951, the Government made it plain that they had no intention of an early appeal to the country; indeed they had no need. In early 1953 there was some expectation that an Election might be called in the autumn,[39] but in October 1953, to the surprise and alarm of many of his colleagues, Churchill denied the possibility for that year, or, as far as he could see, in the next.[40] In his speech on the Address in November 1953, Churchill dwelt at some length on his decision not to seek an early General Election. He argued that Elections exist for the House of Commons, not the House of Commons for Elections, and that the Government's duty was to provide stable administration without constant reference to the electors.[41]

As 1954 advanced, it was increasingly expected that the General Election would come in October 1955. Churchill himself first appears to have begun seriously turning his attention towards timing in mid-March 1954. He told Woolton then that he would like to discuss the matter with him,[42] and at the meeting of senior Ministers held on 13th April he suggested February or October 1955 or even some time in 1956.[43]

On 17th August Churchill invited Woolton and Sir Stephen Pierssené, General Director of the Conservative Office,[44] to Chartwell to hear their opinions on Election timing. They had in mind 1954 as the best date and Churchill asked Woolton to prepare further background information. Woolton accordingly sent Churchill a memorandum a fortnight later containing arguments for and against elections in autumn 1954, spring 1955 and autumn 1955, and said the balance was in favour of the last date. Woolton added that Eden should be given a full six month period as Prime Minister before the Election.[45] In September principal Central Office agents met and also favoured an autumn 1955 Election date. In a letter to Churchill after the meeting, Woolton stressed the unsettling effect on Party morale of uncertainty about the composition of the Government.[46] He told Macmillan at a later date that a survey conducted by 'the most experienced agents' had taken place which revealed that an immediate Election would be a disaster. The only way to avoid a similar result in the following year would be a complete change in the structure of the Government, and a new Prime Minister.[47]

Churchill was not to be moved, and consideration of an Election date was put off.[48] Yet the Queen's Speech, delivered at the end of November 1954, was, in effect, a holding operation, and contained nothing either to delay or to hasten a General Election.[49]

Election timing was not discussed further until a meeting on 22nd December. Churchill opened by reading a letter from Eden in which he urged an early Election. Woolton thought 10th March was the earliest possible date but Butler protested that it would interfere with his Budget arrangements. Woolton left the meeting to consult with Pierssené and on his return declared that May would be a possible date, concurrent with borough elections.[50] The position of Lancashire, where there were nine Conservative M.P.s with majorities of less than 3,000, loomed large in Woolton's considerations. He feared that Peter Thorneycroft's uncompromising policy at the Board of Trade towards the textile industry might jeopardise the whole outcome in a closerun General Election.[51] Churchill, by now quite emotional, said he would not go but if sufficient numbers of his Cabinet resigned this would force an Election. After this pronouncement, the meeting broke up.[52] A Cabinet was held at 5.30 p.m. that same day at which Churchill appeared undismayed (unlike his senior colleagues). At its conclusion, he called back Woolton and appeared uncertain what to do: he announced as his high electoral value had been shown by the size of the eightieth birthday present from the nation (with nearly a quarter of a million sending gifts)[53] he might lead an early Election and asked Woolton to assess possibilities.[54]

With Churchill's pledge in the spring of 1955 to leave Number Ten, Eden became the key man in discussions on timing. In March Woolton wrote to say that an Election could be held in May though it would mean considerable changes to existing plans, but that the Party favoured an October Election.[55] Eden, who had returned early from talks in Singapore, India and Iraq, following the inaugural S.E.A.T.O. conference in Bangkok, on the news of Churchill's impending retirement,[56] said he would prefer a May Election. This was on the prompting of Woolton, who personally felt that the economic position would deteriorate by October and also that the present Government had drifted for too long and needed a complete change.[57]

Woolton announced at the Cabinet meeting on 14th March that the last possible date for the Election would be 26th May; Butler was 'almost savage',[58] and said it should not be until the first week in June, but his temper collapsed and he quickly came round to agree with the May date.[59] Further discussions were held later in the month at Eden's instigation at the Foreign Office with Lord Salisbury, Butler, Harold Macmillan, Woolton and Harry Crookshank (who called the group the 'Big Five'). They discussed Election dates, but reached no agreement.[60]

At a further meeting at the Foreign Office on 4th April with Sir Walter Monckton and Patrick Buchan-Hepburn also present, Eden now felt doubtful about a May Election, as he could not see what explanation could be offered for it, and was supported by Buchan-Hepburn, who said the necessary Budget resolutions could not be passed through the House in time without the use of the guillotine. Woolton and Butler, whose views had by now changed,[61] favoured May, and Woolton passed a note to Eden suggesting he delay the decision until after the results of the Lancashire County Council elections the following day.[62] A meeting in the evening of 5th April revealed Eden still undecided, but wavering towards postponement, which led Woolton to observe: 'Eden cannot make up his mind which isn't a very hopeful sign.'[63] Yet by 6th April he seemed to have almost settled on May.[64] It was a difficult decision, as he related in his memoirs, for he greatly feared the possibility that he might be Prime Minister for less than two months. He ascribed his firm decision to go to the country on 26th May as due to the diminishing likelihood, with the passing days, that an early General Election would be regarded as unwarranted.[65] On 15th April Eden announced that Parliament would be dissolved on 6th May with the Election following on 26th May.[66]

Towards the end of March, Eden and Woolton began to think seriously about the outline Manifesto prepared mainly by the Research Department. Michael Fraser and Goldman had visited the departmental Ministers in turn and made a list of policies the Ministers had in the pipeline, or points they wanted to stress. This provided the bridge between Party and Government,[67] and from their notes the first draft was written. Woolton felt it lacked 'personality', and wrote to Eden stressing his belief that a new Prime Minister's Manifesto should bear the stamp of the man who is leading the appeal to the country.[68] Woolton suggested Eden engage Guy Schofield, who had been Editor of the *Daily Mail*, 1950–4, and who knew Eden's mind well, to help give shape to the document and make it the expression of Eden's personal beliefs. He was duly engaged, though the impact he made was small.[69] On 30th March Woolton and Butler spent an hour and a half together to discuss the Manifesto,[70] and a small number of meetings were attended by senior Ministers at which points were raised. The title, 'United for Peace and Progress' was the result of much disagreement, and another fuss arose over a phrase Eden wanted to insert, saying that at present no war was being fought in the world. The final document, published on 30th April, differed remarkably little from the draft produced by the Research Department, although it was prefaced by 'A Personal Statement by the Prime Minister', which indisputably bore Eden's personal stamp. Any 'personality' it contained was of a bland variety, providing 'a maximum of rhetoric and a minimum of a programme'.[71]

Not that it mattered: for the Conservatives the Election campaign was the easiest of any since the war.[72] At the poll on 26th May they won 344 seats to Labour's 277 and an overall majority of 58, increasing their share of the vote to 49.7% compared with 48% in 1951. The decision to go for an early summer Election had paid off better than anyone in the Party had dared expect.

Chapter 3   Prime Minister and Government II

Part 1   Appointments and Reshuffles

1951 Appointments

Following the 1951 Election victory considerable uncertainty prevailed as to appointments to the Government. The Prime Minister was very much his own man,[1] yielding to no pressure and revealing to no Minister, not even to Anthony Eden, all his thoughts on the subject, although he did discuss the matter frankly with Sir Norman Brook, John Colville and Christopher Soames. Also little formality had existed in either the identity of Parliamentary spokesmen on specific issues from 1945 until 1951 (Winston Churchill and Patrick Buchan-Hepburn, the Chief Whip, often deciding between them who should take business for the following week)[2] or the composition of the shadow Cabinet whose full-scale weekly meetings were to have decreasing importance after 1945.[3] Churchill, moreover, by no means felt that a man who had concentrated on a particular subject in Opposition should take on that job once in power.[4] He had already formed one Administration afresh, the 'Caretaker' of May to July 1945, and had learnt the lesson of not being preached to by ardent Cabinet makers.[5] In 1951 he was determined to have a 'broadly based Government', and referred to this several times during the Election campaign: this accounted for the appointment of a number of men not initially from politics (Lords Cherwell, Ismay and Leathers) and others whose origins were not in the Conservative Party (Lords De la Warr, Simonds and Reading as well as Gwilym Lloyd-George, John Maclay, Sir Walter Monckton and Sir Arthur Salter).

Though there have been few Cabinets that owed so much to the Prime Minister's personal choices, the composition of the Government as a whole bore a notable similarity to the officers of the Party's Parliamentary Committees,[6] whose senior members were appointed by the Party Leader.[7] Among the junior officers, the Vice-Chairmen and Secretaries, far greater change occurred. A number of Chairmen of the Committees were not appointed to their respective Ministries, and in these changes Churchill's hand can clearly be seen.[8]

The senior appointments and the idea of co-ordinating Ministers were mostly settled in Churchill's mind by the time of the General Election. Eden was to be Deputy Prime Minister, Foreign Secretary and Leader of the House; Rab Butler, Chancellor;[9] Monckton, Labour; Lord Salisbury, Colonies; Sir David Maxwell Fyfe, Home Secretary; Lord Woolton, Lord President and co-ordinator for food and agriculture;[10] Oliver Lyttelton, co-ordinator of production and Leathers co-ordinator of the nationalised industries.[11] A few minor problems remained. The title Deputy Prime Minister for Eden raised objections,[12] while Salisbury did not want the Colonial Office, and was made Lord Privy Seal. Lyttelton, disenchanted with his proposed job,[13] was given the now vacant Colonial Secretaryship. Ismay was made Commonwealth Secretary, and of these eight appointments all but Leathers' were announced on 28th October.

Not all those Churchill wanted to appoint agreed to serve. In particular, three non-political figures declined, Sir John Anderson as a co-ordinator,[14] Lord Asquith of Bishopstone as Lord Chancellor[15] and Lord Portal as Minister of Defence.[16] The death of Oliver Stanley in December 1950, at the age of fifty-four, deprived the Party of one of its most experienced and ablest men.[17] He had ranked number three after Eden, and was considered a likely choice as the next Conservative Chancellor.[18] The highly political Brendan Bracken also declined to serve,[19] as he made clear to Churchill at an early stage, much to the latter's regret. Lord Reid (Lord Advocate, 1941–5) left the Commons in 1948 to become a Lord of Appeal and hence was unavailable.[20] Had these six been included, it would have produced in all probability the most talented Administration of the century since the Liberal Government of 1906.

The remaining seven Cabinet posts were announced on 30th October, in time for the first Cabinet held on the same day at 3 p.m. Churchill's wartime colleagues, Cherwell and Leathers, were included as Paymaster-General and Secretary of State for the Co-ordination of Transport, Fuel and Power respectively, similar functions to the ones they had had during the war.[21] Simonds, an apolitical lawyer and a Law Lord since 1944, not personally familiar to Churchill and suggested to him by either Maxwell Fyfe or Salisbury,[22] became Lord Chancellor. Harold Macmillan was surprised and wounded to be given merely Housing, and it is possible that on this one appointment Churchill listened to the advice of Beaverbrook.[23] Harry Crookshank, though never a favourite of Churchill's, could not be omitted, and was tipped for one of the top economic jobs.[24] Instead he was appointed Minister of Health, and also Leader of the House after Eden's announcement on 30th October that he could not manage the post.[25] James Stuart, at one time hostile to Churchill but by now a good friend and Chief Whip (1941–8), became Scottish Secretary instead of Walter Elliot, whom some felt a strong runner.[26] The youngest and most junior appointment to the Cabinet was Peter Thorneycroft, a concession by Churchill to the younger men in the Party, and a man of whose speaking ability in the House he had a high opinion.[27]

The total of sixteen displayed Churchill's preference for a small Cabinet, made possible by the co-ordinating Ministers who supervised more than one Department.[28] This was one less than Clement Attlee's Cabinet. Out went the Ministers of Agriculture, Education and the Chancellor of the Duchy of Lancaster, and in came the Minister of Health (out since January 1951), the Paymaster-General (out since April 1949) and the new Secretary of State for the Co-ordination of Transport, Fuel and Power, all largely for reasons of personality.[29] Churchill's decision to appoint himself Minister of Defence meant one fewer in Cabinet.

Numbers soon began to rise in a complex series of changes. In March they went to seventeen when Churchill gave up the Defence portfolio to Lord Alexander of Tunis but fell to sixteen once more only eleven days later when Ismay left the Commonwealth Relations Office, a job taken on by Salisbury (who was already Lord Privy Seal). In May Crookshank resigned as Minister of Health but remained in Cabinet, taking over as Lord Privy Seal. The new Minister of Health (Iain Macleod) did not sit in Cabinet and therefore numbers remained constant at sixteen. They rose again by one when Lord Swinton, a constant attender since 1951, succeeded Salisbury as Commonwealth Secretary in November 1952. Salisbury became Lord President after Woolton, who was appointed Chancellor of the Duchy and the post reinstated to Cabinet. In September 1953 they rose to a high point of nineteen when Leathers' job was abolished on his retirement and the Ministers of Agriculture, Education and Food were promoted to Cabinet, settling thereafter at eighteen on Cherwell's resignation in November 1953, and the removal of the Paymaster-General's job from Cabinet. The remaining changes during the life of the Government left Cabinet numbers unaltered: in October 1954 the new Cabinet posts of Agriculture and Food were combined, creating one space taken up by the promotion to Cabinet of the Minister of Pensions and National Insurance.

Two non-Cabinet posts were announced on 30th October, 1951: Buchan-Hepburn[30] as Parliamentary Secretary to the Treasury (Government Chief Whip) and the much-sought-after Selwyn Lloyd, captured by Eden for Minister of State (at the Foreign Office).

Three days before the next batch of appointments, sixteen in total,

78

were announced on 31st October, Churchill invited Buchan-Hepburn and Crookshank to Chartwell and both were of considerable help, particularly with the more junior appointments, as many of the younger men were not well known to him.[31] Many of these appointments, though, were Churchill's own: Lord De L'Isle to the Air Ministry,[32] his former assistant on defence matters, Antony Head, to the War Office, Salter, put in to keep an eye on Butler at the Treasury, and John Boyd-Carpenter, a younger man who had made an impression on Churchill, to be Financial Secretary. The appointment of Duncan Sandys, his son-in-law, caused considerable problems, as he was anxious to avoid a charge of nepotism; he was finally placed as Minister of Supply.[33]

Swinton's role also caused difficulty. Churchill apart, he had more ministerial experience than any other, but a position could not be found for him in the Cabinet. Stuart and Buchan-Hepburn, advising at Chartwell with Crookshank on 29th October, suggested Swinton for co-ordination on hearing the news that Anderson had turned it down.[34] But this proposal was not acceptable to Churchill. Lyttelton's appointment to the Colonial Office, however, left a senior job free on the production side and Swinton was offered the Ministry of Materials, a post which Churchill placed outside Cabinet.[35] He was hurt not to be offered more, which his experience merited, and Brook, as an intimate of Churchill and Swinton, was used as an emissary in the course of Churchill's efforts to persuade Swinton to accept the post.[36] The remaining 31st October appointments were either rewards for Party work (Thomas Dugdale), Eden's choices for the Foreign Office (Anthony Nutting, Reading), strategic (Maclay, leader of the National Liberals), or jobs given to unspectacular but proven men (Geoffrey Lloyd, Lloyd-George, Osbert Peake). In addition two first-time Ministers were appointed, Charles Hill after only eighteen months in the House, and Sir Peter Bennett, aged seventy-one, one of the Party's leading industrial experts.

De La Warr, Sir David Eccles and Derick Heathcoat Amory, appointed a few days later to the largely unpolitical Departments, the Post Office, Works and Pensions respectively, completed the list of Ministers. Over the next week announcements followed of four batches of junior appointments, almost all at the suggestion of Buchan-Hepburn, Crookshank and Stuart,[37] or requested by individual senior Ministers. Thus Macmillan secured Ernest Marples at Housing, and Stuart, Lord Home, Tom Galbraith and William McNair Snadden for the Scottish Office. By 7th November all but two positions had been filled, additional Parliamentary Under-Secretaries at the Home and

Scottish Offices, in accordance with pledges given in the Manifesto and for which enabling legislation had to be passed.[38]

Churchill was concerned throughout to prevent hurt feelings, where possible, of both junior men hoping for their first job,[39] and older men expecting a senior post.[40] He was determined to appoint Ministers full of conviction and belief, and also fresh men. Since a number of new faces who had not served in the shadow Cabinet were brought in to occupy senior posts, such as Ismay, Leathers, Monckton and Simonds, there was not enough room for everyone who had been tipped for posts. In particular there was a body of men too senior to be offered just junior positions. Thus Leo Amery,[41] Elliot,[42] Robert Hudson[43] and W. S. ('Shakes') Morrison[44] in particular had to be left out, even though the last three had been Chairmen of the Party's Parliamentary Committees until the General Election, and hence likely contenders for important jobs. Others, as for example Ralph Assheton[45] and Anthony Hurd,[46] were offered posts, but declined for personal reasons. Churchill, as we have seen in the previous chapter, wanted to appoint the Liberal leader, Clement Davies, Minister of Education, but his Party would not agree.[47] Beaverbrook was almost certainly not offered a job, nor did he seek one.[48]

Churchill's choice of Ministers came under immediate attack for containing too many peers.[49] Indeed with the numbers in the Cabinet at six (soon rising to seven with the appointment of Alexander as Minister of Defence), it had twice as many as the 1950 Labour Government. *The Economist* complained: 'It weakens dangerously the Government's ability to expound its main policies in the House of Commons through men who have played a full part in making those policies.'[50] All the same it is hard to see how the Administration was seriously weakened. Churchill answered back by comparing the eighteen peers in his entire Government with the sixteen in the previous Labour Government.[51] Meanwhile the younger men in the Party felt that too many jobs had gone to old hands. Thorneycroft at forty-two was by far the youngest man in Cabinet, which had an average age of fifty-nine[52] and the average age of the whole Government, at forty-nine, was comparatively high. One reason for the high average age, however, was that those who entered the House in 1950 were mostly too young to be given ministerial jobs. Churchill thus had to rely on older men, the previous large influx of Conservative M.P.s having been as long ago as 1935. The feeling of discontent was to an extent mollified by the appointment of Macleod as Minister of Health in May 1952.

In its political stance Churchill further imprinted his persona on the 1951 Conservative Government by giving precedence in appointments to supporters of a moderate empirical conservatism over the 'right' of the Party. Thus four representatives of moderate conservatism gained key positions in the Cabinet: Eden, Maxwell Fyfe, Butler and Macmillan. Few representatives of the 'right' were given jobs, but some became Chairmen of the Party's backbench committees: for example, Assheton (Finance), Charles Waterhouse (Defence) and Lord Hinchingbrooke (Transport).

Reshuffles

In this Government, which lasted for three years, seven months, Churchill made only six minor reshuffles and one major. Buchan-Hepburn came to play an increasingly large part in advising Churchill on appointments. But he, and Churchill, also on occasion sought the advice of Stuart: for example on the appointment of Macleod in May 1952, and a new Minister of Education, Eccles, in October 1954.[53] Churchill also sometimes listened to the advice of George Christ,[54] often a harsh evaluator of people, but a shrewd judge of talent and Parliamentary ability.

The first reshuffle came after only seven months, in May 1952, caused by the resignation, through ill health, of Maclay, and that of Bennett, who decided he was unsuited to ministerial life. Crookshank used the opportunity to stand down as Minister of Health, a job he found an increasing strain.[55] Lennox-Boyd reluctantly left the post of Minister of State at the Colonial Office to follow Maclay as Minister of Transport, and a small number of adjustments had to be made to fill the gaps.

The November 1952 reshuffle followed Woolton's illness and Salisbury's desire to give up the Commonwealth Secretaryship.[56] Swinton was delighted to accept Salisbury's job, and Salter, unhappy at the Treasury, followed him at Materials. Reginald Maudling received the major promotion from Parliamentary Secretary at Civil Aviation to Economic Secretary at the Treasury. This gave Churchill the chance to bring in two talented younger men: John Profumo, who followed Maudling at Transport, and Lord Mancroft, appointed Lord-in-Waiting in succession to Lord Lloyd, who was made Under-Secretary at the Home Office on David Llewellyn's resignation, with special responsibility for Wales. Eden, in New York at the United Nations General Assembly, was displeased at the changes; he disliked Swinton's appointment, and the rest he regarded as mere rejuggling of old hands.[57]

The third reshuffle, of September 1953, was bigger, brought about by the resignation of Leathers, Harry Mackeson and Salter, the first and last through choice. The expectation of a major reshuffle, probably entailing a replacement for Eden at the Foreign Office, had been in the air throughout the summer when both Churchill and Eden were absent through ill health. Moreover, no major changes had taken place since the formation of the Government two years before. But as Eden's health gradually improved, speculation diminished, and disappointment greeted the ensuing changes ('a mere nibble at the cherry' and 'the bare minimum' said *The Economist*).[58] Churchill also formally ended the largely ineffectual system of co-ordinating ministers, but to compensate he increased the Cabinet by three: the Ministers of Agriculture and Food,[59] who were the two non-Cabinet Ministers who had most consistently attended meetings since 1951, were both promoted to Cabinet, as was the Minister of Education.[60] The Minister here was Florence Horsbrugh, the first Conservative woman to be promoted to a job in Cabinet.[61] Butler, Buchan-Hepburn,[62] Crookshank and Swinton were all consulted by Churchill about the changes,[63] Butler in the absence of Eden playing a large part. The most exciting element in the changes was felt to be the appointment of Heathcoat Amory, a rising figure in the Party, to the new post of Minister of State at the Board of Trade.

A minor re-arrangement took place in November 1953, following the resignation of Cherwell, Paymaster-General, and Joseph Gurney Braithwaite, Parliamentary Secretary at Transport. Lord Selkirk, Lord-in-Waiting, succeeded Cherwell, but the Paymaster-General ceased to have a seat in Cabinet. Reading, at one time thought of as a possibility to follow Cherwell,[64] was appointed to the new job of second Minister of State at the Foreign Office. Three new men were appointed: Lord Hawke who succeeded Selkirk, Douglas Dodds-Parker, filling the vacant under-secretaryship at the Foreign Office, and Reginald Bevins, appointed Parliamentary Secretary at the Ministry of Works.

A larger reshuffle took place in July 1954, when Dugdale resigned as Minister of Agriculture after Crichel Down and Lyttelton finally quit the Colonial Office for industry and the City. Lyttelton was succeeded by Alan Lennox-Boyd to the job for which he had been earmarked since 1951. Boyd-Carpenter was given his first departmental Minister's job at Transport, and Henry Brooke followed him as Financial Secretary to the Treasury. Heathcoat Amory was brought into Cabinet as Minister of Agriculture, Toby Low succeeding him as Minister of State at the Board of Trade. At fifty-one Brooke was the oldest new Minister appointed during the 1951–5 reshuffles, and at thirty, Sir Edward Boyle, appointed Parliamentary Secretary at Supply in succession to Low, was the youngest, two years younger than Churchill had been when he had received his first job in 1906. Lyttelton's departure was intended to coincide with Churchill's expected retirement,[65] although in the event this was delayed a further eight months. Large scale changes had also been discussed before the summer recess,[60] but these too were put off, to the disappointment of some of the Government's supporters.

The sixth and major reshuffle, in October 1954, involved a total of twenty-four changes. Many had hung fire for months, but by September with no immediate prospect of Churchill retiring, pressures broke: Maxwell Fyfe wanted to give up the home secretaryship and take up his claim to be Lord Chancellor, Alexander felt uncomfortable as Minister of Defence and had for some months been anxious for a change, Florence Horsbrugh was getting into deeper and deeper water as Minister of Education, and Macmillan, his programme complete, was anxious to leave Housing.

Discussions took place during late September and early October, and though the final decisions were very much Churchill's, he sought the advice of at least Eden, Butler and Macmillan, but not Crookshank, apparently by this time a less influential adviser.[67] That Alexander, Florence Horsbrugh and Simonds would go, however, there was little doubt, but who would fill the offices of Minister of Defence and Home Secretary, and would Eden leave the Foreign Office to gain experience on the domestic front? Viewing this as an excuse on Churchill's part for further delaying his retirement, Eden declined to move. This meant that Macmillan, who Churchill hoped might succeed Eden, was free to take on another job. Churchill's subsequent plan consisted of Macmillan supplanting Crookshank as Leader of the House and Lord Privy Seal, and Crookshank becoming Home Secretary. Macmillan refused, partly out of loyalty to his old friend, who was not keen to make the change,[68] but also probably because he was hoping for higher things.[69] Macmillan, after much deliberation as to where his best interests lay, suggested the Ministry of Defence, which Eden was also keen for him to get, and Churchill agreed. Lloyd-George, no one's rival, was then advanced to fill the gap at the Home Office. Three men thought to have performed well were given new senior jobs, Eccles – Education, Selwyn Lloyd – Supply, and Sandys – Housing and Local Government, Eccles and Sandys also being brought for the first time into the Cabinet. Peake was also promoted to the Cabinet as Minister of Pensions and National Insurance.

A host of lesser changes took place following the resignations of John Foster, Sir Lionel Heald, James Hutchison and Kenneth Pickthorn. Seven men were given their first ministerial positions, two Lords, Fairfax and St. Aldwyn, and five commoners, William Deedes, Lord John Hope, Sir Harry Hylton-Foster, Fitzroy Maclean and Gerald

Wills. A sinecure post was refilled for the first time for seven years, Minister without Portfolio, given to Lord Munster.

The last reshuffle took place on 7th April, 1955, the day after Eden's succession and involved eleven changes. With the General Election only weeks away Eden avoided major changes, a decision that received a mixed reception.[70] Possibly also, Eden, for compassionate reasons, was reluctant to move on Butler from the Treasury so soon after the death of his wife in December 1954.[71] Even among his colleagues there was disagreement. Woolton, a close confidant at the time, had surprised him by saying that the changes should take place before, not after the Election. Woolton also favoured removing Thorneycroft from the Board of Trade, and possibly substituting Heathcoat Amory,[72] but Eden demurred.

As Foreign Secretary Eden would have liked to appoint Salisbury, but later wrote that he felt it would not be possible to have a Foreign Secretary in the Lords.[73] Instead he decided on Macmillan, at one time considered for the Treasury.[74] As Minister of Defence he picked Selwyn Lloyd after first intending the job for himself, at least for a while, and trying, unsuccessfully, to persuade Salisbury. Meanwhile Woolton favoured Lloyd rather than Heathcoat Amory to succeed Thorneycroft at Trade.[75]

Eden earned the praise of many of his Party in Parliament by the determination he showed to advance younger men in his first reshuffle. Not only were four given their first departmental jobs, Frederick Erroll, Jack Nixon Browne, Donald Kaberry and Harmar Nicholls, but also two of the ablest younger Tories were given sizeable promotions, Boyle to Economic Secretary at the Treasury and Maudling to Minister of Supply. Only two senior men were not reappointed: Swinton, whose appointment as Commonwealth Secretary he never liked, and the Postmaster-General, De La Warr, whom Eden also found unsympathetic. On Salisbury's request, Eden appointed Lord Home Commonwealth Secretary,[76] and in another surprise appointment, he offered Hill the Post Office. These changes were beneficial in reducing the average age of the Cabinet from 58.6 to 55.8 years. His first major reshuffle was to take place eight months later: Crookshank and Woolton finally retired, and Buchan-Hepburn, Macleod and Selkirk were brought into the Cabinet.

Part 2   The Cabinet

A total of twenty-five men sat in the Cabinet in the three and a half years under Churchill's chairmanship. Although Churchill was closest to Lord Cherwell, Anthony Eden, Oliver Lyttelton, Sir Walter Monckton and

Lord Salisbury (even if they often disagreed), there was in no sense an inner circle[1] as there had been in the shadow Cabinet when the dominant voices were Churchill, Eden and Oliver Stanley with Lyttelton also being in a position of peculiar authority.[2]

Churchill began each Cabinet meeting by outlining the subject and he then asked the appropriate Minister to open the discussion, which he had to do fairly briefly or run the risk of being cut short. Churchill would then allow a number of Ministers to comment, keeping careful watch on time if he wished either to force a decision, or to procrastinate in order to avoid reaching an issue later in the agenda. He would then sum up on matters he felt of particular importance: other items would be left to the Cabinet Secretariat.[3] He regarded the Cabinet as extremely important,[4] even sacrosanct, and would only rarely ride roughshod over it to get his way. Yet he often proved tenacious in persuasion.[5] Unlike Clement Attlee, Churchill often allowed discussions to run on longer than strictly necessary, irritating some of the older members, who felt his conduct of Cabinet altogether too slack and indecisive.[6] It was not uncommon for non-Cabinet departmental Ministers to find, after a long wait outside, that their topic would be rushed through. But this is normal in any Cabinet. It is wrong to exaggerate the harmful effects of Churchill's erratic behaviour at Cabinet; though not to all the members' liking, business was conducted, and decisions were taken with little delay, at least until the last few months. Indeed until the end he dominated meetings,[7] to the resentment of some Ministers.

When foreign affairs were discussed, few would offer their comments.[8] Indeed, the Cabinet was scarcely used as a forum of discussion on foreign policy,[9] although Eden kept Ministers informed at all times.[10] Salisbury, and occasionally Lyttelton and Macmillan would offer comments on foreign affairs, but on major policy matters Eden preferred to deal with Churchill direct.[11] Eden was never very happy about criticisms of his foreign policy, although it was only after he became Prime Minister, according to Lord Amory, that his sensitivity about this grew.[12]

In Churchill's absence Eden took the chair at Cabinet. On the first occasion, 17th January, 1952, he was generally felt to manage affairs in a businesslike manner.[13] From the start Eden was conscious of the need to keep up with domestic affairs and understand them more fully. But after the first six months, foreign affairs and ill health intervened, so it was only on the approach of the 1955 Election that his thoughts again began to focus on domestic policy. At no time during the three and a half years did he display much interest in Cabinet Committees, in marked contrast to Ernest Bevin, Foreign Secretary during the previous Attlee Administration. Eden believed that a property-owning democracy was preferable to a socialist society,[14] and that the drift towards a collectivist state could be prevented only by spreading property and status as widely as possible. His priorities were housing, full employment, concern to see the growth of schemes for profit sharing, employee share ownership and participation. He was concerned with the general trend in domestic policy from 1951–5.[15] Over the 1952 and April 1955 Budget proposals, he intervened in economic affairs to ensure less harsh measures were put into effect. In 1952, after information on Rab Butler's intentions had been forwarded to him in Lisbon, he even considered resigning.[16] He thought himself as being on the left of the Party, but without many specific policy programmes in mind. He appointed Robert Carr as his Parliamentary Private Secretary, partly in the hope that Carr would help him formulate precise plans and expand his knowledge of domestic affairs, particularly industry.[17]

Eden's closeness to Churchill undoubtedly enhanced his standing in Cabinet. In spite of often serious quarrels,[18] a lasting breach was never likely and there remained a profound bond between them which neither forgot.[19] The relationship was a curious compound of love and envy, and their behaviour towards each other a matter of constant surprise to their intimates.[20] The reality and depth of the bond was revealed at odd moments, such as the spontaneous delight Churchill displayed when Eden told him of his intention to marry Churchill's niece, Clarissa.[21] Observers on the sidelines, witnessing one of the outbursts against Churchill to which Eden was prone, were likely to receive a jaundiced view of the relationship.[22]

Eden had few personal friends in Cabinet, nor did he go out of his way to alter that position: he was fond of Salisbury and, of course, Churchill, and admired Lord Simonds, but a distinct coolness was apparent in his relations with Butler, Harold Macmillan and Lord Swinton, and he must have been aware that Lyttelton and James Stuart had reservations about his ability to become a good Party Leader. His main friendships lay outside the Cabinet: Carr and Anthony Nutting at the Foreign Office, Sir Thomas Dugdale at Agriculture (a member of Cabinet for only ten months, September 1953–July 1954), and Jim Thomas at the Admiralty, and Lord Scarbrough outside politics.[23]

Salisbury, the next most senior figure in Cabinet, had grown in stature considerably in the six years since the end of the war[24] due to his crucial position as Opposition Leader of the House of Lords at a time when the Conservatives' representation in the Lower House was so low.[25] As well as Leader of the Lords from 1951, he was successively Lord Privy Seal (October 1951–May 1952) and Lord President (November 1952–March

1957), both sinecure posts, with additional shortish periods of departmental responsibility (Commonwealth Secretary March–November 1952, and acting Foreign Secretary June–October 1953). From November 1952 he was also a strong Chairman of the highly important Home Affairs Committee of the Cabinet. Salisbury was greatly burdened by responsibility after 1951. Apart from his ministerial and House of Lords duties, demands from his estates and family took much of his time, and, like Eden, frequent bouts of ill health, stemming from his active service during the First World War, impaired his efficiency. He was ill, for example, for much of early 1953.[26] Although he found his departmental responsibilities a burden, he had his eye on the foreign secretaryship,[27] and had Churchill been successful in his attempts to persuade Eden to give up this post and move over to the home front, Salisbury would probably have been appointed in his place.[28]

Salisbury was a man of principle with politics in his blood,[29] and motivated by a high sense of duty. His political views placed him on the right wing of the Cabinet,[30] and on more than one occasion he was on the verge of resignation, particularly after Eden became Prime Minister.[31] Thus he seriously considered resigning over the progress of iron and steel denationalisation in July 1952;[32] from his position of acting Foreign Secretary in August 1953, due to Churchill's interventions in his conduct of policy;[33] in September 1953, to make way for younger men;[34] over the Peter Townsend/Princess Margaret affair in the summer of 1953;[35] and in July 1954, over Churchill's proposal for a summit meeting.[36] This tended rather to devalue his credibility. Not always a wise man, Salisbury could be devious, though he was regarded with affection and respect by most of his colleagues and by Churchill. Thus his voice carried great weight in the Cabinet, and he was highly influential in his private discussions and correspondence with colleagues.[37] Churchill respected him greatly for resigning with Eden in February 1938 over appeasement, and though their relationship underwent some strain throughout 1951–5, particularly after Churchill's stroke in 1953, Salisbury remained one of his closest advisers, and a close personal friend (as was Lady Salisbury). In February 1953, when Salisbury had to give up his duties for a month due to illness, Churchill said: 'He is one of those in my orchestra whose note I value.'[38] Churchill also determined that history should not repeat itself in reverse; in December 1886 Salisbury's grandfather had accepted the resignation of Churchill's father as Chancellor of the Exchequer.

Twice Salisbury took the centre of the stage. When Churchill suffered his arterial spasm in February 1952, the first person John Colville approached for advice was Salisbury.[39] During the far more serious stroke of June 1953, Salisbury was considered, by Churchill's entourage, the

87

most suitable caretaker Prime Minister until Eden recovered his own health. Once more the decision on what action to take devolved on Colville, as the *de facto* senior Joint Principal Private Secretary to the Prime Minister. If Churchill died, as Lord Moran predicted he would, Colville thought it would not be right to recommend that the Queen should send for the next most senior Cabinet Minister, Butler, because he could hardly form a Government and then retire after three months on Eden's return. Accordingly, Colville suggested to the Queen's Private Secretary, Sir Alan Lascelles, that the Queen send for Salisbury and ask him to form a 'Caretaker Government' until Eden was fit to return.[40] Had Churchill not recovered this is almost certainly what would have occurred. How the 1922 Committee and the Labour Party would have reacted is a matter for speculation, but neither is likely to have responded calmly,[41] even though the Sovereign's prerogative to choose the Prime Minister was accepted in the Conservative Party at the time. If Eden himself had not been ill, he might well have been nominated Prime Minister at once by Salisbury and Butler,[42] though this assumes that Churchill, had he still been alive, would have agreed to resign, which cannot be taken for granted.[43]

Butler was Chairman of the Cabinet's Economic Policy Committee and the next most senior Cabinet member. He had been a highly influential Director of the Conservative Research Department since 1945, and his appointment as Chancellor of the Exchequer in 1951 confirmed his position as the outstanding representative of the 'new Conservatism'.[44]

As Churchill warmed to him, gradually removing the 'watchdogs' he had cautiously placed around his work at the Treasury, so Butler's standing increased,[45] not least in the House where he performed far better against his predecessor Hugh Gaitskell, now shadow Chancellor, than had been expected. By the autumn of 1952 he took the chair in Cabinet when both Churchill and Eden were away,[46] and his standing rose considerably during Churchill's and Eden's illnesses in the summer of 1953.[47] In Cabinet, unlike some Chancellors, he contributed little, being as much a thinker as an activist, and rarely expressing decisive opinions on matters outside or even within his own field.[48] Churchill, however, came to trust Butler's judgment increasingly over the months.[49]

Butler had few if any close friends in the Cabinet. He was reasonably close to Monckton and Swinton, but some other relationships deteriorated, in particular those with Eden and Macmillan. He considered Eden (along with Cherwell) responsible for defeating his plan of making the pound convertible in February 1952, and from that point on jealousy and mistrust grew, based on the degree of press coverage given to each, and the jockeying for position as number two in the Government.[50] Similar jealousy was also responsible for the souring of Butler's relations with Macmillan, while those with Lord Woolton were still poorer. This in part resulted from the years in Opposition when Butler became Chairman of the Conservative Research Department (from 1945)[51] and Woolton Chairman of the Party Organisation (from 1946). They quarrelled over methods of fund raising and also the Research Department's degree of autonomy.[52] Three times Woolton intervened in the hope of preventing Butler either becoming or continuing as Chancellor: when Churchill was forming his Government in 1951, again, a year later, and finally when Eden was considering changes to his Cabinet in April 1955.[53] He thought Butler a clever man, but that he had come to believe in the Treasury, as had Sir Stafford Cripps and later Gaitskell, and that its officials had undue influence over him. Woolton was not alone in his views; the day that Churchill retired he remarked in his diary: 'Crookshank says that Butler is a myth.'[54]

Next in seniority came four men of roughly similar standing. Woolton owed his place largely thanks to his success as Party Chairman from 1946 – he was widely acknowledged as the architect of the Conservative victory in 1951 – and also to his departmental duties since 1939 when Neville Chamberlain brought him into politics from business.[55] He returned in 1951 as Lord President and also as co-ordinator of agriculture and food. He was ill for several months from October 1952[56] only resuming active departmental work in September 1953 as Minister of Materials,[57] although without the same vigour.[58] In Cabinet he seldom spoke outside his own departmental responsibilities, but took a keen interest in trade and economic matters, subjects on which he would not infrequently submit well-written papers.[59] He also devoted much time to promoting the case for commercial television,[60] and the need to expand higher technological education.[61]

Woolton never became a Parliamentary politician; indeed he never properly understood Parliament. Having served all his previous ministerial career (bar three months) in a coalition, he found it difficult to adapt to an official Opposition.[62] A poor debater, he usually read his brief without elaboration. Soon after the Election he endured taunts in the House of Lords, particularly about his promise that the Government would provide more red meat. Later he was stunned by the vehemence of Labour's attack on him after Butler cut food subsidies in his first Budget, a move contrary to an Election pledge Woolton had given on behalf of the Party.[63] When Butler told Woolton of his plans, inexperience made him think they could be balanced if he honoured another Election pledge, the revision of pension schemes.[64] Accordingly he

89

offered his resignation,[65] a naive gesture which Churchill brushed aside.[66] Woolton was further wounded by an attack over the food subsidies fracas by Antony Lambton[67] at the 1922 Committee on 27th March, 1952.[68] The episode as a whole left a deep impression on him.

The Cabinet's inner circle never fully accepted him, despite his length of service in the Conservative Party. His different social background (Manchester Grammar School and Manchester University and with Jewish business connections) prevented him being at ease with many of his colleagues, though he also loved to be in the company of aristocrats.[69] He felt closest to Sir David Maxwell Fyfe (they both had Liverpool in common),[70] and was also friendly with Harry Crookshank, Stuart and Macmillan, in particular, but he was never a 'chummy' man who mixed easily. With Churchill, especially, he shared little common ground; each admired the other's ability, but relations remained cool.[71] Churchill would not infrequently speak to Woolton in a peremptory fashion in the company of others, yet he would never be unpleasant about Woolton in his absence. Woolton, for his part, never knew where he stood with Churchill.[72]

But their relationship was soured by Churchill's action during Woolton's convalescence after his illness in October 1952.[73] Churchill, feeling that Woolton was unlikely to make a full recovery, set about choosing a replacement as Party Chairman. He settled upon the printer of the Conservative Party's literature, Malcolm McCorquodale.[74] In this Churchill was forestalled by a letter from Lady Woolton.[75] Eden also strongly objected to Churchill's approach to McCorquodale, made without consulting either the Chief Whip or himself, partly because McCorquodale was considered to be a Butler rather than an Eden man.[76] On Woolton's return to politics in March 1953, he found Churchill still anticipated his early retirement, but Woolton was anxious to remain as Party Chairman for a further six months. Eden and Macmillan both encouraged him not to yield to Churchill's wishes,[77] and in the event he did not retire until July 1955, his successor being Oliver Poole.[78]

The Party was Woolton's power base, the annual conferences the triumphant affirmation of that support. He ran a highly efficient machine,[79] treating it much like a business. He chose the staff in Central Office with care,[80] and let them manage their own affairs unhampered, always ready to offer his backing if required, but he was by no means a policy maker.

His friend Maxwell Fyfe owed his considerable standing in the Party initially to the reputation he had won as Deputy Chief Prosecutor at the Nuremberg trials (1945–6). A keen Party politician, standing rather to the left of the Party's centre, he had a considerable intellect, excelling more in its retentive rather than its creative faculties. In office he became an able Home Secretary, renowned for his prodigious hard work in Cabinet Committees and the quality of his speaking in the House. Few of his Cabinet colleagues possessed his ability to work such long hours without detriment to their performance. With less previous ministerial experience than many of the senior men in the Government,[81] nevertheless Maxwell Fyfe ensured himself a major job by his work in Opposition. His standing, particularly in the House of Commons,[82] where from 1951–4 he piloted through tedious or complicated measures, led him even to consider himself as a possible future Leader of the Party. With the passing months, however, it became increasingly clear to him that he could not rise above third in succession, after Eden and Butler, with Macmillan increasingly important.[83] With no hope of 'doing a Bonar Law' and slipping in between,[84] he altered his sights to the lord chancellorship.[85] Maxwell Fyfe, like Woolton, was by no means an intimate of Churchill's: indeed it is likely that the latter found him, on a social level, uncongenial,[86] although he relied heavily on his advice.[87] One of the three senior lawyers, along with Monckton and Simonds, he would often also express opinions on legal matters in Cabinet.

A man whom Churchill found distinctly unsympathetic, yet unable to ignore, was Crookshank. A somewhat withdrawn bachelor, fastidious (he liked to wear a red carnation in public, with no sprig of green) and a strict observer of protocol, he was little known in the country or even in his own Party.[88] He had held a number of ministerial jobs,[89] without particular distinction,[90] becoming a senior figure in the Party in Opposition, largely through his first-class debating ability. Churchill automatically put him in Cabinet as Minister of Health, and when Eden felt unable to take on the additional burden of Leader of the House, this was passed to Crookshank, to his undoubted pleasure.[91]

He soon dispelled doubts as to his suitability, in particular by a speech on 13th November, 1951, which was well received.[92] It took him a year, though, to gain sufficient confidence to settle down in the job. Despite his unsurpassed knowledge of the rules of the House, his pride in Parliament and her traditions, and the seriousness with which he took his post,[93] he never won Conservative affection, nor fully satisfied backbenchers,[94] although he was good with the Lobby. His qualities were best displayed at the weekly announcements of business, and also in winding up major debates. Unlike Chuter Ede (Leader, March–October 1951), he neglected the legitimate demands of the Opposition, and suffered criticism for interpreting his duties too narrowly and making insufficient concessions to ensure that business ran smoothly. Indeed the Labour shadow Cabinet did not regret his resignation in

91

December 1955.[95] Eden, too, had certain reservations about Crook-shank's performance[96] whereas the Cabinet generally felt he was performing well.

Crookshank took the chair in Cabinet on three occasions during Churchill and Eden's trip to North America in January 1952,[97] though on subsequent occasions when both were away the honour fell to Butler. In Cabinet he spoke infrequently, was not an originator of policy, even acting as a brake on his less cautious colleagues. His main contribution lay in discussions on Parliamentary strategy.

Though Macmillan could be regarded as Crookshank's only close friend in the Cabinet (they had known each other since childhood, being the same age and having been together at Eton, Oxford and in the Grenadier Guards, and Macmillan had even saved Crookshank's life by encouraging troops to dig longer for him when he had been buried alive in the First World War), he was friendly with a number of more junior members, making it his business to get to know several of them better, and frequently inviting them back for meals to his lavish house in Pont Street.[98] He was also close to Patrick Buchan-Hepburn, the Chief Whip (1948–55), who would seek his advice on matters of appointments. It was a particularly happy time for him, the period of his greatest political influence, although his ambition to become Commonwealth Secretary remained unfulfilled.[99]

The last figure in this group, Stuart, owed his position to the influence he had built up during his period as Chief Whip (1941–8), as well as to his friendship with Churchill. A highly able Secretary of State for Scotland, his influence extended far beyond departmental responsibilities. The Cabinet listened to him carefully on account of the confidence Churchill placed in him and because he was respected for being a truly independent voice: having no ambition for higher office, he feared no one in the Cabinet and could be relied upon to speak his mind. He knew he lacked a trained intellect, and would adopt a common-sense standpoint to debunk a fellow Cabinet Minister if he felt the argument had drifted away from reality.[100] He was an almost completely pragmatic politician, without strong doctrinaire views on either domestic or foreign policy issues.

An ebullient figure, he had many friends in Cabinet, in particular Macmillan (a brother-in-law),[101] Monckton, Lyttelton and Dugdale, as well as being one of the most popular Cabinet members within the Party. It is difficult to assess his importance but Stuart's influence on Churchill and Ministers can all too easily be underestimated.[102]

Next in the hierarchy came a further four men, less senior overall than those above, but nonetheless still highly significant. Lyttelton, a colourful man of immense ability, failed to fulfil his potential in politics through always keeping one eye on the business world. Nor did he always disguise his poor opinion of his Parliamentary colleagues which helps to explain, perhaps, why he remained rather an outsider in political circles. He was also a poor speaker in the House of Commons, surprisingly perhaps, given his wit and eloquence in private conversation. Yet he devoted considerable energy to his task as Colonial Secretary. Like Stuart, he had no further political ambition, and hence was unafraid of speaking his mind, and his views on colonial policy usually went unchallenged. Apart from occasional contributions on financial and foreign issues, he rarely spoke in Cabinet on topics outside his own field. But he injected a lighthearted air into Cabinet proceedings, and was greatly missed by his colleagues when he resigned in July 1954. Lord Salisbury wrote that the Cabinet would be a serious and even a tedious place without him.[103]

He had great affection for Churchill, and only agreed to continue in politics out of feelings of loyalty. To say, as did Maxwell Fyfe, that Lyttelton did not care for anyone else in the Cabinet, would be an exaggeration,[104] but his closest friends tended to be outside Parliament, the only exceptions being Macmillan and, to a lesser extent, Salisbury.

Macmillan's gift for friendship was fully employed during the life of this Government, and amongst Cabinet colleagues he felt antipathy only towards Eden and Butler. His ability to make close friends undoubtedly helped him secure not only Cabinet support for his expensive programme as Minister of Housing, but also for his rise from being one of the more junior Cabinet Ministers in 1951 to one of the most senior by the end of 1954.[105] Early on he did not tend to speak in Cabinet outside his own departmental business,[106] but his influence grew steadily. By at least 1954 he was being considered as a possible Foreign Secretary (actually succeeding Eden the following April); yet few in 1951 had foreseen this meteoric rise in his fortunes. Macmillan gained a new-found air of confidence, which, Woolton was to remark in his diary, tended on occasion to become excessive.[107]

Macmillan set out deliberately to cultivate his relationship with Churchill, careful to humour or praise him as the occasion demanded.[108] He felt genuine affection and admiration for Churchill, so it was not merely a case of currying favour to advance his own interests. In his turn Churchill thought highly of Macmillan's intelligence, and when in December 1953 the building target of 300,000 houses a year was reached, Macmillan rose even higher in his estimation; but unlike the remaining two Ministers in this group, Churchill never regarded Macmillan as an intimate.[190] Macmillan's promptings over

Churchill's retirement did not improve relations.

Churchill was devoted to both Monckton and to Cherwell, 'the Prof', as he called him. Churchill felt, quite unfairly, that Monckton at times acted too much like a highly skilled top civil servant, who, having been given his orders to ensure peace on the industrial front, carried them out to the letter.[110] Beyond his own field of employment, Monckton did not like to venture into political matters,[111] although he maintained throughout a keen interest in the legal world and, as has been noted, would proffer his opinion when legal matters came up in Cabinet.

He was one of eight from an original Cabinet of sixteen who had little or no further political ambition,[112] and along with most of these, lacked a doctrinaire set of political attitudes. With over half the Cabinet not actively seeking further political advancement (an unusually high proportion), this was conducive to a harmonious and relaxed atmosphere. Indeed, the original Cabinet of 1951 was one of the most apolitical of the century.

Cherwell, who sat in Cabinet until his long-desired return to Oxford in November 1953, spoke little at meetings. His influence had lessened considerably since the war, but he remained a frequent weekend visitor at Chequers[113] or Chartwell, where Churchill liked to try out ideas on him, especially those concerned with economic or scientific subjects.[114] He also made some impact on economic affairs.[115] Indeed, for the first two years, Churchill saw more of him than of any other Cabinet Minister, including Eden.[116] But Churchill was never strongly impressed by Cherwell's judgment: he rarely took his advice on home politics and never on foreign affairs.[117] Like Lord Beaverbrook, Cherwell was apt to goad him on against his better judgment, and Churchill did not always recover himself in time.[118] Churchill's enthusiasm for Cherwell was not shared by many of the Cabinet: to most of them he remained an aloof figure who made little attempt to win their affection.

Churchill continued to seek Cherwell's company after his retirement from ministerial life in November 1953; indeed for visits to London Cherwell kept on his rooms in No. 11, Downing Street, and found Chequers an easy journey from Oxford. He maintained his interest particularly in atomic matters,[119] continued to send Churchill minutes on a variety of subjects,[120] and took trouble to inform Churchill of his whereabouts (even on holiday) in case he needed him for consultation.[121] He joined the Prime Minister's party to the Bermuda Conference in December 1953, and Washington in June 1954, but his inclusion owed as much to companionship as to any substantive contribution to high policy. He was even summoned to an occasional Cabinet.[122] But overall Cherwell's influence lessened as Churchill's interest in domestic affairs diminished after 1953. Cherwell's political views put him to the right of Cabinet, a position he shared with Salisbury.

Of the remaining four members of the original Cabinet, only Peter Thorneycroft survived beyond the first three years, and it was not until later years that he blossomed into a more dominant figure. Lord Ismay was the first to go, after only four months. A soldier by training,[123] he scarcely uttered a word during his short spell in Cabinet as Secretary of State for Commonwealth Relations, and did not find it easy to adjust. Moreover, Commonwealth affairs were not to the fore at the time. Ismay departed to Paris to become the first Secretary-General of NATO, but like Cherwell, another of Churchill's old and much trusted friends, he attended the Bermuda Conference in December 1953,[124] and continued to be consulted occasionally on defence topics. But after March 1952, he ceased to be an effective presence, though remaining a close personal friend.[125].

Lord Leathers, unlike Ismay, had previous ministerial experience,[126] but did not adapt well to the Party atmosphere of 1951. He was saddled with being an 'overlord', responsible for transport, fuel and power, a difficult job for even the most skilled politician. He had seen little of Churchill or other former Conservative Ministers since the war, and consequently felt rather an 'outsider' in Cabinet.

Simonds, the Lord Chancellor, was new to politics, having spent his life as a lawyer, but he blended well with his colleagues, and Churchill formed a high opinion of him.[127] He was fond of Woolton and a close friend of Salisbury. Many in the Cabinet regarded Simonds as a rather important curiosity: few indeed first entered the Cabinet on the eve of their seventieth birthday, or were appointed to one of the highest offices of state without any political apprenticeship.[128] In Cabinet itself he talked little, except when asked. He much enjoyed his unexpected three years in the Cabinet, but remained an innocent in politics, a fact he freely admitted to his closer associates.

Thorneycroft was the youngest in the original Cabinet, and until fresh recruits arrived in September 1953, retained an air of the 'junior' boy. As President of the Board of Trade he spoke well, in a businesslike manner, but his own subject did not arouse particular interest in the Cabinet (apart from the recession in the textile industry when he made a stand against further protection). Therefore trade and industry affairs were usually dealt with briefly.

The first newcomer after 1951, Field Marshal Lord Alexander of Tunis, in character for this Cabinet, had no political experience, and probably felt less at ease in the Cabinet than any of his contemporaries.[129] Churchill, never at his strongest in matters of appointments, admired Alexander's performance as field commander in the war,[130] and thought him a suitable choice for Minister of Defence when he himself relinquished the post in March 1952. Although on occasion he stood up to Churchill in Cabinet, he was more often out of his depth in the midst of his political colleagues and found difficulty in winning any controversial argument against them.

Swinton did not formally join the Cabinet (as Commonwealth Secretary) until November 1952, though he had been a constant attender before then. Churchill apart, he was the most experienced Cabinet Minister,[131] a factor upon which he capitalised fully. His crisp, sometimes terse voice would be heard a great deal (some thought too much), and he enjoyed giving his views on a wide range of topics. Despite a touch of *folie de grandeur*, he was much respected and enjoyed considerable personal influence. Churchill held him in great regard, as he did many who had fought in the First World War, regarding him primarily as a 'doer', and thus ideally suited to the Ministry of Materials. Few others in the Cabinet were prepared to speak to Churchill as frankly and forcefully as Swinton: Stuart and Lyttelton would, but these were the exceptions.

In September 1953 three Ministers were promoted to Cabinet rank. Florence Horsbrugh, the first woman to sit in a Conservative Cabinet, had been experiencing difficulties as Minister of Education, principally due to a squeeze on resources for education. Churchill accepted the argument that it was desirable to have a woman in the Cabinet, but did not personally care for Florence Horsbrugh. The Ministers of Agriculture and Fisheries, and also Food, Dugdale and Gwilym Lloyd-George, were elevated at the same time. Both were experienced, older men and far from forceful.

The first of the younger men of promise were promoted in July 1954. Alan Lennox-Boyd succeeded Lyttelton as Colonial Secretary, and Derick Heathcoat Amory took over from Dugdale on his sudden resignation in the wake of the Crichel Down affair. Heathcoat Amory was an unassuming man, then as always, and Churchill rapidly formed a high opinion of him;[132] he made more of an impression on his colleagues than any of the other younger men who were promoted.

Of the three new Ministers who arrived in October 1954, Osbert Peake was the oldest, elevated when the Ministries of Pensions and National Insurance merged and his job was upgraded. An efficient Minister with an agile mind, many felt he should have gone further, perhaps becoming Minister of Labour, but Peake was not an assertive man, nor was he intensely interested in politics. To his Cabinet colleagues he remained something of an enigma, of indeterminate political views. The remaining two were hardworking and intensely ambitious: Sir David Eccles, who succeeded Florence Horsbrugh as Minister of Education, and Duncan Sandys, promoted to the Cabinet post of Minister of Housing.

The newer recruits were encouraged to participate by Churchill, though to a man they kept their observations brief. The irritation felt by the older members of Cabinet at Churchill's idiosyncrasies was not fully shared by these younger men, who had not had time to lose their initial excitement at serving in Cabinet under Winston Churchill.

Part 3 Non-Departmental and Junior Ministers

Five non-departmental offices were employed during this Conservative Government. How was Churchill going to utilise these jobs? An examination of their use this century shows he had great scope for variety. For one, they were to chair all important Cabinet Committees with the exception of the Economic Policy (Rab Butler) and the Defence Committee (Churchill).

The Lord President of the Council

The direct duties of the office were limited, and, as always, included responsibility for the work of the Privy Council Office. Under Churchill the Lord President was also charged with general oversight of scientific activities on the civil side, being answerable for the Department of Scientific and Industrial Research, the Medical Research Council, the Agricultural Research Council, and the Nature Conservancy Council. Though important, these duties occupied only a small amount of his time. He also held the post of Chairman of the Lord President's Committee, which under Churchill was renamed the Home Affairs Committee, and discussed matters of social, but not economic policy.

Churchill appointed Lord Woolton his first Lord President, a job he had previously held in the 'Caretaker Government' (May–July 1945). This he combined with the chairmanship of the Party, co-ordinating the Ministries of Food and Agriculture, and also acting as deputy to Lord Salisbury as Leader of the House of Lords. These, plus his Cabinet responsibilities absorbed the bulk of his time, although with Lord Cherwell he helped encourage the development of scientific and technological education.[1]

At the Conservative Party Conference at Scarborough in October 1952 Woolton fell seriously ill.[2] After five major operations,[3] by January he began to feel better. In February Cabinet papers were

97

circulated to him,[4] and in April he returned to active duty, although he never fully recovered his former vitality.[5] By mid-November 1952 Churchill had become increasingly alarmed by doctors' reports that Woolton would not survive. Thus, with the Lord President's heavy responsibilities for the Coronation the following year, Churchill decided to replace him with Salisbury,[6] and to make Woolton Chancellor of the Duchy of Lancaster with a seat in Cabinet.[7] Salisbury was anxious to leave the Commonwealth Relations Office, and his appointment as Lord President was announced on 24th November, 1952.

In January 1954 the Atomic Energy Authority became the Lord President's responsibility after a prolonged feud in Whitehall about its future.[8] Salisbury took up this new burden conscientiously. Not one to advise on organisation, he was nevertheless useful on political matters, such as negotiations with the United States.[9] He worked closely with Sir Edwin Plowden, the Chairman of the new Authority, who found that Salisbury missed a Department and advisers to brief him on Cabinet topics, so he himself would discuss economic topics with Salisbury, which the latter found most helpful.[10]

Despite his other responsibilities, Salisbury took pains over his duties as Lord President, which he continued until his resignation in March 1957. During his tenure of office he encouraged the post-war expansion of Government expenditure on civil scientific research, which doubled from 1952-7.[11] His efforts did not go unrewarded: the Royal Society made him a Fellow for services to science, a relatively unusual honour for a layman.

Lord Privy Seal

Unlike the office of Lord President, incumbents had no specific duties, but were given special responsibilities by the Prime Minister. In Clement Attlee's Government Lord Addison combined it with the leadership of the Lords from October 1947 to March 1951, as did Salisbury's father, the fourth Marquess, from 1924 to 1930. Salisbury combined it with the leadership of the Lords and even, for two months in 1952, with being Commonwealth Secretary; Harry Crookshank, who succeeded him in May 1952, with leadership of the Commons. He was a main stand-in for absent Cabinet Committee chairmen.

Chancellor of the Duchy of Lancaster

The only formal responsibilities of this office concerned certain Crown Estates in the Midlands and the North of England, but these were traditionally considered of secondary importance, and thus the position had been used almost solely as a sinecure, resulting in a rapid turnover of Chancellors, no less than thirty-nine in the first half of the century. Under the Labour Government, John Hynd (1945–7) and Lord Pakenham[12] (1947–8) for example also had special responsibility for the administration of the British Zone in West Germany, but were not in the Cabinet. Churchill's first Chancellor was Lord Swinton whose portfolio also included the posts of Minister of Materials, senior Minister in charge of Government publicity and *de facto* deputy leadership of the House of Lords. He was also a constant attender (though not a formal member) of the Cabinet. Swinton was Chancellor for just a year, being succeeded by Woolton in the Government reshuffle in November 1952.

Churchill, on Woolton's return to London in March 1953 after his illness, told him it was a sinecure, indeed during his own brief tenure of the job (May to November 1915) he had only been to its office once.[13] Churchill exaggerated: the office did include some minor responsibilities, as well as certain functions regarding the Coronation. Woolton, with his businessman's outlook, was unwilling to let pass a chance of good husbandry, especially one which involved an opportunity of serving the monarch, to whom he was devoted. He was determined not to be moved on to another office, and held the chancellorship (November 1952–December 1955) for the longest period since J. C. C. Davidson (1931–7). He devoted considerable energy to learning about the estates and made a number of improvements which resulted in an increase in their value.[14]

At the same time Woolton continued as Chairman of the Party, as well as being from September 1953 Minister of Materials with instructions to wind up the Ministry, which he achieved in July 1954. Though nominally still co-ordinator of agriculture and food until the formal abolition of the 'overlord' system in September 1953, this had effectively ceased to occupy his attention since his illness in October 1952.[15]

Paymaster-General

This was a highly adaptable office with negligible official duties, to which varying ranks of Ministers were appointed. Unlike the other non-departmental sinecures the office was left vacant several times, including three periods between 1939 and 1951. Under Churchill the position was held first by Cherwell, with a seat in the Cabinet, then by the comparatively junior Lord Selkirk, outside the Cabinet. Since 1900 the Lord President had always sat in Cabinet, the Lord Privy Seal for all but three periods.[16] the Chancellor of the Duchy half the time (with the tendency for this office to become a non-Cabinet position), but the Paymaster-General had sat in Cabinet for only three short terms.[17]

Cherwell was reluctant to become a Minister again, accepting only out of loyalty to Churchill. His responsibilities included the co-ordination of scientific research and development,[18] advising the Prime Minister on defence and economic questions,[19] and, at Churchill's request, he revived the Statistical Branch under his key aide, Sir Donald Mac-Dougall.[20] Unlike other non-departmental Ministers, Cherwell possessed a small, but highly efficient personal staff, who supplied him with a number of briefs on economic matters.[21]

Selkirk had been a Lord-in-Waiting since November 1951, so had gained considerable experience speaking on the Government's behalf in the House of Lords. His work changed little after his appointment as Paymaster-General in November 1953, but he received increased status in the Lords where he became responsible for all Treasury matters, now with a small private office to assist him.[22]

Minister without Portfolio

The most flexible of the five non-departmental offices, its number of Ministers varied. For several long periods until the appointment of Lord Munster in October 1954 the post had been left vacant,[23] although since then the practice has been to have either one or two Ministers. Munster's predecessor, Arthur Greenwood, held the office from April to September 1947, and presided over certain Cabinet Committees.[24]

Churchill left the position vacant in 1951, and only appointed Munster on the insistence of Salisbury, who felt he needed more support in the House of Lords.[25] Munster's ministerial career had had a promising start, having first been appointed a Lord-in-Waiting in 1932. After various junior positions he became Paymaster-General, 1938–9. Although he was a man who still carried some weight, he had been an unspectacular junior Minister at the Colonial Office (1951–4). However, his new appointment was seen as an important strengthening of the Government's position in the House of Lords,[26] although his function was merely that of an exalted Lord-in-Waiting.

Junior Ministers

Junior Ministers as a whole counted for much less in the 1951–5 Government than they have since. Many did little more than answer Parliamentary Questions and carry out minor routine departmental work. The workload depended on the individual, and the extent to which his Minister wished to consult him on policy matters.

Junior Ministers fell into two grades, Ministers of State and Parliamentary or Financial Under-Secretaries.[27] The first Minister of State as a junior Minister was Richard Law at the Foreign Office, appointed in September 1943. In January 1948 Attlee added a Minister of State at the Colonial Office. Churchill introduced a Minister of State for Economic Affairs under Sir Arthur Salter at the Treasury from October 1951 to November 1952, but then the job was discontinued, and its functions taken over by the Economic Secretary. As a result of a policy pledge, he added a Minister of State at the Scottish Office in November 1951. A fourth Minister of State was created in September 1953, when as part of the reorganisation at the Board of Trade[28] the Secretary for Overseas Trade was replaced by a Minister of State whose duties were to give special attention to the promotion of exports and the problems of overseas trade. With a fifth Minister of State created in November 1953, the Foreign Office now had two, who a year later became known as Ministers of State for Foreign Affairs.[29] But status varied. Selwyn Lloyd (Minister of State 1951–4), and Anthony Nutting (Minister of State for Foreign Affairs 1954–6) carried considerable weight, Lord Home (Minister of State at the Scottish Office 1951–5) less, and Lord Reading (Minister of State for Foreign Affairs 1953–7)[30] and Henry Hopkinson (Minister of State at the Colonial Office 1952–5)[31] even less.

A similar range of influence can be found in the second category of junior Ministers. Sir David Maxwell Fyfe gave his junior Ministers very little work at the Home Office (1951–4), and this was also the case in smaller and non-Cabinet Ministries where there was little scope for junior Ministers to be involved in policy making. There was, however, a group of junior Ministers whose influence was far greater than average, either through an unassertive departmental Minister,[32] or because the junior Minister was particularly forceful or able.[33]

Parliamentary Private Secretaries

Although not members of the Government, some Parliamentary Private Secretaries had more influence than junior Ministers. The majority played only a minor role, however, keeping the Minister informed of backbench opinion and attending the various Party Committees, though the Minister seldom took much notice of backbench opinion. Of those

Parliamentary Private Secretaries who held considerable influence, some had special relationships with their Ministers and were close friends,[24] often following their Minister when he changed office; some were encouraged by their Minister to play a particular part in the work of their office;[35] and others secured greater influence than most due to forceful personalities.[36]

Part 4   Co-ordinating Ministers

The idea of appointing co-ordinating Ministers with oversight over various Departments, thereby reducing the numbers needed in Cabinet, was Winston Churchill's own, and stemmed largely from his wartime preference for a small Cabinet and a desire to have around him Ministers whom he knew. Although a viable exercise in the machinery of government, and defended as such in Parliament, Churchill's underlying motive was to have the advice of trusted men, without imposing heavy departmental responsibilities on them.[1] But the idea failed to appeal to Anthony Eden, Rab Butler, or other senior Cabinet members.[2] Both Sir Edward Bridges and Sir Norman Brook suspected that Churchill might introduce such a system, and tried hard to dissuade him.[3] It was no more popular with the Ministries who were to be 'co-ordinated', or with the Opposition, whose bursts of criticism were concentrated between November 1951 and May 1952.[4]

Churchill originally intended to appoint four 'overlords', as they soon came to be known, because of their membership of the House of Lords. All four, Lord Cherwell, Lord Leathers, Lord Woolton and Sir John Anderson only came to politics during or just before the war,[5] and had been members of the Coalition Government of 1940–5 (the last two as members of the Cabinet).

With Anderson, however, Churchill struck a problem. The role Churchill had in mind for him is unclear: Anderson's official biographer says Churchill wished him to accept a peerage, become Chancellor of the Duchy of Lancaster, and act as supervising 'overlord' to the Treasury, Board of Trade and Ministry of Supply,[6] while Macmillan recorded in his diary: 'But where is Sir John Anderson? He is to be a viscount and co-ordinate Raw Materials, Supply, etc . . .'[7] Whatever the job, Anderson refused. He considered the Chancellor of the Duchy of Lancaster 'an outrage to his dignity and worth' according to Brendan Bracken[8] but, more serious, he was unconvinced of the value of a co-ordinating system,[9] and reluctant to resign his outside positions and receive only a ministerial salary.[10]

The other three accepted. Woolton was appointed Lord President of the Council (a job he wanted, but which he alleged Churchill had tried to give to Salisbury),[11] with responsibility for co-ordinating the policies of the Ministries of Agriculture and Fisheries, and of Food. An eighth secretaryship of state was created for Leathers, who co-ordinated Transport, Fuel and Power. He stood high in Churchill's estimation as a result of his success as Minister of War Transport (1941–5),[12] but since they had seen little of each other in the intervening six years, the appointment was rather an act of faith. Cherwell was reappointed Paymaster-General (a sinecure post he had previously held, 1942–5), with responsibility for co-ordination of scientific research and development, supervision of atomic research and production, and the direction of the Prime Minister's Statistical Branch.[13] He had not intended to join the Government, having written the previous year, when offering his resignation from Churchill's 'Consultative Committee', that he was 'almost certainly the only one who would not be able to take office in any Government you might form'.[14] Churchill, however, succeeded in overcoming Cherwell's opposition,[15] as with many professing reluctance to serve.

The function of each overlord was not, however, made clear. A number of explanations were offered to Parliament. In the House of Lords, Woolton said, 'the work of the co-ordinators is not a responsibility to Parliament; it is a responsibility to the Cabinet';[16] in the Lower House, Churchill argued that the system was a natural development from the Chairmen of Cabinet Committees as operated during the war, and that 'the co-ordinating Ministers have no statutory powers. They have, in particular, no power to give orders or directions to a departmental Minister.'[17] Yet the extent of confusion about the function of overlords is shown by a letter Churchill received from Woolton the day prior to his statement. Woolton argued that since, unlike Leathers, his task of co-ordination was not entrusted to him by the Crown, he did not feel that he should issue instructions to the Departments, whereas Alexander and Leathers should.[18] In practice, the individual overlord was left to interpret his function in his own way, often with unsatisfactory results.

Woolton's appointment worked most smoothly partly because he attempted little.[19] As he wrote to Churchill: 'I consider that I am responsible to you and to the Cabinet for co-ordinating these two Ministries, and co-ordinating denotes that I secure that they work together in harmony, not that I control their detailed operations.'[20] Churchill replied that he thought his method of handling the co-operation of Departments better than Leathers', who, he said, found it necessary to be in his office at 8.30 a.m. each day.[21] To a large extent

Woolton's method involved leaving the two Ministries of Agriculture and Food to get on with their own work. He had no staff, other than a skeleton Private Office, with C. H. A. Duke as his Private Secretary, to help him keep abreast of policy or discover which questions to ask, and complained that he should be kept better informed.[22] Officials from both Ministries considered his effect on policy to be minimal. A number of minutes which Woolton received from Churchill were also sent to the individual Ministries. In March 1952, for example, Churchill sent a communication to Woolton and the Minister of Food urging an extension of meat imports from new countries and increased scope for free enterprise trade in meat.[23] Gwilym Lloyd-George, the Minister of Food, sent a detailed reply to Woolton, based upon his Department's research,[24] and Woolton replied for both.[25] On other occasions, Woolton appeared to act on his own initiative: in June 1952, for instance, he pressed the Ministry of Food to investigate means of speeding up the derationing of sugar and margarine.[26] But these and other promptings from Woolton did little to hasten the process of derationing, as the Ministry of Food, under the promptings of Lloyd-George, was already moving in that direction at all possible speed. Furthermore, his interest in and influence on the work of the Ministry of Agriculture and Fisheries was almost negligible.

Woolton's likelihood of success in his job was greater than Leathers': intellectually better suited to thinking in 'policy' terms, he also had the advantage of overseeing two Ministries which had natural affinities, as the comparative ease of their merger in 1954–5 showed. Churchill, however, argued: 'Coal, gas, electricity, oil and transport represent a homogeneous group of subjects which calls for co-ordination. Moreover, it includes the basic services which have passed under public ownership under socialist schemes of nationalisation.'[27] This was an over-optimistic assertion, bearing small semblance to administrative realities.

Leathers' failure was largely due to personal factors, though it would have required a remarkable man to co-ordinate such diverse Ministries as Transport and Civil Aviation, and Fuel and Power.[28] Leathers had risen to the top of the shipping world by hard work and attention to detail, but lacked the ability to look at broad policy questions, or to grasp a wide range of material. His strengths were almost the opposite of those needed for a successful co-ordinator, as Churchill should have realised. Too easily he became bogged down in detail, and hence became a considerable irritant to both Ministries. He presented one or two papers to Cabinet, originating from the individual Ministries, and seldom altered by Leathers. He performed poorly in the Lords;[29] he was no good at Parliamentary procedure, and not being judged capable of piloting the Transport Bill through the Committee stage in the House of Lords, it was handled by Lord Swinton.[30]

Relations with both Ministries were never good. Neither John Maclay (Minister of Transport and Civil Aviation, 1951–2)[31] nor Geoffrey Lloyd (Minister of Fuel and Power, 1951–5)[32] was especially happy at the arrangement, and this was not diminished by Churchill's intimacy with Leathers and the substantial weight this added to Leathers' advice.[33] The officials, too, felt their Ministries had been subjected to a downgrading, which led to a certain amount of confusion: some officials at Fuel and Power, though, were pleased to have Leathers, finding it easier to extract decisions from him than from Lloyd. Maclay was less perturbed than Lloyd by Leathers' position, partly because he was less ambitious, though, undoubtedly, the muddled position resulting from the system contributed to Maclay's breakdown of health in the spring of 1952. Alan Lennox-Boyd succeeded him as Minister of Transport and Civil Aviation in May 1952. He, too, found the system unsatisfactory and confusing, partly because Leathers invariably seemed to be working with officials when he wanted to see them, and also because he made public statements which had not been cleared with the Ministry, so adding to the general impression of lack of orderly oversight.[34]

Relations with the Ministry of Fuel and Power were more remote and less important than with Transport. Leathers felt more at home on transport questions, as he had little knowledge of the fuel and power industries; he also got on far better with Lennox-Boyd and Sir Gilmour Jenkins (Permanent Secretary at Transport) than with Lloyd and Sir John Maud (Permanent Secretary at Fuel and Power, 1952–8). In addition, Leathers' small private office initially had a much better understanding of the transport side since the two Private Secretaries, Evan Maude and Patrick Shovelton, came respectively from the Treasury and the Ministry of Transport;[35] Fuel and Power had no such representative.

The position of the third overlord, Cherwell, proved to be somewhat different. He had broader and less defined responsibilities, no specific Departments to co-ordinate, and the staff at his disposal – the Paymaster General's private office and the Prime Minister's Statistical Branch, containing men of the calibre of Sir Donald MacDougall[36] and John Fforde[37] – were more senior and more plentiful than those of the other two overlords. The post was, in effect, a continuation of his wartime position, when he was Churchill's *éminence grise* on scientific questions. As we have seen earlier in the Chapter, the opportunities for him to contribute to his field were, however, considerably reduced.[38] His main efforts between 1951–3 were directed to economic questions,[39] while his major contributions on the 'scientific' side were towards setting up an independent Atomic Energy Authority[40] and promoting technological education.[41] On scientific aspects of defence policy, he was felt to be less effective than he had been in the war: he made fewer appearances at the Defence Committee of the Cabinet, where he mainly concerned himself with questions of atomic energy. Officials in the Ministry of Defence discovered he was out of touch with some post-war developments, although he still retained some influence.

With the Cabinet reshuffle of 4th September, 1953, the overlord system was formally brought to an end, as a result of a combination of factors: resistance from the Ministers under the overlords and the fact that since his illness in October 1952, Woolton, though nominally still a co-ordinator, was being continually bypassed by Lloyd-George and Sir Thomas Dugdale (Minister of Agriculture 1951–4). The officials in the Ministries, as well as Bridges and Brook, were not anxious to see the scheme continued. Labour had maintained a barrage of criticism in both Houses, arguing that it blurred ministerial responsibility, and, since the overlords sat in the Lords, this prevented the Commons from exercising effective control. But for a long while Churchill refused to end the system.[42] Finally, and most importantly, the overlords themselves were becoming restless. Cherwell finally managed to persuade Churchill to release him at the end of October so that he could return to Oxford, promising to continue to advise on scientific questions if needed.[43] Woolton had made it clear to Churchill that his supervisory control over his two Ministries had largely ceased to function,[44] while Churchill wanted him to do urgent work at the Ministry of Materials. It had also become clear to Leathers that he was not carrying enough weight in either the Cabinet or the House of Lords, and he had been anxious to resign since at least March 1953.[45] Thus the Conservatives reverted to the former system of co-ordination of policy in Cabinet Committees and in the Cabinet itself, as had been happening increasingly in preceding months.

Churchill's idea of overlords had proved an ineffective (and largely untested) luxury,[46] but one which that Government could afford.

Chapter 4   Administrative Affairs

Part 1   The Civil Service

The Civil Service has seldom contained as many high calibre officials in the top positions as it did during 1951–5: those who were primarily administrators,[1] as well as those who tended to express their views more forcibly.[2] Some civil servant/ministerial partnerships were particularly effective such as Sir Henry Hancock and Gwilym Lloyd-George at the Ministry of Food, Sir David Milne and James Stuart at the Scottish Office, Sir Godfrey Ince and Sir Walter Monckton at the Ministry of Labour, and above all Sir Frank Lee and Peter Thorneycroft at the Board of Trade. A few Ministers were somewhat eclipsed by far more able Permanent Secretaries, notably Florence Horsbrugh by Sir John Maud at the Ministry of Education, Jim Thomas by Sir John Lang at the Admiralty and Lloyd-George by Sir Frank Newsam at the Home Office after Lloyd-George's promotion in 1954. Only one Permanent Secretary/Minister relationship could have been described as unsatisfactory, that of Sir James Helmore and Duncan Sandys at the Ministry of Supply. Harold Macmillan might have had a difficult time with Sir Thomas Sheepshanks, Permanent Secretary, Ministry of Housing and Local Government throughout this period, had he not been able to bypass him and deal direct with the Deputy, Dame Evelyn Sharp.

Sir Edward Bridges had been the outstanding civil servant in Whitehall since his appointment as Secretary to the Cabinet in 1938, a job he retained until the end of 1946. He became Head of the Civil Service and Permanent Secretary of the Treasury[3] in 1945 in succession to Sir Richard Hopkins. By 1951, however, the year of his fifty-ninth birthday, he was beginning to feel his age, and had lost much of his creative energy. Yet as Lord Redcliffe-Maud remarks: 'Bridges was very widely respected among the permanent secretaries of the day and was a kind of father figure. He was always number one until he retired.'[4] Some disagreed and saw Sir Norman Brook as the effective number one after 1951,[5] others saw Bridges' retention of the headship of the Civil Service until 1956 as an obstacle to progress.[6] The claims of the Permanent Secretary of the Treasury to the title Head of the Civil Service had been regarded during the war as still of recent origin and questionable value.

Sir Horace Wilson (1939–42) lost influence and the power of the office may even have fallen after Winston Churchill became Prime Minister in 1940 but Hopkins (1942–5) did something to restore both the standing of the Treasury and the position of Head of the Civil Service.[7] Bridges continued the trend: his work under Attlee alone justifies him being called the ablest holder of the post this century. He had a greater intellectual grasp than Sir Warren Fisher (1919–39) and was a more impressive figure than Hopkins (1942–5). Though he had less understanding of economics than some later Heads, such as Sir William Armstrong (1968–74) and Sir Douglas Allen (1974–7), his mastery of the machinery of the Civil Service alone justifies the claim. Bridges also managed to avoid the trap for Heads of the Civil Service of becoming over-identified with the Prime Minister and the Government of the day, a snare into which Fisher and Armstrong, and even Brook (1956–62), at times fell.

Bridges had never been on terms of close personal friendship with Churchill during the war, and it is therefore hardly surprising that their relationship did not progress to this level during 1951–5.[8] They saw little of each other after 1951, their contacts being generally written: their relationship was marred by one or two minor disagreements, notably about the Honours List, but Churchill never ceased to have full confidence in Bridges.[9]

Neither were Brook and Bridges especially close after 1951. Brook, ten years his junior, was a protégé of Bridges, advanced by him during the war.[10] They worked closely as colleagues, always in and out of each other's rooms, and had been close personal friends. But an increasingly uncordial atmosphere existed between them during Bridges' last two or three years in the Civil Service, which reached a high point during the build-up to Suez in 1956 when Bridges felt cut off from the developments. It is possible also that Bridges became cooler towards Brook due to his lack of sympathy with the way the job of Permanent Secretary of the Treasury and Head of the Civil Service was split after his departure in 1956. Bridges was inclined to be jealous of Brook, whom he saw exercising the same kind of authority as he had had during the war. Bridges realised that Brook knew Clement Attlee better than he, and did not resent this, but there may well have been some jealousy on account of Brook's intimate relationship with Churchill, and because Churchill increasingly consulted Brook on matters beyond the jurisdiction of the Cabinet Secretary.[11] Though Churchill always regarded Bridges and Brook as his two 'chums' amongst the higher Civil Service, the truth was that after 1951 Bridges ceased to be a major influence at Number Ten. Brook also felt a certain antipathy to Bridges from the early days after the war when he considered Bridges stayed on as

Cabinet Secretary longer than necessary, thus preventing him from becoming full Cabinet Secretary until 1947. Differences also arose over the fraught question of reform of the machinery of government.

The bulk of Bridges' innovatory work as Head of the Civil Service had been completed by 1951. He had taken a keen interest in the Machinery of Government Committee during the war, set up at the instigation of Sir Stafford Cripps to try to prevent a recurrence of alleged deficiencies during the 1930s hampering post-war reconstruction. Though the break-up of the Coalition Government destroyed the atmosphere of political non-partisanship for which the plans were envisaged, Bridges still clung to his belief in the need for reform from the inside. Above all he was concerned to see that economists, scientists and statisticians should be given a proper place in Whitehall,[12] and in this work was greatly helped by Sir Alan Barlow, Second Secretary at the Treasury, 1938–48. Bridges ensured that planning was incorporated into the machine, manifested in the creation under Herbert Morrison of the Central Economic Planning Staff in 1947.[13]

Even after the 1947 changes, Bridges was keen to remodel the Government's economic organisation, believing that the possibility of a future Conservative victory would not remove the need for direction and control. In one of his last acts before the General Election in 1951 he appointed a Group of Three (Brook, Sir Harold Emmerson and Lee), to decide on an order of priorities.[14] This body suggested nine specific problems for investigation, all of which touched upon questions of economic policy and productivity, and four of which subsequently became the subject of enquiry by *ad hoc* committees under Sir Thomas Padmore (known generally as 'Padmore Committees').[15]

After 1951, however, Bridges' attempts at reform were increasingly thwarted. Churchill was deeply suspicious of anything that smacked of planning or attempts to redraw economic organisation which might have resulted in more authority being given to the Treasury. Churchill, besides, had his own plans, such as co-ordinating Ministers, which both Bridges and Brook unsuccessfully tried to block.[16] The new Government was committed to reducing the size of the Civil Service, and would have been deeply suspicious of any proposal involving an increased role for bureaucracy. There was no Minister in the new Administration committed to reform, as Cripps had been: Rab Butler, in a similarly commanding position, was instead convinced of the need to reduce the size of government: his creativity was always geared more to policy than organisational reform.

Meanwhile, among the officials Brook was not alone in being sceptical of the continued need for work on the optimal organisation of economic work throughout Whitehall.[17] He was also cool about Bridges' attempt in March 1952 to resurrect the Government Organisation Committee. Bridges wrote to Brook with the appeal: '. . . if those of us who have lived all our working lives in Whitehall and have studied the Whitehall organisation give up as hopeless all attempts to reform it from inside, then what hope is there of any reform in our time?'[18]

Moreover, the dominant Whitehall officials of the day, Lee, Ince, Newsam and Sir Archibald Rowlands, were preoccupied with other matters and took little interest in broader machinery of government (M.G.) questions. Early on in the Administration, Brook spent several weekends with Churchill, looking at organisation matters, but few specific reforms appeared and after a few months these sessions lapsed. Bridges was also having to swim against the pervading tide at the time, which now favoured the abandonment of physical controls by government and an end to the preoccupation with the organisation of Whitehall. Consequently, the changes in the Government's organisation that occurred during 1951–5, the merging of the Ministries of Transport and Civil Aviation,[19] Pensions and National Insurance,[20] and Agriculture and Food,[21] the winding up of Materials[22] and the redistribution of functions with regard to the Scottish Office,[23] owed more to Ministerial drive and the need for economy than to any moves from officials.

One important 'Padmore Committee', which investigated the allocation of functions between the Board of Trade, Ministry of Supply, Ministry of Fuel and Power and the Ministry of Materials, reported in January 1954. Lord Woolton's comment on the report illustrates how much the atmosphere had changed since the arrival of the Conservative Government in October 1951. Woolton noted that:

In Opposition many of us concluded that the country was suffering under a weight of Government which was expensive both of money and of effort, and we looked forward to a freer society which relied less on either direction or support from Government Departments . . . we failed to agree [during the wartime Coalition on machinery of government] because of deep political divergences – the socialists wanted powerful Ministers and kept them [and] we are doing the same, and since we came into office the Cabinet has never discussed this question, which is not one of economy only but one of principle. The Civil Service gives us devoted and competent service: but the chief officers of the Service, like the Ministers, are so encumbered with a host of problems that very few have time or energy left to sit back and think beyond the passing duties of the day.[24]

Woolton in fact suggested that a Cabinet Committee be set up to see what sort of machinery of government was appropriate for the needs of the day. Bridges' own effort to continue the examination of this problem after 1951 was the least happy aspect of his last years as Head.[25]

The energies which did remain for examining and assessing the structure of the Civil Service became more diffused. An enquiry was held by the Royal Institute of Public Administration under the chairmanship of D. N. Chester,[26] with Maud and Dame Evelyn Sharp as members of the study group, into changes in organisation since 1914, with the intention of investigating how far certain administrative norms influenced actual developments.[27] The enquiry was started in 1952, at the suggestion of civil servants on the Royal Institute of Public Administration research board, who felt the board's original proposal, an economic organisation enquiry, was too similar to the last principal M.G. investigation.[28] A second area of investigation sponsored by R.I.P.A. was the New Whitehall Series, whose first volume, on the Home Office, was published in 1954.[29] The proposal for a revision of the old Whitehall Series was undertaken on the condition that the studies be written in Departments, under the guidance of each Permanent Secretary, so that – in Bridges' words – they would be satisfactory, consistent and unembarrassing.[30] A Royal Commission on the Civil Service was set up in November 1953, under the chairmanship of Sir Raymond Priestley,[31] Butler having announced a few months previously that a comprehensive review of pay and conditions would be undertaken.[32] Attlee queried the need, and Butler replied that it was felt necessary to have a review at least once every twenty years. Its report, published in November 1955,[33] was unspectacular compared with some other Royal Commissions on the Civil Service before it, notably Tomlin (1931), but it made a number of suggestions on pay, conditions and new classes, some of which Bridges began to introduce before his retirement.[34]

The question of equal pay for women in the Civil Service had been an unsettled area for a long time. The desirability of equal pay had been accepted in principle by Governments since resolutions in the House of Commons in 1920 and 1921, subject to economic circumstances permitting the increase. Hugh Gaitskell, in 1951, repeated that the Government still could not afford to finance equal pay, but pressure had mounted steadily, and in March 1954 Butler was presented with two petitions, containing 680,000 signatures.[35] It was no longer feasible to resist the pressure, the more so because the Conservative Party document of 1949, 'A True Balance', contained a recommendation for the introduction of equal pay, finances permitting, which was repeated in the 1950 Manifesto.[36] On 19th May, 1954 negotiations on the introduction of equal pay began, and in January 1955 Butler announced that both sides of the Whitley Council had reached agreement, and that equal pay in the public service would be introduced from 1st January, 1955.[37] To achieve this, Butler had had to argue against strong opposition in the Treasury, and credit is due to the Government for pressing ahead with this reform.

Bridges was anxious, in general, to encourage retirement at the age of sixty, but was sixty-four himself when he retired at the end of 1956.[38] Towards the end of the Attlee Government, he developed a nervous muscular complaint, and at one point seriously considered retiring in 1951,[39] although he later recovered much of his old verve and energy, and ill health seldom kept him away from the office. During his last years in the Civil Service Bridges was fortunate in having in T. J. Bligh[40] a Private Secretary (1949–54) whom he particularly liked, and who was of the highest calibre: Bligh's influence was all the greater as he served his master at a time when he was least strong physically.

Brook, aged only forty-nine when the new Government came in, was Bridges' obvious successor, and was to have been moved over from the Cabinet Office to the Treasury in November 1951 as Chief Planning Officer (in succession to Sir Edwin Plowden) and deputy to the Permanent Secretary to the Treasury.[41] Churchill, however, blocked this move.[42] His desire to retain Brook at the Cabinet Office as long as he remained Prime Minister provided Bridges with a valid reason, as well as a possible excuse, for remaining as long as he did. Had Bridges retired before Churchill, there was no obvious candidate apart from Brook to succeed him.

Throughout the higher echelons of the Civil Service there was undoubtedly some feeling that Bridges was rather delaying his retirement. In his last two or three years he worked a fairly short day (usually from 10 a.m. to 6 p.m.),[43] compared with his own performance in earlier years and in relation to some of his colleagues. He became prickly about discussing the date of his retirement.[44] Like Churchill, he simply did not want to give up; finance might also have provided a reason, as he was never well off, and unlike more recent Heads and senior officials he did not after his retirement take any company directorship. But Bridges had another reason for staying on: he wanted to be Head when Priestley delivered his report on the Civil Service.

One would be wrong to dismiss Bridges' contribution during 1951–6 as insignificant. He was a unifying figure and successful arbitrator between warring Departments. Some respected him without being close, other senior officials were his personal friends, in particular Hancock and Maud, and also Sir Gilmour Jenkins, Lee, Milne and Sheepshanks,[45] but he had a tendency to be introverted, and could never have been called a 'clubable' man. Two officials in particular could stand up to Bridges, Sir John Woods, who had already retired from the Board of Trade by the time of the Conservative Government, and Rowlands, who, though not in a top Ministry, Supply, was particularly influential in committees.

In these last years, Bridges spent up to a third of his time on work flowing from his position as official Head of the Civil Service. The remainder was devoted to his function as Permanent Secretary of the Treasury,[46] but even then Butler on occasion felt that Bridges was not there when he needed him. 'He was terribly overworked . . . the Government ought to have shared out his work before.'[47] The Chancellor tended not to look to Bridges for economic advice; Bridges' influence on Treasury policy was usually greatest in the formulation of Budgets, particularly in 1955.

Bridges had full confidence in Padmore, a highly effective overseer of the Civil Service, to whom he gave a virtual free hand in its day-to-day management. Bridges' main time on the Civil Service side was spent as sole man responsible for Permanent and Deputy Secretary appointments.[48] Churchill never rejected a Bridges' recommendation, nor did he take a great deal of interest in Civil Service appointments, partly because the officers were usually unknown to him. Bridges held informal discussions in a number of official quarters, and, once he had settled on a candidate, would visit the Minister concerned to obtain his approval, which was normally forthcoming.

Bridges was responsible for a number of senior officials changing Departments, notably Sir Alan Hitchman to Permanent Secretary at Agriculture in 1952, Maud to Permanent Secretary at Fuel and Power in 1952, and Edward Muir to Deputy Secretary at Works in 1951. It was more usual practice, though, for the most senior official in the Ministry to be promoted to the vacant job, as Dame Evelyn Sharp at Housing and Local Government in 1955, Sir Gilbert Flemming at Education in 1952, and Sir Ivone Kirkpatrick at the Foreign Office in 1953.

The substantial casualties among civil servants during the First World War and the suspension of recruitment until 1925, meant that Bridges had more opportunity than subsequent Heads to promote able young men, a number of whom he advanced to fill positions normally held by men in the forty-five to fifty-five age bracket.

Bridges' contribution during 1951–6 was of continued importance in ensuring that the Treasury worked in a friendly atmosphere with other Departments, and urging Departments to see that the Treasury should be brought in at the earliest possible stage when new policies were being

113

discussed. He retired in 1956, content with his work as Head since 1945 and with the state of the Service – with the building-up of the scientific Civil Service, the Central Statistical Office and planning divisions, with training improvements and arrangements for ironing out departmental frictions, and even with the eventual reorganisation of Departments, especially those concerned with the social services.[49]

The Conservatives had returned in 1951 with suspicions about the Civil Service.[50] Many felt not only that the country had let them down badly in 1945, but also that the Civil Service by 1951 was in the pocket of the Labour Party. The leanings of the Civil Service and also its sheer volume were viewed with suspicion, and the Conservatives were pledged to prune 'waste and extravagance' in every Department. Yet the Conservatives, as they found again in 1970 and 1979, encountered grave problems bringing about a significant reduction in its overall size, although Butler did report the shedding of 25,460 civil servants in the eighteen months up to 1st July, 1953.[51] When they returned in 1951 they determined to set 'abuses' right, the supposed misuse of the system of Government cars being one notorious example – car numbers were eventually cut from 722 to 444 by February 1953.[52] Many members of the new Government, especially Churchill, Macmillan and Sandys were initially highly suspicious of their officials, though none was as successful as Churchill in making changes (retaining Brook at the Cabinet Office and bringing back Sir Ian Jacob as Chief Staff Officer, John Colville to the Private Office and R. V. Jones to the Ministry of Defence). It was a mark of the impartiality and professionalism of the Service that within two years almost all these suspicions had disappeared.

Part 2   The Cabinet Office

The authority of Secretary of the Cabinet received a considerable boost during this Conservative Government. Sir Norman Brook, as a result of his special relationship with Winston Churchill, and also his master's irregular performance after 1951, was able to exercise a more active role than would have been allowed a Cabinet Secretary with a more vigorous Prime Minister. Sir Thomas Padmore, who was to have become Secretary to the Cabinet in November 1951 had had an outstandingly successful career in the Civil Service. But he did not have Brook's tremendous experience,[1] and it is possible that he would not have formed quite the same close bond with Churchill.[2] Brook remained as Secretary of the Cabinet until 1962, and the Cabinet Office retained the position it gained during 1951–5, helped by Brook's closeness to Macmillan when Prime Minister.

The Cabinet Office, a small organisation in the early 1950s, handled all matters before Cabinet and its Committees and circulated minutes.[3]

Until 1952 there were two Deputy Secretaries, both of whom were joint secretaries of the Defence Committee. The Deputy Secretary (Civil) was Alexander Johnston, until the autumn of 1951, followed by Padmore, until he returned to the Treasury as Second Secretary in mid-1952. The full title was Civil Deputy and Secretary of the Cabinet Designate, and, after Padmore's departure, the job was not filled. The Deputy Secretary (Military), the Chief Staff Officer, who took minutes at Defence Committee only,[4] was a post successively held by Sir Kenneth McLean (1951–2), Sir Ian Jacob (1952) and Sir Nevil Brownjohn (1952–6). The two Under-Secretaries were Sir George Mallaby,[5] who took the minutes at Defence Committee alongside the Military Deputy, and Oscar Morland until 1952 then Ronald Harris. Beneath them worked two Assistant Secretaries, three servicemen and a group of five to seven Principals, on secondment for two years, usually, from other offices. Brook did not want a permanent Cabinet Office staff and so would borrow from other Departments, keeping one or two officers for a longer period to ensure continuity. Mallaby and Harris were two who remained for a longer period. Both had varied careers in the Civil Service and some previous experience of the Cabinet Office.[6]

Brook and one of the two Under-Secretaries would sit in on a full Cabinet to take minutes. The normal practice was for Mallaby and Harris to share the meeting, one changing with the other halfway through, while Brook remained throughout. Prior agreement was reached as to who would take notes on which items on the agenda. Brook himself took the most important items, making very crisp notes about two-thirds of a page in length. He wrote about five minutes behind the discussion, and his notes conformed closely to the final minutes. Mallaby and Harris' notes were usually far longer. These notes formed the basis of the minutes. Brook allowed the Under-Secretaries a free hand in writing the minutes and, after a morning Cabinet, wanted them given to him by 4 p.m. He did, however, make certain stipulations as to the type of minutes produced: not too long and no attribution, unless a Minister had specifically requested it, which was rare.

We went back to the Cabinet Office after the meeting . . . then we examined our notes very carefully and the determination was that we should not miss any point of importance that had been made in the discussion. That we should record very clearly and precisely what the decision of the Cabinet was and that we should not expose even in the Cabinet minutes anything that distorted the collective responsibility of the Cabinet, so that one wouldn't record certain Ministers expressing opinions opposed to the final decision. What we would do, therefore, would be to introduce the paper or discussion with an explanation of what the subject was about and then a series of points made in the discussion, followed by a summary by the Prime Minister leading to a decision. The object of that was to make the Departments understand, who had to act on these things, that the thing had been thrashed out and that their points had not been missed or ignored. Also that the decisions were perfectly clear without giving away that the Minister of Agriculture, for example, disagreed with the whole thing. We thought that would be wrong.[7]

The minutes thus made the meetings appear to be logical discussions, often far from the case. Macmillan once told Mallaby, after looking at the minutes, that Cabinet Office officials were falsifying history: 'Historians reading this fifty or a hundred years hence will get a totally false picture. They will be filled with admiration and surprise to find that the Cabinet were so intellectually disciplined that they argued each issue methodically and logically through to a set of neat and precise conclusions. It isn't like that at all and you know it.'[8]

Brook also exercised much influence in preparing the agenda. Suggestions would come from a number of sources: from individual Departments requiring a decision, from Brook because he knew Churchill wanted the topic discussed, or, if they felt it was time to air certain problems, direct from the Ministers themselves, or, less commonly, from Churchill. Brook then recommended an agenda to Churchill in the form of a forward programme for the coming week, and then the particular agenda for each meeting (normally two in a week). Brook drew together the various suggestions, but Churchill had to give his approval, and he frequently made changes to Brook's proposals, not unusually at the last minute, thereby causing some consternation.[9] Frequently this meant disappointments as it proved impossible to slot in a certain item. Brook used his influence in the preparation of the agenda dispassionately,[10] but it was still a formidable position for one official to hold.

The junior Cabinet Office staff, beneath Mallaby and Harris, took minutes at the Cabinet Committees and Official Committees. The three servicemen would take the Defence and Civil Defence Committees. Apart from the Defence Committee (chaired by the Prime Minister), the main Ministerial Committees were the Economic Policy Committee (chaired by the Chancellor), the Home Affairs Committee (chaired by the Lord President), and the Legislation and Future Legislation Committees (chaired by the Home Secretary). Foreign affairs, on those occasions when they were discussed by Ministers, went to full Cabinet.[11] A number of Official Committees, for example the Atlantic Official and Mutual Aid Committees, many of them *ad hoc*, also met at regular intervals.

The Churchill Government inherited a highly efficient system of Cabinet and Official Committees, but within a few months officials were complaining that the neat system consolidated by Clement Attlee was in disarray.[12] Churchill simply disliked working through Committees, the Defence Committee[13] excepted. In particular he disliked the two-tier system of Committees, Ministerial and Official, with identical terms of reference, and attempted to cut away as many Official Committees as possible – twenty in one day according to a contemporary rumour[14] – and also instigated a review of all committees in Whitehall, and the Cabinet Office. At one tier below Official level were interdepartmental Official Committees which met *ad hoc* without the Cabinet Office providing a Secretariat. These steadily increased in size and importance throughout this period.[15] However a great deal of co-ordination continued to be carried out by informal contacts of Permanent Secretaries, who would meet at their clubs and at the Cabinet Office Mess for lunch.[16]

Churchill's idea of co-ordinating Ministers allowed him to dispense with certain committees since the 'overlords' would now see to the co-ordination. Labour criticised the system fiercely, arguing that during the war and the Labour Government of 1945–51, co-ordination had taken place in committees, whose nature and composition were secret, whereas the identities of the co-ordinating Ministers were well known.[17] The issue flared up most strongly in November 1951, and again in April and May 1952, but, since the Ministers performed little real co-ordination, the fuss was unnecessary.[18] Within a year the former pattern of Ministerial and Official Committees began to reassert itself as Churchill's attention moved away from the machinery of government.

Churchill, though, continued to rely more on Brook than on any other Minister or official.[19] Their relationship during 1951–5 was close, which is, in a way, strange as superficially they had little in common, the one a *bon viveur* and unmethodical, the other ascetic and the embodiment of order, a man who always had everything in place, knew where everything was and had practically no papers on his desk.[20] It is, however, possible to over-exaggerate Brook's ascetic side: he much enjoyed good living in an unostentatious way, and also being at the centre of power

117

and in Churchill's confidence. Bridges would have seemed a much more natural friend for Churchill. Brook's admiration for Churchill[21] was born during their wartime contact,[22] and they remained close during 1945–51.[23] Indeed, Brook's judgment, normally so sound, could be faulted in his attitude to Churchill, as only in lighter moods would he admit Churchill's failings. To Brook, Churchill embodied the excitement of politics in a remarkable man: to Churchill, Brook was a man to be respected for his orderly classical mind. 'When Winston was excited about something,' according to Mallaby, 'Norman Brook was always there as a steadying influence, and Winston came to rely on him enormously. I think this was the strength of the relationship: he was quite sure he could get Norman Brook's wise judgment on any issue entirely untinged by personal considerations.'[24] He looked upon him as a personal friend though they both remained conscious of their official relationship. John Colville wrote: 'Churchill trusted him implicitly, relied on his judgment and listened to his advice with attention. From October 1951 to April 1955 Brook never put a foot wrong and, as Churchill's energies began to flag, Brook filled in the gaps and ensured the competent conduct of business with unerring skill.'[25] Brook wrote summaries of Cabinet papers for Churchill, and was always seated next to him at Cabinet meetings. A frequent weekend visitor at Chartwell and Chequers, he usually accompanied Churchill on official trips abroad, including the United States in January 1952 and Bermuda in December 1953.[26] This was not on account of his expertise in foreign affairs but because Churchill found his calm judgment and advice indispensable.[27] Latterly, Churchill began to consult Brook on matters that were more Bridges' province, such as promotions, which caused tensions.

Brook had had an unusual career. He entered the Home Office in the first post-First World War entry in 1925, and was still a Principal, at a time of unusually slow advance, at the age of thirty-five.[28] He experienced a meteoric rise during the war, emerging as an additional Secretary to the Cabinet in 1945. He was a classical civil servant, always loyal, a tremendous organiser and in no sense a 'political' official. A number of points stand out about his period as Cabinet Secretary. A Cabinet Secretary needs three main qualities: to have the absolute confidence of the Prime Minister, the Civil Service and Ministers. Brook clearly had the first, and the fact that he was accepted as almost certain successor to Bridges implied he also had the second. Hence he could provide the crucial link between Prime Minister and Administration. As regards the third, nearly all Churchill's Ministers liked him and frequently dropped in to see him for a talk, rather more so than had been the case with Attlee's Ministers. Many knew Brook from the war, in particular

Anthony Eden and Lord Woolton, whose Permanent Secretary Brook had been at the Ministry of Reconstruction,[29] and found it useful to talk to him as he knew Churchill's mind so well. He could also advise them on the best way of putting forward their proposals to Cabinet, when to do so and in what form. Observed Lord Moran, '[Brook] has an honest mind, and is on the whole more approachable than Bridges: it is easy to understand how the whole Cabinet trust him and rely on his judgment.'[30]

Without Brook, Churchill's shortcomings in his last period as Prime Minister would not have been so well disguised. He ran a highly efficient Cabinet Office and, although not universally popular with his staff,[31] was for the most part liked and admired for his loyalty to those who worked under him.[32] Yet he was not a readily accessible man, and real friendship developed with only a few intimates. His role as Cabinet Secretary he regarded primarily as one of co-ordinator and presenter of material, rather than as an initiator of policy. He viewed all matters with detachment apart from one area, the Commonwealth, which profoundly interested him.[33] This gave him another link with Churchill, and the Commonwealth Conferences, whose Secretariat was managed by the Cabinet Office, were the high spot of his calendar. Economic discussions held as little interest for Brook as they did for Churchill, and it was chiefly organisational matters that absorbed him, not only of the Commonwealth, but also of NATO and O.E.E.C.[34]

Part 3   The Home Office

The Home Office had been steadily shedding responsibilities to other Departments since the beginning of the century, but in 1951 it still remained one of the most important, with the job of Home Secretary consistently filled by one of the most senior men in the Government.[1] The various responsibilities of the Home Secretary were described by the Permanent Under-Secretary in 1954 as: 'to advise the Sovereign on the exercise of many of her Prerogative powers, to be the channel of communication between the Sovereign and her subjects, to maintain the Queen's Peace, and to discharge the Crown's ultimate responsibility for the internal safety of the realm.'[2] Anything concerning the good order of Britain, then as now, if not allocated to another Department, became the responsibility of the Home Office.

As the main domestic activity between 1951 and 1955 centred on Departments concerned with denationalisation and decontrol, the Home Office was in the main out of the limelight. Most of its responsibilities were apolitical, which meant little change of policy after

119

the General Election, not least because Chuter Ede, who had been Home Secretary throughout Attlee's premiership, was a middle of the road, if not a right-wing Labour Minister, and Sir David Maxwell Fyfe tended to be on the centre left of the Conservative Party. There had also been a heavy programme of Home Office legislation under Ede and this required a calmer period for these reforms to be digested. On the whole under Churchill this was a quiet period, with neither Maxwell Fyfe nor Gwilym Lloyd-George initiating reforms.

The new Government's decision, announced in October 1951, to give the Home Secretary the additional title of Minister of Welsh Affairs marked a change in policy. In this capacity he represented Welsh opinion to his ministerial colleagues but had no executive responsibility in Welsh matters. Maxwell Fyfe also spent much time in his first months on one further departure, reversing the Labour Government's decision that public houses in new towns should be provided and run by the state.[3] The comparatively quiet period at the Home Office was continued under Lloyd-George (1954–7) until the period of fresh reforms later, in particular under Rab Butler (1957–62) and Roy Jenkins (1965–7).[7]

Maxwell Fyfe had not anticipated the post of Home Secretary, and accepted on the understanding that he would be appointed Lord Chancellor at a later date.[5] Winston Churchill, however, wanted him in the House of Commons, indeed Lord Moran quotes the Prime Minister as saying: 'He was so useful in the House of Commons where he was most industrious.'[6] His previous ministerial experience had been as Solicitor-General for the final three years of the war and Attorney-General in the 'Caretaker Government' in 1945; he had been called to the Bar in 1922, another asset for the task of Home Secretary. According to Lord Shawcross, himself a Labour Attorney-General, Maxwell Fyfe had a photographic memory, better than anyone he recalled meeting, and he was a master at handling departmental briefs.[7] However, his lack of depth of ministerial experience, compared, for example, to most of his Cabinet colleagues, became apparent, and Churchill sometimes found his political judgment unreliable, not least, according to Moran, over Crichel Down and commercial television.[8] He lacked a fine political sensitivity, and his colleagues thought him, on occasion, awkward.

Maxwell Fyfe took on a large burden of speaking, and earned the respect of both sides of the House.[9] He was no orator, but a good debater and adept at piloting Bills through the House, including the Television Bill in 1954 as the Postmaster-General, Lord De La Warr, was in the Lords, and the Visiting Forces Bill, 1952, for an overbusy Anthony Eden. His strengths have not been put more clearly than by Sir Norman Brook:

David was very conscientious. What I like about him is that if you have a problem he will at once offer to help and take any amount of trouble to find a solution. He has good judgment, and when his report is ready every aspect is considered. Nothing is left out. It is pretty dull stuff, but when David has done the Cabinet doesn't want to discuss it any further, but is ready to pass on to the next item on the agenda.[10]

Maxwell Fyfe's main interests lay in law and order, and he was highly efficient during the several crises which the Home Office had to manage. He took a stand against the reintroduction of corporal punishment during the debate on the Criminal Justice (Amendment) Bill, and Ede called Maxwell Fyfe's speech more courageous than any he had heard during the life of the Parliament.[11]

Regarded with some admiration by his officials, he was not, however, as popular with junior Ministers, since he kept his own counsel, and was even considered aloof. The position of junior Ministers at the Home Office was not aided by Sir Frank Newsam, the Permanent Under-Secretary, who preferred to deal direct with the Home Secretary.[12] The Attlee Government had just one junior Minister at the Home Office, who dealt with the Parliamentary side. Patrick Buchan-Hepburn put forward the name of David Llewellyn, M.P. for Cardiff North since 1950, who was duly appointed as junior Minister primarily responsible for Welsh affairs. He was not, however, happy as a Minister and suffered from ill health, and after a year offered his resignation.[13] A replacement had to be found, and by thumbing through the pages of *Who's Who*,[14] Churchill hit upon the name of Lord Lloyd,[15] son of his great friend, the first Lord Lloyd of Dolobran. In addition to his responsibility for Welsh affairs he became spokesman for Home Office affairs in the House of Lords.

Lloyd was far better suited to the work than his predecessor. A good spokesman in the Lords, he was nonetheless given insufficient responsibility in the work of the Office. In the October 1954 reshuffle he became Parliamentary Under-Secretary at the Colonial Office in succession to Lord Munster, and his place at the Home Office was taken by Lord Mancroft, thus maintaining the precedent of a peer as junior Minister. Mancroft was active in the Lords, and was highly thought of by some senior figures in the Party.[16] During Lloyd-George's time as Home Secretary Mancroft was much concerned with Welsh affairs, making more speech-making trips than either of his predecessors.[17]

The Parliamentary Under-Secretary on the 'non-Welsh' side could not be appointed until the enabling Ministers of the Crown (Parliamentary Under-Secretaries) Bill was passed in December 1951, which increased by two the number of junior Ministers who could be appointed to the Government. Sir Hugh Lucas-Tooth, who had been acting as unofficial shadow junior Minister for home affairs during part of the period of Opposition, was appointed, almost certainly due to Buchan-Hepburn's influence.[18] His first, and only, ministerial job, he performed it with some distinction. Aged forty-eight on appointment, he was paternalistic rather than sympathetic to the more liberal mood of the younger Tories, but his jocular manner and experience as a barrister equipped him well for the large volume of Parliamentary speaking he undertook. He displayed more administrative than political aptitude in the post, and there was no obvious position for him after his four-year spell at the Home Office. Lucas-Tooth also oversaw the work of the Home Office departments concerned with aliens and Northern Ireland.[19]

By mid-1954 Maxwell Fyfe, realising that his hopes of high office would not materialise, became restless to become Lord Chancellor,[20] one of several factors behind the October 1954 reshuffle. Churchill originally intended to put Harry Crookshank into the Home Office, but after protracted discussions, Lloyd-George emerged as a compromise candidate whose appointment would be welcomed by all interested parties.[21] On the face of it, the choice of such an unassertive and unenergetic figure at a time of intense jockeying for power between a number of Cabinet Ministers appeared strange. But there was no mystery.

His immense popularity both with his colleagues and the Opposition, his successful period as Minister of Food during the previous three years, the fact that he was Welsh, and presented no threat, help explain the appointment.

But it was not a particularly happy experience for him. Lloyd-George performed best as head of a team, leading a strong group of officials and junior Ministers which accounted for his success at the Ministry of Food. Yet at the Home Office his support was less formidable. Neither Lucas-Tooth nor Mancroft were able to exercise the authority of Charles Hill at the Ministry of Food,[22] whereas Nigel Fisher, Lloyd-George's faithful Parliamentary Private Secretary, was prevented by Newsam from playing much part in the Office.[23] Moreover, Lloyd-George, unable to stand up to Newsam, with whom his relations were poor, soon realised that the job held little for him, and his undoubted talents were not put to their best use. Taking decisions on capital cases was loathsome to him, and he found the many routine matters dull, and often failed to keep abreast of his papers. Eden when Prime Minister had great confidence in him,[24] but overall he cannot be regarded as one of the ablest Home Secretaries since the war.

Without question, the dominant figure in the Office was Newsam, Permanent Under-Secretary since 1948, after Sir Edward Bridges and Brook one of the most powerful figures in Whitehall. Appointed Deputy Under-Secretary in 1941, he succeeded the even more impressive Sir Alexander Maxwell seven years later. Newsam was a man of formidable powers, decisive, authoritative, at his best in a crisis of national emergency, such as the East Coast floods disaster, or the preparations for a possible General Strike in 1956. Devoted to the Home Office and its staff, he took enormous pride in the Office as the custodian of the liberty of the individual. But he had drawbacks. He was apt to be impatient of slower or more timid people, which meant they were at times afraid to oppose him. He was not greatly interested in the organisation of the Office and did not strengthen sufficiently the higher levels of the Administration to match the growing pressures of work. He considered himself very much master of the roost. Unable to dominate Ede, who kept him in his place through force of personality,[25] he held his own against Maxwell Fyfe, with whom he worked better than with either of the other Home Secretaries,[26] and he dominated Lloyd-George. A doer rather than a thinker, he originated few ideas. His main interests were the police, and the criminal justice system. He made a significant contribution to the development of the modern police force, especially to their training and technological developments.

Below Newsam were originally two and, after 1952, one Deputy Under-Secretary. Sir William Murrie, a highly able administrator, had only joined the Home Office at the rank of Deputy in 1948. Apart from a spell in the Cabinet Office he had spent his career in the Scottish Office, of which he later became official head (1959–64). He oversaw the Aliens Department and the Children's Department including probation, assisted Newsam with capital cases and undertook a certain amount of co-ordination, for example on building programmes. On his appointment as Secretary to the Scottish Education Department in October 1952 his position was left vacant, and the three Assistant Under-Secretaries responsible to him from then on reported direct to Newsam.[27] Sir Arthur Hutchinson had also been a Deputy since 1948, and on Murrie's departure became the sole Deputy Secretary. Like Newsam he had had a long spell as Private Secretary to the Home Secretary.[28] He was responsible for the Fire Service Division and also for the Civil Defence Division until the appointment of a Director-General of Civil Defence in 1954.[29]

The breadth of Home Office work is illustrated by describing the work of the five Assistant Under-Secretaries. One of these was responsible for criminal matters and the police, another for international affairs, a third for aliens and naturalisation matters, a fourth for the Children's and Probation Divisions, and the final one was responsible, *inter alia*, for the U.K. Dependencies, liaison with the Government of Northern Ireland and for supervision of Private Bills and local bye-laws.[30] A number of these Assistant Under-Secretaries were especially outstanding, including Philip Allen,[31] Sir Austin Strutt, who acted as master of protocol during the Coronation for which he was awarded a K.C.V.O. in 1953,[32] and John Ross.[33]

Not surprisingly with such an uncontroversial Department, Churchill had little occasion to intervene in its work.[34] He allowed Maxwell Fyfe free rein, the only exception being the odd case of apparent injustice which came to his attention, when he would puff up his feathers and act with the old aplomb until the storm had died away. One such occasion was when he took steps to set about a reversal of a Home Office decision to refuse political asylum to a Polish stowaway in late July 1954.[35]

In addition to the routine matters such as police (which Newsam dealt with), children's care and aliens, Maxwell Fyfe's attention was taken up by a number of particular problems. The Home Office was involved in the problems of the aftermath of the East Coast floods on the last night of January 1953. A Committee of Ministers was at once set up under Maxwell Fyfe and a Committee of Officials under Newsam,[36] who excelled at this type of work, and he was the dominant figure co-ordinating the repair work, although Maxwell Fyfe received the public credit and gained in standing as a result. The Government introduced the Coastal Flooding (Emergency Provisions) Act 1953, which received Royal Assent in May and provided for works of defence against sea-water in areas affected by floods, and for the rehabilitation of agricultural land damaged by sea-water.

Maxwell Fyfe again entered the limelight in January 1953, during the Craig/Bentley murder trial, an issue which probably caused as much concern as any during his period as Home Secretary.[37] Derek Bentley (aged nineteen) and Christopher Craig (sixteen) had set out to commit a burglary in Croydon. They were disturbed by the police, and after incitement by Bentley, Craig shot and killed a policeman. Both were convicted of murder but only Bentley was recommended for hanging, Craig being too young. The proposed hanging provoked a great outcry. Maxwell Fyfe refused a reprieve as he did not, apparently, wish to create a precedent,[38] and despite the opposition of two hundred M.P.s to the death penalty in this case, Bentley was hanged on 28th January, 1953.[39] 'A Student of Politics' was not alone in applauding his decision: 'silent, immobile endurance in face of a great ordeal'.[40]

The rise in the crime rate, especially among the young, caused considerable anxiety in early 1953.[41] Total indictable offences known to the police had nearly doubled in the fifteen years up to 1952, the police force was an estimated 8,000 under strength and the 24,000 inmates of prisons and borstals suffered much overcrowding. As a response, the Government introduced the Prevention of Crime Act 1953, which prohibited the carrying of an offensive weapon in public places without lawful authority and was designed specifically to deal with the 'cosh boys'. Maxwell Fyfe made an effective speech in the debate arguing that the purpose of the Bill was to deter violence before it occurred.[42] In September 1953, the Royal Commission on Capital Punishment reported,[43] saying it was impracticable to find a satisfactory method of limiting the scope of capital punishment by dividing murder into degrees; it also put forward a number of controversial proposals.

The issue of civil defence came increasingly to the fore especially after the emergence of the thermo-nuclear bomb in 1953–4. The Government attempted to build up the strength of the Civil Defence Corps, but the Report of the Select Committee on Civil Defence Estimates, published in December 1953, unsettled public confidence, and Maxwell Fyfe, in the Commons in January 1954,[44] more or less admitted that the state of the Civil Defence programme was little more than a façade.[45] Local authorities had always been responsible for the administration and training of Civil Defence, but critics in the Home Office and outside questioned whether this arrangement, which had worked well in the war, was suitable and good value for money in a nuclear age.[46] Within the Home Office Newsam disliked being continually bothered by the subject, and the responsible official, the Deputy Under-Secretary Hutchinson, was not felt to have the experience or qualifications necessary to provide the leadership and drive that many local authorities felt was needed.[47]

Pressure for the Government to make a change to the existing apparatus grew throughout 1954, and in September 1954 Sir Sidney Kirkman, a member of the Army Council from 1945 to 1950, was appointed to the new post of Director-General of Civil Defence, to secure full co-ordination of plans by the military and civil authorities at all levels. Insisting that he had the same right of direct access to the Secretary of State as he had at the War Office when Quartermaster-General from 1947 to 1950, he soon began to make up his own mind and decide what was required. Newsam was delighted to be relieved of responsibility for Civil Defence, and those irksome officials who were initially suspicious and critical of the introduction of an outsider soon moderated their views. A significant improvement was undoubtedly made by having a man in charge who felt he could act on his own initiative and who had greater independence of action than an established civil servant. Recruitment anyway was beginning to improve throughout 1954, and by the end of the year the Civil Defence Corps numbered a third of a million, nearly double the level of three years before.[48]

Another concern at the Home Office during 1951–5 was the law relating to sexual offences. Pressure came from certain backbenchers, Sir Robert Boothby prominent among them, for a review. Boothby wrote to Maxwell Fyfe urging reform of the 1861 and 1886 Acts, to make homosexuality no longer an offence between consenting adults in private, plus legislation to establish the age of consent. He also urged the setting up of a Royal Commission or expert departmental Committee.[49] Maxwell Fyfe was initially strongly opposed to reform,[50] but nevertheless, in response to this pressure, Lucas-Tooth announced in a debate on the subject in April 1954, that a departmental Committee would be set up by the Home Secretary and Scottish Secretary on the subject of homosexual offences.[51] Under the chairmanship of Sir John Wolfenden, then Vice-Chancellor of Reading University, it reported in August 1957 in favour of liberalising the laws governing homosexual behaviour.

Immigration was an issue only just coming to the fore during 1951–5, yet it was not a problem to which the Home Office devoted much time.[52] As a prophetic leader in the *Sunday Times* on 14th November, 1953 recorded: 'The United Kingdom has been spared up till now, a serious colour problem of its own . . . Now, however, we are threatened with the possibility of a serious colour problem here through the persistent immigration of people from the West Indies.' The Home Office felt a larger issue was emigration from Britain to the Commonwealth. The policy statement on the Empire, published in June 1949,[53] said it welcomed the steady emigration flow, and in May 1952, the Empire Settlement Act, 1952, which renewed for five years the Act of 1937, provided assistance for suitable emigrants to the Commonwealth.

Yet anxieties about immigration were just beginning to come to the surface, traceable to late 1953 and early 1954. Public concern about the problem of immigration, particularly from the West Indies, went back to 1945 when some of the West Indians who came to join the Services or to work in munition factories decided to remain. Though it was far from becoming a public issue. Numbers were not recorded, but an estimated 5,000 West Indian immigrants entered Britain in 1953, and over 9,000 in 1954.[54] In February 1954 a Question was asked in the House about whether Churchill would make a statement on the colour bar, and the following month he was asked whether he would set up a committee to report on Commonwealth immigration. Churchill replied that the topic was under consideration,[55] but that he did not think any useful purpose would be served by setting up a committee at that point. In April the Party's Commonwealth Affairs Committee raised the question, as a result of which a letter was sent to Maxwell Fyfe, whose reply intimated that the matter had been under consideration for some time.[56] Anxieties, centring on the pressure on demand for jobs and homes, continued to mount throughout 1954,[57] and in December the Minister of State at the Colonial Office, in reply to a Question, said the Government were very conscious of the need to consider the influx of West Indian immigrants but no statement could yet be made.[58] The Cabinet was reluctant to commit itself to restrictions, and in the event the first legislation did not appear until the Commonwealth Immigrants Act of 1962. The problems of coloured people were one of Churchill's blind spots: it was a major omission of his not to have spoken out against prejudice.

Wales

Only after 1945 did the Conservative Party begin seriously to consider producing a separate policy for Wales. Pressure from Conservative organisations in Wales, culminating in the 1947 Party Conference in Llandudno, provoked action on the part of the shadow Cabinet. A Party panel was set up the following autumn, including Welsh M.P.s Nigel Birch and Peter Thorneycroft, and produced a document 'The Conservative Policy for Wales and Monmouthshire' published on 1st March, 1949. This proposed the appointment of a Cabinet member with special responsibility for Wales, a move which had been foreshadowed by Butler in a speech during the 1948 Welsh Day debate.[59] The document also promised that a Conservative Government would be sympathetic to the preservation of Welsh language and lore.[60] Butler first suggested the title 'Minister of Welsh Affairs' in a speech at Haverfordwest in May 1951, and it was repeated in the policy document 'Britain Strong and Free'. After the Election Churchill assigned the responsibility to the Home Secretary, and defined his responsibilities as being '. . . to inform himself of the Welsh aspect of business by visiting the Principality and by discussion with representatives of Welsh life and to speak in Cabinet on behalf of the special interests and aspirations of Wales'.[61]

Proposals to make the Home Secretary responsible for Wales and to increase the scope of Civil Service machinery with specific responsibility for Wales had been discussed in Whitehall since at least 1945. The Welsh demand for a Welsh Office on the lines of the Scottish Office had been the main item on the machinery of government agenda during 1946, but few concrete changes emerged.[62] The only institutional innovation was a 'standing conference' under the chairmanship of a senior Whitehall official, Sir Frederick Armer,[63] which had the duty of advising Ministers and their Departments on matters of administration and necessary steps to improve co-ordination. In addition, the Government agreed to compile an annual summary of Government action in Wales to be published as a White Paper.[64] The Labour Government in 1948 also set up an advisory body, the Council for Wales and Monmouth,[65] and Herbert Morrison as Lord President was charged with general responsibility for Wales, since, in his capacity as Leader of the House, he already arranged Welsh debates.[66]

Maxwell Fyfe, though a Scotsman, proved to be popular in Wales. He made approximately twenty-five trips a year there, an exhausting additional burden on the already heavy workload of the Home Secretary. He took his Welsh responsibilities seriously, and on his trips aimed to talk over problems with as many Welshmen as he could fit into his timetable.[67] The Parliamentary Under-Secretary with responsibility for Wales also made regular trips, sometimes more than once a week. He had an office in Cardiff, received deputations in Wales or London, and was Chairman of the quarterly conferences of the Heads of Government Offices in Wales.[68] These developments were appreciated by the Welsh, although they did not result in the Conservatives (who after 1951 had six Welsh seats to Labour's twenty-seven and the Liberals' three) capturing more seats in the 1955 General Election.

Although Maxwell Fyfe fulfilled the purpose of the task laid down by Churchill, of visiting Wales and speaking in Cabinet on its behalf, little came of it in terms of practical policy co-ordination or initiatives for Wales. A former Minister of the time later said: 'We used to make speeches to jolly them along, but we achieved virtually nothing. The Home Office had a Welsh speech which we used to give out amending it for certain areas, but when we came to deal with various problems we were able to do nothing as we had no administrative power in Wales.'[69] Responsibility for Welsh affairs was spread between the Ministries of Agriculture, Education, Health and Housing and Local Government amongst others, which produced separate plans for Wales with little attempt at co-ordination or the creation of a coherent strategy. Maxwell Fyfe was able to instigate some changes: he saved the Towy Valley from a forestry scheme which would have dislodged tenant farmers, prevented the Llanllyn Peninsula being devoted to military uses,[70] and encouraged new road programmes, centring on Port Talbot and Swansea. A committee was set up under Lord Lloyd in January 1953 to advise the Government on investment and modernisation in South Wales, especially as a result of the reorganisation of the tin plate industry.[71] The Welsh Department of the Ministry of Education was upgraded in status in September 1954, and the Secretary of the Welsh Department of the Ministry of Agriculture was promoted to Under-Secretary. Special concessions to Welsh interests were made both in the new Charter of the B.B.C. and in the Television Act, 1954. Informed opinion generally felt that further concessions to the Welsh were uncalled for.[72]

The reforms of 1951 were soon superseded. When Harold Macmillan formed his Government in January 1957, he transferred general responsibility for Wales from the Home Secretary to the Minister of Housing and Local Government, and left the post of junior Minister with special responsibility for Wales vacant. This was considered a more satisfactory arrangement because responsibility for Welsh affairs was vested in the Minister already in charge of Welsh planning and local government problems. The explorations and false starts instituted by the Conservative Government during 1951–5, however, were not without value, and helped pave the way for the eventual establishment of the Welsh Office in 1964.[73]

Northern Ireland

The Home Secretary had certain functions in relation to Northern Ireland, mainly to act as the official channel of communication between the Governments of the United Kingdom and of Northern Ireland.[74] In practice, since such wide powers were devolved to the local Parliament in Belfast and to the local departments in Northern Ireland, Irish affairs did not occupy much of the Home Secretary's time. This remained the case until the sectarian strife was renewed in the late 1960s,[75]

Politically, Northern Ireland appeared settled,[76] and Maxwell Fyfe had full confidence in the Prime Minister, Lord Brookeborough (1943–63) and the Governors, Lord Granville (1945–52) and Lord Wakehurst (1952–64). The Conservatives, who dropped a seat in 1951, had nine M.P.s.[77]

Economically the position was not sound: 50% of workers in manufacturing industry were employed in clothing and textiles, and the Government, as the 1955 General Election approached, became increasingly worried by the high unemployment figures, even though these had fallen from 10.4% in 1952 to 7% in 1955, and the need to adopt positive plans, particularly measures to attract new industries.[78] A small department in the Home Office managed relations with the Northern Ireland Government, under the supervision of a Northern Ireland Liaison Officer. Maxwell Fyfe delegated much of the responsibility for Northern Ireland to Lucas-Tooth, who made on average two visits a year.[79] The eruption of violence just fifteen years later was utterly unforeseen.

Part 4   The Scottish Office

The upsurge of nationalism in Scotland in the late 1940s shattered the comparative calm of Scottish affairs. Unlike the fervour in the early 1930s, the Scottish National Party this time played a minor role. In the 1950 General Election their three candidates lost their deposits; at the 1951 Election they ran two candidates who fared similarly, as did the candidate at the Dundee by-election in July 1952. An extra-Parliamentary organisation known as the Scottish Convention[1] lay behind this nationalist zeal and in 1949 organised a mass petition, the Scottish Covenant, which they claimed had two million signatures, and which demanded a Parliament for Scotland, although within a United Kingdom framework.

The Labour Cabinet became alarmed, and in February 1950, Hector McNeil was appointed Secretary of State, replacing the undynamic Arthur Woodburn (1947–50) to try to play out the nationalist feeling. By the time of the 1951 General Election, however, as the economic hardships of the late 1940s began to ease, the tide was starting to turn. The theft of the Stone of Destiny from Westminster Abbey on Christmas Day, 1950 by a small group of enthusiasts, in particular alienated many moderate sympathisers.[2]

Initially the Conservatives reacted to the underlying unrest by publishing a policy statement in 1949 which contained various proposals for securing more effective Scottish control of Scottish affairs.[3] This proposed additions to the Scottish team of Ministers and the appointment of a Royal Commission, later included in the 1951 'Unionist Policy Statement for Scotland'. James Stuart played a major part in formulating these ideas,[4] many of which were later acted upon. A new post, Minister of State for Scotland, was created, and also the Ministers of the Crown (Parliamentary Under-Secretaries) Act, 1951, made possible the appointment of a third Parliamentary Under-Secretary. The appointment of Lord Home as Minister of State, working mostly in Scotland, helped reassure the Scots that they were not being ignored.

Within a month of the General Election, Home announced that the first step to a Royal Commission would be a committee on the financial and economic relations between Scotland and the rest of the United Kingdom,[5] chaired by Lord Catto.[6] This duly reported in July 1952. Its main proposal was for a separate return of Government revenue and expenditure in Scotland to be prepared. In accordance with this a White Paper on 'Revenue and Expenditure' was published in January 1954, showing that Scotland contributed 9.7% of British revenue and that her share of 'local' expenditure was 12.3%. But the conclusions of the Catto

Report disappointed some who favoured seeing a National Income White Paper for Scotland alone. Nevertheless, the Government set up the Royal Commission in the same month under the chairmanship of Lord Balfour[7] 'to review with reference to the financial, economic, administrative and other considerations involved the arrangements for exercising the functions of H.M. Government in relation to Scotland'. The omission from its terms of reference of any suggestion of Parliamentary or political devolution evoked adverse comments from the nationalists.

The unanimous Report of the Commission was published in July 1954.[8] It noted that relations between Scotland and England had been adversely affected by 'needless English thoughtlessness and undue Scottish susceptibilities', but it considered that Scottish difficulties had resulted from economic factors and the general increase in governmental activity. The report roundly attacked the myth of English exploitation: the Catto Report had already demonstrated that Scotland took more out of the national purse for purely local expenditure than it paid into it, and only in the case of road transport did the Balfour Report find any evidence of a British Ministry treating Scotland unfairly.[9] The Report was against dividing the responsibilities of the Secretary of State among further Scottish Ministries, but recommended that the Secretary of State should in future be responsible for comparatively minor matters such as highways, animal health and the appointment of J.P.s. It also recommended an increase in the powers of the Scottish Controller of the Board of Trade, and the maintenance of close links between the Board of Trade and the Scottish Home Department on questions of distribution of industry.[10] A thoughtful report, its recommendations played a part in strengthening the Government against nationalist criticism. Winston Churchill announced on 18th November, 1954 that the Government would implement these proposals, responsibilities for animal health and the appointment of J.P.s being transferred in 1955, and road administration on 1st April, 1956.[11]

Further administrative devolutions also helped overturn the nationalists' argument that Scotland was being run from Whitehall: the Electricity Reorganisation (Scotland) Act, 1954, transferred to the Secretary of State certain functions relating to electricity supply in Scotland and set up a new public authority, the South of Scotland Electricity Board; a separate Scottish regional railway authority was established on 1st February, 1955, and the Minister of Food's Scottish responsibilities were also transferred to the Secretary of State. The arrival of television in Scotland in 1952 similarly helped reduce feelings of isolation.

The Conservatives came to power in 1951 convinced they had the solution to the problem of the nationalists, but their measures played only a minor part in settling the disquiet. The major factor was the improvement in the Scottish economy, especially from 1952, when unemployment varied from 3.1% to 3.6%, compared to the general British average ranging from 1.9% to 2.2% during 1952. Nationalist unrest was to stir again, at the end of the decade, with economic dissatisfaction the main cause, as once again Scottish unemployment rose to a level well above that in England.

The Conservatives were prepared to go further than Labour in concessions to the Scots, but few other changes occurred at the Scottish Office. As in England and Wales, house building had increased priority but this was only a change of degree, a political decision, facilitated by building materials becoming more readily available. Early in 1952 Stuart was instrumental in reversing the decision to extend the state management scheme of public houses, a minor change which had not been anticipated, and which illustrated the difference in Party philosophies.[12] McNeil had been ambitious and intensely interested in some aspects of the work of the Scottish Office, for example, in the industry and employment side, and had he been there longer might well have proved a great Secretary of State. Stuart was temperamentally, and also from a Party point of view, against introducing more new legislation than could be helped, or interfering more than was absolutely necessary.[13] What is striking then is not the change but the continuity of policy at the Scottish Office between the Labour and Conservative Governments.

The Secretary of State for Scotland had charge of four Departments (Agriculture, Education, Health and Home) within the Scottish Office, employing about 5,000 people and working from St. Andrew's House in Edinburgh. The Scottish Office was mainly an administrative Department, whose work generated little controversy in the House. The Secretary of State had to conform to general Government policy or show cause for Scottish reasons for doing differently. There was, however, scope – if rarely used – for independent action, and few policy initiatives emerged. Above all, Stuart, considered by many to be one of the most successful Secretaries of State since the war, was no innovator, as Tom Johnston, for example, had been between 1941 and 1945.

Stuart's appointment as Secretary of State came as a surprise to many, not least to himself. 'Honestly I had never contemplated it,' Stuart recalled in an interview. 'I couldn't pretend to be displeased except my ignorance of the subject – I had never even been a junior Minister in my life.'[14] He had, however, been a highly successful Chief Whip from 1941–8, and in November 1950, Churchill appointed him Chairman of the Unionist Party in Scotland, so it would seem that Stuart's surprise was somewhat exaggerated. Politically unambitious, he had to be persuaded by Churchill to take the office.[15] According to Lord Strathclyde, the Prime Minister overcame Stuart's reluctance by declaring: 'A Stuart shall rule again in Scotland.'[16] The appointment was not a complete surprise to the Scottish Office, however, Woodburn having already speculated that Stuart would be made Secretary of State if the Conservatives returned to power.[17] Many both from within the House and outside expected the job to go to Walter Elliot, who had served with distinction as Secretary of State from 1936–8, but his age (he was by no means a young sixty-three), the general feeling by 1951 that he had become rather a dilettante, an antipathy to Churchill dating from before the war and Stuart's personal popularity with the Prime Minister and the Cabinet – all this worked against him. Elliot remained loyal to Stuart, brushing aside Labour banterings in the House that he should have been given the job. He received some compensation in his election as Chairman of the Party's Scottish Unionist Members' Committee in the House of Commons[18] (a position Stuart had held until the 1951 General Election), but, according to Lord Crathorne, his brother-in-law and formerly Sir Thomas Dugdale, he was greatly disappointed not to have been included in the Cabinet.[19]

Two were short-listed for the new job of Minister of State, Home being Stuart's choice.[20] (Lord Selkirk, the other candidate, became instead a Lord-in-Waiting and in November 1953 Paymaster-General). Stuart was also responsible for all other appointments at the Scottish Office. He first asked T. D. Galbraith[21] (later Lord Strathclyde), an M.P. since 1940 and one of the two Parliamentary Under-Secretaries at the Scottish Office in the 'Caretaker Government' of 1945.[22] He was a natural choice as Parliamentary Under-Secretary, and on Stuart's behalf, he persuaded a reluctant William McNair Snadden, M.P. for Kinross and West Perth since 1938, and well known to the Scottish agricultural community as a stockbreeder and large scale farmer,[23] to accept the second post.[24] Lady Tweedsmuir was considered as third Parliamentary Under-Secretary, but rejected since Stuart thought her comparatively inexperienced and disliked the idea of women Ministers.[25] Instead James Henderson Stewart, a National Liberal, was appointed in February 1952. The three Parliamentary Under-Secretaries were by no means young (on appointment Galbraith was sixty; McNair Snadden, fifty-five; and Henderson Stewart, fifty-four), but they had the benefit of several years' experience on the backbenches. For his Parliamentary Private Secretary Stuart chose a man unknown to him, a Glasgow M.P. and businessman, Jack Nixon Browne, who went on to serve in the Scottish Office for thirteen years as Parliamentary Under-

133

Secretary 1955–9 and (as Lord Craigton) Minister of State, 1959–64.[26] Together, the six made one of the strongest teams ever at the Scottish Office; indeed theirs was the only major departmental team to remain unchanged until the April 1955 reshuffle. They worked well together, and there was a close personal relationship among the Conservative members of the team. Stuart respected Henderson Stewart and their official relations were uniformly good, but he found him, as a National Liberal, less agreeable personally and politically than his other colleagues.[27]

Stuart delegated much of the work to the junior Ministers, and expected them to attend to detail.[28] Home's function was outlined by Churchill in the House, to 'concern himself specifically with industry and development, the peculiar problems of the Highlands and Islands, and general aspects of local government'. This would be in addition to education matters.[29] Much of his time was also spent examining ways of diversifying Scottish industry and the problems of hill-farming,[30] and although he made significant contributions, his role has been exaggerated by his two biographers.[31] He complemented Stuart, excelling, unlike Stuart, in making speeches in the country. Unenthusiastic to take on the job, he was slow initially to find his feet, but after the first year his confidence and effectiveness grew. Although it was his first ministerial post (apart from two months as a junior Minister at the Foreign Office in 1945), he had previously been Parliamentary Private Secretary to Neville Chamberlain from 1937–9. He had also served for a short period as Parliamentary Private Secretary to Noel Skelton at the Scottish Office from 1931, and commented in an interview that he benefited in 1951 from that experience of Scottish affairs. He spent most of his time in Scotland where he was a popular figure, only appearing in the Lords once a month or so, and was given an almost entirely free hand by Stuart. 'I said "What would you like me to do?" Stuart replied, "Do what you like provided you don't get me into trouble." '[32] In retrospect it could be said that Home was too big a man for the limited job, which was better suited to men of the calibre of Galbraith (as Lord Strathclyde), 1955–8, and Nixon Browne (as Lord Craigton), 1959–64, who followed as Ministers of State.

Home also oversaw the work of the three Parliamentary Under-Secretaries under the overall supervision of Stuart. But, as with Stuart's oversight of Home's work, so too this supervision was loose: 'We divided the job and worked as a team,' according to Lord Home. 'There was no formality about it.'[33] In practice, when the three junior Ministers needed a higher opinion, they often went direct to the Secretary of State, bypassing the Minister of State. They each had their own responsibilities, corresponding approximately to the four Departments of the Scottish Office.

Galbraith, the *de facto* senior Parliamentary Under-Secretary, held responsibility for housing, health and local government. Good in the House, enjoying the rough and tumble of debate, unlike Stuart, he was the ablest all-round performer of the three juniors. With the political priority behind the housing drive, Stuart took more interest in Galbraith's work than in that of the others.[34] Galbraith was a well-known figure in Glasgow, and performed as a useful back-up to Home, making speeches to reassure the Scots that they were not being neglected.[35] His reward was promotion to Minister of State in April 1955, a move he did not entirely welcome.

McNair Snadden oversaw agricultural and forestry matters. He was a first-class farmer in his own right, and Stuart scarcely interfered with him on details, but the key decisions affecting agriculture were taken between Rab Butler, Dugdale and Stuart in London. He brought to his work a sound understanding of Scottish agricultural problems, but he was the most lightweight of the three, a poor speaker, who made no impact outside his own specialist area.

Henderson Stewart was responsible for education, fisheries, law and order and other aspects of the work of the Home Department. Not as popular in the House as McNair Snadden, though a better speaker, he dealt with much of the House of Commons work. He was left a relatively free hand in his own field and worked with industry and ability. He took a specialist interest in bringing together the two Scottish education unions (the S.S.T.A. and the E.I.S.)[36] and also in the problems of the Highlands.[37] Together with Stuart, the three Parliamentary Under-Secretaries normally spent Monday to Thursday in London, caught the night sleeper to Edinburgh and spent Friday either at St. Andrew's House or speaking in Scotland, although it was often the practice for one of the Parliamentary Under-Secretaries to remain in London on Fridays as duty Minister.

Stuart was undisputed master of this multi-talented team. The younger brother of the well-known Scottish peer, the Earl of Moray, there was a touch of the Edwardian languor and dilettantism about him of his brother-in-law Harold Macmillan. But Scottish Minister was not a job he enjoyed as much as being Chief Whip (1941–8), which had fascinated him. He found the work of a departmental Minister a constant strain, especially at first when nervous exhaustion forced him to take a rest.[38] Despite his love of the Parliamentary side of the work, he disliked speaking in the House, and Labour complained he took too little part in debates. Yet as the months passed he quite came to enjoy Parliamentary

Questions,[39] and his anxiety about speaking in public decreased. His strength lay in a combination of power of decision, ability to work hard, political instinct and complete absence of personal ambition.[40] 'Do you know why they [the Cabinet] like me?' Stuart once asked Galbraith. 'It's because there is nothing they can give me and there is nothing that I want.'[41] He was also highly able intellectually, though his dry, almost torpid manner made some feel otherwise. He earned the affection of his officials to a degree unparalleled for any Scottish Secretary of State to date. Part of this was due to his personality, but also to the fact that he was close to the Prime Minister, and so could count on his support in Cabinet. Stuart told Galbraith on another occasion: '. . . if the Secretary of State can't get out of the Government what he wants he's got no right to be Secretary of State.'[42] This earned him wide respect in the Office.[43]

Stuart's energies were channelled into a number of different areas. Some issues came direct to him, for example capital decisions from the Home Department, on which he was found to be decisive. Politically sensitive questions, such as unemployment and housing, also occupied him. He took an interest in fishing problems, partly because his constituency contained fishing ports such as Lossiemouth, partly as Henderson Stewart, with his other responsibilities, was unable to devote much time to it. Above all he recognised the need to cool down nationalist fervour, and the appointment of extra Ministers and certain administrative devolutions which he put forward helped in this direction. He was personally responsible for two further measures, the transfer of responsibility for electricity, and the decision to build the Forth Road Bridge,[44] neither strictly crucial in economic terms, but both strengthening the hand of the Government against the nationalists. Labour regarded Stuart with respect, if not admiration, and as policy was so similar, had little grounds for serious opposition. He was undoubtedly aided also by his tenure of the job of Secretary of State coinciding with a mood of optimism in Scottish affairs: not just in the economy was there an upsurge of life, but also in Scottish culture, seen for example in the early years of the Edinburgh Festival.

Churchill's support helped Stuart a great deal: 'He always backed me throughout my time at the Scottish Office . . . if he could, and helped me.'[45] This was not due to any special regard the Prime Minister had for Scotland, for his interest in Scottish affairs was minimal, but rather to his close friendship with Stuart, which stemmed from his days as Chief Whip.[46]

Stuart was also fortunate in his Permanent Under-Secretary, Sir David Milne, whom he liked and trusted, as McNeil had done. Milne had taken over from Sir Horace Hamilton in 1946 and had done a great deal to build up the position of the Scottish Office by 1951. He was a man of considerable ability, one of the dominant Whitehall figures, though he by no means earned the universal respect of his officials. He excelled in political flair and foresight, delegated successfully to his subordinates, and had the considerable gift of understanding his political chiefs. Yet he was less involved with detail than most Permanent Under-Secretaries and rarely drafted anything himself, although he was an assiduous tinkerer with other people's drafts. The other dominant official in the Scottish Office was the Secretary of the Home Department, Sir Charles Cunningham. With Milne, Stuart described them as: 'the two men upon whom I had relied constantly for the best advice in the land'.[47]

Stuart also relied greatly on his Private Secretary, initially George Pottinger (1950–2), a forceful figure whom he inherited from McNeil, and then the mellower and highly adept Ian Robertson (1952–5) with whom he developed a close relationship. In the Scottish Office the job had broader responsibilities than in other Departments, as not only did he have to provide the link between the Minister and the Permanent Under-Secretary, but also with the four departmental official heads, who might be four hundred miles away in Edinburgh when a crisis blew up.[48]

Each of the four Departments was headed by a Secretary, who met with Milne each Monday morning to discuss and co-ordinate policy. Milne did not submit the detailed business of the Scottish Office to Stuart, since each Department consulted with the Ministers directly concerned.[49] The Home Department, regarded by many as *primus inter pares*, partly due to the influence of Cunningham, the Secretary, partly because its scope, covering local government, transport, fisheries and other economic matters, in addition to those responsibilities such as police, prison, civil defence and fire assigned in England and Wales to the Home Office, was broader than that of the other Scottish Departments.

Responsibility for roads, bridges and ferries was transferred to the Scottish Office in 1956, but this by no means meant that the Home Department controlled transport policy for Scotland, since non-fishery harbours, railways and airports remained beyond their purview. Apart from the announcement of the decision to build the Forth Road Bridge, which the Treasury insisted should be a toll bridge, no particular advances took place on the road building programme. Home was a consistent advocate of the need for better roads in Scotland,[50] and the announcement in July 1953 of the decision to spend £1m. more on Highland roads owed much to him. Yet overall Government expenditure on roads was modest; of the £19m. spent on road improvement and construction in 1954–5, only £4½m. was spent in Scotland.

The Government's major priorities for Scotland were to curtail emigration and to stimulate diversification of industry as Scotland's staple industries, especially coal-mining and shipbuilding, continued to decline. Close relations were maintained with the Scottish Council (Development and Industry) a body which strove to attract new industry to areas of high unemployment. The economy improved by 1955, with industrial production up nearly 12% in the first quarter of the year compared with the same period in 1951, and average unemployment down from c3.5% in 1951 to c3% in 1955.[51]

Cunningham, the only Secretary to remain throughout the 1951–5 Government, played a major part in the increase of Exchequer grants to local authorities. By the Local Government (Financial Provisions) (Scotland) Act of 1954, an extra £2m. of Exchequer assistance was given to local authorities, resulting in a relief to rates. This was an interim measure pending the Government's consideration of the Sorn Committee's Report [52] published in August 1954 on the system of rating and valuation in Scotland.[53] Improvements to the rating system, however, continued to pose problems for a number of years.

The Secretary of the Agriculture Department until 1953, when he retired aged sixty-five, was the immensely experienced Sir Patrick Laird, who had held the job since 1934. His successor, Alexander Glen, was not, however, such a strong figure. Most of the Department's efforts went into improving agriculture in the Highlands. The Hill Farming Act, 1954, made it possible for tied cottages to receive improvement grants. Electricity was extended to remoter agricultural areas in an effort to prevent depopulation and increased grants were provided to encourage reafforestation. The Crofters (Scotland) Act, 1955, one of the last measures to be passed before the 1955 General Election, set up a Crofters' Commission to reorganise and regulate crofting, and to look after crofting interests.

Galbraith was responsible for the Department of Health. While he played an important part in one or two major health issues, he took no great interest in day-to-day health matters.[54] The main priorities here were to encourage the building of houses, to continue the battle against tuberculosis and to improve the hospital service by bringing existing hospitals up to date and improving the available services.[55] Expenditure on the N.H.S. in Scotland rose from £41m. in 1950–1 to £49m. in 1954–5, and the number of hospital beds increased by 3,000 between 1951 and 1955.[56] As in England and Wales, both health and education expenditure was held virtually steady in real terms, while finance on housing was increased. In health care, efforts were made to use existing expenditure more efficiently. The tide was turned in the fight against tuberculosis with 66 deaths per 100,000 in 1947 falling to 37 in 1951 and 20 in 1954, but incidence of the disease remained higher in Scotland than in the remainder of the United Kingdom. Initiatives to tackle tuberculosis had been taken by Labour before 1951. One of Galbraith's major contributions on the health side was directed towards the treatment of Scottish tuberculosis patients in Swiss sanatoria.

Scotland's housing problems were more complex than those in England and Wales due to the larger concentration of slum areas, especially in Glasgow, and a poorer per capita income, resulting in lower rents and thus less potential for house improvements. Close contact was maintained with the Ministry of Housing, and at Macmillan's request the Scottish Office joined the Building Committee of the Cabinet.[57] Through encouragement to private builders and local authorities – the Housing (Scotland) Act, 1952 increasing Exchequer subsidies – the number of houses completed increased dramatically. The post-war peak had reached 25,800 in 1949, but this climbed to 30,900 in 1952 and 38,800 in 1954.[58] Attention was then turned to improvements and slum clearance. This was tackled by the Housing Repairs and Rents (Scotland) Act, 1954, which, *inter alia*, required local authorities to submit to the Secretary of State within a year proposals for clearing sums, and made conditions for improvement grants more attractive. In all this work, Galbraith's drive and compassionate approach made a lasting imprint.[59]

At the Education Department Sir William Murrie replaced Sir John Mackay Thompson on his retirement in September 1952. Murrie was foremost an administrator, and he returned to the Scottish Office after spells in the Cabinet Office and Home Office, eventually succeeding Milne as Permanent Under-Secretary in 1959. Education was not a subject that particularly interested Stuart, and neither did Henderson Stewart make it one of his priorities. Due to the different Scottish education system, there was less scope for working closely with their Whitehall counterpart. As in England and Wales, school building and ensuring an adequate supply of teachers constituted the main priorities. To attempt to remedy the staffing deficiency, a committee was set up under Sir Edward Appleton[60] in October 1953, to report on the shortage of mathematics and science teachers in Scottish secondary schools.[61] School teachers' salaries were increased in 1954 and in January 1955 the Teachers Salaries (Scotland) Amendment No. 1 Regulations were issued, which contained the first comprehensive salary system for further education teachers. Yet numbers of students completing training for teachers' certificates were still twenty-five per cent less in 1955 than in 1951.[62] Expenditure on new school building increased by nearly fifty per cent in 1955 compared to 1951, a trend confirmed in late 1954 when local authorities were informed in Circular No. 296 that 'the Government had decided to make additional resources available for investment in educational building.' The number of new school places increased accordingly, from 19,900 in 1951 to 29,300 in 1955.[63]

A minor problem for the Government was filling the two Scottish Law Officers posts, the Lord Advocate and the Solicitor-General for Scotland. There were only five Scottish lawyers in the House in 1953 (one Conservative, three Labour and one Liberal). This meant that William Milligan, the Solicitor-General until he succeeded Lord Clyde as Lord Advocate in December 1954, was not in the House, although he watched from the gallery whenever he could. He was, however, returned at a by-election in January 1955, and moved to the safe seat of Edinburgh North for the General Election the same year. His place as Solicitor-General was taken by the shrewd William Grant, a well-known Edinburgh lawyer, who did not enter the House until the 1955 Election. Clyde was the ablest legal brain of the three, but did not greatly care for being an M.P., and found travelling to London a tiresome distraction from his work in Edinburgh. Though a great figure in the Scottish legal world, his influence on Stuart and policy at the Scottish Office was minimal.[64]

Labour's attention was rarely focused on Scottish problems during 1951–5. Indeed, the Executive Committee of the Scottish Labour Party passed a resolution claiming that the failure of the National Executive Committee to recognise specific Scottish problems had damaged Labour's position in Scotland. But there was also little heat generated, because the Conservative Government simply did not pass controversial legislation.[65] In education, agriculture and health it merely continued Labour's policy, although it tended to lay more stress on the need to make concessions to counter the nationalist threat, on pressing ahead with house building and on the special problems presented by the Highlands. The Conservatives were rewarded at the 1955 General Election by a mild swing in their favour, giving them one extra seat (36 to Labour's 34).[66] Certainly the serious decline in the Conservative vote in the 1960s was not foreseen in 1955.[67]

Part 5   The Post Office

The job of Postmaster-General was primarily managerial rather than political and, although one of the more senior departmental posts in the Government, had ceased to be a Cabinet appointment in 1935.[1] Unlike other Government jobs, it offered little important political activity or involvement, but the holder was required to oversee the largest trading organisation owned by the state, which by 1952–3 had an annual revenue of £250m. Had it not been for the Television Act, 1954, which in setting up the Independent Television Authority made the Post Office the responsible Department,[2] little of political interest would have occurred in the Department in these years. The appointment of Lord De La Warr as Postmaster-General came as a surprise as both Ralph Assheton and Walter Elliot had been offered the job. But Churchill wanted to broaden the base of his Government.[3] De La Warr, a former Labour junior Minister (in the 1924 and 1929–31 Governments) and then a National Labour member until 1943, joining the Conservative Party after the 1945 General Election, was a man thought likely to prove acceptable to the television lobby in the Party and to be able to steer the necessary legislation through Parliament.

A conscientious and enthusiastic Postmaster-General, De La Warr much enjoyed being a Minister and became increasingly devoted to the work. He usually arrived at his office at about 10 a.m. and worked through until lunchtime. The afternoon he spent in the House of Lords when it was sitting and in his office when it was not, and he was anxious that papers for overnight attention be sent to him daily.[4] He was a talented administrator but had never handled a body like the Post Office, and found difficulty in coming to terms with the fact that in a large organisation it is in broad policy directions rather than *ad hoc* decisions that a Minister can most effectively play a part.[5] He was popular in the Department and considerate to his staff, though apt to have bursts of irritability. His close friends in Government included Lord Alexander of Tunis, Lord Salisbury, Sir David Maxwell Fyfe and Sir Walter Monckton, but many of his colleagues still regarded him as a turncoat.[6] A good speaker in the Lords, he succeeded in steering the Television Bill through the Upper House, where some of the toughest debates took place.[7] He also took all important decisions that did not require Cabinet approval.

He was upset when not reappointed by Anthony Eden in April 1955, particularly since at the time some felt that he might be promoted (he was fifty-four), possibly to the Commonwealth Relations Office, an ironic guess as De La Warr and Lord Swinton (Commonwealth Secretary, November 1952–April 1955) were two of the members of Churchill's Government for whom Eden had no further use.[8] David Gammans, the Assistant Postmaster-General, had been hoping for promotion to fill De La Warr's place, and so felt equally disappointed when Charles Hill, a younger man, was appointed.[9] Gammans remained for a few months, but when it became clear that no promotion was forthcoming, resigned in December 1955.[10]

Gammans was not popular with his ministerial colleagues, who regarded him as pushy, nor with many in the Post Office, who found him inconsiderate. One of the few non-public school members of the Government (the others included Reginald Bevins, Harold Watkinson and Patricia Hornsby-Smith), he did not mix easily. He was hard-working, able and ambitious, especially for a position in the Colonial Office or the Commonwealth Relations Office, which reflected his Colonial Service background.[11] He saw more of the work than most junior members of the Government because his Minister was in the Lords, although he performed poorly in the Commons.[12] He supported the Television Bill enthusiastically and became an important influence on his colleagues, in committees and behind the scenes. Maxwell Fyfe, however, carried the main burden of the Bill in the Commons. That aside he spent much time on managerial matters, answering M.P.s' letters and Questions in the House, particularly about telephones. He was ably assisted by Harmar Nicholls,[13] one of the more influential Parliamentary Private Secretaries in this period, and like Gammans a non-public school man.

On matters of policy, and on all Post Office activities, the Postmaster-General was advised by the Post Office Board, consisting of both Ministers and a number of senior officials. At their head was the Director-General, from 1949–55 Sir Alexander Little, a wise, deeply thoughtful man, of a retiring nature, who was highly respected in the office, although few knew him well since he found difficulty in making close friends. His relationship with De La Warr, whom he regarded at times as a novice, was not all it might have been,[14] and neither was he at his happiest with Charles Geddes, General Secretary of the Union of Post Office Workers. Ironically Little's major contribution came on the industrial relations side, where he encouraged closer union consultation with management. According to Sir Donald Sargent, a senior member of Little's team, management/union relations during the early 1950s were said by union leaders to be second to none.[15]

Little's previous experience had been concentrated on the postal rather than the telecommunications side,[16] and he devoted far greater energy to the former.[17] On technical matters he relied in particular on Sir Gordon Radley whose career he encouraged and who succeeded him on his retirement in 1955.[18]

Sir Ben Barnett (Deputy Director-General, 1949–56) lacked the intellectual capacity of Little, and was a more pragmatic and extrovert figure, and hence one De La Warr found more sympathetic. His main experience had been in the field of telecommunications although his interest extended to all aspects of the Post Office's work, and the responsibility for the Television Bill fell to him as deputy responsible, *inter alia*, for broadcasting. He put great energy into it and originated much of the legislation.[19]

De La Warr was only rarely an innovator, but he did oversee the execution of plans already agreed. These included increasing the coverage area for B.B.C. television reception from 63% of the population at the end of 1951 to a planned 97% after completion of thirteen new television stations. In July 1954 the Postmaster-General authorised the B.B.C. to proceed with nine V.H.F. stations giving coverage to 75% of the population in the belief that high frequencies would improve reception. Twenty low-power television transmitters were being installed suitable for the transmission of colour,[20] although colour did not come to the television screens for another fifteen years. An agreement was signed in London in December 1953 between the G.P.O. and the United States and Canadian authorities for the provision of the first transatlantic cable from Scotland to Newfoundland, then the longest submarine telephone cable in the world. De La Warr was also responsible for some of the first policy decisions leading to the establishment of Subscriber Trunk Dialling (S.T.D.), although plans were not fully completed until after his departure. He also showed courage in accepting that a breakaway faction from the Post Office Engineering Union should not be recognised despite the fact that this involved a battle with ministerial colleagues, in particular with Boyd-Carpenter at the Treasury.[21]

The major criticism levelled at the Post Office in these years was the large waiting list for exchange lines. Progress was being made, and the list, which stood at about half a million in December 1951, was reduced to 350,000 within three years,[22] but the position was still regarded as being far from satisfactory.[23] The extent to which the post and telephone services subsidised telegrams was widely criticised, at least until the G.P.O. price increases in 1952-3 (many public enterprises were increasing their charges at this time). Telephone rates were raised less than telegram charges, thereby reducing the amount telephones subsidised telegrams and also other less profitable aspects of the Post Office's work. These price increases were also sufficient to turn a probable deficit into a small profit on commercial accounts.[24]

The Department's major political issue, commercial television, was one of the very few key issues during 1951-5 where the Prime Minister was a genuine waverer.[25] He was rather pushed into supporting commercial television[26] and later, at times, resented it.[27] Churchill rarely watched television or listened to the radio, therefore he had no strong feelings on the subject, although he did have a certain suspicion of the

B.B.C.'s monopoly powers. According to Moran, Churchill was saying in June 1952: 'It is not a subject I feel very strongly about . . . But I am against the monopoly enjoyed by the B.B.C. For eleven years they kept me off the air . . .'[28] Aware that at least half the Cabinet, including Eden, Lord Salisbury, Harry Crookshank and Rab Butler, opposed the plans,[29] he was nevertheless anxious to have a free vote.[30] The Television Act was a result of Party and not Government pressure.

The incoming Conservative Administration had not bargained on having to decide so soon on the future of broadcasting, but one of the first questions that arose was the B.B.C. Charter, due to expire at the end of December. Churchill announced a six-month extension and set up a Cabinet Committee under the chairmanship of Salisbury to formulate a policy, the other members being De La Warr, Maxwell Fyfe and James Stuart. In March, Salisbury was appointed Commonwealth Secretary, and felt he could not cope with the additional burden of the chairmanship of the B.B.C. Committee. Churchill invited Lord Woolton, the Party Chairman, to take over the job,[31] asking him to produce a White Paper on the future of broadcasting which would secure Party agreement. Within six weeks of accepting the job Woolton produced a proposal which he called a compromise: there would be no sponsoring for the B.B.C., which was to be left alone, but competition would come into television, breaking the B.B.C.'s monopoly power with the introduction of commercial television. The conditions of the licence should be laid before Parliament as a safeguard. In forwarding the recommendation to Churchill, Woolton reminded him that the proposals would please those members of the Party particularly anxious to maintain the Conservative principle of opposition to monopolies.[32]

The Cabinet considered the draft White Paper at meetings during the second week of May 1952 and made several important alterations. A key meeting of Conservative backbenchers took place on 8th May, at which Woolton was present, and where they begged him to be definite about declaring that in the Government's view competition in television should be allowed at a later date. As a consequence, Woolton made a major alteration to the draft White Paper, which appeared in the final form:[33] 'might well' in paragraph seven of the draft became 'should', so that it read: 'The present Government have come to the conclusion that in the expanding field of television provision should be made to permit some element of competition.' The Cabinet on 13th May agreed to the change.[34] De La Warr replied accordingly in the debate that month on Lord Reith's motion on broadcasting policy. He delivered the long-awaited statement in July 1953, defining some of the broad principles on which the Government believed that commercial television might operate, and bore the brunt of the heated debate in the Upper House that November. The second reading of the Bill was taken in the early summer of 1954, and received Royal Assent in July.

At the Post Office, credit for preparing the Bill belongs to Barnett, without whom the Bill would have taken a substantially different form.[35] Outside the Department the importance of Mark Chapman Walker (Chief Publicity Officer at Central Office, 1951–5) was central. A powerful operator of people, he was for a number of years Woolton's closest confidant. Chapman Walker early on sensed the prime importance of competitive television, and his partnership with Woolton to secure this end was crucial. At times they pushed Churchill and the Cabinet too hard, as over the publication of the the pamphlet 'There's Free Speech! Why Not Free Switch?' in August 1953, about which Churchill made strong protestations. Churchill wrote to Woolton on 11th August, 1953:

> I am very sorry to see that the enclosed pamphlet has been published by the Central Office. Considering that probably a majority of the Cabinet dislike this process, and that we are trying to stave off the stupid and interested agitation which has brought it into undue prominence, I think the Central Office should have left it alone or consulted the Cabinet beforehand . . . I hope therefore you will recall any of the pamphlets which have not been distributed.

And four days later he added:

> It is difficult to see what good the Conservative Party can get out of this machine-made and, to some extent, interested agitation by members of the 22 Committee . . . On this issue which might [harm us] at by-elections . . . I am sure the only solution would be the free vote and that I understand from Butler is what he is working for.[36]

After the Act was passed in 1954, however, Churchill became more sympathetic to those who favoured a minimum of interference with the Independent Television Authority, as this diary entry of Woolton's makes clear:

> . . . We were discussing the television issue, on which I was opposed to both Salisbury and Eden, and Butler, and supporting Churchill against the P.M.G. Churchill's language to the P.M.G. was harsh indeed. He told him that he thought his political allegiance was getting a little mixed . . . [and that] we should have alienated an important part of the Conservative press . . . the issue was the simple one as to whether we should give instructions to the chairman of the Independent Television Authority, Kenneth Clark, who thought he should

145

not admit any more Conservative intervention . . .[37] We ended up by telling the P.M.G. to write to Sir Kenneth Clark to say we had every confidence in the ability of the I.T.A. to carry out their duties, and we gave them no help at all.[38]

Part 6   The Lord Chancellor and Law Officers

The Lord Chancellor

Winston Churchill had hoped to appoint Lord Asquith of Bishopstone Lord Chancellor, but although urged on by his family, he did not feel well enough to accept. Churchill had known him for a long time, and this fact, rather than a serious assessment of his suitability, accounted for the offer.[1] Asquith, a man of shrewd intellect, had been a Law Lord since earlier in 1951, but was younger and considerably less experienced than Lord Simonds, who was eventually appointed.[2] Asquith's poor health (he died in 1954), and his lack of dynamism made it unlikely that he would have been a good Lord Chancellor, and he almost certainly would have found the political side of the work uncongenial.

Sir David Maxwell Fyfe, some felt, had an undeniable claim, having been Attorney-General in the 'Caretaker Government' (May-July 1945). Churchill decided as early as 1950 that he did not want Maxwell Fyfe as Attorney-General again, having more important work in mind for him. But, as he wanted to retain him in the Commons, the lord chancellorship was out.[3] Instead he appointed him Home Secretary,[4] which Maxwell Fyfe accepted on the understanding that he could become Lord Chancellor at a later date.[5] Some even felt Lord Simon,[6] who had held the post in the War Cabinet, a possibility for the job,[7] but his age (he was a year older than Churchill), effectively excluded him.[8] Simonds himself was not a young man, being appointed a month before his seventieth birthday, his first and only political appointment. He had been an authoritative and decisive Law Lord since 1944, was a distinguished and widely respected lawyer, in a higher class than Maxwell Fyfe or Sir Walter Monckton,[9] and the legal profession expressed great satisfaction at his appointment. It is likely that either Lord Salisbury[10] or Maxwell Fyfe[11] suggested his name to Churchill. Simonds was surprised to be asked, and assumed it would be for the duration of the Administration.

Although an outstandingly good lawyer and judge, and a fierce and formidable cross-examiner, Simonds proved an unspectacular Lord Chancellor. He never felt comfortable involved in politics: 'an exhibition which is distressing to blokes like you and me' was how he described one of Churchill's provocative performances in the House.[12] Simonds, like Lord Gardiner (1964–70), came to the Woolsack without previous political experience, a considerable disadvantage.[13] Churchill had a great liking for him and faith in his advice on law and constitutional principles, but never thought of him as a politician.[14] In Cabinet he was inclined to be diffident, seldom speaking except when asked for an opinion.[15] He tended to be hindered at times rather than helped by the presence of the two other eminent lawyers: both Maxwell Fyfe and Monckton would quite often dissent from Simonds' view, resulting in a difference of legal opinion within the Cabinet,[16] although he never complained about this.

His strength as Lord Chancellor lay in other directions. The key features of his period were the highest standards of probity and correctness he brought to the office. He regarded the integrity of the bench as inviolate, the preservation of that integrity as of cardinal importance and earned the confidence of both the bench and the bar. He looked after the judges and in particular managed to carry his case on their salary, over which he encountered considerable opposition in Cabinet, even though there had been no increase for more than a hundred and twenty years, when the salary of High Court judges was fixed at £5,000. He wrote a Cabinet paper on the subject, a powerful piece of advocacy written in fine language (he was a great stylist), which was responsible for persuading Churchill of the need for the increase.

A Bill was introduced on 13th March, 1953, and the Second Reading in the House of Commons was planned for 26th March. But at the Cabinet meeting on 20th March a long discussion on the future of the Bill took place, and despite a persuasive speech by Churchill in the House on 23rd March, followed by an acrimonious meeting with the officers of the 1922 Committee, the decision was taken by a meeting of Ministers that evening to postpone the Bill until after the Easter recess.[17] The problem was the Government's plan for a tax free allowance which brought opposition from many of its own supporters as well as Liberal and Labour members.[18] The Government solved the impasse by introducing a Bill on 4th November, 1953, which increased judges' salaries by £3,000, an increase of £734 per annum after tax.[19] The Conservative backbenchers remained critical, but did not force a division, and the Bill passed into law in April 1954. As a show of his own personal integrity, Simonds did not take the increase due to him.[20]

Simonds was courteous to all he met, and popular in the small Lord Chancellor's Office, then little more than a large Private Office. He had a happy relationship with Sir Albert Napier, the Permanent Secretary until 1954. Napier had done much to found the modern Lord Chancellor's Office, adapting it to post-war needs with great skill and patience.

He had not enjoyed smooth relations with either Simon (1940–5) or Lord Jowitt (1945–51), so he was delighted that his last years as Permanent Secretary were to be spent with a man he had known since they were at New College, Oxford, and with whom he enjoyed such a warm friendship.[21] When he retired in 1954 the deputy, Sir George Coldstream, took his place.

An important aspect of Simonds' period as Lord Chancellor was his great friendship with Salisbury, by whom he was much influenced. There was complete mutual trust and affection and each frequently sought the advice of the other. They worked together in the House of Lords (Salisbury as Leader, Simonds as Speaker), making a highly effective team. Simonds was well liked in the House, where he made short precise speeches. Along with some other Conservatives, he distrusted the former Labour Lord Chancellor, Jowitt.

As a lawyer Simonds was a conservative traditionalist. Certainly he had no liking for innovators, such as Sir Tom Denning, then a Lord Justice of Appeal, and admired greatly men of more traditional stamp such as the Law Lords Normand (1947–53) and Reid (1948–75). But his judgments, once considered conservative, have in recent years tended to be regarded as less so.[22]

Simonds had the keenest intellect of any Lord Chancellor since the war, on a par with Lord Hailsham (1970–4 and 1979 on).[23] Surprised to be offered the Woolsack in 1951, he was even more surprised when asked to resign in October 1954. He was deeply hurt by the manner of his dismissal – he had no indication it was coming – and felt he was being treated as a pawn to Maxwell Fyfe. Churchill himself was uneasy about it, and asked Salisbury to tell Simonds he was no longer required.[24] Perhaps his lack of experience of the realities of political life made his sudden dismissal more painful than it might otherwise have been. Reverting to being a Law Lord itself (he succeeded Lord Porter as a Lord of Appeal) did not upset him: '[I] am well content to return to my proper sphere. I doubt whether one ever gets really acclimatised to the political world unless one takes to it pretty young,' he wrote to Lord Cherwell.[25] In his memoirs Maxwell Fyfe wrote that when Churchill asked him to become Lord Chancellor in the late summer of 1954, it was 'to my great surprise'.[26] This was probably not so. As early as April 1954 Brendan Bracken had written to Monckton in his forthright style 'remember that [Maxwell Fyfe] is eager to become L.C.'[27] Indeed according to some witnesses it was Maxwell Fyfe's pressure that led directly to Simonds' retirement.[28]

Lord Kilmuir, as Maxwell Fyfe became, was an entirely different type of Lord Chancellor, a more prominent figure and more political. He took an active interest in other issues in Cabinet,[29] and was given a large amount of work dealing with broader fields.[30] He was a well-known figure in the country and was constantly being invited to make speeches on political and legal matters, which he invariably undertook.

Kilmuir, because his appointment came late in the life of the Government, had little opportunity to make much mark before the May 1955 General Election. He had been much respected on the Northern Circuit and proved to be even more popular at the bar than Simonds had been. He was felt to be an able, if not an outstanding lawyer, and to have done a good job at Nuremberg, where he was Deputy Chief Prosecutor, 1945–6. He took to the Woolsack quickly, showing great interest both in his new responsibilities and in the office, where his enthusiasm and personable manner soon earned him the active loyalty of the officials. Both Simonds and Kilmuir enjoyed good relations with Lord Goddard (Lord Chief Justice, 1946–58), though of the two Goddard was closer to Simonds, whose strong support of the judges he greatly admired.

The Law Officers

These were amongst the last offices to be declared after the Election. John Foster was probably the best of the available barristers in the Commons, but he was not chosen. Perhaps the Whips felt a safer man than the rather unconventional, colourful Foster was required, who, to his surprise, was then appointed junior Minister to the Commonwealth Relations Office.[31] Monckton, Solicitor-General in the 'Caretaker Government',[32] had been appointed Minister of Labour so was unavailable, and Selwyn Lloyd, who had concentrated more on politics than law, had been snapped up by Eden for the Foreign Office.[33] Another possibility was Sir Lionel Heald, of whom Simonds had formed a favourable impression as a senior member of the Patent Bar. A distinguished lawyer with a considerable practice, Heald only entered the House in 1950, but immediately made his mark with a Private Member's Bill to abolish the common informer procedure which had received Royal Assent earlier in 1951. He had been engaged in important patent cases after the war and had been a member of the Bar Council since 1947,[34] but had not expected Churchill's offer when it came in 1951.[35]

Dissension arose, however, over the appointment of Sir Reginald Manningham-Buller as Solicitor-General, who was felt to be not well enough known at the bar,[36] but those who disapproved of his appointment soon revised their attitude once his aptitude became obvious. Yet overall, there was speculation in late 1951 and early 1952 as to whether

Churchill's three gifted lawyers could make good their political reputations.[37]

Heald was not an outstanding Attorney-General, but he did good work for the Crown and put up a thoroughly capable performance. Without the political sense or vigour of Manningham-Buller, he did not command the attention of the House, and being a non-political Attorney-General he thus had less influence than others, notably Sir Hartley Shawcross (1945–51), and Manningham-Buller himself (1954–62). Heald had a quiet time: Churchill, with whom he got on well, told him that it was his business to look after the legal side, and said he definitely did not want any legal quibbles. Heald took the view that a Law Officer should not deal with policy but merely with legal questions, and there was nothing during 1951 to 1954 to which he seriously objected.[38] When called to Cabinet to give an opinion, he spoke briefly and to the point and created a good impression there.

Heald worked well with Simonds, whom he liked, though was not as close to him as Manningham-Buller latterly became. The relationship between the Lord Chancellor and the Law Officers of the day is delicate, and not always easy.[39] It appears to have produced few problems for Simonds. Heald worked well with Manningham-Buller, although the combination was perhaps less effective than Shawcross and Sir Frank Soskice before them, or their successors, Manningham-Buller and Sir Harry Hylton-Foster, the team which took over on Heald's retirement in October 1954.

It was entirely Heald's own decision to retire. He had been happy in the job, but feeling that its demands were not those best suited to his undoubted gifts as a lawyer, he had made it known in July that he was ready to resign when convenient.[40] In the spring of 1954 a plan had been mooted to make Monckton Attorney-General with a seat in the Cabinet,[41] as he was finding the Ministry of Labour a strain, and Anthony Eden and Patrick Buchan-Hepburn were anxious to keep him in the Commons. In the event he remained at Labour, and Heald stayed for the time being as Attorney-General.

In the October 1954 reshuffle, Manningham-Buller moved up from Solicitor to Attorney-General, his own place being taken by Hylton-Foster. Some doubts were expressed about whether these changes, along with Maxwell Fyfe's elevation to the House of Lords, would weaken the Government's conduct of legal business in the Commons,[42] but within a few months these were brushed aside. Manningham-Buller had done a good job as Solicitor-General, as he did in all his offices,[43] not because of an outstanding intellect, but due to his ability to put everything he had into the task at hand. He was a man of immense industry, tough and an effective debater, but at this stage not especially popular on either side of the House. One of the adroitest Law Officers since the war, over the years he came to have increasing influence. He worked well with Hylton-Foster, a milder man whose rise from political obscurity had been swift, having, like Heald, only entered the House in 1950. The new Solicitor-General was a highly able lawyer, who had a first-class practice at the bar in the North-East Circuit of which he was Leader. He was able to handle complex legal matters with great skill, and made a good start, being later appointed Speaker in succession to 'Shakes' Morrison.

It is not easy to assess the impact of Law Officers on policy but certainly under Heald and the early months of Manningham-Buller's tenure it was scarcely significant. They had a difficult task, coming so soon after the highly successful combination of Shawcross and Soskice,[44] and were to some extent overshadowed by them.

Part 7 The Ministry of Works

Three factors brought the Ministry of Works into the limelight in the 1951–5 Government: the support it gave Harold Macmillan's housing drive until the building licensing scheme came to an end in 1953; the Coronation; and Sir David Eccles' determination to gain more public finance for the arts, culminating in the Historic Buildings and Ancient Monuments Act of 1953.

The Ministry was created in its new form in 1945, and although its functions as a 'sponsoring' Ministry dwindled with the disappearance of controls from 1950, it was still a 'production' as well as a 'common services' Department.[1] The production authority for the construction and building materials industries, it therefore held responsibility for the Government building programme, repair of war damage, maintenance of Government property, royal palaces and parks, and ancient monuments. In addition, since the war, it was the Department responsible for the licensing system which went with the building industry, for which a regional organisation had been set up in twelve areas.[2]

Eccles was one of the younger men known to Winston Churchill, who he insisted should be given a job.[3] Some of his colleagues felt Eccles was disgruntled to be offered such a lowly post,[4] but this was incorrect. After initial disappointment he was pleased not only to head a Ministry of his own as his first job, but also to be given one which brought him into contact with two great interests, the arts and finance.[5]

Indeed, a profile in the *Observer* at Coronation time summed him up: 'Elegantly groomed in clothes that seem a shade on the small side, with a

151

breast pocket handkerchief well displayed, and a dash of perfume . . . a taste for beautiful things, a lively interest in people, literature, and art, and much administrative gusto' it felt him ideally cast for the job, even if he was to cause upset at Coronation time by referring to the Queen as his leading lady. His service as Economic Adviser in the Ministry of Production (1942–3), where he had gained practical experience of industrial organisation, plus his own business experience, provided additional advantages. He had one of the most agile minds of any Minister of Works,[6] but suffered from an unfortunate habit of appearing conceited and making people feel that he regarded his policy as the only possible one.[7] This was only a mannerism, however, and those who worked closely with him in the Ministry found him a pleasant colleague, and a good Minister.[8] He was also fortunate to have such an able Permanent Secretary, Sir Harold Emmerson, with whom he got on so well.

The main change of direction in the Ministry concerned the support given to the housing drive. The Conservatives in 1951 inherited a number of controls left over from the war which hampered house building, in particular controls over labour supply and materials. When Macmillan arrived at Housing he looked to the Ministry of Works to abolish unnecessary controls and licensing, and to see that the bricks and other components would be produced and distributed correctly.[9] Eccles was only too ready to press ahead and did not need encouragement. The officials responded well to the new political initiative, and in no way resisted. There were frequent meetings between Eccles and Macmillan to investigate ways of improving the organisation and efficiency of the construction industry, and also between officials of both Ministries, with the licensing work being done at the regional offices. Without doubt, Eccles' energy and enthusiasm played an indispensable part in the success of Macmillan's housing drive, as the latter readily acknowledged.[10]

The Ministry of Works was only one of several Departments and organisations working together on the Coronation under the general direction of the Duke of Norfolk, the Earl Marshal. The Ministry was wholly responsible for setting the stage, preparing the Abbey, designing and building the annexe, seating in the Abbey for nearly 8,000 people and erecting stands for 120,000 people along the major part of the route. In this work, considerable use was made of the plans made for the 1937 Coronation, but preparations still took over a year. Eccles managed the job very well, paying especial interest to the artistic side, choosing designs and colours, leaving the Department to work on the details.[11]

This same artistic sensibility accounted for his espousal of the need to support the arts. As Minister he felt art had been greatly neglected since the war and constantly urged the Treasury, the Department responsible, to provide more money. This was by no means popular with many in the Government who felt that available funds should be channelled into less esoteric uses. But Eccles pushed on stubbornly and forcibly, and, after a speech in the House at the beginning of February 1953, Crookshank commented: 'Heard Eccles – he went far beyond Cabinet brief.'[12] On 7th February he announced that the Government wished to spend about £250,000 a year on the preservation of historic houses, and on 14th May added that the Government would spend an additional sum of £500,000 over five years on the acquisition of certain threatened historic houses. He had had to fight a battle in Cabinet against Salisbury and the traditionalists who favoured tax relief for owners to enable them to make improvements. Eccles, however, felt that this would never pass through the Commons, and pressed successfully for his own plan, of awarding grants for specific improvement plans. The Historic Buildings and Ancient Monuments Act was passed at the end of July that year, which gave the Minister certain fresh powers to help preservation work and set up three Historic Buildings Councils for England, Scotland and Wales. These sound achievements owed much to the single-mindedness and foresight of the Minister.

Eccles was promoted to Minister of Education, with a seat in Cabinet, in the October 1954 reshuffle, to be succeeded at the Ministry of Works by Nigel Birch, another highly adept man with a keen interest in economics. But whereas opportunities presented themselves for Eccles to make full use of his talents at the Ministry, Birch was under-utilised. Although surprised and pleased to be appointed, he found little work of political importance.[13] The executive job, which is all it had become, was far better suited to Patrick Buchan-Hepburn, who was appointed in December 1955.[14] Birch was at the Ministry an insufficient time to make much mark, but was found to be an able administrator and was well respected.

The Ministry was one of the larger Departments with two Deputy Secretaries and a non-industrial staff of 12,000, a very high proportion of whom were professional people.[15] There was never much however for a junior Minister to do, as both Hugh Molson (1951–3) and then Reginald Bevins (1953–7) found.[16] Efforts were later made to abolish this post but the Whips insisted on keeping it on.[17]

Chapter 5   Economic Policy I

Part 1 The Treasury

The identity of the Chancellor in the Conservative Government had been a matter for speculation. It is probable – although not certain – that Oliver Stanley would have been appointed, had he not died in December 1950,[1] but thereafter many thought Oliver Lyttelton, who succeeded him as Chairman of the Conservative Party's Finance Committee, the most likely.[2] Sir John Anderson, who had held the job between September 1943 and July 1945, was also considered a possibility after Stanley's death, but since he ceased to be a member of the House of Commons in 1950, he was effectively out of the running.[3] The only other possible contender was Harry Crookshank, a principal Opposition speaker on economic subjects after 1945, but Winston Churchill never regarded him warmly.[4] In the event, Rab Butler was given the job after, apparently, Lord Woolton had turned it down. As Woolton recorded in his diary:

> When Churchill appointed Butler to the office I asked him if he was not making a mistake. He had some doubts about it . . . Winston could not find anybody else. He knew that John Anderson had not been a success there; he dare not appoint Oliver Lyttelton because Oliver's reputation in the City was rather that of a gambler and market operator. He had asked me whether I would go to the Commons and become Chancellor of the Exchequer if he made the necessary law, and I had refused because I knew it would be so unpopular in the House of Commons to bring a peer in to fill a recognised House of Commons job, and so he fell back on Butler.[5]

Lyttelton himself ascribed his rejection to his poor performance in the House, seen in the Finance Bill debate in 1951, with the Chief Whip in particular opposed to his appointment.[6] Yet Churchill, under the heavy influence of Anthony Eden, felt that Lyttelton, with his City interests, would be likely to antagonise Labour. Churchill apparently told Butler: 'Anthony is not going to have Oliver Lyttelton who is absolutely tainted with the City. We couldn't have a Chancellor in the House of Commons

154

who was a City man.'[7] Lyttelton was disappointed, though he says he had for a long time before thought the Treasury unlikely.[8] He supported Butler loyally, and never showed his disappointment, even to those close to him,[9] although this was the second time he had been near to becoming Chancellor, having been considered by Churchill after Kingsley Wood's sudden death in 1943.[10] As he later wrote to Churchill: 'I was furious when the *Observer* said I had groused about not being sent to the Treasury because it was entirely untrue.'[11] Had he been appointed, with his firm character and his business background (he was Chairman of Associated Electrical Industries, whereas Butler was originally an academic).[12] it is possible that economic policy would have followed a very different course.

The position of the Treasury had been considerably enhanced since Churchill's last period as Prime Minister. In particular, when Sir Stafford Cripps was appointed Chancellor by Clement Attlee in November 1947, he retained responsibility for supervision of economic policy and brought with him the Central Economic Planning Staff, the Economic Information Unit and the Regional Boards for Industry from his previous position as Minister for Economic Affairs. For the first time control over the Budget, national economic policy, imports, overseas finance and the investment programme were concentrated in one hand, all the more important once the Government had accepted the responsibility of maintaining full employment. This, however, only served to increase Churchill's suspicion of the Treasury, and he returned in 1951 determined to counter its influence.

On Butler, Churchill had reservations to overcome. He was a man of Munich, distrusted by Party patricians such as Lord Salisbury,[13] and there is no doubt that Churchill found him definitely odd. Butler gave the impression that he was surprised by the appointment,[14] but in fact he had thought it likely.[15] Churchill said it did not matter that Butler was not an economist, since he was going to appoint Sir Arthur Salter, 'the best economist since Jesus Christ', to help him.[16] Churchill brought back Lord Cherwell, partly to provide him with alternative economic advice, and also appointed a new body, the Treasury Ministerial Advisory Committee, containing senior Ministers, to keep a check on Butler, and to provide him with economic advice to supplement what he would receive from official sources.[17] Churchill even tried to appoint Anderson 'overlord' over the Treasury, Board of Trade and Ministry of Supply.[18] Seldom can any Chancellor have been so potentially constrained.

With these safeguards around him, and little background knowledge of Treasury work, it was no surprise that Butler proved a cautious and conservative Chancellor, who according to officials, made little impact on arrival and did not appear to hold any particular point of view.[19] At first he seemed uncertain both of his position and his relationship with Churchill, who made no secret of the fact that he did not have complete confidence in his new Chancellor.[20] But Butler was not to be cowed. He displayed two gifts in particular: his 'Rolls Royce' mind (before he became an M.P. he was a Cambridge don) and his skill in the House. According to Henry Channon (admittedly an admirer), 'He is the ablest Parliamentarian of our time, cold, courteous, suave and seemingly simple, he outwits everyone . . .'[21] His non-economic background (unlike his immediate predecessor, Hugh Gaitskell, who was a trained economist) meant that his political instinct often dictated his choice and led him to reach the right decision.[22]

Butler was popular with his officials because he listened to advice, beginning with the premise that his advisers would probably know more about the subject than he. They, however, objected that he disliked making up his mind too firmly, or taking any decision he could not go back on.[23] Coupled with an ambiguity and a not uncommon liking for appearing incalculable, it could sometimes be difficult to understand what he meant.[24] He also worried his officials, especially towards the end of his time at the Treasury, by his unwillingness to commit himself on policy for the Budget, or to apply his mind to the Budget speech until it was almost upon them.

Butler accepted the view that one should use fiscal and monetary policy to try to keep the economy at a fairly even level of employment. He was in no sense an innovator,[25] and but for the April 1955 Budget, he did not let his desire to lower taxes get the better of him. He brought great intellect and energy to the office, and to the extent to which the growing economic fortunes of Britain from 1951–5 were due to any individual, Butler deserves a large share of praise.[26] He managed to make the most of favourable circumstances, and in terms of economic indicators was the most successful post-war Chancellor. Unemployment never rose above 2% nor inflation above 3% from 1952 to the 1955 General Election.

In many ways too sensitive to be a comfortable Chancellor, Butler was wounded by criticism, displaying none of the toughness of his successor, Harold Macmillan. Like Eden, he was vain, but unlike many vain men could laugh at his own vanity. He was shy, but despite this, many who worked with him at the Treasury grew attached to him, encouraged to do their best for him through his great personal charm. Following on from Cripps and Gaitskell, both of whom earned the wide respect of the officials, it was not easy for Butler, who was perhaps more admired by the Treasury Ministers than by its officials. If there was a powerful

Minister who wanted something, he would not infrequently get his way against Butler, in particular Harold Macmillan and Eden, on those rare occasions they wanted something. But most spending Ministers, Florence Horsbrugh, Osbert Peake, Iain Macleod, Derick Heathcoat Amory, Lord Alexander of Tunis, Butler found entirely manageable.

He suffered under a double blow in 1953–4. His mother, to whom he was particularly close, died after a drawn-out illness in mid-1953.[27] A bigger blow was to come the following year, when, on 9th December, his wife Sydney Courtauld died.[28] Many felt that she added steel to his character which he otherwise lacked. Certainly she was a strong character, dominant although not intellectual, and undoubtedly she did give him an edge, and aided him considerably through her critical faculties. Some think her death created a turning-point in his life, after which he became increasingly indecisive and vain.[29] There is, however, a risk of exaggerating its effect: her protracted cancer put a severe strain on him,[30] which was at least relieved when her suffering ended. But two other factors were more important in explaining the undoubted difference in the pre-1955 from the post-1957 Butler. The lesser was his being passed over in favour of Macmillan as Prime Minister in January 1957, the greater was a serious viral infection which began in 1955 and lasted throughout 1956; afterwards he was unable to work at the same tempo. Some of the fight went out of him, never to return. One can justly say the loss of his wife made him more introverted and sensitive to criticism, but it did not seem to impair his judgment,[31] even in the Budget which followed in April 1955, where he was under pressure from Eden and received conflicting Treasury advice. It is likely it would have proved difficult for Butler even in ideal circumstances.[32]

One of Butler's greatest strengths was his ability to choose the right people on whom to rely (as he proved at the Research Department from 1945–51). Yet he relied less on his able band of junior Ministers, than on some officials. Salter became Minister of State for Economic Affairs, a post which had existed for a while with a different function under the Attlee Government.[33] The job was the same as the Economic Secretary's and after Salter's retirement in November 1952, the office of Minister of State for Economic Affairs was abolished, and Salter's replacement, Reginald Maudling, became, simply, Economic Secretary.[34] Salter had been Independent M.P. for Oxford University from 1937–50 and Churchill persuaded him, against his own wishes, to stand again as a Conservative in 1951.[35] After the Election, Churchill offered him either an independent Economic Ministry of his own (had he accepted, it is difficult to imagine what would have happened) or second Minister in the Treasury. Salter, not keen on administrative upheaval, favoured the latter,[36] which he accepted on condition he could have access to the full Cabinet whenever necessary.[37]

It was not a happy appointment. Although a man of considerable intellectual distinction and broad experience (he had been Director of the Economic and Finance Section of the League of Nations from 1919–20 and 1922–31), he was already seventy years old and clearly past his best. Relations with Butler, who had little use for his advice, were cool.[38] Butler later said: '[He] was very trying, because he didn't really agree with very much I did.'[39] Ideal to work for, Salter did not feel easy with colleagues on the same level nor with superiors. He had, undoubtedly, been a first-class economist in his day, but was no longer fully in tune with modern economic thought, although still an expert on overseas finance matters. Neither did Salter have a private line to Churchill, who, once the appointment was made, forgot about him.[40] He performed poorly in the House of Commons, tending to lecture Members, which meant, in practice, therefore, that he was used less and less.[41] The burden of speaking fell more on the Financial Secretary, John Boyd-Carpenter, and even Maudling, then Parliamentary Secretary at Civil Aviation, the first time a Parliamentary Secretary from another Department was allowed to speak for the Treasury.[42] In the debate in the House on the Finance Bill in 1952 Maudling helped Butler with distinction. Salter undermined his own reputation in the House when in winding up a routine Treasury Bill he gave the Opposition and press the impression that further cuts were on the way.[43]

It was thus no surprise when Salter left the Treasury after only one year, and was appointed Minister of Materials in succession to Lord Swinton. Maudling was appointed Economic Secretary, a disappointment to him as he had been hoping to retain Salter's grander title.[44] Butler had known Maudling since he joined the Conservative Research Department when in Opposition. Although not trained as an economist, he was delegated to look after economic and financial matters, and had more influence on the economic thinking of the Chancellor than many Economic Secretaries; even so, this amounted to little. Officials found him highly intelligent, and painstaking with his work until he became adept at it, but he did not assert himself and saw little of actual policy making.[45] He was good in the House, able to make a speech at short notice, and highly regarded by his fellow Ministers. He showed his calibre mainly on the overseas side: exchange control was then the responsibility of the Economic Secretary, and he undertook a number of overseas missions deputising for Butler.[46]

So highly regarded was he that Eden had intended in April 1955 to appoint him President of the Board of Trade to succeed Peter Thorneycroft, about whom opinions varied.[47] Eden was persuaded against this move at the last moment, partly by Butler, and so instead Maudling received the still sizeable promotion to Minister of Supply. He was succeeded as Economic Secretary by Sir Edward Boyle, at thirty-one years of age the youngest Minister in the Government. Noticed already for his intellect and charm, he had served for nine months as Parliamentary Secretary at the Ministry of Supply. Despite his lack of experience, he was listened to carefully and was closer personally to Butler than any other junior Minister at the Treasury.[48]

The post of Economic Secretary, founded only in 1947, was junior to the long-established job of Financial Secretary, which also carried a heavier burden of work. Butler had originally hoped to appoint Selwyn Lloyd, his recruit, and, one who impressed him as principal lieutenant on 'Britain Strong and Free'.[49] Lloyd had been tipped for an economic job,[50] but Eden, wanting a non-specialist at the Foreign Office, asked him first. So Butler chose Boyd-Carpenter, who had made a name as an acute critic of the Labour Government since 1945.[51] His first post was a successful appointment, Boyd-Carpenter's qualities being admirably suited to the job of Financial Secretary. He was hard-working, extremely competent, good with figures and strong in the House: Butler found him utterly dependable.[52] The job, which dealt with revenue and expenditure questions (except defence expenditure) and had responsibility for contacts with the Boards of Inland Revenue and Customs and Excise, was the forerunner of the job of Chief Secretary, although without the latter's powers. The position did not require a deep grasp of economics, but strength combined with understanding, and an ability to see issues broadly: with his acute, lawyer's mind, Boyd-Carpenter provided these.

In July 1954 Boyd-Carpenter succeeded Alan Lennox-Boyd as Minister of Transport, and Henry Brooke, at fifty-one, was appointed Financial Secretary. It was his first ministerial job, for although an M.P. since 1937 he had been Conservative Leader on the London County Council since 1945. Butler had known Brooke since their schooldays at Marlborough College.[53] Although abler intellectually than Boyd-Carpenter, he found himself out of his depth for the first few months, but came to have increasing influence during his two and a half year period as Financial Secretary.

As his Parliamentary Private Secretary, Butler chose Hubert Ashton, who was fifty-three and married to Gaitskell's sister, but had not entered the House until 1950, having spent most of his career with the Burmah Oil Company. They were fond of each other. Ashton did not take part in economic discussions at all, but Butler liked having him around because he was uncomplicated and Butler could relax in his company. It was a brave choice: some in the Party felt that Butler might have been better served by a younger and more ambitious man.[54]

Ministers carried much less weight with Butler than certain officials. Sir Edward Bridges, the Permanent Secretary and also Head of the Civil Service since 1945, had seriously considered retiring in 1951, but remained, partly after persuasion by Churchill.[55] With his experience also as Secretary of the Cabinet from 1938–46, he was without any doubt the most experienced official in Whitehall. He would attend most general Treasury discussions, especially at Budget time when he was Chairman of the Budget Committee.[56] But his relationship with Butler left much to be desired. Though slightly in awe of his Permanent Secretary, Butler would become irritated if he was not there when he wanted him: at times the dissatisfaction ran both ways.[57] During the Conservative Party Annual Conference in 1954 an unfavourable article appeared in *The Economist*. Butler phoned from Blackpool to speak to Bridges to 'blow-off' about it, late in the afternoon of 9th October. A junior official answered the phone in Bridges' office, told Bridges who it was, and Bridges replied, 'Tell him I've gone home.' The official was left to listen to Butler's stormy protests.[58] Bridges, with his calm and orderly mind, could, at times, find Butler's vagaries somewhat tedious. Whether the job was too much for one man is a question on which witnesses during 1951–5 had different opinions. Lord Armstrong of Sanderstead for example said: 'From the Chancellor's point of view it was ridiculous that when he wanted to see his Permanent Secretary on important business he could not do so because he was engaged on other work.'[59] Lord Croham, however, later commented that the combined job was not too much for one man provided he did not want to travel with the Chancellor, which Bridges did not. Bridges was always there in a crisis if Butler needed him.[60] Bridges was not an economist, and would have found himself ill at ease in a complex economic discussion. Consequently he had little direct impact on the economic thinking of the Chancellor, except in the 1955 Budgets.[61]

Bridges was regarded with a mixture of affection and awe throughout the Treasury. He liked to know what advice was being given to Treasury Ministers and what decisions had been taken, but did not attempt to be sole or principal adviser to the Chancellor on every subject, and accordingly encouraged his Second and Third Secretaries to report direct to the Chancellor.[62] Bridges regarded the economists in the Treasury as the technical experts, and if they could not explain their actions, they were no good. He confined his interventions almost solely to those occasions when he thought advice wrong, or when it had been put forward without sufficient consultation either within the Treasury or with other Departments. His main contributions as Permanent Secretary of the Treasury had come earlier. He persuaded the senior Treasury officials to see the Budget as an instrument designed to control the whole economy, and to accept the attendant integration into the Treasury of the Central Economic Planning Staff and Economic Section.[63] He was without doubt an outstanding Permanent Secretary of the Treasury, at least until 1951.

Four Second Secretaries served under Bridges. The senior, Sir Bernard Gilbert, had held the job since 1944, and was responsible for the supply side. Gilbert, unlike Bridges, was a man full of ideas, a mathematician with a very keen mind, sceptical of both Keynes and controls, and critical of expenditure. But by 1951 he was growing tired, his brilliance turning increasingly towards blocking rather than encouraging new thinking.[64] Gilbert intended to retire in 1951 when he was sixty but Bridges told him that he could not continue himself at the Treasury unless Gilbert consented to stay on.[65] In late 1951 Gilbert, like Bridges, fell ill, but unlike Bridges, Gilbert never recovered his full health.[66] He became deputy to the Permanent Secretary in November 1953, when Butler felt the advice he was receiving too diffuse, so he made Gilbert responsible for co-ordinating economic policy, embracing the work of both the home economy and the overseas finance sides, and channelling their advice to him.[67]

Gilbert was also put in nominal charge of the Central Economic Planning Staff when Sir Edwin Plowden left, but took little interest in it, and also became Chairman of the Economic Planning Board.[68] Butler relied on him more than on any other Second Secretary (apart from Sir Leslie Rowan), particularly on matters of internal finance.[69] Gilbert, however, became increasingly stubborn and dictatorial,[70] though his great experience always proved helpful in unexpected situations. Like Bridges, he remained throughout the Butler chancellorship.

Sir Wilfred Eady, the other 'old man' at the top of the Treasury, a Second Secretary since 1942, looked after home finance until his retirement in April 1952. He had by now little influence, having been in a backwater since the collapse of the early convertibility scheme under the Labour Government, which had rather discredited him. Like Bridges, he never pretended to have a great economic or financial brain, while the war and recovery had also taken a heavy toll on his reserves of energy. Some felt Bridges made a mistake in retaining Eady and Gilbert after 1951.

Following Eady's retirement, Gilbert also took on his responsibilities until Sir Herbert Brittain's appointment in November 1953 as Second Secretary responsible for the divisions concerned with home finance and

161

supply expenditure. He was a tremendous worker, often staying late in the office. He had an acute, if unspectacular, mind and Butler liked him because he was so dependable.[71] Indeed, Butler had a tendency to prefer the reliable type to the man with flair.

Rowan, a man of great flair, was an exception, and influenced Butler more than any other Second Secretary.[72] At forty-three, he was one of the brightest young men at the Treasury,[73] having been a Second Secretary from 1947 to 1949, when he went to Washington as Economic Minister. He returned in 1951 to take over from Sir Henry Wilson Smith as Head of the Treasury's Overseas Finance Division. An athletic,[74] emphatic man with a tendency to be dogmatic, he was undisputed master on matters of overseas finance. 'I would put Rowan's influence on me and on the Treasury as very high,' said Butler, who, in particular, relied on him for advice and speech-writing at international conferences, an area where Butler himself was not strong.[75] Rowan had a marked influence on the 1952 Budget, but when Butler thought he had advised him wrongly on the 1952 convertibility issue, his influence trailed off slightly. On two occasions, his views were of especial importance: the Abadan oil nationalisation issue from 1951–4, and the so-called 'Robot' scheme for convertibility in 1952,[76] to whose title he gave the first two letters (RObot). He was very keen to move ahead to greater freedom on the foreign exchange market and was particularly concerned with relations with the United States and the Commonwealth. He held aloof from general economic discussions except where they touched upon the balance of payments, and in those he did join, expressed scepticism of increasing Government expenditure.

The remaining Second Secretary, Sir Thomas Padmore, had responsibility for establishments; this area after 1968, became the Civil Service Department. Another of the bright younger men, a few months junior in age to Rowan,[77] he had been in the Cabinet Office since September 1951, expecting, until Churchill's arrival, to succeed Sir Norman Brook as Secretary. Early in 1952 Bridges told Churchill he wanted Padmore back in the Treasury, and could not allow both him and Brook to remain in one place. He returned to do the same work he had done as Third Secretary, but now with increased status. Butler did not greatly concern himself with the establishment side, but had complete confidence in Padmore.[78]

As Butler became more experienced his faith in the Treasury Second Secretaries lessened. Indeed it was partly on his advice that when Bridges retired in 1956 he was succeeded by a Foreign Office man, Sir Roger Makins, a factor which may have precipitated the departure of Rowan from the Treasury in 1958, when only fifty.[79]

Butler relied more heavily on Plowden, the Chief Planning officer. Plowden had intended to retire in November 1951, and his place was to be taken by Brook, who was also to be appointed deputy to the Permanent Secretary at the Treasury.[80] Two events happened to prevent this. The first was Churchill's desire not to lose Brook as Secretary to the Cabinet, the other Butler's reluctance to lose Plowden, with whom he had been friendly since before he became Chancellor. The Central Economic Planning Staff had been set up in March 1947[81] to develop long-term plans for the use of the country's manpower and resources. Its staff was small.

> 'All the time I was there, I kept in mind the need to keep the Planning Staff very small,' [Plowden later said]. 'I know from my previous experience in Whitehall that the best way was to work with it rather than against it. My objective was to integrate it into the Whitehall machine and in particular into the Treasury. In that way we did not duplicate the work done by parts of the Treasury and other Departments, but worked with and through them.'[82]

Plowden was also Chairman (until 1953) of the new Economic Planning Board, set up in 1947 to promote contact and understanding between Government and private enterprise.[83] The Planning Staff had a chequered history. When Cripps became Minister for Co-ordination of Economic Affairs in September 1947, they were transferred from the Cabinet Office under the Lord President to Cripps' new Department. That experiment lasted only six weeks; when Cripps became Chancellor in November they moved with him.[84]

The Planning Staff, however, did not develop along the lines that Cripps had sketched in the House of Commons in March 1947, when he visualised a new form of co-ordination.[85] They were much concerned in negotiations for the Marshall Plan, which required forward projections from the countries involved, including Britain, but after 1951, and especially after Plowden left in 1953, the functions gradually withered away or were absorbed in new machinery set up to deal with the O.E.E.C. The Staff were also keenly involved with the annual Economic Surveys,[86] but these became increasingly general,[87] and were eventually abolished in 1962. In practice, the Planning Staff became little more than a division of the Treasury, its main task to scrutinise the possible consequences of specific departmental plans for the economy as a whole. Its effective end occurred when William Strath, the Third Secretary in day-to-day charge of the Planning Staff, left the Treasury in 1955.[88]

163

The Economic Planning Board similarly declined in importance because Ministers were never prepared to delegate real responsibility to it. It was already largely ineffectual when the Conservatives came to power, and it suited them to keep the Board quiet, in an advisory role, until it gradually withered away in 1961.[89] Thus no decisive move away from planning occurred in the Treasury after the arrival of the Conservative Government in 1951, simply because little had previously been instigated.

The absence of real long-term planning by the Labour Government after 1945 could be contrasted to the experience of France, where the Government did try to introduce long-term controls. In the last year of the Labour Government, planning ceased, except in specific limited areas. Informed opinion was increasingly sceptical. *The Times* on 11th September, 1952 said: 'The idea, which was fostered by false analogies drawn from wartime experience that well-being can best be achieved in this complex and advanced economy by means of detailed central planning has become progressively threadbare in the past five years.' And by 1951 many of the instruments through which planning could be realised – rationing, allocations of capital investment throughout individual Departments, bulk purchase, had begun to be dissolved by the Labour Government. The Conservative Government's main objection lay as much in the use of the word 'planning'.[90]

Plowden's function thus evolved into advising Butler on the macroeconomic alternatives and consequences of policy. He retired in November 1953, feeling that six and a half years in the job was enough, and became Chairman of the Atomic Energy Authority. Plowden's position was that of a *de facto* Second Secretary, as was Sir Robert Hall, the Economic Adviser. Plowden worked closely with Hall, and Butler found them on the whole more sympathetic than the *de jure* Second Secretaries. Plowden and Hall would talk together, also with the economic advisers, and Plowden would then see Butler early in the day with a distillation of their advice. Butler was to miss him greatly. 'His departure,' he was to comment, 'undoubtedly weakened my position and that of the British economy.'[91]

November 1953 also saw the Economic Section moved from the Cabinet Office to the Treasury.[92] It had been set up in 1941, and the White Paper on Employment Policy in 1944 stated that the Economic Section would remain as a permanent feature of Government machinery. When Cripps became Chancellor in November 1947, he relied on Hall and Plowden for economic advice, and from then on the Economic Section worked more and more as if it were part of the Treasury. So this formal move merely acknowledged what had already been the practice.

Hall, who had been Director of the Economic Section since 1947, became, after the move and the absorption of the remaining functions of the Chief Planning Officer, Economic Adviser to the Government.

Butler thought highly of Hall, especially his contribution to Budget speeches (one of his strengths was that he wrote well), and referred to him later as 'our strong, silent man who came to have more and more influence'.[93] He trusted Hall's judgment and found that he did not have a particular axe to grind. Hall's influence was exercised more directly after the departures in 1953 of Plowden and William Armstrong, Butler's Principal Private Secretary. He was at his most powerful in 1954 when almost alone he persuaded Butler to produce a cautious Budget. Hall's approach was similar to that of Plowden: both were Keynesian and also 'economic', whereas most of the senior men in the Treasury were 'non-economic'. These men worried about market problems and how to finance expenditure, whereas Hall and Plowden thought more in macro-economic terms about full employment and balance of payments stability. None, however, were monetarists in the sense in which the word is now used, and Hall was one of the earliest advocates of an incomes policy.

Butler found William Armstrong, his Principal Private Secretary until 1953, offered excellent advice. Inherited from Gaitskell, he did not want to lose him and never felt quite as happy with the advice he received from his officials after he (and Plowden) moved on. He was replaced by Louis Petch, a respected and accomplished Secretary, who headed a particularly strong Private Office, with Ian Bancroft[94] and Robert Armstrong[95] as Private Secretaries under him.

Butler's personal preferences for certain individuals carried down below the Second Secretary level, and if he formed a high opinion of a more junior man, he would call him into his office regardless of his rank. Thus he listened carefully to the opinions of Denis Rickett,[96] whose advice he sought alongside Rowan's on matters of overseas finance,[97] and also Otto Clarke,[98] Sir Edmund Compton,[99] C. R. Ross[100] and Burke Trend.[101]

Chief among the many other groups and bodies to whom the Chancellor looked for advice was the Bank of England. Butler would see the Governor, C. F. Cobbold,[102] alone on Friday mornings, and found the meetings helpful although he was never greatly influenced by Cobbold or his advisers (apart from the 'Robot' episode).[103]

Cobbold had seen the Bank through nationalisation, ensuring that it secured a large degree of independence, and was considered the most suitable candidate to become Governor in succession to Lord Catto in 1949. Cobbold's experience at the Bank had been in domestic money, and he concentrated his efforts on the gilt-edged market and funding the Government debt.[104] Matters of foreign exchange and relations with foreign central banks Cobbold left very much to Sir George Bolton,[105] who had considerable influence in these areas. Overall, the Bank's views on matters relating to the management of the currency, foreign exchange market and convertibility[106] carried weight, but it played little part in discussions on general economic policy apart from the impetus it provided to the increased reliance on monetary policy in 1951–2.

Butler regularly saw representatives of the Boards of Inland Revenue and Customs and Excise, who also sat on the Budget Committee. They undoubtedly influenced methods and amounts of taxation, but it was the Treasury (and more specifically Butler) who actually decided how much and of what kind, leaving the Inland Revenue and Customs and Excise to provide the technique.[107] Neither side of industry had much impact on Butler, who had gained first-hand experience of both during his brief spells at the Ministry of Labour, as Parliamentary Secretary from 1937–8 and Minister from May–July 1945, in the 'Caretaker Government'. Representatives from both the T.U.C. and the Federation of British Industries (F.B.I.) came to see Butler before Budgets, but this was a formality and the content had been all but finalised before their visits. The views of the business world reached the Chancellor far more through contacts with individual Conservatives, such as Ralph Assheton, Chairman of the Conservative Finance Committee,[108] Crookshank, Lyttelton and Ashton, than through institutional links. Lunches were organised for Butler to meet City men but the Treasury never liked them and they petered out.[109]

Although the formal trade union representations to the Chancellor seldom affected policy, this does not mean that little attention was paid to them. Two efforts, in particular, were made towards the unions: to keep on as good terms as possible in an attempt to mitigate their power in wage bargaining, and the avoidance of changes which would result in excessive rises in the cost of living. Thus when food subsidies were cut in the 1952 Budget the likely effect on food prices was carefully considered. Avoiding wage inflation, especially after the large wage rises in 1951, was a major concern of Butler's economic policy. He worked closely with Sir Walter Monckton, and was careful to do nothing that might antagonise the unions, and wherever possible he attempted to woo them.[110] At the time some felt this to be his major weakness as Chancellor. Nonetheless Butler was perfectly content to see the system of wage bargaining continue in its present form: had Gaitskell returned as Chancellor in 1951 he might have experimented with a further wages policy,[111] but to Butler and Cabinet there was too much 'planning' about such a step.[112] When the inflation rate began to settle down during 1952–3 at 2%, the Government became increasingly worried about unemployment. Woolton wrote to the Prime Minister,[113] saying that the Government had no policy at all to tackle unemployment, but that since the White Paper on employment policy in 1944, the public looked to Government to provide the answer. Woolton prepared a paper on the subject proposing that a policy should be developed 'while there is time'.[114] However, as few regarded unemployment as a serious problem during Butler's chancellorship, these worries soon died away.

The Treasury Ministerial Advisory Committee proved to be a body of little standing or value. Butler rather scoffed at it, partly because of a personal antipathy to Woolton.[115] The Committee, beginning with just five members, Woolton, Swinton, Lyttelton, Peter Thorneycroft and Sir David Eccles, initially concentrated its energies on looking at public expenditure. They were opposed to economic planning, having long discussions on whether 'forecasting' was worthwhile, and attempted unsuccessfully to abolish the 'Economic Survey'. Popular with neither Butler nor the Treasury,[116] the Committee's membership was gradually increased in size as it came to debate more general economic questions, until after some months it was absorbed into the Cabinet's Economic Policy Committee.[117] Churchill also found less need of this body as his confidence in Butler grew. As Lord Moran was to record: '"Rab is behaving very well," Winston said. "The Party has great confidence in him. He scorns to play for popularity, just does what he thinks is right."'[118]

When Butler wanted the advice of his ministerial colleagues, he asked them personally, relying on Lyttelton far more than on anyone else.[119] Swinton was always friendly to Butler, and he also worked closely with Thorneycroft, President of the Board of Trade. Cherwell's comments, given direct to Churchill on the advice of the Prime Minister's Statistical Office, Butler found a positive irritant.[120] When Churchill became Prime Minister again in 1951 he asked Cherwell to re-create the Statistical Branch of 1939–45, which he did reluctantly and on a much smaller scale. Churchill also announced that Cherwell would occupy the official residence of the Chancellor at Number Eleven, Downing Street. The Opposition was suspicious of this and Gaitskell attacked Churchill[121] for attempting to insert a Minister between the Prime Minister and the Chancellor of the Exchequer. Churchill replied that Cherwell's function related to statistical, not economic advice. This clearly was not so. The main figure in the office was again Sir Donald MacDougall,[122] and under him were J. S. Fforde, M. F. G. Scott and J. R. Parkinson. They worked much more for

Cherwell than for Churchill, providing him with economic briefs and digests.[123] When Churchill's view, however, was required on some aspect of economic policy, Churchill liked a second opinion, so would seek help from Cherwell and also from Lyttelton and increasingly from Macmillan.[124] Churchill was much less interested in economic matters than he had been during the war, so when Cherwell retired in November 1953, the Statistical Branch was wound up, its influence only having significance on the 'Robot' issue in 1952.

Churchill probably surprised himself at how little positive interest he took in economic policy, and how free a rein he gave Butler. Those in the Treasury felt no coherent guiding hand from the Prime Minister, although there were odd interventions in Treasury work, as when Churchill demanded to see in detail the proposals for the 1952 Budget. It was the commonly-held view in the Treasury that Churchill was going downhill and was not up to much, at least on economic policy. The problems of the economy on his return in 1951 he certainly found bewildering,[125] and he rapidly ceased to grapple with its complexities.[126] Churchill's tendency was to look on financial matters in rather general terms such as preferring a freer economy. He was also in favour of the top level of income tax not rising above sixty-six per cent, feeling it reasonable that anyone should be able to retain at least a third of his earnings.[127] His brain, one of tremendous experience and imagination, was not analytical, and was too old to understand the complex aspects of a subject which had changed utterly since his own period as Chancellor, between 1924 and 1929, though his instincts were as sound as ever.

Butler came to feel more and more isolated at the Treasury, with neither the Prime Minister nor the Foreign Secretary paying much attention to his work (on the other hand, he would have resented it if they took too much interest), and he increasingly felt that his achievements were unrecognised by his Cabinet colleagues;[128] this was particularly the case after the death of his wife in 1954.[129] This was unfortunate because his chancellorship appears even more distinguished with the passage of years than it did at the time. Hesitant and irritating though he may have seemed to those who worked with him, relying on intuition rather than an acquired economist's judgment, he chose between conflicting and occasionally bewildering advice (invariably of one kind, namely Keynesian)[130] which resulted in steady growth in the economy from 1952.[131] By 1955 the central position of the Treasury in economic policy had also been assured after the failure of the various Churchillian 'counterweights': not only had the Treasury Ministerial Advisory Committee been effectively dissolved and the independent Prime Minister's Statistical Office wound up, but also the co-ordinating Ministers had been discredited and terminated, the process being formally sealed by the move of the Economic Section to the Treasury in November 1953.

Part 2   Economic Policy

Three periods can be discerned in Rab Butler's tenure as Chancellor.[1] The first was dominated by anxiety about the outflow of gold and dollar reserves and pressure to make the pound convertible. Little immediate change of policy, however, resulted from the new Government other than an alteration in 'attitude', the Conservatives ostensibly being more in favour of freeing controls and restrictions. Indeed, in retrospect, some Treasury officials feel that less change occurred in 1951 than at any other changeover of Administrations in the thirty years following the end of the Second World War.[2] The new policies that the Government did adopt after the Election were in fact either recommended by officials or were forced on the Government by the dire economic position. The increase in the Bank rate, from 2% to 2½% in November, and to 4% in Butler's first Budget (as a result of Bank rather than Treasury pressure, although Sir Edwin Plowden strongly supported it), had already been urged on Hugh Gaitskell. Conservative Ministers accepted the step with considerable reluctance.[3] Likewise, Butler's import cuts in November 1951 and January 1952 (strongly opposed by Thorneycroft and the Board of Trade)[4] had been first mooted by officials when Labour was in office. Food subsidies were cut by forty per cent in the Budget, and this Labour would not have done, although they had begun to cut back on controls and rationing. On tax matters both Chancellors accepted the Keynesian argument for tinkering with levels: Butler had some strong views on this, as over the subsidy and benefit changes in the 1952 Budget, but he often let himself be guided by his officials. The excess profits tax, imposed at Churchill's personal instigation, was a new departure,[5] closer to Labour than Conservative doctrine.

The crisis in the economy inherited by the Conservatives also militated against any significant change in policy. One of the Labour Government's last acts had been to agree to a medium-term defence plan with NATO allies in response to the threat to peace highlighted by the Korean war.[6] The Labour Government knew that the new defence plan would put a strain on the balance of payments, but they hoped, mistakenly, that the U.S. Government would provide dollars to offset this. Although it is probable that, had Winston Churchill been in power, he would have gone as far, if not further, than Clement Attlee, by the end of 1951 the foreign picture looked less threatening, and the Conservative Government found the commitment unnecessarily severe. In addition, the strain on the economy caused by the defence expenditure, about which successive Chancellors since 1945 had complained, was beginning to tell. At the Lisbon Conference of NATO in February 1952, the Government announced that it could not meet the requisite levels; balanced reductions followed a defence review initiated by Churchill in 1952, which recommended reductions to conventional forces.[7] The defence commitment entailed a disruption to the balance of payments, due partly to the redirection of the engineering industry towards defence production. But as this change in direction had had little time to filter through, the strain on the balance of payments was caused mainly by an adverse turn in the terms of trade. This meant the Conservatives' hopes of relaxing controls had to be delayed for over a year.

Throughout January 1952 the Cabinet was considering measures for dealing with the balance of payments position.[8] It was estimated that the sterling area was then in deficit with the rest of the world at an annual rate of about £1,600m. which caused a loss of nearly 40% of the gold reserves since June 1951, and a change in Britain's European Payments Union position from an accumulated credit of over £100m. at the end of June 1951 to a debt of nearly £200m. at the end of December 1951. It was estimated that unless adequate emergency action was taken, Britain's reserves would fall to as little as £500m. – the level at which the pound had been devalued in September 1949. The Cabinet was told that four factors were responsible for Britain's worsening position since the war: the change from being a net creditor of £3,500m. to a net debtor of £2,500m.; the decline in value of gold reserves, from being equal to four or five months' turnover of Britain's external transactions before the war to equalling only three weeks' turnover of transactions by 1952; a marked deterioration in the terms of trade since 1938, entailing each unit of exports bringing in only three-quarters as many imports as it did on the eve of the war; finally, the terrible cost of the war on Britain's capital assets at home and abroad – equalling about one quarter of the country's entire wealth. Most of the internal losses had been made good by 1952, but scars remained. Strange then that more doctrinaire policies were not adopted to tackle this alarming legacy.

At the time officials felt that the individual characters of the Chancellors themselves provided another explanation as to why there was so little change of policy: Gaitskell was to the 'right' of his Party, Butler to the 'left' of his; both men believed in full employment and the necessity of managing the economy to secure this end. Butler was not as inclined as some in his Party to swing the economy over to a hotly competitive 'capitalistic' society, any more than Gaitskell wanted to see an extension of socialism throughout the economy. Indeed Ralph Assheton, the powerful Chairman of the Conservative Party Finance Committee, and some of its attenders such as Richard Law and Lord Hinchingbrooke wanted Butler to do much more to institute a laissez-faire economy.[9]

This congruity of policy would not have been so marked had a policy designed to free the pound gone forward in the spring of 1952.[10] This was the so-called 'Robot' plan, compounded out of the names of the chief protagonists, ROwan, BOlton and OTto Clarke.[11] This issue caused more dissension in Whitehall than any other in the decade apart from the 1956 Suez crisis.[12] The proposal must be seen against the background of the Government's persistent attempts from November 1951 to January 1952 to cut public expenditure, and to reduce imports and domestic spending, which had all seemed to have failed to ease the drain on sterling. The drain itself was due principally to the large sterling balances accumulated during the war: one of 'Robot's' objectives was to have further devalued these, over and above the 1949 devaluation.

The proposal originated with Sir George Bolton at the Bank, who began canvassing the plan of making the pound convertible (to non-sterling area holders at a floating rate of exchange) as early as 1950. He was also concerned to take exchange control out of the hands of Government. His views gained many supporters at the Bank, notably C. F. Cobbold, the Governor, although he was not to play an active part. A group of senior advisers and officials at the Bank worked out a variety of plans which were discussed with senior members of the Treasury principally from the Overseas Finance Division.[13] The proposal was not put to Gaitskell, but in Butler the supporters of the plan found a willing ear, and they were strengthened in their determination by the outflow of the pound in the winter of 1951, and felt that either a devaluation or floating would be inevitable. Their plan, they thought, would take the strain off the gold and dollar reserves, and put it on the rate of exchange. 'I backed it,' recalls Butler, 'because I thought, in my innocence, that, if the pound went down then the politicians would get together and take the necessary measures to restore and re-establish the economy . . . We thought it would be a way of ensuring that anti-inflation measures were not taken, and also we thought we could avoid devaluation.'[14] Despite the opposition of the Economic Adviser (Sir Robert Hall), Chief Planning Officer (Plowden)[15] and his Principal Private Secretary (William Armstrong), Butler nevertheless felt the daring proposal was worth a try. A meeting of Finance Ministers of the Commonwealth took place in London in January 1952, to discuss the balance of payments crisis in the

171

sterling area, and though the communiqué treated convertibility as a main aim of policy, Butler was silent about the 'Robot' plan.[16]

The Budget date was brought forward from April to 4th March so that the plan could be introduced: a minimum period of warning to the United States and sterling area member countries was visualised by the advocates of the proposal. Butler put the proposal to a small meeting of Ministers, including Churchill, Oliver Lyttelton and Lord Cherwell on 20th February, hoping to obtain swift agreement.[17] Surprisingly, Butler's paper arguing for 'Robot' was couched in the most negative idiom, full of the likely disturbing effects of the course of action and was probably written by an official with reservations about the scheme. Yet Churchill was inclined to be in favour, as was Lyttelton, who, there are grounds for thinking, had played a major part in bringing Butler round to accepting 'Robot'.[18]

Brendan Bracken (a friend of Lyttelton) had written to Lord Beaverbrook on 15th January: 'He [Butler] is, I think, converted to the policy of freeing the pound.'[19] All the same Butler ran into two obstacles: not only was Cherwell seriously disturbed by the plan, but a further meeting of Ministers took place at Number Ten on 22nd February, this time including James Stuart, Sir David Maxwell Fyfe and Lord Woolton,[20] which insisted on Anthony Eden being consulted about the plan, due to the impact it would have on Britain's foreign relations.

Eden, however, had left for a NATO Conference in Lisbon, after a delayed departure due to George VI's funeral on 15th February. Sir Eric Berthoud,[21] as a senior Foreign Office official on the economic side, and Sir Herbert Brittain,[22] were instructed to report to him in Lisbon.[23] Eden was told who supported and opposed the proposal, with Berthoud mentioning specifically that both Cherwell and Lord Swinton[24] were doubtful, the latter because of the inflation it was likely to cause in the Commonwealth, as was Hall, and also Lionel Robbins, then Professor of Economics at the London School of Economics,[25] who had been privately consulted.[26] They also brought a letter from Bridges to Plowden in Lisbon saying that Ministers had virtually decided to go ahead with 'Robot', but would not take a final decision without the consent of the Foreign Secretary. Bridges hoped Plowden would persuade Eden that this was the right action to take, and send back a message to that effect. But Bridges also felt that Plowden should know that strong opposition to the proposal came from Hall, and enclosed a memorandum from Hall with his objections. Eden initially felt the plan should go forward, followed by a General Election for endorsement at the polls. Plowden considered such drastic action unwarranted and felt that Butler had let himself be stampeded by the Bank. In fact, late on the evening of Berthoud's arrival, Plowden went to see Eden at the British Embassy in Lisbon. He told Eden about Bridges' letter, and counselled him to ask for a decision on the matter to be deferred until after his return from the NATO conference. As a result, Berthoud returned to London with a cautious handwritten letter from Eden to Churchill suggesting more serious thought be given to the whole idea.

Back in London, the main political protagonists and those in the Treasury began to lose ground as opinion turned increasingly against the plan. Over the weekend 23rd–24th February further discussions took place, and on Monday, 25th February, Harry Crookshank announced in the House that the Budget would be postponed until 11th March to allow more time for discussions. Opposition centred on Cherwell, whose natural inclinations were backed up by minutes based on the solid economic arguments of Sir Donald MacDougall.[27] Support for Cherwell also came from Sir Arthur Salter, although he remained much the junior partner, and in the long discussions which took place amongst Ministers, they and Swinton were the chief opponents ranged against Butler and Lyttelton, supported to an extent by Crookshank[28] and Woolton, who favoured the burden of the deficit falling on the day-to-day rate of exchange rather than on the reserves.[29]

Much turned on what Eden would do, and he, on his return to London, came down firmly against. Churchill, too, became increasingly sceptical, having much faith in the combined opinions of his two special appointees, Cherwell and Salter. A four-hour Cabinet meeting took place on Friday, 29th February, where, after stormy discussions, it was decided to drop the plan.[30] Eden received much of the praise at the time for 'Robot's' defeat, although as much, if not more, of the responsibility lay with the powerful advocacy of Cherwell, who was prepared to resign if the decision had gone against his view.

It had been agreed to reconsider 'Robot' in April, but Butler did not raise the matter, since the reserves were gradually improving. When the proposal was again defeated in June 1952, attention was turned to the 'collective approach to convertibility', a far less radical plan, providing for convertibility at a floating rate, which was canvassed at the Commonwealth Economic Conference in November–December 1952. Gradual moves towards making the pound convertible were taken over the next few years,[31] but with the improvement to the reserves, notably from mid-1952 on, drastic action was no longer deemed necessary.

Butler, in the remedial measures in late 1951 and early 1952, relied heavily on his advisers, but by the March 1952 Budget he had gained more confidence in his own judgment. Since so much action had already been taken, he was able to offer a comparatively mild Budget on 11th March, deciding to cut food subsidies by £160m. from £410m., a move strongly supported by the Treasury, which felt that food subsidies could easily become an open-ended commitment. Neither Eden nor Sir Walter Monckton favoured this policy, although they, along with Churchill, applauded the concessions: a compensatory cut in income tax and increases in pensions and other welfare benefits, which together amounted to over £300m.[32]

Butler's personal standing rose as the economy began to fare better towards the end of the year,[33] aided considerably by better terms of trade, which accounted for almost half of the improvement in the balance of payments.[34] This heralded the second period of Butler's management of the Treasury, characterised by fears of under-employment during 1953 and part of 1954. Butler, throughout his chancellorship, took pains to show that the Conservatives were not a Party of unemployment, and did much to ward off the danger despite the opposition of certain Cabinet colleagues who wished to reduce Government expenditure still further. Butler, unlike Gaitskell, constantly argued against the maintenance of what he considered over-high levels of defence expenditure: in particular he perceived the danger to Britain's export trade if too many resources were diverted from metal industries to rearmament.[35] At the same time, much work was being done in the Treasury about what to do in the event of a United States recession. When planning his 1953 Budget, Butler was confronted by the threat of a productive capacity being under-employed, and he was advised to go for an expansionary policy, advice he willingly followed. He introduced some sensible measures, in particular restoring initial allowances (at twenty per cent) on new equipment for industry, and introducing tax cuts, resulting in an increase of approximately £150m. in consumption income, which coincided with a rise in national output of four per cent over the year.[36]

Butler favoured continuing expansion in his third Budget in 1954, but caution was so strongly counselled that he grudgingly introduced an almost neutral one, 'a tiny, insignificant Budget', said Gaitskell in the House of Commons.[37] This proved generally acceptable to his Cabinet colleagues who were anxious to avoid any indication that an Election was imminent. Woolton recorded in his diary: 'We have just had the Budget, which is the dullest thing that anybody ever created . . . and was done deliberately, so that the Socialist Party would not think there was going to be an Election in October. We have left ourselves plenty in hand to make promises that can be fulfilled.'[38] On this score, at least, the ploy worked: a leader in *The Times* on 7th April, 1954, said: 'It would be difficult to imagine anything less like an electioneering Budget . . .' By now Plowden had left the Treasury and Armstrong the Private Office, so Butler relied to a far greater extent on Hall, who was worried about the recession in the United States and the possible effect this might have on British exports. The Budget contained only one expansionary measure, an investment allowance proposed by the Economic Section. Butler accepted this proposal as he was anxious to increase the low level of investment by industry, despite strong opposition from the Inland Revenue.[39]

As 1954 progressed it became clear that fears over the recession in the U.S. were exaggerated, and a mood of optimism pervaded the Treasury. The third phase of Butler's chancellorship began, which, in its early stages, marked the high-point of his period at the Treasury. Both Butler and his advisers reacted against the caution exhibited in the Budget, and in May the Bank rate was reduced to three per cent, and, in July, hire-purchase restrictions were abolished altogether. In October Butler told the Conservative Party Conference: 'I give you a slogan, invest in success,' and he propounded the vision of doubling Britain's real standard of living in twenty-five years.[40] The stimulation proved excessive, and Butler would have done well to heed Hall's more cautious approach. In early 1955 Butler was forced, to Churchill's annoyance,[41] to reintroduce the credit restrictions and raise the Bank rate by stages to four and a half per cent. In retrospect one can see that Butler was over-optimistic about the value of monetary policy: on 27th January he told the Cabinet that the rise in Bank rate by $\frac{1}{2}$% that morning would be sufficient to check any inflationary tendency.[42] By April Butler was claiming that these measures had proved successful in cutting imports and encouraging exports, and, upholding his argument that a flexible monetary policy would be an effective standby weapon if needed, he argued in his Budget speech that there was room for expansion, and consequently took sixpence off income tax, giving back about £135m. in tax relief.

To have taken such an inflationary step at a time when the economy was rapidly expanding brought forth much criticism at the time, and has since come to be regarded as the major blemish on an otherwise successful chancellorship.[43] To what extent was Butler himself culpable, if blame indeed is to be attributed? Butler was undoubtedly labouring under some strain in the spring of 1955, as commented upon by his colleagues, who found his performance at times erratic.[44] But equally there is a danger that one can overstress personal considerations. Moreover, there is strong evidence for believing that Butler himself was not absolutely convinced of the need to take so much off income tax and would have preferred something more modest. For a long time he hesitated. He was receiving conflicting advice: the Bank and the senior Treasury officials, including Bridges and Sir Bernard Gilbert, thought that income tax was too high and should be reduced; most of the Economic Section was strongly against the reduction, especially the younger members who had little wish to see another Conservative Government elected. Hall was more cautious: he saw that, on Keynesian reasoning, if revenue was high because of pressure on the economy, this was no valid reason for giving it away; but he did not press strongly against the tax cut although he persuaded Butler to insert into his Budget speech a passage mentioning recourse to monetary weapons if the measures proved over-expansionary. William Armstrong stayed the weekend with Butler shortly before the Budget, and advised strongly against so big a tax cut and the reliance upon monetary policy as a fall-back, but his advice went unheeded. On the other hand, both Churchill and Eden made it known to Butler that they favoured an expansionary Budget. Eden was to write later: 'When I consider the surplus at the Chancellor's disposal, I am astonished at his moderation.'[45] Opinion amongst backbenchers in the House, led by Assheton, would not have let Butler get away with another standstill Budget like that of 1954 with so much surplus in evidence.[46]

Butler eventually decided on tax cuts. He was impressed by the views expressed at the Commonwealth Prime Ministers' meeting (31st January–6th February) where it was the general view that the economy was healthy, and he received advice from various quarters to lighten taxation.[47] He felt the measures taken earlier in the year were sufficient to strengthen the pound, and he also appears to have been swayed by the argument that a flexible monetary policy could be used to dampen inflationary pressure if it emerged.[48] Butler also knew if an Election were announced he would have little Parliamentary time to pilot the Finance Bill through the House; therefore he could not afford any measures which would lead to lengthy discussion and thus favoured the simplicity of the tax cut.[49] After the announcement on 15th April that the Election would indeed take place the following month, discussions were held with the Labour Party who agreed to facilitate the passage of the Finance Bill if it was a comparatively simple one.[50]

Butler should not be blamed too heavily for the April 1955 miscalculation. It is naive to blame the Chancellor for the Budget being '[a] striking instance of politics geared to immediate electoral advance'.[51] No Chancellor, knowing that a General Election was imminent, would not have taken this factor into account. Much respectable informed opinion agreed with the move. Norman Macrae wrote: ' "Which sort of Budget

176

would you regard as the more inflationary," one prominent Tory asked me at the time, "a budget that took sixpence off the income tax and kept us in power, or one that was orthodoxly stern and resulted in Labour getting back to power?" . . . At the time, to be frank, many of us agreed with him.'[52] Moreover, to the great majority of Butler's advisers it did not seem to be excessive to give away half the surplus in the Budget. Hall later said: 'I don't think that anyone foresaw that there was going to be a balance of payments crisis later in the year, which was connected more with the position of sterling than with the Budget.'[53]

But crisis there was. The overall effect of the Budget was found to be over-stimulating. The assistance expected from credit control was not forthcoming:[54] several restrictive measures were introduced in July, and an emergency Budget became necessary in the autumn. This, however, should not detract too much from the credit due to Butler for his work at the Treasury. With this one possible exception he was level-headed and careful, and his decisions were usually correct.[55] Exogenous factors made it possible for Butler to achieve what would in later years have been considered a near miracle:[56] the economy was run at full employment with a minimal rate of wage or price inflation; without, after 1952, balance of payments difficulties, and in the absence of a wages policy. A summary of the economic position appeared in a leader in *The Times* on 13th December, 1954, which must have been one of their most optimistic assessments ever:

> There seems to be no [inflation] worth the name in recent movements of prices and wages, [the writer confidently proclaimed]. With production and consumption in this country at the highest levels of all time, the population fully employed and the external balance of payments still to all outward appearances satisfactory, the present state of the national economy gives little ground for complaint.

Butler came to the office at a time when the economy looked bad but was beginning to improve of its own accord. When the price of imports soared in 1951 it produced an adverse balance of payments. Due to the time lag before the price of imports worked through into the price of consumer goods, the automatic offsetting from a change in the terms of trade did not occur in 1951. But by 1952 the price of imports began to fall, counteracting the higher price of oil imports. Thus Butler was getting an advantageous anti-inflationary effect to offset the disadvantageous inflationary effect from which Gaitskell had suffered. Further, British post-war recovery, aided by the Marshall Plan, was firmly under way, despite the strain imposed by the rearmament programme of 1951–2. So with production expanding, and domestic consumption held back, Butler inherited a favourable position, which he had the good sense not to waste.

Part 3 The Board of Trade

The wartime concept of every industry having a sponsoring Department in the Government was retained after 1945, with the Board of Trade consolidating its position by taking over the remaining functions of the wartime Ministry of Production and responsibility for the distribution of industry from the Ministry of Labour.[1] It also became increasingly the body responsible for the protection of consumers.

As President of the Board of Trade Peter Thorneycroft was a surprise appointment, for he had had minimal previous ministerial experience.[2] It was a wise choice, as few others of the younger men in the Party[3] could have held their own against the highly experienced Ministers and officials with whom the President of the Board of Trade had to deal. He exhibited a good mind, lacking in brilliance or great originality, but his main strength was his advocacy of an argument in Cabinet, its Committees and in the House. He was pragmatic, decisive and tended to see matters in terms of black and white.

A liberal by nature, he favoured removal of restrictions and emphasised the need for reducing the burden of taxation on industry, even at the cost of increasing personal tax. He felt strongly that it was not the job of Government to regulate or intervene in industry, but to lay down the ground rules within which industry should make its own decisions. Beyond that, he saw the only function of Government as being the creation of an 'economic climate', through Budgets and other measures, in which business could flourish. Foreign affairs held little interest for him, unless they impinged on Britain's trading interests. He was extremely keen on the Organisation for European Economic Co-operation (O.E.E.C.)[4] and its move to dismantle trade barriers between European countries, and, not surprisingly, perhaps, his enthusiasm for a more united Europe stemmed more from economic than political reasons.

Henry Hopkinson was Secretary for Overseas Trade for the first six months until his departure to the Colonial Office. A comparative newcomer to politics,[5] he settled uneasily into the ministerial mould. Diffident in debate and not good at defending himself, he lacked the wit to make effective retorts. In the Department he was able to use his clear mind to good advantage, but was in the job insufficiently long to make much mark. He was promoted to Minister of State at the Colonial Office in May 1952, a job he found more to his liking. With the need to appoint someone at short notice to succeed him, Sir Harry Mackeson was chosen in recognition of his service in the Whips Office.[6] It was one of the less happy appointments in the Government: the post required a man with first-hand knowledge of the export trade, who understood domestic controls and the ways of encouraging industry to capture fresh markets abroad. The appointment of an ex-army officer,[7] completely out of his element, was unfortunate and did little to help British industry.

It was not until the job, upgraded to Minister of State,[8] was given to Derick Heathcoat Amory in September 1953 that its potential was fully exploited. His appointment also coincided with fresh priority being given by the Government to the export drive.[9] He had some experience of industry, and told Winston Churchill he would be interested in that job though perhaps not in others.[10] A highly intelligent, hard-working, if retiring man, he did not, perhaps, make as much impact as he might have done.[11] Lord Woolton came to have a high regard for his work and was instrumental in encouraging his promotion to Minister of Agriculture following Sir Thomas Dugdale's resignation in July 1954. Toby Low was appointed Minister of State in Amory's place, a step up from Parliamentary Secretary at the Ministry of Supply, where he was felt to have done well. He had a much broader knowledge of industry and business than his predecessors, and brought his lively and incisive mind to bear on a wide range of problems, in particular the question of protection for the British textile industry and the Japanese Trade Agreement.

Henry Strauss, the Parliamentary Secretary until April 1955, had entered the House in 1935 and had some wartime ministerial experience.[12] Felt to be on the right of the Party, he was put in to act as a counterbalance to the Tory reformer Thorneycroft. In the House he was regarded as mildly eccentric, with a fog-horn voice. His two great passions were for individual liberty under the law and for plain English. As a lawyer he concentrated on the legal side and development areas. He never spared himself as a Minister, although as a regulator of departmental affairs and in relations with industrial leaders, he was not at his happiest. Senior among the large number of Parliamentary Private Secretaries was Thorneycroft's old friend Alexander Spearman, who left after a year due to business pressures,[13] and whose job as *de facto* senior Parliamentary Private Secretary was taken by another intimate of Thorneycroft, John Hay. He attended meetings of the Party's Trade and Industry Committee and reported back on feelings in the House,[14] but it is doubtful whether Thorneycroft took much notice of that body's views.

As Permanent Secretary, Sir Frank Lee,[15] whom many considered the

179

pre-eminent official of the day, had succeeded another equally distinguished public servant, Sir John Woods, earlier in the year.[16] Lee was a key figure amongst officials in economic debates,[17] and provided the intellectual muscle behind Thorneycroft so that together they formed a highly effective team. A man of enormous physical and mental energy, he paid more visits abroad than any other Permanent Secretary at the Board of Trade, liking to be on the spot himself. Lee's major weakness, however, his unwillingness to delegate responsibility, was to become even more marked after his appointment as Joint Permanent Secretary at the Treasury (1960–2).[18]

As a Minister Thorneycroft believed he would make little impression unless he focused on one or two key issues at a time (G.A.T.T., the General Agreement on Tariffs and Trade, was the first), leaving the routine matters to the junior Ministers.[19] Throughout their period in Opposition and in their policy statements,[20] an anti-G.A.T.T. feeling had been expressed.[21] Thorneycroft had not been understudying Trade in Opposition, and when he first arrived at the Board of Trade he naturally took the party line favouring Imperial Preference. But within a few months, after the Department's statisticians had illustrated the importance of trade with both North and South America, as well as with Europe, and the steadily declining importance of Commonwealth trade, Thorneycroft revised his views.[22] He was also impressed by how Commonwealth trade was changing and it no longer seemed realistic to assume that Britain could take all Commonwealth goods without restrictions.[23] Lee and the Board of Trade officials also pointed out that preferences with Canada and to a lesser extent Australia were no longer as favourable to Britain as they once had been.[24] Moreover, India and Pakistan had become more interested in trade with the United States, and other Commonwealth countries were increasingly unenthusiastic about the value of Empire trade.

Thorneycroft encountered some problems in persuading Cabinet that Britain's future lay with multilateral trade,[25] but his greatest difficulty lay with his own Party. In the spring of 1952 three separate Early Day Motions were placed before the House, urging the Government to promote as free an exchange of goods as possible between Commonwealth countries, one receiving the support of forty-five M.P.s.[26] The biggest battles, though, took place at the Party Conference. At the 1952 Scarborough Conference L. S. Amery[27] rose to speak for two motions supporting Imperial Preference, passed with negligible opposition. The Cabinet had discussed the future of Empire trade at a meeting on 7th October and had decided in favour of an extension of Imperial Preference in order to increase trade within the sterling area. Oliver Lyttelton, who was to speak for the Government on the motion at the Conference, was instructed to express its belief in the principles of Imperial Preference as a good method of developing the Commonwealth's trade and resources.[28]

By the time of the Margate Conference in October 1953, the position had changed. The Government was less hospitable to criticism of G.A.T.T., expressed in a motion proposed by Lord Balfour of Inchrye,[29] which called for modifications and was passed unanimously. An event had occurred in the meantime which had the utmost significance on the future of Empire trade. At the Commonwealth Economic Conference, held in London in December 1952, only Australia and Southern Rhodesia expressed support for Imperial Preference. This made Thorneycroft's job much easier as his Cabinet colleagues, who discussed the question at their meeting on 8th December, now recognised that Imperial Preference was no longer to be regarded as an effective instrument of Commonwealth economic policy.[30] Thorneycroft was thus able to tell the Conference that although G.A.T.T. required some modification, it had nevertheless come to stay. The crunch came at the 1954 Blackpool Conference, where the decisive blow was struck. The official motion supporting Imperial Preference before the Conference was much too mild for Amery and Sir Victor Raikes, a long-serving backbencher, who put forward a far tougher amendment urging changes to G.A.T.T. in favour of preferences for Commonwealth trading. The Cabinet discussed the matter on 1st October but expressed the view that Thorneycroft would not be able to defeat the Imperial Preference faction entirely, and that it would be better perhaps to play along with them. But 'let him try', Churchill said of Thorneycroft. Then in a powerful speech at the Conference, Thorneycroft argued that the amendment should not be pressed, ironically on the grounds of unity of Commonwealth and Empire.[31] This rather took the ground from under the feet of Amery and his supporters. The amendment was defeated by a substantial majority[32] and the original motion carried overwhelmingly.[33] Support for Imperial Preference continued to be voiced, but with the death of Amery in 1955 the movement quickly withered.

Churchill's own role in the move away from Empire trade was crucial. He was never a dyed-in-the-wool Empire man like some Conservatives and always retained a Liberal's belief in the virtues of free trade. Where he did speak on the Empire, it was to praise the symbolic rather than the purely economic benefits. Thus in the House as early as 1946 he had said:

[Preferences] have become part of our supreme common life and . . . are even more important to us as symbols of our indissoluble union than for their commercial advantages, which are, nonetheless, considerable.[34]

In Cabinet Thorneycroft gained tacit support from Churchill. He later commented:

The Liberal element in Churchill weighed against the deep-seated Tory belief in the value of Imperial Preference. That was why he wasn't fighting on the side of Leo Amery and the 'old guard'. If not actually supporting me, holding himself more in a judicial position as Head of the Government, he was certainly anxious to see that the more liberal economic views developing within the Conservative Party had a fair hearing.[35]

Ever since the Commonwealth Economic Conference in December 1952 held in London, individual member countries had been expressing approval for the gradual restoration of multilateral world trade,[36] and similar views were expressed at the Commonwealth Economic Conference in January 1954, held in Sydney.[37] Other factors also helped make Imperial Preference less attractive to the Conservatives. In September 1953 the U.K. obtained at the Geneva G.A.T.T. Conference a waiver enabling duties on certain foreign goods to be increased without interfering with the duty-free entry of Commonwealth goods. This was mainly the work of Sir Edgar Cohen. Japan's entry into G.A.T.T. also caused anxieties that British manufacturers would be left defenceless. To circumvent this, Thorneycroft began exploratory discussions on what was to become the Customs Duty (Dumping and Subsidies) Act, 1957.

Thorneycroft took much interest in steering through another controversial overseas trade measure: the Anglo-Japanese Trade and Payments Agreement, 1954, whose aim was to restore trade equilibrium between Britain and the Commonwealth, and Japan, and which restricted textile imports from Japan. Thorneycroft had to argue this through some stiff opposition in Cabinet, and it also upset the Eisenhower Administration.[38]

Thorneycroft, supported later by Low, firmly held his ground in resisting pressure from manufacturers and trade unions to impose import controls to protect the Lancashire textile industry from cheap imports from the Commonwealth, in particular India, Pakistan and Hong Kong.[39] Under the terms of the pre-war Ottawa Agreements, Commonwealth imports were free of duty and quantitative restrictions, but since the war imports of Indian textiles, in particular, had increased considerably. Pressures on the Government to introduce import restrictions were greatest during the 1952 textile recession, and again in the later months of 1954 and early 1955. Anxieties mounted in Cabinet as the General Election loomed, since the Lancashire seats, where nine Conservative M.P.s had majorities of less than 3,000, held the critical balance in a close contest,[40] especially as Thorneycroft, through his rigid policies, had failed to ingratiate himself with the powerful voices in the county. On two occasions Woolton voiced the opinion that Thorneycroft should be moved.[41] Churchill responded by arranging to meet the Cotton Board, on 24th March, 1955,[42] where he assured members that urgent consideration would be given to their proposals. The Government also made it plain that safeguards would be applied if competition became too severe. In the event, the Election went well for the Conservatives in Lancashire, although direct comparison with 1951 is difficult as a result of boundary reorganisation.

The reopening of the Liverpool Cotton Exchange was a major event in the textile industry. Closed during the war, it had not been reopened in 1946, but was replaced by the Raw Cotton Commission operating the system of bulk purchase under state control. At the Election the Conservatives had pledged to restore free trading, and in December 1951 set up a committee to examine the question. Despite the many drawbacks of the Cotton Commission[43] the report was cautious.[44] For the first two years of the Government's life, discussions took place between officials at the Ministry of Materials and the Board of Trade, as well as talks with representatives of cotton merchants and spinners. Conservative backbenchers, increasingly restless at the delay, played a decisive part in speeding up the process.[45] The decision to close down the Raw Cotton Commission was taken in the autumn of 1953 amidst Labour criticism that it would produce unemployment. Labour M.P.s, especially from Lancashire seats, felt strongly about the issue[46] and put the Bill, consisting of only a few clauses, through a large number of meetings in Standing Committee. The bulk of the work on the legislation was done by Lord Woolton and the Ministry of Materials officials,[47] while Thorneycroft and Heathcoat Amory saw it through the House. It became law in April 1954 thus clearing the way for the Exchange to reopen on 18th May, 1954.

In a further, and comparatively minor issue, Thorneycroft provided the drive to wind up the 'utility scheme' for clothing and furniture, which was a morass of regulations. The Labour Government had set up the Douglas Committee to examine utility schemes, which reported after the Election,[48] with the conclusion that the utility scheme was little more than a method of allowing purchase tax to be removed from cheaper quality goods. Thorneycroft acted quickly on the Report, ensuring that in his first Budget Butler announced the ending of the utility scheme, and its replacement by the simpler and more flexible 'D' scheme.[49]

It was left to Thorneycroft to implement the policy of increasing East–West (but not China) trade, outlined in the House by Churchill in February 1954. Churchill had said: 'The more trade there is through the Iron Curtain and between Great Britain and Soviet Russia and the satellites the better still will be the chances of our living together in increasing comfort.'[50] This involved confronting the difficulty of self-imposed restrictions which the West had put on trade with the East. The United States raised a stream of objections to opening up trade, and tripartite discussions on the subject of East–West trade took place in London with the U.S. and France in March. As a result of these and further talks, Thorneycroft was able to announce a substantial relaxation of the strategic controls on exports to the Soviet bloc.[51]

He devoted a considerable part of his time to examining methods of expanding exports, arguing in Cabinet that a healthy domestic industry was an essential prerequisite. This involved arguments with the Treasury on the extent to which tax and incentives should be offered to home industry. To encourage exports, Thorneycroft improved the facilities for finance and credit available to British exporters.[52] In particular he pushed for an increase of exports to North America, although the opinion was even expressed in Cabinet that North America was not a feasible market for British exporters.[53] Exports were one-third greater in 1953 than in 1950, and overall U.K. exports in 1954 were the highest ever reached, both in value and in volume, nearly four per cent more than in any of the previous three years. Imports, however, continued to remain well above the value of exports, though by 1954 the visible trade deficit had been nearly halved on the 1951 value. This was in spite of increasing competition from West Germany and Japan. Thorneycroft also recognised that a healthy international trade depended on close involvement with international bodies such as the European Payments Union (E.P.U.),[54] O.E.E.C. and the International Monetary Fund (I.M.F.)[55] and also in reducing such barriers as import quotas as far as possible. Indeed, by the end of 1954, import quotas had been removed on eighty-four per cent of British import trade from Europe.[56]

An interesting development initiated by Thorneycroft was the setting up of what he called his 'informal advisory group on exports', whose members included a number of leading industrialists, Sir Richard Costain, George Dowty, Edward Beharrell (of Dunlop) and Sir Harry Pilkington. They met once a month or so for informal discussions on methods of encouraging exports and removing obstacles to growth. This went some way to meeting public criticism that Thorneycroft's personal relations with industrialists were never close enough.

One major aspect of the Board's work, monopolies and restrictive practices, occupied less of Thorneycroft's time than might have been expected. Pledged to act effectively against monopolies, the Government produced in late 1953 the Monopolies and Restrictive Practices Commission Act. Perhaps in an effort to appear unpartisan, a Liberal, David Cairns,[57] was appointed to succeed the first Chairman of the Commission, an independent body set up by Labour in 1948. Despite repeated Opposition criticism to the contrary, the 1953 Act did produce some strengthening of the Commission, enabling it to sit in groups, which resulted in a large increase in the annual turnover of reports.[58] The most influential of these reports had in fact been initiated by Thorneycroft in December 1952 into certain restrictive practices,[59] which ultimately led to the major Restrictive Practices Act of 1956.[60]

The Labour Government made regional policy a major priority between 1945–7, but then began cutting back on aid to development areas, partly as a result of balance of payments difficulties. The Conservatives after 1951 continued on the same lines, giving regional policy low priority – their wish to reduce intervention in the economy undoubtedly playing a part. In a debate in the House in February 1953 Thorneycroft stressed that the real hope lay in the expansion of industry, which should not be a substitute for Government incentives for distribution of industry, since too great an effort in development areas hampered industrial growth elsewhere.[61]

As unemployment in the regions remained low, with the Welsh economy growing more rapidly in the early fifties than the national average, and with the Scottish and Northern Irish economies reasonably buoyant, it appeared as if the need for any separate regional policy had miraculously almost disappeared.[62]

In industry high expectations had been aroused by the return of the Conservatives, but these were soon dashed.[63] The initial economic measures passed were even more restrictionist than Labour's, and Butler warned the F.B.I. to exercise restraint in the distribution of profits. The introduction of the excess profits levy (E.P.L.) in Butler's first Budget and the maintenance of dividend restraint[64] caused further irritation, as did the Government's refusal throughout the year to reduce public expenditure and taxation. The position, however, was eased by the 1953 Budget, which removed E.P.L., reduced taxation and restored initial allowances, and also by the period of rapid economic expansion between 1953 and 1955. Neither was the Government's labour policy any more popular with industry. As Hugh Massingham wrote: 'In union circles it is often said that [Sir Walter Monckton] is the best Minister of Labour for years – but that is not what some employers think. They feel that he is so anxious to prove that the Conservatives are the true friends of the workers that he will distribute other people's halfpence without a moment's hesitation.'[65] Personal relations between Ministers and industrialists were never close: Churchill, Anthony Eden and Rab Butler seldom spent much time with industrial leaders, and the closest, most fruitful channel of direct communication was between Sir Harry Pilkington, President of the F.B.I., 1953–5, and Thorneycroft.[66]

Part 4   The Nationalised Industries

The Scope of Denationalisation

Between 1945 and 1951 the Labour Government nationalised seven basic industries and services either in part or in their entirety, as well as the Bank of England, although in civil aviation, road transport and the finishing sector of the steel industry, some private operators remained. Nationalisation was strongly opposed by the Conservatives, but only iron and steel and road haulage reverted to private ownership when they returned to power.

To denationalise coal would have been politically unacceptable because of poor output in many coalfields, notably in South Wales. Moreover, the Conservative Party had never been especially friendly to the coal owners. Financial considerations were the more significant: no one, for example, would have been prepared to buy the railways back from the Government. Some uncertainty existed about the Party's attitude to electricity, and also gas, although an attempt to denationalise the latter would have presented formidable difficulties.[1] A committee was set up after the 1950 Election to review Party policy, whose members included Lord Swinton and Sir Arnold Gridley,[2] but it reached the conclusion that denationalisation of gas would be unrealistic and reorganisation was to be preferred.[3]

There was also some controversy on denationalisation of parts of civil aviation. Plans were considered by the Government after 1951 for the denationalisation of at least some of British European Airways' domestic routes, but in the circumstances (lack of suitable aircraft, magnitude of necessary capital investment) the independent operators were unable to agree among themselves on any constructive proposals.

No single operator appeared to have the necessary resources.[4] Instead, increased opportunities were given to independent operators for new services.[5]

The Government was under pressure from their backbenchers in the first months to speed up the process of denationalising steel and road haulage. A motion with forty-six signatures was put down by Cuthbert Alport in the first week in April 1952, critical of the Government's slow progress. Winston Churchill informed the 1922 Committee on 9th April that bills for denationalising steel and road haulage would be initiated that Session.[6] In fact little progress was made and the influence of backbenchers in speeding up the process has been exaggerated.[7] The Government did not introduce the Steel Bill in the first year. Instead Churchill announced at the Conservative Party Conference in October 1952 that the denationalisations would now take place within the next twelve months. This time his promise was fulfilled.

After the denationalisations were complete, Churchill gave the following explanation of the Government's policy: '. . . where we are preserving [nationalisation], as in the coal mines, the railways, air traffic, gas and electricity, we have done and are doing our utmost to make a success of it . . . It is only where we believed that a measure of nationalisation was a real hindrance to our island life that we have reversed the policy, although we are generally opposed to the principle.'[8]

Road Transport

This proved to be the more difficult to unravel, although there was more of a Party lobby pressing for denationalisation of road haulage than for steel and also more constituency pressure. These factors, and Churchill's own preference for pushing ahead with road haulage, explain why this was taken first and steel denationalisation postponed until the 1952–3 session. The Labour Government had intended, in their 1947 Transport Act, to provide an integrated system of public inland transport by nationalising road and rail services under the British Transport Commission, which the Conservatives pledged to modify. 'Both public and private enterprise will be needed in transport . . . Private road hauliers will be given an opportunity of coming back into the business and the crippling restriction of the 25-mile limit of operation on private lorries will be modified,' said 'Britain Strong and Free'. Road haulage nationalisation never worked satisfactorily: British Road Services (B.R.S.) was expected to become a national fleet with a statutory monopoly in public long-distance general haulage, but as a result of take-over difficulties, the Commission never owned more than about one-twentieth of the nation's goods vehicles.

Churchill interfered far more on the denationalisation of road haulage than on iron and steel.[9] Not only had he complete confidence in Duncan Sandys, responsible for the latter, but he decided, somewhat precipitously, that John Maclay, the Minister of Transport, was moving too slowly on road haulage. Public indignation, much of it justifiable, at this nationalisation, made him feel that road haulage should have the most urgent priority.[10] He took considerable interest in the Transport White Paper, going through it line by line in the Cabinet for over two hours which Harry Crookshank thought intolerable.[11] The White Paper itself, issued in May 1952, proposed major changes to the 1947 Act, and received a poor reception.[12] The details were worked out not by the Ministry of Transport but by an *ad hoc* Cabinet Committee, who also prepared the Transport Bill.

The White Paper proposed that road haulage be denationalised and the Road Haulage Executive abolished. It suggested a levy be paid by road users to compensate the railways for loss of traffic due to competition, and insisted that railways must not own any long-distance road transport.

The Transport Bill, published in July 1952, was felt to be an improvement on the White Paper, allowing the railways to own some road transport. It was still felt to be inadequate, however, chiefly because of the levy, and also the crude methods envisaged to dispose of road haulage to private concerns.[13] Crookshank announced that the Bill's Second Reading would not take place until after the summer recess,[14] to allow the Government time to reconsider. The Cabinet, after prolonged discussion, finalised their plans at the meeting on 29th October.[15] A second Bill was introduced in November,[16] differing from its predecessor in the amount of freedom given in fixing charges and introducing a modified form of levy.[17] Crookshank announced that the Bill would be subject to a Guillotine,[18] and in early December the House in Committee began a detailed examination of just the first two clauses, which dealt with those aspects of road haulage (relating to disposal after denationalisation) improved least since the initial White Paper, and therefore most in need of examination. The passage of the Bill proved to be stormy, especially the consideration of the House of Lords' amendments, and the Guillotine was finally brought down on 27th April, 1953.[19] The Bill became law on 6th May, 1953.[20] Important changes had arisen in the course of the discussions, foremost among them being the railways' freedom to decide on the matter of charges, and the greater degree of competition permitted with road haulage.

Unexpected difficulties were encountered in selling off the B.R.S. assets.[21] Vehicles offered in small lots sold well, but demand proved relatively small for the units large enough for potential buyers to be able to maintain the long-distance trunk services. Lennox-Boyd had been sensitive to accusations that low prices would be charged to those wishing to purchase transport units. He therefore asked the much respected Lord Portal to take on the chairmanship of the Road Haulage Disposal Board: he declined and Sir Malcolm Trustram Eve[22] was chosen in his place.[23] He proved a good choice as he was respected by Labour and helped take much of the sting out of their campaign: indeed, much of the unrest about the disposal operation came from the Government's own backbenchers who were anxious to force the pace.[24]

Pressure also came from the constituencies to sell off bus companies in municipalities, but the Cabinet were never keen on this. Lennox-Boyd, in particular, felt that such a policy would be too easily and assuredly reversed by Labour.[25] In its place the 1953 Act repealed the powers to nationalise municipal and private bus services under area schemes. The Act also gave the Minister powers to require the Transport Commission to divest itself of majority shareholdings in bus companies.

Iron and Steel

This had been the last industry to be nationalised,[26] the decision to end private ownership being the subject of particularly strong criticism from many quarters,[27] prominent among them the then Conservative Opposition. Plans had not had the chance to progress far so the physical operation of denationalisation was unlikely to cause many problems. The King's speech of November 1951 announced that the Iron and Steel Act would be annulled and the industry reorganised under free enterprise, with an adequate measure of public supervision.[28] In the debate on the Address,[29] George Strauss (Minister of Supply, 1947–51) stated that on their return to power, Labour would once again nationalise the industry, and that in this event the total compensation already paid out would not be increased. Sandys issued a directive on 13th November, 1951, preventing the Board from changing any part of the publicly owned steel companies without consulting him, thus shelving the plans for reorganisation of the industry on a regional basis.

The Government, amidst much speculation, appeared to hesitate in producing an Iron and Steel Bill. Partly, they were holding off denationalisation until the capital market was more willing to buy steel shares, but there were also divisions inside the Government about the timetable for the Bill, and the decision was taken at Cabinet on 24th April, 1952, to drop it for that session.[30] The Conservative backbenchers created a fuss about this, and the delay proved no more popular with the industry at large.[31]

The physical task of denationalising the industry was not technically difficult. The Government, however, given that it had decided to accept in large measure the mixed economy inherited from Labour, had to decide how much control should be retained over iron and steel after denationalisation. Relations between all interested parties were, for the most part, good, a situation helped by the awareness that steel industries in other countries were beginning to advance much more rapidly than in the U.K., and that if progress in an atmosphere of harmony was not achieved, steel might fare as poorly as other staple industries, such as coal-mining and ship-building.

The major decisions on how the industry was to be denationalised were taken initially by the Cabinet, and then at its Steel Committee,[32] often acting on the recommendations of the Ministry of Supply. The Department itself and its Ministers were responsible for dealing with the Corporation, the iron and steel trade, the unions, preparing the detailed legislation, and steering the Bill through the House. In his relations with the Corporation, Sandys was extremely tough. Steven Hardie, the Chairman, resigned in February 1952 and it was no secret that their relations were less than cordial. Sandys also summoned the new Chairman, Sir John Green, and the whole Board to his room when he felt they were being difficult about holding up reorganisation. Oliver Lyttelton wanted to press on with denationalisation at the earliest opportunity.[33] Others of a similar mind, such as Crookshank and Lord Woolton, wanted to see a wider measure of denationalisation. Rab Butler and Harold Macmillan, meanwhile, preferred the 'halfway' solution favoured by Sandys, who felt the Government would have to retain some degree of responsibility for the industry after denationalisation.[34] He wanted to produce a piece of legislation which would endure, and not be immediately reversed by Labour. Lord Cherwell had some serious reservations about steel denationalisation,[35] and Lord Leathers expressed concern about going ahead with the denationalisation due to the difficulty of finding private purchasers.[36] Lord Salisbury, who steered the Bill through the House of Lords, was very much in favour of it in the more moderate form, and in July threatened to resign when he disliked the way discussions were going in Cabinet.[37] Churchill, himself, was unenthusiastic. Lunching with Lord Beaverbrook early in September, he remarked that the sale of companies was impossible and that the best solution was to leave control to private enterprise, but ownership to the Government.[38] Drafting the Bill caused great difficulties,[39] not because of legal intricacies, but due to Sandys' determination to produce a well-expressed and clear-cut piece of legislation. In this respect it was much better than the original Iron and Steel Act of 1949, the drafting of which no one in the Ministry had much liked.

As far as future growth and price stabilisation were concerned, there was small change in policy,[40] and the Bill did little to stimulate competition in the industry. It specified that the new creation, the Iron and Steel Board, would be responsible for supervising the industry 'under competitive conditions', but this entailed minimal change from the existing practice under the Iron and Steel Federation.[41]

A White Paper on steel appeared in July 1952,[42] and like its transport counterpart was poorly received.[43] The Iron and Steel Bill, introduced that November, containing a number of modifications, was a considerable improvement on the White Paper. The passage of the Bill aroused far less opposition in the House than did the Transport Bill. The Second Reading even had to be adjourned at one stage as less than forty members were present.[44] The Third Reading, too, passed by with the minimum of fuss in February and March 1953, one day ahead of its timetable,[45] although Strauss, in his final speech, repeated the promise to renationalise the industry when Labour returned to power.[46] The general lack of fuss owed much to Sandys' careful management. The new Act, which became law on 6th May, 1953, repealed its 1949 predecessor, dissolved the Iron and Steel Corporation, established an Iron and Steel Board for the supervision of the industry[47] and provided for the return of iron and steel to private ownership. Sandys and Toby Low made a more than competent job of the denationalisation. Sandys showed firmness in the preliminary tussle with industrial interests, in which he brought the foundries under the Iron and Steel Board's supervision.

Disposal was entrusted to the Iron and Steel Holding and Realisation Agency (I.S.H.R.A.), which presented some difficulty, especially at first,[48] and took ten years to complete. It appeared impossible to sell off the main state holdings, Richard Thomas and Baldwins, and in the interim the Government was required to invest substantially in the firms remaining in its hands. By January 1955, steel companies accounting for some 50% of steel output had been disposed of, the figure rising to 86% by 1957.[49] The membership of the Iron and Steel Board was announced in May 1953, the Chairman being Sir Archibald Forbes.[50] Its main efforts were concentrated on prices and development, and in both fields made a decisive contribution to the industry's future, although the Board's impact took some time to work through.

Steel, unlike road haulage, was renationalised by Labour in 1967. It is not possible to assess the impact of the first nationalisation, as the Corporation had such little time to make progress on reorganisation. One can, however, see that in the fourteen years up to 1967, investment when compared with international competitors had been low, and technological advance slow.[51] Some have blamed the lack of authority given by the 1953 Act to the Board to promote investment and reorganisation.[52] In any event, the idea of having a body to supervise but not dominate a privately owned industry, plus the spectre of renationalisation, proved unconducive to allowing natural market forces to have their sway.

Select Committee on Nationalised Industries

Throughout their period in Opposition, Conservatives frequently drew attention to the need for public accountability of the industries nationalised by Labour, and at the 1951 Election they spoke of the need for stricter Parliamentary oversight. On 4th December, 1951 a Select Committee was appointed to consider the methods by which the House was informed of the affairs of nationalised industries and to make suggestions for improvements. In its Report (July 1953) the Committee recommended the appointment of a special Committee of the House to keep the nationalised industries under examination.[53] A discussion took place in the Commons on 8th February, 1954, and as a result, on 13th July, the Government announced that a Select Committee on the Nationalised Industries would be set up in the next Session. It was appointed on 16th March, 1955, and at its first meeting decided that its terms of reference were inadequate, and, with the support of the Conservative backbenchers, the Government agreed to expand them.[54]

Assessment

Labour vehemently opposed both Bills, yet it was impossible to argue that the Conservatives were attempting wholesale denationalisation. Many of the industries and services nationalised by Labour between 1945–51 were left in state hands, British Road Services was only partially dismantled, and the Iron and Steel Act retained a substantial measure of Government control. Indeed, it became obvious after 1951 that nationalisation was bringing few of the benefits claimed by its enthusiasts. It had not prevented a regular succession of acute balance of trade crises as some had hoped it might. There had been little revival in the coal industry, rail recovery had been modest, and the integration of road and rail transport, envisaged by Labour, had hardly begun by 1951. Lavish investment in electricity had tended to produce cheap power for domestic consumption rather than acting as an encouragement to the export of industrial manufactures. A leader in *The Times* in early 1953 put the position plainly: 'Nationalisation has lost the attraction it had in 1945.'[55]

Sir Norman Chester, in his mammoth study *Nationalisation of British Industry, 1945–51*, concluded that there were five areas concerning the industries which had not been fully settled when the Conservatives came to power in 1951: the relation of the Boards and Parliament (discussed above); the structure of the industries; the role of the Minister in relation to prices and wages; financial objectives and the treatment of non-commercial elements in the Boards' activities.[56] Two further areas may be added: relations between Ministers and Boards on the general conduct of their industry and the extent of consumer participation in the industries. In all but the non-commercial elements, important changes were initiated during 1951–5.

Over the structure of the industries the Government displayed little consistency. A number of enquiries into the organisation and administrations of the Boards were instituted, thus following the policy laid down by Herbert Morrison, when Lord President. The Government appointed an independent Committee on the supply and distribution of electricity and would have liked a similar enquiry into the National Coal Board, but were fearful of the National Union of Miners' reaction, and instead they left the Coal Board to arrange its own enquiry.[57] Thus a Committee was established under the chairmanship of Sir Alexander Fleck, whose Report favoured a strong central Board acting as a team with a powerful technical headquarters organisation. Most of the recommendations were immediately accepted and implemented by the Government.[58] This involved two departures from the previously expressed Government view on the organisation of nationalised industries: consultation on Board appointments and direct access of part-time members to the Minister.[59]

The Government took a different line on the organisation of the railways. The British Transport Commission under its powerful first Chairman, Lord Hurcomb, wished to centralise responsibility. The Government rejected this and in its Transport Act 1953 required the Commission to draw up a reorganisation scheme providing for decentralisation through area authorities.[60] The Government would not agree to an enquiry into railways before proceeding with its reorganisation plans, but it did agree to an independent enquiry in 1952 for London Transport, which was to remain virtually unchanged.[61]

As for the role of the Minister in relation to prices and wages, and the financial objectives the industries should pursue,[62] again the Government was inconsistent. In transport, the Government proposed a wide measure of competition: the railways would have minimum restraint on the fixing of charges. In the steel industry, however, where the range of competition was bound to be limited in an industry where large firms were needed for the sake of efficiency, competition was further circumscribed by the new Iron and Steel Board which could not only fix maximum prices and sanction or forbid investment, but could also import and allocate raw materials.

In the fuel industries, the Government boldly proclaimed the need for competition.[63] Thus in the debate on the gas and electricity industries on 9th November, 1954, Geoffrey Lloyd said he wanted the Boards to be venturesome and enterprising, and since every venture could not always be successful, he considered it his duty to defend the Boards if a sound enterprise failed. But as the Government never accepted the need for price policies which would have allowed the fuel industries to compete realistically with each other (in particular it pressurised the oil industry to sell its product at an unrealistically low price to power stations for electricity production) its advocacy of the virtues of competition in fuel appeared somewhat unconvincing.

Greater ministerial responsibility for increased capital investment was employed, a position that stemmed from the state of the development programmes of the nationalised industries. The Gas Council, Electricity Authority and Transport Commission were all approaching the statutory limits of their borrowing powers, and the Government therefore introduced legislation to produce increases. With the exception of steel and transport, the Conservatives did not appear to interfere any more than had Labour with the day-to-day management of prices and wages. The Government did however intervene, following a precedent set by the Attlee Government, over wages and working conditions, when dispute threatened on the railways.

In the sixth area, ministerial interference with the Boards on the general conduct of the industry was greater. In the industries which remained nationalised, the Ministers' statutory powers were not exceeded, although they were more broadly interpreted. But in the industries subject to denationalisation, Government intervention was felt to have gone beyond what had generally been considered the limit of statutory powers. This was particularly the case with the use of the power of the Minister to give a 'general direction', which had been envisaged by the nationalisation statutes for use in exceptional circumstances. It was first used by Sandys to prevent the Steel Board from making further reorganisations. Its second use aroused even more controversy as it could have been argued that the Government was setting a precedent for the exercise of directional power for political purposes. On 15th April, 1952 a directive was issued to prevent the Transport Commission raising certain fares. When the Minister's power to issue a directive was challenged in the House of Commons, Sir David Maxwell Fyfe justified its use on the grounds that the 'national interest' was affected by the cost of living. But in the Ministry of Fuel and Power, the Minister's attempts to produce greater co-ordination were frustrated precisely because the three Chairmen (of the Coal, Gas and Electricity Boards) knew the Minister only had power to give general, not specific directions on the running of the industries.[64]

The final aspect of the nationalised industries that had not been settled by 1951 was the extent of consumer participation in the industries. This was an area where Conservatives, with their philosophic belief in the merits of making nationalised concerns more responsive to consumers, might have been expected to introduce radical innovations. The 1953 Transport Act did indeed extend the scope of some of the Consultative Committees, but this was a rather half-hearted step which was not even attempted to the same extent in other nationalised industries.

The Conservatives, while still in Opposition, would have benefited from putting more into the framing of a consistent policy towards the nationalised industries. They returned in 1951 with little clear idea of how they wanted ministerial supervison arranged. Churchill originally hoped to appoint Leathers Minister for Nationalised Industries,[65] but had to settle for Leathers as co-ordinator over fuel and power and transport and civil aviation, which went at least some of the way.[66] There was also a certain irony which should be noted that, despite the Government's ambivalent views towards nationalised industries, it decided to transfer responsibility for atomic energy from the Ministry of Supply to a public corporation.[67] In short the Conservatives were ambivalent towards the industries, having a political distaste for their success, but fearful of the industrial and financial consequences of their failure.

Chapter 6   Economic Policy II

Part 1   The Ministry of Labour and National Service

In the conditions of full employment existing after 1945, the main emphasis of the Ministry of Labour and National Service, established in December 1916,[1] shifted to industrial relations. The Ministry remained responsible for a wide range of areas, such as safety, health and welfare, but by the 1950s it had become a conciliatory force, intervening, when required, to settle disputes. Its active economic role did not come until early in the following decade.[2]

The appointment of Sir Walter Monckton as Minister came as a surprise to many, not least to himself. When he entered the House after the Bristol West by-election in February 1951, which had been caused by the death of Oliver Stanley, Winston Churchill made it plain that he was earmarked as the next Conservative Attorney-General.[3] In the following months, however, he formulated other plans for Monckton, offering him the Ministry of Labour, a position Monckton did not particularly want.[4]

Churchill, who had longer experience of relations between Government and unions than any other politician or senior union leader, and who was anxious to avoid a repeat of the hostility between Conservative Governments and the unions between 1924–39,[5] insisted that if Monckton could not maintain close relations with the unions, he should resign.[6] Sir David Maxwell Fyfe, who had shadowed the Ministry of Labour in Opposition, was thus passed over for the Labour portfolio, due in part to the unions' alarm at his opinions on the 1927 Trade Union Act, which had been repealed in 1946. (He believed that the law in relation to the political levy should be changed, from 'contracting out' to 'contracting in'.)[7]

Monckton enjoyed the challenge presented by the Ministry and put his skills as a lawyer to good use in deciding the merits of each case, even if he did find the job a great strain. Nevertheless, it is an exaggeration to suggest, as does his official biographer, that he often sought advice on resignation.[8] Though he found the work taxing, he did not seriously consider the possibility[9] until 1954. Early in the New Year his health broke down during the rail crisis,[10] and as the year advanced he became more and more anxious to move to a new post.[11] His health remained poor, and by the end of the year the press was speculating that he would resign, although Monckton issued a firm denial.[12] In January 1955 he was ordered to take a complete rest for a number of weeks,[13] and as a result felt he must offer his resignation, though 'he was not in the least wanting to leave the Government'.[14]

There was the possibility that Monckton might become Lord Chancellor, but once Minister of Labour he set his sights on the post of Lord Chief Justice in succession to Lord Goddard.[15] This was almost certainly promised to him by Churchill on his appointment to Labour,[16] and by 1953 enquiries were being made as to Goddard's intentions.[17] Lord Simonds (Lord Chancellor 1951–4) suggested Monckton as a Law Lord as a vacancy was expected in the summer of 1954. In another plan Monckton was mentioned as Attorney-General in succession to Sir Lionel Heald. Meanwhile Brendan Bracken felt Monckton was right to leave Labour because of the strain, but strongly disapproved of Monckton as Attorney-General,[18] even with a seat in the Cabinet, and favoured Simonds' suggestion as the next step towards becoming Lord Chief Justice.[19] In the event Monckton stayed where he was, since his divorce in 1947 was always a handicap to his becoming Lord Chancellor.[20] Maxwell Fyfe was duly appointed to the job in October 1954, and Goddard remained firmly entrenched, being prepared to retire, Bracken considered, only 'if he thought that the comrades were coming back and would fill his place with a man he disliked.'[21] Indeed it was widely assumed that Goddard was not anxious to make way for Monckton.

Monckton's conduct of the Ministry attracted some criticism. Sir Wilfred Neden, for instance, was concerned at the persistent shortage of skilled workers, and advocated Government initiatives in retraining schemes.[22] But retraining was generally unpopular, and as Monckton had a precise remit to ensure there were no difficulties with the unions,[23] this effectively prohibited him from being an innovator.[24] His strength lay in other directions. He read papers and mastered arguments at great speed, had an excellent memory and incisive judgment, 'the best departmental civil servant of us all without doubt' according to one contemporary.[25] He was superb at dealing with people,[26] better even than Iain Macleod (Minister of Labour and National Service, 1955–9). He would always listen to his senior officials, even down to the third and fourth level, and would take seriously their suggestions, making them feel he much appreciated their point of view, even if he did not agree. This naturally created good morale, and he was popular in the Department, because it was soon obvious that he regarded himself as a member

197

of the team.[27] He was also a good advocate in Cabinet, which the Ministry respected, particularly since it came as a welcome change from the five and a half years of George Isaacs (Minister, August 1945 – January 1951).

Monckton in turn received good service from his officials, with whom he always retained the upper hand. He was fortunate in his Permanent Secretary, Sir Godfrey Ince.[28] Ince was a strong, even obstinate man, who had been widely recognised as an exceptional civil servant during the war,[29] with definite views on the functions of the Ministry of Labour. However, after the war – having become Permanent Secretary in 1944 – he wanted to hold on to the Department's wartime functions and this involved disagreements with the Treasury. Under Ince, the Ministry continued to play an important part in the life of the nation, although he personally became a controversial figure in Whitehall.[30] A planner by nature and a master of statistics, his orderly approach was better suited to questions of manpower supply than to industrial relations.

Monckton also worked well with the two Deputy Secretaries. Sir Harold Wiles, in charge of manpower and national service, played an invaluable part. His achievement was the more noteworthy because he laboured under the handicap of a speech difficulty, a legacy from the Great War. Sir Guildhaume Myrddin-Evans was theoretically responsible for industrial relations though these were largely left to the Chief Industrial Commissioner and the Minister. He devoted much of his energy to the International Labour Organisation (I.L.O.), and it was in this work that he made his greatest contribution. A past President of the I.L.O.[31] it was due largely to his influence that it became a specialised agency of the United Nations. Although important, his work had no immediate relevance to the problems of Britain's economy and industrial relations.

Three Chief Industrial Commissioners worked consecutively under Monckton, ranking amongst the most senior officials in the Ministry. Sir Robert Gould held the post when the new Government took office and remained until the end of 1952, taking a great deal of weight off Monckton in his first months. Hubert Gee, the most able intellectually of the three, succeeded him, though due to ill health he resigned prematurely. Neden followed in 1954, and achieved this position as a result of his reliability rather than his intellectual qualities. Monckton experienced no major differences of opinion with him, as there were later to be between Neden and Macleod. Monckton worked closely with his two Private Secretaries, Anthony Sutherland and, after 1953, Conrad Heron.[32]

Monckton's first Parliamentary Secretary was Sir Peter Bennett, who possessed one of the best understandings of industry among the Conservatives, and this almost certainly explained his appointment.[33] He did not, however, carry much weight as a junior Minister in the House, tending to be impatient with its workings, a factor responsible for his resignation after just seven months. His decision to retire was confirmed by a debate on unemployment in the Western Isles, where the House eventually adjourned at 7 a.m.: he found he had little sympathy with discussing the topic of herrings and lobsters at that hour.[34] By then over seventy years of age, he felt he had made his contribution. His replacement in the May 1952 reshuffle, Harold Watkinson, also had practical experience of industry and developed a close relationship with the Minister. More than many Ministers Monckton needed a strong Parliamentary Secretary and found his ideal complement in Watkinson.[35] Very much the up and coming young man, keen to make his name and acquire experience, he was anxious for as much of the Ministry's material as possible to come through him. During Monckton's absences due to ill health, his workload increased and he came to be seen eventually as a possible successor to his Minister.[36] But apart from Monckton's absences, neither he nor Bennett contributed a great deal to the work inside the Ministry, their main contribution consisting of a supportive role to Monckton and speaking in the House.

Monckton's main energies as Minister were devoted to the settlement of industrial disputes, the aspect of his work in which the Cabinet took most interest.[37] The strikes that concerned Monckton most were undoubtedly those which had the greatest impact on the economy, hence his particular anxiety over the railway disputes.[38] As a result he spent much less time on questions of safety, health and welfare, the international labour and manpower sides, which became, in the main, the province of his officials.[39] Thus the Baking Industry (Hours of Work) Bill of 1954,[40] one of the few pieces of legislation to emerge from the Ministry during 1951–5, was written by a junior civil servant. It nevertheless provided a telling example of Monckton's style as Minister, for on completing the speech, he made a point of warmly congratulating the official who was present in the House.[41]

Churchill, having given Monckton his instructions, tended to leave him alone, but backed him in Cabinet.[42] In private Churchill did much to cultivate personal relationships with individual union leaders,[43] but rarely intervened directly in disputes. He scarcely made himself felt in the Ministry, although nominally in charge during Monckton's absences, and he thought it tactically wise to avoid detail. His interest in the unrest in the electrical industries in September 1953,[44] in the railways at the end of 1953 and 1954,[45] and the newspaper strike in his last weeks in office were the only major exceptions.[46] Despite some personal antipathy to Churchill amongst trade unionists,[47] the T.U.C. was not opposed to seeking Churchill's direct intervention if it thought it to its advantage.[48]

The Cabinet seldom exercised much say in the conduct of industrial relations, though many soon became anxious about the continuous yielding to union demands.[49] Crookshank records how the Cabinet, discussing the dock strike which had resumed in October 1954, decided 'no troops as there may be a settlement',[50] but available evidence suggests that the Cabinet was not encouraged to offer its views on strikes, the two railway disputes being exceptions.[51] Woolton, discussing the railway unions' pressure on the Government to persuade the Transport Commission to meet their pay demands, wrote in late 1954: '. . . A year ago precisely similar circumstances arose, and as a result of the intervention and pressure of the Prime Minister, the Transport Commission gave way . . . It emerged . . . that [Sir Brian] Robertson [Chairman of the Transport Commission] had been opposed to giving way last Christmas.[52] I took that view.'[53] Turning to the position in the present, he continued: 'The cabinet was unanimous against giving a subsidy [to the Transport Commission], but not unanimous against letting Brian know that he could run into debt. The Prime Minister said that a strike now might ruin our Election prospects and also the Budget . . . I said that I didn't think that the Government ought to be prepared to intervene with a union that had not first gone through the appointed process of arbitration.'[54] Monckton, uncharacteristically, was against giving way: 'He said it would start off another series of demands from the miners, postmen, engineers, etc. Eden was very much against giving way. Churchill was unconvinced. He's frightened of a strike . . . Macmillan was all for appointing a committee of investigation which would postpone any decision until the summer when we could let them have a strike.'

This entry from Woolton's diary[55] provides a rare glimpse into the views of the senior Cabinet members on the question of strikes. In this particular case, a Court of Enquiry headed by Sir John Cameron was set up just before Christmas and its interim Report, published on 5th January, 1955, came down in favour of paying the railwaymen a 'fair and adequate wage', and contained the classic statement that in deciding to provide a nationalised rail service the nation had willed the ends, and would now have to will the means by paying the rail workers. Crookshank recorded how he 'Stood in for a Cabinet at 5.30 but the rail strike talks went on and on – eventually we stood down at 8 or so,'[56] and on the 6th January the strike was called off. Churchill recited to Lord

Moran the dire results which would have flowed from a strike, and finished by shouting: 'Do you realise all the things that were bound to happen, the change in the nation's life?'[57]

Monckton's methods of dealing with industrial unrest were not dissimilar to those used by his predecessors; the setting up of an enquiry if the unions and employers could not find a satisfactory compromise. The unions felt these enquiries were by and large independent of Government and were content for their members to sit on them, and, with very few exceptions, accepted their verdict. But enquiries were a last resort. Monckton would first try to settle disputes between interested parties, often at the Ministry of Labour's office in St. James's Square. He would seat the employers in one room, the union men in another, and the Chief Industrial Commissioner would move between the groups. Monckton preferred the informal approach, and was always available for consultation should it prove necessary. He later wrote:

> One's task was not to give judgment as in a law court, it was much more to examine and explore the field of conflict and reduce it patiently to its narrowest limits and then to indicate a way in which in that smaller field the parties might find a way of getting together.[58]

It was precisely in this process that Monckton's gifts of conciliation were employed to the full.

Until earlier in 1951 official strikes remained illegal, a hangover from the wartime Conditions of Employment and National Arbitration Order, which had been continued after 1945 with the agreement of the unions. Labour replaced it in their last months in office by the Industrial Disputes Order, which continued the provision for compulsory arbitration but permitted strikes after an award had been made by the Tribunal. On both sides of industry this fostered a readiness to compromise in the interests of industrial peace. This system only broke down at the end of 1953 when in four separate disputes, in the electrical, mining and engineering industries, but principally the December railway dispute, unions refused to be bound by arbitration.[59]

Relations between employers' organisations and trade unions had yet to become institutionalised. Consultations between unions and Government had been greatly expanded during the war and afterwards by the Attlee Government, and the Conservatives were anxious to continue the practice.[60] Indeed, to foster a relationship of confidence with the unions, Monckton took pains to keep the T.U.C. informed of action taken on major issues, particularly where the repercussions of a dispute might cause widespread lay-offs, or where an inter-union element existed, as with railway disputes.

201

Both sides of industry consulted regularly under the auspices of the National Joint Advisory Council (N.J.A.C), founded in 1946 to consider problems submitted to it by the Ministry of Labour, although individual industrial disputes lay outside the scope of their discussions. Monckton chaired the meetings of the N.J.A.C., a job he executed well and gained the trust of both sides.

The British Employers' Confederation (B.E.C.),[61] which dealt with labour relation questions, was dominated by its long-serving Director, Sir John Forbes Watson, until his death in August 1952.[62] It realised that the Government was following a conciliatory policy towards the unions, and that the settlements were the price to pay for industrial peace. The B.E.C. felt dissatisfied with the level of these settlements and also with the number of official strikes, but did not want the Government to introduce a wages policy. Monckton enjoyed good relations with its leaders, but not nearly so close as with their union counterparts. Despite their contact, especially after George Pollock took over from Forbes Watson, relations could, with profit, have been far closer and consultations more regular.

The T.U.C. issued a statement immediately after the 1951 General Election to say that it would of course work with the Government,[63] a pledge reiterated on later occasions. But it made clear its opposition to many Conservative policies. Several union leaders found relations easier with Monckton than with any other Minister of Labour in the early post-war years, even including those of the Attlee Administration, the rapport he developed with them being the more remarkable as they were all unknown to him in 1951. Recalled Sir Vincent Tewson, T.U.C. General Secretary throughout the period, 'He was liked by us all, and was friendly and helpful. His cool lawyer's mind never diminished the warmth of his personality.'[64] At a speech in Southsea on 15th July, 1953, Arthur Deakin, General Secretary of the T.G.W.U.,[65] said: 'I believe Sir Walter Monckton has given us a square deal and we have been able to do things that were difficult to do under our own people.'[66]

Some Conservatives disagreed with Monckton's appointment because, as he was not a member of the Committee that produced the 'Industrial and Workers' Charters', he showed little interest in implementing its proposals.[67] Instead, Watkinson announced[68] that the Government would, place before the N.J.A.C. an 'Industrial Code', embodying the principles set out in the Workers' Charter, namely that industry should provide workers with three general rights: security of employment; incentives to do the job well and get a better one; and status as an individual no matter the size of the firm. The unions, however, gave these ideas a cool reception, and modified proposals were put before a subcommittee of the N.J.A.C., set up in July 1953.[69] Meanwhile the Conservative Party formed a special committee to consider how individual trade unionists might best be wooed.

Its report was welcomed at the Margate Party Conference in October 1953 where Watkinson said: 'Today in the Conservative Party there is plenty of room for any and every trade unionist.'[70] Only two innovations, prohibiting the closed shop[71] and introducing postal ballots,[72] urged by certain sections of the Party, were not adopted because of this policy of deliberate courtship with the unions.

In many ways Monckton's was a wise appointment. A more doctrinaire man might well have upset the unions. Churchill saw the importance of keeping the unions sweet so that his Government could pursue its urgent tasks unhampered by labour troubles. Monckton's instructions were explicit. 'Winston's riding orders to me were that the Labour Party had foretold grave industrial troubles if the Conservatives were elected, and he looked to me to do my best to preserve industrial peace. I said that I should seek to do that by trying to do justice . . . without worrying about Party politics.'[73] Monckton's strength lay in the fact that he was accepted as neutral by both sides in a dispute, and that the union leaders had great confidence in him, appreciating that he had a special relationship with the Prime Minister. The unions still harboured suspicions about Churchill, although the war had done much to destroy the antipathy they felt towards him as a result of the General Strike of 1926, when he was Chancellor of the Exchequer. Monckton's work, aided by the popularity of Rab Butler as Chancellor, did much to allay the widespread fears amongst union members about the new Government.[74]

The policy of steering clear of trouble with the trade unions, regardless of cost, has since been widely criticised[75] as the major error of this Government. Even at the time, many in the Conservative Party and some Ministers found the levels of concession unpalatable. It meant, for example, an almost automatic enquiry if conciliation in a major dispute was unsuccessful. It meant also that, in order not to prejudice the Government's posture of impartiality, the Minister and other Government spokesmen refrained from comment on the substance of a dispute, even if it was widely held that the union claim in question was unrealistic. It meant further that when an enquiry reported, its recommendations were pressed on the parties as a basis of settlement, even if Ministers privately disagreed with them. More often than not, this entailed leaning on the employers to increase their last offer.[76]

Monckton, however, saw some measure of concession to the unions as an inescapable consequence of the Churchill instruction to avoid conflict. The risk always existed that 'standing up to the unions' would undermine the trust and confidence which the Government sought to build up and that a series of major industrial upheavals would be seriously damaging to the programme of post-war reconstruction. Yet, without question, the unions felt that they had got the better part of the bargain.

Monckton followed his remit to the letter. Lord Woolton recorded how, when discussing the railway dispute of December 1954 in Cabinet 'I was interested that Monckton – for the first time in my experience – was against giving away.'[77] However, few of Monckton's colleagues in Cabinet protested, at least not until 1954: they saw all too clearly the advantages of the Monckton policy. Wrote Harold Macmillan: '. . . it may well be argued that with the critical state of financial affairs, and in view of the slender majority by which we governed, any extensive or prolonged industrial dispute might have proved disastrous.'[78] Woolton himself reflected from the quiet of his retirement:

> It could so easily have happened that a strike that began on the industrial level, with a demand for more wages, could have become a strike against the Government's political policy. The fact that this issue was avoided was due to the wisdom shown by the trade union leaders and the determination of the Government, inspired by Mr. Churchill and executed by Sir Walter Monckton, to confine the issue to the industrial field, even at the risk of entering into compromises that could only have an inflationary effect.[79]

Butler himself saw the advantages, despite the inflationary consequences. 'It was all free collective bargaining, and that, of course, delighted Winston, who took no interest in any other system . . . If he'd gone on for ever, it would have been disastrous, but during my period it was extremely convenient. It didn't do me any harm.'[80] No one in Cabinet tried to have Monckton replaced, nor suggested a constructive alternative to his policy. 'Walter Monckton was so popular with Churchill and so affable and so able intellectually that no other policy was tried.'[81]

The conciliation policy was peculiarly well suited to the conditions of the early post-war years but would not have worked in more recent times. A number of factors accounted for its success. The trade union movement had grown immensely in stature during the war, when its leaders had closer contact with the Government than ever before with the result that their most senior figures[82] had become, in effect, part of the establishment. Their experience and prestige gave them confidence that they could take a reasonable line, and receive support from their rank and file. Their leadership was respected and they did not feel the need constantly to justify their actions: neither were they troubled by the consistent pressure from their members which in later years encouraged union leaders to ask for more sweeping concessions from successive Governments.

Even whilst Monckton was Minister of Labour, however, the trade union picture began to change. A new generation of union leaders clearly felt that more needed to be done by the leadership to reflect increasing shop-floor pressures that were already making themselves felt, particularly in the car industry and in the docks. Frank Cousins' appointment in 1956 as General Secretary of the Transport and General Workers' Union typified this trend.[83] Governments, responding to this, became increasingly interventionist, which in turn made relations more complex and less easy to handle. It is thus most unlikely that the policy that Monckton pursued in the early 1950s would have been applicable to the changed circumstances of later years.

Monckton was fortunate in having Alfred Robens as his opposite number on the Labour frontbench, a strong man, with whom he was personally friendly, and who greatly respected him. Robens felt relations were far better than would have been the case if the Government had had a less moderate Minister of Labour.[84] Another Labour politician, Harold Wilson, said: 'Monckton could do almost anything in the House, and it seemed as if he could do anything with the unions as well. He was certainly one of the most impressive of that Cabinet.'[85] Monckton's continuous insistence that politics should be kept out of industrial relations strengthened this relationship. He did not go out of his way to make friendships with his more doctrinaire and 'political' colleagues, and avoided, where he could, the Party Conferences, feeling that to appear too partisan might jeopardise his relations with the unions.[86] The state of the economy, which steadied the unemployment rate at nearly two per cent, and brought steady growth, helped Monckton's position.

Several factors, however, worked against him. In 1951 he arrived at the office with a heritage of outstanding and awkward wage claims, involving some six million workers. He also had to overcome initial misgivings at his appointment from much of industry and from both sides of the House. Suspicion was prevalent among some trade unions during these years about new productivity methods, and the British Productivity Council, formed in 1952 to continue the work of developing industrial efficiency, inevitably led to some redundancies. Skilled labour was in short supply, which caused constant pressure on wages as firms competed for those with the requisite skills. To help combat this,

Monckton introduced the Notification of Vacancies Order, 1952,[87] which went some way to ensuring that employees used Employment Exchanges, rather than offering their services direct to firms on their own terms. Finally, though the underlying growth trend in the economy relieved inflationary wage pressure, inflation had been exacerbated as a result of the Korean war boom, which presented an additional stimulus to wage demands.[88]

The Treasury was keen on instituting a policy which would moderate the level of wage settlements, though it did not always find a willing ear in Butler, who had suggested, shortly after becoming Chancellor, that wage increases might be linked to productivity, but the T.U.C. demurred.[89] Treasury pressure was responsible for Butler's homily to the N.J.A.C. in July 1953 about the danger of wage increases to British exports: a 10% rise in wages in manufacturing industry without a corresponding increase in productivity would raise the price of exports by $4\frac{1}{2}\%$.[90] Sir Robert Hall, Butler's chief economic adviser, became increasingly worried by the risk of inflationary pressure. But the Treasury's anxiety, although echoed in the Cabinet by Woolton and others, carried little sway with Churchill.[91] By the end of 1953, the policy of support for free collective bargaining backed by conciliation came under increasing threat. Disputes in the engineering and ship-building industries were settled after Monckton set up Courts of Enquiry, both of which recommended increases of about five per cent. The threatened strike on the railways at the end of 1953 was similarly deflected after a promise of increased pay. The policy was more severely strained by the N.U.R.'s threatened strike on the railways a year later, although this was resolved by the Court of Enquiry under Sir John Cameron, referred to above. But it was not until 1955 that the policy began to break down under the collective effect of three national strikes of political significance: the docks; the newspaper industry and the third railway dispute.

There existed, however, little fundamental questioning of the system of free collective bargaining or any measure of agreement in these years about any possible alternative.[92] In the later 1950s, when a relationship of trust had been built up between the trade unions and the Conservative Government, the time may well have been ripe for wide-ranging talks, and possibly even a Royal Commission. Issues such as the closed shop, restrictive practices, legal immunities, secret ballots, and an agreement on a policy for wage settlements could then have been discussed. But this would have needed the active consent of the unions. As it was the issues were ducked, an opportunity missed.

Monckton achieved at the Ministry of Labour what he had been asked to do. Industrial peace was, with a few interruptions, the order of the day, and it was not until 1955 that working days lost through industrial disputes rose much above the average for 1946–51. The cost was of course some degree of 'wage push' inflation. The arguments for and against the wisdom of the policy of conciliation are nicely balanced. It would, however, be wrong to blame Monckton: he was acting on the express direction of the Prime Minister, and neither Churchill nor the Chancellor wished to alter the policy, nor did Monckton's junior Minister, Watkinson. The Conservative Party's Labour Committee[93] was in the main content with the Monckton line, but the B.E.C. made anxious noises, as did the Cabinet after the first two years. Yet Monckton's conduct of industrial relations was not only, up to a point, inevitable: to a considerable extent it was a collective policy.

Part 2　The Ministry of Food

The Ministry of Food had existed between 1916 and 1921, under the title Ministry of Food Control, and was set up again in 1939 on the outbreak of war. It introduced rationing, first of butter, bacon and sugar in January 1940, followed shortly afterwards by meat, margarine, cooking fat, tea and cheese, and later sweets. The Labour Government initially retained the Department to administer rationing of basic food-stuffs and the bulk purchase of overseas supplies. The experience was not entirely happy: the attempt to deration sweets was unsuccessful, as were two other projects, John Strachey's ground-nut plan and the Gambian egg scheme. However, by the spring of 1950 Clement Attlee was asking the Ministry what steps could be taken to end rationing and control,[1] and as a result some food-stuffs, such as jam, were derationed, and other items, such as butter and sweets, had their weekly allowance increased.

Labour might well have kept the Ministry in existence, whereas, to the Conservatives, the winding up of the Ministry was always inseparable from ending food control.[2] But in terms of policy, there was little change after the General Election, no more than an increased emphasis on the need to end controls on both buying and selling.[3] The governing factor for the new Government was the same as it had been for the old, namely what was practicable in terms of available food supplies. Indeed, for the first year, the Conservatives had to tighten controls, cut down imports, and were forced to take the unpopular step in 1951 of cancelling the customary Christmas bonus of rations. In the early summer of 1952 they even thought it might be necessary to cut the butter ration the following autumn.

As a Minister of some experience it was widely expected that Gwilym

Lloyd-George would be given a more senior job. Lord Llewellin, Food Minister for the last eighteen months of the war, had been thought more likely for the post, having been tipped for it by as reliable a source as Geoffrey Cox in the *News Chronicle* two days after the Election. But Lloyd-George it was to be. He had been Parliamentary Secretary at Food before being promoted to Minister of Fuel and Power in 1942–5. Yet in his second spell at Food he was highly successful, in marked contrast to his performance later at the Home Office. An impressive figure, the younger son of David Lloyd George, he was always well dressed, had a beautiful Welsh voice, and although a poor speaker, was one of the most popular Ministers in the House. As a profile in the *Observer* recorded the week he left the Ministry: 'Like Sir Walter Monckton, Gwilym Lloyd-George is that rare bird in politics – a thoroughly nice man. He has no airs, no conceit, no secret snobberies.' But throughout his period at Food he was essentially only a front man; the ideas and drive in the Department were not his own. He was not a hard worker, even sometimes lazy and indecisive, and his officials found him reluctant to commit himself to paper, although they all greatly liked him. His main strength, his political instinct, enabled him to head a Ministry whose record was one of the best of that Government. He was promoted to the Cabinet in the September 1953 reshuffle with Sir Thomas Dugdale, Minister of Agriculture. This made no difference to the Department as he had previously attended Cabinet meetings whenever food matters were being discussed. Nor did it make much difference to the Cabinet, as Lloyd-George seldom spoke outside his subject.[4]

Lloyd-George relied most on Charles Hill, the Parliamentary Secretary, and Sir Henry Hancock, the Permanent Secretary. Hill, who only entered the House in 1950 after six years as Secretary to the British Medical Association, was yet another surprised at his appointment made at the request of Lloyd-George.[5] Hill had made his name as the 'radio doctor' during the war. His new job could hardly have been tougher as Lloyd-George delegated a great deal of speaking in the House to him, and food policy was a controversial area, especially in the early years. He spoke mainly on the lower-level arguments, such as rationing orders, which he did well; indeed he could make a good speech with little warning. But it was on policy that he had his biggest impact. Early on he sensed that it would be possible to decontrol various foods, and the political pressure within the Ministry to accomplish this came from him far more than from Lloyd-George. His influence as junior Minister was thus more than most, a result not only of his own ambition and hard work, but also of Lloyd-George's lack of assertiveness, and a reluctance to dampen Hill's enthusiasm, provided their views did not clash.

Hancock had a wider experience than most senior officials, having served at the Ministries of Labour and Supply and the Home Office. He arrived at Food shortly before the Election in 1951, after two years as Permanent Secretary of the Ministry of National Insurance. He was a professional administrator of high quality, and the Ministry was delighted that someone of his mark was appointed. He oversaw both branches of the Ministry, the supply and commodity (the 'buying' side), and the service, distribution and rationing (the 'selling' side).

From Hill came much of the political initiative for decontrol, from Hancock much of the administrative drive which made it possible.[6] They were helped by one of the ablest groups of civil servants in any Department.[7] Recruited in 1939 from other Ministries, the universities and the food trade, they had built up an *esprit de corps* not always found in larger or older Departments. Of the two Deputy Secretaries, Sir Laurence Helsby worked on the selling side, where much of his effort went into the chain of distribution prices, a complex business, the prices being fixed after intricate accounting surveys. He was outstandingly efficient, able though not universally popular, and had the additional advantage of having served as Attlee's Principal Private Secretary (1947–50).[8] On the buying side was the ebullient but shrewd Sir Albert Feaveryear who did a great deal to find world food supplies for Britain until he died in office in April 1953.

Before derationing could begin, various problems had to be overcome. Above all, food-stuffs had to be found (and there were still world shortages of many foods, as Labour had found) so that the extra demand which would follow derationing could be met. Meanwhile bulk purchase, which was responsible for two-thirds of food imports in 1951, was ended.[9] Finding the currency with which to pay for the food was a major concern, especially in the first year when sterling was in short supply and the Treasury was reluctant to let extra sterling leave the country.[10] As Lord Woolton wrote to Winston Churchill: 'The amount of rationed meat we can bring in from the Continent is . . . limited by currency difficulties.'[11] However, the position eased gradually during the year. On 7th May the Economic Policy Committee of Cabinet decided to limit the import of South American meat for 1952–3 to £30m., but this was overriden six days later by the Cabinet which decided that no financial limit was necessary.[12]

Re-establishing markets was an added difficulty. Apart from the meat trade, most food groups were reluctant to see an end to state control, as in the years since 1939 they had become accustomed to the security of guaranteed supplies and margins. Many of the younger managers in the

209

trade had little experience of competition, and others did not want altered their share of available trade which had been maintained at pre-war levels.[13] Moreover, a whole generation had grown up who had no experience of a free market in food: the position was epitomised by the young journalist who at the press conference where Sir Thomas Dugdale announced egg derationing, said: 'But Minister, in a free market, who will fix the price of eggs?'[14]

A further problem was political: derationing could only take place after subsidies had been reduced, since, for most food-stuffs, subsidies without rationing would mean an unlimited Exchequer liability. But the Government was wary about the political consequences.[15] Food subsidies were first introduced in 1941 at a level of £63m. to stabilise the prices of basic foods during the war. By 1945–6 the cost of these subsidies had risen to £265m., and was pegged at £465m. by Stafford Cripps in 1950, being reduced later that year to £410m. In his 1952 Budget Rab Butler proposed to reduce the annual rate of food subsidies from £410m. to £250m. by the end of the financial year 1952–3, partly to facilitate decontrol. This provoked a major row in the House,[16] and cuts in food subsidies continued to provide fuel for Labour criticism for many more months. Their anger was not fully justified, however. Food subsidies for 1952–3 still totalled £334m., although by 1955 they had been removed from most foods, except bread and milk. Yet the rising cost of support prices and deficiency payments to farmers, plus welfare subsidies, all included in the food subsidies bill, meant the sum paid on this form of expenditure was still as high as £330m. in 1954–5.

Each sector of food to be derationed needed a precise timetable. This was simple enough with a self-contained item such as tea, where the buyers' market did not have to be complex. But with a food-stuff such as meat, with many interrelated commodities, enormous difficulties arose, as decontrol had to be synchronised with other substances such as animal feeding-stuffs with which it was linked.[17]

Undoubtedly, the pace at which derationing took place was aided by Churchill's enthusiasm, since it was one of the issues that concerned him most on the domestic front.[18] In the first months of the new Government, when Lloyd-George was becoming established, a number of Minutes came from Churchill, urging extensions of meat imports,[19] or crisp messages such as: 'Would it be possible to make a plan to deration pork and let it rip?'[20] Churchill was more doubtful about egg derationing as we shall see.[21] But Churchill's interest was usually erratic.[22] Once items began to be derationed he saw their great propaganda potential, meat in particular being regarded as a major item in contemporary newsreels, and backed Lloyd-George all the way, and was further enthusiastic about winding up the Ministry. He played a major part in pressing for sugar derationing,[23] against the initial caution of some officials in both the Ministry of Food and the Treasury.

Before items could be derationed they had to be returned to private trade as with tea at the end of 1950; it was then derationed in October 1952. Sugar was partially returned to private trade in October 1952, and derationed in September the following year. There had been disagreement with the Ministry of Agriculture, who wanted to increase domestic sugar beet production, while the Ministry of Food wanted to import and so deration sooner, but in the end the problem was much more one of securing funds to buy the sugar than of finding supplies.[24] With sugar decontrolled, sweets could be derationed in February 1953. The Conservatives, in fact, in underestimating demand, nearly repeated Labour's mistake of derationing too early, and were only saved by buying large quantities of Cuban sugar.[25] Cream followed in April 1953, though the Government were cautious about this as they were sensitive to possible Opposition attacks that they were giving priority to foods for the rich.[26]

Eggs were derationed in March. They had been the subject of much discussion in the Cabinet, partly because the popular press had speculated that eggs would, as a result, double in price. Churchill was worried: 'Oh my poor people, they can't pay a shilling for eggs.' But Dugdale, backed by his officials convinced him to the contrary,[27] and in the event egg prices fell. Little else was derationed in 1953, but in May 1954 butter, cheese, margarine and cooking fats followed.

Meat was the last major item. Woolton was especially anxious to see an end to rationing as the Opposition had picked up a phrase he had made in an Election broadcast about 'red meat', and used it to taunt him by arguing that Woolton had meant there would be more red meat immediately.[28] Churchill was similarly enthusiastic, to see meat derationed, believing meat to be vital for his 'island people'.[29] The problems were again ones of finding adequate supplies (especially as imports of Argentinian meat had been discouraged after the war) and persuading the Treasury to pay for imported meat. In the event the decontrol of animal feeding-stuffs in May 1953 facilitated a great increase in the supply of pork and paved the way for derationing.[30] There remained the question of how domestic livestock would be supported when control came to an end. The Ministry of Agriculture and the farmers favoured a monopolistic producers' marketing board for home suppliers and a fixed price; the Ministry of Food and the traders a return to the former marketing methods with the addition of a deficiency payments scheme, the solution the Cabinet adopted.[31]

211

As rationing and bulk purchase came to an end, the Government began to think more specifically about the future of the Ministry. Not all its functions would simply disappear: the nature of food administration had changed radically since 1939, there was continuing work to be done on the administration of financial assistance to farmers, work on food hygiene and maintenance of nutritional values as well as overseas commitments to be wound up. There were three choices. To keep in existence an independent Ministry, called perhaps the Ministry of Nutrition, an option not favoured by the Government with its preference for reducing the number of Departments. To close it down, transferring its functions to the Board of Trade, which had had responsibility for emergency food administration in the interwar years. But it was widely felt that the Board of Trade was large enough already, and, as it turned out, the Board of Trade itself did not care for Food's leftovers. The scheme had, however, been favoured by Hill[32] and also some Ministry officials themselves (who as a first choice had hoped to keep the Ministry in existence as an independent Department). This group of officials were rather more the 'old guard', who were especially opposed to the third option – the one eventually adopted – of merging the Ministry's remaining functions with the Ministry of Agriculture and Fisheries. They felt that if the Ministry of Food joined Agriculture, the consumers' interest would lose out to the producers', while the Ministry had been a strong balancer of both interests. Neither Lloyd-George nor Hancock, however, had serious objections to the merger.[33]

Over the last few years, relations between both Departments had at times distinctly lacked harmony, with Agriculture urging high guaranteed prices as the basis for home-grown commodities, and Food pressing for more imports so the process of derationing could be hastened and prices kept down. Resistance to the merger was not confined to Food; some officials in Agriculture[34] and other interested parties, including the N.F.U.,[35] felt unhappy about it. A leader in *The Times* on 18th October, 1954 said that the remaining functions of the Ministry of Food 'should have gone anywhere rather than to the Minister of Agriculture. It is asking too much of any Minister to be able to hold the balance fairly between the interests of the consumer and the powerful agricultural interest . . .' The *Manchester Guardian* was even more outspoken in its opposition to the merger: in a leader on 18th October, 1954, it suggested consumer interests might fall prey to Agriculture's 'restrictionist mentality and their insatiable demand for high food prices'.

A joint Minister for both Departments, Derick Heathcoat Amory, was appointed on 18th October, 1954, and a draft Order providing for

212

amalgamation was approved by the House of Commons on 28th March, 1955. Hill remained as junior Minister for a few months to pilot through the Food and Drugs (Amendment) Act, before his surprise appointment in April 1955 as Postmaster-General.

Despite qualms on both sides, the merger was executed smoothly, and it was to the credit of the Whitehall system that differences were sunk so speedily. Fears that the consumer interest might be submerged did not, however, prove totally without foundation. But the merger was in fact by far the best of the possible solutions. Conflicts between the producers and consumer interest were now settled in one Department, and very often in one part of that Department.[36]

Labour opposed every derationing Order, but not in earnest as they realised decontrol was bound to come.[37] Neither did food prices soar, as the Opposition predicted. In fact the retail price index, of which food items constituted 40% of the total, rose by only 15% from October 1951 to May 1955, with coffee, meat, tea and margarine having slightly higher price rises.[38] Factors in the world economy[39] were ultimately responsible for making derationing possible. Labour was moving in the direction of more freedom, but it is unlikely that it would have capitalised on the favourable conditions as quickly as Lloyd-George and Hill.

Part 3   The Ministry of Agriculture and Fisheries

The prominence of this Ministry increased considerably during and after the war as a result of the commitment to maintaining agricultural production.[1] In 1945, the prospect of a world food shortage for many years, coupled with the need to maintain reserves of foreign exchange, made all political Parties accept the need for Government action to ensure high domestic food production,[2] unlike after the First World War when the machinery and measures for increasing home food production were soon dismantled. In particular, the important decision was taken in 1947, on Sir Edwin Plowden's advice, to increase agricultural output by 50% on the pre-war, and 20% on the 1947 level, in an effort to prevent a balance of payments crisis. Plowden argued that Britain would reap a greater return on capital spent on agriculture than elsewhere. When devaluation was forced on Britain in 1949 the original basis of the agricultural expansion programme was shaken (although neither Attlee nor Churchill later fully examined the programme to see if it was still on course).[3] All the same a prominent position for the Ministry was assured amongst the economic Departments in Whitehall; even though the Conservative Minister of Agriculture did not sit in the Cabinet until 1953, this was not an indication of downgrading, rather that in Lord

Woolton there was an 'overlord' in the Cabinet responsible for food and agriculture.

The Agriculture Act, 1947, based on the conclusions formed by the Coalition Government during the war that agricultural policy should be based on guaranteed prices and assured markets, also laid down the method of conducting relations between the Government and the farmers. The Act, in addition, made permanent the wartime system of County Agricultural Executive Committees, charged with the duty of promoting agricultural development and efficiency. Initially these Committees played a considerable part in the expansion of domestic food production, albeit gradually, but the removal of controls after 1951 caused their powers to dwindle.[4]

Labour's Minister of Agriculture throughout 1945–51 was Tom Williams, who held the job longer than anyone else this century and enjoyed high personal prestige with the farmers and in the House. There was uncertainty about his Conservative successor. Robert Hudson, Minister during the Coalition Government (1940–5), was certainly in the running, but was passed over and resigned his seat in the Commons the following year.[5] The post was instead offered to a man influential in Party circles, a former Chairman of the Party (1942–4), and in the last Parliament Chairman of the Conservatives' Agriculture Committee, Sir Thomas Dugdale.[6]

Dugdale had been Stanley Baldwin's Parliamentary Private Secretary from 1935–7.[7] His political sense was astute, he was hard-working, amiable, very well liked by his staff, and took a keen interest in the work of the office. He also earned the confidence and respect of the Labour Party to an extent achieved by few other Ministers during the period.[8] He deserves much credit for the way he succeeded in securing the farmers' agreement on the move away from guaranteed prices and markets for their produce. But he was handicapped by his lack of previous ministerial experience, and his resources were fully stretched as Minister, allowing him little play for outside interests or for taking a broad view of policy. When he first arrived at the Ministry he gave the impression that he had more familiarity than Williams with the way the economy worked, but officials soon found this was not so.[9] On matters of policy his judgment was good, although invariably based on the advice of his officials. As a landowner he was more interested in broad questions of land than in details of derationing and payments, which he never entirely mastered.

Derick Heathcoat Amory (1954–8), who succeeded Dugdale after his resignation in July 1954, was altogether a more adept Minister. He told Winston Churchill on his appointment that he had had little experience of agriculture (a typically self-deprecating remark) to which Churchill responded that the Department was crammed with hundreds of experts[10] and he did not want another. He had a good mind, coupled with an understanding of the way the economy worked,[11] but was uncertain of himself at the beginning, and relied a great deal on the experienced Richard Nugent, his Parliamentary Secretary in the Commons. He was disappointed by the way his speech on agriculture went at the October 1954 Party Conference at Blackpool, but his confidence in his undoubted abilities began to return with the New Year.[12]

The practice of having two Parliamentary Secretaries, one in the Lords the other in the Commons, had grown since 1940 (only the Home, Colonial and Foreign Offices operated similarly). Both were assigned specific areas to oversee, although, as any question on the Department's work could be raised in either House, the junior Minister would deal with it, regardless of whether or not it fell within his special field of interest.[13] Neither Nugent nor Lord Carrington, the two Parliamentary Secretaries appointed in 1951, had previous ministerial experience. Nugent, however, had been on the Council of the National Farmers' Union (N.F.U.) and on its General Purposes Committee. They were both considered highly promising younger men (Carrington was thirty-two when appointed, Nugent forty-four, but had only entered the House the previous year), and played a larger part in the work of the Ministry than many junior Ministers in other Departments. Carrington dealt with the landowner and travelling side, which involved visits to the Agricultural Executive Committees, and Nugent concentrated on the N.F.U.[14] Carrington, who had yet to mature into the accomplished Minister of his later years, was regarded by the Ministry as promising and exceptionally pleasant to deal with. Anthony Hurd, a farmer and agricultural journalist, had originally been offered the job of Parliamentary Secretary,[15] but turned it down because he could not afford to become a Minister and preferred a country existence.[16] Instead he became a strong Chairman of the backbench Agriculture and Food Committee. In the October 1954 reshuffle Carrington's place – he was appointed junior Minister at Defence – was taken by Lord St. Aldwyn, another newcomer to ministerial life.

The Permanent Secretary since 1945 was Sir Donald Vandepeer. A man of great drive and energy, the undisputed master of the Department, he had been in the Ministry of Agriculture all his life and had a considerable understanding of the subject.[17] He retired in 1952, and was succeeded by Sir Alan Hitchman. No immediate change was obvious in either administration or policy, although the two men were very different. Hitchman came with little initial knowledge of agriculture, and was the less forceful character. But where Vandepeer's horizons barely stretched beyond the work of the Ministry, Hitchman had a much broader view of agriculture in relation to the rest of the economy. He had worked in the Ministry of Labour for twenty-one years before moving to the Treasury in 1947 (latterly as Third Secretary), and from 1951–2 had been the first Permanent Secretary of the new Ministry of Materials. Initially he found N.F.U. leaders difficult in negotiation but this passed and he was soon to be esteemed both by farmers as well as by Ministry officials. Dugdale tended to find him more sympathetic than he had the sterner Vandepeer.

Beneath the Permanent Secretary worked two Deputies. Until 1947 there had been just one, but in that year, with the expansion of the Ministry's work, Sir Edward Bridges decided a second Deputy should be appointed. After the merger with the Ministry of Food, the number of Deputy Secretaries was increased to three: Deputy A managed the old Ministry of Food Divisions; Deputy B the scientific side, at first presided over by Sir George Dunnett, and Deputy C, the economic, Sir Reginald Franklin.[18] There was also a Fisheries Secretary[19] with the grade of Under-Secretary who until the merger reported direct to the Permanent Secretary, but whose work afterwards fell within the jurisdiction of Deputy C. The two main aims of the Government's fishing policy during 1951–5 were to take action on over-fishing in the North Sea, a problem which had come to the fore since 1950, and to act on the state of the near and middle-water fleets. In 1953 the Over-fishing Convention of 1946 was ratified, and a permanent Commission set up. Little could be done immediately and the total tonnage of fish landed in the U.K. fell from 930,000 tons in 1951–2 to 820,000 tons in 1953–4. The White Fish and Herring Industries Act, 1953, supplied grants towards the cost of new engines and boats for the run-down near and middle-water fleets.[20]

The creation of the Forestry Commission in 1919 relieved the Ministry of its responsibility for forestry work, but regular contact was maintained, in order to reconcile the interests of agriculture and reafforestation. The important decisions in forestry had, however, been taken before 1951. The Report of the Forestry Commissioners on post-war forestry policy,[21] published in 1943, recommended more than doubling the forest area in Great Britain to five million acres after the war. The Forestry Acts of 1947 and 1951 were designed to help realise this, and in January 1954 new and amended grants for replanting and maintenance were announced.

Agriculture was not a particularly controversial subject between the Parties and disagreements were invariably about means rather than ends. As Churchill was to say in the House early in 1953, 'British agriculture is no Party issue. It is a national issue.' This bipartisan approach continued in the main until Christopher Soames' period as Minister (1960–4).

Agricultural policy between 1951–5 was based on two broad aims: to maximise food production, and to devise a new marketing system which would continue to provide stability for farmers in the conditions of freedom made possible by the end of shortages and state trading.[22]

The 1947 target of a 50% expansion in agricultural production had not been realised by 1951, despite rapid growth initially. The 1949–50 figures were 13% up on the 1947 level, but there was scarcely any further improvement during 1950–1.[23] In the agriculture White Paper, of May 1952,[24] eight objectives were set out to raise production above the pre-war level: the basic problem it diagnosed as a lack of financial resources, especially amongst the smaller farmers. To compensate, substantial awards at the 1952 and 1953 Annual Price Reviews[25] were given in the form of production grants and in assistance to small farmers and to those cultivating difficult land. As a result of these efforts, net agricultural production was raised on the 1947 level to the desired 20% by 1952–3 and 22% by 1953–4.[26] By the 1954 Price Review[27] the emphasis had moved to the importance of improving efficiency, and thereby making possible a steady reduction in cost to the Treasury.

The second aim was to devise a system of price guarantees for farm products which would operate after the ending of food rationing and controls. Under the Labour Government, the practice had been for prices to be fixed annually by the Ministry in consultation with the Treasury and also the Ministry of Food, the Government's main buying agent. After 1951 various systems of price guarantee were considered by the Conservatives, but eventually a system of deficiency payments was evolved, whereby the Ministry of Agriculture fixed a guarantee price, and if the market price the farmer received was below this level, then he would receive a deficiency payment to make up the difference.[28] It was a complicated process as prices had to be worked out individually for each product at the time of each Annual Price Review.

The main ministerial work on this was done by Nugent, and Basil Engholm, who ran the Marketing Division and was later Permanent Secretary at the Ministry, 1968–72. The Government's plans were laid out in a White Paper 'Decontrol of Food and Marketing of Agricultural Produce', published in November 1953.[29] State purchase of home-produced food could no longer continue, it maintained, but the Government nonetheless firmly adhered to the principles of the Agriculture Act, 1947,[30] and accepted their obligation to provide a stable and efficient system.

The system of deficiency payments came about as the result of extensive talks with farmers and traders during 1952–3. The N.F.U. in particular was worried about the new arrangements,[31] preferring a producers' marketing board, and won various allowances and concessions from the Government. The 1954 Annual Review promised Exchequer support of £200m. a year for home agricultural production, though a steady reduction in this sum was envisaged for following years. Unease amongst the farming community declined visibly after this. The value of guarantees as a whole was raised by £28m. in the 1955 Annual Review, largely because the 1954 harvest had been the worst for fifty years.

The deficiency payments scheme worked in different ways for each commodity. For milk, the determination of monthly prices for producers fell to the Milk Marketing Boards, who had their marketing powers restored in April 1954. Eggs, on the other hand, after being decontrolled in March 1953, could be sold to packing stations which would pay producers the best price they could receive in the light of market demand, and farmers would be sure of receiving at least the guaranteed basic minimum price fixed after the Annual Review. Deficiency payments were, on the whole, a good scheme, but they had one major drawback which was never resolved: they did not correlate home and foreign produce. If imports of agricultural goods came in at a low price, the farmers were dependent upon the Treasury for support.[32]

Relations between the Government and the N.F.U. were good throughout these years despite the latter's initial opposition to the system of deficiency payments.[33] This relationship was aided considerably by the Ministry being concerned with only one industry and, even after the merger with Food, only two. As a result contact was much closer than was possible in some other economic Departments, notably the Board of Trade, which dealt with a number of industries. The N.F.U. was well led by Sir James Turner, President 1945–60,[36] with Joshua Knowles, General Secretary, 1945–70, a key figure in the background, but some in the Ministry felt its actions not always in the best interests of the nation. The Treasury official in charge of agricultural prices was initially quite junior and consequently unable to stand up to the farmers, while Turner was one of the few people whose arguments could, in the last resort, prevail against Rab Butler's.[35]

Price settlements were undoubtedly more inflationary than they need have been, but this was not just the fault of the N.F.U.: Conservative Governments were always more susceptible to pressure from the farm lobby, and conscious of the importance of votes in agricultural constituencies.[36] The influence of the N.F.U. was at its height under

218

Dugdale, and greater than it had been under Williams, but it gradually decreased after the arrival of the tougher Heathcoat Amory, who was responsible for stabilising relations with the farmers in a way that had not been achieved since the 1947 Act.[37]

The philosophy that food production was paramount overrode landowner rights and was responsible for the affair of Crichel Down,[38] the issue over which Dugdale resigned in July 1954. Land in Dorset, compulsorily purchased by the Air Ministry for war use, was transferred to the Ministry of Agriculture in 1949, and by them to the Agricultural Land Commission for development as a single farm. A local resident, Lieutenant-Commander George Marten, whose wife would have inherited much of the land but for the compulsory purchase order, and who had important political connections, protested that they were not given the opportunity to purchase back the land. As a result of prolonged agitation, Dugdale, in October 1953, appointed Sir Andrew Clark, Q.C., to hold a public enquiry into the affair. He recalled, '. . . All sorts of rumours were being bandied about in the press and elsewhere about the evils of the civil servant . . . to such a state that people were saying that there was corruption going on . . . Directly that situation developed I saw the only thing to do was to set up a completely independent enquiry to look into the whole matter.'[39] Some informed opinion felt that Clark was not sufficiently impartial. His Report, published in May 1954, severely censured certain officials in the Ministry, but found them not guilty of corruption.[40] Dugdale told the House on the same day that no further action need to be taken, but his attitude was considered complacent by some.[41]

On 17th June Dugdale faced a group of about one hundred and fifty backbenchers at the Party's Agriculture, Fisheries and Food Committee, under the chairmanship of Hurd. Dugdale said that he recognised the gravity of the errors of certain officials, but did not feel he should be out for 'their blood', and that he fully accepted responsibility for mistakes of his officials. From the floor Robert Crouch, M.P. for North Dorset and prominent behind the agitation, felt some action should be taken against the officials, and Sir Waldron Smithers said that if Dugdale would not dismiss them, he should resign. Most backbenchers, however, in particular Antony Lambton and Harry Legge-Bourke, felt Dugdale should remain as Minister.[42]

The promised debate on Crichel Down took place in the House on 20th July after a delay to await Churchill's return from Washington. Dugdale repeated that his officials were not guilty of wilfully deceiving him, but said that as a result of the decision of a Committee[43] set up by the Prime Minister the worst offenders were now working elsewhere. He concluded by announcing his resignation, which earned him respect and sympathy on both sides of the House. Labour were not anxious for Dugdale to resign, and Williams even declined to take part in the debate, out of personal friendship.

By his honourable resignation Dugdale revived the principle of ministerial responsibility. This had been disregarded by Labour during 1945–51 when no resignations followed the failure of the ground-nuts scheme nor the serious miscalculation of health service expenditure. The blame lay to an extent with Dugdale who was late in seeing the importance of the issue (as was the Ministry), and in reporting it to the Cabinet. But Dugdale was adamant that it was entirely his own decision to resign. He had, however, not been thought an outstanding success at Agriculture, and it is unlikely either that he would have been given a new appointment, at a time when younger men were being encouraged, or that he, rather than Heathcoat Amory, would have become Minister of the enlarged Ministry after the merger with Food. Dugdale confessed that he should have brought the issue before the Cabinet at an earlier stage but did not because, 'events were very much hurried in that particular year and again I didn't realise the importance of this particular event down at Crichel and I had more important things to attend to, and I just let it slip by.' The floods on the East Coast were also very much on his mind.[44]

Churchill himself played little part in the episode,[45] relying on Sir David Maxwell Fyfe and the Cabinet Committee, though he felt instinctively that the land should be returned to its original owners, which was in fact the eventual outcome.[46] Indeed agriculture was not a subject which much interested Churchill, though he commonly expressed anxiety lest 'his people' should not have enough to eat, and was particularly worried about the poor potato crop in 1954. He did, however, support Dugdale against the Treasury which wanted to introduce an import levy which would have increased the cost of domestic agricultural production.[47] But in discussions on the all-important Annual Price Review, he had little to contribute. Indeed, at one critical meeting called by Churchill in his room at the House to resolve a deadlock between the Ministry of Agriculture and the Treasury on prices, he sat in his chair looking despondent without uttering a word.[48]

Crichel Down had a long-term effect throughout Whitehall in alerting officials and Ministers to the dangers of high-handedness in their relations with the public,[49] and also making Governments agree to the principle that when land had been taken for one purpose and was no longer required, it should be offered back to the original owners. As the trouble was highly localised in one ministerial Department, and did not have a wider impact, Heathcoat Amory found that it had few repercussions on the Ministry.[50] Indeed Crichel Down had one main beneficial effect: the Ministry sold as much as possible of the agricultural land acquired by the Government for special usage.

Part 4   The Ministry of Materials

The Labour Government had decided that the control of raw materials after the war should be entrusted to those Departments responsible for each particular industry. In 1946 they further decided that bulk purchase and distribution of raw cotton should be entrusted to a non-departmental body, the Raw Cotton Commission. Early in 1950 this decentralisation of control over raw materials was carried a stage further when the raw materials organisation in the Board of Trade was split up. This trend, however, was reversed the following year, largely as a result of the Korean war, which made the price of raw materials soar and convinced the Government that a separate organisation for these commodities needed to be re-established. Originally Richard Stokes, then Labour's Lord Privy Seal, was given a watching brief over the supply of raw materials, but in July 1951 he was appointed the first Minister of Materials with his own Department.

The new Ministry was created partly in the belief that it was better to have one Department which dealt with all aspects of raw materials, but also to give Britain muscle in the international market place,[1] particularly where the United States and France were concerned.[2] The British were fortunate in their new appointee as representative, Lord Knollys,[3] on the International Materials Conference, the chief international body dealing with raw materials, who held the job until 1952.

Most of the Board of Trade's raw material business, including relations with the Raw Cotton Commission, was to be managed by the new Ministry, which was generally responsible for the supply of materials up to the point at which they entered the manufacturing industry. These materials included lead, zinc, aluminium, copper, magnesium, hemp, sulphur, tungsten, leather, timber and jute, as well as cotton.[4] The Ministry of Supply remained the central authority concerned with iron, steel and certain other metals.[5]

The change of Government in 1951 brought about no immediate change of policy. If anything, Lord Swinton, the new Minister, was, by force of circumstance, a more enthusiastic controller than Stokes, a far from doctrinaire socialist. The new Government had pledged to reopen the Liverpool Cotton Exchange and to remove restrictive controls over raw materials, but for the first year made little headway. The change, which coincided approximately with the appointment of Sir Arthur Salter as Minister in November 1952, owed less to a new political initiative than to the easing of the world position in raw materials as a result of the ending of the Korean war. A new impetus to winding up controls (and hence also the Ministry) was given by the replacement in September 1953 of Salter by Lord Woolton, who arrived with the specific idea of removing controls, as the Ministry had expected.[6]

Stokes and the Treasury had jointly decided that the initial senior officials should come from neither the Board of Trade nor the Ministry of Supply. Sir Alan Hitchman was appointed from the Treasury to be Permanent Secretary,[7] Edward Muir, from the Ministry of Works, Deputy Secretary (though of the five Under-Secretaries, only two did not come from Trade or Supply). Together they worked out the organisation of the Department. Hitchman was an ideal appointment as the first Permanent Secretary: he was a persuasive yet tactful civil servant, popular with his junior officials, and managed to delegate successfully the vast amount of work to be done in the early months. By the time he left to become Permanent Secretary at Agriculture he had set the Ministry on a firm footing. His replacement, Sir James Helmore, did an effective job and was undoubtedly highly able, though some in the Department considered him not entirely reliable. He had hoped to continue in this job, and was by no means sure that he would be asked to succeed Sir Archibald Rowlands at the Ministry of Supply, although the succession did in fact take place, and after only a year. Sir Eric Bowyer, a rather cautious Scot, took his place. He worked closely with Woolton,[8] helping to wind up the Department and taking great trouble to see that the staff were happy with their new appointments. In retrospect it can be seen that the regular changes of both the political and official heads of the Ministry showed that it was not viewed as a major Department.

Stokes had been an immensely able and energetic, though occasionally erratic, first Minister, and a difficult man to follow. Swinton, however, was one of the most exceptional of Churchill's team. There had initially been considerable doubt about whom to appoint. Churchill wanted Sir John Anderson as a co-ordinating Minister responsible for, amongst other things, materials and supply.[9] Anderson, however, turned him down, so Churchill approached Swinton, but had difficulty in persuading him to accept Materials combined with the chancellorship of the Duchy of Lancaster.[10] It was greatly to Swinton's credit that he never let his disappointment at being offered such a comparatively lowly job affect his contribution to it, and he devoted all his energies to the task of being Minister.

Top: Conservative Party Chairman Lord Woolton with Winston and Clementine Churchill the night the 1951 Election victory was declared. Bottom: Four senior Ministers outside Number Ten after the first Cabinet meeting: (*left to right*) Harold Macmillan, Oliver Lyttelton, Lord Ismay and Lord Leathers.

Gwilym Lloyd-George.

Florence Horsbrugh.

Sir Edward Bridges.

Osbert Peake.

Sir Walter Monckton.

Alan Lennox-Boyd.

James Stuart.

Lord Swinton.

Rab Butler about to leave for the House of Commons to deliver his first Budget, accompanied by his wife, Sydney Courtauld.

Sir Thomas Dugdale, leaving for the House of Commons to announce his resignation over the Crichel Down affair.

Above left: Lord Cherwell (*right*) in the United States in 1953, accompanied by the British Ambassador, Sir Roger Makins. Above right: Sir David Maxwell Fyfe, later Lord Kilmuir. Below: Anthony Eden with Lord Salisbury at London airport on his return from the Mediterranean following his illness in 1953.

Above left: Harry Crookshank leaving after Churchill's last Cabinet meeting.
Above right: Lord Moran.

NATO meeting in Paris: (*left to right*) Reginald Maudling, Lord Alexander of
Tunis, Anthony Eden and Duncan Sandys. Sir John Harding is behind, to the left
of Sandys.

Above left: Winston Churchill on his way to Buckingham Palace to hand in his resignation to the Queen. Behind him are Christopher Soames and John Colville. Above right: The Graham Sutherland portrait.

Man goeth forth unto his work and to his labour until the evening.

The cartoon which appeared, under Malcolm Muggeridge's editorship, in *Punch*.

Photograph taken after the final Churchill Cabinet meeting: (*left to right, back row*) Osbert Peake, Peter Thorneycroft, Sir Walter Monckton, James Stuart, Gwilym Lloyd-George, Alan Lennox-Boyd, Duncan Sandys, Derick Heathcoat Amory, Sir David Eccles, Sir Norman Brook. (*left to right, seated*) Harold Macmillan, Lord Woolton, Lord Kilmuir, Sir Anthony Eden, Sir Winston Churchill, Lord Salisbury, Rab Butler, Lord Swinton, Harry Crookshank.

Swinton had long experience of the field, dating back to his periods as President of the Board of Trade (1922–3, 1924–9 and 1931). His officials found him a good Minister to work with, and appreciated his knowledge of economics and commodities, as well as of the Government machine.[11] All four Ministers of Materials were men of great quality and experience, and three, excluding Salter, were also men of great force, but Swinton was generally felt by officials to be the ablest. As Minister he liked to talk to the official involved with a particular policy in which he was interested, right down to Principal level. He would usually grill the particular official quite fiercely, but finish by saying how much he liked his work, an approach which helped create good morale. He was not particularly patient, although he was seldom bad tempered without cause, and the Ministry was sorry to lose him.

Under Swinton little progress was made either to end controls or to wind up the Ministry,[12] although softwood was returned to private trade in January 1952, and lead that October. Swinton's drive was also largely responsible for persuading the United States to re-enter the tin market, an essential prerequisite for the end of state trading in that commodity.[13]

More progress was made under Salter. He had a great knowledge of and interest in the background to problems of raw materials, but was found to be not sufficiently practical and too much of a theoretician in the Ministry. He had good relations with his officials, but tended to have favourites, which they found tiresome. He could also be less than impartial in questions of policy, suggesting on one occasion that *The Times* should have priority in available supplies of newsprint. Although a hard worker, it was felt a man with more drive was needed and, if he had not tendered his own resignation, it is likely he would have been dropped in the September 1953 reshuffle.[14] He decided that the work was becoming too much for him,[15] and as he wrote to Woolton: 'I came to the conclusion myself early in the summer that I didn't want another winter of the combined strain of departmental duties by day and division obligations at night . . .'[16] Some liberalisation of controls had been achieved during his term of office; zinc, for example, had been returned to private trade in January 1953, aluminium in July and copper in August, but the appointment of Woolton gave this process a decisive boost. As Salter wrote in his resignation letter, by August 1953 nine-tenths of the public trading activities in which the Department were engaged when the Conservatives came to power had been handed back to private enterprise.[17] But the most difficult task still remained.

Winston Churchill asked Woolton to try to close down the Ministry in six months, though Woolton soon found that the time scale simply was not possible.[18] Woolton, an economic liberal by nature with a suspicion that the Ministry had not been strictly necessary, typifying Labour's belief in bureaucracy,[19] was an ideal man for the job. He was also a first-class administrator, again an indispensable requirement for the post, essentially an executive one.[20] Woolton soon found, like Gwilym Lloyd-George at the Ministry of Food, that traders had fast become accustomed to the security of state control, and many were reluctant to return to the risks of ordinary commercial trading.[21] But he pushed forward firmly and ran the Department on a businesslike footing, able to talk to traders in their own language. This was the first departmental Minister's post Woolton had held for over eight years. He was unknown to the senior officials in the Ministry and they were naturally curious to see how he would perform. They were not disappointed, and found him courteous and immensely impressive in his conduct of business, though apt to be aloof. He was highly literate, could write a first-class Cabinet paper, had as good an understanding of the economy and business as anyone in that Cabinet, and was also one of the few Ministers who would overrule Sir Norman Brook's advice.

Woolton was confronted by a number of important problems as soon as he become Minister in September 1953. A decision had to be taken almost at once on the reopening of the Liverpool Cotton Market and the future of the Raw Cotton Commission, in preparation for the 1954–5 cotton year.[22] The future of public trading in jute and jute goods, no longer justifiable on supply grounds, had to be examined. Timber and newsprint were still under Government control for import saving reasons, but policy remained to be determined.[23] In addition, the whole question of the future of the Ministry was in the air.

By June 1954 the bulk of the work of ending state trading in raw materials had been completed. Hemp, magnesium and sulphur had been returned to private trade in January, the London Metal Market was in operation and the Liverpool Cotton Exchange reopened. There remained only tungsten, which was returned in August 1954, and raw jute, returned in January 1955. The future of jute and jute goods had caused considerable problems. It made sense on economic grounds to return the whole trade to private hands, and it was the only significant piece of public trading left at the beginning of 1954. But efforts to find another way of safeguarding the Dundee jute industry from cheap Indian jute goods, for which import duties were debarred, failed and so control of manufactured jute goods was left in Government hands. Reluctance to increase unemployment in Dundee, where both seats, held by Labour, were near marginals, played a part. Woolton produced a scheme whereby the Government became the buying agent for raw jute on behalf of the manufacturers, charging them a commission for

doing so and then leaving them to face market prices;[24] textile manufacturers bitterly resented this preferential treatment.

Woolton had to tackle a number of other problems. Large stocks of
strategic materials had accumulated under previous Governments,
which, excluding jute and cotton, were valued at over £100m. Neither
Woolton nor the Treasury had any great belief in the value of a strategic
stockpile in the event of war. A great deal of public money had been
invested without any clear idea of what was involved in keeping large
quantities of materials in good shape.[25] Woolton noted in a letter to
Churchill that it would be 'folly' to throw these on to the market at any
price speculators would pay for them,[26] so he personally ensured that
good prices were achieved,[27] the sale of timber stockpiles causing him
the most problems.[28]

Finally there was the question of the future of the Department. A
Committee of the Permanent Secretaries of the Ministries of Fuel and
Power, Materials, Supply, and Board of Trade had been sitting since
early summer 1954 under the chairmanship of Sir Thomas Padmore to
produce a report on the allocation of functions between the Departments. The report recommended the Ministry should continue its existence fortified by the addition of responsibility for chemicals, iron and
steel and the Atomic Corporation. Woolton, however, was not in favour
of this plan, and told Sir Edward Bridges he thought it politically
important that the Ministry should disappear, and favoured absorption
of its remaining functions into the Board of Trade.[29] Woolton also
feared that if the Conservatives continued with the Ministry, it would be
a 'dangerous temptation' to a future Labour Government.[30]

The officials spent February and March reconsidering the proposals,
and by early April came up with a new plan, to amalgamate the Ministry
of Materials with the Board of Trade, to transfer responsibility for the
engineering industry from the Ministry of Supply to the Board of Trade
also, and to transfer responsibility for iron and steel to the Ministry of
Fuel and Power.[31] Woolton readily agreed, emphasising the importance
of making political capital out of these departmental economies.[32] At
this point Churchill made one of his rare impressions on the work of the
Ministry. He wrote to Woolton in June urging that the Ministry be
wound up formally sooner rather than later, arguing that the limited
disposal operations could be left in the hands of the Chancellor of the
Duchy of Lancaster, and that 'full publicity should be given to this very
creditable story'.[33] Thus Harry Crookshank moved the Ministry of
Materials Dissolution Order in the House on 26th July, and the remaining functions were finally transferred to the Board of Trade on August
16th, 1954.

225

Churchill for the most part had little influence on policy at the Ministry. He offered support when needed in Cabinet and believed deeply in restoring freedom, but there was no consistent prodding and urging to speed up the process.[34] Not that this was necessary: the three Conservative Ministers were all convinced of the need to restore private trading, and the pace at which this could be done was dictated, to a large extent, by exogenous factors. In this they were loyally served by a highly able group of officials, who at no time displayed a reluctance to carry out the policy which was going to lose them their jobs.[35] The work fulfilled an important part of the Conservatives' Election promises, resulted in the saving of public money and encouraged enterprises in the markets which had been atrophying under the system of state control of raw materials.

Woolton's fear that had Labour returned in 1955 they might have used the Ministry as a springboard for further experiments in state control was, however, exaggerated. There is no evidence to suggest that the creation of the Ministry in July 1951 was for other than purely pragmatic reasons, and it is also probable that had Labour won the 1951 Election, they would have continued their policy of winding up controls, although more slowly.

Part 5 The Ministry of Transport and Civil Aviation

Britain's transport system suffered badly from neglect and enemy action during the war, and little progress had been made by Labour during 1945–51 to rectify the position. The Attlee Government had retained two separate Departments, but officials in the Ministry of Transport and the Ministry of Civil Aviation had anticipated a merger.[1] The appointment of a single Minister, however, came as a surprise to John Maclay, who thought he had been appointed just Minister of Transport.[2] Indeed, the first Maclay knew about his appointment to both portfolios came when he saw the announcement coming through on the ticker-tape machine in the House of Commons. After a few months it became clear to both Departments that amalgamation was indeed on the way,[3] a process undoubtedly hastened as a result of the ineffectiveness of the transport 'overlord', Lord Leathers, and the enthusiasm for the merger of Maclay's successor, Alan Lennox-Boyd, on grounds of administrative efficiency.[4] Despite some deep-seated fears in both Ministries,[5] in particular in Civil Aviation, the merger went ahead in October 1953.[6] But it proved far less happy than the merger of Pensions and National Insurance, or even than Agriculture and Food, and a separate Ministry of Aviation was re-established in 1959.

226

Maclay had wide experience of shipping, and Leathers had a high regard for his work on merchant shipping during the war: this rather than his position as Chairman of the National Liberals accounted for his appointment.[7] But it was not a happy experience for him: Churchill gave Leathers far more of his attention and backing than Maclay, which was an error of judgment considering Maclay's ability and Leathers' own difficulty in making a success of the position of overlord.[8] Churchill, in a rare display of callousness, harassed Maclay on a number of issues, especially on what he considered to be the slow pace of progress towards denationalisation of road transport. Churchill's interventions were undoubtedly a major factor in Maclay's breakdown of health in April 1952 and his resignation the following month.[9] But other factors played a part: Maclay found himself supervising two Ministries, both requiring a great deal of his time in administrative decisions, yet separated geographically (Transport in Mayfair's Berkeley Square, Aviation two miles away in Holborn), and further problems were caused by the lack of forethought given to the appointment of a single Minister.[10]

Churchill had hoped to leave the post vacant for a while, pending Maclay's return to health, until informed by Sir Lionel Heald, the Attorney-General, that nothing could be done in the Ministry of Transport's name unless there was a Minister in the post.[11] It had been announced that Maclay was too ill to transact business, and that the Parliamentary Secretary at Transport, Sir Joseph Gurney Braithwaite, would be temporarily in charge of both (though little was in fact done by him, especially on the Civil Aviation side). But on Heald's prompting, Churchill looked for a new Minister and settled on a decidedly reluctant Lennox-Boyd, a past Chairman of the Party's Civil Aviation Committee in Opposition, who accepted the job in May 1952 on condition he would be made Secretary of State for the Colonies when Oliver Lyttelton retired. '. . . I didn't want to leave the Colonial Office at all though I was number two there, and I didn't want to leave it even to be number one somewhere else.'[12] In the end he had to put in two years in the job, during which time he gained useful experience of a domestic Department before his critical five-year stint at the Colonial Office (1954–9). He was exceptionally popular, being appreciated for his sound common sense and his ability to carry legislation through the House. The *Sunday Times* described his handling of the Transport Bill as 'spirited, good-humoured and skilful'.[13] In the first year most of his time was spent on preparing road haulage denationalisation, but he always managed to keep on top of all aspects of the Ministry's work.[14] He never felt fully at home there, however. As one of Lennox-Boyd's Private Secretaries at Transport told the Private Office at the Colonial Office: 'Lennox-Boyd's body might be with us, but his heart is with you.'[15] He was delighted, therefore, when in July 1954 he was finally appointed Colonial Secretary.[16]

John Boyd-Carpenter was promoted from Financial Secretary, Treasury, to replace him.[17] Lacking the flair of Lennox-Boyd, he was nevertheless a steady and enthusiastic Minister who worked long hours as a matter of principle, but did not always find it easy to delegate. He was not uncreative, but his strength lay in his administrative ability more than in the formulation of new policy initiatives.

Just one junior Minister, Gurney Braithwaite, had been appointed to the Ministry of Transport after the 1951 General Election. In some ways it was an odd choice as he had been in the House for twenty years without ministerial experience or other particular distinction, and he lasted just two years as a Minister before returning to the backbenches. But during the Conservatives' period in Opposition he had been a trenchant frontbench spokesman on transport, and spoke well in the House during 1951–3. But ill health had been plaguing him for some time,[18] and he was succeeded in the November 1953 reshuffle by Hugh Molson, a bright man who like many others in the Government could find little scope in the role of junior Minister to make any great contribution to the work inside the Department.[19]

At first no Parliamentary Secretary was appointed at Civil Aviation,[20] although the post had existed under the Attlee Government. This omission was rectified in April 1952, although the Minister, Maclay, had no foreknowledge[21] – illustrating the extent to which he was isolated at the Ministry. This was despite the fact that he, amongst others, had voiced the opinion that the gap should be filled. The appointment of Reginald Maudling also came as a surprise to the officials, who had not expected such a high-flier to be chosen for a Ministry not in the front rank.

Maudling, who had been a Vice-Chairman of the Party's Finance, Trade and Industry Committee since the 1951 Election, showed in his first job his capacity for covering his work at high speed, although he never pretended to be much interested in civil aviation problems. Thus he was delighted when Rab Butler, who had been Chairman of the Conservative Research Department where Maudling worked from 1945 to 1950, asked for him as Economic Secretary at the Treasury in November 1952. John Profumo, a more experienced politician than Maudling, who had already made his mark in the Party, was appointed in his place.[22] Although not as outstanding a Parliamentarian as his predecessor, he was respected in the House, and the officials were impressed by his work in the Department. After the amalgamation in

October 1953, Molson concentrated on the inland transport side and Profumo on civil aviation, although he also took some of the work connected with shipping.

The Permanent Secretary at the Ministry of Civil Aviation, Sir Arnold Overton, had been an outstanding official in his earlier years (Permanent Secretary at the Board of Trade, 1941–5, and Head of the British Middle East Office, Cairo, 1945–7), but was past his best by the time he was appointed official Head of the Ministry in 1947. He still had the intellect to be a first-class Permanent Secretary, but was too shy and aloof to establish easy relations with his colleagues.[23] Most of the work was carried by the two men of Deputy Secretary rank. Sir George Cribbett had been Deputy Secretary since 1946 and covered the Air International Relations, Air Services and Safety Departments. He had great energy and personality, knew the work intimately and was in Overton's latter years in many ways *de facto* Head of the Ministry. The other side covered all ground technical services and state-owned airfields and was presided over by the Controller of Ground Services, since 1948 Sir Alfred Le Maitre.[24] After the merger in 1953, Cribbett and Le Maitre continued with the same responsibilities at the new, enlarged Ministry. Overton, who was sixty in 1953, was quite content to retire with a seat on the board of British European Airways (B.E.A.). The Ministry of Transport itself was divided into two main departments, shipping and inland transport (which became four when, after the merger, Civil Aviation's two were added).[25] Each was headed by a Deputy Secretary[26] who reported direct to Sir Gilmour Jenkins, Permanent Secretary since 1947.[27] The shipping side was Jenkins' major interest and he devoted considerably less time to other aspects of the Department's work.[28]

Many changes in civil aviation followed the General Election in 1951. Whereas the Labour Government had given limited scope for private enterprise in air transport, permitting certain specialised services and charter work, it regarded their participation in scheduled services as abnormal. But the Conservatives did not envisage such limited scope for private operators: as Lennox-Boyd told the House in May 1952, the Government aimed 'to improve the position of independent companies'.[29] Charter services were held to be mainly for independent companies, who were also able to apply on equal terms with the two state corporations, the British Overseas Airways Corporation (B.O.A.C.) and B.E.A. for certain scheduled services. In addition, the Government provided some relief for the independent operators' capital problems. Labour was highly critical of these moves, feeling that the Government was undermining the position of the two public corporations. The independent operators themselves had initially urged denationalisation on the new Government, but these plans came to nothing.[30]

The Minister of Transport, however, was adamant that despite increased priority for private operators, nothing would be done to impair the strength of B.O.A.C. and B.E.A.[31] Throughout 1951–5 these two state corporations aroused less controversy than almost any other nationally-owned industry, but their financial position did cause some concern.[32] Although for the first time, in the financial year 1952–3, no Exchequer grant was made to B.O.A.C., a net loss for 1950–1 of £4.6m. being turned by 1953–4 into a net profit of £1.1m., B.E.A. continued to make a net annual loss of about £1.5m.[33] Meanwhile, Lennox-Boyd's time was also taken in his first few months by the question of a second London airport. A White Paper[34] of July 1953 recommended that Gatwick should be developed as the main alternative to Heathrow.[35]

The British aircraft industry suffered a major setback in early 1954 when disaster befell the De Havilland Comets, the pioneers of jet propulsion in civil aviation and the pride of B.O.A.C.'s fleet. The Comet, having gone unscathed through all its trials and its first, highly successful year in operational service on routes to Africa, India and the Far East, suffered five crashes in short succession. Two were thought to be due to pilot error, one to bad weather, but the most worrying were two crashes caused by design faults. On 10th January one aircraft appeared to explode in mid-air over the Mediterranean near Elba,[36] and on 8th April a second went down off the Southern coast of Italy in similar circumstances. As a result the Comet was withdrawn from service and much of Britain's early initiative in jet airline travel was lost.

On the shipping side policy hardly changed after 1951. The Conservatives, like Labour before them, had to cope with the perennial problem of maintaining Britain's position in world shipping – a position under attack from flags of convenience, and also because British ship-builders were not building enough large tankers.[37] On the question of pollution, there was a fresh initiative but this stemmed far more from officials than from Ministers,[38] and in particular from one Under-Secretary, Percy Faulkner, Chairman of the British Committee on the Prevention of Pollution of the Sea by Oil, 1953–7, and Government Delegate at the International Conference on Oil Pollution of the Sea, 1954.[39] In 1952 the Minister set up a Committee to recommend practical measures to prevent oil pollution around the U.K. coasts. It recommended an international conference to reach agreement on remedial action, and in late 1953 the Government invited maritime nations to send representatives to London. The international conference was held there in 1954, attended by forty-two countries, which drew up a convention creating specific zones where discharge was prohibited. The Oil in Navigable Waters Act, 1955, a major item of legislation in the battle against pollution, gave effect to the convention, and came into force in July 1958.[40]

On the inland transport side, the three main areas of concern were road transport,[41] highways and railways. On 8th December, 1953 Lennox-Boyd announced the first major programme of road improvement and construction to be initiated since the war. The Opposition, in the person of Herbert Morrison, called this a 'pretty miserable effort',[42] a viewpoint endorsed by *The Times*: in a leader it criticised both Labour and Conservative Administrations for their 'niggardly policy' towards road-building. The Labour Government had produced a ten-year programme for roads in 1946 but felt compelled to withdraw it within a year because of economic difficulties. The sense of financial stringency continued: Lennox-Boyd later reflected that in his first months at the Department, the Treasury were economising 'right, left and centre' on road construction.[43] A considerably enlarged programme, to cost an estimated £150m., was announced in the Queen's speech on 30th November, 1954, and outlined in detail by Boyd-Carpenter the following February.[44] The plans included a national motorway programme, for which embryonic plans had existed since Alfred Barnes' period as Minister (1945–51), although the scheme finally announced by Boyd-Carpenter differed much from Labour's, being geared to industrial and economic purposes whereas Labour's earlier scheme, with its emphasis on Wales and Scotland, was more socially orientated.[45]

The roads programme took a large part of Boyd-Carpenter's attention as Minister, especially in securing funds and approval for specific projects, such as the M1 and the Hyde Park scheme, both regarded as controversial.[46] Undoubtedly in his eighteen months as Minister he did much to accelerate road construction, and in this was aided both by his skilful deployment of statistics and his ability to argue against the Treasury because of his previous experience as Financial Secretary (1951–4). Amongst his other major preoccupations were railway modernisation and electrification, the post-Comet development of aviation and the initiation of Gatwick Airport.[47]

On inland transport the Conservatives had made the following pledge: 'Both public and private enterprise will be needed in transport. Publicly owned transport will be reorganised into regional groups of economic size.'[48] This was implemented in the Transport Act, 1953 which *inter alia* provided for the denationalisation of British Road Services and the abolition of the Road Haulage Executive. It also gave new terms of reference to the British Transport Commission, which had been set up by the 1947 Transport Act to provide 'an efficient, adequate, economical and properly integrated system of public inland transport and port facilities within Great Britain'. Problems had arisen, partly because the first Chairman, Lord Hurcomb, had interpreted his function as a relationship of 'non-co-operation' with the Ministry.[49] By the 1953 Act, the Commission's maximum membership was increased from nine to fifteen, it was relieved of its duty to integrate the nation's transport services, and its powers to nationalise bus and dock undertakings were repealed. The Commission retained responsibilities for road transport, docks, canals and railways. The Railway Executive, one of the six 'Executives' established in 1947 under the Transport Commission, was abolished. From 1947 until 1953 railways had been run by two bodies, the Transport Commission and its subordinate body, the Railway Executive, a clumsy arrangement. Relations between them had never been happy and the Commission itself pressed for the abolition of the subsidiary body.

The Conservatives were faced by formidable problems with the railways; they were subject to steadily increasing deficits, with the position of the railways being undermined both by rising costs and decreasing demand for carrying freight.[50] The Government had to act decisively. Decentralisation was one main aim of their policy. Plans were outlined in the 1953 Act, introduced as a White Paper in July 1954,[51] and approved by Parliament in November. Management at area level was strengthened, and greatly increased autonomy within the regions was permitted. Lennox-Boyd was especially concerned to encourage this, partly to revitalise the regional pride of the independent railway companies, such as the Great Western Railway, which had existed before nationalisation. Their other main answer to the railways' difficulties was a modernisation plan,[52] at an estimated cost of £1,200m., and an overhaul to the charging system, based on economic costs.[53] This policy owed much to the drive of General Sir Brian Robertson, the Chairman of the British Transport Commission, whom the Government had appointed in September 1953 to succeed Lord Hurcomb.[54]

After Churchill's early interventions when Maclay was Minister to speed up the denationalisation of road haulage, his interest in transport questions abated. His attention was subsequently caught just by ephemeral transport issues, such as the possibility of an air accident depriving him of his majority in the House: he even set a maximum limit on the number of Conservative M.P.s who could fly at any one time. Thus he once forbade a party of Conservative M.P.s to fly on a special flight to an international conference, despite being balanced by an equal number of Labour M.P.s. This was the occasion on which Churchill remarked that he could not afford to lose 'so many baskets in one egg'.[55] Railways, however, always captured his romantic interest: he was especially willing to yield to demands for more money for railwaymen, and even attempted (until the Treasury blocked him) to sweep away the annual interest charges the railways bore on loans.[56]

By any standards, Conservative transport policy was one of the weakest aspects of the Government's work. Wisely dispensing with the Transport Commission's impossible ideal of an integrated transport system, the Government could, nevertheless, have done more to pursue a balanced and rational transport policy. Efforts made, at least in the first three years, such as the denationalisation of road haulage, were largely prompted by doctrinaire considerations and were irrelevant to the nation's transport needs. The Government should have directed its attention earlier to the immeasurable damage the transport system had suffered during the war especially in the light of the scant replacement or modernisation that had been achieved by Labour from 1945 to 1951.

Railways were perhaps the most in need of capital investment. The track and rolling stock were in such poor state of repair that train speeds had to be kept considerably lower than they were during the 1930s. Roads were little better off. The number of cars had increased from three million in 1938 to five million by 1953, but the roads themselves had been held in more or less static condition. A leader in the *Observer* called this state: 'an appalling tax on national welfare'.[57]

Even the road and railway modernisation plans of 1954–5 were somewhat inadequate to meet needs: the railway plan to spend £1,200m. over 15 years and the road plan to spend £147m. spread over four years made an average of £117m. per annum to be spent on Britain's inland transport – just 7% of Britain's annual gross capital formation. The *Sunday Times* castigated the Government for its part in permitting the inland transport system to become 'alarmingly out of date'. The railways, it said, possessed equipment 'old fashioned and uneconomic more than a generation ago', whilst on the road front 'this country possesses no single modern motor road of any length'.[58] The Government was hard pressed with many urgent claims on expenditure, but it could, nevertheless, have been quicker to see the economic and social importance of providing an efficient and modern inland transport system. Two opportunities in particular were missed: the Government could have raised further revenue by the introduction of tolls on new main roads, as in France and Italy, although on a number of new bridges, such as the Forth Road Bridge,[59] tolls were authorised. In addition, as the *Sunday Times* estimated,[60] if the funds spent on 50,000 houses built during 1954 in excess of the 300,000 target could have been diverted to transport, this would have provided more funds than the railways were asking for in one year for their whole capital programme.

Civil aviation was in little better state. In early 1953 Vickers announced it was to build a jet of 100–150 seats, derived from the Valiant bomber, but the Cabinet decided to cancel the order,[61] partly on advice that public demand would be fully met by turbo-prop planes which would cross the Atlantic in twelve hours. The early failure of the Comet, delays in the production of the turbo-prop Britannia and B.O.A.C.'s declaration in early 1955 of its intention to buy planes from the United States, all contributed to the sense of despondency. As a leader in the *Sunday Times* put it: 'From a feeling of pride that in [Britain's aircraft industry] we were leading the world there seems to be developing a spirit of denigration.'[62]

Part 6   The Ministry of Fuel and Power

The Ministry of Fuel and Power was created in June 1942, as a response, almost entirely, to the problems of securing adequate fuel supplies.[1] Whether the Ministry would continue to operate in peacetime was by no means certain, but its valve was soon realised. Shortly before the end of the war, a brief piece of legislation, the Ministry of Fuel and Power Act, 1945 became law, giving statutory authority for a permanent Department.[2] The structure of the Ministry changed little until January 1957, when it became the Ministry of Power, taking over responsibilities for iron and steel from the Board of Trade,[3] and for liaison with the Atomic Energy Authority from the Lord President's Office.[4] It continued until 1969, re-emerging as Energy in 1974.

Although ceasing to be a Cabinet position after 1947, when Hugh Gaitskell succeeded Emanuel Shinwell as Minister, Fuel and Power had been at the very centre of the stage during the 1947 fuel crisis, and its position in Whitehall was steadily gaining in importance. It also had the benefit of senior Permanent Secretaries: Sir Frank Tribe (1942–5) had been Secretary at the Office of Production and went on to become Permanent Secretary at the Ministry of Aircraft Production and Food; Sir Donald Fergusson (1945–52) made his name as Permanent Secretary at Agriculture (1936–45); Sir John Maud (1952–9), later Lord Redcliffe-Maud, had been Permanent Secretary at Education (1945–52).

The Ministry was responsible, *inter alia*, for the three nationalised industries, coal, gas and electricity, and one uncontrolled fuel source, oil. The Ministry of Fuel and Power Act, 1945 gave the Minister power to develop fuel and power policy as a whole. But the scope of the job was never entirely satisfactory. It called for an ability to influence, not to control the four industries, and in practice there was little scope for the Minister to co-ordinate them. Much of the Ministry's time in the early years after the war had been taken up with nationalisation and its ensuing problems, and it was not until the last months of the Labour Government that Fergusson, after pressure from certain sections of the House of Commons and the trade unions, decided that an overall strategy for fuel was called for. Philip Noel-Baker, the new Labour Minister (February 1950–October 1951), accordingly set up a Committee under Lord Ridley[5] in July 1951. The moment could hardly have been more propitious. The country was in the wake of the rearmament crisis, and there were serious anxieties about the continuous coal shortage and drastic load shedding by the British Electricity Authority in the coming winter; the Committee's task was to examine whether, in the light of increased demand and technical developments, steps could be taken to promote the best use of fuel and power resources.

The Report, completed when worries about fuel had decreased, was signed in July 1952,[6] offering forty recommendations. It generally favoured a market solution, recommending that the best pattern of fuel and power usage could be promoted by the customers' exercise of free choice between competing sources. But this was not what the adherents of a single fuel policy wished to hear. A proposal had been forcibly put to the Committee, with strong trade union support, for a new planning authority with executive powers to co-ordinate the nationalised fuel and power industries. But this the Committee rejected as being incompatible with 'maintaining competition'.[7]

Recommendation number forty did, however, suggest the establishment of a Joint Fuel and Power Planning Board, an advisory body with an independent Chairman. But this was rejected, principally for two reasons: the Conservative Government was anxious to avoid anything which smacked of planning, and the individual fuel industries had no desire to lose their autonomy or become part of a central 'strategy'; they had grown up having taken autonomy for granted, and they were not going to sacrifice it now without a struggle.[8]

As a minor genuflection to the idea of co-ordination, suggested in the Ridley Report, the Conservative Minister, Geoffrey Lloyd, set up a ministerial co-ordinating Committee, consisting of himself, the Permanent Secretary (Maud), the highly respected Chairman of the British Electricity Authority (Lord Citrine),[9] the Chairman of the Gas Council (Sir Harold Smith) and the Chairman of the National Coal Board (Sir Hubert Houldsworth). This group met regularly in the Minister's room, but did not produce a co-ordinated policy: not only was the oil industry left out of the discussions, but also the Minister and all three Chairmen strongly believed in competition as the only practicable regulator. Highly diplomatic Minutes were taken, the meetings proving most valuable as an informal forum. Each industry thus retained a large degree of autonomy, with the Minister rarely exercising influence in 'the national interest'.

Little change of policy resulted from the new Government in October 1951, although with Labour, in the person of Alfred Robens, saying in the House in July 1952 that the nationalised industries should be free from Party conflict, this perhaps was not surprising.[10]

Lloyd's problems came more from his own hot-blooded backbenchers, in particular Gerald Nabarro,[11] author at this time of two works on fuel policy, and Colonel Claude Lancaster,[12] a prominent colliery owner until nationalisation. Unrest, at its highest point in 1952 and 1953, came from the Party's Fuel and Power Committee, under the chairmanship of Sir Victor Raikes,[13] with Nabarro as Joint Secretary. Apart from criticism of increased fuel prices, the largest single issue concerned pressure for a root and branch enquiry into the workings of the National Coal Board, and a motion to that effect was signed by over one hundred and twenty Conservative M.P.s. A major row was in the offing. After Lloyd and Lord Leathers attended an inconclusive meeting of the Committee on 31st March, 1953,[14] the stage was set for a showdown before the 1922 Committee on 23rd April. But against all the odds, Lloyd acquitted himself well,[15] and the rejection of the case for an enquiry was to be a major defeat for the Fuel and Power Committee's caucus.[16] After this, the unrest fell away.[17]

Lloyd was the natural choice for the job of Minister, although he only accepted it with some reluctance. He had shown much promise in his early political and ministerial career, not least as Parliamentary Private Secretary to Baldwin, 1931–5, and had gained wide experience of the problems of fuel and power from a variety of ministerial appointments during the war.[18] But he found the job a frustrating task, having deftly to guide and influence the heads of the four fuel industries, since he performed best when he had a concrete problem to solve. Part of the problem lay with the job itself: after the first two forceful Ministers, Shinwell and Gaitskell, the next three, Noel-Baker, Lloyd and Aubrey Jones all found difficulties thanks mainly to the indeterminate nature of the position. Not only did they suffer from having all been excluded by the original nationalisation statutes from being able to give the industries specific instructions, but further they had to contend with the job's comparatively small influence in the Whitehall machine, at least until its upgrading in January 1957 with the appointment of Lord Mills. Lloyd also had to manage for the first two years with the additional handicap of having Leathers as a co-ordinator, by no means a happy arrangement.[19] Lloyd took the view that Leathers was not to interfere in the House of Commons work, and Fergusson had some tough words when he thought Leathers was encroaching too far into the Ministry's work. Some officials, though, were sorry to see Leathers go, feeling that his decisive and forceful manner would be missed by the Ministry. Lloyd had a good intellect and was capable of hard work, but became restless with affairs he found uncongenial.

Lloyd took direct responsibility for oil, which he managed with notable success, and shared electricity with Lancelot Joynson-Hicks, the Parliamentary Secretary, whose appointment had not been predicted: a solicitor, when appointed he knew next to nothing about the fuel and power industries, as against a whole list of Conservative M.P.s who did.[20] However, he became an effective junior Minister, who worked hard in his own areas of responsibility, safety in mines, gas, as well as parts of electricity. The second son of a long-serving Conservative Home Secretary,[21] he resigned in December 1955, moving to the Upper House in 1958 as Lord Brentford, in succession to his brother.

The organisation of the Ministry followed the pattern for smaller Departments. Fergusson, the Permanent Secretary, was conservative by nature, yet had presided over the nationalisation of coal, gas and electricity with absolute loyalty to his Labour masters, and with single-minded efficiency. He was a tough man, sometimes even fierce, and belonged to a generation of officials who believed it their duty to put only major policy decisions to the Minister; he was fearless in telling Ministers if he disagreed with their plans.[22] He knew little about the Department and its policies when he arrived, but did much to unify it into a working entity, and left behind him in 1952 a coherent and efficient organisation. His place was taken by Maud, and again the Ministry had as official head a novice in the highly specialised work of the Department. Maud, in his turn, was representative of a younger breed of Permanent Secretaries, less authoritarian than their elders, excelling in intellectual qualities and with a broader economic understanding.[23] Maud was more of a reactor to events and less of an initiator than Fergusson. But he adapted himself to the job in an imaginative way and was exceptionally good when listening to the technical arguments, knowing the wider economic and political implications, and then advising the Minister.

Beneath him was just one Deputy Secretary, Sir Laurence Watkinson. Like many of the officials in the Ministry, he had a Board of

Trade background, joining Fuel and Power in 1947 as deputy, with a reputation as an expert on rationing gained during his war experience at the Board of Trade. He was not a forceful man, nor one with strong ideas of his own, but had a very good manner with people, and excelled at ensuring that the wishes of the Minister or Permanent Secretary were executed. In a Ministry that tended to be centrifugal, Watkinson was a great unifier and mollifier. His own specialist field was coal though the more influential voice on coal matters was R. Kelf-Cohen,[24] a particularly authoritative Under-Secretary.

Equivalent in rank to the Deputy Secretary was the post of Chief Scientist, created in 1948. Sir Harold Roxbee Cox, widely known as having played a major part in the development of the jet engine,[25] was the first holder of the office. A dynamic force, he considerably expanded the amount of Government research undertaken at the Ministry, previously concerned mainly with fuel economy. Working in close touch with the Department, he presided over a number of forward-looking projects such as work on coal-burning gas turbines and the underground gasification of coal.[26] Despite increasing Treasury criticism that most research work should be undertaken by the nationalised industries themselves,[27] Roxbee Cox's work continued unabated after the arrival of the Conservative Government in October 1951. But as he increasingly felt that further promotion in the Civil Service, with its bias against scientists, was unlikely to transpire, he decided in 1954 to leave for private enterprise, having first recommended Kelvin Spencer, a man keenly interested in applied science and its interaction with Government, as his successor.[28]

In 1947 the Ministry had gained another new senior office. In that year Fergusson reluctantly decided that the Ministry needed an economist[29] to liaise with the Central Economic Planning Staff. But the work of the Ministry's Economic Adviser, Philip Chantler, changed considerably after the arrival of the Conservatives in 1951, with their general move away from planning. There was much less co-ordination with economists in other Departments, and he increasingly concentrated his attention on economic aspects of specific work within the Ministry.[30]

Coal

The structure of the coal, gas and electricity industries was broadly similar. Coal was nationalised first, on 1st January, 1947,[31] when the National Coal Board (N.C.B.) was set up. This relieved the Ministry of operational control of the industry, as the N.C.B. took over the day-today management of the mines. Ultimate responsibility to Parliament for the conduct of the industry, however, remained with the Ministry. It was by far the most important of the nation's fuel sources, providing over ninety per cent of all its energy in 1951. The fact that the National Union of Mineworkers (N.U.M.) sponsored no less than thirty-six M.P.s in 1951 also contributed to coal's political importance.

The coal division of the Ministry was divided into a number of branches. One maintained contact with the N.C.B. on matters of broad policy, a second controlled open-cast coal production, and other branches were concerned with distribution, both at home and abroad. The new Government favoured more decentralisation in the industry[32] yet was cautious. It changed its anti N.C.B. attitude of Opposition days, and tried to be sympathetic, but was not impressed by the Chairman, Houldsworth, who had been appointed by Labour shortly before the General Election.[33] They would have liked to remove him, but feared the problem this would cause with the N.U.M. Houldsworth was not popular on the Coal Board itself,[34] nor with many Conservatives: Brendan Bracken, in a letter to Lord Beaverbrook, described him as a 'pleasant second-rate lawyer with left-wing affiliations'.[35] But Houldsworth, meanwhile, stayed in the job until his death in February 1956, although the Minister had planned to replace him that July.

Trouble was brewing in the coal industry. By 1953 total output was beginning to fall for the first year since 1947, absenteeism was at its highest levels,[36] and statistics for the previous year showed that the industry accounted for over a third of all days lost in industrial disputes. No wonder then that the Government supported the Coal Board's decision in October 1953 to set up a Committee to investigate organisation, which became known generally as the Fleck Committee, after its Chairman, Sir Alexander Fleck, Chairman of I.C.I.

Its Report, the subject of sharply conflicting submissions from within the N.C.B. organisation, was published in February 1955 and was well received,[37] and Lloyd announced the Government's immediate intention to act on its recommendation that the Board be reconstituted to comprise twelve members, including a new post of Vice-Chairman. As part of the reorganisation, a new man was appointed Deputy Chairman,[38] James Bowman, who succeeded Houldsworth on the latter's death the following year. The Board, after prolonged wrangling, announced in March that it accepted most of the other recommendations of the Fleck Committee, which stressed the need for decentralisation and also better management.

As *The Times* noted in May 1953 none of the great hopes held out for nationalisation had so far materialised in the coal industry.[39] By July the

Coal Board agreed that coal had to be imported for the first time, though only half a million tons were required. The industry's outlook did not improve in 1954, and the Government, to avoid a possible fuel crisis, authorised further imports, this time of four million tons. It was the Ministry's coal division which initiated the idea, and twice the Coal Board turned down their suggestion, only reluctantly agreeing when it became unavoidable. The Treasury, especially Sir Leslie Rowan, the Second Secretary for Overseas Finance, disliked having to agree to imports because of a shortage of dollars, but they, too, had to admit the need. Heavy imports of coal continued throughout 1955 and 1956, but by 1957 domestic demand for coal began its long downward turn.

One aspect of Conservative policy towards the coal industry to which the Opposition did not object was the passing of the Mines and Quarries Act, 1954, which attempted to consolidate all existing legislation relating to safety in mines and to introduce new safety measures which took account of new techniques and machinery. This was the first major legislation on the subject since the Coal Mines Act of 1911. It relied much on the findings of the Royal Commission on Safety in the Mines set up in 1935,[40] whose recommendations had been placed in abeyance as a result of the Second World War. A progressive and thoughtful piece of legislation, the 1954 Act was one of the few major Conservative Bills to find a warm response with Labour, with Noel-Baker remarking in the House: 'I join with all my heart in the congratulations . . . to the Minister on having introduced the Bill . . . we can be sure that the Minister's connection with the Bill will be remembered to his lasting credit for the rest of his political career.'[41]

The original Bill was modified considerably as a result of pressure from the N.U.M.[42] When Labour had been in power, the N.U.M. carried considerable weight with the Government, but this influence was substantially reduced after the Conservatives came to power.[43] The Ministry of Fuel and Power, rather than the Ministry of Labour, had traditionally been responsible for relations with the miners, but at first Lloyd was instructed to leave them to the Chairman of the National Coal Board. It took a year before formal contact between the N.U.M. and the Government was resumed. Lloyd later recalled: 'When he appointed me Churchill said, "Geoffrey, remember, no trouble with the miners." In fact we got on with them very well.'[44]

Electricity

The electricity industry was flourishing, and was easily the most efficiently run of the three nationalised industries. Indeed, there was concern that it should not use its near-monopoly of light and power supply to dominate gas, then the Cinderella of the fuel industries, even if it was a more efficient converter of coal into heat.[45] From 1945–55, electricity output from power stations almost doubled, and this was accompanied by improved efficiency. In the ten years after nationalisation in April 1948 the price of electricity rose by only 34%, compared with a 60% rise in the general retail price index.[46]

The industry was nationalised by the Electricity Act, 1947, which set up the British Electricity Authority with overall responsibility for general policy, finance and the generation and main transmission of electricity, as well as fourteen Area Electricity Boards, which looked after distribution. The creation of the new authority carried forward the work of the Central Electricity Board, set up by the Conservative Electricity (Supply) Act, 1926, and the nationalisation was accepted as inevitable by all but a few diehards in the Conservative Party.[47] With the Conservatives' traditionally greater responsiveness to rural needs, rural electrification became a major priority in the early 1950s. In 1953 the Electricity Authority was asked by the Government to undertake a considerable expansion of its plans as so many rural areas were still without electricity. The response was immediate, and by 1955–6 nearly 15,000 outlying houses and farms were connected to the mains for the first time.[48]

Electricity was to confront Lloyd with a number of other problems. He had to fight Harold Macmillan, who felt that power stations were taking away too many bricks from his house-building programme.[49] As a result a Committee was set up in August 1952 primarily at the instigation of the Ministry of Works,[50] to see what economies could be secured in the building of power stations.[51]

The industry received larger public funds for investment than any other single industry, a fact which aroused some opposition among Conservative backbenchers.[52] In a debate in the House in July 1954, Lloyd announced that, though it was Government policy to leave responsibility for the operational and engineering questions to the Electricity and Gas Boards, Parliament had also decided that periodic enquiries should be conducted into the Boards' conduct. Thus in 1954 the Government set up an independent Enquiry into the working of the nationalised electricity supply industry, presided over by Sir Edwin Herbert, a distinguished solicitor and later President of the Law Society. It did not report until December 1955,[53] but its recommendations, favouring decentralisation and operation on a more commercial basis, were considered too radical by the Government, with the new Minister, Aubrey Jones, being reluctant to commit himself.[54]

241

In February 1955 the Government presented to Parliament its 'Programme of Nuclear Power',[55] proposing a ten-year programme to bring into operation twelve nuclear power stations producing electricity equal to that produced by five to six million tons of coal a year (the programme was tripled in April 1957, but later cut back).[56] This was part of the British Electricity Authority's expansion plan, with nuclear-powered rather than coal-fired stations. The 1955 announcement was in fact motivated by the Government's desire to be free from the clutches of the N.U.M., just as the 1957 boost to the programme was prompted by the desire to be free of the dependence on oil, whose vulnerability as a fuel source had been highlighted by the Suez crisis.[57] Together, the announcements heralded the age of nuclear power, although it was publicly proclaimed that coal would be the life-blood of British industry for the following twenty-five years.[58]

Gas

Gas was the last of the three to be nationalised, on 1st May, 1949. This was an important period for the industry. There were increasing problems with gas' basic input, coal, in particular its quantity, quality and price, and there were plans for turning over to oil. There was also concern about the industry's loss of markets to electricity and oil.

The Permanent Secretary and Parliamentary Secretary had regular meetings with the Chairman and the Gas Council,[59] but left them a large amount of autonomy. Sales of gas were increasing by less than one per cent per annum, and the market for gas changing gradually: sales to the domestic consumer were steadily declining, whilst industrial concerns were increasing their demand. The Heyworth Committee of 1944–5[60] had noted the weaknesses of the industry, and since nationalisation a programme of modernisation and reconstruction had been taking place. In May 1954 the Gas Council published a programme of development, 'Fuel for the Nation', visualising a twelve and a half per cent increase in domestic consumption in the seven years to 31st March, 1960 and a similar increase in industrial consumption.[61] Investment, at an average of £40m. per annum, was small in relation to electricity, though large for an industry which had almost ceased to grow.[62]

Oil

The oil industry, consisting of large international private companies, was naturally handled in a different manner by the Ministry than

242

nationalised coal, electricity and gas. Yet even British Petroleum, in which the Government had a fifty-one per cent holding and on whose board two Government-appointed directors served, was treated as an independent concern and there was an understanding that, commercially, the Government would take no action.[63]

British oil refineries were rapidly increasing their output, from 6.3m. tons of refined oil products in 1951 to 11.1m. tons in 1953,[64] and more use was being made of oil as a substitute for coal in power stations and in producing gas. The Government was anxious, according to Lord Brentford,[65] to persuade industry and private consumers to convert from coal to oil on the argument that oil supplies were reasonably assured. (Coal as we have seen presented a monopoly threat from the N.U.M.) The Electricity Authority, encouraged by Lloyd, decided to equip seven of its large new power stations with dual firing apparatus which could utilise either coal or oil.[66] Of the oil companies, Esso was interested and co-operative in the plan of converting power stations to oil, B.P. and Shell less so.[67] With Treasury concern about effects on the balance of payments, the development of home refining was partly to reduce the foreign exchange costs involved and partly to avoid dependence on overseas refineries in politically unstable countries. Exports of refined oil products, almost non-existent before the war, were becoming an increasingly important factor in the balance of payments, rising from 0.4m. tons in 1946 to nearly 8m. tons in 1954.[68] The Ministry was concerned in the Abadan oil refinery problem of 1951–4, and the Permanent Secretary, with officials from the Treasury and Foreign Office, sat on a special Cabinet Committee, though major policy decisions were taken by senior Cabinet Ministers. As with the Suez episode of 1956, the Ministry was kept in the dark about issues of vital concern to its work.

Lloyd was allowed a relatively free hand in his administration of the Ministry, and apart from problems with the coal industry, Abadan, and the development of the nuclear power programme, the Cabinet rarely had cause to discuss fuel and power questions. Churchill, in fact, was not much interested in Lloyd's work, though he was prone, characteristically, to throw out the occasional suggestion, as for a large bonus for extra coal output,[69] without necessarily thinking through the consequences carefully.

Chapter 7   Social Policy

Part 1   The Conservatives and the Welfare State

The Labour Government of 1945 tended to claim that it alone was responsible for the establishment of the welfare state, and during the 1950 and 1951 Election campaigns asserted that if the Conservatives were returned, social services would be drastically cut back. 'Would the social services be safe under the Tories?' proclaimed Hugh Gaitskell's Election Address at Leeds South. 'They boast of cutting further expenditure. If they mean to cut anything at all they mean to cut the social services.' Both Labour claims were false, even if it seemed initially that there must be some substance in Labour's warnings when in his first Budget Butler cut food subsidies and imposed some health service charges. Labour protested vigorously (a difficult task, as Gaitskell himself had imposed N.H.S. charges in 1951), but no further comparable cuts or charges were introduced throughout the life of the Government.

The foundation of the modern welfare state, building on the work of pre-war Governments, was largely initiated by the wartime Coalition Government, supported in Parliament by a Conservative majority. This work included the appointment of the Beveridge Committee in June 1941 to review arrangements for social insurance and allied services, and the subsequent publication in 1942 of proposals for a new comprehensive national insurance scheme and a new industrial injuries scheme;[1] the Butler Education Act of 1944 following on the Education White Paper of the previous year, finally, the publication in 1944 of proposals for a National Health Service,[2] the need for which Conservatives had accepted since before the war. These initiatives were naturally all developed and refined by the Labour Government after 1945, but the origin of its social policies remained firmly rooted in the work of preceding Governments.

Far from cutting back social services after 1951, as Labour had predicted, or indeed as many felt inevitable in view of the economic crisis, the Conservative Government expanded them. Indeed the fact that it had done so became a proud boast: Churchill proclaimed in 1954 that: 'We have improved all the social services and we are spending more this year on them than any Government at any time. That is true of education, health, housing, family allowances and the whole field of the social services.'[3]

The figures for public expenditure on social services show not only a steady increase in money (and real) terms, but also an increase during 1951–5 in expenditure on social services as a percentage of total public spending.[4] Much of the increase of expenditure was naturally due to rising costs and to factors beyond the control of Government, such as the large increases in numbers of school children. But some of the higher spending was due to deliberate Government policy, in particular its decision to make house-building a priority, to raise social security benefits to the level envisaged in the Beveridge proposals, and latterly to promote reorganisation of schools still undivided between primary and secondary levels.

More forethought had gone into considering the Conservatives' economic rather than their social policy during the period of Opposition. There was no 'Social Services Charter', and the Conservatives would have benefited from more constructive discussions of their policies towards the welfare state.[5] Policy statements at the 1951 General Election contained definite proposals for housing, and also specific plans for health, some of which could not be implemented.[6] But there were only vague commitments – to provide better services – made for education, a review of benefit rates for pensions and social security.

The time was ripe for a critical reassessment of Conservative social policy. As the *Sunday Times* noted in an editorial: 'The fact is that the Welfare State, thanks to the mismanagement of our finances and the lack of clear thought among its Socialist exponents, has got into a muddle.'[7] The article called for a profound re-examination of the whole system, to look at anomalies whereby, for example, more people were getting national assistance ('poor relief', subject to a means test) in 1950 than received it at the beginning of the century. Further those people who received this minimum subsistence money in fact were receiving, on the eve of the 1951 Election, 50% more money a week with rent (64 shillings) than those on unemployment or sickness pay (42 shillings a week). The *Sunday Times* regarded it as iniquitous that 'the best type of man or woman', who strove to avoid going to the National Assistance Board, should receive much less than the 'feckless type' who sought as much as he could get on assistance benefit. Moreover, the new national insurance scheme, designed to be financed by workers' contributions, was at fundamental variance with the basic concept in the social services of redistribution from rich to poor. Further, following the abandonment of the pre-war system of payment for secondary education, parents nevertheless receiving the low levels of family allowances still paid back some of this money for their children's education through tax.

A radical reconsideration of Conservative policy would indeed have been a desirable step. But this was not to be. Instead the Government's social policy was guided too often by expediency; for example, preferring housing where there were more votes to education; not pressing for rent increases sufficient to enable landlords to put their houses in good order for fear of risking electoral unpopularity, or postponing the provision of a proper financial basis for pensions for fear of upsetting the unions. Moreoever, the Government made little attempt to think out a coherent and balanced social policy. The Cabinet's Social Policy Committee fell into disuse, and there was markedly little co-ordination between the Departments concerned with social policy. What contact there was tended to be at Under-Secretary level or below, on an *ad hoc* basis. A leader in *The Times* on 2nd February, 1952 had commented that there was 'not yet much evidence' of a 'consistent social policy'. There was to be no improvement over the next three years.

The Conservatives did, however, proclaim three broad principles in their attitude towards the social services:[8] that waste and inefficiency should be minimised; that help be concentrated on those most in need, and finally that those who wished to create more security for themselves and their families should not be penalised.

Their efforts to reduce waste were responsible for the setting up of the Guillebaud Committee on the N.H.S.,[9] a reduction in the numbers of officials in the social service Departments, and the amalgamation of the Ministries of Pensions and National Insurance. Efficiency was one thing, but the new Government was less successful in providing aid to the areas that most deserved help. Had they instituted more charges for those who could afford to pay, better services could have been provided and more resources directed towards the needy. A pamphlet written by Iain Macleod and Enoch Powell, 'Social Services: Needs and Means', was published in January 1952. It concluded, 'rightly' said a leader in *The Times*, that the question to be asked was not 'Should a means test be applied to a social service?' but 'Why should any social service be provided without a means test?'[10]

Perhaps the greatest social policy difference between the Parties lay in the third of the three guiding principles, the Conservatives' insistence that those families and individuals who wished to pay for a better social service should be allowed to do so. While the Conservative Government was anxious to maintain and in some cases extend the provision of private facilities in housing, health, schooling and pensions, so the Labour Party was moving in the opposite direction.[11]

Churchill had little detailed interest in the work of the social policy Ministries, although he gave strong support at Housing to Harold Macmillan, by far the most senior of social service Ministers to remain at his post for any considerable length of time. At Education (taken out of the Cabinet after the Election in 1951) and at Health after Harry Crookshank's departure in May 1952, Churchill appointed Ministers who did not carry much political weight. Education, in particular, declined in political importance,[12] until Sir David Eccles' appointment as Minister in October 1954. Meanwhile as Minister of National Insurance, Osbert Peake was one of the more established Party figures, but the political importance of his Ministry altered little under the Conservatives.

Labour was certainly gestating more radical proposals for the social services during 1951–5 (which would of necessity have been modified in office), but the policies of the Conservatives under Churchill and Labour under Clement Attlee between 1945–51 showed remarkably few differences. The welfare state was an expensive new addition to the responsibilities of Government, a dominant fact of life for both Parties, and increases in benefits or the provision of better services could scarcely be afforded without reducing expenditure elsewhere. At the same time, introducing further charges in health, raising contributions to the national insurance scheme or making cuts would have involved considerable political difficulties. In social policy – in as far as the Churchill Government could be said to have had one – 'Butskellism' was the order of the day.[13]

Part 2   The Ministry of Housing and Local Government

The Ministry – the senior social policy Department not the least because it was the only one to have had its Minister in Cabinet throughout the life of the Government – had recently gone through a confusing sequence of names and functions.

The Ministry of Local Government and Planning had been formed in January 1951 out of the Ministry of Town and Country Planning, which was felt to be too small and detached, and that part of the Ministry of Health concerned with the local government system and the environment services of public health and housing.[1] The change in title to Ministry of Housing and Local Government chosen by the new Conservative Administration came about 'to emphasise the importance of housing',[2] Winston Churchill being insistent that the name 'Housing' should appear first in the title.[3] The Ministry, like the Home Office, was essentially a residual Department, dealing with matters for local authorities not covered elsewhere. Its function in relation to housing, as Harold Macmillan soon came to realise, was to advise and supervise the one and a half thousand local housing authorities in England and Wales, who were themselves responsible for licensing private enterprise houses and for ordering, programming and helping to subsidise council houses.

With the election commitment to build 300,000 houses a year, the Ministry inevitably became a priority Department of the new Government. The figure owed its origin to the pressure of a small group of backbenchers, prominent among them Harmar Nicholls and William Robson Brown,[4] who had been pressing for the adoption of the high target of 300,000 houses but who had met with little encouragement from senior party men except Walter Elliot. A small Committee had been set up under the chairmanship of the shadow Minister of Works, Duncan Sandys, to consider this target, but they had reported back that it was not feasible. The pressure group were not to be defeated so readily and decided on a change of tactics, hitting on the idea of organising delegates to shout out '300,000' during a speech in the housing debate at the 1950 Party Conference at Blackpool.[5] The platform were at first taken aback by this display,[6] but the senior figures, Lord Woolton prominent among them, quickly realised the electoral possibilities and accepted the commitment.[7] Churchill in his speech at the mass meeting at the conclusion of the Conference on 14th October said: 'You have demanded that the target that we should put in our programme should be 300,000 a year. I accept it as our first priority in time of peace . . .'[8] This pledge was repeated in the 1951 Election Manifesto: 'Housing is the first of the social services. It is also one of the keys to increased productivity. Work, family life, health and education are all undermined by overcrowded houses. Therefore a Conservative and Unionist Government will give housing a priority second only to national defence.' It is of note, however, that no date was put on the attainment of the target.[9]

Woolton, feeling he had saddled the Party with the commitment, and that 'many of my colleagues in the shadow Cabinet thought I had been unduly rash',[10] felt he should become Minister of Housing himself.[11] Churchill, however, had other plans for Woolton, and instead – apparently on the advice of Lord Beaverbrook[12] – chose Macmillan, who had been Chairman of the Party's Housing Committee in Opposition, and so, in a sense, was the natural choice. Churchill also felt the need for a tough man, not only due to the importance of realising the target, but also to stand up to those in the Ministry and local authorities who had told the Labour Government that 200,000 houses annually was the maximum possible figure. But the press were doubtful about the appointment: 'No forecaster was rash enough to suggest Mr. Harold Macmillan for the Ministry of Housing,' proclaimed the *News Chronicle*, 'surely he is miscast.'[13] Macmillan himself was disappointed not to be given a more senior position (ideally he would have liked the Foreign Office),[14] and failed at first to see the personal kudos that would follow if he achieved the 300,000 target. Macmillan had not in fact excelled during the period in Opposition: he had appeared rather florid in the House and had a reputation of being somewhat effete.

But the job was to prove the making of Macmillan. Within three years he emerged from being one of the more junior members of the Cabinet to one of the most influential, capable of demanding, and receiving, the highest offices. It was also one of his happiest ministerial posts[15] where he made more impact than in any other office he held outside the premiership.[16] Though frequent references can be found in which Macmillan expressed a wish to leave Housing,[17] these occurred in moments of dissatisfaction and did not reflect his calmer judgment, which, after an initial period of anxiety, was one of great satisfaction at the progress he was making. At first he failed to appreciate the fact that the Ministry was not a production Department: this he felt acutely, especially having served as Parliamentary Secretary at the Ministry of Supply during the war, where he had learnt so much from the Minister, Beaverbrook.[18] The civil servant at the Ministry responsible for housing remarked: 'I think Macmillan in 1951 was under the mistaken impression that houses were produced by direct contract between the Ministry and the builders, working hardly at all through local authorities.'[19]

In fact council houses were built by the local authorities themselves; all they needed from the Ministry was approval for their plans and numbers, and finance in accordance with the subsidy arrangements laid down by statute. Housing was the first Ministry which Macmillan had sole charge of for any length of time, his only previous experience as head of a Whitehall Department being as Secretary of State for Air in the 'Caretaker Government' of 1945. He had never shown a marked interest in housing policy before 1951,[20] but he quickly mastered both the subject and the Ministry's organisation. Moreover, Macmillan was relatively rare for a Minister in that he took a keen interest in both the language and the structure of Government legislation. His ability to master these details helped him to carry his busy legislative programme during 1951–4 through the House with both considerable skill and wit.[21]

Macmillan soon became undisputed master of Housing, admired for his efficiency and regarded highly by most officials, partly because he knew what he wanted and was able to get it. As was natural, he drew heavily on the proposals of his predecessor Hugh Dalton (Minister of Town and Country Planning, 1950–1) and his officials, and acquired a gift for making the policy appear to be his own.[22] He had a flair for publicity, for the act which would catch the public's eye, as with his trips after floods to Lynmouth in August 1952, and to the East Coast in February 1953.[23] These forays revealed little which could not have been as usefully discovered by an official, but earned him a great deal of press coverage. A dramatic picture of cloth-capped Macmillan, for example, appeared on the front page of the *Daily Mail* on 20th August, 1952. Beside it the headline: 'Mr. Harold Macmillan, the Housing Minister, will report to the Cabinet today on his tour of flood-damaged North Devon.' He had a similarly sensitive nose for warding off trouble. In his early days at the Ministry he held a monthly lunch to which he invited Nicholls, Enoch Powell and others who might be critical of his policy on the pretext that he wished to hear their views. They were naturally flattered at his courting of them, and did not appreciate that Macmillan by his gesture was effectively defusing their potential opposition.[24] Housing became one of the two great success stories of the Government, the other being derationing. Macmillan made the most of the regularly published and steadily improving official figures. He also made the most of the publicity facilities offered him by the Conservative Research Department.[25]

Macmillan was one of several departmental Ministers with a business background, and he ran the Ministry like a commercial concern.[26] He set up a small Minister's Council[27] which met initially once a week in the Ministry and was the main discussion body, although by 1953 it was meeting no more than once a month. The Minister's Council was an entirely new idea and was at first not favoured by two senior officials bred in a different tradition, Sir Thomas Sheepshanks and Sir John Wrigley. At these meetings Macmillan was superb. He did little of the talking himself and would listen carefully until the end. In this way he let everyone feel that they were contributing.[28] His custom was to ask the opinion of the youngest present first so the most senior spoke last and this procedure was liked by most officials once they got accustomed to it and to him.[29] In a similar spirit Macmillan instigated the establishment of the *ad hoc* Cabinet Committee on Building, whose members included Sir David Eccles, the Minister of Works, and James Stuart, the Secretary of State for Scotland.[30] Its function was to co-ordinate all aspects of the building programme.[31] This business ethos was also seen in Macmillan's choice of two aides, Sir Percy Mills and Ernest Marples.

As soon as Macmillan saw the magnitude of the task before him, he decided he needed someone to act like a director-general in the wartime production Ministries, and Mills, although not his first choice, seemed ideal.[32] During the war he had held key posts at the Ministry of Production. Now he agreed to come for one year as 'Honorary Adviser on Housing to the Minister'. But, despite his past association with Whitehall, the appointment of an outsider was disliked by some: apparently Sir Edward Bridges even complained to Churchill. In particular it was resented by Sheepshanks, the Permanent Secretary, who was jealous of the powers and responsibilities of his position and thought Mills would detract from the single-mindedness of the relationship between the Minister and his senior adviser.[33] No other senior civil servant felt as strongly, and most officials felt the obvious course was to win Mills' confidence if they could, given that Macmillan had made up his mind that Mills would be a useful asset in his crucial battle to convince his Cabinet colleagues that, regardless of expense, the housing commitment must be adhered to.

Mills established ten Regional Housing Production Boards, a move that at first frightened the Department.[34] These were built upon the already existing regional office organisation of the Ministry which during the war looked after the Department's many domestic responsibilities, from hospitals to the homeless. Their purpose was to speed up house-building by reducing shortages of materials and land. The Treasury was opposed to the retention of the regional system, let alone its revitalisation, but this was one of several battles between them which Macmillan won.[35] There was much argument in the Ministry as to whether the Regional Production Boards achieved any purpose. But officials who felt that their contribution was nil, failed to appreciate the considerable impact of the Boards on the suppliers of bricks, metal, wood and other commodities. Macmillan himself had no doubt as to the value, and wrote at the time: 'The Housing programme still largely depends on the local authorities; and their extraordinary success . . . is due to the work of the regional staff.'[36]

The regional offices remained throughout Macmillan's time, but after 1954 were progressively dismantled, partly as an economy measure but also because by then the housing targets had been reached and it was felt that local authorities should now be allowed greater independence.[37]

Macmillan systematically visited each region during 1952–3, but left the detailed running of the Boards to Mills, who kept to his word to hold the post for only one year. Macmillan was unhappy to lose him, yet respected his wishes: he left in December 1953, but continued to give advice and attend certain meetings. According to Macmillan, 'There was no step which Marples and I took without consulting him and getting

251

the advantage of his experience and judgment.'[38] Mills liked to get things done, and much of the boosting of production was due to him. Nevertheless, Macmillan exaggerated in his diary[39] when he wrote: 'I could have done nothing without him' and in his memoirs,[40] 'without him we could have achieved little'. Many of those interviewed felt that the chapter 'Building The Houses' in Macmillan's memoirs did not always accurately portray how he felt at the time, and that he had relied over-heavily in compiling them on the written evidence available (his diary and Minutes). When discussing his advisers, he overestimates the importance of Mills and Marples, and omits altogether to mention others, such as Sydney Wilkinson, Under-Secretary and chief housing aide.[41] Wilkinson submitted a draft Paper to Macmillan in November 1951 for submission to the Cabinet which detailed many items of policy subsequently adopted. The Cabinet did not accept the Paper in one go, and Macmillan had to go back to it more than once for authority to proceed. But, overall, one can fairly say of the Ministry as a whole that officials were invariably responsible for the making of policy, Ministers for its implementation.

As Parliamentary Secretary, Macmillan secured his own choice, Marples.[42] A comparative newcomer to politics, he had already made his mark in the construction industry as managing director of an engineering and building company. He was the author of a booklet on housing which received wide attention and had been Secretary of the Party's Housing Committee in the latter period in Opposition. Marples displayed a lively mind, great common sense and energy and was highly publicity conscious: his was the idea to stage an exhibition of three houses in Holles Street near Oxford Circus in London showing what could be done to improve existing houses with the aid of improvement grants.[43] Macmillan, through his connections with the Palace, managed to persuade the Queen to come and open them.[44] A skilful engineer, Marples was responsible for initiating the design of a house which required practically no timber, and used cement as a substitute, which saved one of the scarcest resources.[45] He was particularly useful in dealing with deputations from local authorities, thus saving Macmillan much work in that time-consuming field. But to the overall housing programme his was not a major contribution: he would attend the meetings but was not a dominant voice,[46] and neither was he a particularly effective Parliamentary spokesman. Macmillan was progressively to lean more on others.[47] As his Parliamentary Private Secretary, Macmillan chose Reginald Bevins, an ambitious new M.P. who saved Macmillan being troubled by his own backbenchers, and, unlike many Parliamentary Private Secretaries, was given small jobs in the Ministry.

Indeed Bevins himself has written: 'Within about a year I had established myself for all practical purposes as a second junior Minister.'[48]

Macmillan was fortunate in having in the Ministry a particularly able body of officials. Some of the elder ones, more set in their ways, found some difficulty, as we have seen, in adapting to his methods, but in general they were extremely anxious to help. Sheepshanks, the Permanent Secretary, had been appointed at the Ministry of Town and Country Planning in 1946, when aged fifty-one, and remained there until transferring to the new Ministry of Local Government and Planning (subsequently Housing and Local Government) in 1951. By then, however, he was already past his prime, his health having suffered from the strain of excessive work during and after the war.[49] Nonetheless a first-class administrator, negotiator and draftsman, it is doubtful if Macmillan got the best from him. It was unfortunate that one of the more reserved, traditionally-minded of Permanent Secretaries should have been coupled with one of the most dynamic, iconoclastic of Ministers. Sheepshanks' major weaknesses in Macmillan's eyes were his orthodox methods and lack of dynamism, and Macmillan came to regard him merely as a figurehead. Sheepshanks would complain about Macmillan's methods, but never ran a campaign against him. Macmillan for his part soon found that he could successfully bypass him, and came to rely increasingly on the advice of Dame Evelyn Sharp, as Sheepshanks himself had been doing for some years. When Sandys became Minister in October 1954, he soon decided that Sheepshanks was not the Permanent Secretary he wanted,[50] although in the event Sheepshanks retired in his own time in 1955 at the age of sixty, and knowledge of Duncan Sandys' frustration with his Permanent Secretary never became generally known in the Department.

Initially there were two Deputy Secretaries, Sir John Wrigley and Dame Evelyn Sharp. Wrigley was a man who had enormous experience of housing as a result of eight years at the Ministry of Health, and provided useful continuity as the senior representative from Health to join the new Ministry of Local Government and Planning in January 1951. But some felt his retirement was already overdue. His eventual departure, in 1952 aged sixty-four, was precipitated by a quarrel with Mills: Wrigley was a quiet man, and after one or two curt remarks from Mills, who tended to regard all civil servants as socialists, he decided it was time to go.

Dame Evelyn Sharp became Deputy Secretary at the Ministry of Town and Country Planning in 1946. Her particular field was planning, and she had long established herself as pre-eminent in her field, earning high praise from previous Ministers.[51] She succeeded Sheepshanks as

Permanent Secretary in 1955, but had long been the effective number one voice in the Department.[52] Macmillan had great admiration for her intellect and mental agility and relied on her more than on any other official, although she had little to do with the housing drive itself. Much of the shape of post-war planning – and the new towns in particular – were the product of her fertile mind. She was the most accomplished female civil servant since the war, possibly one of the most able of either sex. Macmillan was close to few other officials at the Ministry, in contrast to later offices which he held where he was to form close bonds with several of his top civil servants. Neither was he as close to his Principal Private Secretaries at Housing as he was to be at, say, the Foreign Office or Number Ten, although he did insist that at all times his two able Private Secretaries (Jack Beddoe until February 1953, then John Rogerson) should know all that was going on.

As a result of Macmillan's concentration on housing he was unable to devote as much time as he would have liked to his other ministerial responsibilities, in particular the problems of rates, housing subsidies, requisitioned houses, local government and public health. In this latter category, the Ministry had to cope with the notorious 'smog' of December 1952[53] – when the death rate suddenly shot up by 4,000 a week – and the public health implications of the East Coast flooding in February 1953. Macmillan also found a great deal of his time taken up by two large and technically difficult Bills in 1953–4, Housing Repairs and Rents, and Town and Country Planning.

The housing drive came in two phases: accelerating the rate at which new houses were being built until the target of 300,000 houses a year was reached, and then attempting to clear slums and improve unsatisfactory housing.[54] Shortage of materials, steel, timber and bricks proved a problem until 1954, but the situation was eased by economies in house construction: Marples' design using a minimum of timber helped, and still more savings resulted from Dalton's plan for a small house, which Macmillan successfully exploited.[55] Supplies were boosted by the ending of price controls, at the prompting of Sir David Eccles, on certain key building materials, but throughout 1953 imports of timber and bricks were found to be essential. Lord Swinton's ingenuity as Minister of Materials was particularly helpful in overcoming the steel shortage of 1951 which had forced Labour to slow down their school-building programme.[56] Swinton was to comment on Macmillan's stint at Housing: '. . . He was realistic and practical and did not try to overbid or overinsure. I always gave him what he wanted, though there were plenty of rival claimants baying like hounds at feeding time.'[57]

As the production of subsidised houses by local authorities increased,

Macmillan turned his attention to private building, which in turn would also relieve the burden on the Treasury. A Cabinet paper in November 1951 argued that private building must be made to make a substantial contribution to the target, if only to reduce the financial burden that local authority houses put upon the community (let alone the desirability of establishing the Conservative ideal of a 'property-owning democracy'). Under the Labour Government, local authorities kept being compelled to change the ratio at which they granted licences to private builders, and by the time of the 1951 Election it was one private licence to every four local authority houses. In November 1951 this ratio was changed to one to one, and progressive liberalisations occurred in August 1952, the major turning-point,[58] then again in December 1952,[59] and January 1954[60] until controls were finally abolished in November 1954.[61] The number of houses built for private owners increased dramatically, and on 1st December, 1953 Macmillan was able to announce that the target of 300,000 houses a year had been reached.[62]

Home ownership was encouraged in a number of ways. In August 1952 the Minister gave local authorities consent to sell council houses under certain conditions. Numbers however remained small, little more than 3,000 council houses being sold by local authorities in England and Wales before the 1955 General Election. In May 1954 a new policy was announced to help young married couples with deposits. Local authorities in their turn were encouraged by the Housing Act, 1952, which increased housing subsidies to balance the increased interest rate charged following the rises in the Bank Rate in 1951–2.

By mid-1952 Macmillan was already beginning to turn his attention to the second arm of the housing drive, the improvement of existing dwellings,[63] which received what appears with hindsight to have been a grossly exaggerated title, 'Operation Rescue'. The plans were outlined in a White Paper[64] and were implemented in the Housing Repairs and Rents Act, 1954. This still left untouched millions of substandard dwellings, but Aneurin Bevan's comment that landlords were getting 'a mouldy old turnip',[65] was unfair in view of the Labour Government's poor record on house improvement. Thus the problem of bad housing was largely left to Macmillan's successors to solve. Many in the Ministry felt, with some justice, that Macmillan was to blame for the lameness of the Housing Repairs and Rents Act: they had urged a far higher increase in rents to allow for repair work than Macmillan felt politically feasible, and as a consequence, landlords had insufficient money to spend.[66] Indeed the landlord could not claim a rent increase unless he had already and recently actually spent money on repairs, and put the dwelling into 'good and tenantable repair'. As most landlords could not afford to do this, they were bound to fall at the first fence. The *Sunday Times* noted in a leader on 8th November, 1953, entitled 'Homes or Politics': 'Mr. Macmillan has grasped the nettle, but not firmly enough.' Many agreed.

Macmillan was not alone among Conservatives in being suspicious of new towns, with many in the Party regarding them as a device for moving Labour voters out of the towns into the traditionally Tory countryside. They had burgeoned after the Ministry of Town and Country Planning, under the New Towns Act, 1946, was empowered to approve the construction of new towns to take the overspill from London and other big cities. Under this Act twelve new towns were established,[67] with by the end of 1954 more than 27,000 houses and 131 factories.[68] At first Macmillan was undecided about what attitude to adopt,[69] but he soon came to see their positive side, not least the houses they built. He also thought them more attractive to live in than many of the towns of the industrial revolution.[70] Rab Butler and Peter Thorneycroft, however, took a different view. Butler thought new towns were taking too large a share of national resources, and officials at the Board of Trade convinced Thorneycroft that the new towns should be discouraged because they were attracting industry and finance from development areas. Macmillan triumphed on this, as on other issues: four measures in successive years from 1952 were passed voting new towns more money, and in 1954 11,600 new dwellings were completed in them. The new towns were not, however, viewed with unqualified approval. A leader in *The Times* noted that: '. . . The programme is getting further and further from fulfilling the expectations with which it was launched immediately after the war.'[71] A related measure was the Town Development Act of 1952, which Macmillan had inherited from Dalton: this provided a framework for large and overcrowded towns to export population and industry to smaller ones.[72] The main large conurbations concerned were Birmingham, Manchester and Liverpool, though the scheme never worked as well for these three as it did for London.

A distinctive change of policy did occur in one particular aspect of new towns: their public houses. Pubs were the responsibility of the Home Office, and Chuter Ede, Labour's Home Secretary, 1945–51, thought they should be under state control in the new towns. Sir David Maxwell Fyfe, under the stern prodding of his colleagues, especially Stuart,[73] set about reversing this plan in the Licensed Premises in New Towns Act, 1952.[74] The fact that the brewers were major subscribers to the Conservative Party undoubtedly stiffened the Government's resolve to carry through this particular piece of legislation. Indeed the Opposition argued that the Government was currying favour with the brewers, who had a strong financial interest in the Party. The Government strongly resisted this criticism. They brought down the Guillotine on the Bill on 21st July, which Ede called a 'constitutional outrage'.[75]

It also fell to Macmillan to amend the Town and Country Planning Act, 1947, drafted by Lewis Silkin, the Minister, 1945–50. This had involved a fiscal instrument known as the development charge whose unforeseen effect was to retard development. Neither Sheepshanks nor Sharp, who had played a major part in the 1947 Town and Country Planning Act, were at first keen to see the development charge abolished. The Treasury felt it would be a mistake to remove the development charge altogether, and would have preferred to see it remain at a reduced rate as it provided a useful source of income. Macmillan believed the Silkin Act was a drag on the housing programme because it dried up the land market for private developers and was incomprehensible to most people, himself included. He gave it scant attention for the first year,[76] until in December 1952 he set about piloting through the House the preliminary Town and Country Planning Bill,[77] a holding operation until further legislation could be passed. He also abolished the collection of the charge on all development and repealed the Government's obligation under the 1947 Act to pay out £300m. in compensation by mid-1953. A White Paper[78] dealt with arrangements for paying compensation, and was embodied in the Town and Country Planning Act, 1954. The passage of this Bill involved considerable difficulties, and occupied much of his attention throughout the first half of 1954. Though the details of the Bill were the work of his officials,[79] he displayed skill and perseverance in seeing it through the House. Dame Evelyn Sharp congratulated Macmillan on his indispensable contribution, saying she had seldom seen anything as brilliant as his handling of the Bill.[80] It was indeed a necessary piece of legislation, but many of the problems it attempted to tackle have proved intractable.

Bombed towns provided a further problem on the planning side. Labour had made little headway with redevelopment, and six years after the end of the war bomb-sites and derelict spaces were still a common feature in many towns. Here Macmillan stuck out hard for more money for the eighteen cities which had suffered particularly badly from bombing,[81] and this paid dividends. In 1954 27,500 houses were built in blitzed town centres compared with 20,000 in 1951.

The third aspect of the Ministry's work, local government, Macmillan left very much to his officials. After the war local authorities acquired a number of new functions relating to housing and town planning, but at the same time also lost others to the National Health Service, the nationalised industries and the Ministry of National Insurance. The time was ripe for a radical re-examination of the whole structure and functions of local government, and to build on the limited progress that had been made in the inter-war years in the direction of rationalising and strengthening the powers of the local authorities. Like the Attlee Government before them, the Conservatives pledged themselves in 1951 to institute some reforms, but the Government complained that it could not find the Parliamentary time.[82] In truth, though, the Conservative Government were anxious to avoid – as Labour had been before it – offending local vested interests, whose support they regarded as of major political importance. A number of minor pieces of legislation were passed, such as the New Valuation Lists (Postponement) Act, 1952,[83] and the Local Government Superannuation Act, 1953: Macmillan was prone to complain that politically unimportant Bills created more problems because people would raise niggly points. As his period of office was drawing to a close he circulated a paper of possible reforms, headed by the reorganisation of local government. He realised the problems in the structure of local government as well as its functions, but had few concrete ideas as to a solution. In the event over ten years were to pass before Labour appointed the Royal Commission on Local Government under the chairmanship of Sir John Maud, whose Report was published in 1969 (London's local government was reformed in 1963).

One of Macmillan's greatest difficulties was to secure finance from the Exchequer to facilitate house-building, a continuous battle exacerbated by the economic crisis of late 1951 and early 1952.[84] The first serious approach Macmillan made to Butler was for the increase of the exemption limit for stamp duty on the purchase of a new house – a request costing little but which was nevertheless refused. A small but significant spur to the speculative builder was thus lost early in 1952. Macmillan continued to fight hard against Butler, whose Treasury officials were cautioning restraint, and through perseverance, and ultimately force of character, his will prevailed. Realising that he would have to be released from control of the Treasury's capital investment programme if his housing target was to be attained, Macmillan enlisted the support of Churchill,[85] and got his way; Butler could effectively be ignored. The major victory for Macmillan came at the end of July 1952, when he won a battle in the Cabinet against Butler. In a perspicacious article in the *Observer* on 3rd August, Hugh Massingham asked himself why Macmillan had won: 'The answer is partly to be found in the able personality of Mr. Macmillan himself, whose furious enthusiasm and quickness in argument make him a formidable opponent. There may even be a weakness in Mr. Butler's own make-up . . . he is not quite the Iron Chancellor that the late Sir Stafford Cripps was.' The quarrelling was seldom bitter, but was constant, and did nothing to improve their already fragile relationship. Indeed, Macmillan was one of the very few figures during 1951–5 whom Butler found difficult to oppose.[86] As Butler later reflected: '. . . He used to press me like hell . . . it may have been my fault really. You don't notice these everyday things do you? I mean money passes, but your officials are doing it really. I had been told that I really ought not to have let it through . . . it was my fault that I didn't realise what a terrific strain on the economy this was.'[87]

Churchill took a keen interest in the housing drive[88] – indeed at the 1950 Blackpool Party Conference he had declared: 'Houses and homes come before health, because overcrowding and slum dwellings are fatal to the family life and breed more illnesses than the doctors can cure'[89] but he never interfered internally in the Ministry.[90] Macmillan also undoubtedly benefited from the support of other Ministers apart from Churchill: amongst his friends, Harry Crookshank, the Leader of the House, in arranging the Parliamentary timetable for his business, as well as backing in Cabinet for his programme from Oliver Lyttelton, Swinton, Lord Salisbury, Stuart and Maxwell Fyfe.[91]

Many in the Ministry at the time felt that the scale of the housing drive was unwise, and agreed with Sheepshanks' view that the Conservatives had over-reached themselves, or that the priority given to new houses was at the cost of deliberately prolonging the long-standing neglect of rent-restricted houses in need of repair or improvement. Indeed the figures bore this out: the numbers of building workers on existing houses fell from 220,000 to 170,000 from the summer of 1951 to the summer of 1953. Those working on construction of new houses rose from 260,000 to 340,000.[92] Others have since criticised the level of house-building as being opportunistic, and sacrificing the long-term well-being of the nation for the sake of short-term electoral advantage.[93] This can be accepted up to a point, although the Conservatives' action should also be seen as perhaps the inevitable consequence of wooing voters in the electoral market place of representative democracy. The Conservatives under Macmillan at Housing were merely more successful at achieving what Labour (with less efficiency and drive) had tried to do under Dalton. Indeed Dalton had written in his diary on 29th October, 1951, just after the Election: 'He [Macmillan] won't be able to build any more, if as many, as I. My last month [September] showed more than 17,000 completed – a good month. But there'll be steel, dollar [sic], softwood, cement and bricks [shortages] . . .'[94]

Labour at the time raised objections to what they considered the neglect of other forms of building due to the stress on houses. Bevan, on the top of his form, maintained that earlier in 1953 there had been an argument between Butler and the spending Ministers, which they had lost to Macmillan, who had said '. . . stand back a bit. I am advancing here.'[95] Thus a debate was staged on 1st July, 1953 on the level of school-building, where Florence Horsbrugh was able to make a strong case. The number of new school places brought into use had in fact risen from 159,000 in 1951 to 262,000 in 1953. Macmillan made one of the most powerful and commanding speeches of his career up to that point in winding up the debate, and was well able to ridicule the Opposition:

> It must be still more irritating [to the Opposition] to see the [housing] figures rising month by month. I do not know what the final figure for 1953 will be, but if it should be a good one . . . Will there be compliments and good wishes, perhaps a little token, to the Minister – a specially bound copy of 'Challenge to Britain' [Labour policy statement] or, better still, a year's subscription to the *Tribune*? Alas, I can expect nothing so gracious. Curiously enough, no sooner have we begun to prove that building on this scale can be done, than our critics turn round and say that it really ought not to be done.[96]

All good knock-about stuff, but Macmillan's oratorical gifts and indignation at what he considered Labour's dishonest attack obscured the fact that there was substance in their case, especially in the comparative neglect of industrial building at a time when, in this area, Britain's competitors were forging ahead. Macmillan was able to show that spending on new factories was increasing at about four per cent per annum,[97] but this figure, when compared to international standards, makes Macmillan's confidence appear like complacency.

At Housing Macmillan proved himself a highly effective Minister, and it is unlikely that many others in Churchill's Cabinet would have had the industry to achieve the housing target. By mid-1954, as the Housing Repairs and Rents Bill was passing through its final stages in the House, Macmillan began to look around in earnest for a job to which he might, with profit, move: Foreign Secretary,[98] and Lord Privy Seal combined with Leader of the House[99] were two possibilities mentioned by Churchill, but these had to be dropped after objections from the incumbents[100] – Anthony Eden and Crookshank. Eventually it was decided he should become Minister of Defence, a job for which he had been in the running in 1951.[101]

Sandys, the new Minister, was appointed in October 1954. He had managed well that large and unwieldy Department, the Ministry of Supply, and had made a success of piloting the Iron and Steel Act of 1953. Sandys, delighted by the appointment, which also meant a seat in Cabinet, had gained immeasurably in confidence and experience during the previous three years, and came to Housing a determined and accomplished Minister. Unfortunately, he did not learn from his mistakes in personal relations, which he proceeded to repeat at his new Ministry. He was imbued with the idea (probably inherited from his father-in-law, Churchill), that it was absolutely essential to get on top of one's officials from the start, often failing to appreciate that a halfway house could be found. But Sandys was a strange compound: he was one of the few Ministers who on appointment asked the senior staff to his home for drinks.

Certain officials resented the way Sandys interfered with their work, in contrast to Macmillan who had left them a free hand. Others felt that his painstaking concentration on one issue at a time was at the cost of ignoring or dropping equally important items. Yet few could deny, as officials had also found at Supply, that the thorough if laborious work he put in on crucial issues meant he learnt the argument backwards and would thus often win his case in Cabinet, and give a strong performance in the House. He continued his habit of enormously hard work, and would frequently work until the small hours and even at times beyond dawn.

To most of his officials he was a cold man, incapable of letting his hair down, yet his junior Ministers frequently found him an excellent boss.[102] Sandys used to say that as a Parliamentary Secretary during the war he had been ignored by his Minister, and was determined the same should not happen again.[103] Despite his eccentricities and his excessive attention to unimportant detail – during his first week he spent a great deal of time reorganising the filing of Parliamentary Questions, putting in the 'double tag' system which he particularly liked – he was in his peculiar way a very effective Minister of Housing. The Opposition respected his command of the subject, and throughout he had a clear idea of his aims.

Failing promotion, Marples had wanted to remain in his post as Parliamentary Secretary but a last-minute objection was raised as a result of his association with the contractors Marples Ridgeway, and he was moved on to National Insurance. William Deedes was a Whips' choice for the new Parliamentary Secretary: Powell had been approached first but had turned it down.[104] Unlike Marples, Deedes had special areas of responsibility assigned to him, and took local government, clean air, water and sewerage. He was thought to have performed well in his first ministerial post, and was marked out for high office.[105]

Part 3   The Ministry of Health

When in 1951 the Attlee Government split the former Ministry of Health to produce the Ministry of Local Government and Planning and the new Ministry of Health, the latter's political importance inevitably fell. The new Minister, Hilary Marquand (January–October 1951), though a pleasant and able man, by no means possessed the force of Aneurin Bevan (1945–51), a dominating figure and inspirational force on the work of the Department. With the accession of Marquand the job was also taken out of Cabinet, further depriving it of political weight.

Senior officials at the new Ministry of Health did not as a whole feel that the incoming Conservative Government would make major changes to the National Health Service (N.H.S.), freshly created by the Attlee Government, or that the Service was anything but firmly established, but there were in certain areas fears that Conservative tendencies were likely to be even more political than those of Labour.[1] The public displayed considerable interest in how the Conservatives would deal with the N.H.S., and Labour, as was perhaps natural, prophesied the worst. These fears were, however, soon shown to be out of place. At a meeting of the Cabinet's Economy Committee on 7th December, 1951, Ministers decided not to press ahead with plans for hospital charges, and a month later dental charges for children were also dropped.[2] Indeed the new Government held expenditure on health at a similar percentage of G.N.P. as had been the case since its inception in 1948. That there was not more change owed much to the two Conservative Ministers, Harry Crookshank (1951–2) and Iain Macleod (1952–5), and also to the momentum which the N.H.S. had acquired in the first three years of its existence.

The Conservatives did introduce some minor charging (for drugs, medicines, certain appliances and dental treatment) in the National Health Service Act, 1952,[3] but the origin of this was more a need to stretch funds than party dogma. The Act was designed to reduce the annual Exchequer health bill for England and Wales by £18m.–£20m., but the saving from the charges, which became effective from June 1952, made little difference to total health expenditure, which, at constant prices was almost exactly the same per head in 1954–5 as in 1949–50. Moreover, the notion of 'charging' was not a new departure. The charges in the 1952 Act had been written into Labour's 1949 Bill but had not been implementèd, and they supplemented those on spectacles and dentures (which precipitated Bevan's resignation as Minister of Labour in April 1951, to which post he had been appointed from Health that January).

Within the Ministry of Health's sphere the new Government faced

262

two immediate issues: doctors' pay, and whether the N.H.S. gave value for money. Its response helped set Conservative attitudes to the N.H.S. which were to endure until the electoral defeat in October 1964.

The question of doctors' pay had been a running sore since 1948 and few disputed that they were poorly treated. The Labour Government eventually decided to appoint a High Court Judge to adjudicate on pay levels for doctors. Marquand and Hector McNeil (Secretary of State for Scotland, 1950–1) set up an Enquiry under Mr. Justice Danckwerts in August 1951. Relying heavily on evidence supplied by doctors that critics felt unduly favourable to their own case, Danckwerts reported in the spring of 1952, recommending that doctors should be given nearly as much as they had asked, at a cost of £40m. spread over four years. The size of the recommendation was a blow to the new Government (although Conservatives as a whole tended to feel that doctors had been unfairly done by), and there were qualms about accepting Danckwerts' award – though it had no real alternative. Crookshank played an important part in persuading the Cabinet to allow the increase, despite Government hopes of cutting public expenditure.

In Opposition the Conservatives had conducted an anti-waste campaign and had repeatedly criticised the form taken by the N.H.S. Once in Government they set about turning their words into deeds. Was the N.H.S. giving good value? In April 1953, Macleod set up a Committee under the Cambridge don, Claude Guillebaud,[1] to review the expenditure of the N.H.S. and to examine whether the most efficient use was being made of Exchequer funds. The establishment of the Enquiry was attacked by Labour in extravagant language, with Bevan going so far as to say that Macleod was 'seeking another instrument by which he might mutilate the National Health Service', and that Macleod was its 'avowed enemy',[5] but there was nothing overtly political in its creation, and it is likely that had Labour still been in office, they, too, would have felt a need to set up a similar enquiry, perhaps justifying it in different language.[6] When the Committee reported in January 1956, it found little evidence of waste, and remarked on the substantial improvements made in the scale and quality of service provided.[7] In effect it rebuked politicians for their suspicions, and made it clear that the N.H.S. was indeed providing good value.[9] The key to the Guillebaud Report was the work prepared for it by R. M. Titmuss and Brian Abel-Smith, two exceptionally well informed and influential witnesses, and both noted for their 'left-wing' views.[8] Whatever hopes the Conservatives may once have had of making substantial savings at Health were thus lost.

Realising that the Ministry of Health was a highly sensitive area, Winston Churchill appointed Harry Crookshank, one of his most senior colleagues, and gave him a seat in Cabinet. Though he had not before served in a Ministry connected purely with social policy, he had wide experience of a number of Departments, and his experience as Financial Secretary to the Treasury (1940–3) and Postmaster-General (1943–5) was felt by many to qualify him for a top 'economic' job. He was a wealthy man and a benefactor[9] who had taken considerable interest in different aspects of health care.[10] It is uncertain whether Churchill originally intended Crookshank to remain at Health for a long period, or merely as a holding operation until it was decided which of the promising younger men in the Party would be most suitable for the task. However, from the moment that Anthony Eden declared in the first few days after the General Election that he could not take on the leadership of the House, and this additional burden fell on Crookshank,[11] it was clear that he could not combine both duties for long, particularly in view of the strain on his health.[12] Early in November 1951 Churchill told Crookshank to let him know if the two offices were going to prove too much for him.[13] In February 1952 the press speculated that a new Minister of Health would be appointed, although Crookshank recorded in his diary that there was, 'Not a word of truth in it so far as I know.'[14] He did, however, find the burden increasingly difficult. On 5th May Churchill asked him to give up Health to allow him to concentrate on the leadership of the House. Some of his colleagues, Eden in particular,[15] felt he had not up to that point proved an especially effective Leader, and hence would benefit from being able to give it his exclusive attention. Labour M.P.s had also complained that Crookshank could not fairly combine the job of Minister of Health, a departmental position, with the need to consider the position of all three Parties, the duty of the Leader of the House.[16] As part of a small reshuffle, he was appointed Lord Privy Seal on 7th May. Two days later he recorded in his diary: 'To bed early as I am so tired, but dropping Health will help.'[17]

Crookshank had none of the flamboyance or power of Bevan, but he brought to the office tremendous zeal and sense of commitment. Combined with his powerful intellect and serious personality, he was set to become a most distinguished Minister of Health, and in his seven-month spell earned the admiration and affection of his senior officials. He quickly came to understand, far better than most, the complex relationship in the Ministry between professionals and administrators. He said he found an analogy with the War Office helpful: the Chief Medical Officer was akin to the Chief of Imperial General Staff as head of the professionals, in relation to the Permanent Secretary as head of the administrators.[18] But it was not just in his grasp of how the machine operated that his qualities displayed themselves: he also had a deep knowledge of problems of health care. He was particularly interested in mental health, and refused to let it be neglected. He was determined to right abuses: early on he presented the Permanent Secretary with a list of items that were unpopular with the public or on which he thought the public felt particularly strongly, and asked for an analysis to be made of the way that grievances might be redressed.[19] But he laboured under a major handicap: he needed to be in or near the House when it was sitting because Labour would engineer a fuss when they saw that the Leader of the House was away from London on ministerial business. In consequence, his ministerial work and visits had to be concentrated into Fridays and occasionally Saturdays, and this inevitably limited his effectiveness.[20] When he left the Ministry in May 1952, he took with him his Parliamentary Private Secretary, old friend and confidant, Robert Cary.

The appointment of his successor, Iain Macleod, has been well documented.[21] He came to the job with little political following, largely on the evidence of his debating skill in one key speech, which proved beyond doubt that he could face up to Bevan. After becoming Chairman of the Party's Health and Social Services Committee in February 1952, his appointment as Minister of Health at some stage was always a strong possibility, but his intervention in the Second Reading debate on the N.H.S. Bill in March 1952, in which he also displayed his deep knowledge of health matters and great memory, helped make it a certainty. Called to follow Bevan, Macleod began in fighting style which caught the attention of the House: 'I want to deal closely and with relish with the vulgar, crude and intemperate speech to which the House of Commons has just listened.'[22] With a keen interest in health care since his period at the Conservative Research Department, and with his medical background (his father was a G.P. from Skipton), he could hardly have been better suited, and the appointment also went some way to quell the feelings of younger M.P.s that their interests were under-represented in the Government. The Department no longer had its Minister in the Cabinet, but this did not necessarily entail a lowered priority for health: Macleod attended on those few occasions when health questions were discussed, and it was quite natural for such an inexperienced Minister not immediately to sit in Cabinet.

Without the usual preliminary period as a junior Minister, it is not surprising that Macleod was at first found by his officials to be modest and unsure of himself. Unlike many new Ministers though, he was not found to be at all suspicious by many of his senior officials, and they worked well with him.[23] Some indeed came to regard him more as a friend than a boss. Others, however, found him a cold man, reluctant to give them his trust and certainly unwilling to form friendships.[24] But, without exception, all found that he was decisive and that when his mind was made up, he would not have his will circumvented in any event. His phenomenal memory, and the speed and thoroughness with which he read and digested his departmental briefs soon ensured that he became undisputed master in the Department. Indeed, *The Economist* noted that Macleod was by far the best informed answerer on departmental Questions in the House of Commons.[25]

Macleod was happy to have a comparatively quiet period at the Ministry, partly because he felt the N.H.S. needed time to settle down,[26] and also because he was not prepared to court trouble by pressing too hard for more funds. In some quite senior quarters in the Ministry there were fears that Macleod had ideas, if not for the wholesale abolition of the N.H.S., then at least for its radical reorganisation, and that he was waiting for Guillebaud to report before striking.[27] But this is most unlikely. Macleod certainly possessed imaginative ideas for the finance of welfare services, and it appears at first a puzzle as to why he did not do more to implement them. The most plausible explanation is that, once in office, he realised their impracticality.

Macleod was a conscientious worker, but did not spend overlong hours at the Ministry: his usual pattern was to work in the office until midday, before going to the House.[28] It is interesting that the fellow Minister whose work and style Macleod admired most was the moderate and affable Sir Walter Monckton. He tried to ensure that the existing apparatus could perform as well as possible, rather than introduce innovations. His influence was exerted in many diverse directions: he encouraged the formation of group practice (many doctors were opposed to the alternative, health centres),[29] was adamant, like Crookshank before him, that mental hospitals be given priority on available funds; did much to reduce the backlog of work needing to be done on thoracic surgery, in March 1954 launching a new drive to eliminate tuberculosis, and, finally, did more than any other Minister since the war to encourage voluntary services. The Labour Government had tended to frown on these, but Macleod was quick to grasp their vital role in a service where funds were always likely to be scarce. Thus he gave every encouragement to bodies such as the League of Hospital Friends and the Multiple Sclerosis Society, as well as supporting public events, such as blood transfusion rallies. Not loath to make new departures if he felt them necessary, he was the first Minister brave enough to acknowledge the existence of the Family Planning Association and visit its headquarters. He also did much to encourage work being done in Whitehall in 1954–5 on assessing the needs of old people, the results of which were published in 1956.[30]

The one Parliamentary Secretary throughout was Patricia Hornsby-Smith, the more successful of the two women in Government.[31] At thirty-seven, Patricia Hornsby-Smith was the youngest woman ever to be appointed to a job in a Conservative Government. A Private Secretary at the Ministry of Economic Warfare during the war, she had been M.P. for Chislehurst since 1950. Initially apprehensive about how the somewhat 'Edwardian' bachelor, Crookshank, would take to a young woman M.P., she was surprised and gratified by his consideration and guidance, particularly as he entrusted her with clearly defined areas in the Department.[32] With little new legislation produced by the Ministry under Macleod, she had less work to do in the House than many junior Ministers, but she was a willing worker and performed a good job as his back-up. Macleod's Parliamentary Private Secretary, Graeme Finaly,[33] on the other hand, found his boss so independent that the Minister had little need for his services.

Within the Ministry there was a clear division of responsibility between the administrative and medical officials. Since the new Ministry's formation in 1951, the Permanent Secretary (an administrator) had been Sir John Hawton. His succession was unexpected partly on account of his comparative youth (he was forty-seven), though many in the Ministry had hoped for it. He had been the real author of the 1944 White Paper, and had got on well with Bevan. With Sir Wilson Jameson, Chief Medical Officer, 1940–50, Hawton had done more than any other official to set up the N.H.S. He had the potential to be a most effective head of the Ministry, but was beginning to feel the effects of the illness which was to plague him increasingly throughout his years as Permanent Secretary, in which office he remained until 1960.[34] His relationship with Macleod was thus not as satisfactory as it could have been.

The medical (professional) branch of the Ministry was headed by the Chief Medical Officer, who held the same title at the Ministry of Education and Home Office, although most of his work was done at Health. It was a job that was graded at Permanent Secretary level, with right of access to the Minister, though the Permanent Secretary was acknowledged head of the Department. On the retirement of the highly influential Jameson in 1950 his place was taken by Sir John Charles, not such a forceful figure, who devoted much of his time to international aspects of the work. Beneath him were two deputies: George Godber (who succeeded Charles in 1960), the dominant man on the N.H.S., even while Macleod was Minister, and Sir Weldon Dalrymple-Champneys, an expert on the control of drugs, who took care of environmental matters.

The Conservatives, on their return in 1951, were faced with more formidable problems than just questions of value for money and doctors' pay. Shortages of hospital facilities were still severe, the number of dentists inadequate to meet demand, conditions in mental hospitals deplorable, and many doctors were being forced by economic pressures, prior to the Danckwerts award, to accumulate dangerously excessive lists of patients. In all these areas solid progress was made during 1951–5.

The number of hospital beds available in England and Wales rose by only 14,000 from 462,000 in 1951 to 476,000 in 1955.[35] Labour's energies had been devoted to establishing the overall Service, and no new hospital had been completed from 1945–51. For his first three years at the Department, with the available building materials being taken by the Ministry of Housing, Macleod put his energies into ensuring that the annual sums for capital expenditure on hospitals were being used as efficiently as possible. Not until February 1955 could he announce any real increase in the hospital-building programme: a three-year plan for major new hospital-building schemes, with the Treasury spending some £13m. on hospital capital expenditure in England and Wales by 1956–7, rising to £18m. by 1957–8.[36]

The 1951 statement of Conservative policy declared that although there would be too few dentists for many years, priority should be given to mothers and children, and to preventive work.[37] As a result of the N.H.S. Act, 1952, and appropriate adjustment of fee schedules, the number of children receiving dental courses rose dramatically, and in 1954, of the approximately six million courses completed, about half were on persons under twenty-one. In addition the drift away from the school dental service was discouraged, but total numbers of dentists on the list in England and Wales fell, from 9,694 in 1951 to 9,359 in 1955;[38] only one quarter of the number needed to provide a comprehensive service. The Ministry's annual Report published in December 1954 showed that there had, however, been a remarkable transformation since pre-war days. Before the war one in ten adults went to the dentist each year, but by 1953 this had improved to one in five for those in their twenties. Improvements among children being even more apparent. The shortage of dentists was partly due to the inadequate salaries and partly to the age structure of the profession. The so-called '1921 dentists' were all coming up for retirement at a time when those with modern training were too few. The age structure was adverse because when dentists were first given a register in 1921 established ones, however trained, were admitted, causing a large influx into the profession. It was not until April 1955 that Macleod could announce a dental salary review. Macleod's only Bill as Minister, introduced in late 1955, was based on an Enquiry into dental recruitment which had been set up in December 1954. This went some way to relieving pressure on dentists by making more use of dental assistants[39] and making it easier for dentists from abroad to work in Britain.

Much was done in the field of mental health to reduce waiting lists. After some experimentation with day hospitals, by the end of 1953 five such hospitals were in operation, saving money as well as producing some advantages in treatment. In addition nearly 30% of total hospital capital expenditure for 1954–5 was devoted to mental hospitals, as opposed to 17% in 1950–1, and in May 1954 Macleod laid the foundation stone of only the second new hospital to be started since 1945,[40] a Mental Deficiency Hospital at Southport. To help examine the problem in more depth, Macleod in February 1954 set up a Royal Commission under Lord Percy of Newcastle, whose Report in 1957 was to do much to enlighten mental health care in Britain.[41]

The problem of over-working by doctors was partially relieved by improving the system by which doctors were paid. After the Danckwerts award, which gave doctors more pay, a new system introduced in April 1953 encouraged doctors to go where they were most needed, discouraged too large lists of patients and stimulated the formation of partnerships. The maximum number of patients permitted on a doctor's list was reduced from 4,000 to 3,600, and as a result of these measures the average number of patients per doctor fell from 2,431 in 1952 to 2,283 in 1955.[42] Macleod was less successful, however, as seen above, in encouraging the new concept of health centres in an effort to increase the efficiency of the G.P. service, but his efforts to increase the number of group practices fared better, and during 1953 alone, over 1,000 additional doctors entered partnerships as a result of the supplementary payments provided for groups. The total number of doctors on the list in England and Wales also rose, from 17,298 in 1952 to 18,817 in 1955,[43] which in turn relieved pressure, although much of the increase was the result of assistants becoming partners. The British Medical Association, who had fought the Attlee Government hard over the introduction of the N.H.S., were delighted by the return of the Conservatives in 1951, and with the additional factor of their pleasure at the size of the Danckwerts' award, it is hardly surprising Macleod enjoyed better relations with the doctors than almost any other post-war Minister of Health. A survey conducted on behalf of the B.M.A. in mid-1953 found that the Danckwerts' award had removed the underpayment that led doctors to complain they could not improve their service to patients.[44]

All these developments owed much to Macleod himself, and to his ability to work purposefully and in harness with his officials. Macleod enjoyed good personal relations with both Marquand and Bevan, and earned their respect. Labour continued to protest against charges and hospital pay beds, but these criticisms were not regarded as too much of a threat, and under the circumstances it is difficult to imagine that Labour would have managed the N.H.S. very differently, or even better, in these years. Macleod made a big impact in his first ministerial post and was able to show a record of sound progress combined with general popularity with the doctors and with his own backbenchers. Indeed, he was the most effective Conservative Minister of Health until his ex-Research Department colleague, Enoch Powell, was appointed in July 1960. This was achieved despite little support or encouragement from the Prime Minister, who regarded health as secondary to housing.[45] Crookshank and Macleod buried once and for all the notion that the Conservatives were out to destroy this most sacred cow of the welfare state, and in so doing gained the grudging respect of many of their opponents.

Macleod could be criticised for not going far enough along the line indicated, for example, in his booklet written with Enoch Powell, advocating, *inter alia*, charges for hospital beds and for prescriptions.[46] At the time of the Election in May 1955 there were still serious shortages of doctors in certain areas, of hospital beds, and mental health care. An expansion of the system of charging those who could pay would have been politically possible with the Conservative majority in the House, and would have provided extra finance at a critical time. Statistics show that during 1954–5 gross outlay on the N.H.S. was £550m., of which contributions from patients came to only £24m., or 5% of the total.[47] But there were drawbacks: charging would have involved an expensive increase in bureaucracy and unpopular arrangements for means testing.

Part 4   The Ministry of Education

In the 1950s education lacked the prominence in public and political life that it was to develop in the next decade, but it still had more importance than the Prime Minister realised. Indeed, as during the war, Winston Churchill did not regard education as a major concern. Churchill had hoped to appoint Clement Davies (Liberal Leader, 1945–56) as Minister, but the Liberal Party objected.[1] Not feeling this to be a Ministry whose work would be of central importance to his Government, he was guided by Patrick Buchan-Hepburn, the Chief Whip, and gave the job to Florence Horsbrugh, although not without some opposition. Oliver Lyttelton and Brendan Bracken were reluctant to see an elderly and conservative spinster as Minister and tried to intervene, the latter pushing the claims of Walter Elliot.[2] But their efforts were abortive.[3] Meanwhile the Ministry itself remained in the dark about who their new master was to be. Indeed, the first they heard of Horsbrugh's appointment was when two men arrived from the Ministry of Works to convert the bathroom facilities into use for a lady![4]

Her appointment was generally thought an error. She had been a good backbencher, and though she lacked the charm of some other women politicians, notably Nancy Astor, the first woman M.P. to take her seat in the Commons, or the quickness of Ellen Wilkinson (a particularly good Minister of Education from 1945 until her death in February 1947), she was nevertheless one of the ablest women party politicians in the House. She had served as the member for Dundee for eight years before her appointment as Parliamentary Secretary at Health in 1939, a job she held until the end of the Coalition Government in May 1945, and in opposition was Chairman of the Party's Education Committee.[5] By 1951, no longer so vigorous or resilient (she was already in her early sixties), she lacked the intellectual, administrative and debating qualities necessary for a first-class departmental Minister. She had no previous experience of education and did not master the subject as well as many of her successors, notably Sir David Eccles (1954–7 and 1959–62) and Sir Edward Boyle (1962–4). Despite the *Sunday Times*' claim that: 'She brings to her task the quality that it needs above all – humanity,'[6] diplomacy was not her strong point; the Opposition did not care for her, and her personal relations were never particularly good with local education authorities[7] nor with the various teachers' bodies, in particular the National Union of Teachers (N.U.T.), who became increasingly exasperated by her 'do nothing' attitude.[8] Some of the younger, more progressive and idealistic officials in the Ministry became impatient, too, with her. They had hoped for an energetic and imaginative Minister in 1951, and had to bide their time until Eccles' appointment in October 1954.[9]

Florence Horsbrugh had a difficult job. Her predecessor, George Tomlinson (Minister of Education, 1947–51) was a hard Minister to follow: he not only had a seat in Cabinet, but was also widely liked and respected. Florence Horsbrugh's initial exclusion from the Cabinet (although the press proclaimed her to have Cabinet status) set her off to a bad start with the education establishment (it was in fact only the third occasion since 1919 that the Minister of Education was not in the Cabinet).[10] To counter the undercurrent of criticism, Churchill reaffirmed in the House that the Minister would have access to Cabinet whenever any subject 'directly or indirectly' affecting education was to be discussed.[11] Eventually she was promoted to Cabinet in September

1953, but the damage had already been done. One Labour M.P., a former headmaster, Horace King, called it 'a disastrous setback'[12] to education. Florence Horsbrugh received little support or encouragement from Churchill, who did not care much for her personally, and displayed less interest in the subject than probably any Prime Minister since the war.[13] It was Florence Horsbrugh's misfortune that her period at the Ministry coincided with the post-war population 'bulge', caused by the sudden increase in the birth rate just after the war. These children were just beginning to enter nursery and primary schools. Inevitably she came to be criticised for what was considered the excessive size of classes.

The Government, however, would not increase the supply of funds for education, and so she had to defend restrictive measures which were beyond her power to alter.[14] Some colleagues acknowledged her difficulties. Harold Macmillan wrote in kindly vein: 'You have made a great success of your Ministry: it only remains now to make that success known to the public in the true perspective,'[15] and Anthony Eden, in a valedictory note, that: 'I think that I understand something of the formidable problems with which you have had to wrestle.'[16] But at the time, neither they, nor their colleagues, gave her support in Cabinet. Rab Butler, Minister of Education, 1941–5, and responsible for the seminal 1944 Education Act, was, perhaps surprisingly, not as enthusiastic in support of resources for education as might have been expected. On the other hand, Florence Horsbrugh later told the Treasury Financial Secretary, Henry Brooke, on more than one occasion, Butler had been enormously considerate and appreciative of her problems.[17]

Florence Horsbrugh made the most of her difficult position. It is possible that an abler Minister could have weathered this period more successfully, as have other Ministers of Education, notably Shirley Williams (1976–9), facing a similar position of financial stringency. But Florence Horsbrugh's contribution should not be dismissed too lightly. She proved herself a good, if routine and unoriginal Minister, and did not expect her dismissal in October 1954, when the press gave her a warmer assessment than she had received as Minister. *The Economist* noted that although under her the Ministry had been poorly served politically, she had more courage and administrative ability than she had been given credit for.[18] *The Times* said in a leader: 'She has been as good a Minister of Education as Government policy allowed her to be and she had more courage than many of her backbenchers.'[19] Bracken, meanwhile, was full of spleen. In a judgement far too harsh, but nevertheless of interest as it was the view of a man close to the Prime Minister and several senior Cabinet members, he said: 'I have always regarded

Mother Horsbrugh as a disastrous Minister of Education and the Tories will pay a very high price for her services. She is a good old girl who doesn't conceal her disbelief in education.'[20] But of her own departure, Florence Horsbrugh wrote simply and somewhat pathetically: 'I am very sad to have left the Ministry.'[21]

The Parliamentary Secretary, Kenneth Pickthorn, went in the same reshuffle. An unusual choice for office, a man nearly sixty years of age who had served in the House for sixteen years without being given a job, his selection in 1951 was probably attributable to his knowledge of education and his position as an influential backbencher. One of the most distinguished constitutional historians of his day,[22] he had been the Member for Cambridge University from 1935 until University seats were abolished in 1950, and he was now M.P. for Nottinghamshire Carlton. Yet there was little to occupy a junior Minister, who found himself dealing mainly with Welsh affairs and cases of teachers' misconduct.[23] Parliamentary Secretaries were seldom involved in policy discussions, and Pickthorn had few opportunities to make much impact in his one ministerial job. He was appointed without her consultation, and Horsbrugh made it plain that she had not wanted him. Their partnership was neither a happy nor a strong one.[24] Pickthorn's main strength had been his skill as a backbench critic, but he was temperamentally unsuited to serving in Government where he was bound by collective responsibility to support policies with which he disagreed. In common with some other academics who later joined the Ministry of Education, Pickthorn, who had been a Fellow of Corpus Christi College, Cambridge, since 1914, lacked an innate political instinct. A poor ministerial speaker, like Horsbrugh, he was also not good with officials, whom he tended to lecture, appearing to be the schoolmaster correcting their English rather than listening to the message they were trying to convey. Nevertheless, he fulfilled his duties tirelessly, and his knowledge of teaching commended him to many in the profession.

Sir John Maud had been the Ministry's Permanent Secretary since 1945. Succeeding Sir Maurice Holmes,[25] at the age of thirty-nine, Maud was regarded as one of the outstanding younger men in Whitehall. A colourful, outgoing person, he had been an academic and administrator until his appointment as Deputy Secretary to the Ministry of Food in 1941. From 1939–43 he was Master of Birkbeck College, London, and widely respected in the education world. He had worked well with the Labour Ministers of Education, but after the arrival of Florence Horsbrugh the uncomfortable position arose where Maud's speeches began to attract more publicity than the Minister's. In a sense she was operating under her powerful Permanent Secretary's shadow, and relations were not always easy. After seven years in the one post he was considered ripe for a move, and at Sir Edward Bridges' suggestion went to Fuel and Power, having been considered at one stage as a possible successor to Sheepshanks at Housing.[26] Yet his personal relations with Florence Horsbrugh were mostly satisfactory, and they parted on good terms. Indeed his farewell letter suggests more than mere formality: 'No Permanent Secretary could ever ask for better treatment from his Minister than I've had these last nine months from mine.'[27]

Sir Gilbert Flemming, one of the two Deputy Secretaries, who had made his name working on the system of emergency teacher training, succeeded him. A more withdrawn, austere figure than Maud, and less domineering, he nevertheless displayed a more penetrating intellect. Flemming's logic, it was said, was unchallengeable in an argument, provided one accepted his premise: all one could do was to challenge that premise. He was highly knowledgeable and well known throughout education circles, being the only one of the Ministry's Permanent Secretaries in the twenty-five years after the war, until Sir William Pile's appointment in 1970, to have spent his career in the Department.[28] Less well known either at home or abroad than Maud,[29] and unlike his predecessor having no great love of speech-making, he was devoted to his work which he saw as being centred more at the Ministry. An outstanding administrator and official head of the Department, he remained Permanent Secretary until 1959.[30]

The guidelines to education policy for the following twenty years were laid down by the 1944 Act of the Coalition Government, which had been largely bipartisan. Though the Minister (Butler) was a Conservative, Labour were as committed to it as much as the Conservatives. Any new direction in education policy could only have come from one of two factors: economic circumstances and political preconceptions. The latter were only a minor factor in the first decade after the war. The change of political colour in 1951 did not make as much difference as the pinch on financial resources, which had begun to be felt in Labour's last years of office, precipitating Tomlinson's major education cut-backs of October 1949.

Austerity was the order in education in the early 1950s. The charge for school meals was increased from seven pence to nine pence, the Ministry ensured cheaper and simpler methods were used in new school-building, and local education authorities were asked in December 1951 to reduce the expenditure forecasts by economising on administration, transport and less essential services.[31] The directive was withdrawn in December 1954, having achieved an annual reduction in forecasts of just two per cent. Further cuts were announced by Florence Horsbrugh at the beginning of February 1952,[32] envisaging a drastic revision of the building programme for the coming year. (In fact between 1st June, 1951, and 1st June, 1954, the number of schools under construction fell from 1,204 to 993.) At the time there was widespread relief that the school-age limit had not been reduced – at either end of the scale – as had been feared in certain quarters.[33] Expenditure on education overall, however, increased at the similarly modest rate it had done since 1945, with total expenditure on education in England and Wales increasing very little in real terms, from £318m. in 1951–2 to £405m. in 1954–5.[34] Most of this increased expenditure was accounted for by inflation, rising numbers of school children (from 3.7m. in 1951 to 4.4m. in 1955 in primary education and 1.7m. to 1.9m. over the same years in secondary education),[35] as well as salary increases for teachers in 1952 and 1954. Not until after 1954 was there any significant increase in expenditure per head.

The two dominant issues at the Ministry remained, as they had been under Labour, the supply of sufficient school buildings and teachers.[36] The great surge in school-building needed after the war had not been fully anticipated. The raising of the school-leaving age to fifteen in the 1944 Act (implemented in 1947) and with it the need for more facilities had been taken into account, but the 'bulge' in post-war births had not. The Ministry reacted quickly, but was confronted by shortages of building labour, and certain essential materials, in particular steel and timber. A range of often highly imaginative techniques had to be devised to build the schools in as short a time and as cheaply as possible. After 1949 increasing attention was paid to cost effectiveness, and within the next two years total costs had been cut by twenty-five per cent. The building rate increased under the Conservatives, as materials became more readily available (despite the cut-backs announced in February 1952) with 1,500 new schools being completed between October 1951 and October 1954, providing a total of 650,000 new school places. Undoubtedly the policy of reducing the cost of new buildings stretched funds further, and the Government's decision to delay new projects helped speed completion of buildings actually under construction. By 1955 over 2,500 new schools had been built since the war, not just to replace those damaged by bombing, but also to cater for the new housing developments and increased numbers. This was a considerable achievement, but still, according to regulations, over half the schools were overcrowded in 1955. Indeed, a leading article in *The Times* at the end of 1953 stated that: 'Overcrowding in the schools is becoming steadily worse,' and called for urgent action to be taken to reduce class sizes.[37]

The supply of teachers, the other dominant issue, was similarly not

Party political. The National Advisory Council on the Training and Supply of Teachers, set up by Tomlinson in 1949, had been considering whether it would be feasible to lengthen the teacher-training course from two to three years, but reported against this in 1952 because of the rising birthrate. Increases in teachers' salaries helped make the career look more attractive, and by 1955 shortages had eased: total numbers in full-time teaching service in that year increased from 220,000 in 1951 to 244,000.[38]

Education was not, however, bereft of controversy during this period. The organisation of secondary education, which covered ninety-five per cent of all children aged eleven or over, had not been definitively tackled in the 1944 Act, and by the early 1950s serious debate was beginning in the Department and in education circles on the value of comprehensive schools. The subject was not yet the national political issue it was to become ten years later, and discussions took place in a relatively dispassionate atmosphere. Many of the younger officials in the Ministry felt that, largely because of fallibility in judging merit in the eleven-plus examination system, experiments in comprehensives were worth a try, but endless discussions took place about the optimum size of schools. The Attlee Government had refused to push for the development of comprehensives as the main form of secondary education, so in terms of practical policy there was little difference between Tomlinson and Florence Horsbrugh. By mid-1954 out of about 5,000 secondary schools, only thirteen were comprehensive – nine in London, two in Middlesex, one in the West Riding of Yorkshire and one in Anglesey. A further twenty-one were under construction in England and Wales, of which eighteen had been included in approved building programmes since 1951. Both Florence Horsbrugh and Eccles followed the policy of allowing limited experiments, provided there was not too much local opposition and parents had a fair choice of secondary schools within an area. On these grounds Florence Horsbrugh prevented two secondary schools being included in comprehensive experiments, Eltham Hill Secondary School for Girls and Bec County Secondary School for Boys, both in 1954. In fact, few of the 146 local education authorities at this time were enthusiastic about the idea: by 1955 only twenty-three had proposed any comprehensives in their development plans, and only six (4%) proposed an all-out comprehensive system.[39]

Enthusiasm for comprehensives was also lacking in other quarters: the N.U.T. had doubts, and in 1948 a large majority at their annual Conference refused to condemn the tripartite division of secondary moderns, technical and grammar schools; the Assistant Masters were by 1951 firmly opposed to comprehensives, and officials at the Ministry were by no means unanimously convinced of the benefits. The Conservative Party Conference in 1952 passed a motion, with one dissentient, deploring the attempt to replace the tripartite system with comprehensive schools. Florence Horsbrugh, having assured delegates of her determination to deal with the subject 'purely as an educational matter' went on to detail a number of benefits of experiments in comprehensive education.[40] The next year a similar motion, proposed by Angus Maude, was passed unanimously. Shortly after coming to office in 1954, Eccles made the unequivocal statement to a joint meeting of the Associations of Assistant Masters and Assistant Mistresses: 'My colleague and I will never agree to the assassination of the grammar schools. We want you to continue and flourish.'[41] A leader in the *Sunday Times* on 2nd January, 1955 called it a 'very important statement of policy which bears repeating'. It was mainly in the Labour Party that support for comprehensives was growing in these years. A policy statement of 1953 declared: 'Labour will abolish the practice of selection at 11-plus for different types of [secondary] school,'[42] and Party pamphlets showed they were thinking in terms of mixed ability classes, whereas most comprehensives at this time had some form of streaming. The way was thus paved for Anthony Crosland's (Secretary of State for Education and Science, 1965–7) Circular 10/65 of 1965, which 'requested' authorites to reorganise secondary education on comprehensive lines.[43]

A major problem in the 1944 Education Act had been the denominational schools, a question which continued to occupy a large amount of the Ministry's time. It was a highly complex subject, one where feelings ran high. The Conservatives pledged themselves in 'Britain Strong and Free' to discuss with the Churches and other bodies the problems of denominational or voluntary schools to see what solutions could be found to their difficulties, particularly with finance. Discussions had already begun before the 1951 Election, resulting in the Education (Miscellaneous Provisions) Act, 1953. This provided increased financial support for the building of voluntary schools, allowing the Minister to make a fifty per cent grant for the purchase and adaptation of buildings bought for voluntary school premises. This Act owed much to the tenacity of Florence Horsbrugh, and was her main achievement as Minister, earning her the gratitude of the religious authorities.[44]

The scope for a Minister of Education was limited. Florence Horsbrugh was dependent upon the support of teachers and the local education authorities, but had neither. Ministers in every Department are subject to influences from Cabinet, Parliament, the Ministry and outside bodies, but few, if any, operated under as many pressures as the Minister of Education. The local education authorities were represented collectively by a number of associations, not least the Association of Education Committees (A.E.C.) whose influence at this stage owed a great deal to its long-serving General Secretary (1945–77), William Alexander, later Lord Alexander of Potterhill, then at the height of his career. The education system then ran on a broad consensus involving the Ministry's senior officials, the local education authorities, and representatives of the teachers, in particular Sir Ronald Gould, General Secretary of the N.U.T. (1947–70), like Alexander a man who had an extraordinarily long-term and beneficial effect on the shape of post-war education. Gould was the milder and more sympathetic, respected through education circles as he was with Ministry officials. Although he relied on the support of those he represented, he had the necessary backing from the teachers, and knew the limits beyond which they would not go. Florence Horsbrugh took Gould's advice on the rare occasions when she asked him directly for it,[45] but overall the influence of the N.U.T. was not high for at least the first two years of the Government, and the Government, to its later regret, paid scant attention to their demands.

Improvements in teachers' salary scales in 1952 and 1954, and improved pensions in the Pensions (Increase) Act, 1952 helped ameliorate an underlying tension that existed between the teachers and the Government, because of cut-backs in education, as did the later promise to women teachers (sixty per cent of the total) in March 1955 of equal pay, to be introduced over seven years. But a major fuss over teachers' pensions in 1954 shattered the comparative calm. The Government had introduced a Teachers (Superannuation) Bill at the beginning of 1954 designed to replenish the funds of the Teachers Superannuation Scheme.[46] Florence Horsbrugh, who never much liked the Bill, had no alternative but to accept it as the price for avoiding severe cuts.[47] The teachers, however, were furious, considering their contributions to have been badly managed by the Treasury. The Bill also came at an unfortunate time following shortly after the 1954 rise in pay, which increased most teachers' salaries by £35 per annum, regarded widely as inadequate. The teachers built up a formidable lobby against the Bill, flooding their M.P.s with letters as part of a nationwide campaign, one of the biggest of its kind. Churchill continually delayed acting on the Bill, and the Cabinet postponed it at least twice.[48] The row was responsible for Horsbrugh's eventual departure in October 1954, partly because the Party did not wish to confront the teaching profession, and because she again showed, as she had done over the Education (Miscellaneous Provisions) Act of 1953, her incapacity for lucid exposition.[49] The Bill was consequently postponed,[50] having aroused the interest and also antagonism of Conservative backbenchers in a way that no other education issue did in the decade. It was left to her successor, Sir David Eccles, to pick up the pieces.[51]

The October 1954 reshuffle resulted in a far stronger team, with Sir David Eccles as Minister and Dennis Vosper[52] Parliamentary Secretary. Eccles was a much tougher and more imaginative Minister, with one of the ablest minds in the Party. Unlike Florence Horsbrugh, he also had an acute interest in and understanding of economics, and was anxious to take part in the broad economic discussions in Cabinet. There was pleasure among education circles at the change of policy indicated by the appointment, and at the appointment of a Minister who carried weight in the Cabinet despite the fact that up to that time he had certainly not been known for his views on education.[53] Eccles was to emerge as one of the outstanding post-war Ministers of Education in his two periods (1954–7 and 1959–62). Although he was only Minister for a short time before the Election in May 1955 (where this study ends) his impact by then was already felt. Eccles' arrival was associated with two important changes of direction, the reorganisation of all-age schools, the first part of proposals to carry out what he called the central promise of the 1944 Education Act,[54] and a shift in emphasis in the Ministry towards technical education.[55] The latter took longer to reach fruition. The decisive impetus came in 1956 with the publication of the White Paper[56] and the appointment of Antony Part to succeed Frederick Bray as head of the Ministry's Further Education Branch.[57]

Some all-age schools were in remote villages, but many were city slum schools, often housing hundreds in bad conditions. The numbers of these schools had been steadily falling (from 8,755 in England and Wales in January 1948 to 4,588 in January 1953), but they were still responsible for over 200,000 children in 1954, 25% in rural areas.[58] Eccles wisely chose this as his starting-point, and he carried with him the full support of the education service and his own Party.[59] Under his guidance the Ministry issued Circular 283 in December 1954, which declared that all-age schools in rural areas must be completely reorganised into separate primary and secondary departments. Priority was thus given to rural all-age schools, while those in urban areas were assisted by the removal of the ceiling on local education authorities' expenditure for improvements to old schools.

Universities were the responsibility of the University Grants Committee (U.G.C.), set up in 1919 and appointed by the Chancellor of the Exchequer, which had the responsibility for recommending and allocating public funds needed for the universities. The U.G.C. being under the aegis of the Treasury meant that university policy was handled by

Government separately from the national education service as a whole. Sir Richard (Otto) Clarke later wrote that this separation throughout the 1950s must have distorted priorities in education expansion, though hardly anyone was saying so at the time.[60] The responsibility of the Treasury for the universities continued until the seminal Robbins Report of 1963[61] and the creation of the Department of Education and Science in 1964. This took over responsibility for schools at one extreme, and also supervised the Government Research Councils at the other, which in the early 1950s had been overseen by the Lord President.

Little thought was put into another aspect of further education, the expansion of technical education before the 1955 Election. The question was not a new one to the Government. While in Opposition the Conservatives had criticised Labour's White Paper on higher technological education[62] for not going far enough, and at the 1951 Election pledged themselves to create higher technological colleges with academic independence. This cause was pursued earnestly by Lord Cherwell and Lord Woolton, the two members of the original Cabinet with a scientific education. The latter's thinking on the subject had been greatly influenced by the nuclear physicist and Nobel prizewinner, Sir James Chadwick,[63] who had impressed on him the lack of British technical scientists to translate scientific discovery into industrial practice. Woolton, in large part responsible for the Election pledge, had as Lord President official responsibility for the Department of Scientific and Industrial Research.[64] Lord Salisbury, who succeeded him in November 1952, initially neutral,[65] became increasingly in favour of developing technological institutions. Cherwell, the 'overlord' responsible for the co-ordination of scientific research and development, had been much impressed by the German technical Hochschule, and wanted these as a model for a new type of national educational institution. He made a number of speeches in the Lords and wrote on the subject.[66]

Cherwell and Woolton felt that technical colleges under the Ministry of Education were unsuitable for training the technologists Britain so urgently needed. Newly built technological colleges in 'green fields' (Cherwell's expression) were needed, each containing 3,000–4,000 students. They should be in the hands of the U.G.C., but independent of universities, with the possible exception of Imperial College, London.[67] Woolton wrote to Sir Edward Bridges immediately after the 1951 Election suggesting a working party to explore the field. Butler and the Treasury, however, were not in favour of independent technological colleges,[68] and nor was the Ministry of Education, who strongly favoured the development and upgrading of the existing technical colleges within their purview, citing their good links with local industry and commerce.[69] Woolton put forward a Cabinet paper[70] as a result of which a decision was taken in Cabinet on 20th November, 1952 to develop a small number of these higher technological institutions alongside Imperial College, amongst other places at Glasgow (James Stuart, naturally, was particularly enthusiastic)[71] and at Manchester.[72] But these ambitious and sensible plans were not to be realised on anything like the scale these advocates wanted. The combined opposition of the Treasury, the U.G.C. and the Education Ministry to the idea of developing separate institutions, rather than building up technical colleges on the existing university faculties, and the resignation of Cherwell from Cabinet in November 1953, combined to defeat their more ambitious plans. The development of the Imperial College of Science and Technology, part of London University, and the Manchester College of Science and Technology were the sole, though by no means insignificant, results of the efforts of Cherwell and Woolton, although neither had the independence which Cherwell at least had favoured. Churchill was sympathetic but took little interest in the affair whilst it was being debated in Whitehall. Yet two weeks after his resignation, he was to consider his lack of support the most serious omission of his premiership.[73]

Although there had been little change at the Ministry of Education after 1951, Labour, nevertheless, made criticism of education policy one of the main thrusts of their attack. Yet by April 1953 a leading article in *The Times* noted: 'Except for some equalitarian [sic] and extraordinarily expensive adjustments wished for by Labour there is little to divide the two Parties. Either in office would be faced by the desperate task of getting enough roofs and enough teachers for the swollen numbers now passing through the schools.' Labour might argue, the leader continued, about the *rate* of improvement, but not convincingly, because in truth both Parties had found the pace too hot: 'It is possibly the absence of genuine political differences which causes educational debates in the Commons to incline to dullness.'[74] All the same Florence Horsbrugh, in particular, suffered from Labour's attention, and neither she nor Pickthorn defended the Government's policy well in the House. In terms of constructive policy, however, Labour remained divided, for example, in their attitude towards raising the school-leaving age to sixteen, to comprehensives and to the continued status of independent schools. The most intense debate came on 1st July, 1953 after the Select Committee on Estimates published a Report on British schools drawing attention to rapidly deteriorating buildings, which led 200 Labour M.P.s to put down a censure motion. Florence Horsbrugh made an untypically good opening speech, the Government's case also being aided by the outstanding closing speech by Macmillan. They produced figures which showed the

281

increase in spending on school-building since 1951, the attack was repulsed, and the Government won with a majority of thirty-three.[75] Yet Florence Horsbrugh's published reply to the Select Committee's Report was strongly criticised by the teachers. 'A very disappointing document,' said Sir Ronald Gould.[76]

The Conservatives' record at Education was generally adequate, apart from their failure with both teachers and local education authorities in public relations, which reached a low point in mid-1954, and in the low priority given to the Ministry until Eccles' appointment in October 1954.

Part 5 The Ministry of Pensions

The Ministry of Pensions, which dealt with war pensions and war widows' pensions, was the smallest and least politically important of the 'social policy' Departments. Set up in 1916, its structure came out of decisions taken during and after the First World War. Although subject to some political pressures during the interwar period, it was an area of entrenched interests where innovation would have been political and administrative folly.[1] Thus it commanded neither first-rate Ministers nor officials after its first few years. The Beveridge Report[2] of 1942 had suggested that it should be merged into a new Ministry of Social Security, but the Government had different plans and set up a separate Ministry of National Insurance in the closing stages of the war. In 1953, under the Conservatives, Pensions and National Insurance finally came together, but not as a Ministry of Social Security in the way Lord Beveridge had envisaged as welfare functions were still widely scattered between a number of Ministries and non-ministerial Departments.[3]

To head the still separate Ministry of Pensions in 1951, Winston Churchill chose a disabled ex-serviceman, Derick Heathcoat Amory, who gladly accepted the job, although he was not unduly ambitious for ministerial office.[4] He had been severely wounded during the Arnhem operation in September 1944, although he would normally have been exempted on grounds of age, with characteristic courage he insisted on going into action with the men he had trained.[5] His business training and the special interest he had shown by serving as a representative of the disabled on the Central Advisory Committee which advised Government on questions of war pensions did, however, make him especially suitable for the job.[6] Sir John Smyth was appointed as Parliamentary Secretary, a man with the Victoria Cross, interested in war pension work and selected because of the confidence he would evoke amongst ex-servicemen.[7] In particular he did a great deal on his own initiative to speed up the money due to the Far Eastern prisoners of war,[8] and together with Heathcoat Amory made a strong, sympathetic team.[9] The Parliamentary Private Secretary, Richard Wood, found his main work was in looking after Heathcoat Amory in the House, and attending meetings of the Party's Health and Social Services Committee.[10] The youngest son of the first Earl of Halifax, Wood had lost both legs in the Second World War and was a key spokesman of the British Limbless Ex-Serviceman's Association (B.L.E.S.M.A.). He followed Smyth as Parliamentary Secretary in December, 1955. Wood was a man of the greatest integrity and neither as Parliamentary Private Secretary nor as Parliamentary Secretary did he show B.L.E.S.M.A. or other pension interests any especial favour. Indeed it must have been rare for any Department at any time to have had a group of three such compassionate and honest politicians.

The new Government made no changes in pensions policy, and, as a result, the Ministry's work generated little heat in the House. Criticism inevitably centred on the levels of pension benefit, but it did not strike the Minister that these were attacks on particularly Party lines.[11] The lack of controversy was helped by Heathcoat Amory's refusal to make Party points in the House. He preferred to look at questions from a national rather than a Party standpoint, even complimenting the Opposition for the good work they had done when in power at the Ministry. This approach explains why he was one of the most popular Government members with Labour.[12]

Heathcoat Amory made an impressive job of his first ministerial post. Like Sir David Eccles, Lord Ismay, Antony Head and Sir Walter Monckton, he was appointed as a departmental Minister in 1951 without any previous ministerial experience,[13] but his officials did not find this an undue handicap. He viewed his task as trying to secure the highest pensions and compensation that the Treasury could be persuaded to grant, and to run the Department as sympathetically as possible with a minimum of red tape.[14] Popular in the Department and felt to be able and balanced, he was a man who worked well as the head of a team, unlike some of his Labour predecessors, who were individualists. Morale in the Department was high, the general feeling being that it was managed better under Heathcoat Amory than under Labour, and far better than it had been before the war.

The fact that the Ministry's work was bound to decrease (even after the decision in 1948 that it should handle service disablement pensions resulting from peacetime as well) posed special problems for its Civil Service staffing, as it could not offer a proper career structure. The practice had grown up between the wars that its staff should be officials who, whatever their nominal rank, were not members of the Administrative Class trained for policy work. The Permanent Secretary was invariably brought in by the Treasury from another Department. The same was true after the Second World War and this unsatisfactory administrative position pointed to eventual amalgamation with another Ministry, whatever the political pressures.[15] The Permanent Secretary, Sir Arton Wilson, had a Ministry of Labour background, joining Pensions as Secretary in 1948. He was a sound administrator, but had little experience in political or policy work. Beneath him was one Deputy Secretary, Dame Marjorie Cox, a long-serving War Pensions civil servant, highly knowledgeable, decisive and full of common sense in her own field. Beneath her was just one Under-Secretary; together they comprised the smallest number of officials in the top three grades in any Government Department.

The main pressure to increase benefits both inside as well as outside the House came from the British Legion, which regarded itself as the sole spokesman for ex-servicemen, though it was in fact one of several groups. Its National President since 1947 had been the blind Conservative M.P., Sir Ian Fraser,[16] whose position in the House ensured that its interests were well represented.

As a result of the decision of the Coalition Government of 1940–5 and subsequent Labour legislation, there could be no question of a general increase in war pensions except hand in hand with National Insurance benefits. Though the Labour Government had in some cases improved the special allowances for the seriously disabled, there had been no rise to take inflation into account. In 1951 Hugh Gaitskell had specifically said Labour could not afford any increase, but the Conservatives, anxious to appear sympathetic towards the war pensioners, and realising that inflation was causing genuine hardship, gave a pledge in the 1951 Election campaign to reverse this decision. Thus, in the 1952 Budget the standard weekly rate of disability pension was increased from forty-five shillings to fifty-five shillings.[17] The decision owed little to Heathcoat Amory's pressure, but it was his task to administer these changes smoothly and impartially.

Despite efforts by interested parties to retain the Ministry, Churchill announced its winding up in the House in February 1953.[18] The British Legion in particular was anxious lest its special relationship with the Ministry of Pensions would cease under the new arrangements and that its interests would not be as well represented.[19] On the other hand various unions with which the Ministry of National Insurance dealt were happy to see the merger because they felt that war pensioners were in some ways in a privileged position.

284

The impetus for the merger, which had previously been considered by Labour,[20] came from Heathcoat Amory, who foresaw substantial administrative economies and certainly no detriment to the Ministry of Pensions or its work.[21] The suggestion appealed to Churchill and Sir Edward Bridges, both of whom were in favour of rationalisation. The arguments for amalgamation were many. There would be clear administrative savings both in Whitehall and in the provinces where local offices could serve both for war pensions and for Ministry of National Insurance benefits. The need for a separate Department for war pensioners had anyway been reduced when the new National Insurance Scheme and the National Health Service were introduced, as war pensioners were covered by both. The special Ministry of Pensions hospitals were merged into the general hospital service, ensuring fullest use of available hospital accommodation. Above all, as the number of war pensioners declined, so the Ministry would, stressed Heathcoat Amory, become too small to offer satisfactory promotion prospects for its staff.

In both Departments there was a certain amount of feeling against the move, and disagreement as to which name should come first in the title of the new Department. The Permanent Secretary, Wilson, was due for retirement in 1953, and facilities were made for the Deputy, Dame Marjorie Cox, to move over to the new Ministry where she now had senior responsibility for the war pensioners. Opposition was much more serious in the House, where the Government felt at one time that the merger would be overthrown.[22] The debate there was often acrimonious, and it owed much to Heathcoat Amory's sensitivity and persuasive powers that on 1st July, 1953 he managed to carry the Transfer of Functions Order with a majority of fourteen.[23]

The move was entirely sensible and the war disabled did not lose out, though, undoubtedly, the feeling that they had a special position was gradually being eroded. Smyth transferred to the new Ministry, and in October 1954 the Minister, Osbert Peake, was promoted to Cabinet. This move, though well deserved on personal grounds, was dictated partly by a desire to conciliate the war pension interest. In December 1954 the standard basic rate for war disability pensions was increased to sixty-seven shillings and sixpence per week, which was matched by an increase in other pension and insurance benefits. This was the biggest single increase of war pension benefits, a substantial increase in real terms on the 1951 basic rate of forty-five shillings per week. The Government managed never to depart from the principle of equal treatment for war pensioners, and such minor advantages as war pensioners had had preserved from the pre-1939 system were not added to or enlarged.

Though there was little of 'political' nature in the Conservatives' conduct of war pensions policy, it did display two important trends in their thinking. First, their determination not to appear ungenerous in their level of welfare benefits, though Labour, too, would undoubtedly have increased pension rates when national finances improved after 1951. Secondly, it also exhibited their preference for reducing the number of Government Departments, and it is unlikely that Labour, had they been returned in 1951, would have encouraged the merger at such an early date.

Part 6   The Ministry of National Insurance

Although one of the youngest of the 'social policy' Ministries, responsibility for its work was not new to Governments. It was set up as the Ministry of Social Insurance (National was substituted for Social after six weeks) in October 1944 in the wake of the Beveridge Report of 1942 to handle insurance contributions, payment of benefits for sickness, maternity, industrial injury, retirement and death, and also to administer a new scheme of family allowances. Unemployment benefits too were the responsibility of the new Ministry, although their day-to-day administration continued in the Ministry of Labour's Employment Exchanges. The Minister also had responsibility for the National Assistance Board, which, it was decided in 1944, should be retained as a separate organisation to deal with all non-contributory pensions and *ad hoc* financial assistance.[1] The following year workmen's compensation matters were transferred from the Home Office. Thus by 1951, the Ministry was settling down into its largely routine and administrative work, a period of calm felt to be necessary to consolidate the recent and major changes.

Some areas, however, still needed to be settled, in particular, the vexed question of retirement age and pensions which led to the appointment of the Phillips Committee in 1953. As a leader in *The Times* on 5th October, 1953 noted: 'The truth is that leaders in both Parties are frightened by the mounting cost of pensions. Some of them must be regretting their past disregard of the view of the Beveridge Report that, while subsistence pensions (in return for appropriate contributions) could reasonably be offered to those retiring a couple of decades after the war, they could not safely be granted to the existing generation of retired old folk.' This factor explains why pension increases announced by Labour in 1951 were so limited, and why Osbert Peake, the Conservative Minister, said in 1952 that it would be some years before

286

increases in retirement pensions matched increases in sickness and unemployment benefit.[2]

Peake proved the right man for the tasks ahead. He had been Parliamentary Under-Secretary at the Home Office from 1939–44 with responsibility, *inter alia*, for workmen's compensation. His brief spell as Financial Secretary at the Treasury in the last months of the war and during the 'Caretaker Government' made him a likely candidate for a senior appointment, as did his work as spokesman on social security matters during the Attlee Government.[3] A shy man, diffident, but firm in his decisions, his experience as a coal owner before nationalisation had given him an understanding of certain aspects of the Ministry's work, in particular industrial injuries. The miners held him in high regard, as did the unions generally, and he also had good contacts with Labour members. Some in the Ministry felt that Peake played as big a part as Sir Walter Monckton in gaining the confidence of the trade union movement after 1951. Its liking for Peake stemmed in part from his coal-mining firm's good reputation with the National Union of Miners. He had a stammer, but this, if anything, helped in his relations with the unions and in Parliament. He was popular with his officials, sympathetic to their problems and could be relied on to support them. With a great fund of common sense, he was a capable administrator but one who had little opportunity for innovation.[4] Peake became Minister of the amalgamated Ministry of Pensions and National Insurance in September 1953, and in October 1954 was promoted to Cabinet in part to show that the Government was giving full consideration to pension questions. The *News Chronicle* noted in acid style in a leader on 18th October that: 'There has been much talk about pension reform, but too little action.' Many on personal grounds felt Peake's promotion overdue, although when in Cabinet he seldom spoke on issues outside his own field. He was not over ambitious, but had been anxious for a change of Department,[5] even hoping to be appointed Home Secretary.[6] When, in December 1955, it became clear that this was not to be, he offered his resignation. In the opinion of certain colleagues, he had been undervalued. Lord Butler, for example, told the author: 'I don't think that Osbert Peake ever had his day. I don't think he was ever given his opportunity really.' But Patrick Buchan-Hepburn, the Chief Whip, felt differently: in his opinion Peake had insufficient drive, and some minor differences with Anthony Eden may also have contributed to his departure. Others felt a difference of view with Treasury officials in the autumn of 1954 had unfortunate if delayed repercussions.[7]

Junior Ministers seldom played much part in a comparatively minor Department such as National Insurance.[8] Peake regarded junior

Ministers very much as trainees, an attitude shared by the Permanent Secretary, Sir Geoffrey King. For Robert Turton, initially the only Parliamentary Secretary at National Insurance, this was his first job, although not one he either sought or expected.[9] He had been a Vice-Chairman of the Party's Agricultural and Food Committee and of the backbench 1922 Committee until the 1951 Election and in Opposition he had been a junior spokesman on food.[10] After the merger, Turton and Sir John Smyth, from Pensions, stuck to their previous specialisations. An efficient and experienced team, both junior Ministers had a high respect for Peake.[11] Ernest Marples succeeded Turton in October 1954, a move which, following the important task he had fulfilled as Parliamentary Secretary at Housing, looked like a demotion. Harold Macmillan, his former boss, later explained that the Pension Bill was to be the main piece of legislation in the 1954–5 session and would prove useful experience for him.[12] But Marples was less interested in social security than in house-building, and it caused little surprise when Eden dismissed him in December 1955.[13] Meanwhile, John Arbuthnot, who had been Parliamentary Private Secretary to Smyth at Pensions, came over to the new Ministry ostensibly to serve Peake, though in fact he continued to specialise on war pension matters.[14]

The work of the Ministry of National Insurance occasionally caught the Prime Minister's eye, but he showed no sustained interest. He was, however, responsible for family allowances being increased to eight shillings rather than the planned seven shillings and sixpence in 1952.[15] In fact during the passage of the 1946 National Insurance Act through Parliament, Jim Griffiths (Minister of National Insurance, 1945–50) had considered raising family allowances to seven shillings and sixpence but this was not taken up by the Labour Government. Yet Harold Macmillan's claim that during the fuss surrounding the autumn 1954 pension-rate increases, 'The Prime Minister took a special interest in this and was unceasing in his effort to bring matters to a head,'[16] would appear an overstatement. At this time Churchill's attention was absorbed by foreign affairs, in particular his plan for a summit meeting with the Soviet Union. Churchill had general feelings about pensions, stemming in part from his period as Chancellor of the Exchequer (1924–9), when he laid down the structure of contributory pensions,[17] but he never concerned himself to any extent with detail.

Peake worked well with the Permanent Secretary, King, and tended to regard the relationship as if he was the Chairman and King the managing director. Like many in the Ministry, King came from the pre-war Ministry of Labour, where he had been an Assistant Solicitor in charge of the Assistance Board's legal work. Though an impressive lawyer, it was not until the war that his career blossomed, and in 1944 he emerged as Secretary of the Assistance Board. He was 'borrowed' from the Board in 1946 and became a *de facto* Deputy Secretary at National Insurance,[18] a position that was formalised in 1949, concentrating his attention on the inauguration of family allowances and the legal intricacies of workmen's compensation and industrial injuries. King's appointment as Permanent Secretary in 1951 followed an unexpected change in the postings of a number of top officials, including the departure from National Insurance of its official head, Sir Henry Hancock.[19] King had a clear financial mind coupled with a good deal of humanity. He was a powerful figure who liked to concentrate responsibility at the centre. He took charge, in particular, of the Industrial Injuries Scheme, and tended to regard it as his own territory rather than an Under-Secretary's.[20] He had weaknesses, in particular the lawyer's common failing as an administrator – a facility for mugging-up a case and then forgetting about it, and also found difficulty in working as a member of a team. Some quarters felt he kept Peake too much in his own hands, which inevitably restricted Peake's access to more junior officials.[21]

Sir Nicolas de Villiers, Deputy Secretary since December 1951, arrived with the firm expectation of succeeding King when he retired, but this was not to occur. Instead, King's place in 1955 was taken by Sir Eric Bowyer (Permanent Secretary at Materials, 1953–4). De Villiers was one of the brightest young men at the top of the Civil Service, and had been appointed Deputy Secretary at the young age of forty-three.[22] He oversaw the work of all the Ministry's departments, except those concerned with matters of finance, establishments and the medical and legal offices. For the first year after the merger with the Ministry of Pensions there was a second deputy, Dame Marjorie Cox, responsible for war pensions. But on her retirement in 1954 this work was taken over by an Under-Secretary. (Only one other woman contemporary reached Deputy Secretary level, Dame Evelyn Sharp.)

The most prominent official on the national insurance side was John Walley,[23] one of the seven Under-Secretaries. He had played a prominent part with Hancock in the handling of the main national insurance scheme in the early years of the Ministry under its first Permanent Secretary, Sir Thomas Phillips (1944–8).

With no immediate change of policy discernible at the Department after Peake's arrival, officials did not feel that either he or the new Government was any less sympathetic than Labour to the problems of social security. The Conservative Government, highly sensitive to its public image, was, if anything, more aware than Labour of the need to increase benefits in line with inflation. At the Treasury, which had the dominant hand over the level of benefits,[24] Rab Butler was personally more sympathetic than many Chancellors, but highly conscious, nevertheless, of the cost of increases and their effect on the rest of the economy. As the insurance scheme was designed to pay for itself, increased benefits meant increased contributions, which in turn caused trouble with the Opposition.[25]

There was no lack of pressure on the Ministry to increase benefits.[26] The unions, not surprisingly, were the most influential, but tended to concentrate their attention on the industrial injuries scheme. Their pressure did not extend to national assistance increases, although politicians (of all Parties) were always willing to support those most in need. Peake, King and Walley were on good personal terms with the General Secretary of the National Union of Mineworkers, Arthur Horner, who once told Peake that he found it much easier working with him than with Edith Summerskill (Minister of National Insurance, 1950–1). Horner was chiefly interested in the establishment of the miners' pension scheme and in redundancy payments. Although a Communist, he earned the respect of civil servants and Ministers by his sincerity and his willingness to stick by his word once given.

The Conservative Party Conferences were constantly pressing for increases in pension benefits; a unanimous motion was passed in 1952 and there was only one dissentient in 1954. At the 1953 Conference, however, a motion urging the appointment of a Committee to enquire into the distress of those on fixed incomes and pensions was defeated by a large majority after a forceful speech opposing it by Peake.[27] In the House, individual Labour M.P.s, notably Ellis Smith, would speak on the subject and lobby Peake; miners' interests were especially well represented due to the large number of M.P.s sponsored by the N.U.M.[28] Despite the weight of pressure, however, the Government was never forced to increase benefits against its will: it was not to be rushed.

The work of the Ministry fell in three main areas: national insurance, industrial injuries and family allowances, and a fourth, war pensions, was added after the merger with Pensions.

National Insurance, the largest of the four schemes, covered retirement pensions, widows' benefits, unemployment, sickness and maternity benefits. The basis had been laid down by the National Insurance Act, 1946, but Labour had let the cost of living rise by nearly a third before the Cabinet decided in 1951 that Edith Summerskill should raise retirement pensions,[29] and even then the other main insurance benefits were left at the rates of 1946, except for some improvements for widowed mothers and for children. Peake, when an Opposition Front Bench spokesman, had criticised these Summerskill proposals as being contrary to the original Beveridge plans, accepted in the national insurance structure in the 1946 Act, and was determined to get them right when in office. The Family Allowances and National Insurance Act, 1952,[30] costing about £60m. per annum, provided, *inter alia*, for a general increase in retirement pensions, unemployment, sickness and widows' benefit, thereby restoring uniformity of rates. They were raised on average by twenty per cent, unemployment benefit for men rising from twenty-six shillings to thirty-two shillings and sixpence per week. Peake believed, unlike King and most Treasury officials and economists, in the financial and political importance of preserving the independence of the insurance concept from budgetary considerations. Butler did not announce the increase to thirty-two shillings and sixpence in his Budget, but said that this was the figure the Minister, who would make his own statement later, had in mind.[31] A proposal to increase the benefit to thirty-six shillings had been put in confidence to unions and employers' leaders, conditional on their agreement to support moves to be embodied in the Bill towards a higher pension age, on which the Treasury was keen. The T.U.C. said it was not something they could support without an independent Enquiry. The extra increase to thirty-six shillings was thus temporarily shelved.[32] Maternity benefits were increased by the National Insurance Act, 1953, costing about £2.5m. a year and were made without any increase in the weekly contributions.

Labour as has been shown had left unresolved the question of retirement age and pensions. They, too, had hoped to set up an Enquiry but were diverted by Trade Union opposition, principally from Arthur Deakin, General Secretary, Transport and General Workers' Union from 1940 until his death in May 1955. Yet Labour's plans were sufficiently developed by the time of the Election in 1951 for a Chairman to have been selected, Sir Charles Morris, the Vice-Chancellor of the University of Leeds. Peake, after 1951, also saw the need to go ahead with the Enquiry, but was stalled by the caution of the Treasury Ministers. Sir Edward Bridges was responsible for reactivating an idea, which had first emerged from meetings between himself, Dame Mary Smieton[33] of the Ministry of Labour, and Walley (representing Hancock). They proposed having two Committees, one to investigate the general question of financial provision for old age, the other to remove obstacles which prevented old people continuing to work.[34] The Government liked this idea, but more time was lost while it decided who should approach the unions, as Deakin was continuing to make it clear that he felt individual unions should negotiate pensions for their members. Monckton offered to make the approach, but then demurred and handed the responsibility to Peake, who decided, quite correctly as it turned out, that it would be best to tell the unions outright that the Enquiries were to be set up, and to ask for their nominations.[35] The Treasury, which had the task of selecting a Chairman, put forward Phillips.

There can be little doubt but that the Government mishandled the issue, first by their lack of decisiveness and their unwillingness to back Peake's judgment,[36] and then by Butler's announcement[37] that there would be no increase in rates of benefit until after both the Government Actuary's first major statutory Review of the insurance scheme, completed in 1954,[38] and the Phillips Committee had reported. This unduly rushed the work of the Committee. The 1952 increases had not fully restored to insurance pensions their original purchasing power of 1946 and there had since 1952 been a 3–4% rise in the cost of living: to raise benefits to the level of subsistence standard would have involved an increase of 15–30%.[39] Moreover, Labour were becoming increasingly restive, and saw the reduction of food subsidies in the 1952 Budget as a prime justification for immediate increases in pensions. All this put the Committee under pressure to make its Report, which was unfortunate because it had weighty issues to consider.

Its Report, *The Economic and Financial Problems of the Provision for Old Age*,[40] appeared at the end of the year. A leader in *The Times* on 4th December, 1954 delivered a harsh but deserved judgment: 'Throughout its report there are signs of unfinished thinking and deficient factual knowledge. This is presumably because of the rush in which the Committee, for purely expedient and ephemeral political reasons, was obliged to work.' In the debate in the Commons on 8th December, 1954, Summerskill criticised Peake for treating the Phillips Committee in a grossly inconsiderate manner, and repeated the accusation that the Report had been rushed. This criticism apart, the Report made a number of interesting proposals, such as increasing the pension age to sixty-eight for men and sixty-three for women (the T.U.C. at its 1954 Congress was, however, hostile). But in the fuss over the increase in pension rates, it was never properly debated in the House of Commons.

The pressure for an increase in pension benefits had built up during 1954 to become one of the major political issues of the year. Following the Budget, when there was general disappointment that Butler had not announced a rise in pension rates, the issue soon began to dominate domestic politics. A motion put down by Labour in mid-July 1954 calling for a rise in pension rates brought from Peake a pledge for an increase soon.[41] Macmillan, in a party political broadcast in September said, 'The

Government's full proposals on pensions will be announced before the end of this year.'[42] In November Labour urged Peake to speed the raising of rates[43] and when nothing was forthcoming after two weeks put down a censure motion against the Government. *The Times* on 16th November called this insincere and 'pensioneering'. In the debate in the House the same day Peake produced one of the best speeches of his career, and held out the hope of details before Christmas. Undoubtedly the likely proximity of the next General Election was responsible for much of the heat generated by the issue. The increases, eventually announced by Peake in the House on 1st December, 1954, became the National Insurance Act, 1954, and increased benefits by 23% (although contributions rose by only 17%). The new rates, by which a man would now receive forty shillings a week, affected 6 million people of whom 4.5 million were retirement pensioners. The Government thereby fulfilled its pledge to restore the purchasing power to insurance benefits that Parliament had intended when creating the scheme in the 1946 National Insurance Act.[44]

In industrial injuries, the second area of the Ministry's work, Peake took a particular interest.[45] The old system of workmen's compensation was gradually replaced by a new scheme, based on medical assessment of the degree of disability. The Industrial Injuries Act, 1946, was the main piece of legislation in this field. Benefits were improved by nearly fifty per cent altogether under the Family Allowances and National Insurance Act, 1954, and these increases affected about one million people. In addition, Peake was particularly anxious to help the seriously disabled whose special position Conservatives felt had not always been fully recognised by the Labour Government.[46] Peake thus carried through the Pneumoconiosis and Byssinosis Act, 1951, allowing various sufferers from these diseases who had formerly been excluded to receive benefits from the Industrial Injuries fund. Eligibility to benefit was further extended by the National Insurance (Industrial Injuries) Act, 1953, and the Industrial Diseases (Benefit) Act, 1954.

Family allowances, the smallest of the four fields for which the Ministry was responsible, were received by three million, in respect of second and subsequent children. The 1952 Act increased the benefit from five shillings to eight shillings a week per child, and various extensions to eligibility were made in July 1953.

The Ministry was also responsible for the National Assistance Board, which administered non-contributory pensions, payable at the age of seventy (forty for a blind person), subject to a means test. The National Insurance Act, 1946, increased the weekly rate but provided that no more non-contributory pensions would be granted after 1961, by which time everyone participating in contributory schemes would qualify for the full national insurance pension on reaching retirement age. In addition the Board gave money to any person over the age of sixteen not in full-time employment if, after a means test, he showed personal need. The rates for national assistance were increased in 1952 and 1954, and about one in four pensioners received help from the Board, whose rates increased by 50–60% from 1948–54.[47]

Peake had a difficult job, especially following so closely after Griffiths, who had been so important and respected a figure in the early years of the Ministry. Peake built on that work and played an invaluable – and underestimated – role in consolidating the social security system. He should not be held responsible for the major failure of the Government to anticipate the later breakdown of non-partisan policy-making in the field of pension benefits. Much had been settled by the time Peake came to National Insurance in 1951, but not the question of a satisfactory financial basis for retirement pensions. Relevant proposals put forward during 1951–5 included (from Sir Alfred Roberts and Walley) a scheme for earnings-related pensions, long before R. M. Titmuss had thought of a similar idea and launched it through Richard Crossman. Peake also had thoughts for solving the problem of pension finance but was waiting for the right moment to put them across. He himself was keen on raising the pensionable age, but realised at the same time that this should not be done unless employment prospects for old people were improved.[48] The Cabinet did not wish to tackle this issue since it was one that ran the risk of antagonising trade union leaders. Neither did the Treasury fully appreciate the difficulties that lay ahead. A non-partisan solution to the financial problems of pensions might have been found in these years but the opportunity was missed.

Chapter 8   Defence Policy

Part 1 The Ministry of Defence

The Ministry of Defence was officially established on 1st January, 1947, with A. V. Alexander, later Lord Alexander of Hillsborough, as Minister. The experiment, begun in 1936, of having a single Minister for co-ordination of Defence, had not worked well,[1] since the Minister had no departmental staff to assist him and all the power was vested in the Service Departments, his task being to co-ordinate them through interdepartmental Committees. When Clement Attlee became Minister of Defence at the beginning of his Administration in July 1945, the same position that Winston Churchill had held since May 1940, he determined to re-examine the whole defence structure.

The 1946 White Paper,[2] which Attlee produced and whose recommendations were adopted by the Government, stressed one major defect of the previous arrangements in particular, the absence in the pre-war Committee of Imperial Defence of a 'guiding hand' to formulate a unified defence policy for the three Services. The Government did not wholly reject the concept of amalgamating the three Services and placing them under a single Minister, but did not want to do so at the time. Instead it decided to establish at the top level a Defence Committee of the Cabinet, under the Prime Minister's chairmanship, replacing the Committee of Imperial Defence which had been in existence since 1903. Responsibility was devolved on to the new post of Minister of Defence, acting as deputy for the Prime Minister at Defence Committee, helped by a number of other Committees.[3] The individual Service Ministers were to continue to be responsible to Parliament for administering their own Service and its Service Ministry.

Under the new system the Minister of Defence now had a small Ministry to support him, he was executively responsible for certain limited functions and expenditure, and the Service Ministers no longer sat in Cabinet. The new Ministry of Defence was to have three major functions: the apportionment, in broad outline, of available resources between the three Services in accordance with strategic policy laid down by the Defence Committee, the settling of questions of general ad-

295

ministration where a common policy was thought desirable and the administration of inter-Service organisations.[4] In 1951, after the refusal of Lord Portal (Chief of Air Staff, 1940–5) to accept the post of Minister of Defence, since he had no wish to become involved in politics,[5] Churchill decided against giving the job to Lord Ismay[6] and immediately reappointed himself Minister of Defence.[7] Quite how long he envisaged retaining the post is not clear, nor whether from the beginning he intended that Lord Alexander of Tunis, then Governor-General in Canada, should take over as soon as he was able to step down. In response to criticism from Attlee that the combined jobs of Prime Minister and Minister of Defence were too much for one man, Churchill had said: 'I am well aware of the burden of both these offices, but I feel that I must, at any rate at the outset, master the situation in the sphere of defence . . .'[8] The evidence slightly conflicts.[9] There is no doubt, however, that Churchill, who found Alexander's company particularly congenial, felt that if he appointed his old friend, he could then still play an active part in defence matters.[10]

Despite Churchill's declared desire to be a peacetime Minister of Defence, he never fully got to grips with the job and in the event only held it for four months. The officials at the Ministry saw much less of him than they had of Labour's A. V. Alexander (Minister of Defence, 1946–50) or of Emanuel Shinwell (Minister of Defence, 1950–1), and the political heads of the Service Ministries had correspondingly greater influence.[11] Churchill seldom went to the Ministry, and concentrated more on broad strategy than on the problems of resources and allocations between the Services.[12] He instigated a major strategic review by the Chiefs of Staff, which became known as 'The Global Strategy Paper'[13] of 1952, but rather lost interest in it after it had been established. Those who worked with him found him vastly changed from the war, and unable to master the peacetime functions of the Ministry.[14] He still thought very much in terms of the problems and outlook of 1940–5 and had not adapted himself to the strategic position of Britain in the post-war world.

The lack of sufficient troops in Britain to defend the country against a possible Russian attack was his first concern.[15] This possibility was not taken too seriously by the Service Chiefs, but, on Churchill's insistence, there emerged the Home Guard Act, 1951, which re-established the Home Guard on a limited basis in peacetime. Sufficient numbers to build up a reliable force were not forthcoming, however,[16] and the move was generally regarded in defence circles as anachronistic.[17]

In contrast to Attlee he was felt to be a poor Chairman of the Defence Committee, and complaints also arose that he called insufficient meetings.[18] Nor was he decisive enough. Indeed, in an interview Lord Harding was to recall that, 'With the passage of years it seemed to me that as Chairman of the Defence Committee Churchill had lost some of the outstanding powers of decision that had characterised his brilliant leadership throughout the war.'[19] In addition his performance varied widely, from poor and anecdotal to absolutely first class, using his unrivalled experience of defence to stunning effect, exhibiting a depth of understanding far beyond the capabilities of those in attendance. Sir William Dickson, Chief of Air Staff, 1953–6, later wrote: 'The Prime Minister indulged in many of his old tricks of trying to divide in order to rule, and his chairmanship of the Defence Committee was sometimes explosive and unreasonable, but both Ministers and Chiefs of Staff understood him and did not allow such performances to detract from the leadership which his experience and authority was still able to give.'[20] On occasion he chaired the Committee after Alexander's appointment, in line with the principles laid down by the 1946 White Paper, although he usually delegated the responsibility to his successor.

While Minister of Defence, Churchill relied greatly on the advice of Ismay,[21] whom he had appointed Secretary of State for Commonwealth Relations, partly so that he could continue to benefit from the advice of his former Chief of Staff.[22] Had Alexander refused the Defence portfolio, Ismay would probably not have been allowed to leave the Government to become Secretary-General of NATO in the spring of 1952. Churchill also sought Lord Cherwell's advice on defence matters, and although still regarded as an expert on nuclear subjects, on some other aspects 'the Prof' was felt to have become out of touch.

Churchill insisted on taking both Cherwell and Ismay, plus Sir William Slim (C.I.G.S., 1948–52) and Sir Rhoderick McGrigor (First Sea Lord, 1951–5), with him on his first United States trip in January 1952, where his major preoccupation was to attempt a reversal, against the unanimous opinion of his own advisers, of a decision to appoint a United States Admiral as Commander-in-Chief of the Atlantic.[23] The Truman Administration, for their part, were only too relieved that Churchill did not suggest re-creating the wartime Combined Chiefs of Staff, as had been feared.[24]

It was on this same Atlantic trip that Churchill travelled to Ottawa to invite Alexander to be Minister of Defence. Like Lord Simonds, the Lord Chancellor, he lacked any previous experience or particular understanding of politics, and the necessary insight and toughness needed to make a success of his post. Alexander, unlike Simonds, however, was prone to making the occasional gaffe in public. At the beginning of July 1952, in an after-dinner speech, he divulged some secret information on

British anxieties concerning the state of the reserve forces in Korea. In the fuss that followed Churchill had to spend an hour answering Questions in the House the following day.[25] Even more of a handicap was Alexander's total ignorance of the Whitehall machine. As he was removed from a job he enjoyed greatly and in which he performed well, and put into one where he felt out-of-place and ill-at-ease, it is perhaps unfair to blame him entirely for his poor performance as Minister. The fault lies partly with Churchill, who chose such an ill-equipped man for the task.

In minor matters of co-ordination between the three Service Departments and the Ministry of Supply Alexander had some success. But he never attempted proper co-ordination and was poor at giving clear directions. All his colleagues found him immensely likeable, though some detected a streak of vanity. He did, however, take his responsibilities as Minister seriously, if inclined to laziness about reading papers and dealing with routine office work. Conscientious about visiting establishments and inspecting troops, he would do this whenever possible, but scrupulously showed no special favour to his own Service, the Army.[26] He coped well with 'managing' Churchill, soothing him whenever he was upset about any aspect of defence. External relations presented few problems since he was so highly respected abroad; during his trip to the United States, in July 1954, he was treated with great deference, and the NATO countries, too, would listen to him carefully and appreciate his views.[27] He enjoyed a high reputation both in the House of Lords and in the country, founded on his outstanding war record. He always looked elegant, very much the part, and was a tremendous public figure.[28]

But there his suitability ended; his deficiencies far outweighed his merits. Popularity at home and abroad was insufficient a credential for a Minister of Defence. He never escaped from a soldier's mentality and was at his best when, as a field commander, he was under orders. He had no experience of finance, an integral part of the job, and as Minister was also required to create policy. He played only a small part in discussions on strategic matters; careful not to assert his military past with the Chiefs of Staff, he tended to stand aside from discussion on strategic questions. Churchill envisaged Alexander as a type of super-Chairman of the Chiefs of Staff Committee, akin to the position he himself had held in the war.[29] But Alexander never tried to pull his weight and left them a free hand, giving no positive direction. His relations with the Service Ministers were similarly loose, and he had not the will or the strength to stand up to either Lord De L'Isle and Dudley (Secretary of State for Air, 1951–5) or Antony Head (Secretary of State for War, 1951–6), despite his good personal relations with them.

Alexander was weak in Cabinet, and the Ministry suffered a number of disappointments when papers were rejected since he had no experience or taste for explaining and defending his policy. In the House of Lords he fared adequately provided he was well briefed and suffered few interruptions. Some in the Ministry felt that their position was weakened by not having the Minister in the House of Commons. His contribution to policy was negligible on equipment questions, though he coped better with personnel matters. He regarded Service pensions as a major question, feeling he had a personal responsibility to ensure the Services were properly treated, and wrote to the Chancellor on this matter. Unusually, he argued the case for higher pensions well in the Cabinet, where he was defeated, and was then unhappy defending the Government's policy in the House of Lords.[30]

Alexander invariably followed Churchill's line, having few ideas of his own. His Chief Staff Officer during 1952, Sir Ian Jacob, jotted down his impressions after giving up the job:

> I found Alex an enigma. No one could achieve the highest in war without considerable qualities. His were courage of a very high order, a fine appearance which made him look all over a fine soldier, a fund of common sense and an ability to meet and talk with everyone on level terms. This is quite a formidable list but there seems to be lacking the equivalent mental equipment. His thought was by no means profound and he didn't seem to have any original ideas. He didn't seem to impose his thinking on the development of ideas when he became a Minister . . .[31]

Churchill was disappointed by his lack of initiative,[32] though he would have been highly reluctant to put someone stronger in his place.[33] Thus Churchill's practice was to bypass Alexander and deal direct with the Services, so much so that he was regarded almost as *de facto* Minister of Defence, and even appeared to take more interest after he had relinquished the post. Said Sir William Dickson: 'Churchill had a high personal regard for Lord Alexander, but he treated him more as his deputy than as an independent Minister of Defence. Thanks to Lord Alexander's qualities of character and his affection for the Prime Minister, and to all the Chiefs of Staffs' respect for Alexander, and to our own understanding of his position, the arrangement worked.'[34] Certainly throughout Churchill's last three and a half years as Prime Minister, though his interest in domestic matters steadily waned, this was not so in defence (or foreign) policy.

It is perhaps no surprise that Alexander never felt happy at the

Ministry of Defence.[35] After two and a half years, aware that he was not making a success of the job, he asked to be released. On the great issues of the day, whether Britain should join the European Defence Community, deployment of troops east of Suez, and the extent to which Britain should rely on the nuclear deterrent, he was effectively silent.[36] Indeed it would be fair to say that he was more at home in his ceremonial role than at his desk in Whitehall. He put the matter succinctly when on his retirement he wrote to Cherwell: 'As you know I only came back from Canada to serve our old Chief and do a job for the Services and not to start a new career.'[37]

Harold Macmillan, who had requested the post from Churchill, succeeded him in October 1954. But the increased responsibility he had demanded was not forthcoming until after Duncan Sandys became the Minister in January 1957.[38] Indeed the job did not hold out the promise that Macmillan had anticipated, and he suffered from greater interference from Churchill than he would have liked. To Lord Moran he complained: 'Winston ought to resign. He didn't interfere in my housing, just left it all to me. But since I became Minister of Defence I have found that he can no longer handle these complicated matters properly.'[39] Macmillan's irritation may have stemmed in part from a feeling prevalent in informed circles at the time, and expressed in a journal (*The Economist*) normally favourable to Macmillan, that he '. . . gave the impression that his undoubted capacity for the imaginative running of his own show melted away when an august superior was breathing down his neck'.[40] The article felt that Macmillan at Defence was disappointing; and that he had unnecessarily riled Labour by appearing to carry the idiom of a largely political housing drive into the problems of peace and war. Nevertheless he quite enjoyed working at the Ministry[41] alongside the senior Service figures, and helped write the 1955 Defence White Paper with great enthusiasm,[42] though it was later the subject of long discussions involving changes before the Defence Committee. Throughout these talks Churchill interfered, but for the last time. Having realised that his final hopes of a summit meeting with the Russians would not transpire, he devoted considerable energy to the Paper, channelling into it all his available strength. Meanwhile, Macmillan found the position of co-ordinator lacking in sufficient clarity or power, and this experience was largely responsible for his decision to change the defence apparatus when he himself became Prime Minister in 1957.

Macmillan's appointment pleased the Ministry and he was highly popular with his officials,[43] but there was insufficient time for him to make any real mark. The job required more knowledge than most on technical matters, and Macmillan, though quick, continually had to ask questions, and never had a chance to master the field. Three years for a Minister of Defence was considered to be an optimum time. Macmillan had only six months.[44] On Churchill's retirement in April 1955 he was appointed to the Foreign Office, and was succeeded at Defence by Selwyn Lloyd, of whom Eden had formed a high opinion as his Minister of State at the Foreign Office. It was a happy posting for Lloyd, who had been interested in military problems since the war.[45]

Churchill at first continued the Labour Government's practice of not having a junior Minister of Defence. However, since Alexander sat in the Lords (for the first time since 1940 the Minister was not in the Lower House), he therefore felt it necessary to appoint a junior Minister in the Commons. Nigel Birch was thus transferred from Parliamentary Under-Secretary at the Air Ministry. On a personal level he worked well with Alexander but became increasingly disillusioned with his lack of interest in new ideas. To Birch, a man of great energy and activity, this was a frustrating experience. He played an important part in relationships with the NATO countries and excelled in debates in the House, but, in common with other junior Ministers, there was little for him to do in the Ministry. He was rewarded for his work by being made Minister of Works in the October 1954 reshuffle. The practice of appointing a junior Minister continued, but with the Minister now in the Commons, a spokesman in the Lords was appointed, Lord Carrington, an able deputy but not the commanding figure of his later years in politics.[46]

The Department was the smallest in Whitehall and contained only a small number of senior officers. The Permanent Secretary (1948) was Sir Harold Parker, in succession to the first head, Sir Henry Wilson Smith, who had been recalled to the Treasury as Second Secretary.[47] Parker was a somewhat unusual choice. He had a Treasury background[48] until called to the Ministry of Pensions in 1941, where he was Permanent Secretary from 1946–8. He was appointed to succeed Wilson Smith so as not to appear to be favouring any one of the three Services, but with the inevitable result that he had little experience of defence matters. A highly professional administrator, he was perhaps not the best man to head the new Ministry, which required not only a skilled diplomat, but also an 'ideas' man.

Parker concerned himself primarily with administration and personnel, and with the less important parts of NATO policy, such as the provision of infrastructure. In these matters he was excellent. The Ministers of Defence, however, felt they wanted something more. Shinwell relied to a greater extent on Sir Kenneth McLean, the Chief Staff Officer. Churchill liked Parker but seldom saw him, but Macmillan was not over-impressed, though he appreciated him as an 'experienced administrator'.[49] The problem arose from Parker's conception of his role not as advising on broad strategy to the Minister, but as an administrative exercise. In an interview he recalled what he saw as the aim of the Ministry: 'It was a problem not really of broad strategy, but it was a problem, as of course the White Paper said, of allocation of resources and priorities and an overall appreciation.'[50]

The key figure in the Ministry was, in effect, Sir Richard Powell, who enjoyed correspondingly far more appreciation from the various Ministers of Defence.[51] He had an Admiralty background, and joined the Ministry of Defence as Under-Secretary in 1946. He was recalled to the Admiralty in 1948, but, owing to the Korean crisis in 1950, Shinwell brought him back to Defence as Deputy Secretary, the office he held for the next six years. A more impressive figure than Parker, he had a strong, creative mind. Powell focused on the defence budget and allocation of resources, and acted as a link with the Chiefs of Staff Committee on broad issues of strategy and defence policy. Powell was a practical realist, at his most effective when bludgeoning the military into taking decisions, and keeping them within the Treasury expenditure limits.

Sir Maurice Dean had been a second Deputy Secretary since 1948, concerned with the administrative and personnel side. When in 1952 he moved to fill a vacancy at the Treasury and then the Board of Trade, there was not felt to be sufficient work to merit the continued appointment of a second Deputy.[52] The Ministry had two Under-Secretaries since its establishment, who were directly responsible to the Permanent Secretary. One oversaw manpower questions, both quantitative and qualitative (John Newling, until 1957); the other concentrated on the 'material' side (Powell until his departure in 1948 for the Admiralty, when his place was taken by Geoffrey Wheeler).

During the early 1950s Powell, with his interest in policy and finance, was far more concerned than Parker with the Defence Committee of the Cabinet, the senior of the many Committees in the defence field. It was responsible to Cabinet both for reviewing current strategy and for co-ordinating departmental action in preparation for war. Unlike the Committee of Imperial Defence which it replaced, the new Defence Committee had executive authority.[53]

Alexander of Tunis, when he took the chair at Defence Committee in place of Churchill, was frequently needled by Sandys (Minister of Supply, 1951–4), who had quickly formed a low opinion of the new Minister of Defence. For all his intransigence, though, the most influential voice was not Sandys', but Head's. A professional soldier, Head had served on the planning staff during the war.[54] He also benefited from a close relationship with Churchill, having assisted him on defence Questions when in Opposition. Overall, the most powerful exponents of their respective Services at interdepartmental Committees were Sir John Lang (Permanent Secretary, Admiralty, 1947–61), Sir John Slessor (Chief of Air Staff, C.A.S., 1950–2) and Head for the War Office. Throughout the period 1951–5, the Defence Committee met less frequently than during 1946–51, and was felt to be less effective as the central co-ordinating body.

As a result of the 1946 reforms, the Chiefs of Staff Committee, which was retained after the war, prepared strategic military plans for submission to the Defence Committee. The 1946 White Paper stressed the necessity of the Cabinet and the Defence Committee having direct access to the Chiefs of Staff on all technical matters of strategy and defence, and for that reason they submitted their plans direct to the Defence Committee and not first to the Minister of Defence. The Chairman of the Chiefs of Staff Committee was the senior Service Chief: in turn, Slim (1951–2), McGrigor (1952–5) an 'accommodating Chairman' according to one witness, and Sir John Harding (1955), until in 1955 Anthony Eden provided for a permanent Service Chairman on account of the increased work caused by international defence organisations such as NATO.[55]

The Chiefs of Staff organisation lay within the Ministry of Defence, but the Ministers did not act as the mouthpiece of the Service Chiefs. This arrangement led to a number of problems. A. V. Alexander (Minister of Defence, 1946–50) lacked firmness in his dealings with them, which resulted in much unnecessary discussion and squabbling, particularly from Lord Montgomery of Alamein (C.I.G.S., 1946–8). Alexander of Tunis, as we have seen, was ineffectual with the Service Chiefs and Macmillan resented the Chiefs' direct access to the Prime Minister, bypassing the Minister of Defence.

Under Churchill this problem became more pronounced since he regarded his relations with the Chiefs as personal, inviting them frequently to Chequers at weekends for individual and collective talks.[56] Dickson later wrote:

Our relationship with Churchill as Prime Minister was on the whole a happy and satisfactory one. His experience in the war had given him a high opinion of the Chiefs of Staff organisation and he regarded and used the Chiefs of Staff as his principal military advisers, both individually and collectively. His interest and concern over defence matters remained paramount and he controlled the Chiefs of Staff and the Ministry of Defence as closely as he had done in the war years.[57]

But Churchill showed complete disrespect for the Chiefs of Staff Committee system he inherited from Labour, and caused great consternation by his insistence on inviting Ismay and Cherwell to the first Chiefs of Staff Committee meeting during his Administration.[58] Churchill had initially been put out to discover he was scarcely familiar with the new team: Slim (C.I.G.S., 1948–52) he knew slightly, while Slessor and McGrigor (First Sea Lord, 1951–5) he had scarcely met. He quickly decided that McGrigor did not match up to his ideal of a First Sea Lord,[59] and was never impressed by him. Slim he did admire,[60] likewise his successor, Harding (C.I.G.S., 1952–5). Slessor, however, he did not greatly care for and, partly because of their personal coolness, Slessor did not prolong his tenure as C.A.S., which he could have done.[61] Of all the Chiefs of Staff whom Churchill saw in his last years at Number Ten, he had the highest opinion of Slessor's successor, Dickson.[62]

Until the appointment of a Chief of Defence Staff in 1958, the Chairman of the Chiefs of Staff Committee found problems in reaching a consensus, partly on account of a succession of ill-balanced teams of Chiefs. Of the earlier combination, Slessor was able to dominate McGrigor, and Slim too on occasion found problems holding his own against him.[63] A more balanced team existed from 1953 with Harding, Dickson and McGrigor, but again McGrigor weakened the Admiralty's case by not being sufficiently strong.[64]

Links between the Chiefs of Staff and Minister of Defence were principally maintained by the Chief Staff Officer. The job originated with that of Ismay, who had a special relationship with Churchill (as Minister of Defence) during the war. After the 1945 General Election, Ismay remained as Chief of Staff to Attlee, and played a major part in setting up the Ministry of Defence. The job of Chief Staff Officer thus became formalised and was continued by Sir Leslie Hollis after Ismay's departure for India as Chief of Staff to Viceroy Lord Mountbatten of Burma. The position – a high-level liaison officer between the Minister and the Services – varied in importance depending upon its incumbent, but during 1951–5 never recovered the influence it had during the special circumstances of Ismay's tenure. Military advice, co-ordinated by the Chiefs of Staff Committee and by its subcommittees, was brought to the Minister by the Chief Staff Officer, who attended these meetings as the Minister's personal representative. One incumbent described the job as follows:

I had to ensure that the Chiefs of Staff and the Minister of Defence were in close harmony. Now that was comparatively simple with Alex who didn't think much anyway, but with Winston it was a bit of a job.

Also to make certain that the Chiefs of Staff were tackling the right things, that the machine was running properly, and one had to make sure that they got on with everything they should have dealt with and soon, and that the staff were doing their job and the Secretariat were working properly.[65]

The Chief Staff Officer was also Deputy Secretary (Military) to the Cabinet, having direct access to the Prime Minister at all times and directing the military side of the Cabinet Office. Churchill inherited McLean (Chief Staff Officer, 1951–2) from Shinwell, who later wrote: 'McLean was one of the most intelligent officers I met, a skilful soldier and a wide-awake man whom I admired greatly.'[66] Churchill, however, did not know him, so from the beginning McLean was at a disadvantage, and his relations with Churchill remained uneasy.[67]

They deteriorated further when McLean failed to take action after Churchill had protested, because of his obsession about the defenceless state of Britain, about the despatch of certain troops to Germany.[68] Churchill decided within a few weeks that this unknown McLean was unsuitable, and made efforts to bring back Jacob, whom he knew from the war.[69] This presented a number of problems – Jacob since 1947 had been Director of Overseas Services, B.B.C., and further he had retired in 1946 with the rank of Major-General, not Lieutenant-General, the rank necessary for the Chief Staff Officer.[70] Moreover the Chiefs argued against Jacob's appointment, not wishing an ex-officer to be brought back into a job for an active serviceman. Churchill however prevailed, and in May 1952 McLean returned to the War Office and his place was taken by Jacob, although ironically by the time he arrived Churchill had ceased to be the Minister of Defence.

Jacob, like many others at the time, did not have a high opinion of the new Minister of Defence. Jacob was almost too bright and full of ideas for the job, displaying his originality most notably during the preparation by the Chiefs of the 1952 'Global Strategy Review'.[71] He left at the end of the year to succeed Sir William Haley as Director-General of the B.B.C., and in December 1952 Sir Nevil Brownjohn became Chief Staff Officer. Not a man of the same intellectual quality as Jacob, he nevertheless performed well, in the manner of an efficient military staff officer.[72] His relationship to the Chiefs of Staff Committee was similar to that of Sir Norman Brook to the Cabinet.[73]

The Chiefs of Staff were responsible for advising the Government on overall strategy, and the Service Departments on the necessary personnel and material to carry it out. These needs were discussed in the Standing Committee of Service Ministers, who were responsible for the maintenance and administration of their Services within the resources allocated to them.[74] The Minister of Defence presided over the Standing Committee, where again Alexander found difficulties asserting himself against the more articulate Service Ministers eager to promote their own charges. Certain conclusions of the Standing Committee were forwarded for submission to the Defence Committee which was then able to form an overall view on expenditure to submit to Cabinet.

A Committee which increased in importance throughout this period was the Ministry's Defence Research Policy Committee. It contained those responsible, both operationally and scientifically, for research and development in the Service Ministries and the Ministry of Supply. It was chaired by the Scientific Adviser of the Ministry of Defence,[75] Sir Henry Tizard, who had managed the job superbly since 1946. He left in early 1952; having initially intended to remain in the job only five years he had begun to feel the strain (he was aged sixty-six when he retired).[76] Not so much was seen of his successor, Sir John Cockcroft, who was heavily occupied at the Atomic Energy Research Establishment at Harwell, where he had been Director since 1946. Much of the work was done by Sir Frederick Brundrett, Deputy Scientific Adviser since 1950, who became full Scientific Adviser in 1954. More the modern administrative type of officer than Tizard or Cockcroft, he ran the research side much more effectively than the latter. Brundrett was not a great scientist or creative genius, but excelled as a committee Chairman, obtaining decisions and keeping people happy. The importance of the job increased in particular as weapons technology assumed more importance, and Brundrett regularly attended Chiefs of Staff meetings[77].

Part 2   The War Office

The three Service Departments began to lose much of their independent power after the creation of a separate Ministry of Defence in 1946. Much depended, however, on the weight carried by the new Ministry in relation to the political heads of the Service Ministries. The War Office still retained considerable potential authority over defence matters after 1946, particularly during Emanuel Shinwell's tenure of office (1947–50). The Secretary of State would argue the War Office's case in Defence Committee and the Service Ministers' Committee, and could even argue against the Minister of Defence when asked to attend full Cabinet. The situation was highly fluid. Since the creation of the modern War Office directed by an Army Council in 1904, and modelled on the Admiralty,[1] the Secretary of State for War had sat in Cabinet until 1946, apart from the duration of the War Coalition.[2]

Antony Head was by far the most influential of the three political heads of the Service Departments after 1951. He had gained some experience of defence organisation during the war,[3] leaving the Army in 1945 with the rank of Brigadier and entering Parliament. During the period of Opposition he served Winston Churchill, whom he knew from the war, as a *de facto* shadow junior Minister on defence questions.[4] Churchill asked Head to become Minister of State at the Ministry of Defence in October 1951 under him, but Head, who felt this new position was unlikely to work in practice, refused. Churchill had envisaged Head presiding over the three Services at meetings, but the latter felt that it was not practicable to suppose a junior Minister could dictate to the three Service Ministers.[5] Duncan Sandys, who had initially been considered for the War Office,[6] was eventually brought in at Supply, and Churchill appointed Head, whose special relationship with the Prime Minister on defence questions continued.[7]

Head's appointment was particularly popular with the soldiers, and he quickly earned their respect as Minister, his previous experience of the Army as a career soldier from 1934–45 serving him well. He possessed a sharp mind, and although some initially found him slightly aloof, on better acquaintance they came to esteem him highly. He had a superb memory, and would learn the facts and figures in his important speeches, for example the Army estimates, by heart, speaking literally without a note. He developed into a highly effective Minister who was able to dominate his counterparts for the Air Force and Navy because of his superior intellect and his relationship with Churchill.[8] Within a year 'A Student of Politics' in the *Sunday Times* (on 20th December, 1952) was talking of him as one of the 'ascendant' Ministers.

The War Office traditionally had two junior Ministers, a Financial Secretary and a Parliamentary Under-Secretary, but in April 1947 these offices were combined.[9] The creation of the Defence Ministry made this an obvious rationalisation and even after 1947 there was not a great deal to occupy the single junior Minister. He had some ceremonial and inspection duties, relieved the Secretary of State of the more routine House of Commons speaking, oversaw the Territorial Army, and was Vice-President of the Army Council, but as far as work in the Office was concerned, he played little part. James Hutchison was appointed Under-Secretary and Financial Secretary in November 1951, a man known to Churchill because of his distinguished war work in Special Operations Executive (S.O.E.).[10] The office found him an extraordinarily pleasant and straightforward man, but like many who entered

Parliamentary and ministerial life at a late age (he was nearly sixty on his appointment), he did not find the transition easy, and this proved to be his only job. Fitzroy Maclean, another with a distinguished war record, replaced him in the October 1954 reshuffle. He joined the Special Air Service (S.A.S.) in January 1942, and had been Brigadier commanding the British Military Mission to the Jugoslav Partisans, 1943–5.[11] Maclean was a favourite with Churchill, who ideally would have liked to have given him an appointment in 1951. Despite Maclean's friendship with Head, it was in fact Churchill who instigated his appointment in 1954.[12] He was an abler Minister than Hutchison, and might have gone far had he not been prematurely dismissed in January 1957, in the wake of Suez. His main weakness was his inability to be as effective in the House as he was on paper and in meetings.

Sir George Turner, the Permanent Under-Secretary since 1949, retired in 1956. He was a remarkable man, not least for being one of the very few Permanent Secretaries to rise from the lower levels in his Department. He joined the War Office in 1911 where he remained throughout his career apart from a spell from 1939 to 1948 in the Ministry of Supply. He possessed great wisdom about the Army, and had a knack of coming up with the right answer, though he could also be harsh and uncharitable in his judgment of others. Despite his state-school education and completely different background from Head (Eton and the Guards), their relations were excellent. So too were Turner's with the soldiers; indeed, his major contribution as Permanent Under-Secretary was helping to break down the barrier which still existed between soldiers and civilians after 1949. This he saw as one of his prime aims as official head of the Department. An extremely hard worker, like Sir Archibald Rowlands, the Permanent Secretary at the Ministry of Supply. Both men combined good living with working inordinately long hours. Turner's colleagues in the Office liked him and he always provided strong leadership. His command of the work was seldom seen more clearly than in his evidence to the Public Accounts Committee, where he was regarded by M.P.s as one of their best witnesses.

Beneath Turner were two Deputies, Deputy Under-Secretary (A) was Sir Thomas Cash until his retirement in early 1954 when he was succeeded by Sir Charles Key. Cash oversaw all matters concerning establishments and all other non-financial aspects relating to the Army.[13] Deputy Under-Secretary (B), Sir David Roseway (1945–55),[14] dealt with all matters of finance. One of the brightest of the younger men, Richard Way, worked under Roseway and was Turner's choice to succeed him as Permanent Under-Secretary in 1956. At the time, however, Anthony Eden considered him too young (he was forty-one), and as no one else from the War Office seemed suitable, Edward Playfair was brought in from the Treasury.[15]

The Army Council nominally directed the War Office. The Secretary of State was President, and the Parliamentary Under-Secretary was Vice-President, making him theoretically, though not in practice, senior to the Permanent Under-Secretary and the Chief of the Imperial General Staff (C.I.G.S.). The Army Council debated matters of specific concern to the Army, and discussed proposals before they went forward to one of the various inter-Service Committees. The full Army Council met once a month, and most of the routine work was done by its Executive Committee, containing all members apart from the two politicians and the C.I.G.S., which met weekly under the chairmanship of the Permanent Under-Secretary. It screened material before deciding whether it need go to the full Army Council, and dealt with most matters that did not raise political factors.[16]

The Office regarded Sir William Slim (1948–52) as an outstanding twentieth-century C.I.G.S.[17] (unlike Lord Montgomery of Alamein, 1946–8), to a large extent because of Slim's tremendous fund of practical good sense and the way he kept the interests of defence in all its aspects in mind, not just those of the Army.[18] Sir John Harding was his natural successor when Slim retired in November 1952. Indeed, a profile in the *Sunday Times* said no man came to the job with a more distinguished record in peace and war.[19] He had had a number of command posts since the war, culminating in his appointment as Commander-in-Chief (C.-in-C.), British Army on the Rhine (B.A.O.R.), 1951–2. He, too, was regarded by the office as outstanding, more for his judgment and manner than any great qualities of flair or insight. Sir Brian Robertson held hopes of becoming C.I.G.S. like his father before him (1915–18), but despite the backing of the Foreign Office he was never more than an outsider, largely through lack of command experience before his appointment as C.-in-C., Middle East Land Forces (M.E.L.F.) in 1950. Realising that by the time of Harding's retirement he would be too old to succeed him (he would be sixty in 1956), he retired from the Army in November 1953 to become Chairman of the British Transport Commission. In the event, Sir Gerald Templer, who had distinguished himself as High Commissioner in Malaya, was appointed in succession to Harding in October 1955.[20]

The War Office during 1951–5 was mainly concerned to increase the fighting power of the Army, especially in the light of the commitment of forces to Europe as a result of Western European Union, 1954,[21] the fighting in Kenya and Malaya,[22] and the problem of the future of the

British base on the Suez Canal. Two brigades were committed to fighting the Mau Mau in Kenya, the unrest of the Kikuyu tribe having increased considerably during 1952. Due to the unsatisfactory relationship between the Governor, Sir Evelyn Baring, and the C.-in-C. of the East Africa Command, Sir George Erskine, frequent referrals back for instructions from the War Office became common, at least until the establishment of the War Council, in the wake of the visit by Oliver Lyttelton and Harding in March 1954.[23] In 1951–2, 25,000 British troops were committed to Malaya, and by 1953 the total number of security forces engaged in combating the terrorists had risen further, once joined by Gurkhas. In addition, 10,000 British troops were committed to Korea. By 1954, however, the position eased. The war in Korea was over and the evacuation of the Suez base from 1954 led to the release of further troops.[24] Thus the creation of a strategic reserve in Britain became possible,[25] and the easing of pressures outside Europe meant the Chiefs of Staff raised no objection to the pledge given by Eden to maintain four divisions as well as a tactical air force on the continent.[26]

As a result the overall size of the Regular Army was reduced by two per cent from 1951–5, although its numerical strength far exceeded that of the Navy or R.A.F.[27] Allied to the question of size was the problem of morale, common to all three Services, and this topic frequently came up for discussion before the Executive Committee and the Army Council. Various ameliorating measures were introduced, including less cross-posting between units, increased leave and travel concessions for servicemen overseas.

Withdrawal from the Suez Canal base and the search for a replacement in the Middle East naturally involved the War Office. Though the decision to leave the base was taken by Eden for political reasons,[28] the War Office, albeit far from unanimously, felt that the maintenance of the large fixed base on the Canal was no longer justified in view of the drain on finances and men. At the request of Eden, Head went to Egypt to discuss final plans for the withdrawal, and he was largely responsible for the form taken by the Heads of Agreement,[29] signed in Cairo in July 1954.[30] Various alternative bases were considered; Gaza was put forward as a possibility though dropped at the end of 1952,[31] Haifa was offered by Israel in 1950 but was turned down by the Foreign Office on political grounds.[32] Cyprus was chosen despite doubts about its internal political position and the absence of a deep-water harbour, though the facilities at Malta were put forward as a compensatory factor. The War Office was content with Cyprus, but the Air Ministry decried its lack of a modern airfield. Harding was sympathetic to their point of view: 'As C.I.G.S. I accepted the transfer of our Middle East headquarters and garrison from the Suez Canal Zone to Cyprus as the only practicable alternative. But I was in full agreement with the R.A.F. that it was essential to provide in Cyprus an airfield capable of taking all military aircraft.'[33]

Equipment programmes were continually being frustrated through lack of adequate finance. The main questions concerned the extent to which Army equipment and training should be changed to cope with nuclear warfare. In 1953 the decision was taken to adopt a United States ground-to-ground missile for the Army, and units to operate it were formed in 1956. To meet the possibility of nuclear war, two 'nuclear formations', able to fight independently, and excelling in mobility and toughness, began training in Germany in the summer of 1955.[34] Among conventional weapons a new infantry anti-tank gun 'The Bat', was introduced, details of which were released in May 1953, and the completion of a new heavy gun tank was also announced in 1953.

Churchill's interventions in War Office work were idiosyncratic. As usual, he was prone to interfere with appointments, and thus tried to prevent Gerald Lathbury succeeding Erskine as C.-in-C., East Africa Command, not because he disliked Lathbury, but because he did not know him, and he thought Erskine was doing a good job. Churchill was prevailed against, and Lathbury duly took up his post.[35]

On first becoming Prime Minister again Churchill, as we have seen above, felt extremely anxious about the position of Britain, which he thought would be defenceless against a sudden attack of Russian paratroopers.[36] His insistence on the reactivation of the Home Guard was responsible for the Home Guard Act, 1951, one of the first pieces of legislation introduced by the new Government. It involved a row with the Treasury, and many in Whitehall thought the Act unnecessary. The aim was to build up a force of 125,000 but in the first year only 25,000 were forthcoming,[37] and many thought the whole plan best forgotten. Shinwell taunted Head by saying that '. . . His attempt to enrol the Home Guard in face of advice given him has proved a complete flop.'[38] A leader in *The Times* on the following day, however, was more appreciative, calling the Home Guard a 'useful addition to the armed forces'.

Part 3   The Admiralty

The Navy was the least resilient of the three Services between 1951–5, partly as neither the First Lord of the Admiralty (James P. L. Thomas) nor the First Sea Lord (Sir Rhoderick McGrigor) was sufficiently assertive, but also through uncertainty about the Navy's strategic role.

311

The pattern of warfare as it had unfolded since the end of the Second World War seemed to indicate less need for a large Regular Navy. Consequently, not only was its manpower being reduced, at a time when the Army's remained static and the R.A.F.'s grew, but also expenditure, though increasing more rapidly than for the Army, was a long way behind the R.A.F.[1]

The appointment of Thomas as First Lord did not affect the Navy's decline. He had previously served as Financial Secretary at the Admiralty (1943–5) and his appointment was partly a reward for his services as Vice-Chairman of the Conservative Party (1945–51), where he had made a particular success of his job in which he was responsible for supervising the selection of candidates. His close friendship with Anthony Eden, whose Parliamentary Private Secretary he had been for a number of years (1937–8 and 1940), also helped ensure the appointment, for which he had long hoped, as did his period as Chairman of the Conservative Party's Naval Committee when in Opposition.

Thomas did not prove an effective First Lord, however, though he by no means acquitted himself poorly, and was perhaps unfortunate to hold the post at a difficult period in the Navy's history. He was slow at tackling problems, and not at his best when controlling a group of Admirals, Ministers and civil servants. Neither was he an initiator of policy. To be fair, however, it would have taken a remarkable First Lord to bring about much change in policy. Most decisions at the Admiralty involved technicalities and so it would have been a bold First Lord who cast aside the advice of his Sea Lords. A good mixer and conciliator, a role not to be underestimated, Thomas performed his ceremonial duties well, but tried to avoid making decisions unless the Admiralty was in unanimous agreement.[3] He supported the Naval Staff in their policies, and at those Cabinet meetings he was called upon to attend would frequently defer to his attending Service colleague in doubt.[4] Before meetings, he was very carefully briefed, itself not a quick process, and no one quite knew what would happen if discussion went beyond his notes. He seldom became involved with technical matters where he realised his lack of knowledge. He worked well with the Permanent Secretary, Sir John Lang, who had known Thomas when Financial Secretary. Indeed, without such a strong man behind him, Thomas' shortcomings would perhaps have become more obvious in Whitehall. Yet one of Thomas' major strengths was his wide range of friendships throughout Whitehall. Churchill also liked his company. Sir Norman Brook once told Sir Harold Kent (Treasury Solicitor, 1953–63) that when anything remotely connected with the Services turned up, Churchill would say: 'Let's have J.P.L. along, shall we?'[5]

The Attlee Government reverted to the practice of having two (rather than three) junior Ministers at the Admiralty,[6] a Parliamentary and Financial Secretary, who reported to Parliament as the First Lord's main deputy on political matters and matters of finance, and a Civil Lord, regarded as his junior. This was a Department where there was scope for an exceptionally able junior Minister to stand out, as James Callaghan (Parliamentary and Financial Secretary, 1950–1) had shown.[7] Callaghan's successor was Allan Noble, a Commander on his retirement from the Navy and entry into the House of Commons in 1945. He had been picked out from the younger men in the Party to be Eden's Parliamentary Private Secretary (1947–51), although this fact was not immediately made public.[8] An appointment was thus likely after the General Election and the Admiralty an obvious choice. Simon Wingfield Digby, the Civil Lord, was given oversight of works and buildings, dockyards and airfields, and was also responsible for the Admiralty's industrial employees. Both were felt to have performed well.[9] The Parliamentary Private Secretaries saw little of the work inside the Admiralty, though they would accompany Ministers on tours. Richard Stanley, a friend of Thomas, was initially appointed Parliamentary Private Secretary to all three Ministers, but from 1952 worked solely for Thomas, and Rupert Speir was appointed to serve the others.[10]

The Permanent Secretary since 1947, Lang was the most influential civilian in the post-war history of the Admiralty.[11] Like Sir George Turner (at the War Office) he joined as a clerk without a university education, and spent his entire career in the one Department. He possessed an extremely quick analytical brain, and an encyclopaedic memory. More persuasive than Sir James Barnes (Air Ministry) or Turner (War Office) he was especially adept in putting forward the Admiralty's case for more money to the Treasury.

The Board of Admiralty was the governing body, although many decisions were taken without reference to the full Board. The individual Sea Lords enjoyed a great deal of autonomy in their own particular fields: Second Sea Lord, personnel; Third Sea Lord, known as Controller, ship-building and materials; Fourth Sea Lord, supplies and transport; Fifth Sea Lord, Fleet Air Arm. Matters tended to come to the Board only where there was disagreement among the Naval Staff, or where a unanimous policy needed to be developed. The Board, which discussed all matters other than Naval promotions, met normally once a month.[12] As Chairman, Thomas proved adequate, and his main strength lay in his smooth running of affairs, avoiding any major rows. Sir Michael Denny (Third Sea Lord, 1949–53), the great thinker where materials were concerned, and Lang were the dominant voices. Sir

Alexander Madden, the Second Sea Lord (1950–3)was well liked but not especially influential, while his successor, Sir Guy Russell (1953–5), exercised more power. Lord Mountbatten of Burma (Fourth Sea Lord, 1950–2) carried great authority as might have been expected given the onerous posts he had occupied,[13] although he took care not to push himself forward beyond his rank in his spell on the Board,[14] until his appointment as C.-in-C., Mediterranean (1952–4), when he was kept away from policy decisions at the Admiralty.[15] Indeed, when Mountbatten later became First Sea Lord he felt the more junior Sea Lords should display the same deference to him that he had shown when Fourth Sea Lord to his superiors.[16]

Lord Fraser of North Cape (First Sea Lord, 1948–51) had recommended that McGrigor should succeed him. He held great respect for McGrigor's work during the war, protecting convoys to North Russia, and regarded him as a fine sailor. Churchill, however, did not take to McGrigor any more than he had to Fraser.[17] Compared with most other post-war First Sea Lords, McGrigor's performance was unimpressive. His tenure of office coincided with a period of cut-backs in several programmes, which he did not fight, although he did make great efforts to impress upon the Navy that the cut-backs were inevitable and they must adapt to them.[18] Not an innovator, he did have the advantage of being liked and trusted by the Navy, and managed to keep them contented during a difficult period. McGrigor was never at his happiest as First Sea Lord, but loved the Navy and preferred to be at sea, where his qualities displayed themselves to far greater effect than in Whitehall.[19]

The Admiralty expected that Mountbatten would return as First Sea Lord,[20] a post he was very keen indeed to occupy and for which he had been tipped as early as the end of 1953.[21] Thomas, too, was anxious for Mountbatten to succeed McGrigor, which he did in April 1955, and for the first time since 1948 there was a First Sea Lord capable of thinking in broad strategic terms.[22]

Many thought that as Churchill had twice been First Lord (1911–15 and 1939–40), he would be especially sympathetic to the Navy's interests. But this was not to be. He fought desperately hard with the Truman Administration in January 1952 to secure the post of Supreme Allied Commander Atlantic for a British officer, but after losing the argument appears to have lost his enthusiasm for the Navy. Dating from his early disenchantment with McGrigor,[23] he had more sympathy for the other two Services[24] and on more than one occasion spoke vehemently against the Navy in Cabinet.[25] In common with the other Service Departments, appointments very often caught his attention. Early in 1952 he wanted to appoint Sir Philip Vian as Commander-in-

Chief, Portsmouth, but was overriden by the Board of Admiralty, and instead Vian was created an Admiral of the Fleet, a most unusual appointment, since this title was normally reserved for only the most senior officers.

Much Admiralty policy was of an apolitical nature, and those changes that occurred after Thomas succeeded Lord Pakenham as First Lord were not in major policy fields[26] but in matters such as the officer structure[27] and recruitment of officers to the Navy. Callaghan (when junior Minister) had changed the age of entry to Dartmouth from fourteen to sixteen, but by the time Thomas arrived as First Lord it was clear that this was not working out. The idea had been to encourage the entry of boys from state schools, including the secondary moderns, but they were rarely able to compete with public-school boys at the age of sixteen. The Admiralty also disliked the sixteen entry-age, as did the Navy. Thomas accordingly set up a Committee under Ewen Montagu (Judge Advocate of the Fleet, 1945–73). Its Report suggested restoring the fourteen entry while retaining the sixteen entry as well, appealing to Labour in the House as well as to the Navy. Thomas, however, decided against the plan, and instituted a new idea (probably at the instigation of his senior officials), of having just a 'special entry', of sixth-formers with 'A' levels (as the Air Ministry had been doing at Cranwell and the War Office at Sandhurst). Scholarships were thereby given at the age of sixteen for boys to stay on another two years at school, and this proved more successful in increasing the grammar-school entry. Dartmouth therefore ceased to be a naval public school and became akin to Cranwell or Sandhurst.[28]

Recruitment presented only a minor problem during these years. The Admiralty improved both its publicity and its conditions of service, introducing general service commissions in 1954, but largely because the Navy appeared to be a more attractive proposition in peacetime than either the Army or R.A.F., it experienced less difficulty in approaching its recruitment targets. Civilian intake rose from 12,000 in 1950 to 18,500 in 1951, steadying at about 14,000 per annum from 1953.[29] 'The Explanatory Statement on Navy Estimates, 1955–6',[30] however, referred to a shortage, particularly the small numbers remaining for longer engagements. The modernisation of training to suit the modern weapons that the Navy was then envisaging, was an inevitable result of scientific advance during and since the war. The development of new weapons themselves posed a further problem. Guided missiles were being developed throughout these years and by 1955 ships were being converted to carry them.[31] Initially ship-to-air missiles were to be installed, although plans were in progress for eventual modifications to allow the use of ship-to-ship versions. Propulsion was another matter to which much thought was devoted. Gas turbine engines were introduced,[32] but at this period their use was restricted to smaller vessels.

The Admiralty's view of the role of the Navy and the need for the development of fighting ships can be seen in Thomas' 'Explanatory Statement of the Navy Estimates for 1955–6,'[33] which showed a three per cent drop in expenditure on the previous year's estimates. His introduction made clear that he felt the time ripe for a comprehensive White Paper to examine the role of the Navy. 'The Global Strategy Paper' of 1952[34] had visualised only a minor role for the Navy in the event of atomic war, which had caused speculation as to its function.[35] The 1955 Naval White Paper was a firm statement which helped dispel doubts about the future of the Navy. In peacetime the Navy's role was seen as supporting national policy overseas and ensuring world-wide trade continued unmolested. In the event of nuclear war, it was to destroy enemy ships, protect communication lines and provide direct air support for operations which could not readily be supplied by shore-based craft. To realise this, emphasis was to be laid on two types of vessels: battle groups of ships and guided-weapon ships with their escorts. The 'fists' of the fleet would be provided by the two existing heavy aircraft carriers, *Ark Royal*[36] and *Eagle*, while two light carriers, *Albion* and *Centaur*, were to be added to a modernised *Victorious* and the new *Hermes*. Thomas announced that to increase the carriers' strike power, replacements had been ordered for the present fighter aircraft, the Sea Hawks and Sea Venoms. The replacement for the present 'strike aircraft', the Wyvern, would be capable of carrying an atomic bomb. The guided-weapon ships were to replace the ageing cruiser fleet, and while this changeover was taking place, the Navy would press ahead with modernisation of three Tiger Class Cruisers.[37]

Part 4   The Air Ministry

Of the three Service Departments, the Air Ministry expanded the most rapidly during 1951–5, and was the Service most favoured by Winston Churchill. Not only did the expenditure increase more than on the other two Services (thirty-four per cent from 1951–5), but also over the same period, the R.A.F. was the only Service not to suffer a net loss of personnel. An air of optimism pervaded the Department, and developments in the R.A.F. were much in the public eye. It was chosen as the obvious vehicle for the delivery of Britain's steadily growing stockpile of strategic nuclear weapons, which consequently became its main priority during 1951–5. Important developments were also taking place in guided-weapons, Coastal, and, later on, in Fighter Command.

Churchill chose a peer, Lord De L'Isle and Dudley, as the new Secretary of State.[1] His previous ministerial experience was restricted to the post of Parliamentary Secretary at the Ministry of Pensions during the 'Caretaker Government', although he also served the Party as joint Treasurer (February 1948–March 1952). More important to Churchill, however, De L'Isle was one of the few younger men in the Party known to him, and had also been awarded the Victoria Cross. De L'Isle proved considerably more able than his predecessor, Arthur Henderson (1947–51), and more persuasive in the various Defence Committees than Jim Thomas at the Admiralty. But his lack of depth in party politics was a handicap: inexperience in the House of Lords prevented him being a strong spokesman there, and he soon settled into an administrative rather than an innovatory role.[2] His personality proved his main strength, smoothing over disagreements and finding acceptable compromises, and he enjoyed popularity with both the R.A.F. and Ministry officials, many of whom thought it unjust when Anthony Eden dropped him in December 1955.

De L'Isle relied a great deal on his junior Minister, who, being the sole spokesman in the House of Commons, carried more weight than his counterparts in the other Service Departments. The first Parliamentary Under-Secretary was the sharp and extremely bright Nigel Birch, who had made his mark during 1945–51 as an acute critic of Labour on financial matters but who held the job for just four months until he left to become Parliamentary Secretary at the Ministry of Defence (and spokesman in the House of Commons) to coincide with the arrival of Lord Alexander of Tunis. George Ward, who like Birch had entered the House in 1945 and thus had no previous ministerial experience, succeeded him (until his promotion, he had chaired the Party's Civil Aviation Committee for over a year). Ward had served from 1932–7 and 1939–45 in the R.A.F., to which he was devoted, and quickly mastered his post, performed well in the House, and was considered one of the best junior Ministers in the Department in the post-war years.[3]

The Secretary of State, as President of the Air Council, was the titular head of the Air Ministry and answerable to Parliament. Responsibility for the administration of the R.A.F. was vested by statute in the Air Council, with a membership of nine, on whose authority all business was transacted. The body met once a week to consider internal matters affecting the Ministry, policy questions and the development of new weapons and armaments.

Apart from the Chiefs of Air Staff, Sir John Slessor (1950–2) and Sir

William Dickson (1953–6), there were several prominent Service members of the Air Council, Sir Ralph Cochrane (Vice C.A.S., 1950–2) in particular, who would have been Lord Tedder's choice to succeed him as C.A.S. in 1950.[4] But there was also strong backing for Slessor, who was appointed. The two men subsequently came to terms, with Cochrane becoming Slessor's number two.

Slessor, C.A.S. since Tedder's departure in 1950, had had a wide range of experience in the field and in Whitehall since joining the Service in 1915. In terms of intellect and inter-Service planning ability he was regarded as the outstanding Service Chief during 1950–2.[5] A rapid and voluble speaker, full of ideas, he tended to monopolise meetings: indeed some felt he upset the balance of the Chiefs of Staff by his domineering manner. According to Lord Cherwell he was:

> . . . Undoubtedly one of the ablest men I ever met in the Air Force . . . As Chairman of the Chiefs of Staff Committee he played a notable part in formulating and justifying many very important decisions, having a thorough grasp – and what is perhaps more important – sympathy with the problems and needs of the other services.[6]

He studied problems intellectually and produced lengthy but well-argued papers on a wide range of subjects, invariably written in his own hand. His major contribution as Chief of Air Staff was to press the case for deterrence, notably in the 1952 'Global Strategy Paper',[7] although he could be criticised for spending too much time on fighters and bombers, and paying too little attention to transport planes, which the Army wanted, and to helicopters, which he considered too vulnerable.[8]

He completed his appointment in December 1952, at the early age of fifty-five. He was asked by the Secretary of State to stay on for at least another year, but declined, partly at least because he did not greatly care for Churchill.[9] Dickson, another in the long line of distinguished Air Chiefs since Lord Portal during the war, succeeded him. A more modest man than Slessor, and with a less grandiose conception of Britain's role in the post-war world, he was regarded as a first-class administrator, if not such an original thinker. He went on to become Chairman of the Chiefs of Staff Committee, 1956–8, and the first holder of the new job of Chief of Defence Staff, 1958–9.

Sir James Barnes, the Permanent Under-Secretary, had succeeded Sir William Brown on the latter's death in February 1947. A man who had spent his entire career in the Air Ministry, he enjoyed equal popularity with the R.A.F. as did Sir George Turner with the Army. Barnes did not possess the commanding personality of Sir Arthur Street (Permanent Under-Secretary, 1939–45), one of the great civil servants of the day, or Brown's exceptionally wide experience of Whitehall, but he had served in the Air Ministry since 1919 and practised as well as preached the gospel of close co-operation with the R.A.F. at all levels. (Indeed, close contacts between officers and civil servants was far more in evidence at the Air Ministry than at the War Office or Admiralty.) In consequence he commanded the confidence of his Service colleagues and the support of his Civil Service juniors, and capably held his own with his counterparts, Turner, and Sir John Lang, as well as with the Treasury. The effects of years of hard work were, however, beginning to show and being sixty in 1951, he was one of the older Permanent Secretaries on his retirement in 1955.[10]

The Conservative Government perhaps surprisingly initiated virtually no important changes to policy at the Air Ministry. From 1945 until the Korean war, the R.A.F. had been in a condition of 'accelerated run-down'. The Air Ministry had issued specifications to the aircraft industry in January 1946 for the development of a jet bomber to be ready by 1957[11] (later changed to three types, the Valiant, Victor and Vulcan),[12] the priority at this time being the development of a jet fighter force. Not until the Korean war did the Attlee Government seriously commit itself to a nuclear bombing force, placing its first production order for a V-bomber, the Valiant, in early 1951. Britain's decision to develop three bombers, in contrast to the United States' decision to build a single one for the medium and heavy categories, was due to Slessor, who recalled the experience of the late 1930s when the R.A.F. were developing three bombers, the Manchester, Stirling and Halifax, and believed that had it been necessary to have made a choice between them, the wrong one might well have been chosen.[13] The Labour Government undertook a three-year build-up of the R.A.F., including expansion of personnel, construction of new airfields and facilities, and increased numbers of fighters and tactical bombers. Thus the Conservative Government's policy, giving priority to the R.A.F. rather than to the other two Services, and building up the nuclear bombing force, had already been laid down.

A shift in emphasis did, however, take place in 1952, when cut-backs in jet fighter production were announced, and priority given initially to Canberra tactical bombers and to Valiants, and in December to the long-range Victors and Vulcans. Birch told the House in March 1953:

. . . In the Vulcan, the Valiant and the Victor we have medium long-range bombers which we believe will be the best in the world. It is for that reason that we have decided to build up our light bomber forces to a lower peak than we had originally intended and to go into immediate production with the new long-range medium bombers. We shall not have a very large strategic Air Force, but it will be a highly effective one.[14]

Thus over the next two years the Canberra programme was steadily cut back in favour of the long-range bombers, with the Canberra squadrons gradually converted into heavier bombers. The decision to concentrate on deterrence (with bombers) rather than defence (through fighters) was to an extent based on the Defence Review undertaken at Churchill's instigation by the Chiefs of Staff in 1952,[15] where Slessor provided the major ideas on the likely shape of future conflicts and the attendant need to rely on deterrence.[16] One should not exaggerate, however, the extent to which after 1952 the R.A.F. ignored defence for the sake of concentrating on the policy of deterrence. For example, Ward in the defence debates in the House of Commons in March 1955 said:

> . . . I am quite confident that Fighter Command as it stands today provides an extremely efficient and powerful defence capable of dealing with any type of bomber which the Soviet Air Force now has in service, and when it is fully rearmed the Command will have day and night fighters well capable of destroying the new jet bombers which the Russians will then have in service.[17]

Close relations were maintained throughout with the United States Air Force (closer than between their respective Armies and Navies) who encouraged the R.A.F. to build up their own strategic nuclear bomber force. The Americans also depended on Britain for providing bases for her own bombers: indeed, this caused Churchill concern that in a war the Soviet Union might strike Britain first to eliminate the United States Air Force. After his trip to the United States in January 1952, Churchill was able to report back to the House on 26th February that he had obtained assurances that atomic bombers would not be used from East Anglia bases without Britain's consent.

In 1955 the first Valiant squadron (equipped to carry atomic bombs) came into service,[18] followed by the more sophisticated Vulcan squadrons in 1957 and Victors in 1958. The first generation of Victors was not, however, fully operational or equipped with hydrogen bombs until 1961, and by that year the United States was putting most of its strategic efforts into long-range missiles. Fighter Command meanwhile had lagged behind, hence a separate White Paper,[19] in addition to the

320

normal Defence White Paper, was published in February 1955. According to Harold Macmillan, by then Minister of Defence: 'On the bomber side we were in a good position: but the fighters were in a sad state of confusion. The simplest method appeared to be to come out with a frank statement of the facts . . .'[20]

The main decision announced in the White Paper was to abandon the Swift, found wanting in seven different models, and to concentrate on the Hunter. Decisions on the development of fighters, as of bombers, were guided by earlier experience. The experience of the Second World War had shown that great benefit had been derived from the development of two fighters, Hawker's Hurricane and Vickers' Spitfire. With the Korean scare in 1950, it was again decided to press ahead with two fighters, the Hawker Hurricane and the Vickers Swift, and that it would be unwise to put all available resources into just one model. But in the following years, as the danger of war decreased, the Government, after much deliberation, decided that one, the Swift, should be dropped, Despite the logic of the Government's case, the Public Accounts Committee was nevertheless highly critical of the decision to build two separate fighter models.[21] At the same time, it was announced that the planned 'Blue Sky', the first air-to-air missile, would go ahead.[22] To Coastal Command was added the 'Seamew' aircraft for inshore maritime reconnaissance work; in Ward's words, the 'Seamew' was required because of 'a gap in our maritime defences which no existing aircraft filled precisely'.[23]

An unfortunate (and possibly inevitable) consequence of the concentration on deterrence and nuclear weapons was that requirements for conventional war tended to be overlooked. This showed itself possibly most noticeably in the comparative neglect of Transport Command, seen only too obviously in the problems encountered moving troops during the Suez campaign in the autumn of 1956.

Part 5 The Ministry of Supply

The Ministry of Supply steadily decreased in importance during the early years after the war, although the nationalisation and denationalisation of iron and steel brought it into the limelight, and served temporarily to check this trend. In October 1945 Attlee had decided to merge the wartime Ministry of Aircraft Production with the Ministry of Supply, and to make the new Department the sponsor of the engineering and heavy metal industries, irrespective of whether these industries were engaged in civilian or military production.[1] In addition, arms development and responsibility for atomic energy were entrusted to the Ministry. Thus the Army and the R.A.F.[2] (but not the Admiralty) looked for the bulk of their supply needs to the Ministry. From 1951, however, the Ministry's functions began to be distributed to other Departments. A start was made when in July 1951 the Labour Government transferred most of the responsibilities for raw materials to the new Ministry of Materials.

The Ministry's decline accelerated after the Conservatives came to power. While in Opposition they had decided that the Ministry should not continue in its present form, and in the 1950 Election Manifesto even suggested it should be abolished and its functions redistributed amongst the Service Departments. The delay in implementing these changes suggests that, despite the Ministry's unpopularity in many quarters, and the strong case to be made for changes once rationing had disappeared, it performed its civil job sufficiently well for reorganisation not to be a priority. In the event, the Ministry's responsibilities for atomic energy passed to the Lord President in January 1954, who was given responsibility for the new Atomic Energy Authority.[3] Iron, steel, engineering and non-ferrous metal industries were transferred to the Board of Trade in July 1955. The Ministry thus became primarily a Department concerned with defence provisioning; apart from its responsibilities to the Service Departments from then till its eventual demise in 1959 it dealt in addition only with the aircraft, electronics and light metal industries.[4]

Churchill appointed Duncan Sandys Minister of Supply, a familiar Department to him and a field in which he had considerable experience. He had been Parliamentary Secretary at the Ministry of Supply, 1943–4, and Chairman of the War Cabinet Committee for defence against German flying bombs and rockets, 1943–5.[5] Nevertheless some felt that his marriage to Churchill's eldest daughter, Diana, meant that he owed his appointment to nepotism, a hypothesis he strongly denied. In fact Sandys had proved himself a capable Minister during the war, and as Minister of Works, 1944–5, might have expected high office in 1951. Furthermore, during the period of Opposition he had also been Chairman of the Party's Works Committee. Yet Sandys was not especially popular with the Conservative Party, and for the first few months had to battle in the House; after his first major speech, he said he felt that all Parties were against him.[6] But by the end of his three-year period at Supply few doubted his ability to administer a large Department or to carry legislation through the House. As a profile in the *Observer* on 30th October, 1954, recorded: 'He is now a politician in his own right and needs no Churchill to give him a helping hand.'

His officials found him unsympathetic; but Sandys, unfortunately, was a man who needed sympathy. He was far more popular with his junior Ministers and personal staff (including his official Private Secretaries), to whom he showed consideration and even kindliness, than with some senior officials. His experience as a Minister in the war had encouraged in him the erroneous belief that abrasiveness was necessary to achieve results. As a Minister he wanted to reach his goals and was prepared to irritate people and create a fuss to get his way. Like many of the incoming Ministers in 1951, he suspected officials,[7] especially those whom he considered had a lazy bureaucratic outlook. In part, this accounted for Sandys' unsatisfactory relationships with his two Permanent Secretaries, Sir Archibald Rowlands and, after his retirement in 1953, Sir James Helmore. Opinions vary about how poor Sandys' relationship was with the former, but there can be no doubt that their relations were far from cordial. Rowlands did not disguise the fact that he had not wanted to see Sandys as the Minister and his attitude remained distant, although he loyally supported Sandys on issues of major importance.

Sandys worked inordinately long hours and paid extreme attention to detail, which may also explain his difficult relations with his officials. His lack of consideration for his senior civil servants was epitomised by his tendency to ask to see them just as they were about to leave work. They would remain behind in the office, only to be informed later in the evening, without any explanation, that the Minister no longer required their presence. Since Sandys' work output bore more relation to his own formidable banks of energy than to any concept of 'the working day', he felt no compunction in asking officials to remain working with him until the late evening or early hours of the morning if he felt it necessary. Whereas Sandys could easily return to his Westminster home in Vincent Square after a late night in the office, it created considerable difficulties for his officials, many of whom lived in the Home Counties. He spent hours on minutiae, to everyone's irritation. For example, he once spent hours cross-examining officials because two reports of the monthly output of tanks varied by a very small figure, and he was convinced he had discovered a 'cover-up'. Nowhere was his meticulous word-by-word approach more fully displayed than in the preparation of the Iron and Steel Bill.[8] This careful preparatory work meant that Sandys always had a detailed knowledge of any issue before Cabinet, Defence Committee[9] or the House concerning the Ministry, which helped him gain support for his case. On only one occasion did he lose an argument in Cabinet, over the Vickers 1000 aircraft, which was eventually cancelled.[10] The Vickers 1000 was a long-range jet airliner which the Ministry were keen to see developed. B.O.A.C., however, preferred to concentrate resources on the development of a turbo-prop airliner, the Britannia. Some feel that this was a fatal error. It allowed the U.S. Boeing company to capture the market with their 707s, and by the time the British developed a long-range jet liner, the VC10, the market had been cornered by Boeing. Sandys' skill in Whitehall arguments earned him the respect, if not the affection, of his senior officials at the Ministry. One of them summed up the position to the author: 'Sandys was difficult, obstinate, distrusted by his officials, a bit of a bully, and put his officials to an enormously unnecessary amount of work – but he was also the most effective Minister you could possibly wish to have.'[11] His qualities, therefore, despite his faults, helped make him one of the most successful new Ministers in the Government.[12]

Sandys always favoured a *chef de cabinet* system, which he operated in embryo. After a few days he brought his constituency secretary, Freda Smith, into the office, whose field of activity extended far beyond mere constituency work. Initially her arrival created slight unease but she was swiftly accepted. Sandys also wanted to replace his Private Secretary, Henry Walker, who had worked with George Strauss (Minister of Supply, 1947–51), and whom he therefore considered unsuitable. Sandys, however, was persuaded to try Walker for a few weeks; he remained for nearly two years and an association of mutual trust developed between them. So good was their relationship that when a few months later Sandys announced he would like Colonel Kenneth Post as his own aide,[13] he accepted the Private Office's argument that this was unnecessary.

Toby Low, the Parliamentary Secretary, had shown his interest in defence by sitting on the Army subcommittee of the Conservative Defence Committee in Opposition. He was exceptionally well suited to Sandys, and, being liked and well regarded by the Ministry, was able to smooth the ground between them. Low left the Ministry three months before Sandys, being promoted in the July 1954 reshuffle to Minister of State at the Board of Trade. His replacement, Sir Edward Boyle, was Sandys' rather than the Whips' choice, having come to his notice in a Party Committee, discussing details of the Iron and Steel Bill.[14] Boyle had backed Sandys in the discussions and argued that foundries should come within the ambit of the Iron and Steel Board, whereas many other Conservative M.P.s' felt they should be left without supervision.[15] Sandys had to fight for him, as many, including Churchill, thought him, at thirty, too young, although he had previously been Parliamentary Private Secretary to Nigel Birch at the Air Ministry, 1951–2, and Ministry of Defence, 1952–3. Boyle's ability soon became obvious to all in the new Ministry, and within a year he had been snapped up by Butler as Economic Secretary at the Treasury.

When Sandys was appointed Minister of Housing in October 1954, the rising star of the day, Selwyn Lloyd, took his place. He had served as Minister of State at the Foreign Office since 1951 and he owed his appointment at Supply to Anthony Eden who wished to see the promotion of his ally, of whom he thought highly, in advance of his own arrival at Number Ten, thought to be imminent. Lloyd, who entered the House in 1945, had practical experience of the defence field from the war.[16] Initially the sheer size of the Ministry overwhelmed him, since he had no experience of managing such a large body. But he soon mastered the job and was found to be a highly competent administrator, which the Ministry felt was required at the time.[17] Yet he remained at Supply for less than six months, during which period his attention was concentrated on the future of the Swift and Hunter fighter aircraft.[18] He therefore had insufficient time to make much impact on other issues, before being promoted as Minister of Defence in April 1955. His place at Supply was taken by Reginald Maudling, who had not anticipated this particular appointment, having been tipped for a top economic job.[19]

Rowlands, one of the dominant Whitehall figures of the day, had been Permanent Secretary since 1946. He was a tough, hard-living and hard-working man with great intellectual ability and tremendous drive: indeed, it was his custom to work right through Saturday night into Sunday morning to keep on top of his work. Widely admired, he was to an extent held in awe by most in the Ministry.[20] He left the senior officials much freedom in their own, often highly specialised, areas; indeed, the sheer size of the Ministry allowed him little chance to do otherwise. On Friday afternoons he invited all the Deputy and Under-Secretaries into his room for a couple of hours to talk about problems generally.[21] Undoubtedly, however, by 1951 he was showing some signs of the years of overwork, and his performance did not match up to what it had once been. He retired in his own time in 1953,[22] and Helmore came in from the Ministry of Materials as the new Permanent Secretary.[23] He was earnest and highly able, though not universally popular in the Department. He soon quarrelled with Sandys, accusing him of tampering with the system, and only began to enjoy the work after Lloyd became Minister.[24] In Maudling's view Helmore was a very good Permanent Secretary for a Minister who knew his own mind. He was in fact a man of markedly different style to Rowlands. Helmore had two main themes during his period at the Ministry: the first was to shed to other Departments as much of the Ministry's work as possible, and he consequently played a major part in relieving the Ministry of responsibility for engineering, iron and steel and atomic energy.[25] Secondly, he determined to concentrate his attention on one side of the Ministry's work which particularly interested him, aircraft production. In order to do this, he initiated the creation of a new job, that of Deputy Permanent Secretary, whose responsibility was mainly internal affairs and management.[26] The job went to Sir Cyril Musgrave, who succeeded Helmore on his retirement in 1956.

Two main changes of policy at the Ministry of Supply followed the Conservatives' victory in 1951, the cutting back of the Attlee Government's rearmament programme,[27] and the denationalisation of iron and steel.[28] The latter occupied a large proportion of Sandys' time in his first two years, but he retained one other main interest within the Ministry, advocating the policy of 'deterrence' with nuclear weapons; the ideas he was later to expound so ably as Minister of Defence (1957–9) were refined during his years at Supply.[29] The crippling expense involved in maintaining the necessary range of up-to-date conventional weapons increasingly concerned him, and he came to believe that the future lay in nuclear weapons and their means of delivery.

Sandys was also deeply involved in a row that developed over the organisation of atomic energy.[30] Sandys, who wanted responsibility to remain with the Ministry of Supply, clashed with Lord Cherwell, who wanted to transfer it to a separate organisation.[31] Feeling in the Ministry ran high on this issue, partly because to lose it might have been construed as criticism of the Ministry's stewardship since 1945, but also because its loss would accelerate the break-up of their already declining empire; and atomic energy represented a particularly glamorous portion at that.[32] Cherwell battled so hard as he felt that everything in Government Departments was stifled by regulations. Sandys, for his part, came to the office in 1951 believing it a sensible move, as did the majority of his colleagues. But he changed his views, doubting whether defence interests would be best served by an independent body – doubts which incidentally many feel have since been endorsed by events – and querying whether a separate Atomic Energy Authority would be under sufficient control. He therefore came to feel that, in the public interest, atomic energy should remain within a Ministry large enough to have the necessary range of services to control it. On this basis there was no obvious home for it other than the Ministry of Supply.

In the Department most supported the Sandys' line, apart from Friston How, the Under-Secretary since 1945 in charge of atomic energy, who as a result virtually lost his channels of communication with Sandys. The Ministry at first tried to prevent How from appearing before the Waverley Committee (chaired by the former Sir John Anderson) which had been set up in April 1953 to consider the matter. This was perhaps not surprising, as neither Sandys nor Rowlands were anxious to entrust the official presentation of the Ministry's case to someone who made it clear that he did not share their views.[33] Churchill failed to understand why the issue was causing so much fuss. Although he had full confidence in his son-in-law, he never went out of his way to favour him.[34] Indeed he could be decidedly formal with Sandys when conducting departmental business. Sandys for his part always felt strongly that if he did not work hard, the accusation of favouritism which plagued his appointment would be resuscitated. Meanwhile the atomic energy issue rumbled on with the position changing after Rowlands' departure, as Helmore felt some sympathy towards the Cherwell case. When Sandys realised the issue was going against him, he fought a rearguard action for Supply to retain at least the military research station at Aldermaston, but was again defeated. Sir David Eccles introduced the Atomic Energy Bill into the House in February 1954[35] and the Atomic Energy Authority was established in July that year with responsibility to the Lord President, How being Secretary and Sir Edwin Plowden[36] the Chairman. The set-up as it emerged has since been criticised with some justification for being neither fully independent nor within the Whitehall net, under Parliamentary control.

The final transfer of functions of the engineering and heavy metals side to the Board of Trade soon after the General Election of 1955 also upset many officials in the Ministry, unhappy to see their Department become almost solely one of defence procurement. This reallocation came about as the result of a Report produced by a group of officials under Sir Thomas Padmore, in January 1954, and whose recommendations Cabinet Ministers substantially accepted.

Part 6   Assessment

Whitehall Organisation of Defence

The machinery for defence as it developed from 1946 under a co-ordinating Minister of Defence meant that by the time of the 1955 General Election Britain had a reasonably efficient fighting force at not excessive cost. But the organisation was still far from satisfactory. Looking back over twenty-five years, many of those who worked in Whitehall and the Services told the author that they were unhappy with the defence arrangements.[1] Some like Lord Mountbatten of Burma saw the idea of a co-ordinating Minister of Defence as inherently unsatisfactory, and believed that the position could only be resolved by amalgamation of the Service Departments into a unified Ministry of Defence, which he himself precipitated in 1964.[2] Others, such as Sir John Lang and Sir Ian Jacob, felt that the 1946 arrangement was a necessary stepping-stone to the unified Ministry. Still others thought that the Ministry of Defence managed reasonably well after 1946 although two important areas remained unsettled: whether Service Chiefs should have direct access to the P.M., and whether the Ministry's officials should, in the main, be recruited from the three Service Departments, which exposed them to the charge that they could never be fully impartial. Some even felt that the Treasury hampered the work of the Ministry by changing at frequent intervals its senior officials, which hindered the Ministry's ability to argue with the Treasury over finance. The distinguished scientist, R. V. Jones, who returned to Whitehall, September 1952–December 1953, as Director of Scientific Intelligence, later wrote that the Ministry had become an 'administrative jungle' compared with the streamlined Chiefs of Staff organisation during the war.[3] Sir Richard Clarke, a most cogent critic of the machinery of government, also thought the post-1946 arrangement an unsatisfactory compromise.[4]

Considerable flexibility in the defence world was displayed in the relative importance of various Whitehall jobs, Committees and even whole Departments. During Lord Alexander of Tunis' period as Minister of Defence (1952–4) the Service Departments retained a great deal of autonomy, far more than later under Duncan Sandys (1957–9), whose increased authority was due both to a strengthening of the power of the office and to his forceful personality.[5] Indeed, Sir Harold Parker, Permanent Secretary of Defence (1948–56), later said: 'There is no doubt that in, I would say, the ten years after the war, the way in which the Ministry of Defence functioned or didn't function depended to an enormous extent on the personality of the Minister.'

The office of Permanent Secretary in fact carried far less weight under Parker than under his successor, Sir Richard Powell (1956–9). Another key job, Chief Staff Officer, was much more influential under Jacob (1952) than under the versatile but less acute Sir Nevil Brownjohn (1952–5). In the Alexander of Tunis/Parker regime the Ministry carried weight on matters such as Service pay, standardisation of equipment and co-ordination of expenditure requirements. But on the broader strategy and the question of size and shape, the views of the Ministry of Defence came second to the desires of the Service Chiefs and the Service Ministers.

The post-1946 system had the basic flaw that the Minister of Defence, until his hand was progressively strengthened, had to depend entirely on asserting his own personality over fellow Ministers, and further that, given the fluid position resulting from imprecise allocation of responsibility, decisions were of necessity compromises. This did not always lead to decisions which were in the overall national interest.[6] It was also a problem that a small Ministry of Defence, as envisaged by the architects of the 1946 White Paper, had not actually been maintained. The Ministry had grown for a number of reasons: in particular its work on NATO infrastructure and other related international organisations. In practice, it tended to become the dumping ground for problems that could not be tackled elsewhere as well as for those that needed an immediate response.[7] Gradually, over the years following 1946 as the Ministers of Defence desired more effective control of the defence budget, they became increasingly concerned with the framing of military appreciations and plans, and the control of the research and development programme, which came to form an ever-expanding part of Britain's comprehensive defence policy.[8] One can conclude by saying that the 'co-ordinating' Minister of Defence, a position which had worked relatively well in wartime when there was agreement on common ends, did not adapt himself well to the conditions of peace and retrenchment.

Dissatisfaction had been expressed by top serving officers in Whitehall ever since the defence apparatus was introduced in 1946. In 1948 Lord Montgomery of Alamein, then Chief of the Imperial General Staff, told Jacob he was in favour of the latter's proposal for the amalgamation of the Service Departments, but Lord Tedder, the Chief of Air Staff, was opposed.[9] Sir John Slessor, who succeeded Tedder in 1950, was an enthusiast of rationalisation, and made an unsuccessful overture to Lord Fraser of North Cape, then First Sea Lord, to suggest moves took place towards the ultimate merger of the R.A.F. and Navy because the strategic role of both in war seemed increasingly similar.[10] Eventually it was decided to appoint a formal Chairman of the Chiefs of Staff (meetings formerly had been chaired on an *ad hoc* basis by the Chief who was longest serving) as a minor step in the direction of more Service co-ordination: Selwyn Lloyd, then Minister of Defence, wrote to Lord Ismay that he was confident the arrangement would work well with the much respected Sir William Dickson as the first Chairman. But a more difficult matter, he continued, was the relationship of the Minister of Defence with the three Service Ministers, where he admitted that there was growing pressure for a change. Lloyd said he was anxious to avoid the issue, at least until Dickson had had a chance of settling in.[11]

The Minister of Defence's position was strengthened decisively after the White Paper of 1958 when the effective power of policy decision shifted to him, working closely with the Permanent Secretary, Chief Scientific Adviser and the newly created Chief of Defence Staff.[12] This did, however, produce a number of new and awkward problems, principally that the Defence Committee now ceased to function in the way envisaged by the architects of the 1946 White Paper. Sir Norman Brook later told Jacob that a number of factors were to blame: Harold Macmillan as Prime Minister disliked working through committees, and the Defence Committee in particular, preferring to deal direct with the individuals concerned, and further, senior Ministers were just too busy to attend the Defence Committee regularly.[13]

Nuclear and Conventional Policy

The military authorities were slow in the immediate post-war years to appreciate the changes in Britain's position brought about by the Cold War and nuclear weapons, and the need to develop an appropriate defence policy.[14] The decision had been taken by the Defence Committee in January 1947 to build a British atomic bomb,[15] although this fact was not publicly recognised until Churchill's announcement in February 1952 that: 'I was not aware until I took office that not only had the Socialist Government made the atomic bomb as a matter of research, but that they had created at the expense of many scores of millions of pounds the important plant necessary for its regular production.'[16] Churchill further announced that the weapon would be tested later in the year.[17] This major event in Britain's history occurred on 3rd October, 1952, with remarkably little public interest. The bomb was exploded on board a ship off the Monte Bello Islands (near Australia) under the direction of William Penney.[18] Exchange of information with the United States had almost completely ceased by 1952, and consequently no U.S. observer was in attendance.[19] Indeed, one of Churchill's main aims on his return to power in 1951 was to see nuclear collaboration with the U.S. returned to its pre-1945 level. He believed that the Monte Bello test would inaugurate a much closer relationship on exchange of information,[20] and soon after Eisenhower's arrival at the White House in January 1953 Churchill began pressing him in this direction. Churchill discussed it with Eisenhower at the Bermuda Conference in December 1953.[21] Eisenhower agreed to ask Congress to permit a greater sharing of legislation, and the U.S. Atomic Energy Act of 1954 permitted limited liberalisation in this direction – primarily motivated, it would appear, by a desire to facilitate the training of allies with tactical nuclear weapons to compensate for manpower deficiencies in Europe.[22] Churchill meanwhile allowed his annoyance at what he considered Labour's error in allowing nuclear co-operation to lapse after the war to get the better of him, as seen in the hot-tempered hydrogen bomb debate in the House of Commons in April 1954,[23] in which he riled the Opposition by saying that 'the abandonment of our claim to be consulted and informed as an equal was the act of the Socialist Administration.'[24]

Little consideration, however, had been given by the British to the circumstances in which the bomb might be used.[25] This sense of drift in thinking on strategic matters was paralleled by a lack of clarity of thought on the deployment and shape of conventional forces. The outbreak of the Korean war in 1950 found British forces widely dispersed and lacking in preparedness. The rapid build-up of defence instigated by the Labour Government entailed a doubling of defence expenditure, which the Conservatives in 1951 found hard to maintain. The strain this placed on the economy coupled with the growing feeling in defence circles, emanating from the Chief of Air Staff, Slessor, that the time was ripe for a reconsideration of defence strategy, was responsible in early 1952 for setting in motion what became the first major post-war Defence Review. The Chiefs had conducted a less important Review the previous year at Bracknell, also at the initiative of Slessor, who later said:

> I was rather astonished when I became Chief of Air Staff [in 1950] to find there had been no general Review [since the war]. There was an awful tendency then if any problem came up for the Chiefs of Staff to say 'refer this to the Joint Planning Committee for examination and report'. I said, 'This is not a thing which we should shelve off, this is a thing we ought to do ourselves . . . we must go away from Whitehall and get together with no other thoughts, and tell our deputies to deal with anything that comes along.'[26]

Churchill, who was intensely concerned by the impact of atomic and then thermonuclear weapons on foreign relations and defence policy, had independently come to the conclusion that the time was ripe for a fresh assessment of defence priorities, and can be regarded as an initiator of the 1952 Review.[27]

The three Chiefs set to work on the paper in the spring, travelling to the Royal Naval College at Greenwich to produce the final text, which was considerably improved by Sir Ian Jacob,[28] and the Report was endorsed by Churchill and the Cabinet in July 1952. The basic theme of the paper was that increased effort would be needed to win the Cold War, that success would be achieved by a policy of deterrence, and that

Britain should therefore concentrate on complementing American nuclear strength. The paper also advocated a decrease in the number of overseas commitments and a reduction in troops devoted to conventional warfare. Important though the paper was, there has been a tendency for defence commentators, relying on the opinions of those who had left Whitehall by the end of 1952, to over-play its significance.[29] The 1952 paper was itself an expansion of the views expressed by the minor Defence Review conducted by the Service Chiefs in 1951. A long series of talks in Whitehall took place throughout the remainder of 1952 and 1953 on the defence strategy, during which some of the more radical conclusions of the 1952 paper were toned down. A feature of the discussions of the Chiefs of Staff during these years was their willingness to accept, albeit on occasions reluctantly, the need for economies in defence expenditure. Defence after the war had become more expensive. In the mid-1930s there were 350,000 men in the armed forces; in 1952 there were 850,000 (due to rise to 900,000) of whom 300,000 were serving overseas. In the years immediately preceding the war, defence accounted for 5% of the national product: in 1952 it had risen to 10%.

After the Election of 1951 it was widely accepted, both in Whitehall and by informed opinion outside, that the strain imposed by the three-year defence programme announced by Labour in September 1950 could not be borne. This factor, coupled with the decrease in international tension, was responsible for the 1952 White Paper declaring: 'It was made clear at the outset that such a programme could be achieved in three years only if the labour, raw materials, machine tools and other manufacturing capacity were available as and where they were needed. It is now clear that these conditions cannot be fully satisfied.'[30]

Pressure was applied on NATO member countries[31] to reduce the unrealistically high targets set for armed forces agreed at the Lisbon Conference in February 1952, and in December the NATO Council approved major reductions.

The 1953 Defence White Paper revealed some limited new thinking on strategic questions. Although there was to be no overall increase in expenditure in real terms,[32] the R.A.F. was to receive more money, the Navy less. The prevailing tenor was that preparations should be made for global war, but its likelihood was now thought less immediate, hence the concept of a 'prolonged pull': it talked of the need to build up a deterrent and the ensuing need to strengthen forces for global war should the deterrent fail. Overall it was surprising that its tone should have been so conventional in outlook, and that it did not bear more trace of the innovative thinking of the Chiefs of Staff during 1951 and 1952. It is ironical that it was only after Slessor's departure from active service in

December 1952 that his thoughts were crystallised into policy statements, the more so as none of the three Chiefs of Staff who served during 1953–4 possessed creative minds of Slessor's calibre.

By the time of the 1954 Defence White Paper, the arguments of the 1952 Defence Review had begun to filter through to a much greater extent into policy statements.[33] This White Paper was a watershed, not for its comments on conventional weapons, where the trend towards favouring the R.A.F. at the expense of the Navy and Army was continued, but for its remarks on defence strategy, because of the stress given to the importance of nuclear weapons. In plain terms it stated that '. . . The primary deterrent . . . remains the atomic bomb and the ability of the highly organised and trained United States strategic air power to use it.'[34] The White Paper further declared the need for more haste in equipping the R.A.F. with a force of modern bombers capable of using atomic bombs to full effect.[35]

The intention to build up an independent nuclear force, hinted at previously, was confirmed by the major White Paper in 1955, 'a milestone in our history' as a leader in the *Sunday Times* on 20th February, 1955 described it. The decision to construct a British hydrogen bomb had been taken the previous year with minimal dissent from officials or Ministers, although Harry Crookshank records their discussions were 'stormy'.[36] The first United States hydrogen bomb test had been conducted at Eniwetok Atoll in 1952 (the Soviet Union following with their own in 1953), and although Churchill knew about the American bomb from at least August 1953,[37] information about it was not generally made known until six months later.[38] Having decided to rely on a deterrence strategy and to build up the V-bomber force, the hydrogen bomb was seen as the inevitable step forward. The White Paper declared that maximum effort should be put into the development of nuclear weapons and the means of delivery, and that in the allocation of resources 'even higher priority' should be given to 'the primary deterrent'.[39] The justifications for an independent British force were aired in the debate on the White Paper. Macmillan, then Minister of Defence, attacked the view that an independent nuclear role was not necessary for Britain, calling it: '. . . A very dangerous doctrine . . . Politically it surrenders our power to influence American policy and then, strategically and tactically, it equally deprives us of any influence over the selection of targets and the use of our vital striking forces.'[40]

Churchill's powerful and deep thinking on the impact of these new weapons of mass destruction was of key importance in stimulating discussion. His highly praised speech in the defence debate of March 1955 was one of his last major contributions before retirement. He told

Lord Moran that he had taken twenty hours preparing the speech and a further eight checking the facts.[41] A significant slice of his time in his crucial last weeks in office had been spent working on the speech, which was an expansion of the views he had expressed at the Commonwealth Prime Ministers' Conference in February 1955.[42] The result was a highly articulate and beautifully expressed statement of the need to rely on a policy of deterrence; indeed, he believed that the avoidance of a third world war after 1945 was due solely to the deterrent nature of nuclear weapons. But it is of note that Ministers as a whole did not play a significant role in the evolution of this strategy. Some like Sandys and Antony Head made important contributions, but they were in the minority. Lord Swinton too had been very anxious for Britain to have its own nuclear deterrent. Neither in the main did civilian officials in the Service Ministries, with the notable exception of Powell at the Ministry of Defence. The important work and thought was put in by senior officers of the Services, principally Slessor, and also Jacob, and the supporting scientists.

Developments in conventional forces, although given a lower priority in some Departments like the Air Ministry, were not of course ignored. Tactical weapons, fitted with atomic warheads, bridged the gap between nuclear and conventional weapons, and began to be supplied to NATO by the United States from 1954.[43] Public discussion about the role of conventional forces, and in particular that of the Navy, was on the increase after 1951. Of the three Services, the role for a large Navy in the age of nuclear warfare was the most in question. The R.A.F., as the bomb carrier, was assured of a role, the Army was rather more vulnerable, although few disputed the likelihood that situations would continue to arise where conventional land forces were required. The Army would thus be needed not just to man the new tactical weapons, and to act as a defensive bulwark in Western Europe, but also to defend Britain's position overseas, as in the emergencies in Kenya and Malaya.

The period under study was one where the notion of 'broken-backed' warfare was in vogue, as seen in this passage in the 1954 Defence White Paper:

> It seems likely that a [global war] would begin with a period of intense atomic attacks lasting a relatively short time but inflicting great destruction and damage. If no decisive result were reached in this opening phase, hostilities would decline in intensity, though perhaps less so at sea than elsewhere, and a period of 'broken-backed' warfare would follow, during which the opposing sides would seek to recover their strength, carrying on in the meantime as best they might.

This concept had originated from the deliberations of the Chiefs of Staff in the early 1950s. Slessor despite some exaggeration was being substantially accurate when he said in an interview: 'It was essential that we had all three Chiefs of Staff behind us and the broken-backed war thing I never believed in, and neither did Bill Slim. But we had to put it in for the sake of little Rhoddy McGrigor because otherwise if there was no broken-backed war then there was no case for keeping a large Navy.'

Atomic weapons had made little initial difference to the scale of conventional forces required for NATO, but the arrival of the hydrogen bomb precipitated further discussion. The 1955 White Paper did not mention 'broken-backed' warfare, and by the end of 1955 the concept had yielded to the plan for a 'firm shield' of troops and tactical aircraft in Western Europe.

The relative importance of the three Services, in particular the gradually increasing priority given to the R.A.F., can be readily seen in the figures for size of troops and expenditure. From 1951–5 the strength of the Army fell by 2%, the Navy by 12%, but the R.A.F.'s increased by 2%. The figures below are in thousands:[44]

	1951	1952	1953	1954	1955
Royal Navy	136	141	138	128	122
Army	427	445	435	437	416
Royal Air Force	241	262	268	252	246

The expenditure totals provide an even clearer picture of the rising importance of the R.A.F. with production and research expenditure taking a rapidly increasing slice of the total defence budget.[45] The Army throughout 1951–5 was the biggest spender of the three Services, although it was also the Service to have its spending cut back most drastically from a high point in 1952–3. Expenditure is in millions of pounds.[46]

	1950/1	1951/2	1952/3	1953/4	1954/5	1955/6
Army	309.0	422.3	525.0	487.8	477.0	462.9
Navy	190.0	271.3	333.4	324.1	345.8	337.7
Air Force	225.1	322.3	421.3	416.4	463.6	431.1
Ministry of Defence	4.0	11.3	12.2	17.1	16.5	15.3
Ministry of Supply	49.3	83.0	111.8	119.1	133.0	157.9
Defence-Total	777.4	1,110.2	1,403.7	1,364.5	1,435.9	1,404.9

These figures should be viewed alongside the increase of a quarter from 1950 to 1955 in the percentage of public expenditure devoted to military defence.[47]

Chapter 9   Commonwealth and Colonial Policy

Part 1   The Commonwealth Relations Office

The Conservatives' policy in few other Departments was watched as closely as in the Commonwealth Relations Office. How would their policy differ from Labour's on pressing questions like the enlargement of the Commonwealth as Colonies progressed towards independence, the move away from recognition of the British Crown amongst the new Commonwealth, the future of empire trade? Would the Conservatives under Churchill try to re-establish the Commonwealth as a vital political and economic force with Britain as its undisputed head? In the event, however, Conservative policy was to differ little from Labour's during 1945–51 – despite at least one of their Commonwealth Secretaries, Lord Salisbury, having markedly old-fashioned views.

The Department, formed out of the Dominions Office and the India Office, had only existed in its present form since 1947.[1] Winston Churchill regarded the post of Secretary of State at the Commonwealth Relations Office (C.R.O.) almost as a sinecure, certainly not a full-time job. He appointed the non-political Lord Ismay, his old colleague and friend, because he wanted someone in Cabinet whom he trusted and who would help him with defence matters, having appointed himself Minister of Defence again in October 1951. Ismay, who from 1940 to 1946 had been Chief of Staff to the Minister of Defence (Churchill throughout the War coalition), had since collaborated closely with Churchill in the writing of his history of the war. Not only was Ismay well known to the Prime Ministers of Australia, Canada and New Zealand, but he also knew India and the various Indian Leaders, having served as Chief of Staff to Mountbatten as Viceroy of India from March to November 1947. Indeed, 'Pendennis' in the *Observer* on 28th October wrote that Ismay's appointment, announced the same day, had 'one enormous merit': 'No other Conservative would be so trusted in India.'

Yet, despite his qualifications for this important job, to the surprise of senior officials in the Office, Churchill within a few days gave Ismay NATO work, and asked him to attend the Lisbon NATO Conference in February 1952 as acting Minister of Defence.[2] Churchill further invited him to the Truman–Acheson talks in the United States in January 1952 to assist on the defence side, and frequently summoned him to Number Ten for 'after hours' consultations. *The Times* even went so far as to enquire whether Ismay could be spared sufficiently from defence matters to make good his appointment as Commonwealth Secretary.[3] For a few months his wartime relationship with Churchill appeared to have re-established itself.

Ismay later admitted to having felt some shock when he heard of his appointment. In his memoirs he describes how he was awakened in the night of 26th October and summoned to Number Ten to be offered the job: 'I thought that the cold tap had failed to do its work and that I was still dreaming . . .'[4] He was not alone in his surprise. Should, it was widely asked, a General with administrative experience[5] but no professed interest in politics be appointed to a top Cabinet job? The C.R.O. itself was initially apprehensive that Ismay might only be Chief of Staff to Churchill, who would effectively be in charge of the Office, but these fears proved groundless.[6]

Ismay's biographer states that his staff were uncomfortable having a Minister with a mind of his own who wrote his own speeches,[7] but this exaggerates Ismay's contribution. Although well liked and a man of great charm and warmth, he was not suited to the position of Minister, making little impact either in Cabinet[8] or on the work of the C.R.O.,[9] due to his absences on defence matters and the brevity of his appointment, which lasted only four and a half months. Churchill had led him to expect a minimal work-load, therefore he was somewhat daunted when he realised that the Office required a good deal more.[10] His House of Lords' responsibilities he enjoyed least of all, especially when required to make speeches, which he found difficult. His opinions, however, carried great weight in the Upper House on account of his relationship with Churchill. Ismay's strength clearly lay not in his oratory, or intellect, but in his common sense, and, above all, his good manner with people. Contacts with High Commissioners and Commonwealth leaders he managed well, and he would have excelled at Commonwealth conferences, but unfortunately none took place during his period as Secretary of State.

His undoubted qualities were better suited to his subsequent post as Secretary-General of NATO, to which he moved in March 1952. At the Lisbon Conference the previous month the member countries decided to appoint a full-time Secretariat and to create a new post of Secretary-General. The delegates wanted a British appointee, their first choice being Sir Oliver Franks, the widely respected Ambassador to the United States, but he declined, and after some frantic international negotiations, Ismay was eventually selected.[11] Churchill didn't want him to go, and it was only after heated discussions that Anthony Eden persuaded a reluctant Prime Minister to part with his former aide.

Churchill therefore had to find a replacement at short notice. Lord Salisbury, the Lord Privy Seal, of whom Churchill was fond, was the obvious choice. He had much experience of the Commonwealth,[12] and was known to all senior members of the former Dominions Office, including Sir Percivale Liesching and Sir Stephen Holmes. His appointment, however, was not a success. The overburdened Salisbury found he had too many responsibilities: he was Leader of the House of Lords, his main preoccupation, and an active member of the Cabinet. He also had to manage his estates, a task he took seriously, and which demanded much of his time.[13] He delegated a large amount of work, but, with all the demands on his time, often fell behind, returning to the Office with red boxes he had not been able to deal with overnight. In common with many Ministers, he found this particular aspect of ministerial life irksome. After a few months the strain began to tell, especially since his health was poor, and he told Churchill he could not cope with the job. Churchill considered him to be of more value as Leader of the Lords, and so appointed him to the less onerous post, departmentally speaking, of Lord President of the Council.[14]

Salisbury had enjoyed the work, and in his short stay was especially keen on encouraging the formation of the Central African Federation. He believed implicitly in the Commonwealth, but saw more clearly than most that its expansion would weaken the ties holding it together. He envisaged it containing only the white Dominions or those – unlike India – who were prepared to recognise the Queen as their Sovereign. An agreeable Minister to work for, he was much liked in the Office, although – as a Marquess and the senior member of one of the most distinguished families in British politics – held somewhat in awe. His aristocratic background inclined him towards being somewhat distant and impersonal with officials, but his invariable courtesy and charm more than compensated. His personal affection for Eden made the C.R.O.'s relations with the Foreign Office easier than they had been under Ismay, or than they were to become under Lord Swinton, Salisbury's successor.

Salisbury and Swinton could hardly have been more different. Swinton, although a kinder man than he had once been, showed considerably less sensitivity to his officials' feelings.[15] He was always on top of his work, but his relations with the Foreign Office deteriorated, partly due to mutual antipathy for Eden. Swinton had quite possibly been Churchill's choice for Colonial Secretary in preference to Oliver Lyttelton,[16] since he had already worked there as Secretary of State in the National Government of 1931–5. But his appointment as Commonwealth Secretary in November 1952, with a seat in the Cabinet, delighted him.

Swinton quickly proved his ability in the job. He worked immensely hard and was devoted to the Commonwealth, especially the older Dominions. Southern Africa in particular interested him deeply. Not negligent of the new Commonwealth, however, he did much to promote trade with India, despite his personal lack of sympathy for Nehru (Prime Minister and Minister for External Affairs, 1947–64). Firmness was an important quality to Swinton, and one that he displayed at every opportunity.[17] But some members of staff, and even High Commissioners, regarded this as intransigent and offensive.[18]

Being a strong believer in the value of personal contacts with Prime Ministers and leading figures in the Commonwealth, he relished the opportunity to travel. His major trip to the Commonwealth took place in the autumn of 1953.[19] In small part its purpose was to placate the ruffled feelings of Robert Menzies (Prime Minister, 1949–66) due to Churchill's attitude of hostility to the A.N.Z.U.S. Pact[20] and to his delaying Sir William Slim's departure to Australia to become Governor-General in early 1953.[21] Principally, however, a tour by the Secretary of State was long due, since neither Ismay nor Salisbury had travelled abroad on Commonwealth business. Of little diplomatic import,[22] the trip nevertheless was considered a valuable exercise in public relations. Swinton was a tremendous admirer of the Prime Minister, and on the tour it was noted that he had a habit of 'apeing' a Churchillian manner in speeches.

Like Salisbury, Swinton, too, had time-consuming demands outside the Office. His other main concern was the House of Lords, where, due to Salisbury's various bouts of ill health, he acted as effective Leader.[23] This meant that he not only arranged general business in the Lords and liaised with the Commons, but much of the burden of speaking in key debates also fell to him.[24]

Although sixty-eight on his appointment, Swinton's performance did not slacken over his two and a half years at the Office.[25] Eden's decision not to ask him to serve in his Government in the April 1955 reshuffle distressed him, although, given their mutual dislike he could hardly have been surprised. There was clearly no love lost: Swinton later described Eden as having become 'addicted to clichés, ambiguities and homilies' and how 'latterly behind the front of the professional diplomat he began to show too many signs of irritability, often of bad temper'.[26] His successor – and surprised to be given the job – was Lord Home,[27] whom Eden had previously, and unsuccessfully, tried to persuade to join the Foreign Office.[28] Selwyn Lloyd, also in the running for this job, was instead appointed Minister of Defence.

Swinton had performed well, although without providing new diplomatic or constitutional initiatives, and neither did he consider deeply how colonies' independence would affect the Commonwealth. He was at his best in organisational and trade matters, where he was able to capitalise on his previous ministerial experience.[29] Many officials regarded him as an outstanding Secretary of State,[30] and were sorry to see him go.

Only one Parliamentary Under-Secretary was attached to the Office. Since many young men in the Party had made the Commonwealth their specialist interest, the appointment of John Foster, a Fellow of All Souls and one of the ablest lawyers in the party, came as a surprise. He had first entered the House of Commons in 1945 and had proved himself a vigorous critic of the Labour Government from 1945 to 1951, distinguishing himself in particular in the prolonged proceedings of the Standing Committee on the Gas Bill. His intellectual abilities were not, however, vital equipment for the C.R.O., and his relations with both Salisbury and Swinton were never particularly happy. He had little involvement in the work of the Office, and spent most of his time in the House of Commons, where he was sole departmental spokesman.[31] A fair speaker, he also drafted much of the Rhodesia and Nyasaland Federation Bill in 1953. The post proved to be Foster's only ministerial experience; no position could be found where his specialist knowledge of constitutional and international law could be put to better use.[32] Douglas Dodds-Parker, a former official in the Sudan Political Service (1930–8),[33] replaced him in the October 1954 reshuffle, but like Foster he was not ideally suited to the ministerial requirements.

From the formation of the single Department in 1947 there had been two Permanent Under-Secretaries, Sir Eric Machtig (division A) and Sir Archibald Carter (division B), these divisions corresponding to the former Dominions Office and the former India Office respectively. An inevitable consequence was that the Department tended to be disunited and it was felt that a single official head should be appointed. When Carter and Machtig retired at the end of 1948, Liesching was considered the natural successor and took up the post on 1st January, 1949.[34]

Liesching possessed impeccable qualifications, having served in the High Commissions in Canada, South Africa and Australia before the war. Since 1946 he had gained further administrative experience as Permanent Secretary of the Ministry of Food.[35] A formidable character and first-class administrator, he successfully repaired the damage caused by the jealousies between the two divisions. As Permanent Under-

Secretary he was mainly concerned to build up an efficient machine, but to a lesser extent was anxious to resist Foreign Office encroachments, having a chip on his shoulder about that Department, and even appeared to go out of his way to recruit non-Foreign Office 'types'. Although Liesching did not work well with Philip Noel-Baker, Secretary of State, October 1947–February 1950, he enjoyed good relations with his four successors, Patrick Gordon Walker, 1950–1, then Ismay, Salisbury and Swinton. With junior Ministers he could be impatient and brusque, and amongst the officials inspired fear rather than affection. Yet a weaker man might have been unable to maintain the smooth running of the C.R.O. through four changes of Secretaries of State within as many years. His main achievement lay in his reorganisation of the Office, so successful that no further changes were necessary until its eventual merger with the Foreign Office in 1968.[36]

At the age of sixty, Liesching was appointed High Commissioner in South Africa, and Sir Gilbert Laithwaite, on the recommendation of Swinton, succeeded him in February 1955. Laithwaite had an India Office background, and since 1948 had served first in Ireland[37] and then as High Commissioner in Pakistan (1951–4), therefore he possessed a better first-hand knowledge of the Indian sub-continent than his predecessor.[38] Although he worked closely with Swinton, their time together was to last only two months.

Liesching believed in delegating work, having decisions taken at the appropriate level, and was one of the comparatively few administrators who practised this consistently. Beneath him there was a single Deputy Under-Secretary, whom Liesching considered as his troubleshooter and Chief of Staff.[39] Liesching laid great stress on putting the most suitable men in key posts.[40] Everything passed through the deputy, but more junior officials frequently reported direct to Liesching. Holmes held the job from August 1951 to August 1952. Like Liesching, he had a Dominions Office background, having served a short spell at the Board of Trade (1946–51). Traditional in his outlook, he was a thorough rather than an outstanding administrator. Sir Alexander Symon, a former India Office official promoted from Assistant Under-Secretary to acting Deputy Under-Secretary, succeeded him for eight months. An industrious and capable worker, he did not, however, inspire the necessary confidence in his staff. In April 1953 Sir Saville Garner returned from India, where he had been Deputy High Commissioner, to take over the post that Symon had held pending his return.[41] Promoted to Deputy Under-Secretary when only forty-five, he soon proved himself to be a far abler deputy than his predecessors, and Liesching found it a relief to have a man of Garner's calibre.[42]

During these years the merger of the Commonwealth Office and the Colonial Office was first mooted,[43] although it was not until 1966 that this took place. At the ministerial level, Swinton worked closely with Oliver Lyttelton (Colonial Secretary, 1951–4), and official relations were, in the main, cordial, although Garner later wrote that both offices were drifting apart during this period: 'In particular in dealing with the new Asian countries, the C.R.O. did not wish to be tarred with the colonial brush.'[44] Legal aspects spanned both offices, headed by the Legal Adviser, Sir Kenneth Roberts-Wray.[45] He devoted the bulk of his energies to Colonial Office work,[46] where he had a staff of nine,[47] rather than to the C.R.O. where his staff numbered two.[48] Neither Lyttelton nor Swinton had a great deal of time for lawyers and legal advice: other Ministers such as Alan Lennox-Boyd, who succeeded Lyttelton at the Colonial Office, were far more amenable to advice and the legal advisers enjoyed working for them.[49]

Two Commonwealth Prime Ministers' meetings and four main economic conferences, an unusually large number, took place during 1951–5.[50] These seldom reached precise conclusions, but, nevertheless, facilitated the smooth management of the Commonwealth, offering an invaluable forum for its leaders to discuss, informally, a wide range of subjects, and to meet and understand each other better.[51] Communiqués were usually issued at their conclusion, but were of little consequence, reinforcing diplomats' scepticism of their value.

The Commonwealth Economic Conference, the most important of the four economic conferences, to review broad policy and discuss economic development and commodity policy, was held in London between 27th November and 11th December, 1952.[52] Prime Ministers of all member countries attended, except India and South Africa, who sent their Finance Ministers.

These were the years when Prime Ministers' conferences still took place in the smallish Cabinet room in Number Ten, a far cry from the large bustling meetings held in Marlborough House of only fifteen years later. The Prime Ministers' Conference of 3rd–9th June, 1953, consisted of mainly informal talks which coincided with the Coronation. According to witnesses, high spirits pervaded the discussions and no firm decisions were taken. The final communiqué discussed the need for peace and security in the Near and Far East, and expressed hopes for the early establishment of the European Defence Community. Two further economic conferences were held, both in 1954, at Sydney in January[53] and at Washington in September, where the Commonwealth Finance Ministers were assembled for a meeting of the International Monetary Fund. At the final Commonwealth Ministers' Conference of the

Churchill Government – held in London between 31st January and 8th February, 1955 – defence topics, in particular nuclear weapons, dominated the discussions. Churchill discoursed on the strategic import-ance of the latest form of atomic bombs, and Britain's decision to manufacture the hydrogen bomb was first announced.[54] The Govern-ment felt it essential that Britain should share her knowledge and convince the Commonwealth that Britain was correct to develop nuclear weapons.[55]

As Chairman, Churchill put up a good performance, although he also found the Conference a severe strain on his limited reserves of energy.[56] Indeed, Nehru wrote to his daughter Indira Gandhi that during the 1955 Commonwealth Conference Churchill appeared to be in 'a kind of second childhood'.[57] Another witness, Harold Macmillan, felt that Churchill put up 'a wonderful performance for his age',[58] a somewhat ambiguous compliment. Lester Pearson, the Canadian Foreign Sec-retary (1948–57), on the other hand had unreserved praise. Churchill displayed 'sweeping imagination and range of mind' in his discourse on the impact of the hydrogen bomb.[59] But in the day-to-day affairs of the C.R.O. Churchill had little to contribute, much less than, for example, Attlee.[60]

Member countries, to varying degrees, regarded membership of the Commonwealth as a benefit, and did not grumble about the prospect of increasing membership from the third world colonies. Indeed, Lester Pearson later remarked that once the decision had been taken to admit the first country, India, as a republic, thus breaking an institutional bond within the Commonwealth, self-interest would increasingly be the only bond holding the new Commonwealth together.[61] No former colony was in fact to join the Commonwealth between Ceylon in 1948, and Ghana, the former Gold Coast, in 1957. (Burma, which was also granted inde-pendence in 1948, chose to become a republic outside the Common-wealth.) However, Dean Acheson (U.S. Secretary of State, 1949–52) told Ismay during the January 1952 talks in Washington that some Commonwealth countries resented having to deal with the United States through London. Acheson also complained that the content of confidential Anglo-American talks had been passed on to Common-wealth members. Ismay appeared 'utterly dumbfounded' by Acheson's remarks.[62]

Canada, the senior Commonwealth country, approved of the new enlarged Commonwealth, although expressed some reservations about the process of decolonisation. She was indeed perhaps the least pleased of all the old Commonwealth countries at the Conservative victory in the 1951 General Election. More than most, Canada regarded the Commonwealth as a complete entity of international importance, not merely as a vehicle for good relations with Britain. Lester Pearson was especially keen on fostering the Commonwealth bond, supported by Louis St. Laurent (Prime Minister, 1948–57).[63]

The possibility of renewed threats from Japan, or from the Communists in Indo-China, particularly concerned Australia and New Zealand. They thus leant heavily on United States' sea and air power in the Pacific provided by the A.N.Z.U.S. Pact, a political organisation agreed to in September 1951 between the United States, Australia and New Zealand and which came into force in April 1952. The exclusion of Britain from the treaty caused Churchill some resentment and pain (a feeling not widely shared throughout Whitehall). Indeed, Churchill felt more keenly and perhaps realised more deeply the symbolic importance of Australia and New Zealand's turning towards the United States. In early October 1952 Churchill sent Menzies a cable in which he made these feelings clear. Richard Casey, Australian Foreign Minister (1951–60), wrote in his diary as a result: 'What the U.K. people fail to understand is that the A.N.Z.U.S. Treaty is of great *political* importance to us . . . The fact is that the Americans are the only people who can in fact help us in South-East Asia or the Pacific.'[64] Churchill was unable to find a sympathetic ear for his views and was thus forced to acknowledge the *fait accompli* of British exclusion.[65] Despite public pronouncements by Australia on the wide-ranging benefits it derived from membership of the Commonwealth, it tended to see the Commonwealth as little more than a special relationship with the mother country, to which it attached especial importance, even after the formation of the A.N.Z.U.S. Pact.[66] Menzies' personal standing increased its importance,[67] although like Salisbury he regretted the enlargement of the Commonwealth, and never got on very well with Nehru of India.[68] The approval given by the Commonwealth Prime Ministers in April 1949 to India remaining in the Commonwealth as a republic particularly displeased him. He later wrote: 'In one stroke, the common allegiance to the Crown ceased to be *the* bond of union, and the "British Commonwealth" became "the Commonwealth" . . . for the republicans, the relationship is in a sense functional and certainly external.'[69] New Zealand under Sidney Holland (Prime Minister, 1949–57) set great store by the Commonwealth, and her relationship with Britain in particular, which at this time was of even more importance to her than her relations with Australia.

Of the two African Commonwealth members, Southern Rhodesia was by far the friendlier. Sir Godfrey Huggins,[70] Prime Minister for twenty years until 1953, and of the Federation of Rhodesia and Nyasaland, 1953–6, was regarded as a key figure in Whitehall, particularly by Swinton, being the only important leader in Southern Africa whose ideas accorded with his own. The Union of South Africa, on the other hand, contributed little to the Commonwealth during these years. A leader in the *Observer* three days after the 1951 Election noted that the new Commonwealth Secretary's 'most awkward problem, as it was his predecessor's' would be relations with South Africa. It pointed out that 'short term military advantage points to closer relations with the Union,' but this would lead to immediate problems with British black Africa, in particular with Nigeria and the Gold Coast. A further difficulty was likely to be South Africa's demand for incorporation into the Union of the three High Commission Territories. Jan Smuts (Prime Minister and Minister for External Affairs, 1939–48), a great friend of Churchill, had always supported the Commonwealth, but Dr. Daniel Malan, his elderly but still vigorous successor (1948–54), and the Nationalist Government had been looking for a way out for some years before they actually left the Commonwealth in 1961.[71] At the same time, they were disturbed by the rapid progress towards decolonisation in the Gold Coast, and felt that Britain must remain in Africa and save it for the West.[72] Meanwhile, Swinton (with Lord Alexander of Tunis playing second fiddle), managed to negotiate the Simonstown Agreement with the South African Government, allowing Britain limited use of their ports in the event of war.[73]

Amongst the new Commonwealth countries, Don Senanayake, the Prime Minister of Ceylon (1947–52), was a popular and respected figure, although difficulties arose at conferences when attenders grappled to understand what he was talking about: 'His command of English, or at any rate of a recognisable English accent, was so imperfect that we in the Secretariat had very great difficulty in recording his oracular statements,' recalled one former Cabinet Office official.[74]

Pakistan, whose opinions tended to produce more controversy than those of her fellow members during these years, considered that the Commonwealth could help settle the question of Kashmir, since the British Government anxiously tried to preserve the balance between India and Pakistan.[75] At the 1955 Conference Pakistan announced that they were about to adopt a republican form of constitution, as India had done five years before, but wished to remain a full member of the Commonwealth. A militant Islamic feeling had grown inside Pakistan over the previous years, much influenced by events in the Middle East, which made the Government decide it must drop allegiance to the British Crown. By so doing, Pakistan undoubtedly strengthened the precedent set by India.

Pakistan, unlike India, had welcomed the return of Churchill and the Conservatives in 1951. India's preference for the British Labour Party had been kindled both by the fact that the transfer of power in 1947 was effected by a Labour Administration, as well as by Churchill's anti-pathetic views expressed in the 1930s to India's independence.[76] A post-Election leading article on 28th October, 1951, in the *Observer* stated: 'India will be waiting anxiously to see whether the Tories, and particularly Mr. Churchill, are now fully reconciled to her independence and prepared to co-operate with her on a basis of free partnership.' Yet, within a few months of the Conservatives' return to power, the Indian Government saw that there was to be no change from the friendly relations that had existed when Labour had been in power: 'It is rather odd that on the whole our relations with the United Kingdom are in some ways more friendly than those of almost any other country,' Nehru, the Prime Minister, wrote to the new Indian High Commissioner in London in August 1952. 'I have great sympathy for England in her present plight,' he continued.[77] Churchill had in fact been determined, ever since independence was declared, to build a relationship of trust with Indian leaders, and went out of his way to pay attention to Nehru's views after his return to Number Ten.[78]

Nehru looked upon the Commonwealth in part as an agreeable club which should not interfere, but which might be of use to him, in addition to the underlying but unexpressed feeling that if Pakistan was a member, then so too must India. Despite Nehru's sympathy for Britain, his country was becoming increasingly critical of the West, and in 1952 he sharply attacked American policy in Korea, and began to criticise NATO as a supporter of European colonial interests. Incensed by the inclusion of Pakistan in the South-East Asia Treaty Organisation (S.E.A.T.O.) in 1954, and in the Baghdad Pact in 1955, India became openly hostile to 'defence pacts', extolling the virtues of non-alignment.[79] Yet in spite of all these outbursts, and her unrest at what she considered the slow progress towards independence in British col-onies, India remained anxious to stay close to the Commonwealth: in the Korean Armistice of July 1953, India and other Commonwealth members showed active interest, and also co-operated closely with Britain at the July 1955 Geneva Conference.[80] All three Commonwealth members in the India sub-continent were greatly relieved by the British military presence in Malaya.

Britain herself also gained a great deal from the Commonwealth and the pre-eminent position she enjoyed in it.[81] Thus it acted as a prestigi-ous political reinforcement to her foreign policy, strengthening her hand against United States' intentions in Korea and Indo-China by demonstrating that the British Government spoke not only for itself. On the military side the Commonwealth provided a ready source of military bases. Australian and New Zealand troops helped reinforce the British in Malaya from 1953 and a Commonwealth brigade took part in the Korean action. Economically, although of declining importance, the Commonwealth still conferred undoubted benefits on British trade, through its protected markets. The percentage of British exports taken by the Commonwealth fell by about 5% between 1951–5, but still accounted for nearly half the total. Peter Thorneycroft, speaking at the Conservative Party Conference at Blackpool on 7th October, 1954, said Commonwealth imports were 54% of Britain's total, compared with 39% before the war. Exports were 53% of the total, compared with 49% before the war.[82] Not until after 1955 did the value of these benefits begin seriously to decline.

Part 2   The Colonial Office

The Colonial Office experienced many changes following its constitution as an independent Department in 1854. In 1907 a Dominions division was created which became a separate Department in 1925 (the Dominions Office, later part of the Commonwealth Relations Office). Freed from these preoccupations, the Office underwent extensive reorganisation to establish closer relations with Governors in the colonial territories.[1]

The Office was as taken aback as Oliver Lyttelton at his appointment as Secretary of State.[2] Originally Winston Churchill wanted Lord Salisbury to do the job,[3] and had decided before the Election that, if victorious, he would place Lyttelton as Minister of Materials and Rearmament.[4] But unfortunately for Churchill, his carefully-conceived plans went awry and at one point Brendan Bracken was also offered the Colonial Office.[5] Lyttelton had been expected to go to the Treasury; indeed, there has since been wide speculation about how he would have fared in contrast to Rab Butler. But a more interesting conjecture is the possible outcome if Salisbury or Bracken rather than Lyttelton had been appointed to the Colonial Office. Neither Salisbury nor Bracken enjoyed good health; they would never have been able to devote as much energy as Lyttelton did to the job, and, arguably, did not possess the flexibility which Lyttelton was to display after 1951. Salisbury in particular was to become increasingly uncomfortable about the swift progress to self-government in a number of territories. Lyttelton was one of Churchill's oldest and most trusted friends, whom Churchill was intent on having in the Cabinet. Lyttelton's disappointment at the post of Materials and Rearmament produced the new offer of the Colonial Office, which he only too gratefully accepted.[6] Happy though he was with his new Department, he agreed to become a Minister once more only for a limited period, and then chiefly out of loyalty to his old friend and master.[7] Lyttelton's own previous ministerial experience had covered mainly the production and trade fields (during the war he had been Minister of Production and President of the Board of Trade),[8] and he had considerable experience of some commodities, having been managing director of the British Metal Corporation Ltd., and Chairman of the London Tin Corporation. The widespread assumption that he would devote himself principally to economic development rather than political affairs[9] was not borne out by subsequent events, as his attention was continually drawn to political developments in the various colonies. Initially there was the deteriorating position in Malaya, then after a brief lull in early 1952 the Mau Mau unrest exploded in Kenya, to be followed by a succession of time-consuming problems in Uganda, the Central African Federation, British Guiana, Nigeria and Cyprus. Lyttelton liked to concentrate on the problem in hand, and he accordingly gave much less attention to colonial territories, such as the Gold Coast, Tanganyika, and those in the West Indies, with less pressing problems.

Lyttelton carried considerable weight in Cabinet[10] and once he had decided on a particular course of action, he ensured that he won the Cabinet's support. This earned him the respect of the Office, who appreciated his calibre and the high esteem with which he was regarded by his Cabinet colleagues in contrast to his three Labour predecessors, George Hall, Arthur Creech Jones and James Griffiths,[11] none of whom possessed Lyttelton's degree of authority in the highest councils of state. He kept an open door in the Office, liking to talk to whichever official, however junior, was best acquainted with a certain problem. From the beginning he worked with great energy,[12] and his approach boosted the Department's morale and efficiency. A determined man, it was his policy to be decisive about military action if he felt it necessary, but also to be radical about political change: 'You always knew which was the really tough decision and what must be done about it,' Anthony Eden later wrote to Lyttelton.[13] He worked on the principle of government by consent rather than by force, and if this could not be achieved, then handing over to another party was the only practicable solution.

Lyttelton did possess an Achilles' heel: his performance in the House of Commons. He came to the House comparatively late in life in 1940, aged forty-seven. He refused to indulge in popularity-winning tricks and on occasion allowed irritability to get the better of him.[14] Although normally an excellent mixer, he could never reproduce in the House the light-hearted manner which he used to such great effect with, for example, the Nigerians.[15] He disliked speaking there, and became nervous before major speeches, thus giving the Opposition an altogether different impression of his abilities from that of his officials.[16] As 'A Student of Politics' wrote in the *Sunday Times* on 20th December, 1953: 'The Opposition does not hide its hostility to Mr. Lyttelton. To them he is the personification of the industrial tycoon, and any stick is good enough to beat him.'

From 1953 his discomfort in the House was a major factor in making him think seriously of retiring. In December he wrote to Churchill: 'The time is drawing near when I must resign my office, leave politics.'[17] He put forward two reasons: that he only had enough money to last a few more months, and that the Chairman of his company, A.E.I. (Associated Electrical Industries), was retiring the following March. He wrote that he hoped Nigeria, the Northern Rhodesia Constitutional Conference and Uganda would have settled down by then, the pacification of Malaya would be nearly complete and the Central African Federation have become settled. The possibility of losing his old friend and supporter greatly disturbed Churchill, who discussed with Eden whether he could be dissuaded.[18] Lyttelton intended to leave at the end of May,[19] but agreed to remain until July 1954, provided Churchill could persuade the A.E.I. directors to accept his delayed return. He offered further reasons for his departure: his lack of relish for red boxes and other wearisome aspects of ministerial life,[20] the lull in disturbances in the colonies (other than Cyprus),[21] but the principal reason, which he divulged only to his close friends, was financial: 'I now have to think a bit of my family . . . I am not lured away from my job by comfort and leisure, but more by overdrafts.' There is no doubt Lyttelton derived enormous pleasure from life in the business world, and was anxious to return to it.[22]

Alan Lennox-Boyd, chief Opposition spokesman on colonial affairs until the Election,[23] had not hitherto served in the Colonial Office, but his earliest ambition had been to become Colonial Secretary. Since 1938 he had held a number of junior positions at the Ministries of Labour, Food, Home Security and Aircraft Production. Lennox-Boyd first met Churchill after coming down from Oxford in 1928, when Lord Cherwell introduced him at Chartwell, and knew him better than most young men in the Party, an additional factor which helped mark him out for high office. In the event Churchill appointed him Minister of State for Colonial Affairs, as second-in-command, which he was happy to accept, being an admirer of Lyttelton. This post had been created in 1948 to cope with the growing volume of business during and after the war, and to meet the increasing need for Ministers to travel to various parts of the colonial Empire.[24] But on important policy questions the Minister of State could not exercise authority independently of the Secretary of State, to whom it was left to decide the areas of responsibility of his deputy.

Lennox-Boyd had only been Minister of State for seven months when Churchill asked him to take over from an ailing John Maclay as Minister of Transport in May 1952. He enjoyed working with Lyttelton and was initially reluctant to accept Churchill's offer, which he did only after much persuasion and the promise of the colonial secretaryship on Lyttelton's retirement, thought not to be far distant.[25] A replacement at the Colonial Office had therefore to be found at short notice, and Henry Hopkinson was selected. His only previous ministerial post had been Secretary for Overseas Trade, a position he had held since the Election. Hopkinson was, however, a man of wide experience. He entered the Diplomatic Service in 1924 and retired in 1946 when British Deputy High Commissioner in Italy. Politics in Britain particularly interested him, and he became a joint Director of the Conservative Research Department until his election as M.P. for Taunton in 1950.[26] Hopkinson's hopes of being a successful Minister were never realised. His long period as a diplomat and his late entry into ministerial life at the age of forty-nine were disadvantages, but he should not be dismissed too readily. He was diligent and thoughtful, but, like Lyttelton, and for similar reasons, he was weak in the House. Under Lyttelton, much of his time was spent on the economic side, the Mediterranean colonies, and on preparations for the Central African Federation.[27] Later, when Lennox-Boyd became Colonial Secretary, he also dealt with other African territories. He continued in office until December 1955, but his position was greatly weakened as a result of a remark made in the House on the day of Lyttelton's retirement,[28] when he said that Cyprus would never receive independence. It was an unlucky slip, especially as many greater ones have been treated less severely, but it touched a raw nerve in Cyprus. Exactly what Hopkinson did mean, however, has never been established.[29]

The Parliamentary Under-Secretary, Lord Munster, had wide experience of Government speaking in the Lords as a junior Minister since 1932, but never achieved major office.[30] Colonial spokesman in the House of Lords, he also had responsibility for the West Indies and Malta, under Lyttelton's supervision. Lyttelton liked him and found him reliable,[31] but he did not carry the weight of Lord Lloyd, his successor in November 1954.[32] Lyttelton liked to give his junior Ministers specific areas of minor responsibility where he allowed them a fairly free hand while he concentrated on the main issues.[33] As his Parliamentary Private Secretary he appointed Hugh Fraser,[34] a family friend to whom he was closer, both socially and in the work of the Office, than any of his junior Ministers apart from Lennox-Boyd.[35] Fraser attended Lyttelton's weekly meetings in the Ministry with Heads of Departments where they discussed particular problems, and travelled with him to Malaya to examine first hand the unrest there in November–December 1951, staying on after Lyttelton's departure for London to write a paper on intelligence aspects of the battle to overcome the terrorists.[36] Fraser also made several trips to Kenya, where Lyttelton used him as an intermediary with the Kenyan leaders.[37]

The only immediately discernible change following Lennox-Boyd's appointment in July 1954 was Fraser's departure. Since Lennox-Boyd had worked closely with Lyttelton during his seven-month period as Minister of State, and had kept in close touch with colonial affairs during his two-year period at Transport, the direction of policy remained unchanged. Both men were passionately devoted to their work, and advocates of steady progress towards self-government in the colonies. Their methods of work, however, showed little similarity. Lyttelton was highly selective about whom he would see, and would only make essential appointments, which left him the time to do most of his paper-work during office hours, leaving about 6 p.m. with only a few papers in his red box, for the most part Cabinet papers and speeches. When Lennox-Boyd arrived three more red boxes had to be ordered. Charm and friendliness were Lennox-Boyd's distinctive characteristics, and on his colonial travels he constantly invited people to call on him when next in London. Fortunate in having private wealth, he was able to put it to very good use in entertaining guests. Always busy, meetings and talks filled his day, and he would leave in the evening with several full boxes to be ready early the following morning.[38] He took great pains with everyone he met, and was regarded warmly in the Office and the colonies, being the most popular post-war Secretary of State with the Overseas Service. The announcement of his appointment produced a chorus of approval throughout the Office and the Colonial Service, and he received nearly 4,000 letters of congratulation, the vast majority from personal acquaintances.

Less decisive and self-confident than Lyttelton,[39] his interest in people to an extent compensated for this, as he inspired great loyalty. His strength as a speaker, both inside the House and out, was another factor in his favour, and, like Lyttelton, he was able to make his will prevail in Cabinet. Political settlements interested him more than economic af-

351

fairs, which he delegated to Hopkinson and Lord Lloyd, unless important economic decisions had to be taken.[40]

Both Secretaries of State worked well with and admired the Permanent Under-Secretary, Sir Thomas Lloyd. A shy, modest man, he had risen through the ranks of the Colonial Office, which he had first entered in 1921. He had made a solid mark in each of his jobs, and few were surprised when Arthur Creech Jones (Colonial Secretary, 1946–50) appointed him to succeed Sir George Gater as Permanent Under-Secretary in 1947, passing over the more senior Sir Arthur Dawe.[41] Unimpressed by philosophical ideas, Lloyd dealt with each problem as it occurred in a calm, methodical manner,[42] content to accept the Secretary of State's decision even where it did not accord with his own. He possessed all the attributes of a traditional non-political civil servant: industrious, an efficient manager of the Office, popular with subordinates, steady and with an overall grasp of the Department's work. He showed his firmest side when championing the interests of the Colonial Office and its staff in Whitehall, while in the Office he managed to separate his friendships from his official duties to perfection. Lyttelton was extremely content with him, but might have preferred a more imaginative and combative personality.[43] Lennox-Boyd too found him a shade over-deferential.

Of the two Deputy Under-Secretaries, Sir Charles Jeffries, who had held the post since 1947, was a traditional and highly experienced official who concentrated on administrative affairs. He presided over the reorganisation of the Colonial Service announced in June 1954 which attempted to safeguard its members' interests as colonies reached independence.[44] This rapidly approaching event caused great concern at future career prospects. But the reforms were insufficient to allay the widespread fear of the Colonial Service in the field and two years later a new scheme giving more effective guarantees was announced in a White Paper.[45]

Sir Hilton Poynton was the second deputy, responsible for the economic division and the social service department, the job being upgraded to Deputy Secretary level in 1947. Sir Sydney Caine, the first deputy on that side until his transfer to the Treasury in 1948,[46] did much to build up the economic division's work. Creech Jones then advanced Poynton over a number of senior colleagues to become deputy at the young age of forty-three, a move that seems to have been prompted by admiration for his administrative ability rather than sympathy for his political views, which were unpartisan. Poynton was a man of considerable intellectual force, who shared a mutual affection with Lyttelton,[47] stemming from a spell as his Private Secretary during the war,[48] and in his rather specialised field was allowed a wide degree of initiative by the Colonial Secretary and by the Permanent Under-Secretary.[49]

Colonial economic policy was a major aspect of the Department's work, and the responsibilities of the economic division were wide-ranging. The 1945 Colonial Development and Welfare Act for which Oliver Stanley (Colonial Secretary, 1942–5) did so much, made available an initial sum of £120m. for a ten-year period for schemes of economic and social development. The dearth of finance and ideas that had bedevilled colonial development plans before the war had given way to new difficulties in the early 1950s – in particular the continuing problem of finding skilled manpower to undertake the schemes in the individual territories, and a shortage of raw materials from Britain with the inauguration in Britain of the 1950 rearmament programme.[50] A further Act, passed in early 1955, was designed to give, on average, £24m. per annum. In addition, individual colonies received substantial aid direct: in 1953 Britain promised £6m. to Malaya and also £4m. to Kenya, together with an interest-free loan of £2m. to help meet the cost of operations against the Mau Mau. The Colonial Development Corporation (C.D.C.), set up by an Act of Parliament in February 1948, and originating from a White Paper sponsored by Stanley when Colonial Secretary, provided a further source of finance. Relations between the new Government and the C.D.C. were, however, not entirely satisfactory,[51] due to a feeling, expressed on several occasions by Lyttelton, that insufficient care had been taken in the evaluation of projects.[52]

The production and marketing of colonial produce was also crucial, especially the politically sensitive bulk-buying arrangements, started at the beginning of the war and continued thereafter by Labour.[53] The return to ordinary free markets accelerated under the Conservative Government, encouraged by Lyttelton, who was unsympathetic to bulk purchase.[54] Poynton, too, felt the position unsatisfactory.[55] Great tensions had resulted from the bulk-purchase scheme: the virtual one-crop colonies such as the Gold Coast (cocoa), Barbados, Mauritius (sugar), and other colonies with more diverse produce like Malaya (tin and rubber), would try to persuade the Colonial Secretary to pay the highest price for their produce, whereas the Ministry, representing the British consumer, Food, Materials, Supply or the Board of Trade, and acting through the agency of the Treasury, would endeavour to secure the lowest price. Where agreement could not be reached between the individual Departments, a decision had to be taken in the Cabinet. Much time was also spent on commodity negotiations, the corollary of ending bulk purchase.[56]

A critical question in Whitehall throughout the early 1950s was the status that would be afforded colonial territories which, on obtaining full independence, desired to remain within the Commonwealth. A joint Colonial Office–Commonwealth Relations Office working party which reported in March 1951 put forward a list of territories where advance to full Commonwealth membership was likely to be a live issue 'in the near future', including the Gold Coast, Nigeria, the Federation of Malaya with Singapore and the prospective West Indian Federation.[57] In April 1953 the Cabinet appointed a Committee of Ministers under the chairmanship of the Commonwealth Secretary, Lord Swinton, to consider again the question of status, in view of impending self-government in a number of territories, which submitted a unanimous Report in October 1954. The Committee moved away from its initial bias in favour of a 'two-tier' system of Commonwealth membership on the grounds that few countries would be content accepting inferior status, and their discontent was likely to be exploited by influences hostile to Commonwealth solidarity. The Committee thus decided that all members of the Commonwealth should be on equal terms, although this would not mean that all would carry equal weight in Commonwealth councils. The Cabinet concurred in principle with the Committee's proposals and agreed that private conversations should be held with the Prime Ministers of Canada, Australia and New Zealand at the forthcoming Commonwealth Conference in February 1955.[58]

No evidence suggests that Churchill actively discouraged the political advance towards independence in the colonies.[59] He had deep misgivings about the reduction of British influence in Iran, Egypt and the Sudan, and was tempted to drag his heels with regard to the colonies,[60] but in fact bowed to the inevitable, without enthusiasm.[61] He believed implicitly in the value of Empire, and though still apt on occasions to grumble about the loss of India, realised the futility of fighting against the admission of the newer nations into the Commonwealth.[62] Generally content to leave all to Lyttelton, he took some interest in any crisis where military force was required, as in Malaya, Kenya and British Guiana, and also in appointing a new Governor or High Commissioner.[63] When he had himself been at the Colonial Office, as Parliamentary Under-Secretary, 1905–8, he had found the work there as uncompelling as any ministerial work throughout his career.[64] Eden, who, as Foreign Secretary, was responsible for the Anglo-Egyptian Condominium of Sudan until its independence in 1956, seldom interfered on colonial issues. In Cabinet meetings Lyttelton and then Lennox-Boyd appear to have been given a wide degree of freedom in determining colonial policy. Doubts were increasingly expressed by members on the wisdom of progressing so far and fast with helping dependent peoples to attain self-government, as in the Cabinet meeting of 7th December, 1954,[65] but there was no serious disagreement on colonial issues there until the Hola camp row in Kenya in 1959.[66]

Part 3   South-East Asia

Malaya

The Conservative victory in 1951 made a decisive difference to the position of Malaya, where the guerrilla war, which had begun in earnest in June 1948, had escalated throughout 1951, culminating in the murder of the High Commissioner, Sir Henry Gurney, in October, a severe blow to civilian morale. Sir Gerald Templer, Gurney's successor, went so far as to say that the country would have been lost if swift and strong action had not been taken.[1] In a confidential talk after the General Election, James Griffiths had confided to Oliver Lyttelton that the Labour Government had been baffled as to how to treat Malaya and found the military problem insurmountable.[2] In Opposition, the Conservatives had consistently stressed the prime importance of Malaya, pointing to its key strategic position in highly sensitive South-East Asia, and also the value of its twin exports, tin and rubber, as dollar earners for the Commonwealth. Like Templer, Lyttelton feared Britain was on the verge of losing Malaya,[3] and tackled the guerrilla problem as his first priority.[4] Without his swift action, his fears might well have been realised.[5]

Lyttelton knew the country well and his experience of the tin industry gave him added impetus and background knowledge with which to tackle the problems. On his own initiative, on 29th November he departed for a three-week visit, taking with him a small party, among them his Principal Private Secretary, Angus Mackintosh, and Parliamentary Private Secretary, Hugh Fraser[6] – despite Churchill's reluctance to let Fraser go in view of the slender majority in the House.[7] After touring the country and talking to key figures, Lyttelton came to several conclusions. Foremost he felt that one man, a General, should be in charge of both civilian and military affairs,[8] even though this decision was contrary to the advice of the United Kingdom Commissioner-General in South-East Asia, Malcolm MacDonald, who favoured a civilian head with a military deputy.[9] MacDonald felt a civilian would be better able to fight the political war and that it would seem less like a military dictatorship.

355

MacDonald and Lyttelton were, however, at one on the creation of the new post of Deputy High Commissioner, to be a civilian appointment. Before making a short trip to Hong Kong, Lyttelton secured the resignation of two high-ranking officials, the Commissioner of Police and the Head of the Special Branch. On his return he settled down in Kuala Lumpur to write a critical Cabinet paper, in which he argued that British control could not be regained without the support of the local population, especially the Chinese, and this would not be obtained until they began to win the war against the terrorists.[10]

Lyttelton took the initiative over Malaya without much detailed interest being taken either by Churchill[11] or the Cabinet, who in the midst of the economic crisis scarcely had time to consider the position before Lyttelton's departure at the end of November. At Lyttelton's meeting with Churchill, two days after his return on 21st December, they discussed whom to appoint to be in charge. Lyttelton favoured Sir Brian Robertson, but he refused to go, preferring to remain in the Canal Zone.[12]

Lyttelton then consulted the Secretary for War, Antony Head, and settled on Sir Gerald Templer,[13] then General Officer Commanding-in-Chief, Eastern Command. It was a brave choice: as a profile of Templer in the *Observer* on 20th January, 1952 commented: 'To place a soldier in supreme charge of such delicate and complex political problems as those of Malaya today is unprecedented in modern British colonial administration.' Churchill had, however, already left for the United States, but in view of the matter's urgency, Templer flew to Ottawa to obtain his approval, a step reminiscent of the wartime practice. Churchill immediately saw in Templer a soldier of exceptional quality; he told him that law and order must be restored, that Malaya must not fall to the communists, and further, that he hoped Malaya would soon achieve independence within the Commonwealth.[14] Before Templer left Canada, it was arranged that he should give a press conference, much to Eden's annoyance, since he felt that they should only be given by politicians.[15] Sir Donald MacGillivray, the Colonial Secretary in Jamaica, was chosen as Deputy High Commissioner, and so rushed were the appointments that he only met Templer for the first time the day before their flight out to Malaya.[16] It was Templer's belief that he had benefited from his previous experience as Director of Military Intelligence at the War Office (1946–8) and as Vice-C.I.G.S. (1948–50), which familiarised him with the types of problems he encountered in Malaya.[17] This is why so soon after hearing about the job, he was able to tell Lord Moran on 11th January in Ottawa: 'The military problem is nothing. The police question can be set right; the Civil Service difficulty can be solved. What we have to do is to get the Malay and the Chinaman, with their different languages and religions, the followers of Confucius and of Islam, to say "This is our country".'[18]

Once Lyttelton had drawn up his plan for overall direction of military and civil forces, the reorganisation of the police and administration, and increased protection for resettlement areas, and once Templer and MacGillivray had taken up their posts, his most important task was accomplished. Sir John Harding, by now C.I.G.S., insisted Templer be given the right of direct access to Churchill to boost his authority.[19] Lyttelton left the man on the spot a free hand, and every fortnight received from Templer, in whom he had complete confidence, long letters which Mackintosh also read.[20] The Office found this reliance on letters a somewhat unconventional channel of communication, since Templer never sent back a single despatch.[21] Although Templer would occasionally seek Lyttelton's advice, Lyttelton never suggested policy unsolicited, nor did Templer ever receive interference from the Chiefs of Staff or the War Office.[22] Templer's appointment thus not only helped to ensure victory, it also enabled the Secretary of State to devote more time to other colonial problems.

The groundwork in the war against the guerrillas had been laid by the 'Briggs' plan, formulated by Gurney and Sir Harold Briggs,[23] which in 1950 began to move 400,000 Chinese living in open areas into over 400 protected villages. Templer was able to expand on this, thereby isolating the Chinese from the guerrillas. The war itself was stepped up; in 1951–2 there were 25,000 British troops and 10,000 Gurkhas, by 1953 over a quarter of a million were engaged in the battle against the terrorists. Templer envisaged a threefold campaign, which played a decisive part in winning the war: to win the 'hearts and minds' of the people (his expression) in order to dissuade them from supplying food and support to the terrorists; the centralisation and unification of the intelligence system; and the reorganisation of the police.[24] Templer's highly skilled back-up team made this possible. Foremost among them was his deputy, MacGillivray, who executed all administrative decisions and took the civil side, Arthur Young, who was seconded from duty as Commissioner of the City of London Police for a year to reorganise and retrain the Malayan police, and Sir Hugh Stockwell, whom he selected as his G.O.C. Stockwell, the sole survivor of the triumvirate,[25] had high praise for his boss: 'Templer was basically at his best then. In Malaya he was able to impose his personality on everyone in a way he was unable to, I think, when C.I.G.S. (1955–8). He was full of fire and energy, and possessed the great gift of knowing what was going wrong and being able to put his finger direct on the problem.'[26] Advance was steady and by May 1954 it was felt that Templer's presence was no longer required and so MacGillivray was able to succeed Templer as High Commissioner.[27]

Although the new Government was able to increase military action, there was at first no new political initiative.[28] In the early years after the war Malaya expressed little desire for independence as the native Malays were in a slight minority among the Chinese and other non-Malay communities. At MacDonald's instigation a Committee began meeting in early 1949 with representatives from the six main races, and over the next two years they worked out their future relations in an independent Malaya. The Conservative Government made plain its belief in ultimate independence for Malaya,[29] and discussions at Kuala Lumpur continued with MacDonald's role reduced in Malaya's internal, but not external, affairs after the arrival of Templer and MacGillivray.[30] The first Elections to a new federal legislative Council took place in July 1955. Lennox-Boyd visited Malaya in August 1955 and fixed a target date for self-government with MacGillivray, who remained as High Commissioner until after independence was declared on 31st August, 1957.

Singapore

As plans proceeded for Malaya's independence, the British Government began to consider whether Singapore should achieve separate independence or unite with Malaya. At MacDonald's instigation a joint Committee of leaders of both countries met, but rejected union. MacDonald then explored the possibility of a Federation of North Borneo, Sarawak and Brunei which could join a Confederation of which Malaya and Singapore would also be members, but after MacDonald's departure as Commissioner-General in 1955 the plan was shelved.[31] Instead a modified form of representative government was introduced for Singapore, and the first elected Premier, David Marshall, said he would resign if he did not secure a commitment to early independence from the British Government. But at a constitutional conference in London in 1956 he failed to convince Lennox-Boyd of an independent Singapore's viability, and so carried out his promise to resign. His successor, Lim Yew Hock, agreed in April 1957 to a revised constitution which would grant Singapore independence after 1st January, 1958. Singapore eventually joined the Malaysian Federation in 1963, but seceded from it in 1965.

Hong Kong

Perched in the midst of the turbulent Far East, the British Government always attached peculiar importance to its relationship with Hong Kong. During the early 1950s the territory was undergoing a period of great domestic activity, with rapid expansion of social services and housing facilities to meet the increase in population from 1.5 million in 1946 to 2.5 million in 1951. Since the Chinese Civil War Hong Kong had maintained a defensive stance, and because representative bodies had not been developed as in most other colonies, greater authority rested in the hands of the Governor. When Lyttelton paid the colony a brief visit in December 1951, he was the first Secretary of State to do so for fifty years.[32] He had full confidence in Sir Alexander Grantham (Governor of Hong Kong, 1947–57), whom he thought 'one of the ablest and most successful of all the colonial governors,' and rarely interfered.[33]

Commissioner-General for the United Kingdom in South-East Asia

This was the sole co-ordinating position of its kind. In 1946 Clement Attlee had offered MacDonald,[34] while he was still serving as High Commissioner in Canada, the job of Governor-General of Malaya, Singapore and British Borneo. His purpose was to co-ordinate and initiate policy in Malaya, Singapore and the three Borneo territories in the light of developments in India and throughout Asia as a whole.[35] In 1948 the post was combined with the duties of a Special Commissioner, which had been introduced after the war in Singapore, responsible to the Foreign Office, with the purpose of advising the British Government on problems and policy in an area which included Burma, Siam, Indo-China and Indonesia.[36] It was only then that the full title of Commissioner-General for South-East Asia was adopted. After Templer's arrival there was speculation in London about whether there would be room for both him and MacDonald, particularly due to the distaste in certain quarters for MacDonald's progressive ideas.[37] But doubts were dispelled when it became clear that MacDonald filled the job with conspicuous success, and was much happier there than he was to be as U.K. High Commissioner in India, which he became in 1955.

Part 4   Africa

The British Government had responsibility in the early 1950s for some fifteen territories of different status throughout Africa. A study of

British policy in the most important of these[1] reveals a wide range in approach as well as in the degree of guidance given to Governors from London, and clearly shows that the Churchill Government had a pragmatic piecemeal approach to problems in each area.

Central Africa

The area comprised three countries over which Britain exercised some degree of jurisdiction: the colony of Southern Rhodesia, in which whites had exercised virtually unlimited power for over twenty years, the responsibility of the Commonwealth Relations Office, and the protectorates of Northern Rhodesia and Nyasaland, less prosperous territories where the prime aim of British policy was to act as trustee for the predominantly African inhabitants. The Colonial Office was the responsible Department for these. By the time the Conservatives came to power in October 1951, the important decisions on the future of the area had been taken by the Labour Ministers concerned, James Griffiths, the Colonial Secretary, and Patrick Gordon Walker, the Commonwealth Secretary, who had both served since the General Election of February 1950. On 21st November Oliver Lyttelton made a statement in the House supporting the plan for a federation of the three territories along the lines of the recommendations of the Victoria Falls Conference in September 1951. But to the surprise of many on the Government side, Labour M.P.s, including Griffiths, became increasingly critical of the idea, and on 4th March, 1952 forced the first division of several on the subject. After much opposition in Parliament, a motion approving the federation proposals passed the House in March 1953, and the Rhodesia and Nyasaland Federation Act received the Royal Assent on 14th July, 1953.[2]

Of particular interest is that Conservative Ministers took up what was originally an officials' initiative. In the Commonwealth Relations Office, Philip Noel-Baker (Commonwealth Secretary, 1947–50) disagreed on the federation plans with Sir Percivale Liesching, who, like his subordinate officials George Baxter[3] and Arthur Clark,[4] supported the proposal. Lord Ismay (Commonwealth Secretary, 1951–2) expressed enthusiasm for the Federation, and took part in informal talks in London early in 1952 with Sir Godfrey Huggins, Southern Rhodesia's Prime Minister since 1933, and a main proponent of federation, and the Governors of Northern Rhodesia (Sir Gilbert Rennie) and Nyasaland (Sir Geoffrey Colby).[5]

A newcomer both to African affairs[6] and to politics, dependent on his officials, Ismay could not have been expected to have made much original contribution. Both his successors as Commonwealth Secretary, Lord Salisbury (1952)[7] and Lord Swinton (1952–5), however, were active supporters of Central African Federation, as it was to be called, in fact devoting more time to it than to any other policy objective.[8] Lyttelton, the only responsible Cabinet Minister remaining throughout the period of negotiations, bore the brunt of responsibility for developments. But apart from Sir Andrew Cohen,[9] the leading intellectual in the Colonial Office until his appointment as Governor of Uganda in 1951, and a main architect of the federation proposals, officials from the Colonial Office showed less enthusiasm for the Federation than their opposite numbers from the Commonwealth Relations Office.[10] Certainly Sir William Gorell Barnes,[11] Cohen's successor as Assistant Under-Secretary responsible for African affairs, felt less strongly, though he supported the experiment in so far as it followed the detailed plans set out in the 1953 White Papers.[12]

Churchill took little interest in the affairs of Central Africa,[13] giving his Secretaries of State free rein; nor were strong views expressed in Cabinet, which accepted the arguments in favour, and entrusted the conduct of negotiations to the two senior responsible Ministers. Anthony Eden, who was preoccupied with other matters in 1952 and was absent through illness during most of the final preparations in 1953, raised no objections.

Lyttelton showed little enthusiasm for the original conception, although he followed the Office line in his 21st November statement in the House.[14] At that time the Colonial Office saw the main purpose of pressing for the Federation as the best method of power-sharing between black and white and avoiding the spread of apartheid from South Africa,[15] not just the political and economic advantages Lyttelton lists in his memoirs.[16] Lyttelton, however, soon came round to the idea and thought multi-racial (as opposed to all-African) government in Central Africa genuinely possible. He admired Sir Roy Welensky, the leading European in Northern Rhodesia and Prime Minister of the Federation in succession to Huggins, 1956–63, who, in league with Huggins, had a profound influence in lobbying Conservatives to support the federation proposals.

Once the Act was passed in July and the Federal Government had come to power in autumn 1953, relations with the Federation no longer directly concerned the Colonial Secretary. He retained responsibility for the territorial affairs of Northern Rhodesia and Nyasaland, while the Commonwealth Secretary acted as the channel of communication between the British and the Federal Government, as well as the territorial Government of Southern Rhodesia. Regular contact was maintained between the respective departments in the Colonial Office and the Commonwealth Relations Office, but never proved entirely satisfactory, because of the difference in outlook. Indeed, Welensky, less than four months after succeeding Huggins as Federal Prime Minister, went so far as to write to Lord Home (Commonwealth Secretary, 1955–60) suggesting the creation of one Department to avoid the different outlooks and policies of the C.R.O. and Colonial Office.[17] Swinton and then Home became the key figures in conducting relations with the Federation. Alan Lennox-Boyd, who had succeeded Lyttelton as Colonial Secretary in July 1954, accepted the organisation of the Federation, although he felt the choice of Salisbury as capital, which gave rise to suspicions about domination by Southern Rhodesia, was unwise.[18]

The federation concept was not to be repeated by Britain in Africa, though further federations and amalgamations of territories were being considered by the Government throughout the 1950s. The Central African Federation in all probability was doomed from the start. Had Labour after 1951 thrown their weight behind it then it might have stood a better chance: as it was the majority of the Opposition – apart from a small group, including Gordon Walker – became increasingly hostile to the plan. They justified their *volte-face* on the grounds that no constitution should be imposed on a dependent people against their will: this stance was never entirely convincing, and there was an element both of Labour not having thought out the implications of their policy when in power, as well as of political opportunism in almost overnight proclaiming themselves the champions of the native Africans in the three territories. Their criticisms did however express the main problem with the Federation, that it did not in fact introduce multi-racial Government: the 1953 Act put legislative control almost entirely in the hands of the white community, comprising less than 4% of the total population (the territories contained approximately 200,000 Europeans, compared with 6 million Africans). In the first Election for the Federation Assembly in 1953, the Federal Party led by Huggins and Welensky won twenty-four of the twenty-six seats: almost no constitutional political activity was open to the Africans. The Federation was plagued with difficulties throughout the ten years of its history as the Africans became increasingly articulate in their demands for political power, and the Federation was eventually brought to an unhappy end in December 1963. Nyasaland (as Malawi) and Northern Rhodesia (as Zambia) both became independent. Southern Rhodesia declared unilateral independence in 1965 under the white leader Ian Smith and had to wait until 1980 when a Conservative Government engineered full independence for the former colony under the name Zimbabwe.

East Africa

British East Africa, consisting of the Colony and Protectorate of Kenya, the Protectorate of Uganda, the trust territory of Tanganyika, and the protected island state of Zanzibar were all some distance from attaining self-government. The region as a whole was thought to stand out as a testing-ground for the possibility of multi-racial or non-racial development as it lay geographically between the Union of South Africa and the Federation of Rhodesia and Nyasaland, on the one side, and the anti-colonialist influences of the Middle East and the sub-continent of Asia Minor, on the other. The Cabinet felt that failure in the area would produce an important zone of instability.[19] Kenya, an economically more advanced colony than Uganda or Tanganyika, had problems arising from the comparatively large number of white settlers and their entrenched political and economic position. Indeed, the country was seen as the chief symbol of British white settler rule in the African continent. Lyttelton was to devote more time to Kenya, where he played a decisive part in its political development, than to any other colony. He worked in conjunction with the Governor, although did not hesitate to override his authority when he thought it necessary. Perhaps Lyttelton's greatest triumph as Colonial Secretary was persuading the white settlers to accept the inevitability of representative government.

On Lyttelton's appointment as Colonial Secretary, all appeared to London to be well in the colony.[20] The new Governor, Sir Evelyn Baring, was highly regarded and had extensive knowledge of Africa (he had been Governor of Southern Rhodesia, 1942–4, and High Commissioner for the U.K. in the Union of South Africa and the three High Commission territories, 1944–51), and the final reports of Sir Philip Mitchell, the Conservative Governor who retired in June, 1952, implied that nothing was amiss. But Henry Potter, the acting Governor until Baring's arrival, on 29th September,[21] alerted the Colonial Office to the dangers of unrest among Kenya's Kikuyu tribe. In his first week, Baring toured the troubled areas, and later that month was joined in Nairobi by Lyttelton who wanted to see for himself the 'confused and worsening' position.[22]

As a result, a state of emergency was declared on 21st October, 1952, but over the following months the position continued to deteriorate further. Lyttelton and General Sir Brian Robertson,[23] the senior British soldier responsible in the field, persuaded Baring that a Commander-in-Chief with direct access to the War Office and no longer subordinate to the British headquarters at Cairo,[24] was essential. Sir George Erskine, formerly General Officer C.-in-C. Eastern Command,

1952–3, was appointed at Churchill's own suggestion[25] in June 1953. This was to prove the turning-point of the campaign. 'You have revolutionised the military situation in Kenya,' later wrote Lyttelton to Erskine.[26] By the time he was succeeded by Gerald Lathbury[27] in April 1955, the worst of the Mau Mau rebellion was over. A more subtle character than Erskine, much of the credit for the final settlement was due to Lathbury. The Army withdrew from operations in November 1956, although the emergency did not officially end until January 1960: by that time nearly 10,000 Africans and Europeans had lost their lives as a result of the Mau Mau troubles.

Baring's governorship aroused considerable controversy, both among the white settlers in Kenya, who felt him altogether too civilised to deal with the Mau Mau, and back in London in the House of Commons. In particular, critics felt Baring mishandled the Kikuyu leader Jomo Kenyatta's[28] trial and conviction in 1953 (removing from the scene the one African leader in the country capable of negotiating peace). In response to criticism of his governorship, a Parliamentary delegation under the respected Conservative M.P. and elder statesman Walter Elliot visited Kenya in January 1954. Their Report criticised the Kenya Government for not sufficiently rallying the Kikuyu to law and order, and recommended a complete reorganisation of the police force.[29] As a result, Arthur Young was appointed Commissioner of Police in 1954, to perform the same task as he had just completed in Malaya. Despite his undoubted charm, Baring's relationship with Young was poor, as it was with John Whyatt, the unyielding Attorney-General (1951–5), and also Erskine. Young felt he should have had the position of right-hand man to the Governor, as in Malaya. He also disliked the way the military side was being run, and resented not being in the War Council, so it was no surprise when he resigned in early 1955.[30]

Baring suffered from recurring ill health, and spent March to June 1954 in Britain on sick leave. A scholarly man, his qualities were used to better advantage in his later years as Governor when he was able to concentrate more on constitutional and land reform. Lyttelton at one time had doubts about Baring's suitability, apparently telling Young in early 1954: 'He is too intelligent for his job. He sees too many possibilities and can't choose any of them.'[31] Yet he always admired and supported him. As Baring wrote to Lyttelton in July 1954: 'I am afraid that Kenya has given you some bad headaches and that we, especially I, have made lots of mistakes. But to receive such complete and such fearless support on absolutely every question without exception, once you were convinced, was something that in my wildest dreams I had never hoped for.'[32]

Lyttelton worked in close alliance with William Gorell Barnes, the senior Whitehall official directly concerned, who visited Kenya once a year. Lyttelton made a second visit in February 1954, this time with Sir John Harding (C.I.G.S., 1952–5). Lyttelton had been concerned at the constant disagreements between Baring, responsible to him, and Erskine, responsible to Antony Head, the Secretary of State for War. Lyttelton, however, felt that the solution employed in Malaya, where the civil and military authorities acted as one, was unsuitable for Kenya due to his conviction that the country should be run as normally as possible despite the Mau Mau problems. After a series of talks Lyttelton proposed the creation of a War Council with representatives from both civil and military sides, thereby dispensing with the need for constant referrals to London.[33] Baring was appointed Chairman, Sir Frederick Crawford (the Colony's Deputy Governor since June 1953 and a former Governor of the Seychelles) Deputy Chairman to relieve Baring of some of the strain, and members included Erskine and Michael Blundell, the liberal-minded white settler leader. The War Council had a Secretariat, set up by George Mallaby, the urbane and experienced Under-Secretary from the Cabinet Office in London. The War Council functioned well and succeeded in its objective of thrashing out disagreements on the spot.

Baring was responsible for much of the content of the 'Lyttelton Constitution'[34] but the credit for persuading the European, African and Asian leaders to accept it lay with Lyttelton. Before he set out for Kenya on his February 1954 visit he had resolved to establish a multi-racial Government[35] and, after ten days of intensive sessions with the interested parties in Nairobi, by a mixture of persuasion and cajoling, and above all by his sheer force of character, he secured their agreement, a tremendous achievement. Lyttelton had particular difficulty overcoming opposition from the conservative white settlers, opposed to any form of multi-racialism in Kenya. Blundell himself launched a European party to support the multi-racial principle: as he acknowledged in a valedictory letter to Lyttelton on the latter's retirement: 'I must confess that I do not think that there has been a Secretary of State for the Colonies who has made more contribution to events in the colonies than yourself since the days of Leo Amery.'[36]

Lyttelton announced the proposed changes in a statement on 10th March, 1954, later embodied in a White Paper.[37] Although the multi-racial Lyttelton Constitution later broke down after Elections to the new Legislature in 1956 and 1957, and both the African and European communities had to endure a long and at times painful period of negotiations before independence was eventually granted in 1963, Lyttelton's contribution to policy between 1951–4 had nevertheless been indispensable in preparing both communities for self-government in Kenya.

Kenya was unusual during the early 1950s in being the only African colony to undergo widespread violence. There is little doubt that this increased the pace of political advance in the colony: not only did the British Government have to find the money and troops to combat African opposition, but it also helped destroy the ambitions of those white settlers who did not follow Blundell and who hoped to gain the political position enjoyed by the whites in South Africa.[38]

In 1951 Uganda was noted both for its dearth of white settlers and thus serious racial rivalries and for its economic prosperity, with its coffee and cotton produce ensuring ready exports; it therefore seemed the best suited of the East African colonies for constitutional advance. Sir Andrew Cohen, appointed as Governor by Griffiths earlier in 1951, had sought some practical experience in the field, and Uganda had presented a ripe testing-ground for his progressive ideas. But unfortunately Cohen's vision of Uganda as a unitary state clashed with the ideas of the Kabaka, Frederick Mutesa II (later Sir Edward Mutesa), the young native ruler of Buganda, the largest of the four provinces in the protectorate. The Kabaka was a leader and active participant in the struggles of Buganda against the protectorate Government, and eventually emerged (after independence in 1962) as the first President of Uganda when the last British Governor resigned late the following year.[39]

The Kabaka's stance typified the unusual internal position of Uganda amongst British colonies: in Uganda it was the colonial administration which was trying to develop a modern centralised Government and a sense of national unity, the African leaders, the Kabaka amongst them, who were holding back, fearing that under a centralised democratic system of Government they would lose their traditional position.

Cohen enlarged the Legislative Council with the object of providing a link from each district to the centre by electing an African member, and also managed to persuade the Kabaka to implement former promises to elect more men to Buganda's own Parliament. All looked well for advance when an incident occurred which was to strike at the heart of Cohen's hopes for smooth progress. Speaking during the summer of 1953 at a London dinner, Lyttelton referred to the possibility of establishing an East African Federation.[40] The speech attracted less attention in England than in East Africa, particularly in Uganda. Despite reassurances from Lyttelton, widespread fear and suspicion were aroused lest a federation be imposed on reluctant Africans – as was being done at that very time in Central Africa – which might place them under the control of Kenya's white settlers. Co-operation between the Kabaka and the Governor abruptly ended. The former made a number of impossible demands: transfer of Buganda affairs from the Colonial to the Foreign Office, and a time limit for Buganda independence within the Commonwealth. Subsequently, he refused to nominate members to represent Buganda in the protectorate's new Legislative Council. Indeed, the Kabaka, who had resisted reform even before the Lyttelton speech, whipped up opposition to the Governor and his policies to such a pitch that Cohen refused to accept responsibility for law and order in Uganda as long as the Buganda ruler remained. Cohen had a series of talks with the Kabaka in November, but policy as well as personality differences combined to defeat the possibility of agreement.[41] Meanwhile, back in London, Lyttelton felt that, given his common upper-class connections with the Kabaka[42] and his own persuasive charm, he might convince the Kabaka of the urgent necessity of maintaining the protectorate's unity.[43]

The Colonial Office felt that Cohen had mishandled the situation. Gorell Barnes thought Lyttelton should go ahead and follow his inclination to talk to the Kabaka. But after consultations with Sir Thomas Lloyd, Henry Hopkinson and Lord Munster, Lyttelton decided not to intervene but to support Cohen, although he urged him to make one last attempt to persuade the Kabaka to change his mind. Cohen agreed, but this final talk proved abortive.[44] Consequently the Kabaka was deported on 30th November on the grounds that his refusal to allow Bugandan delegates to sit on the Legislative Council left Buganda without representation, and his behaviour constituted a breach of the 1900 Agreement by which Kabakas were bound to co-operate with British Governments.

These events prompted an emergency debate in the House of Commons at the beginning of December. Fenner Brockway, the radical backbench critic on colonial policy, opened for the Opposition, and sought to tie the crisis in the protectorate to Lyttelton's speech during the summer on the possibility of an East African Federation. Lyttelton, in one of the best speeches of his career, revealed his deep personal concern for the problems of Uganda and the plight of the Kabaka. The speech had a profound effect on the House, and as a result Jim Griffiths felt compelled to postpone the vote of censure promised by the Opposition leaders before the debate.[45]

Meanwhile, the deportation of the Kabaka failed to improve the position in the protectorate; indeed Africans in Uganda were deeply shocked by the action (heightened no doubt by the death of the

Kabaka's sister on hearing the news). Cohen's standing both inside and outside the colony suffered, although he pressed on with internal reforms, including the introduction of a ministerial system and the allocation of a number of portfolios to Africans. In June 1954 Sir Keith Hancock, Director of the Institute of Commonwealth Studies, was invited to discuss various constitutional questions with representatives of Buganda. These talks resulted in a number of agreements, among them that Buganda should continue to be an integral part of the protectorate. The consequent reforms, coupled with the changeover of Colonial Secretary in July 1954, provided Cohen with the opportunity to request the Kabaka's urgent return. Lennox-Boyd, who like Lyttelton had always doubted the wisdom of sacking the Kabaka, consulted his predecessor, who told him he must do what he thought right.[46] Gorell Barnes was firmly of the opinion that the Kabaka should not be returned as it would make the position difficult not only for Cohen himself but also for certain Ugandans. Lennox-Boyd, however, like his predecessor, decided to back the Governor, and the Kabaka returned to his Kampala palace in October 1955, one of the conditions being that Buganda should send members to the Legislative Council. The intention that he should however become a constitutional monarch did not transpire, and his return heralded a new phase of Buganda separatism.

Uganda had an able and imaginative Governor in Cohen, and had it not been for the constitutional crisis, the Colonial Secretaries would have exercised little influence over the internal affairs of the colony, particularly since its importance was limited, neither suffering from white settler dissension, nor yet ready for immediate independence. Lyttelton himself respected Cohen, as he did any man of intellectual ability, although he had doubts about the wisdom of his political views on the advancement of Africans.[47] But these reservations did not find their way into a farewell letter to Cohen, in which Lyttelton wrote: 'I hate putting my friends in the firing line – and you are certainly one. I believe it is realised here what a particularly difficult situation has faced you in Uganda.'[48]

Tanganyika, not a high priority, and presided over by a strong Governor, took little of the Colonial Secretary's time. Second in size only to Nigeria, Tanganyika had consistently been one of the most peaceful though poorest of African colonies. Sir Edward Twining, appointed Governor by the Labour Government in 1949, remained in office for the next ten years.[49] He encouraged much needed advance in the economic field, being an advocate of African involvement in their country's prosperity, and presided over the consolidation of a strong system of

368

local government. In his policy of striving for multi-racialism as a stage towards self-government, he also achieved notable success in breaking down the social barriers between the three communities living in Tanganyika (Europeans and Asians as well as the predominant native black Tanganyikans – ninety-eight per cent of the total).[50]

Twining, however, possessed an ingrained paternalist attitude, and was certainly no zealot for constitutional change. When in 1954 the native black Tanganyikans began to organise themselves into an active pressure group, he reacted badly. According to Judith, Lady Listowel,[51] 'Twining was horrified by the very thought of an African demanding rights instead of being grateful for the efforts the British Administration generally, and he personally, were making on Tanganyika's behalf.'[52] In 1954 Julius Nyerere[53] had returned from Edinburgh University, and in July founded the Tanganyika Africa National Union (T.A.N.U.). The arrival the following month of the United Nations Visiting Mission gave much encouragement to T.A.N.U.,[54] and further infuriated Twining, who as a consequence uttered the sweeping and inflammatory statement that the Africans had neither a national organisation nor an articulate spokesman.[55] The following year, however, T.A.N.U.'s initial momentum slackened, and in March 1955 the Legislative Council was reconstituted leaving ultimate control firmly in official hands, while at the same time introducing a limited system of racial parity.[56] But in the latter half of the decade development was swift: independence was granted in December 1961 (with Nyerere the first Prime Minister); it became a republic a year later and in April 1964 entered a union with the former colony of Zanzibar to become the United Republic of Tanzania under the presidency of Nyerere.

South Africa

The two High Commission territories in South Africa – Basutoland and Swaziland – and a third, the Bechuanaland Protectorate adjoining South Africa, were the responsibility, through the High Commissioner, of a separate department headed by Arthur Clark in the Commonwealth Relations Office. Some in Whitehall felt that responsibility for the protectorates should be transferred to the Colonial Office, although this only occurred in 1961, precipitated by South Africa's departure from the Commonwealth.[57]

The question of transferring the territories to South Africa was pre-eminent during these years. In the House of Commons, soon after the Election, Churchill had already reaffirmed pledges given to the territories,[58] and further declared that any transfer would not take place until the inhabitants had been consulted and the British Parliament given an opportunity to express its views.

In 1954 Swinton felt it necessary to repeat this pledge.[59] The British Government had no more wish to transfer the three territories to a South African Government pursuing a policy of apartheid than the territories themselves wished for transfer, and it was not until the end of the 1950s that any serious attempt was made to consider constitutional developments.[60] The undeniable fact of the three territories' economic dependence upon South Africa was a major reason for British policy towards them being quite different from that towards other colonies.

Bechuanaland was the most important of the three territories: although not as wealthy in natural resources as Swaziland, its large size and strategic importance north of South Africa more than compensated for its lack of affluence. Moreover, it had been spotlighted throughout the world due to the Seretse Khama affair.[61] A judicial enquiry in 1949 on the protectorate's internal position resulted in the Labour Government banishing both Seretse Khama, the first in succession to the chieftainship of the Bamangwato tribe, and his uncle, Tchekedi, the regent. The origin of the difficulties in the protectorate, which made it such a *cause célèbre*, had been Seretse's marriage to an Englishwoman, Ruth Williams, in 1948. Not just the South African Government, outraged at the open challenge to its apartheid policy on its very doorstep, but also opposition within the Bamangwato tribe itself had forced the Labour Government to act. Their banishment decisions produced a maelstrom in Britain, focusing partly on Tchekedi's banishment for which it was felt there was no justifiable reason, and as a result Gordon Walker, who had become Commonwealth Secretary in 1950, suffered a loss in reputation. The Conservative Government allowed Tchekedi to return provided he refrained from political activity. This move was sanctioned by John Foster, the Parliamentary Under-Secretary at the C.R.O., who acted in Salisbury's absence, and without his knowledge.[62] The Government took a less liberal line on Seretse Khama, however: it uncompromisingly announced in March 1952 that he would not be allowed to go back until an alternative Chief was firmly established.[63] He eventually returned in October 1956 and later became a figure much respected by the British Government.[64]

West Africa

The crucial discussions on independence in the Gold Coast (which became Ghana after independence in 1957) took place between the

Governor, Sir Charles Arden-Clarke, Colonial Secretary Lyttelton and the Prime Minister since March 1952, the black African Kwame Nkrumah.[65] Events had moved quickly.[66] The pace had been set by the radical Report of the Watson Commission in 1948,[67] but even then, when Arden-Clarke, a man with considerable experience of Africa,[68] was appointed Governor the following year, few expected that within eight years the Gold Coast would receive its independence. His brief from the Labour Government was to channel the forces of nationalism, not thwart them, a task to which he willingly and immediately set himself. As he told the American journalist C. L. Sulzberger: 'Where you have plural societies, a number of mixed races as in East Africa, it will take longer to put nations on their feet as natural units; one race tries to dominate the other. In West Africa the problem is simple . . . There are few foreign 'settlers'; thus land was not taken and a clash was avoided.'[69]

Plans for the Gold Coast had thus been settled by the time Lyttelton arrived, with Griffiths taking the key decisions prodded by Cohen. Certain senior officials in the Office felt the advances in the Gold Coast during 1948–9 had been precipitate, and even that these advances had lost the cause of smooth transition to independence ten years, not just in the Gold Coast, but in other British colonies in Africa. Cohen himself later wrote: 'Some have criticised the decisions of 1948 and 1949, by which the point of no return was passed, on the ground that the advance was too rapid. The official view at the time was that no constitution which did not give a real share in the Government to the people of the Gold Coast had any chance of succeeding.'[70]

An illuminating survey of the constitutional position in each colony, prepared for the Cabinet in July 1957, confirmed what some officials in the Colonial Office had long suspected. It noted that the Watson Commission Report of 1948 had sold the pass in British West Africa; successive Governments had since then considered the risks of going too slowly were rather greater than the risks of proceeding too fast.[71] Indeed, after Watson the question became not whether but how soon the Gold Coast would follow Burma and Ceylon, which gained independence in 1948.

Lyttelton therefore had only to keep matters on a steady course and encourage Arden-Clarke to move cautiously. Lyttelton visited the Gold Coast in June 1952 as part of a four-week tour of the four West African colonies, and had talks with both Arden-Clarke and Nkrumah. Lyttelton had come to believe that, if the Gold Coast was to continue to be governed by consent, further changes were inescapable.[72] It was agreed that once proposals for constitutional reform had been prepared by the Gold Coast Government, they should be forwarded to the Secretary of State. Their proposals were published in a White Paper in June

1953 and went beyond what the British Government considered wise or desirable. The Cabinet – with both Churchill and Eden absent through ill health – debated the matter in July. It realised it was in a tight spot. If too lenient, its answer could jeopardise smooth progress in the colonies through the creation of an unfortunate precedent: if too restrictive, a rapid deterioration of the position might ensue and hasten the demand for an immediate grant of independence. Lyttelton, delaying his reply until after the return to the Cabinet of the two invalids, announced in October that, except for the suggestion that Gold Coast affairs should be dealt with by the Commonwealth Relations Office before self-government was attained, the Gold Coast Government's proposals were broadly acceptable. The new Constitution, effective from 8th June, 1954, after a General Election in May, provided *inter alia* for an all-African Cabinet and a directly elected Legislature. Hopkinson, announcing the proposals in the House in April, said: 'Under these changes, the powers retained by Her Majesty's Government are the minimum which they must retain, so long as they have any responsibility for the Gold Coast. These changes must therefore be regarded as the last stage before the Gold Coast assumes full responsibility for its own affairs.'[73]

A number of points of interest emerge from the passage to self-government in Ghana. Ghanaian independence saw the Conservative Government accepting the plan laid down by its predecessor at the encouragement of certain Colonial Office officials, principally Cohen, and at the same time attempting to move marginally more cautiously, on the advice of other Colonial Office officials. Anxieties increased after 1950, both in the Colonial Office and in the Gold Coast, about the lack of preparedness of the native Africans to take over the administration: whereas Ceylon, for example, had an extensive highly-trained native corps, at least three-quarters of the administrative and professional staff in the Gold Coast were Europeans.[74] However, against this was countered the argument that the colony was in a special position – having no racial problem, considerable natural wealth and a popular African Government.[75] Lyttelton's advocacy in Cabinet was crucial in obtaining agreement to the Gold Coast's proposals of self-government.[76]

The importance of the stance of the Governor was also displayed. Arden-Clarke played a key role in working with Nkrumah[77] to guide the Gold Coast through the various constitutional changes, helping shape their political demands into an acceptable form, and thus training the Africans in the skills of government.[78] The emergence of an independent Ghana in 1957 was of particular importance because in many ways it was the catalyst for the torrent of African nationalism in the following decade.

In Nigeria's progress towards independence, which the Government felt must proceed at a slower pace than in the Gold Coast,[79] both the Colonial Secretary, Lyttelton, and the Governor, Sir John Macpherson, played significant parts, although there was no single African leader with the position and influence of Nkrumah. Macpherson was appointed Governor in 1948 at the time when Nigeria received its new Richards Constitution.[80] Quickly realising that the Constitution's regional emphasis failed to take account of nationalist feeling, he embarked on further talks with Nigerians at the national and local level. A new and somewhat cumbrous Constitution in 1951 was the result, very much the fruit of Macpherson's labour and giving considerably more powers to the central government. This proved no more successful than the earlier Constitution, and in May 1953 Lyttelton regretfully announced in the House[81] that the Constitution would have to be redrawn. In fact he was secretly relieved: Lyttelton had been worried by the strains between the politically more advanced and restive Southern Region and the Northern Region, whose fourteen million Moslems were more pro-British. The collapse of the Constitution enabled Lyttelton to grant more autonomy to the North.[82]

Lyttelton accordingly invited all the parties to meet him in London, and a Conference was held from 30th July to 17th August, 1953, attended by Lyttelton and nineteen Nigerian delegates.[83] Though Lyttelton relied heavily on the advice of his officials, especially Gorell Barnes and the legal advisers, his crucial contribution lay in his masterly chairmanship of the Conference, and in the combination of good humour and strength of personality with which he led the three regional delegations to agreement on all points. He had expected to dislike the Conference; instead he warmed to the Nigerians more than to any other African race, particularly to Abubakar Tafawa Balewa[84] (the future Prime Minister of Nigeria until his assassination in 1966). The Conference resulted in a federation with increased responsibilities devolved to the regional government and legislatures.

The choice of a federal capital threatened to upset the Conference. As the Nigerians could not agree, the Secretary of State was asked to reach a verdict, and on the advice of Gorell Barnes and Macpherson decided on Lagos.[85] The Nigerian desire for a firm promise of self-government by 1956 presented a further, though lesser, problem. Lyttelton eventually persuaded them to accept the compromise of another Conference to review the position, meeting not later than August 1956.[86] In order to settle final problems relating to the public service and revenue divisions between the central and regional governments, which could not be resolved in London, it was agreed to reconvene the Conference in early 1954.[87] As Lyttelton himself acknowledged, the London Conference proved to be the most successful of the many negotiations in which he was engaged as Secretary of State.[88]

Lyttelton travelled to Lagos in January 1954 with his new Principal Private Secretary, John Johnston, when the remaining problems were cleared up, including relations between the regions and the centre[89] and the states' rights of secession (which were not adopted). The problem of European officials in Nigeria, who wanted guarantees from the British Government of their future employment, remained unsettled. This was one of the most important practical issues, as Nigeria (like Ceylon, Malaya and the Gold Coast) would have been crippled if the Europeans departed in force on independence, which they threatened to do if they did not receive satisfactory guarantees. Colonial Service reforms in June 1954, creating Her Majesty's Overseas Civil Service,[90] served as a temporary measure to overcome this problem, though more effective guarantees had to be introduced in 1956.

The Report of this second Conference, less significant but which cleared the final obstacles to independence, was published in a White Paper.[91] The changes were laid before Parliament and published on 3rd September, 1954. After the successful conclusion of the January talks, the Secretary of State's attention was diverted to more pressing matters[92] until the run-up to the London Conference in May 1957, where Lennox-Boyd agreed that the East and West Regions be given self-government in regional affairs.

Nigeria continued to be troubled by tribal worries even after its inception as an independent state. These became increasingly serious in the mid-1960s, and in May 1967 the Eastern Region proclaimed its independence under the name of Biafra. Civil war followed, which lasted until the federal victory in January 1970.

Developments in neither of the remaining two West African British colonies,[93] Gambia and Sierra Leone, occupied much of Lyttelton's time, although he visited both on his West African tour in June 1952. Progress towards self-government in neither colony was considered a priority, despite the feelings of jealousy that inevitably were being aroused by political development in Nigeria and the Gold Coast, as well as in the neighbouring French colonies, Guinea and Senegal. Constitutional developments introduced up until 1955 were nevertheless significant stepping-stones to independence. In June and July 1953 Lyttelton

374

agreed to an enlarged Legislative Council for Gambia, to be presided over by a Speaker, and for changes to the Executive Council, which came into effect in 1954. Sierra Leone was the more important colony strategically, with its harbour facilities. Lyttelton agreed to the introduction of a ministerial system, and the first Ministers were appointed in April 1954. Compared with the other two British West African colonies, the native Africans were far less advanced politically and administratively, and there were considerable doubts in the Colonial Office about the eventual granting of independence to Sierra Leone in 1961.[94] Gambia followed in 1965, and became a republic in 1970, the year before Sierra Leone.

Part 5 Assessment

The relatively swift progress towards independence in Britain's colonial territories had not been foreseen before the war. But the terrible cost of the Second World War, in terms of loss of influence, men and money (capital assets at home and abroad equal to one quarter of her entire national wealth were lost), made that progress inevitable.

Colonial policy was one of the more successful aspects of the work of the Government.[1] The actions of Oliver Lyttelton, Colonial Secretary for most of the period, were decisive and often imaginative, his task being very different from that faced by his Conservative predecessors before the war, and even from that performed by the last Conservative to hold the job, Oliver Stanley (1942–5). The status of the office had changed in a remarkably short space of time from being one of the less important Cabinet posts to one squarely in the limelight. Parliament was beginning to take note of colonial affairs in a way it had seldom done before the war. 'Pendennis' put the point graphically in the *Observer*: 'For many decades, Colonial debates used to empty the House: now matters have gone to the opposite extreme and they arouse most undignified acrimony.'[2] Public opinion, which was increasingly well informed,[3] frequently criticised Government policy,[4] and the Colonial Secretary was faced by a barrage of critical pressure from the colonies, unknown to his pre-war predecessors.[5] Not just political development and upheavals took the attention of the post-war Colonial Secretary, but also to a far greater extent he had to devote his time to their economic and social development.

Yet the colonial territories' rate of progress towards independence in the early 1950s was not a burning issue in Party politics. One of the most remarkable aspects of Lyttelton's period as Colonial Secretary was the way in which the Conservative Party accepted his forthright views on the subject. Those right-wing elements who might have been expected to have been critical instead channelled their feelings into opposition to the withdrawal from the Suez base and moves away from Imperial Preference.[6] The stampede towards decolonisation of the later 1950s and early 1960s was not foreseen, and the leadership of both major parties differed little on how quickly progress could take place. Thus, after surveying the main events in the colonies that caught the public's attention between 1951–5, Seretse Khama in 1952, the Kabaka of Buganda in 1953, the Mau Mau in Kenya and the Central African Federation, David Butler wrote: '. . . None of these issues produced a fundamental clash between the official leadership of the two parties. Labour spokesmen did stress increasingly the importance of advancing underdeveloped territories, but . . . no clear distinction appeared between the specific policies recommended by the parties.'[7]

Labour put forward the proposal that a date be fixed for the transfer of power in each territory, but had they been in power they would in all probability have found such an arrangement unworkable.[8] In fact because of the succession of crises faced by Lyttelton, he had little opportunity for implementing carefully conceived plans: he was essentially reacting to events rather than forging them. It is thus not surprising that his colonial policy was remarkable for its variety rather than its standardisation.

The Labour Party made much of the supposed breakdown of bipartisan policy in the colonial field. In so doing they seriously overstated the case. Lyttelton throughout his three years as Colonial Secretary had two guiding principles, which he inherited from his predecessor:[9] continued decentralisation of power to the local community of whatever race, sometimes successfully, as with the Gold Coast, at other times disastrously, as with British Guiana; and the building up of groups of smaller territories into larger ones, such as the federations in Central Africa and the West Indies,[10] and the care and hard work he put into healing sectarian wounds in Nigeria.

The events in British Guiana aroused more anger in the House than any other (except the Central African Federation) during Lyttelton's period as Colonial Secretary. Lyttelton, acting on the advice of the Governor, Sir Alfred Savage, who was concerned at the British Guiana Government's irresponsible and undemocratic policies, withdrew the Constitution in October 1953 and authorised the dispatch of a British cruiser and troops to reinforce local security forces. Labour overreacted without being in full possession of the facts, but their fury gradually petered out as it became clear that the Government of Dr. Cheddi Jagan had been neither as good socialists, nor as responsible as they had been led to believe. Lyttelton published a justification of the Government's action in a White Paper on 20th October.[11] A Commission was later appointed under Sir James Robertson (Governor-General of the Federation of Nigeria, 1955–60), whose Report, published in October 1954,[12] fully justified Lyttelton's action.

Continuity, not change, was therefore the order of the day at the Colonial Office after Lyttelton's arrival there in October 1951. Labour in their internal weakness after 1951 appeared to be making efforts to unite themselves in their indignation at the Government's colonial policy, which they considered was being guided by a conservative and insensitive businessman. Their fury was to an extent a sham and informed opinion was unconvinced by the polemic of Labour's more fervent backbenchers.[13] The stance of the Opposition Frontbench was little more impressive. In the words of *The Times*, its members had 'no well-defined policy attitude towards Africa or the colonies generally, far less a policy'.[14] The *Sunday Times* went further: the British Guiana debate, it said in a leader on 25th October, 1953, had been 'at heart, hollow and artificial . . . The real division of substance lay between the Socialist Frontbench and the extremists behind them'.

The Conservatives after 1951 faced far more problems with the colonies than Labour had in the early years after the war. Then the British Government held the initiative in Africa, but by the early 1950s they were already moving onto the defensive. The Conservatives inherited transitional constitutions introduced by Labour and had the difficult task of trying to make them work, hoping that these would be an educative preliminary to full-scale independence. Such optimistic hopes were not, however, realised. Lyttelton was confronted by the gathering pace of settler impatience and African nationalism which in many cases proved too strong to be restrained by the slender constitutional checks provided. Lyttelton was therefore constantly confronted by the choice of giving way prematurely or putting his foot down.[15] When Alan Lennox-Boyd became Colonial Secretary, however, he had requests from representatives of many colonies not to accede to their public demands for an early increase in the pace of change as they realised their countries were not yet sufficiently prepared for independence.[16]

On the economic side the aim was to encourage friendship and the active loyalty of the colonies. But already by 1951 it had become clear that the schemes were not developing as anticipated: the African in many cases showed himself intensely suspicious of Britain's efforts, especially where land was concerned, and also where it entailed importing capital and personnel. It was partly in response to this cool reception to British aid that Lyttelton, contrary to expectation, did not allow economic development to be a major demand on his time. Public bodies like the Colonial Development Corporation, initiated by Labour,[17] were allowed to run down unobtrusively, although the marketing boards, with their egalitarian and stabilising functions, appeared to have become a permanent feature. New economic problems were looming which were to trouble successive Colonial Secretaries, not least the economic relationship of self-governing colonies to the United Kingdom and the growth of competition in colonial markets.[18]

Colonial issues came before the Cabinet with increasing regularity during the early 1950s. Some Ministers felt insufficient consideration was being paid to colonial problems, and further that their Departments were constantly being confronted by situations of great urgency because the Colonial Office had failed to let them have advance information of developments which were taking place. As a result Sir Norman Brook in August 1955 suggested the creation of a Cabinet Committee to decide on and co-ordinate policy: this was accordingly established under the chairmanship initially of the Prime Minister.[19]

The Conservatives were fortunate to have had three outstanding Conservative Secretaries of State for the Colonies since the 1930s – Stanley, Lyttelton and Lennox-Boyd. But Lyttelton's farsightedness, his readiness to listen to advice, persuasiveness and knack of reaching the right decision qualify him for being judged the most effective.

Chapter 10 Foreign Policy

Part 1 The Foreign Office

That Churchill regarded the Foreign Office as his principal instrument of policy was proved, a leader writer in the *News Chronicle* asserted just after the Election, by the quality of the men he appointed to senior posts in the Department.[1] Of one of these appointments there was no doubt; Anthony Eden would be Foreign Secretary. Apart from his two previous periods as Secretary of State for Foreign Affairs (1935–8 and 1940–5), he had been shadow Secretary since 1945, and had kept in close personal touch with Ernest Bevin (Foreign Secretary, July 1945–March 1951),[2] with whose aims he was in broad agreement.[3]

Eden's presence was felt immediately, the Foreign Office being relieved at the return of a professional they knew after the unskilled and brusque Herbert Morrison (Foreign Secretary, March–October 1951), whose success as a Minister in other Departments had not been repeated at the Foreign Office.[4] Eden's return engendered a new air of authority, but not merely in the Office. Within a few days of taking charge Eden addressed the United Nations in Paris[5] where it was clear that he commanded wide respect.

More has been written about Eden than about any other Minister except Churchill in the 1951–5 Government, much of it unfavourable.[6] This is unjust: with his skills in negotiation and his diplomatic successes during 1951–5, he must be considered one of the most accomplished post-war Foreign Secretaries, second only to Bevin in the eyes of many Foreign Office officials.[7] As Foreign Secretary he knew and was able to talk with authority to almost all major international figures (Truman, Acheson, Molotov and many senior European statesmen he knew from earlier contacts, mostly during the war); he was an excellent negotiator,[8] relying more on instinct than on logic;[9] he had a great command and unrivalled knowledge of the subject, which had been his life's interest. Apart from his periods as Foreign Secretary, he had also served as Parliamentary Private Secretary to Austen Chamberlain when Foreign Secretary, 1926–9, as Parliamentary Under-Secretary at the Foreign Office, 1931–3, and also as Secretary of State for Dominion Affairs, 1939–40. Eden had a good sense of timing, and a broad vision which

379

ensured that he considered the wider implications of a particular course of action, rather than only its likely effect on Britain.[10] He also had great charm, to which many were susceptible[11] and was quick to size up a position. These qualities far outweighed his weaknesses, of which there were likewise a large number: he had too many personal likes and dislikes (about individuals including Nasser and Dulles and even countries, among them Spain and Hungary), which he allowed to affect his policy more than they should have done;[12] he was quick tempered and touchy about criticism, unlike Bevin, although both hated being let down by anyone; he was not an originator of policy, but used the ideas of others, often to good advantage;[13] he worried inordinately about detail and fussed over minutiae, such as the punctuation or style of a telegram, could not always distinguish the important from the trivial, and was often poor at expressing himself, either in print or in speech. This lack of skill at articulating his feelings manifested itself in particular in his relationship with Churchill. Decisive up to a point, in the last resort he needed Churchill to back him up.[14]

His performance in the Commons varied widely: apart from a few sparkling speeches during 1951–5, as a rule he was inclined towards dull delivery. In winding-up debates, however, his ability to make quick off-the-cuff remarks won him admiration. Jo Grimond, thinking of Eden during 1950–6, wrote: 'It is true that his speeches lacked the wit of Oliver Stanley or the telling phrase of Churchill . . . But he held the House of Commons. He made Foreign Affairs appear important and British foreign policy as explained by him seemed of weight and significance. No one else could do it as well.'[15] Eden took his Parliamentary work seriously, taking as much pain preparing for Parliamentary Questions as he would for a speech to the House. When out of the country, as he was during the Geneva Conference (May–July 1954), he would frequently telephone the Chief Whip to learn the mood of the House.[16]

Those who knew Eden from the war noticed how his health declined during the six year interval up until 1951.[17] Within a month of taking office he was complaining of stomach pains before his speeches to the United Nations in Paris and at the NATO meeting in Rome. The problem continued throughout 1952, compounded when he was away from the Office for most of July with jaundice.[18] After his marriage to Clarissa Churchill in August 1952[19] he was persuaded to have a series of medical examinations where gall-stones were diagnosed. His health deteriorated throughout March 1953: towards the end of the month an observer noted that 'For the first time [Eden is] really beginning to show his age and is thin and drawn as well as white.'[20] On 30th March, it was

380

announced he was unwell and a week later that he would have to undergo an operation, which meant postponing his forthcoming trip to Italy, Greece and Turkey.[21] A first operation at the London Clinic on 12th April was not entirely successful, nor was a second on 29th April. By now a weak man, he left London on 19th May to stay at Chequers at Churchill's invitation[22] before leaving for Boston on 5th June where a third operation took place five days later. The surgeon, Dr. Richard Cattell, told Sir Roger Makins, the British Ambassador, that there was only a relatively small chance of Eden recovering completely.[23] But by the end of the month it was clear he was much better. He left the hospital on 29th June for Rhode Island to convalesce, and the following day wrote to Eisenhower: 'It feels almost strange to be free again of doctors and of hospital after all these months.'[24] Returning to London for a few days on 26th July, he was relieved by Lord Salisbury's capable management of the Foreign Office, and left for a recuperative holiday in the Mediterranean on 8th August. While in London he was also reassured by Patrick Buchan-Hepburn, Oliver Lyttelton and Macmillan (who found him 'restored to his old self')[25] that he was the undisputed successor to Churchill. They were convinced the Prime Minister would be retiring in October.[26] Eden returned to London on 30th September, taking up his duties again at the Foreign Office on 5th October, after an absence of six months.[27] Opinions vary as to his state of health after 1953,[28] though his judgment and general ability to conduct business seemed unimpaired. On balance it would appear that Eden, like Churchill after his illness, had both good and bad days, and that there was considerable fluctuation in his performance.[29]

A bulletin had announced that the Prime Minister would take over responsibility for the Foreign Office in Eden's absence. But he was no mere cipher, making it immediately clear to officials that he would run the Egypt discussions in his own way.[30] Highly selective in the topics he considered, he was not interested in many official papers, which went direct from the Permanent Under-Secretary, Sir William Strang, to the Minister of State, Selwyn Lloyd. Nor did he use the Foreign Office as his base, preferring to deal with Strang, and John Colville, his joint Principal Private Secretary responsible for foreign affairs, whom he saw at Number Ten.[31] So in his stand-in capacity Churchill did not feel he was required to have a day-to-day administrative role. He had not only managed the Foreign Office during Eden's absence with jaundice the previous year, but had been reinvigorated by the experience of dealing with work which he enjoyed. But as the weeks of Eden's absence in 1953 continued, Churchill's enthusiasm for the work of the Foreign Office steadily dwindled.[32] It did, however, provide the opportunity for his most significant speech of his last premiership, in which he called for talks at the highest level between the leading powers without being constrained by 'a ponderous or rigid agenda'.[33]

When Churchill was struck down by his major stroke on 23rd June, the House was quick to object to there being no Foreign Secretary. Salisbury was therefore appointed, with Rab Butler the spokesman in the Commons.[34] The Office was delighted with Salisbury and the calm aristocratic manner he exuded, not just because life was quieter as he was in the House of Lords but also as he brought to the Office a welcome note of continuity, experience and competence.[35] The Cabinet also discussed foreign affairs far more fully than when Eden was in charge.[36] Salisbury visited the United States for talks with the Secretary of State, John Foster Dulles, and the French Foreign Minister, Georges Bidault, returning to London on 21st July, a meeting that took the place of a Bermuda Conference, delayed due to Churchill's illness. Salisbury, whose intellectual abilities were admired by Dulles,[37] was able to secure United States agreement to a Foreign Ministers' meeting with the Russians, with a precise agenda.[38] On his return, Salisbury's visit was harshly attacked in the House of Commons by Kenneth Younger, who had been Minister of State at the Foreign Office, 1950–1: 'I am afraid that, in the limp hands of the acting Foreign Secretary, Lord Salisbury, the Prime Minister's policy [of a summit meeting without agenda] has been sunk without trace.'[39] The Foreign Office felt the agreement to hold four-power talks at Foreign Secretary level that Salisbury obtained, especially taking into account the adamant view expressed by Eisenhower that he personally would not attend a summit, was the most he could possibly have got from the Americans (the French, too, did not seem very keen on a meeting with the Soviet Union).[40] *The Times* noted, however, that the Foreign Ministers' meeting, 'has been received in many places with disappointment, as a step back from the Prime Minister's idea of a four-power meeting at a higher level still'.[41] Salisbury was unable to defend himself in the Lords until the week following the Younger attack, when he delivered a well-received speech, written largely by himself. Salisbury was a skilled negotiator, and his progress on other topics discussed at Washington, including Germany, the E.D.C. and Egypt, was better received.[42]

Having two aspirant Foreign Secretaries in the background was a major problem for Salisbury: Churchill constantly interfered over the discussions on summits and Egypt, and Eden was anxious to make his presence felt from the sidelines – and even held a press conference on foreign affairs on his return to England on 26th July, despite a marked lack of enthusiasm from Conservative Central Office as well as from

Salisbury.[43] Eden throughout his absence was most anxious for his views to be known,[44] but because of his close friendship with Salisbury and the latter's tolerance towards Eden there was a minimum of tension. Not that Salisbury was by any means entirely happy in his temporary post: indeed disapproval of both the British line favouring recognition of Red China, and Churchill's policy on top-level talks with Russia, made him at one point consider resignation,[45] and it is quite possible he would have put his foot down more firmly had Eden not returned to the Foreign Office in early October.

Butler was less successful in his job as spokesman in the Commons. He delivered a poor speech in the House on 21st July, which had been written for him by the Foreign Office: even his admirer and former Parliamentary Private Secretary 'Chips' Channon (1938–41) considered the speech 'a flop'.[46] The Opposition was especially irritated by statements which argued that the Washington talks had been a success, for example: 'When we look on the results of the Washington Conference, I think we must agree that it has not only successfully established and consolidated the absolute unity of aim and purpose of the great Powers involved but has also marked a notable step forward towards the relaxation of tension.'[47] Butler was considerably overstretched with extra responsibilities that summer: in Churchill's absence he was also acting Prime Minister, which meant a stream of extra red boxes and endless decisions to be taken in addition to his work as Chancellor. Butler, who had appeared over the previous months to be increasingly invincible, had at last met his match: the extra burden simply proved too much for one man to bear.[48]

Throughout his last period as Foreign Secretary, Eden remained very much his own man. Although always accessible, he often relied on junior Ministers less for policy advice than to find out what his colleagues in the House were thinking, and where Churchill stood.[49] He allowed Selwyn Lloyd a relatively free hand at the United Nations' discussions on disarmament,[50] and generally, the Ministers of State played a more important role, but the Parliamentary Under-Secretaries, apart from Nutting, in practice seldom saw him.[51]

Initially only one Minister of State was appointed. As a barrister with no previous ministerial experience, Selwyn Lloyd had been anticipating a job in an economic Department[52] (indeed Butler wanted him as Financial Secretary at the Treasury).[53] Eden, however, was anxious to have someone with no previous foreign service[54] and for this reason decided against the experienced Henry Hopkinson.[55] But he had gained a favourable impression of Lloyd's performance in the House since 1945, particularly in economic debates.[56] Eden quickly appreciated

Lloyd's ability to work hard and effectively, and delegated an increasing amount to him, although on matters which Eden considered of prime importance, Lloyd played little or no part. As well as the United Nations and disarmament, Lloyd also had responsibility for the Middle East, where Eden accepted Lloyd's assessment of the position in the Sudan and was content to let him handle policy there. He did, however, disagree with Lloyd's preferred solution for the Suez Canal base treaty areas, with a reduced number of troops in the base;[57] Eden wanted to leave the Canal Zone altogether on as good terms as possible and try to make a friendly bargain with Nasser.

During Eden's six months' absence in 1953 Lloyd's authority dramatically increased, as he played in particular an important part over policy towards Persia.[58] He soon established himself as one of the most successful 'number twos' in the Government, though his reputation at this time in the House was never as high as it was at the United Nations.[59] His strength lay not in thinking out long-term plans or new ideas, but in the execution of policy, where his legal mind was invaluable in unravelling complex matters. In Eden's frequent absences he attended nearly as many Cabinets as his Secretary of State, gaining rich experience in this, his first job, not just of foreign affairs, but also of the governmental machine. All this was to serve him well in his later career, as Minister of Supply (1954–5), Minister of Defence (1955), and then as Foreign Secretary himself (1955–60) and subsequently Chancellor of the Exchequer until Harold Macmillan's Cabinet purge of July 1962.

Two Parliamentary Under-Secretaries were appointed in 1951, one in each House. Lord Reading, junior Minister in the Lords, had no previous ministerial experience. Already in his sixty-third year, he was an unusual choice, but acquitted himself well on a narrow front. He also had protocol responsibility, oversaw Foreign Office work connected with Latin America and the Far East, and at the Geneva Conference on South-East Asia in mid-1954, he was a highly competent and respected spokesman,[60] although his influence on policy was virtually nil. An imposing figure, although not an intellectual, he was at his best when conducting relations with foreign diplomats: indeed some in the Office felt he could have managed more work than Eden gave him.[61] In November 1953 he was upgraded to Minister of State, Foreign Office,[62] as it was felt a more senior spokesman was needed in the Upper House and at international conferences.

The second Parliamentary Under-Secretary, Anthony Nutting, was a young man, at thirty-one exactly half Reading's age when appointed in 1951. He had known Eden since the war (he was his Private Secretary in 1942) and after entering the House in 1945 had been marked as a young man ripe for promotion.[63] Eden undoubtedly felt more warmth for Nutting than for any other in his ministerial team, recognising in him some of the dash and charm of his own youth and a potential future Conservative Leader. Eden, however, regarded Lloyd as more of a heavyweight, and the special relationship with Nutting in no way detracted from Lloyd's position as Minister of State.[64] On Lloyd's promotion to Minister of Supply in October 1954, Nutting became a Minister of State, taking over Lloyd's responsibilities for the United Nations, the Middle East and disarmament.[65]

Douglas Dodds-Parker, who had been Chairman of the Party's Imperial Affairs Committee since the Election, became Under-Secretary on Reading's promotion in November 1953. He came with a wide experience of the Middle East, having served in the Sudan Political Service, 1930–8. But he stayed less than a year, before being moved sideways to the Commonwealth Relations Office in the October 1954 reshuffle, and hence made little impact.[66] A double change of Under-Secretaries followed in October 1954. Robert Turton came in from the Ministry of National Insurance at Eden's request because he was thought to be a good Parliamentarian.[67] He inherited Nutting's responsibilities for Europe and also took on economic questions working under Reading. Lord John Hope, Vice-Chairman of the Party Foreign Affairs Committee since the Election and a newcomer to the ministerial team, took over information services and protocol. Both were able men, anxious to contribute, but it was not until Harold Macmillan succeeded Eden in April 1955 that notice began to be taken of their views.[68]

Two of the several Parliamentary Private Secretaries who served Foreign Office Ministers were of particular note. Robert Carr, who accompanied Eden on a tour of the United States in the summer of 1951, had originally been appointed as his Parliamentary Private Secretary early in 1951 as he wanted someone to keep him abreast of industrial and social policy, selected from the post-war vintage of young Conservative M.P.s.[69] It was, in fact, on domestic matters that Carr made his major contribution, and he also had a beneficial, calming effect on Eden.[70] Lloyd's Parliamentary Private Secretary, David Ormsby-Gore (later Lord Harlech),[71] was more involved in the conduct of foreign affairs, travelling with him to the United Nations General Assembly in 1951 and 1954 to act as an aide and speech-writer.[72] A more urbane man than Lloyd, Ormsby-Gore also performed a valuable service in smoothing over some of his master's rougher edges.

Eden thought the same way as the Foreign Office on most policies, and thus there was little friction. Among those whose company and advice he particularly liked were three of his Deputy Under-Secretaries, Sir Pierson Dixon, Sir Ashley Clarke and Sir Harold Caccia, as well as the Principal Private Secretary, 1951–4, Evelyn Shuckburgh.[73]

Sir William Strang had been Permanent Under-Secretary since 1949. A quiet scholarly man, reserved about putting forward his own opinions and by nature cautious and dispassionate, he was regarded by many as the perfect official.[74] He would outline options, leaving the decision to Eden, and they evolved a good, though not a particularly intimate relationship, to the extent that he stayed on at Eden's request for a year following his sixtieth birthday. Strang, however, tended to be rather reticent about arguing with his superiors,[75] and even against his more forceful deputies, in particular Dixon and Sir Roger Makins, he sometimes failed to hold his own. Sir Ivone Kirkpatrick, who succeeded Strang in the autumn of 1953, was more extrovert and definite in his statements. His previous post had been U.K. High Commissioner in Germany (like Strang he specialised in German affairs), and he retained a rather high-handed manner. Opinions about Kirkpatrick were mixed: few doubted his intelligence or quickness, but some objected that he was interested only in certain countries, not least Germany, and also that he was too rough with people. Kirkpatrick was not at his best as a judge of character, and was over-quick to dismiss men as no good. Lord Gladwyn, for instance, thought Kirkpatrick intelligent and courageous, but that he had a tendency to score points and lacked an understanding of the French mind.[76] Wherever possible, it may be said, Kirkpatrick liked to take a strong line on both men and events: this was seen nowhere more clearly than during the Suez crisis in 1956 when he was one of a small minority at the Foreign Office who favoured the use of force against Nasser.

Foremost among the Deputy Under-Secretaries, Sir Roger Makins (1948–52), had a fine intellect, quick grasp, forceful character, and a great influence on promoting Anglo-American relations. Due to this and also to his strong feeling for the importance of the Commonwealth relationship, he was not in favour of closer economic links with Europe. Makins, who specialised in economic and also atomic affairs, was the dominant official at the Foreign Office throughout his period as deputy, and after his return from the United States, where he was British Ambassador (1953–6), he was seen as an obvious choice as Permanent Under-Secretary.[77] Dixon (1950–4) had known Eden well since the war (he was Principal Private Secretary from 1943–7), and they remained close.[78] He was highly able and clear headed, and his influence rested more on the close relationship he developed with successive Foreign Secretaries (in particular Bevin and Eden) than on original ideas of his own. Two other deputies were particularly outstanding, Sir Harold Caccia (1954–6) later Permanent Under-Secretary, 1962–5, and Sir Frank Roberts (1951–4), who ended his Foreign Office career as Ambassador to West Germany, 1963–8, though they did not exert the same influence on Eden as either Dixon or Makins.[79]

A number of senior men served abroad throughout this period. Sir Gladwyn Jebb, the United Kingdom Permanent Representative at the United Nations since 1950, had a special position due to his ability to argue successfully with the head of the Soviet delegation, Andrei Vyshinsky, which led *The Times* to remark that he '. . . has contributed perhaps as much as any man in making this country's policy in the United Nations known to the public in many countries'.[80] In December 1953 he was offered the Paris Embassy (but Eden would not make him U.K. representative to NATO as well, as he had hoped)[81] and though he would have preferred to return to London as Permanent Under-Secretary, he accepted.[82] Just as Eden and Churchill found Jebb somewhat abrasive, so Jebb, for his part, had little regard for the Foreign Secretary – although with his appointment as Ambassador to France he was effectively isolated from main-stream policy discussions in Whitehall. Taking up the Paris post in March 1954, he succeeded Eden's wartime Principal Private Secretary (1941–3), friend and admirer, Sir Oliver Harvey, whose period at the Embassy was remarkable for his industry, and conscientiousness, although some felt excessive his enthusiasm for the left in France. Sir Oliver Franks, British Ambassador in Washington since May 1948, was a political appointee of Clement Attlee. Having entered Whitehall in 1939 from academic life, his Home Civil Service career culminated in his appointment as Permanent Secretary at the Ministry of Supply, 1945–6, followed by two years as Provost of Queen's College, Oxford. The Foreign Office had a very high opinion of him as did the State Department, with Acheson, for example, considering him of far greater stature and ability than Kirkpatrick.[83] Yet when asked by Eden if he would like to serve another term he declined for personal reasons.[84] Churchill initially wanted to appoint another non-career man to Washington,[85] but was prevailed against and Makins was given the job on Franks' departure in December, 1952.

Part 2 'The Special Relationship'

The 'special relationship' between Britain and the United States during 1951–5 may not always have been harmonious; it was organic but full of friction.[1] Yet despite the severest of strains the bond was never fundamentally damaged, remaining deep at least until the shattering disagreements over the Suez episode in 1956. The continuing strength of the relationship owed much to Churchill's own determination to nurture it. In his last major speech in the House as Prime Minister, in March 1955, he said (perhaps reflecting his hopes rather more than the reality): 'One thing stands out in my mind above all others; that is the increase of our friendship and understanding with our ally the United States.'[2] It was a mark of how highly Churchill valued this relationship that in the closing minutes of what he must have known was to be his last major speech as Premier, he brushed aside provocative jibes from Labour members about the conduct of his other great foreign passion, summit meetings, and used his remaining words to explain American policy and defend Eisenhower's actions.[3]

The years after the war saw the trend in the balance of power tipped further in the direction of the United States as Britain lagged behind both in her economic recovery and, *vis-à-vis* the Soviet Union, in the manufacture of atomic weapons. The Labour Government, guided by Ernest Bevin, had maintained close links with the United States, although clashes arose over the questions of tariffs, nuclear weapons, the Middle East and the nature of security arrangements, especially after the defections of Foreign Office diplomats Guy Burgess and Donald Maclean in May 1951.[4] The return of the Conservative Government in October 1951 did little to alter the *status quo*,[5] despite Churchill's even greater enthusiasm for the relationship than his predecessor. Churchill wished to renew the intimate relationship with the presidency which he had encouraged during the war, though not to re-establish the close exchange of letters he had had with Roosevelt. Churchill 'let it be known' that the U.S. Ambassador, alone of foreign Ambassadors, had direct access to Number Ten.[6] The Truman Administration suspected that Churchill's major objective in the January 1952 talks would be to strengthen and re-emphasise the Anglo-American partnership. In background notes to these discussions, the Americans noted that Churchill had been critical in Opposition of the Labour Government for impairing the relationship. They determined to reassure Churchill that the relationship remained a cornerstone of American policy while at the same time pointing out the pitfalls of making it too obvious, not least because of the adverse effect on other nations, especially France, and the disadvantage to the United States of becoming tarred by the 'colonial brush'.[7] On balance, relations were closer with the Truman Administration than they were to be with Dwight D. Eisenhower.

Affectionate remarks were afterwards uttered concerning friendship,[8] although in reality the Truman Administration often remained cool and detached over policy discussions in the heat of the moment as well as being disappointed in the stance taken by the Churchill Government on several issues – including China, NATO and advancing the cause of a United Europe.[9] Their background notes for the January 1952 talks described Churchill as being still robust and vigorous at seventy-seven, but 'hard of hearing' and 'prone to fall asleep'.[10] At the talks themselves, Churchill surprised the Americans by the highly emotional arguments he deployed over the oft-quoted issue of the appointment of the Supreme Allied Commander of the Atlantic, who should, Churchill argued, be a British naval officer. Averell Harriman, Special Assistant to Harry Truman, 1950–1, a wartime U.S. Ambassador to Moscow (1943–6) and a friend of Churchill and Eden, remarked: 'I found in all this Churchill was thinking back to . . . World War II.'[11] The Americans quickly formed the opinion that he was no longer as much in command as he had been during the war. However, between Churchill and Truman (President, April 1945–January 1953) there was definitely a friendship of some warmth.[12] At the end of Truman's presidency they were both anxious to say a personal goodbye to each other.[13]

Relations between the Government and Dean Acheson (Secretary of State, 1949–January 1953), so good during the Bevin period, were less close beneath the surface cordiality. Acheson and Eden were, perhaps, too much alike, in their outlook and even physically, to get on well together. In talks at Paris during early November 1951, Acheson was distinctly irritable about Britain's position on Persia, and bluntly told Eden's Principal Private Secretary, Evelyn Shuckburgh: 'You must learn to live in the world as it is.'[14] Not only did he feel that Eden talked down to him, but he was also jealous of him for stealing the limelight at the United Nations General Assembly, then in session in Paris. At dinner on 6th January, 1952, at the British Embassy, Acheson in turn upset Eden by saying that the business of a Foreign Minister was very different from in the days of Lord Palmerston, and now they had to know about business and commerce, a deeply offensive remark.[15] It was left to the British Ambassador, Sir Oliver Franks, to patch up that dispute.

The friction, however, continued: Eden felt Acheson misbehaved (as he did) in an audience at Buckingham Palace in February 1952.[16] In April *Newsweek* published a full-page article on the bad blood between the two men entitled, 'A Clash of Personalities: Eden vs Acheson'. This boldly stated that the two 'have found personal co-operation as difficult as agreement on policy',[17] and, as a result, both parties felt it necessary to exchange letters of reassurance.[18] Relations reached a low point in New York in November when Acheson was distinctly unpleasant to

Eden and Selwyn Lloyd during discussions over the Indian resolution on Korea.[19] It is possible to exaggerate this abrasiveness, but it is, nevertheless, true that their relationship was considerably less good than either of them afterwards claimed.[20]

The special relationship floundered further with the accession of the Eisenhower Administration in January 1953, and was not encouraged over the next few months, as a result of the testing by the United States of the hydrogen bomb, disagreement over recognition of Communist China and the desirability of East-West trade.[21] Earlier doubts about Churchill's performance as Prime Minister were confirmed by the new Administration. Churchill and Eisenhower's friendship had been forged in the war when Eisenhower was Commander-in-Chief, Allied Forces, North Africa, 1942–4, and Supreme Allied Commander of the Expeditionary Force in Europe, 1944–5. Since 1950 he had been Supreme Commander of NATO Forces in Europe. But as early as December 1951, after his first meeting with Churchill since he again became Prime Minister, Eisenhower had written that '. . . He simply will not think in terms of today, but rather only those of the war years . . . My regretful opinion is that the Prime Minister no longer absorbs new ideas . . .'[22] On 12th February, 1953, Eisenhower, having recently been inaugurated President, lunched with Walter Gifford, the retiring U.S. Ambassador in London. Gifford expressed his 'complete conviction' that Churchill was no longer a real power in the Conservative Party, and pointed out that in the opinion of many he had outlived his usefulness.[23] In New York in January 1953, on his second visit to the United States, Churchill had received a far cooler response from the Americans than he would have liked and left a disappointed man. In John Colville's view, 'The fact was that Churchill now realised, to his bitter disappointment, that he was welcomed and revered in America much more as Winston Churchill than as the Prime Minister of the United Kingdom.'[24] And in his diary Eisenhower wrote of that Churchill visit:

Much as I held Winston in my personal affection, and much as I admire him for his past accomplishments and leadership, I wish he would turn over the leadership of the British Conservation [sic] Party to younger men . . . I assured him that I am quite ready to communicate with him personally, on our old basis of intimate friendship, where discussions between us could help advance our common interests. But I made it clear to him that when official agreement or understanding must be reached, it must be done through those channels that will establish proper records for the future and that will make certain of the proper domestic collaborations that our form of government requires . . . he had developed an almost childlike faith that all of the answers are to be found merely in British-American partnership.[25]

Eisenhower told Churchill that in his view, with world communism on the march, it would be far better for the two strongest Western powers not to appear to be ganging up together. The following month he wrote in his diary:

. . . No such special relationship can be maintained or even suggested publicly. In public relationship all nations are sovereign and equal. This means that on the personal and informal basis we must find a way of agreeing with our British friends on broad objectives and purposes. Thereafter, each must pursue its own detailed methods of achieving these purposes.[26]

Eisenhower also felt that the August 1952 joint Truman–Churchill message to Dr. Muhammad Moussadeq (Prime Minister of Persia, 1951–3), about which Churchill had been delighted, was a mistake and that it would have been more effective if forwarded purely as a British proposal.[27] But it must be said that underlying all Eisenhower's impatience with Churchill was a genuine and deep affection,[28] which remained undiminished. Churchill, it turned out, still exercised a formidable influence over Eisenhower, of which the President's advisers were all too well aware. Over the months, a softening in Eisenhower's original rigid conception of the special relationship could be detected.

The new British Ambassador, Sir Roger Makins (1953–6), had a close relationship with John Foster Dulles (Secretary of State, 1953–9), making as good a job as had Franks in ameliorating the underlying tension. But the new U.S. Ambassador in London, Winthrop Aldrich (1953–7), was kept out of the mainstream by Dulles[29] and was not as skilled an envoy as his highly accomplished predecessor, Gifford (1950–3),[30] whom Churchill and Eden wished to stay. Some upset was also caused by Washington's premature announcement of Aldrich's appointment before the customary consultation had taken place.[31] At his January 1953 meeting with Dulles Churchill decided that he disliked him and considered his influence over Eisenhower pernicious.[32] There was also some dimming of Churchill's own enthusiasm for the new President. But because of his unwillingness to appear critical of his old friend, he would make Dulles the scapegoat for all that went wrong in discussions between both countries.[33]

The most unsatisfactory of personal relationships during the

Eisenhower Administration was between Eden and Dulles. Eisenhower alleged that Eden had expressed the hope that Dulles would not be appointed Secretary of State in a Republican Administration.[34] Eden later denied this,[35] and it would seem implausible that a British Foreign Secretary would ever have dared tell a man likely to be elected President of the United States whom to choose as his principal foreign policy adviser. Yet there was certainly general disappointment in the Foreign Office when Eisenhower's victory was declared in early November 1952, and dismay lest Dulles be appointed Secretary of State,[36] and his reputation over policy on the Far East – he had negotiated and signed the U.S.–Japanese Peace Treaty – was poor.[37] Eisenhower was aware at the time of anxiety about the appointment of Dulles on the grounds that he was unsympathetic to the British,[38] and for that reason had even considered not selecting him. Dulles, too, recognised the problem: on 11th November, 1952 he attempted to obtain an audience with Eden while at the United Nations General Assembly in Paris, but Eden stalled, thinking correctly that Dulles was seeking to ingratiate himself in an effort to be appointed Secretary of State.[39] Dulles persisted and his efforts were rewarded: on 13th November the meeting took place. Dulles gave Eden various assurances that policy would not be changed under a Republican Administration.[40] Dulles himself was pleased by the talk and wrote to tell Eisenhower how cordial and relaxed it was.[41]

Yet the relationship between the two Secretaries of State was not initially as bad as has often been portrayed. Livingston Merchant (Assistant Secretary of State for European Affairs, 1953–6), who, according to several colleagues was closer to Dulles than any other State Department official, said that in Eden's memoirs (where he speaks of Dulles with some bitterness),[42] 'He attributed to Foster a dislike of himself which I am satisfied never existed. Foster Dulles was genuinely fond of Anthony Eden.'[43] In fact, it is the twenty months of Eden's premiership that have tended to be responsible for the unduly jaundiced view of their relations. Both men came to know each other increasingly well during the Bermuda Conference of December 1953, in particular during informal bathing expeditions. After a private talk with Eden during the Conference, the American journalist C. L. Sulzberger wrote: 'Eden professes to like Dulles a lot and finds him a good man to work with.'[44] Jim Hagerty (Press Secretary to President Eisenhower, 1953 – 61) wrote in his diary an enlightening observation during the Churchill-Eden visit to Washington in June 1954. He is discussing a photograph of Dulles, Eden, Aldrich and Makins being taken in Dulles' garden: 'All agreed that such a photograph was necessary to again offset the stories that were constantly being printed that Dulles and Eden are very cool toward each other. While they disagree on many subjects, particularly Red China, I have seen no coolness between the two men throughout the meetings.'[45]

Each grumbled incessantly about the other to his own colleagues but in their private and public relations, at least until mid-1954,[46] they showed a great deal of sympathy and respect towards each other. After the London Conference in September 1954, Dulles wrote to Eden on 3rd October of the 'wonderful leadership' he gave, and how he felt that they were both working more closely together than ever before. Eden sent back a message the following day, remarking how much he appreciated Dulles' unwavering support during the critical week of the Conference.[47] There was, of course, the problem of a difference of temperament and style, yet the extent that both men determined to put such personal differences behind them should not be underestimated.

Relations were certainly not improved by a number of State Department officials and diplomats never even pretending to be neutral in their attitude to Britain, in particular Herbert Hoover Junior (son of the former President, 'Special Adviser' to Dulles in 1953 and Under-Secretary, 1954–7); some were even actively antagonistic to Britain's interests.[48] Eden apparently detested Henry Byroade (Assistant Secretary of State for the Middle East and Africa), whom he felt knew 'absolutely nothing' about the Middle East.[49] He also strongly disliked the American Ambassador to Cairo, Jefferson Caffery, whom he thought 'anti-British' (which was largely true).[50] Men in senior positions and actively sympathetic to Britain, such as Merchant[51] and Walter Bedell Smith, Under-Secretary of State, January 1953–September 1954, were in the minority. Indeed, when the latter retired, Eden wrote to him: 'The idea that you will not much longer be at the State Department fills me with gloom . . . I just hate to think of our work without you.'[52]

These tensions between individuals were reflected and fanned by the disagreements between both Governments on many policy questions. The State Department, and Dulles in particular, were suspicious (Oliver Lyttelton spoke of 'pathological hatred')[53] of any British policy that seemed to support colonialism.[54] To the United States, the containment of world communism was their main aim, and with this went a distrust of neutralism. Britain had no such clear-cut overriding aim, and to an extent conflict was therefore inevitable. Both American Administrations hoped Britain would make a large contribution to Europe, either to NATO or by pledging forces to the European Defence Community (E.D.C.). Only after Britain's pledge of troops to the Western European Union (W.E.U.) in September 1954 was harmony restored on this front. The United States wanted Britain to unite and lead Europe, thereby providing a strong forward bulwark against the Soviet Union. But to Churchill and Eden, the objective of maintaining good relations with the Commonwealth and the United States was just as much a priority as Europe. Meanwhile, the importance Dulles attached to relations with West Germany and with Konrad Adenauer, its Chancellor throughout the period, led to tension between Britain and America as each vied for influence with the Federal Republic. The Labour Government had supported the Social Democratic Party, and Adenauer, who became Chancellor in 1949, was a Christian Democrat. Under Churchill and Eden, however, Anglo-German relations much improved. Eden in particular earned Adenauer's lasting gratitude for saving the situation after the collapse of E.D.C. in 1954.[55] In the Balkans disagreements were constantly arising over the best way of settling the Trieste problem, also a legacy from the war, where Italy and Yugoslavia were in dispute over its possession.

The Middle East was another area of endless differences between the two countries. Over Persia the Attlee Government had felt that the United States was determined to win a share of the oil from Abadan, the last Middle East country where the oil interests remained exclusively British;[56] it was also concerned that if Moussadeq fell, Persia would become communist and that any change of Government would be for the worse. Within two weeks of the Conservatives coming to power, Acheson was expressing irritation at the British officials'[57] attitude that Moussadeq's nationalisation of the Anglo-Iranian Oil Company's oil wells at Abadan was an attack on British foreign investments, and thus his effort at nationalisation had to be thwarted. Eden and the Foreign Office argued that one should never give in and that the Persians would abandon their plans if only Britain stood firm, especially as the Persian economy was crumbling; but the State Department became increasingly anxious about this inaction with each passing week, and irritated at what it considered British 'time-wasting' ploys such as the appeal to the International Court at the Hague.[58] They were anxious for Britain to settle on any terms, which Eden and the Foreign Office were not prepared to do. Further disagreements took place over Egypt, where the State Department had little sympathy for Britain's extremely difficult problem: the future of her Canal base.[59] British requests for U.S. forces to support her troops there were politely but firmly rejected by both Truman and Eisenhower Administrations,[60] the Americans being intent on gaining the friendship of Egypt's new military rulers.[61] British attempts to build a Middle East defence pact, which Dulles refused to join,[62] led to further disagreements and bitterness.

Relations in the Far East were no better. Objectives were the same, the containment of communism, but there was little co-ordination of policies. Relations started off badly with Churchill and Eden unhappy at the exclusion of Britain from the A.N.Z.U.S. Pact.[63] Messages were sent to Robert Menzies (Prime Minister, Australia, 1949–66) who sent back placatory but unmoved replies, since he was reluctant to jeopardise U.S. support in the Far East. No action was taken, and this remained a grievance.[64] Over the Korean armistice talks there were bitter clashes which reached a climax in November 1952 over the repatriation of prisoners. The U.S. did not want an armistice on terms Britain thought right, and Eden and Lloyd had to work hard to persuade Acheson to see their point of view. The two countries differed on the importance of the French defeat at Dien Bien Phu and the attendant need to provide military support, over the likely value of discussions on Indo-China at the Geneva Conference, of which Dulles remained extremely sceptical, and the timing and composition of the South-East Asia Treaty Organisation. Britain felt the United States policy of 'non-recognition' of Communist China illogical and unrealistic, whereas the Americans felt equally strongly that they could not recognise the Peking Government.[65] Disagreement came to a head in early 1955. Eisenhower wrote to Churchill: '. . . Although we seem always to see eye to eye with you when you contemplate any European problem, our respective attitudes towards similar problems in the Orient are frequently so dissimilar as to be almost mutually antagonistic.'[66]

The differences still did not end with the Far East. Even after Stalin's death the American attitude to the Soviet Union was distinctly antagonistic, whereas Britain felt much more could be gained by more contact including trade with the communist bloc.[67] The United States, however, still believed in strategic lists and having a minimum of trade and contact with Russia. The militant anti-communist line prevalent in the U.S., displayed, for example, in the McCarthy campaign of the early 1950s, was responsible for a number of differences of outlook between both countries.[68] Differences also arose over relations with neutral countries such as India, over exchange of information on atomic matters,[69] and over policy at the United Nations, where, as Sir Pierson Dixon, the U.K.'s Permanent Representative at the United Nations, was to write in August 1954, policy was dominated by Henry Cabot Lodge (U.S. Representative, 1953–60) who, as a member of the President's Cabinet, was virtually independent of the State Department. He added that Lodge had virtually no use for the United Nations except as an anti-communist alliance, and that his interests were diametrically opposed to Britain's.[70]

The early 1950s were indeed the time when Britain stood up to the

United States as strongly as she was ever to do in the post-war world.[71] It was a testament to the quality of the special relationship, and the dedication of Churchill and Eden, that differences were weathered and that the underlying bond remained.

Part 3 Churchill's Proposal for a Soviet Union Summit

The main thrust of Winston Churchill's drive to seek a summit meeting between East and West – either with the Soviet Union alone, or on a multilateral basis, including the United States and possibly France – was divided into two stages: March–December 1953 and April 1954–February 1955. In Churchill's mind was a meeting of world leaders on the lines of the Yalta and Potsdam Conferences of 1945.

It is not possible to say exactly when Churchill first thought of seeking a summit meeting.[1] Throughout the period in Opposition he had been seeking an overriding policy objective which he could pursue when and if he again became Prime Minister. His mind kept on returning to a prophetic telegram he had sent Stalin in April 1945 in which he warned of the futility and ultimate danger of the communist and non-communist blocs failing to communicate with each other. Indeed he never forgot this telegram and quoted it on several occasions.[2] One of his first public utterances of his idea of talking to the Soviet leaders came during a speech in Edinburgh on Saint Valentine's Day 1950, during the Election campaign. 'Still I cannot help coming back to this idea of another talk with Soviet Russia upon the highest level. The idea appeals to me of a supreme effort to bridge the gulf between the two worlds, so that each can live their life, if not in friendship at least without the hatreds of the cold war.'[3]

At dinner on 10th September, 1951 at the British Embassy in Paris, Churchill expanded on the theme. He told the assembled company that if elected Prime Minister he would seek a personal meeting with his old wartime ally Stalin[4] to help reduce East-West tension in Europe. Churchill expressed his feeling that the United States might not wish to continue its presence in Europe for ever. He also hoped that the Soviet Union could be encouraged to withdraw from their 'forward positions' in Poland and Czechoslovakia.[5] During the 1951 Election campaign, at a public meeting at Home Park Football Ground, Plymouth, on 23rd October, he returned to his theme:

If I remain in public life at this juncture it is because, rightly or wrongly, but sincerely, I believe that I may be able to make an important contribution to the prevention of a third world war and to bring nearer that lasting peace settlement which the masses of the people of every race and in every land fervently desire. I pray indeed that I may have this opportunity. It is the last prize I seek to win.

In the United States, as early as October 1951, Dean Acheson had reported that Churchill was pressing for a meeting of the 'Big Four' – including Stalin. President Truman disliked the idea, saying any such discussion should take place in the United Nations, which had been set up specifically for that purpose.[6] If Churchill raised the matter (which it appears he did not), they should reply that it would be unrealistic to try to solve the major problems between East and West until a position of equal strength was reached, and that the attendant propaganda surrounding such a summit meeting proposal would probably harm rather than help the West by raising false hopes and giving rise to public demand for unwise concessions.[7] Thus from the beginning the stage was set for an inevitable confrontation of views across the Atlantic.

Once in power, Churchill wasted no time before launching his campaign. In the debate on the Address on 6th November, 1951, he said: '. . . Our great hope in foreign affairs is, of course, to bring about an abatement of what is called the "cold war" by negotiation at the highest level from strength and not from weakness.'[8] The Labour Party were particularly enthusiastic, and during the following months made periodic calls for talks.[9] Surprisingly perhaps, little more was heard from Churchill until after Stalin's death on 5th March, 1953.[10] In the Soviet Leader he had seen much that was evil in the Soviet Union, but after his death he felt there was real hope for a fresh start.[11] Lord Moran tells us that, 'The P.M. feels that Stalin's death may lead to a relaxation in tension. It is an opportunity that will not recur, and with Anthony [Eden] away he is sure he can go straight ahead.'[12] A fortnight later Churchill was encouraged to hear the Jugoslav Prime Minister, President Tito, on a visit to London, say that he did not think the new Soviet regime would want war any more than the old one.[13] A number of minor Soviet concessions followed, which helped foster the belief in a change of heart in the Kremlin:[14] General Chuikov's suggestion of talks on air safety in the 'Berlin corridor' (the Russians had recently shot down a British bomber), Soviet agreement to the appointment of Dag Hammarskjöld as United Nations Secretary-General, and, above all, a far more constructive attitude to armistice talks in Korea.[15] Not only Churchill, but also Eden, who was in Washington with Rab Butler for talks at the time Stalin died,[16] became increasingly keen, in private, on the idea of a meeting with the new leaders in the Kremlin.[17] They had animated discussions on the subject, during which Churchill said to Eden: 'If it is Mol, you go, if it is Mal,* it's me.'[18] Sir William Strang was instructed to set up a Committee to establish a Foreign Office view on a Molotov-Eden meeting. Sir Pierson Dixon, Sir Paul Mason (Assistant Under-Secretary, 1951–4) and Henry Hohler (Head of the Northern Department, 1951–6) met, and all were opposed, although they prepared a list of issues that could be discussed if the talks were to go ahead.

A key meeting was held on 1st April between Eden, Strang, Sir Alvary Gascoigne (the British Ambassador to Moscow) who had been recalled to London for consultations,[19] and other Foreign Office officials. Eden was still highly enthusiastic about a meeting,[20] and suggested Vienna. Although Eden later became so opposed to Churchill's plan for a summit meeting, it should not be forgotten that, initially, he was as keen as Churchill. That his enthusiasm waned owed much to Eden's fear that, with Churchill at the helm, too much would be given away to the Russians, and with insufficient regard for its effect on the Western allies.[21] Gascoigne was in any case doubtful if Molotov would agree, but although all the Foreign Office team were opposed to the idea, they did not press their objections, solely because they felt that Eden was so keen. Afterwards Eden was left alone with Strang and Evelyn Shuckburgh, both of whom argued forcibly against the proposed meeting, bringing forward the probable detrimental effect it would have on Britain's allies. As a result Eden agreed not to pursue the idea without first consulting the Americans.

The next day Eden's initial enthusiasm was further dampened by doubts of Dixon and Sir Frank Roberts. Churchill also agreed that direct contact with the Soviet Union should not be made until the United States, whom the Foreign Office felt were certain to be hostile to the idea, had been consulted.[22] Churchill, however, was much encouraged by a paper sent by President Eisenhower and John Foster Dulles in April 1953, saying that if Churchill wished to make a 'solitary pilgrimage' to Moscow, though they would not advise it, it was all right by them. The message ended: 'Of course you have the right to go whenever you wish.'[23] At this critical time, as Eden began to have severe reservations about summits, his failing health finally gave way. He was instructed by his doctors to remain indoors at his official residence at Number One, Carlton Gardens. Visitors (including Churchill and Strang on 7th April) were allowed, but his health was gradually weakening and he was admitted to hospital on 11th April.[24] With the major obstacle to his plan

*Molotov, Foreign Minister of Soviet Union, 1946–9 and 1953–6 (previously People's Commissar for Foreign Affairs, 1930–46). Malenkov, Chairman of Council of Ministers of Soviet Union, 1953–5.

on the sick-list Churchill knew it would now be much easier to isolate potential opposition from the Foreign Office. Within a week of Eden's entry into hospital Churchill was coming out far more strongly in public in favour of high-level meetings. In Glasgow on the evening of 17th April Churchill welcomed in glowing terms a speech made by Eisenhower the day before in which the President had pleaded for Russian leaders to come to terms with the West. In a non party-political speech in the House on 20th April Churchill made the suggestion that private and informal talks be held at the highest level amongst 'some of the principal Powers concerned'.[25]

Over the next few months secret talks took place at the Russian Embassy in London[26] between Churchill's private envoys John Colville and Christopher Soames, and Jacob Malik, the Soviet Ambassador from 1953, with the object of discovering the Kremlin's attitude to the possibility of a summit meeting.[27] The usual channel for such communications would have been through the British Embassy in Moscow, but in this case the British Ambassador, Sir William Hayter, was not informed, although Churchill did confide his desire to go to Moscow.[28] It might well have been that the Prime Minister, realising the Foreign Office's opposition to summits, sought to conduct negotiations outside their orbit. Julian Amery and Sir Robert Boothby also had informal talks with the Soviet Embassy,[29] although it does not appear that they were acting officially as Churchill's intermediaries.[30]

The United States Government, however, was becoming increasingly alarmed by all this activity in London. Even before the death of Stalin the Eisenhower Administration was alarmed by Churchill's plans, and was no more enthusiastic about the idea of summits than Truman's had been. They were thus relieved that for the first two months of 1953 Churchill appeared quiescent on the subject. Then on 21st February Eisenhower said he would be perfectly willing to meet Stalin at a point halfway between both countries if he could feel the remotest chance of such a meeting doing any good. Labour jumped on Churchill to elicit his response, and they recalled his speeches about the desirability of talks, but in the House on 2nd March he refused to commit himself. Three days later Stalin was dead. With rumblings of a possible meeting continuing from London the United States was compelled to act. On 16th April Eisenhower made his appeal to the new Soviet leaders to turn the tide of history and to give tangible evidence of goodwill through specific actions, such as in Korea or Indo-China. The Soviet reply came on 25th April when Moscow broadcast a leading article in *Pravda* which looked sympathetically on Eisenhower's statement and displayed a far more reasonable tone than had been usual when Stalin was alive.[31] The following day Molotov announced that Moscow was prepared to negotiate with the other great powers for a five-power pact.

Churchill was fortunate that Eden's deputy, Selwyn Lloyd, was more favourably disposed to the idea. Lloyd later said: 'I got the feeling very strongly with my time at the United Nations from 1951 to 1954 that in dealing with the Russians day-by-day that we had to keep the talk going with them, that we had everything to gain and nothing to lose.'[32] As was his manner, Churchill announced his proposals in Parliament. His speech on 11th May, in the debate on foreign affairs, had been expected to include an important statement on the subject. In the event the extent of his commitment to such a plan came as a surprise. Churchill gave a broad survey of developments since the last debate on foreign affairs the previous autumn. Most of the speech was taken up with this summary, but towards the end he talked of the 'supreme event' in the intervening six months, the change in attitude in the Kremlin following the death of Stalin. The key passage ran:

> I must make it plain that, in spite of all the uncertainties and confusion in which world affairs are plunged, I believe that a conference on the highest level should take place between the leading powers without long delay. This conference should not be overhung by a ponderous or rigid agenda, or lead into mazes and jungles of technical details, zealously contested by hordes of experts and officials drawn up in a vast, cumbrous array. The conference should be confined to the smallest number of powers and persons possible. It should meet with a measure of informality and a still greater measure of privacy and seclusion. It might well be that no hard-faced agreements would be reached, but there might be a general feeling among those gathered together that they might do something better than tear the human race, including themselves, into bits.[33]

The following day Harry Boardman wrote in the *Manchester Guardian* that the Prime Minister's speech was 'by any test, the greatest he has made in the House of Commons since the war', an opinion with which many witnesses concurred. The speech became quickly known for its passionate plea for an ending of the suspicions and misunderstandings dividing East and West. It is unclear whether or not Churchill spoke with the Foreign Office's prior knowledge or support. Lloyd (who was himself sympathetic) maintained that the Foreign Office had approved the speech: 'I remember going with Sir William Strang . . . to Number Ten. Sir Winston was in bed. We went through every word of that speech and all the time he was saying: "Now are you quite sure that the Foreign

Office will agree with this?"[34] Colville, however, denies that the Foreign Office agreed to the speech.[35] The picture is further complicated by the evidence of Anthony Nutting, who later wrote that the Foreign Office received copies of the speech just before lunch on the very day Churchill was due to deliver it – thus too late to object.[36] It was certainly the popular mythology at the time that Churchill had not consulted the Foreign Office.[37] Yet it is beyond doubt that the speech caused wide dismay behind the scenes in both Europe and the United States,[38] as well as at home among his Cabinet colleagues whom Churchill had not consulted beforehand.[39]

The Eisenhower Administration, alarmed at how close Churchill's speech had brought the prospect of a summit to actually taking place, responded by sending him a cable requesting an early meeting, along with the French Prime Minister, to hammer out a common approach, fearful for the effects that Churchill's speech might have on the ratification of the European Defence Community.[40] After further confidential exchanges, Churchill was able to announce in the House on 21st May that Eisenhower had expressed a wish for a personal meeting to be held at Bermuda in mid-June.[41] In the event, the inability of the French to produce a Government in June led to a postponement until July. Churchill planned to leave in H.M.S. *Vanguard* on 30th June and the prospect of talks with the Soviet Union was to be his favoured theme for discussion.[42] The United States, meanwhile, were preparing to dampen Churchill's enthusiasm. Advance warning of this attitude came from Bernard Baruch, who wrote to Churchill on 24th June to say that on the preceding Monday he had talked to Eisenhower, Dulles and Walter Bedell Smith; at stake was whether the whole concept of Europe and allied unity would fall prey to the Soviet talk of 'peace'. The Bermuda Conference, he continued, would be a failure unless the common determination to press on with NATO rearmament was clearly demonstrated.[43] Churchill's stroke on 23rd June, however, put an abrupt end to all these plans. Churchill later saw this as the turning-point, believing that if the Bermuda Conference had taken place in the summer of 1953, he might have been able to persuade Eisenhower that a meeting with Malenkov would be useful.[44] This, however, is most unlikely; the Conference might well have produced a head-on clash between the two leaders, with Churchill possibly going ahead with his own, bilateral, talks with the Soviets.

During the summer of Churchill's convalesence, attitudes hardened further. Before he left for his operation in Boston in early June, Eden telephoned Nutting to air his anxieties, and said: 'Try not to allow too much appeasement of the Russian bear in my absence'[45] (though the word 'appeasement' was prohibited). Over the months, the issue became increasingly contentious between Churchill and Eden,[46] who closely followed the developing saga during his own convalescence in the Mediterranean. The Foreign Office had grown ever more implacably set against both the 'appeasement' policy and the possibility of a summit meeting, and in Lord Salisbury they had an acting Foreign Secretary very much on their side.[47] During Salisbury's Washington visit in July 1953,[48] Eisenhower, who was even more hostile to the Soviet Union than Dulles,[49] felt it would be undignified for the President to attend talks involving bargaining and negotiations. To Churchill, he wrote: '. . . I do not like talking informally with those who only wish to entrap and embarrass us. I would prefer, at any rate in the first instance, to leave the initial approach to the Foreign Ministers on limited and specific lines . . .'[50] It was hardly surprising, therefore, that the Washington meeting proposed a conference of Foreign Secretaries to discuss first steps to finding a solution to the German problem, a decision not at all to Churchill's liking; he wanted the Heads of Governments to do the talking[51] and saw his initiative being swamped by complex diplomatic negotiations presided over by Foreign Ministers.

Meanwhile, Churchill, convalescing from his stroke, had begun to ponder a date for a four-power meeting, at top rather than Foreign Secretary level, seeing September as a possible date.[52] Over the next two months, he considered a number of schemes: meeting Malenkov in Zurich,[53] travelling to the United States to see Eisenhower,[54] and for a while he even hoped that Eisenhower might visit London.[55] Churchill again put *Vanguard* on notice and in late September began suggesting the Azores as a place for a preliminary bilateral meeting with the Americans, but early in October Eisenhower flatly refused. The date Churchill envisaged was, he said, quite impossible for him. Moreover, Eisenhower continued that he was very anxious for the French to be included as 'we believe Laniel [the French Prime Minister] is doing a good job'.[56] This appears to have been a ploy on Eisenhower's part to dilute the attendance at the proposed talks and thus to take the steam out of Churchill's initiative.

Throughout the autumn Churchill and Eden remained at odds over the issue. A statement issued from Number Ten on 28th September had in effect to deny that differences of opinion existed with Churchill's colleagues.[57] Churchill persisted in his wish to meet Eisenhower before a summit with the Soviets, anxious lest the initiative on summits pass to the Opposition – as Attlee claimed it had done at the Labour Party's annual Conference on 1st October. Eden did not want Churchill to talk about a change of heart in the post-Stalin Soviet Union in his debate on the Address on 3rd November, 1953, as neither Eden nor the Foreign Office thought there was any evidence supporting this.[58] But Churchill was not to be diverted. His speech contained a passionate statement of the view that the hydrogen bomb, through its terrible destructive potential, would render war less likely, and that it provided a unique opportunity, through the desire of all nations for peace and prosperity, for an easing of international tension between East and West.

Eden and the Foreign Office were uncertain quite what attitude to adopt: they disliked the idea of bilateral talks with the Americans but went along with it as they realised that only Eisenhower could convince Churchill of his opposition to the plan. They had qualms, however, about a summit taking place for the same reason the Truman Administration had been doubtful – it might arouse public expectations which could not be fulfilled.[59] Eden himself was by now inclined to oppose the idea in any form.[60] Churchill persisted in his pressure for a meeting, and in the end the Americans reluctantly agreed, under no illusion that Churchill had much support in his Government. In a telegram to Dulles on 6th November Aldrich said that Eden told him of Churchill's latest proposal for a Bermuda meeting, and that although Eden did not mention his own feelings, Aldrich was sure that many members of the Government, and probably Eden himself, were very much disturbed over Churchill's initiative, and hoped some way could be found to avoid the meeting. Aldrich continued that he thought Churchill was in very poor physical condition, but was determined to make one last gesture towards world peace, acutely aware that his time was running out. Aldrich counselled avoidance of the meeting on the grounds that it could prejudice ratification of E.D.C.[61]

Yet by 10th November, Eisenhower had agreed to a meeting, to be held at Bermuda on 4th December.[62] Bedell Smith appears to have played a major part in persuading Eisenhower that Churchill would not again be turned down, especially due to the high opinion polls in favour of such a conference, and despite the possible prejudicial effect on the signing of E.D.C.[63] Throughout the planning stages Eden and the Foreign Office did what they could to ensure the Soviet Union was kept at the bottom of the agenda, and that the Far East should be the main business. In the event, however, the character of the conference was changed by a Russian note of 27th November which agreed to the proposal for a four-power conference at Foreign Secretary level which the Western Powers had been making since Salisbury's U.S. trip in July, and suggested Berlin as a possible meeting place. As Sir Frank Roberts said at the time: '. . . The Russians made this conference. There would have been virtually nothing to do if they hadn't proposed the four-power

403

Berlin meetings. Now Bermuda can produce an answer.'[64] Agreement on an allied reply had to be the first priority. Churchill did raise the broader question of East-West relations,[65] and many other matters were discussed, among them Indo-China, E.D.C. and Trieste. However, acceptance of the Russian proposal and the harmonising of the allies' policy towards E.D.C. and Germany were the chief outcome of the Bermuda Conference. During the formal and informal talks, Churchill had little encouragement from either the French or the U.S. delegations on his proposed top-level talks with the Soviet Union, and so had little alternative but to fall in line with the agreed reply to the Russian note.

Churchill, personally, was disappointed by Eisenhower's and Dulles' opposition to his plans, and by the overall results of Bermuda.[66] For the next few months, though, while the Berlin Conference (25th January–18th February) and run-up to the opening of the Geneva Conference on 26th April were in full sway, he let the topic rest. Very little positive progress in fact came out of the Berlin Conference, except for the agreement to hold a conference in April of five powers, including China, to discuss Korea and Indo-China.

By April the second and last stage of Churchill's drive for a summit meeting had begun to unfold fired by the most recent U.S. revelations about the impact of the H bomb, which he publicised to both the Cabinet and Parliament.[67] During the debate on 5th April, 1954, Churchill announced that the Government would accept the Opposition motion suggesting an immediate initiative to bring about a meeting between Britain, the U.S. and the Soviet Union to consider disarmament afresh.[68] At the end of the month he suggested privately a meeting with Eisenhower to discuss issues of 'great importance' to both countries, a grandiose pretext of Churchill's for the proposed talks, which he hoped would disguise his real motive for seeking U.S. agreement to summit talks. Eisenhower sent a non-committal reply, saying he would have to await the return to Washington of Dulles, but mentioned also his concern at the wide differences between both countries. Eisenhower was concerned to know why the two countries 'seem to reach drastically differing answers to problems involving the same sets of basic facts'.[69] Yet by mid-May he agreed to talks in Washington.[70] Eden was not enthusiastic about the meeting,[71] having an entirely different conception to Churchill of what the talks would entail. Eden saw the main purpose as discussing ways of giving the French a chance to reach a settlement at Geneva in the next few weeks.[72] There were dissenters, too, in the Cabinet,[73] who insisted that Eden accompany the Prime Minister. Cabinet enthusiasm for the trip increased, however, as they became more aware of the rift that was opening up between both countries, particularly on policy towards the Far East.[74] The Americans doubted if any good would come from the talks. Hagerty quotes Eisenhower: 'Winston really wants this conference, although I don't know how much good will come out of it, but I decided to go along with him once again and play it more or less by ear.'[75]

Talks duly took place between 25th and 29th June. At an early stage in discussions, Churchill reached some form of agreement with Eisenhower on the question of summits, though the sources disagree about the details. Colville writes that on the first day of talks Eisenhower agreed to a meeting with the Russians but later, under pressure from Dulles, retracted his own willingness to participate.[76] Moran narrates how Churchill appeared to believe that Eisenhower liked his idea of meeting the Russians, and that he would go to the Soviet Union, possibly in July.[77] A note of a conversation between Churchill and Eisenhower on 26th June, 1954, tells how the latter would not agree to a meeting anywhere under the present Soviet rule, but did not object to Churchill meeting them in either Stockholm or London. Eisenhower urged Churchill to make the first move through diplomatic channels and to include France. Churchill said: 'Two is company, three is hard company, four is deadlock.' Throughout Eisenhower stressed the importance of Dulles being consulted on the subject, and also the danger in raising expectations from such a conference. Eisenhower said he had little experience of these matters and was uncertain exactly what to do, but could conceive of going to the first day of such a conference, coming home and leaving the Vice-President and Secretary of State there, and then perhaps returning for the last five days.[78] Thus it does appear that Churchill managed to charm Eisenhower into going along at least some way with his plans.

Dulles however remained implacably opposed to Churchill's plan, and poured cold water on it. Hagerty recorded in his diary: 'Dulles later told me that in his private conversation with the Prime Minister from 12.30 to 1.30 the Prime Minister was still obsessed with the idea of going to Moscow for a meeting and had tried to get Dulles to urge the President to do likewise. Of course we are unalterably opposed to such a trip but it may be if we do not go, Churchill will go anyway.'[79] Both sides expressed themselves well pleased with the results of the Conference:[80] harmony was restored on a number of threatening differences over policy in Europe and the Far East, and the U.S. secured British agreement to abstain in the United Nations vote on Guatemala, which gratified them,[81] and Churchill left satisfied with the state of Anglo-American relations,[82] and with the joint Anglo-American Declaration released on 29th June.[83]

A row, however, broke out between Churchill and Eden on the return journey on the *Queen Elizabeth*. Churchill wished to send a message to Molotov from the ship asking whether the Russians would like him to visit them. Eden protested that the Cabinet should be consulted before it was sent.[84] It is not clear whether the Cabinet was asked for their comments or not, as sources differ.[85] There is no doubt, though, that the telegram was dispatched, proposing an informal meeting. It was probably sent on 3rd July, and Molotov sent back a friendly reply on 5th July.[86] When Churchill confronted the full Cabinet with the facts on 7th July there was uproar. The great majority, especially Harry Crookshank and Salisbury, were indignant. They objected to the lack of consultation, and to action being taken without U.S knowledge. Churchill protested that he had made his intentions clear whilst in Washington, but later that day did send a message to Eisenhower to clarify the situation. The Americans themselves could not seem to agree what exactly had been said at the Washington meeting, or indeed what opinion they held about Churchill's proposed bilateral talks.[87] They were clearly distressed and somewhat confused by Churchill's initiative.

Eden returned to the Geneva Conference in a state of some anxiety, and for a few days Churchill was unrelenting and considered resigning if he could not secure Cabinet approval.[88] Attitudes in the Cabinet hardened and for two weeks it was uncertain what would be the outcome. Eden, Crookshank and Salisbury throughout were the most ardent opponents.[89] A letter from Lyttelton to Eden, written between 8th and 20th July, says that Woolton also was considering resignation. Lyttelton described the problem in the Cabinet in characteristic prose.

> I am no less worried about the situation than H. [Macmillan]. I think I see one thing clearly which is that we can't possibly draw back from the W.S.C./M. [Molotov] meeting unless some event at Geneva were to show up Russian intransigence in an unmistakable light. Otherwise we should be represented as a party of shell-shocked Tories headed by a reactionary Marquis [Salisbury] who had gone out shooting before September 1st and had shot down the Dove of Peace as it got up from the turnips.[90]

The crisis came in the Cabinet on 23rd July. Crookshank wrote on that Friday of a 'terrible Cabinet', with Salisbury and Churchill threatening to resign.[91] In some undated jottings amongst Woolton's private papers, Salisbury is quoted as objecting to the Prime Minister taking action without consulting the Cabinet. Churchill fell back on the case that the resolution in the House of Commons (of 5th April) had called for such action to be undertaken. Eden retorted that nothing of value would come of a conference and that the Russians' attitude on Europe was closed. Woolton himself favoured consultation with the United States in the light of the last Russian communication. Churchill thought this would waste time.[92] Colville said that Churchill, who never liked being bullied, was, the preceding weekend, seriously considering an appeal over the heads of his Cabinet colleagues to the conscience of his countrymen.[93] Macmillan later wrote that this was the time when the Cabinet began to have serious doubts about Churchill's judgment. There was a feeling that a top-level summit conference, with Churchill at the helm, might have a 'tragic ending'.[94] The position, however, was considerably eased by a Soviet note of 24th July to the United States, Britain, China and France, proposing a general European collective security treaty and a conference of all European countries desiring to take part along with the United States. Crookshank noted of the morning Cabinet on Monday 26th July that the crisis was solved by the Russian note, so there were no resignations.[95]

The Russians, for their part, were anxious not to bury the idea of a personal visit from Churchill but, somewhat ironically, he now felt that this would be impossible at least until the Western powers had replied to the Soviet note of 24th July.[96] At the very moment when the Soviet initiative appeared to open up the possibility of top-level talks taking place, the combined arguments of the Cabinet and Foreign Office had eventually succeeded in dimming Churchill's enthusiasm for going ahead with his plan.[97] He also felt that Clement Attlee's visit to the Soviet Union *en route* to China in early August reduced the novelty and likely impact of his own mission.[98] The Western replies to the Soviet note, delivered on 10th September, indicated a refusal to attend a conference unless Russia would agree to sign the Austrian Treaty and allow free elections throughout Germany. This effectively aborted Churchill's initiative.

Churchill struggled for the next few months to keep alive his hopes of a top-level summit,[99] but the moment had passed. His confidence in the plan had begun to wane, and he saw no chance of further exploratory gestures until the future of European defence was settled. Labour's constant jibing about the lack of progress towards a summit meeting must have been a bitter pill.[100] On 1st January, 1955, Malenkov, in a press conference, responded unfavourably to a question about diplomatic talks leading to a four-power conference, and early in the following month Churchill's hopes were further crushed by the resignation of Malenkov from the premiership.[101] Moran put it succinctly: 'When

Malenkov went, the bottom fell out of Winston's plans.'[102] In truth, however, the bottom had fallen out of them six months before.

Churchill's last major speech in the House of Commons on 14th March was, indicatively, about summit meetings.[103] The debate had been occasioned by an Opposition motion which deplored 'the Government's delay in implementing' the unanimous motion of 5th April, 1954. In the speech Churchill gave a long account of the discussions about high-level meetings that had taken place in the preceding two years. The saddest moment for Churchill must have come when two Labour M.P.s, James Hudson and Emrys Hughes, asked him why he had changed his mind since his powerful speech at Edinburgh on 14th February, 1950. He was at a loss to know what to say.

It had been a noble plan. Churchill saw the hydrogen bomb as a qualitatively more lethal and dangerous weapon than the atomic bomb,[104] and the threat of it being used in war provided the backbone to his enthusiasm for summits. He wanted to see if he could establish a new and lasting accord between East and West, so warfare might be rendered redundant and Governments could spend the revenue which would otherwise have been devoted to defence purposes to raise living standards.[105] His feeling about the need for a top-level summit meeting did not change. Over two years after the 11th May speech of 1953, he wrote to Eisenhower:

> I have never indulged in extravagant hopes of a vast, dramatic transformation of human affairs, but my belief is that, so long as we do not relax our unity or our vigilance, the Soviets and the Russian people [Churchill's underlining] will be increasingly convinced that it is in their interests to live peaceably with us. There is a strong reaction from the post-war mood of Stalin. Abundance for hundreds of millions is in sight and even in reach. These processes of growth require time, and one improvement can easily lead to another.[106]

With hindsight one can see that Churchill was inclined to exaggerate the change in Russia after the death of Stalin, although undoubtedly the removal from the scene of such a despot provided an opportunity for his successors to make a clean break in policy and open out. At the same time the viewpoint of the senior Foreign Office officials, who felt a rash move by Churchill might jeopardise the delicate position of British long-term policy in Europe, deserves some respect. In a sense their more cautious piecemeal approach and Churchill's visionary one both have right on their side. Conjecture is futile about what might have happened if circumstances had not prevented Churchill's high-level, informal meeting, but the experience since of the alternative, carefully planned meetings at number one or two level, has scarcely proved an outstanding success.

Part 4 Assessment

Anthony Eden may well be considered one of the most skilled and competent Foreign Secretaries Britain has had since the war, and certainly the most knowledgeable. As Iverach McDonald, Foreign Editor of *The Times*, 1952–65, has written: 'Eden was to conduct British foreign policy . . . during one of its most effective and successful periods in modern history.'[1] On the grounds of having solved some problems and thereby having left Britain's external relations in a happier state when he retired as Foreign Secretary in April 1955 than when he was first appointed in October 1951, he was an undoubted success. His guiding theme, which was a wise one, was disengagement, but without leaving a vacuum. In place of untenable positions he wished to internationalise responsibilities, preferably with the involvement of the United States, through the agency of defence organisations.[2] Various writers have emphasised the 'three overlapping circles' – Empire, Western Europe and Atlantic alliance – as being the cornerstones of Eden's policy,[3] and when in power he does indeed appear to have thought consciously in terms of this concept, although expressions of the objectives of policy and the reality were very different. Within the context of wishing to reduce Britain's responsibilities overseas, he dealt with problems as they arose, holding two or three in his mind as the issues of the moment. His preferred style as Foreign Secretary was not only to conduct open negotiations in secret, but also to nibble away at the edges of a problem, rather than biting off a whole issue at once, and to get agreement on a number of minor points in the hope that a climate of confidence would be established in which to conduct further negotiations.[4]

His two major triumphs both came in 1954. His skill in conducting the Geneva Conference, with Molotov as his co-Chairman, brought the Indo-China war temporarily to a halt: 'By any standard Geneva was a great success for Eden,' wrote McDonald. 'To him goes the chief credit for getting the Americans to hold back at that time.'[5] Praise for his role at Geneva poured in from all sides. Richard Casey, the Australian Foreign Secretary, commented at the time on Eden's 'almost inhuman good humour and patience'.[6] Eden also played a key role in the foundation of the Western European Union following the collapse of what was in fact a less good plan, the European Defence Community.[7] The former's purpose was, as he wrote to Lord Ismay, 'to provide a forum rather different from the NATO forum in which the so-called European idea . . . can be fostered. This is not possible in NATO because of the presence of the United States and also of countries with rather different backgrounds and interests such as Turkey, Greece and Portugal.'[8] He also argued with members of the Cabinet, his Party and influential opinion outside Parliament to secure the Sudan and Canal base Agreements, realising that change was inevitable. To Lord Hankey (Cabinet Secretary, 1919–38), the leader of a number of distinguished former officials, including Lord Vansittart (Permanent Under-Secretary at the Foreign Office, 1930–8), who were opposed to the policy of evacuating the base, he wrote in February 1953:

> I am anxious that you should know that what we are trying to do in Egypt is not to run away from a regime which often says crude and hostile things, but rather to lay the foundations of security in the Middle East in the new and changed circumstances that now prevail there. By this I mean of course not so much the new regime in Egypt as the changes in our own position in the world. It is a case of 'new times, new methods'.

He defended the Sudanese Agreement with similar verve.[9] This required tenacity and courage, as it added to his difficulties with his own Party. For as Hugh Massingham wrote in the *Observer* on 15th February, 1953, the outburst against Eden by Conservative backbenchers was not directed just against his Sudan policy: 'It was the culmination of a growing feeling of exasperation with Mr. Eden's performance as Foreign Secretary.' Eden made a significant contribution towards the settlement of the protracted Persian problem in 1954, an achievement of which he was proud,[10] and also played an important role behind the scenes in the talks in London from February to October of that year which culminated in the signing of an agreement ending the Allied Military Government in Trieste.[11] This was a significant example of 'an open covenant secretly arrived at', '. . . an example of a method of diplomacy which I prefer', as Eden said at the 1954 Conservative annual Party Conference.[12]

Several considerations should be borne in mind when assessing Eden's performance during his last period as Foreign Secretary. For much of the time he was often battling against Churchill. Lord Moran records Harold Macmillan putting it most forcibly: 'For fifteen years, according to Harold, Winston has . . . butted in on his work, until poor Anthony is afraid to make a decision on his own.'[13] But Lord Soames remarked that whereas Churchill would push other men to the limit he was not prepared to do so with Eden.[14] There is no doubt, however, that Churchill's constant interference was a considerable irritant to him. As a result it often appeared that Britain had two distinct foreign policies, which were not always in harmony,[15] a situation that appeared to reach a climax during the Geneva Conference in the spring and early summer of 1954.[16] According to Moran, Churchill seemed more interested in his proposed trip to see Eisenhower than in the critical state of affairs in the Indo-China war (where the communists were besieging the French at Dien Bien Phu). Eden, however, had expressly left Geneva in order to discuss with him. Both remarked how frequently they saw issues the same way, but this is an over-optimistic reflection of the truth. Churchill said in his reply to the vote of thanks after his speech at the annual Party Conference at Blackpool on 9th October, 1954[17] that he had worked together with Anthony Eden for sixteen to seventeen years, and if they were at opposite ends of the hall when a complex point in foreign affairs came up, it would be four or five to one that they would come up with the same answers. 'He and I also are very good friends, and we have a family relationship which I value very much indeed.'[18] For a more impartial view though there is Moran: 'The P.M. always claims that Anthony and he agree on most things in the field of foreign affairs, though it is not often very noticeable; they don't seem, for instance, to have much in common about Suez, or China, or in their approach to Americans.'[19] Underlying it all was Eden's justifiable unhappiness at being kept waiting outside the front door of Number Ten by Churchill for an indefinite time.[20]

As Eden cavilled at Churchill's two favourite policies, summits and fostering the special relationship, Churchill in his turn was often out of sympathy with Eden's major enthusiasms – in particular over the policy in the Middle East. In between were topics which Churchill left very much to Eden as he had little or no interest in them, namely, European defence, the Trieste problem, South-East Asia, and United Nations affairs.[21] Churchill frequently expressed his boredom to secretaries at having to inform himself on places, for example in South-East Asia, of which he had hitherto remained ignorant. They disagreed over the Sudan (to the extent that Eden threatened to resign if he did not have Churchill's support for his policy of Sudanese independence)[22] and Persia (Churchill early on made it clear that had he been in power at the time, they would never have been thrown out of Abadan in what he thought was a humiliating way, and that 'there might have been a splutter of musketry').[23] But the most contentious issue between them during Churchill's last premiership was the decision to evacuate the large military base in Egypt.[24] According to Anthony Montague Browne their relationship was never quite the same after the Government began to consider seriously the Suez Agreement.[25]

Churchill himself, who had always been sympathetic to the Jewish cause, tended to side more with Israel. In a letter to Eisenhower a year after his retirement he wrote: 'I am of course a Zionist, and have been ever since the Balfour Declaration. I think it is a wonderful thing that this tiny colony of Jews should have become a refuge to their compatriots in all the lands where they were persecuted so cruelly, and at the same time established themselves as the most effective fighting force in the area.'[26] To Hugh Dalton he said privately in the House of Commons: 'I won't allow the balance to be tilted against Israel. I've always been a Zionist, and I've often had a very heavy time of it.'[27] Churchill disliked the new military rulers in Egypt in 1952 because he was sure they would want Britain to leave the Canal Zone, and also because they had overthrown a King, and although he did not feel warmly towards the high-living King Farouk (who was deposed in 1952) he was nevertheless still a King, and as such worthy of some respect. He was more concerned than Eden of the possibility that if Egypt fell it might come under Soviet influence, taking the view very early on in the life of the Government that the Soviet Union was going to support the Arabs, in particular against Israel, instancing anti-Jewish activity in Czechoslovakia as evidence. He was thus most anxious not to loosen British influence over Egypt.[28]

Churchill returned from his holiday in Jamaica in January 1953 with a new determination, possibly influenced by his Caribbean host, Lord Beaverbrook, not to have a policy of 'scuttle' in Egypt, and this date marks the beginning of the serious rift between Churchill and Eden on the issue, which lasted for the next eighteen months. He never fully reconciled himself to the policy, and consoled himself that the evacuation would mean financial economies and the release of troops for other purposes.[29] It is not clear why Churchill yielded: undoubtedly the news of the effect of the hydrogen bomb helped make him realise the impracticability of a large fixed base in the age of nuclear war,[30] and he also saw the logic of the Chiefs of Staff's argument, that there was little point in maintaining the base when such a large amount of time and effort was spent defending it against the Egyptians rather than preparing the troops to confront the real enemy.[31] The Chiefs themselves performed something of a *volte-face* on the subject, having originally argued that the base was essential.[32] But in his heart it is doubtful if he ever fully accepted the need for the evacuation. At a much later date he told Moran: 'I made a great mistake giving in to them when we left the Canal. I feel responsible. All the Cabinet were for withdrawing. They persuaded me that we must get out of Suez. But if I had been in better health, if I had been stronger, we might have stayed on the Canal and all this [i.e. the Suez crisis of 1956] would not have happened.'[33] Only Sir David Maxwell Fyfe and Sir Walter Monckton originally supported Churchill's line.[34] In addition the U.S. were putting considerable pressure on him to leave the Canal, and he was worried lest anything should jeopardise his proposed summit meeting, about which he cared even more deeply.

Eden has been severely criticised in recent years for failing to seize the European option.[35] Yet it should be remembered that this was a policy also favoured by the Prime Minister. They were in agreement in being opposed to a British contribution to one of the early attempts at integration on the military front – the European Defence Community – the proposal for a European Army entailing fully integrated units from different nations. Eden wrote plainly to Churchill soon after taking office in 1951: 'I have never thought it possible that we could join such an Army.'[36] Churchill himself viewed it as 'a sludgy amalgam'.[37] Eisenhower, then Supreme Commander, NATO Forces in Europe, complained in his diary in December 1951 that Churchill was quite prepared to admit that in the long run a politically unified Western Europe was essential, but that he baulked at the idea of a single European Army, which Eisenhower himself favoured.[38] What he wants, Eisenhower wrote, is to go back to the loose arrangement they had in the war, but merely multiplying the number of participating nations.[39] Churchill's seminal speech at Zurich in September 1946 had been a foundation stone of the United Europe Movement,[40] but his enthusiasm for Europe had never been very clearly thought out. He disappointed enthusiasts for the European movement who expected great things from him when in office, but it is most unlikely that he ever envisaged Britain becoming part of a Federal Europe.[41] His vision was conceived in abstract terms: by the time he became Prime Minister in October 1951 he was too old to undertake the translation of his general feelings into concrete policy.

Not only Churchill and the bulk of Eden's Foreign Office advisers[42] but also a majority in the Cabinet were opposed to closer economic or defence ties with Europe. Yet there were two main enthusiasts in Cabinet, Macmillan and Maxwell Fyfe, whose disappointment was at its height in November 1951, when they felt their hopes had been sabotaged by Eden.[43] But their enthusiasm was soon tempered once this became absorbed in departmental responsibilities after 1951 and they realised how tough the going was to be.[44] Indeed, the question of closer economic ties with Europe was hardly ever discussed in the Cabinet

413

during Churchill's last years as Prime Minister.[45] A later advocate amongst Cabinet Ministers in favour of closer European integration was Peter Thorneycroft, strongly encouraged by his Permanent Secretary, Sir Frank Lee, and his friend Lady Rhys-Williams, Honorary Secretary of the United Europe Movement, 1947–58 (and Chairman, 1958–64). Thorneycroft wrote a powerful Cabinet paper on the subject of closer economic integration, but that was not until 1955. The Board of Trade was virtually alone amongst Whitehall Departments in favouring closer economic co-operation with Europe: the Treasury, influenced by the Foreign Office, was ambivalent and cautious; the Ministry of Agriculture was similarly wary as it felt that a move towards Europe would not be in the interests of British farmers; the C.R.O. was mostly opposed. Amongst non-Cabinet Ministers Duncan Sandys,[46] Sir David Eccles and John Foster were also keen enthusiasts, but they, too, were fully occupied with departmental duties, and were also too junior to be an effective pressure group after 1951. From the backbenches Sir Robert Boothby, a British delegate to the Consultative Assembly of the Council of Europe, 1949–57,[47] was the most prominent supporter of Europe, a cause to which he gave unwavering support. Few, either in the Conservative Party or in the country, would have favoured a policy of embracing the European partners any more warmly. Indeed on the eve of Britain's first application to join the Common Market, a Gallup poll in July 1960 found support for joining from less than half those interviewed.[48] Eden was no little Englander; he liked Europeans, especially the French and their culture, but he did not see closer integration as a practical reality in the early 1950s.

To an extent Eden was bound by the tradition of the day to follow closely the policy of his predecessor. Many of Britain's external policies in the post-war world, to support the NATO alliance, to pledge forces to Korea, and to work in close harmony with the United States, had already been laid down by Labour. At the time of the General Election in 1951, the *Spectator* noted: 'Foreign affairs has been kept reasonably well out of party controversies since 1945.'[49] Indeed, Eden was repeatedly to argue that in his foreign policy he was repeating precedent set down by the Attlee Government. Thus he told Party delegates at the 1954 annual Conference, flushed by the success of his recent diplomatic successes: 'I never try . . .to bring Party politics wilfully into foreign affairs, because I always believe that the more bipartisan our foreign policy can be the stronger the authority of the Foreign Secretary of the day. That is why we always brought to the late Mr. Ernest Bevin all the support we could when we were in Opposition.'[50] Clement Attlee himself after 1951 frequently referred to the need for a bipartisan foreign

414

policy. It was, he said, 'desirable, wherever possible, that in foreign affairs particularly, Government policy should have the support of all.'[51] During 1951–5 the Labour leadership (as opposed to the backbenchers) disagreed with the Government on only a small number of foreign issues, and these were mainly a question of priorities: on the primacy of the need for immediate high-level talks and for the reunification of Germany through free elections, and in the Far East on the need for the early evacuation of the off-shore islands held by Chiang Kai-shek's forces and the admission of Communist China to the United Nations. But on the great majority of issues, frequently (one suspects) to their regret, Labour had to admit little difference with the policies pursued by Eden. Even the left-wing *Tribune*, at the start of the Geneva Conference, was to say: 'Eden speaks for Britain.'[52]

Finally it must be said that no individual could be expected to have performed at anywhere near his best when suffering from constant ill health, and without any clear idea about how long he would remain in the job, thanks to Churchill's prevarication over the date of his departure.[53] Long-term plans were thus made far more difficult. At least twice, supported by his wife, Eden considered packing up the whole game of politics, so depressed did he become by Churchill's vacillation. Under such circumstances it is not surprising that here was a Foreign Secretary who tended to react to problems as they arose without carefully thought out long-term plans.

Epilogue I   The Legacy: May 1955

Exaggerated prophesies and fear-mongering are a common feature of General Elections, but few have produced quite the range of wild predictions that occurred in October 1951. The preceding pages show clearly quite how inaccurate Labour's statements were to prove in the succeeding three and a half years. Within just a year of taking office the press had already begun to comment that the absence of the extremist policies foretold by Labour was one factor in the rise of the Government's fortunes.[1]

On the domestic front, the Conservatives fell far short of introducing a full-blooded capitalist economy. On the contrary, the Government almost immediately introduced a tax on 'excess' profits and industrial leaders felt constantly aggrieved at how little was being done to help them. On the other hand, the Government, under Winston Churchill's prompting, leant over backwards to conciliate the unions: no sign here of the grave industrial relations problems envisaged by Labour. Indeed, following a statement by Churchill in the House of Commons in January 1954, 'A Student of Politics' in the *Sunday Times* wrote: 'It is no longer the Tories who threaten trade union liberties, but the Socialists.'[2] Neither did the Conservatives go out of their way to favour the better off: as the *Observer*, a newspaper often critical of the Government, noted at the time of the 1955 Election: 'In the economics field Britain is very prosperous, the prosperity is widely diffused, with full employment and higher wages than ever before.'[3]

Social services were not drastically cut back: instead the Government expanded them. Houses were built at a quicker rate than under Labour, and pension and other welfare benefits were increased to become worth marginally more in real terms. The National Health Service was left untouched: any plans it may have had for reform came to nothing. Some minor charging was introduced in 1952, but this had already been foreshadowed by Labour and did not impair the fundamental fabric of the free service. Admittedly, until the appointment of Sir David Eccles in 1954, education received a lower priority, but on his arrival reform sped ahead every bit as fast as might have been expected under Labour. The welfare state thus had three and a half years not of further reform

416

and upheaval, but of consolidation, and was arguably in a stronger state in 1955 than in 1951.

In defence policy, far from using the armed forces in an aggressive fashion, the Government actually presided over their cutting back. The only item of its policy that could be regarded as remotely 'Colonel Blimpish' was the re-establishment, soon after the Election, of the Home Guard, an anachronistic and unsuccessful enterprise. But that aside, the Government displayed a refreshing willingness to re-examine defence policy in the light of the changed circumstances of peacetime. In 1951 it inherited a defence structure that had been allowed to run down, and in certain areas such as fighter aircraft to become obsolete. Moreover, there was no clear agreement on what function the Services were being expected to fulfil. The rearmament programme inspired by the Korean war had breathed fresh life into the three Services, but they were still far from an effective let alone an efficient force. By 1955 much had changed. The White Paper of that year went a long way towards a fundamental reassessment of Britain's defence policy in the light of developments since the war. Its main thrust was that Britain should have an effective deterrent, which it would be prepared to use, and that this necessitated a wholesale re-evaluation of the roles of all three Services. Their function, henceforth, was far more clearly defined: to resist aggression other than total war. The reduction in numbers of servicemen was a step along these lines, and many other changes throughout the armed forces were in train by 1955 in accordance with the changed role envisaged for each Service.

Policy towards the Commonwealth and Empire displayed none of the reactionary fervour imagined by Labour. The Government acceded as willingly to Pakistan's request to become a republic as it did to progress towards independence in the Gold Coast and Nigeria. It is true that in both Malaya and Kenya the Government employed substantial military might to quell insurgence, but in both cases it considered it to be suppressing not the legitimate voice of the native inhabitants, but subversive elements within the country. The alacrity and even relish with which the Opposition attacked the Government for its decision to suspend the Constitution in British Guiana in 1953 showed almost a desperation in their attempt to see the Government behave with the old-fashioned gun-boat mentality it had long maintained was the Conservatives' natural instinct. The episode proved to be a humiliating defeat for the Opposition when the Government was able to show it had clear justification for its action. Not that the Conservatives by 1955 had solved every problem. Of considerable concern was South Africa's hostility to the admission of coloured African countries to full Commonwealth membership, and increasing unrest from the local population in Cyprus and in the Central African Federation. Nevertheless, both Commonwealth and Empire, which might well have suffered severe upheavals *had* the Conservatives pursued a hard-line policy after 1951, were arguably in as steady a state in 1955 as at any time since the war.

The Conservatives' foreign policy bore none of the resemblance to the warmongering behaviour predicted by Labour in its bitterest attack during the 1951 Election campaign. Persia was not invaded, but a number of peaceful tacks were adopted before Britain finally acquiesced to the American C.I.A. plot which led to the restoration of the Shah in 1953.

That same year saw the successful conclusion of armistice talks on Korea, a war in which Britain did not play a leading political role but where the Churchill Government showed no zeal to increase its involvement. The following year, not only were Churchill and Anthony Eden responsible for restraining American support for the French in the war against the communists in Indo-China, but they also refused to allow British troops to become involved. In another sphere it is hard to imagine a less provocative gesture than disbanding the huge military base on the Suez Canal and moving to a much smaller base in the British colony of Cyprus.

Churchill was ultimately unsuccessful in his pursuit of a summit meeting with the Soviet Union, but he was tireless in his efforts to move towards peace through that means. Britain's more secure and peaceable position in the world in 1955 compared to 1951 was in no small part due to the efforts of the Churchill Government. Labour, with its warmonger cry of 1951, had been made to look somewhat foolish.

No longer was there talk of crisis and comparison with the grim war years, as had been prevalent during the 1951 Election campaign. Although much aided by favourable circumstances, as we shall see in the following section, it remains true that no Government this century was able so to improve the country's fortunes from such a bleak starting point. The crisis of 1951, so grave that according to the *Spectator* it needed 'no demonstration',[4] had turned into the prosperous and optimistic outlook of 1955.

Epilogue 2   Conclusions

No single theme: Churchill's intractability: Churchill's fitness for office: continuity of policy: the ascendancy of pragmatic Conservatism: the role of the media: departmental policies: policy co-ordination: missed opportunities: exogenous factors: state of the Labour Party: the significance of 1953: Parliament: role of civil servants: ministerial relationships: Britain's position in the world: the Government assessed.

Some historians, such as Robert Skidelsky in his *Politicians and the Slump*[1] on the Labour Government of 1929–31, have found an overriding theme for a particular Administration, but years of Conservative Government between 1951 and 1955 are not susceptible to any such straitjacket. Undoubtedly the most attractive theme of those years would have been 'set the people free', describing how the Conservatives steadily abandoned the wartime restrictions retained by Labour after 1945. No doubt books will be written in due course with this as their motif. But such an interpretation would be incorrect, not least because from at least 1949 Labour had, of their own accord, begun to dismantle many of those restrictions.

A main conclusion, nevertheless, is the inability of a Cabinet, although united on the desirability of his retirement, to induce a determined Prime Minister to resign. This theme can be seen highlighted in the writings of Hugh Massingham, a man who, unlike many contemporary commentators, was not given to making exaggerated claims on Churchill's behalf.[2] As he noted in the *Observer* in August 1954: 'Sir Winston holds all the trumps. He cannot be hurried, and there is no one, inside or outside the Cabinet, who is strong enough or tough enough to make him leave one moment before he wishes.'[3] At the end of the year he was writing in the same vein, but with even more assurance, that: 'No power on earth can make Sir Winston leave one hour before he wishes.'[4] Though it is doubtful if any Prime Minister in the post-war world has possessed the personal standing of Churchill, his ability to remain at the helm nevertheless speaks of the formidable *potential* of a Prime Minister to hold on to power, even though surrounded by hostile critics. This point has particular relevance for a Conservative Party Leader: Neville Chamberlain, Anthony Eden, Harold Macmillan, Alec Douglas-Home and Edward Heath were all subject, in varying degrees, to pressure from their own supporters to resign.

Churchill's performance as Prime Minister is discussed elsewhere, notably in the second Chapter. But what of the widely held view that Churchill was not physically or mentally fit for the job of Prime Minister? 'Of course, it was a great pity he ever came back after the war,' was a

419

frequently expressed view from those interviewed for this study: 'He was of course ga-ga, you know,' would be added confidentially.

Let us separate the two points: his sanity, and the correctness or otherwise of his prolonged tenure at Number Ten. The first can be dealt with briefly. Even in his worst days following the June 1953 stroke he maintained possession of his mental faculties. He never behaved irrationally (if 'ga-ganess' means anything, it must surely mean this). He was, however, apt on occasion to become extremely tired, a propensity that increased dramatically with the passing months. This would incline him towards verbosity and remoteness from the point at hand. Some incorrectly ascribed this to drunkenness, but it was no more that than senility. So tiredness and lack of energy became an increasing problem, and this was coupled with growing deafness. Yet only in his last six months in office did they prove sufficient handicap that his qualifications for office could be justly challenged on this ground.

Should he have retired earlier, let alone ever returned to Number Ten after the war, for which period of office he has received (often) unqualified praise? Most of those who knew him during the war would have agreed with the assessment of the Australian Foreign Secretary, Richard Casey, in November 1951, that the old man was 'more calm and cautious than he was six years ago'.[5] Many indeed would have gone much further in maintaining that he had considerably slowed up since the war. This is undeniable. But the problem with many of those who go on to say that he never should have come back is that they fail to appreciate the kind of Prime Minister Churchill was: not in the Clement Attlee or Harold Macmillan mould of superb administrators and chief executives, nor like Anthony Eden or Harold Wilson wanting to know everything that was going on. Churchill was the man of vision who gave the lead, and then stood back and let others handle the detail. Kept informed by his astute Parliamentary Private Secretary, Christopher Soames, he knew what was going on throughout the Party, and by Sir Norman Brook and his secretaries throughout the Government; when the occasion demanded, he stepped in. This was his style as Prime Minister, and it worked well – at least until about October 1954, a half-year before he retired.

His stroke in June 1953 is likely to be seen as the time history will judge he should have retired, but was he really wrong to go on? It was not just that Eden himself was unfit to take over at that time; Churchill, too, made an excellent recovery and was able to give a further year and more of good service. According to Hugh Massingham in the *Observer* in June 1954, 'Now that he is on his last lap, Sir Winston seems to have acquired an ascendancy over his Cabinet that he certainly did not have during the early days of his Administration.'[6] Two weeks later, having remarked that '[Churchill's] performance at Question Time is still the star turn in the House,' he concluded that there was 'no reason, at least in theory, why he should not lead his Party at another General Election.'[7] Hardly the comments, from the pen of arguably the astutest political writer in Fleet Street, that one would have expected of a man thought to be 'ga-ga'.

By the autumn of 1954, however, as Sir Norman Brook wrote,[8] his performance was declining dramatically, and he was no longer providing sufficient leadership. He should have retired then, though he could still manage the big occasion. Following his speech in the defence debate in March 1955, a leader in the *Sunday Times* noted that '[Churchill's] powers, as he has so brilliantly demonstrated, are still of the highest order'.[9] A leader in the *Scotsman* on 6th April said his recent Parliamentary performances were 'as brilliant as those of any stage of his career'. In the light of such authoritative statements once more one can see how unfair is the widely held belief that he was 'ga-ga' during his last years at Number Ten.

One of the most remarkable features of the Government was the extent that Conservative policy followed on logically from Labour policy in the preceding six years. Although during the 1951 Election campaign Labour foretold that, if elected, the Conservatives would introduce an inegalitarian economic and financial policy, cut back the social services, antagonise the trade unions, hold up political advance in the colonies, and pursue an aggressive and militaristic foreign policy, in fact none of these prophecies was fulfilled.

When one examines the record of the Labour and Conservative Governments in the decade after the war it is the propaganda and justifications for policy that differed far more than the actual content. Only minor shifts of emphasis were to be seen on defence, the colonies and foreign policy. More remarkable is the continuity in economic and social matters. Indeed, some officials later felt there was less new policy at the Treasury after the Conservatives returned to power in 1951 than at any other change of Government in the thirty years following the war. The Conservatives gave a boost to the ending of wartime controls and rationing, retained by Labour after 1945, but this process had already begun. The Conservatives denationalised only two of those industries nationalised by Labour, one of which, iron and steel, still retained a large measure of control by a central body, the Iron and Steel Board. The other, road haulage, was only partially dismantled as a result of the problems of selling nationalised concerns back to private enterprise. The welfare state was left largely untouched.[10] Minor charges were introduced in health, but little serious attempt was made to introduce charging on a large scale to supplement revenues in order to provide better services. The shift of resources towards housing was not so much a reflection of underlying philosophical differences (although there was a move towards private housing) as an astute gamble by the Conservatives for electoral gain, which could equally well have been attempted by Labour. Public expenditure in certain sectors was in fact reduced appreciably after 1951,[11] but this was not done without protests from even the most cost-conscious members of the Cabinet. Within two months of the 1951 Election, Woolton was writing to Churchill to say that he had no doubt of the wisdom of reducing Government expenditure, a Conservative pledge in the Election, but felt that this should not reduce the electorate's standard of living.[12]

That there was so much continuity was in part due to Churchill's own determination to avoid Party controversy and trouble with the unions. His ministerial appointments in 1951 also ensured that a high proportion of moderate figures were placed in key positions. But the momentum of events and the aspirations of the electorate were the greater influence. The post-war world was a very different place from the 1930s, when the Conservatives had last been in power. It would no more have been feasible to make wholesale cuts in the welfare state than consistently to deny the colonial territories their ambitions for independence or to behave internationally as a Super Power to whom other countries must behave with deference.

Had Labour been re-elected in 1951 they would, in all probability, have pursued a far more radical policy than in their previous six years in power. Constrained by economic difficulties, they had been unable to introduce much legislation of a deeply controversial nature in 1950 and 1951. The convergence of both Parties, led by two patriarchal and moderating figures, continued after 1951, and as we shall see they were closer still by 1953, then to slowly drift apart.

The pragmatic Conservativism that came to the fore during 1951–5 was born during the war and even earlier, preparing the way for Labour's introduction of the welfare state and mixed economy during 1945–51.[13] This direction was confirmed by the work after 1945 of the Conservative Research Department and the policy committees it served, which showed how the Party might play a more interventionist role in economic and social policy: its views were embodied in a series of forward-looking policy documents of which the most celebrated was the 'Industrial Charter'. Macmillan later described this work: 'We had to convince the great post-war electorate that we accepted the need for full employment and the welfare state; that we accepted equally the need for central planning and even, in times of scarcity, physical controls. We had to devise and publicise a position in between the old Liberalism and the new Socialism.'[14]

What observers wondered at the time was how the Conservative leadership were able to impose with comparative ease their moderate views on the more radical rank-and-file. In part the traditional respect reserved for the Party leaders in policy formation was responsible, but also the change in the social background of M.P.s after 1945: increasingly they were drawn from the middle classes who became professional politicians and were far more interested in progressive reforms than their upper-middle-class predecessors.[15] This latter factor was certainly thought by *The Times* to be responsible for the dominance of the pragmatic element in the Party after 1945.[16] But the newspaper was wrong about another issue which it thought responsible for changing attitudes. It maintained that the Maxwell Fyfe reforms of 1948–9 had helped strengthen the power of Conservative Central Office over the constituency associations, resulting in turn in a strengthening of the more moderate Party leadership at Westminster. This factor it said was of key importance in explaining why right-wing leaders, who might have wielded considerable influence before 1939, were comparatively powerless – men such as Charles Waterhouse[17] over foreign affairs and Ralph Assheton[18] on economic affairs. But a notable result of these reforms, as Maxwell Fyfe himself to his regret later came to realise,[19] was that the Party leadership virtually abrogated control over the selection of Parliamentary candidates.[20] If a constituency association decided that it did not want an individual as its candidate, there was little the party headquarters or the Leader could do about it. Even Churchill's own standing was not sufficient to secure seats in the early 1950s for his friend Roy Harrod[21] or his son Randolph.[22]

Not only did Churchill's choice of Ministers in 1951, in particular Butler at the Treasury and Monckton at the Ministry of Labour, help to consolidate the hold of moderate Conservatism over the Party, but by 1953, the four men being mentioned as possible Party Leaders at some stage in the future were also all leading moderates, Butler, Macmillan, Maxwell Fyfe and the heir apparent, Anthony Eden.

A right-wing reaction never looked a serious likelihood in the early 1950s. One of their leading figures, Salisbury, was considered as a possible Prime Minister during 1953 if neither Churchill nor Eden recovered from their respective illnesses. His unwillingness to accept such a mantle, even if offered, was in large part due to his own ill health and membership of the House of Lords, and his lack of ambition was effectively revealed by his humble speech at the 1953 annual Party

423

Conference in the foreign affairs debate.[23] Neither was Assheton willing to become a leader of disaffected right-wing Tories: indeed, the *Sunday Times* commented in early 1952 that 'the very idea' of being seen as a possible leader of a backbench revolt, 'alarms him'.[24] The *Observer* commented of another Conservative backbench critic, Walter Fletcher,[25] 'that he was certainly not a rebel'.[26] Moreover, there was little attempt by the various pockets of discontent to join forces: differences in age, social background and policy objectives all played a part. Conservative politicians such as Assheton who wanted to see cuts in Government expenditure and taxation thus showed little sustained inclination to join forces with those younger Conservatives, among them some of the One Nation Group[27] who favoured an extension of charging and selective rather than universal welfare benefits, or those in the powerful lobby who pressed for the break-up of the B.B.C. monopoly. All these factors account for the triumph of the pragmatic element in the Party, a position consolidated further with Eden's accession in 1955.

Few aspects of political life have changed more dramatically in the post-war world than the transmission of information from Government to the media.[28] Today it would be incredible if hardly anything appeared in the media about a Prime Minister's stroke or his retirement plans. Yet that is what occurred in Churchill's last years in power. If James Margach, formerly of the *Sunday Times*, went too far when he later asserted, concerning Churchill's stroke in the summer of 1953, that 'Fleet Street teamed up with Downing Street to preserve an official secret,'[29] nevertheless more than one Lobby Correspondent reported that his editor had restrained him from revealing information about Churchill's state of health.[30] The Premier's physical health was not the only area in which Fleet Street's reportage was limited: a leader in the *Observer*, which in terms of in-depth political coverage led other newspapers at that period, said, '. . . Any attempt to give regular news of divergent opinions at Cabinet meetings would be wrong, for it would undermine the principle of joint [collective] responsibility on which the whole Cabinet system depends.'[31] The senior Ministers in Churchill's Government – Eden, Macmillan, Alexander of Tunis, Salisbury, Simonds and Woolton – were temperamentally not prone to leak Government secrets. They regarded themselves as being on a different social plane to Lobby Correspondents,[32] and seldom mixed informally with them. Paul Einzig of the *Financial Times* later wrote of his regret that after 1951: 'The new Ministers were not so communicative to Lobby Journalists as their Socialist predecessors.'[33] Even Butler, with his mastery of innuendo a major source of information for journalists

424

during the Conservatives' period in opposition, was far less garrulous in office.[34] Journalists seldom met civil servants, let alone were confided in by them.

Moreover many of the journalists themselves, compared to their successors a decade later, were comparatively docile and deferential to establishment figures. Newspaper profiles, for example, were a relative rarity, and where they did occur, as in the *Sunday Times* and the *Observer*, they scarcely made any adverse comment. Two factors in particular were responsible for changing attitudes: the Suez crisis of 1956, when the media were often highly critical of the Government, in contrast to the experience of both world wars; and the gradual change in the climate of public opinion, intensified and accelerated in particular after the end of the decade by the irreverent stance taken by the television programme *That Was the Week That Was*. The gradual replacement of the predominantly non-university Political Correspondents of the immediately post-war Lobby by a new breed of journalist, far better educated and thus less deferential and uncritical in judgments, also helped in the same direction.[35] More important, perhaps, was the development, particularly by Robin Day in the early years of Indepenent Television News, of the probing interview on television, an innovation, which, incidentally, weakened the role of the Lobby by undermining its position as chief link between politicians and the public.[36] Yet before 1955 the Lobby Correspondent still enjoyed considerable authority and exclusivity, with no more than forty at the Lobby's largest meetings. The Lobby was also the funnel used by the information offices of the Whitehall Departments and Ministries, then less sophisticated than today. Not only was investigative journalism only just beginning on radio, but the one television channel, which in 1951 had played for the first time an important part in a General Election,[37] was still not considered a major factor in politics. The role of the B.B.C.'s Lobby Correspondent, E. R. Thompson, was to report political news, not offer penetrating political comment. Outside Elections and Party political broadcasts, Ministers seldom spoke on the air and Churchill was never publicly interviewed on either radio or television. The Government, without this direct access to the public, was thus far more dependent than its successors upon a sympathetic interpretation by journalists, to whom this gave a peculiar influence.[38] The press thus had, for the last time, a unique position at the very heart of political report and comment.

The distinguished political scientist Harold Laski[39] was fond of emphasising the importance of the individual Department's own policy. The Treasury was predominantly Keynesian, and sceptical of reliance on monetary policy; the Foreign Office had a strong dislike of summit meetings, and even managed to woo Anthony Eden away from supporting them in the spring of 1953; nor was it enthusiastic about closer economic ties with Europe; the Ministry of Labour preferred voluntary wage agreements rather than statutory ones; the Ministry of Food, which was responsible for obtaining supplies from abroad at a reasonable price, broadly represented the consumer interest; the Ministry of Agriculture on the other hand stood for the home producer's interest, to the extent that, in 1954, a leader in the *Manchester Guardian* spoke of its 'insatiable demand for high food prices'.[40]

A feature of the Conservative Government, and a recurring criticism of the way it operated, was the poor state of interdepartmental co-ordination. As we have seen, little co-ordination took place between those Departments concerned with social policy. In the absence of a Cabinet Committee dealing with colonial affairs, Ministers outside the Colonial Office suffered from being insufficiently aware of developments in the colonies. The Departments concerned with defence were often at odds, and the ability of the Ministry of Defence to act as a co-ordinator was severely curtailed by the presence of a weak Minister for much of the period, Lord Alexander of Tunis, who did not make his will prevail against the Service Departments.

The analysis of the Government Ministry by Ministry reveals how much work went on independently of co-ordination. Indeed, the former Head of the Civil Service, Lord Armstrong of Sanderstead, used to argue that Conservative Administrations, to a far greater extent than Labour, were Governments of Departments.[41] The years 1951–5 certainly witnessed a strong sense of departmental autonomy. Co-ordination at Cabinet Committee level declined rapidly after the arrival of the Conservatives. The 'overlord' experiment was an attempt to replace co-ordination at Cabinet Committee level by a system of co-ordinating Ministers: it broke down not least through resistance from the Departments themselves. After the war, the Cabinet Office, under the guiding hand of Sir Norman Brook (1947–62), was steadily increasing in influence as the main co-ordinating body in Whitehall, but this process still had a long way to go in the early 1950s.

Churchill himself far preferred co-ordination to take place at full Cabinet rather than at Committee level. In April 1953 he boasted to Lord Moran that he had held 110 Cabinets in the preceding twelve months, compared with Attlee's 85 in a comparable period. He went on to say: 'I am a great believer in bringing things before the Cabinet. If a Minister has got anything on his mind and he has the sense to get it argued by the Cabinet he will have the machine behind him.'[42] Yet inevitably this meant less interdepartmental discussion and long-term planning than under Attlee's elaborate Cabinet Committee structure.

It is not feasible for even the most accomplished Administration consistently to be wise, and, sure enough, the Conservative Government can be seen, with hindsight, to have missed a number of opportunities. Not to have moved to explore closer economic links with Europe was a major omission (although there were formidable difficulties, not least the Commonwealth). Not enough thought was given to education policy until Sir David Eccles' appointment as Minister of Education, and, at Housing, the priority to the housing drive diverted attention from other aspects of the Ministry's work, such as consideration of local government reform. In its last six months, insufficiently clear leadership and direction was given, and too much thought to electoral considerations. Further missed opportunities were the failure to have taken up fully Lord Cherwell's initiative for the expansion of technological colleges to redress Britain's shortage of applied scientists; the slowness with which the Government began to invest in Britain's appallingly neglected inland transport system; its unwillingness to force the three nationalised fuel industries to agree to the need in some measure for a co-ordinated fuel policy was matched by its failure to work out a clear coherent policy towards the nationalised industries; the opportunity of finding a sound financial basis for retirement pensions was discarded partly through electoral considerations; and a final omission was the Government's reluctance to extend charging, not just in the welfare state but also in other public services such as road tolls. Had it done so, more money would have become available to provide better facilities, but, instead, the free service principle became more deeply embedded.

The Government should, however, be absolved from two accusations commonly made against it: that it failed to strengthen the position of industry, and that the Government was in some way responsible for Britain's industrial decline. More could have been done to provide incentives, and to encourage training and research,[43] but such measures would have been only marginal; the malaise of Britain's industrial weakness went far deeper, and cannot be laid at the door of any one Government. The monopoly powers of the trade unions and their opposition to modernisation also played a critical part. Again it has been said of the Government that their policy towards the unions was one of appeasement, which led to unnecessary inflation. But, surely, this was precisely the right policy for the time? Acting under Churchill's express instructions, Monckton, at the Ministry of Labour, built up a relationship of trust with the unions. This was desperately needed, given such vivid memories of antagonism during the interwar years.[44] No reform could then be possible, nor will it be now, without an atmosphere of trust between Government and unions. The right time for reform would have been in the later 1950s or early 1960s, in particular after the convincing victory at the 1959 General Election, when the Government could have capitalised on some of the store of goodwill which had been consolidated as a result of Churchill's initiative, and when it had a far larger majority in the House to secure the passage of necessary legislation.

Throughout this study one has seen the benefit the Government derived from factors outside its control. The most important was undoubtedly the state of the economy. On assuming power in October 1951, the Conservatives inherited a major financial crisis, but the following year the situation began to improve, largely through improved international trade. Indeed, it is probable that no Government this century has benefited from such a dramatic change in the economic climate. It was also fortunate to be in power at a time when there was a general desire to be rid of controls and restrictions, a prevailing attitude which the Conservatives had carefully fostered, in particular during the 1950 and 1951 Election campaigns. A reaction had set in against over-government, which had been in existence since the early days of the war; the predominant mood of the country was thus in harmony with the philosophy of the Conservative Party at the time. As a leader in *The Times* had put it the day after the announcement of the 1950 General Election: 'There is a real and mounting distaste for restrictions, whether needed or not, and a resentment of bureaucratic meddling.'[45]

During 1951–5 the Government derived immense benefit from what *The Times* described as 'the lack of an efficient Opposition'.[46] The Labour Party[47] was weak due to its absence of agreement on policies, the tiredness of its Leader, Attlee, already sixty-eight at the time of the 1951 General Election, and above all, because of its own internal divisions, focused on Aneurin Bevan. This meant that Labour caused the Government far less problems than might have been expected given an initial majority of only seventeen, and in particular it failed to extract significant concessions by exploiting the Conservatives' own severe internal problems during much of 1952. The brunt of Labour's attack came in those areas on which it was united, such as opposition to the reduction of food subsidies and to the denationalisations. Its constructive criticism of other aspects of economic and social policy, as well as of defence and colonial affairs, fell far short of what one might have expected from a responsible Opposition. Altogether the Labour Party was in a sorry state. As Robert McKenzie wrote:

> It is inevitably a matter of national concern if the leaders of one of the two major Parties become so preoccupied with internecine Party conflict that they cease to fulfil their duties of Her Majesty's Opposition, and if they fail to behave collectively like a potential Government. There can be no doubt that this was the condition of the Labour Party during much of the lifetime of the 1951 Parliament.[48]

Historically, 1953 is likely to be seen as a critical year in the early post-war period. As the distinguished American political scientist, Samuel Beer, wrote: 'By the early 1950s Labourites and Conservatives seemed well on the way toward executing a classic movement of a two-party system. From positions widely separating them on issues of substantial, even fundamental, importance, they had moved markedly toward one another.'[49] 1953 was the year when both Parties probably came closest together, stared warily across at each other, before starting to drift apart. Both Parties had completed programmes, Labour by its innovative work during 1945–51, Conservatives during their first two years in office in reversing what it considered the worst excesses of socialism. Each had to decide what to do next: both to become more radical or to concentrate on policies of the centre, accepting the economic and social reforms to date, but without wishing to change them significantly? In the event, while Labour settled for a qualified leftism, the Conservatives adopted a middle-of-the-road stance.

Labour's drift to the left was not nearly as radical as it could have been, given the presence in the Party of the large Bevanite faction, who from 1951 to 1955 held the strategic advantage.[50] Hugh Gaitskell's succession to Attlee in December 1955 helped secure the dominance of the moderate majority in the Party, yet it remains true that Labour, largely due to the influence of its left-wingers, was offering the electorate an extension of the socialist advance as reached by 1951. Labour's policy document, 'Challenge to Britain', was issued in 1953, promising further doses of nationalisation – the chemical, electrical, machine-tool and parts of the aircraft industries being specifically mentioned – as well as reiterating George Strauss' 1951 pledge to renationalise the steel industry; for education and health services it offered more state control in the form of an extension of comprehensives, the phasing out of independent schools and the abolition of all charges for health care.

The Conservatives, on the other hand, decided to hold the status quo on the position of 1953; there were to be no more denationalisations and no cutbacks in the welfare state. By so doing they helped ensure clear victories at the 1955 and 1959 Elections.

If only passing references have been made throughout to Parliament, this is not because the Party contest there was unimportant. The 1952–3 Session in the House of Commons, for example, had been an exhausting one for M.P.s. On at least forty-eight days members had to be present continuously from 3.30 to 10.30 p.m., unless 'paired' by a member of the opposite Party, and on fifteen days no pairs were available. Partly this was due to the Government's preference for taking major legislation – including the Transport and Steel Bills – on the floor of the House rather than sending them 'upstairs' to Standing Committees, where the Government had only the most meagre majority, and hence risked defeat.[51]

This gives a clue to the importance of Parliament during 1951–5. Through pressure on Parliamentary time, the Government was prevented from introducing as much legislation as it would have liked. This, for example, was one reason why the Government did not succeed in bringing nationalised industries within the purview of the Monopolies Commission, as they had pledged.[52]

Three factors, however, were responsible for limiting Parliament's significance in political life during the early 1950s, most stemming from the tightness of Party discipline. Strict whipping meant that the scope for individual M.P.s was much curtailed: as 'A Student of Politics' wrote in the *Sunday Times* in November 1952: 'The lot of most [M.P.s] is to sit, listen, and vote when required according to party direction. As things are, with so fine a balance between Government and Opposition, they are . . . virtually "political prisoners" when the House of Commons is sitting.'[53] The Government, indeed, never came anywhere close to a defeat caused by defections of its own backbenchers. The only occasion when this seemed a possibility was over the Suez base agreement in 1954, when twenty-seven Conservatives and one independent Conservative (Harry Legge-Bourke)[54] voted against the Government. But Labour officially abstained from voting on the withdrawal from the base (although six of their number, including left-wingers such as Fenner Brockway, actually voted for the Government) and the result was an overwhelming Government majority, 257 to 28 votes.

A factor much commented upon at the time was that, again due to the domination of Party Whips from about 1952 onwards, in the words of a leader in the *Observer* 'the real policy discussions no longer take place on the floor of the House but at party meetings behind the scenes'.[55] Finally, the divisions within the Labour Party meant that the Opposition was far less formidable in Parliament than it might otherwise have been. Censure motions, as over the conduct of colonial policy in 1953, could thus be repulsed by the Government without undue difficulty. In the House of Lords Conservative dominance was such that debates seldom attracted wide attention in either the House of Commons or in the press.[56] A notable exception was the discussion over the introduction of commercial television,[57] often brilliant and fiery, which showed the immense potential of the Upper Chamber as a deliberative assembly. Yet, tellingly, the debate was on non-Party lines.

It would, however, be easy to dismiss too readily the importance of Parliament during 1951–5. Although it had a limited value as a deliberative assembly or one that encouraged the Government to modify its legislation, it nevertheless had immense value not least because of the forum it provided for the Government to explain and justify its policies and as a testing ground for ministerial reputations.

The examination of each Department in the Government shows quite how much responsibility is carried by officials. The inability of Ministers even to be aware of, let alone affect, the vast majority of their Department's work has been a common finding. There were, for example, just three Ministers at the Board of Trade, covering fields which by 1981 at the Departments of Industry, Trade and Consumer Protection were managed by ten or more. At the Home Office one junior Minister was responsible for oversight of immigration, aliens and Northern Ireland, the latter since 1972 the responsibility of a separate Department with four Ministers. The civil servants, with their power to influence Ministers, to act independently and execute policy, thus had an effect on events which, although difficult to divine, was of the utmost importance.

Most books about the political history of this century, however, consign civil servants to mere passing reference, if they are mentioned at all. This omission appears all the odder when one considers, as we have seen, that senior officials were often far more capable and even creative than the Ministers they served, officials such as Sir John Maud, Permanent Secretary at Education to Florence Horsbrugh, or Sir John Lang, Permanent Secretary at the Admiralty to Jim Thomas. Can one fairly assess the performance of Rab Butler at the Treasury without looking at the influence on him of Sir Leslie Rowan, Sir Robert Hall or Lord Plowden? Or Peter Thorneycroft at the Board of Trade without examining the role of his Permanent Secretary, Sir Frank Lee? Or Gwilym Lloyd-George's work in ending food rationing divorced from the contribution of his Permanent Secretary, Sir Henry Hancock? Here we have

431

been able only to touch on the importance of these and other equally important partnerships. But the need for historians to consider the contributions of civil servants becomes all the more pressing when one considers the critical impact that some officials had on various areas of major importance largely independently of their Ministers: one thinks for example of Dame Evelyn Sharp's influence on the development of new towns and planning, Sir Roger Makins' pre-eminence over economic questions involving the Foreign Office, or Sir Edgar Cohen's passion for multilateral free trade. It is not just the top two or three grades of officials who deserve special study, but also Principal Private Secretaries: there are many examples in the preceding pages of such creative relationships, of which John Colville to Churchill, William Armstrong to Butler and Evelyn Shuckburgh to Eden are merely the more important ones.

This is an area where oral history, the practice of interviewing those involved in events, has an invaluable role. To highlight the role of civil servants is not to imply criticism: indeed, far too often in histories, politicians have received praise owing to officials. If balanced history is to be written of the post-war years, the contribution of civil servants will have to be discussed. I hope a small start has been made in that direction.

Another area where oral history has a major role to play is in providing information about relationships between Ministers. The decline of letter-writing has made such information harder to uncover. And yet these relations play a critical and infinitely subtle role in politics, as I have attempted to show.

Part of Macmillan's success in securing funds for house-building was due to his talent for friendship: Florence Horsbrugh on the other hand had no close friends to support her in the Cabinet (her positon as a woman was undoubtedly a handicap). Lloyd-George's popularity with senior colleagues helped ensure his appointment in October 1954 to Home Secretary, a job that Osbert Peake, who was considerably more talented, would much have liked, but he had few friends in high places.

The succession question is intricately tied up in a cobweb of loyalties to Churchill and Eden, and cannot be properly grasped without an attempt to understand who supported which man, and why. Had Eden cultivated more friends during 1951–5, he might have been able to ride out the crisis in 1956. As it was these were the years when Macmillan was blossoming from the rather awkward man of Opposition days: he talked and drank with all the right people and cultivated their friendship. Butler, meanwhile, remained rather aloof: it was almost fashionable amongst certain Party figures such as Crookshank and Woolton to be dismissive about him. When the contest between both men occurred in January 1957, these relationships played a part in Macmillan's success.

Historians have tended to shy away from making precise statements about these relationships. Yet they are the clue to much of the politics of the post-war, as of any period, and deserve more study by historians than received to date.

A belief, still widely held by many leaders in the former colonies, is that Britain nurtured great power illusions after the war, a position she was utterly unable to maintain, and that this narrow-minded attitude held until the shattering effect of the Suez episode in 1956.[58] At last she realised, so the view goes, that she must learn to live in the real world and how unimportant a nation she had become: the final break up of the Empire followed, and Britain reluctantly decided she must enter the European Community.[59]

Such a view does not concur with events. The movement towards joining the European Economic Community (Britain had already made a defence commitment by joining NATO, followed up by a substantial pledge of troops to the Western European Union in 1954) was a long and complex process involving a shift of outlook in Westminster, Whitehall, the country and Commonwealth with which the Suez episode, as far as I can see, was only remotely connected. Moreover, Britain had begun to withdraw from her responsibilities in the Empire long before 1956, a process which the arrival of the Conservatives in 1951 did little to alter. Many diverse factors were responsible for speeding up the progress, but as the pattern of inevitable passage to independence had been laid down long before Suez, the crisis could hardly have been of major significance.

On the other hand, there seems little evidence to suggest that post-war Governments harboured exaggerated ideas about Britain's position in the world, ideas in excess of her actual standing with other nations or of her financial position to pay her way. A main plank of Eden's foreign policy was withdrawal from untenable overseas positions such as the Sudan and Suez base, substituting defence pacts instead. This does not suggest unrealistically grand illusions. The Government accepted (albeit with some reluctance from Churchill) the *fait accompli* of the A.N.Z.U.S. Pact, and with it the decline of British influence in Australasia. British interests were under attack in Persia, but no expeditionary force sailed for Abadan. The refusal to become directly involved in Indo-China hardly spoke of a nation boastful of its own prowess. In Macmillan's first broadcast to the nation as Prime Minister, just two months after the Anglo–French invasion of Egypt, he spoke of his anxiety to be rid of 'any more defeatist talk about second-class power'.[60]

433

The 1957 Defence White Paper that followed shortly after, and which provided for Britain 'an appreciable element of nuclear power of her own', showed Suez had not dented British aspirations.

The Suez episode could be more clearly understood not as a culmination but as an aberration.

Many Conservatives look to the Churchill Government of 1951–5, not merely as the most successful Administration since the war, but to support their own views. The pragmatic moderate faction, which held sway in the Party, with the exception of Edward Heath's leadership between 1970–72, until the election of Margaret Thatcher as Party Leader in 1975, points to the way the Government accepted much of the semi-socialised state inherited from Labour and adopted a middle of the road position. The 'new' right in the Party also seek inspiration from this Government. Here Conservatives such as Margaret Thatcher herself and Sir Keith Joseph have opinions which can be traced to Ralph Assheton and others, who wanted to reduce public expenditure, rather than to the other radical wing, the 'old' right, those, such as Leo Amery and Charles Waterhouse, who wanted to hold on to Empire. Thus the political writer Patrick Cosgrave states: 'Historically, the most interesting aspect of the emergence of the new right is that it tends to select for praise the only genuinely successful Tory Government since the war . . . the last Churchill Government.'[61] There is much this faction can find to praise and seek to emulate, such as the abolition of restrictions and controls, the two denationalisations, the drive against waste in the Civil Service and the cutting of public expenditure.[62] It should be noted, however, that the Government gave little succour to those, for example in the One Nation Group, who wanted to extend the principle of charging as a means of reducing Government expenditure. Indeed, the debate in the Party in 1951–5 was not so much between the pragmatic path and the 'new' i.e. laissez-faire right, as between the pragmatic option and the 'old' imperialist right.

These two approaches offer different ways of praising the work of the Government, and many other examples of laudable acts (as well as, inevitably, criticisms) are given in preceding pages. Another less conventional case, however, can be made for stating that Churchill's was a quite exceptional Government. Guided by him, and containing a large number of genuinely wise and honest men in the Cabinet, many of whom had witnessed the terrible slaughter of the First World War and the suffering of the interwar years, the Government often pursued policies it regarded as being in the national rather than Party interest, without the searching by Ministers for personal gain, sometimes characteristic in more recent years. This is not to say that every Party once in power has a duty to seek the middle ground or act uncontroversially. In a democracy different options must and should be offered to the electorate. But if elected to government, Parties should act in a responsible fashion and strive for the truth of each issue, rather than as an *a priori* (and often unconscious) assumption calculate what course of action would favour Party interests, and hence offer best chances of re-election, before considering each question.

Such considerations were, understandably, present during 1951–5: the spring Budget just before the Election for example, and the pension increase question of 1954 were two such examples. But this tendency was to increase considerably in later years.

Epilogue III   Churchill 1951–5: His Place in History

For the quarter of a century since his resignation in April 1955, Winston Churchill's reputation as a peacetime Prime Minister has not been high, declining still further after the publication in 1966 of the diary of his doctor, Lord Moran.[1] The credit for his Government's success has been given to Rab Butler, to Anthony Eden, or even to Lord Woolton, but not to Churchill. The popular picture of him, the half 'ga-ga' and even drunken figure who lives on in the memories of a few of his surviving contemporaries, the pathetic old man of the now extinct Sutherland portrait,[2] the ailing struggler for survival who plods his way unsuspectingly through Moran's diary, all this is quite wrong. The time is thus ripe for a complete reassessement of his role. Indeed, far from being a lamentable failure, he has some claim to be regarded as the most considerable British Prime Minister since the war.

His qualities as a Party Leader and head of a successful Government were significant enough. But there is an altogether deeper and subtler reason for his unique position after the war.

The left tell us all we need is more planning, more centralisation, less Friedman, more Marx; the right that all will be well if only we could have more law and order, less government, more liberty, less Benn, more Hayek. The rest of us sit back, silent witnesses to this non-dialogue of abuse, while Britain's deep-seated problems remain largely untouched.

Our leaders possess a belief that these problems can be solved through a particular ideology. But ideology is always a mask, a mirror that distorts understanding of what action is required for the benefit of all; the more radical and coercive the ideology, the greater the distortion. It will always fail to solve problems in the long run, because action fired by ideology, be it political, economic or even religious, as opposed to a clear perception of events, is always divisive.

Where then is Britain in the early 1980s? Virtually all the indicators of the 'health' of a nation, from crime rates and racial harmony to unemployment figures and days lost through industrial disputes, show that the country is not in a good way. Although the picture is far from being completely black, few would agree that Britain today is in a happy state.

It is not possible to allocate precise blame. Nevertheless one feels that had there been more inspired leadership, and even a better example from the top, then that good influence would, to some extent, have permeated throughout the rest of society.

Post-war premiers have all displayed particular qualities: Clement Attlee excelled in integrity, as did Sir Alec Douglas-Home; Anthony Eden had notable courage, Harold Macmillan embodied calm efficiency. But on few occasions could it be said that they actually exerted a strong positive example: even less of those they selected as their principal aides, whose self-seeking and internecine behaviour perhaps reached a nadir in the late 1960s. It is hard to recall occasions when any British leader actually uplifted any but his most partisan and uncritical supporters. They could move, but not inspire.

Talking from their intellects, or worse, those of their advisers, their words could not penetrate beyond the intellect of the nation. Their cries, arising from self-interest, appealed to self-interest, and when appeals were made beyond, to national interest, their words left a not entirely convincing taste on the palate. Of no post-war Prime Minister could it be said that he really knew himself: how then could he know those in the nation he professed to serve?

Churchill similarly, like Lear, did not slenderly know himself.[3] His faults extended far beyond a paucity of self-knowledge. His views on such topics as education were so old-fashioned as to be lamentable. Selfish in obtaining his own way, he was often vain and inconsiderate of the feelings of others. These shortcomings were nevertheless far outweighted by his immense humanity and wisdom, seen in this extract from his first major speech in the House of Commons after being elected Prime Minister in 1951:

> We meet together here with an apparent gulf between us as great as I have known in fifty years of House of Commons life. What the nation needs is several years of quiet, steady administration, if only to allow socialist legislation to reach its full fruition. What the House needs is a period of tolerant and constructive debating on the merits of the questions before us without every speech on either side being distorted by the passions of one Election or the preparation for another . . . Controversy there must be on some of the issues before us, but this will be a small part of the work and interests we have in common.[4]

Churchill anticipated the futility of the two-Party contest, of what has become known as adversary politics. And yet he was not advocating a mere middle of the road position, a centre Party of so-called 'radicals' and 'liberals'. He had a deep understanding of the futility of any attempt at social engineering beloved by our 'progressives'. He realised that any alteration to society could not be imposed from above, as our well-meaning social democrats and not so well-meaning socialists have been attempting since the end of the war, but could only come through a change in men's hearts. He understood the supreme need to stress the liberty of the individual, though in a moral and compassionate context lacking from the arguments of latter-day advocates of free enterprise. His experience of international affairs told him correctly that the only lasting hope for an easement of world tensions would not be by complex meetings of scores of officials tied to a complex legalistic agenda, but by personal contact at the very highest level between East and West.

Margaret Thatcher has been the first Prime Minister since Churchill to understand deeply the threat to the individual from collectivist policies from within, and the threat from without of the Soviet Union. But to her it is an intellectual conviction. Unlike Churchill she does not feel the difficulties before the nation in her heart. Hence her pleas and policies, well founded, will divide, not unite, and in the long run they will fail.

Churchill, when he was not overtaken by considerations of personal or Party gain, did have the power to inspire and unite. The House sat up and listened. For a while differences were forgotten, he reminded the House and the nation of a unity of purpose as he had done in the war. A unity of purpose is indeed far easier to detect in wartime opposition to the common enemy. But in peace there exists also a common desire, though it is veiled. It is for safety from foreign aggression, security from anti-social elements in society, and for freedom to pursue one's interests and life with a tolerable degree of material well-being.

On the eve of the Election in 1951 he promised:

> If the Government of Britain is entrusted to us . . . we will do our best for all without fear or favour, without class or party bias, without rancour or spite, but with the clear and faithful simplicity that we showed in the days of Dunkirk. We did not then think about party scores . . . We shall go forward without fear and with unconquerable hope that our ancient and mighty people . . . are not confronted with any problem they cannot solve, or with any difficulty or danger they cannot overcome, if only they act with wisdom and courage, and above all, if they act now.[5]

It was a measure of the imperfect nature of Churchill, as well as the formidable difficulty of working for all in peacetime, that he allowed his high ideals of 1951 to be swamped by lower thoughts and corrupted by lesser men. Nevertheless, his vision remained, even if he could not live up to his own ideals in practice. This profound advice was the peroration of his penultimate major speech in the House, and may be considered his legacy to the nation:

> To conclude, mercifully, there is time and hope if we combine patience and courage . . . The day may dawn when fair play, love for one's fellow men, respect for justice and freedom, will enable tormented generations to march forth serene and triumphant from the hideous epoch in which we have to dwell. Meanwhile, never flinch, never weary, never despair.[6]

But, one might say, a Prime Minister is no more than the Leader of his Party: expecting him to act in a statesmanlike manner is to cry out from beyond the boundaries of good reason. There is no conclusive retort to such a view, which is widely held. And yet, if Britain *is* to regain a sense of purpose, an ability merely to see what is, and hence what needs to be done, she will have to find leaders who possess some of that same vision and understanding (as opposed to intellect and ideology) so imperfectly understood yet nevertheless exhibited by Winston Churchill in his last years in office.

Appendix I

GALLUP POLITICAL BAROMETERS: 1951–5

Year & Month	Voting Intention					Govt. Record	PM
	Cons.	Lab.	Lib.	Other	DK		
Col. 1	Col. 2	Col. 3	Col. 4	Col. 5	Col. 6	Col. 7	Col. 8
1951 Jan.	51	38	10	1	(13)		
Feb.	51½	37½	9½	1½	(13)	31	44
March	51	36½	10½	2	(14)		
April	50½	38½	9	2	(13)	32	49
May	49	40	9½	1½	(13½)	35	57
June	48	41	10	1	(12)		
July	49	39	10½	1½	(13)	31	43
Aug.	50½	38	10½	1	(11½)		
Sept.	52	41	6½	½	(11)	35	44
Oct.	50½	44	4½	1	(11½)		
Nov.							
1951 Dec.	47	45	6½	1½	(9)	44	55
1952 Jan.	44½	48	6	1½	(10½)		
Feb.	41	47	10½	1½	(14)	44	53
March	41½	48	9½	1	(9)		
April							
May	43½	49	7	½	(9)	40	51
June	40½	49	9½	1	(6½)		
July	40	50	8½	1½	(9)		
Aug.	40	48	6½	5½	(8)		
Sept.	41	48½	9	1½	(9½)	44	48
Oct.	41½	48	9	1½	(11)		
Nov.	43½	46½	9	1	(12½)	47	51
1952 Dec.	44	45½	9½	1	(11½)	51	
1953 Jan.	42½	46	10	1½	(11)	46	51
Feb.	42½	46	10	1½	(11)		
March	46½	44½	8	1	(11½)		
April	47	45	7½	½	(13)	60	
May	47	45	7½	½	(12½)		
June	46	46	7	1	(11½)		
July							
Aug.	45	46	8	1	(13)	49	
Sept.	44½	47½	7	1	(12)		
Oct.	45	47½	7	½	(11½)	54	56
Nov.							
1953 Dec.	45	47	7	1	(12½)		

GALLUP POLITICAL BAROMETERS: 1951–5

Voting Intention							
Year & Month	Cons.	Lab.	Lib.	Other	DK	Govt. Record	PM
Col. 1	Col. 2	Col. 3	Col. 4	Col. 5	Col. 6	Col. 7	Col. 8
1954 Jan.	45½	46½	7	1	(14)	50	
Feb.	45½	47	7	½	(13)	50	I
March	46½	45½	7	1	(12)		
April	46½	46	7	½	(13)		48
May	45½	47½	6½	½	(12)		
June	45	47½	7	½	(12½)	47	
July							
Aug.	42½	48½	8	1	(11)		
Sept.	43	48	8	1	(11)		
Oct.	45	45½	8	1½	(16)		
Nov.	46	47	6	1	(15)		
1954 Dec.	48	49½	2½	–	(13)		
1955 Jan.	46½	45½	7	1	(14)	53	52
Feb.	46½	44½	8	1	(13)		
March	46½	44½	8	1	(13)		
April	48	44	7	1	(14)		73
May	51	47	2	#	(12½)	57	71
June							
July	47	43	9	1	(11)		68
Aug.	44½	47½	7	1	(14)		
Sept.	48	44	7	1	(10)		70
Oct.	46½	44½	8	1	(13)		63
Nov.	44½	45½	9	1	(12½)		61
1955 Dec.	45½	46½	7½	½	(12)	44	60

Key to the Tables

Barometer	Cols.	Notes
VOTING INTENTION	2 to 5	The answers to the question: 'If there were a General Election tomorrow, which party would you support?' *including* the answers of the 'don't knows' to an additional question: 'Which would you be most inclined to vote for?' but *excluding* those who remain 'don't knows', even after the incliner question.
	6	The percentage of the total sample answering 'Don't know' to the incliner question, excluded in computing the figures shown in Cols. 2–5.
GOVERNMENT RECORD	7	The percentage answering 'Approve' to the question: 'Do you approve or disapprove of the Government's record to date?'
PRIME MINISTER'S POPULARITY	8	The percentage answering 'Satisfied' to the question: 'Are you satisfied or dissatisfied with . . . as Prime Minister?'

443

Appendix II   Ministers and Senior Officials

There follows a list of Ministers, Parliamentary Private Secretaries, Permanent, Deputy and Senior Private Secretaries, and also some other top officials like the Chiefs of Staff and the Chief Medical Officer. A gap instead of a date indicates that the official or P.P.S. held his position through the period under study. A dash either before or after a date (e.g. –1953 or 1953–) indicates that he held the position either up until or from that date. With Ministers, the assumption is that he held an office until the date his successor took over. If there is no successor or date mentioned beneath him, then he continued in the job until after the 1955 General Election.

MINISTERS IN CABINET

Prime Minister and First Lord of Treasury	Winston Churchill	26 October 1951–5 April 1955
	Anthony Eden	6 April 1955
Secretary of State for Foreign Affairs	Anthony Eden	28 October 1951
	H. Macmillan	7 April 1955
Lord President of the Council	Viscount Woolton	28 October 1951
	Marquess of Salisbury	24 November 1952
Lord Privy Seal	Marquess of Salisbury	28 October 1951
	H. F. C. Crookshank	7 May 1952
Lord Chancellor	Lord Simonds	30 October 1951
	Viscount Kilmuir	18 October 1954
Secretary of State Home Office & Minister for Welsh Affairs	Sir David Maxwell Fyfe	28 October 1951
	G. Lloyd-George	18 October 1954
Chancellor of Exchequer	R. A. Butler	28 October 1951
Minister of Agriculture and Fisheries	Sir Thomas Dugdale	3 September 1953 (promoted to Cabinet)
	D. Heathcoat Amory	28 July 1954 (18 October combined with Minister of Food)
Secretary of State for Colonies	O. Lyttelton	28 October 1951
	A. T. Lennox-Boyd	28 July 1954
Secretary of State for Commonwealth Relations	Lord Ismay	28 October 1951
	Marquess of Salisbury	12 March 1952
	Viscount Swinton	24 November 1952
	Earl of Home	7 April 1955

Minister for co-ordination of Transport. Fuel and Power	Lord Leathers	30 October 1951 (office abolished 3 September 1953)
Minister of Defence	Winston Churchill	28 October 1951
	Earl Alexander of Tunis	1 March 1952
	H. Macmillan	18 October 1954
	(J.) S. B. Lloyd	7 April 1955
Minister of Education	Miss F. Horsbrugh	3 September 1953 (previously Horsbrugh held the job as a non-Cabinet position)
	Sir David Eccles	18 October 1954
Minister of Food	G. Lloyd-George	3 September 1953 (promoted to Cabinet)
	D. Heathcoat Amory	18 October 1954 (combined with Ministry of Agriculture and Fisheries)
Minister of Health	H. F. C. Crookshank	30 October 1951 (7 May 1952 when Macleod becomes Minister post taken out of Cabinet)
Minister of Housing and Local Government	H. Macmillan	30 October 1951
	D. Sandys	18 October 1954
Minister of Labour and National Service	Sir Walter Monckton	28 October 1951
Chancellor of the Duchy of Lancaster	Viscount Woolton	24 November 1952 (office promoted to Cabinet)
	(also Minister of Materials	3 September 1953– 15 July 1954)
Paymaster-General	Lord Cherwell	30 October 1951 (11 November 1953 Earl of Selkirk and office not in Cabinet)
Minister of Pensions and National Insurance	O. Peake	18 October 1954 (office promoted to Cabinet)
Secretary of State for Scotland	J. G. Stuart	30 October 1951
President of Board of Trade	(G. E.) P. Thorneycroft	30 October 1951

CABINET OFFICE

Permanent Secretary and Secretary to Cabinet	Sir Norman Brook

Civil Secretary and Secretary of the Cabinet Designate	Sir Thomas Padmore	–1952 (Office abolished)
Under Secretaries	G. Mallaby	–1954
	R. M. J. Harris	1952–
	K. L. Stock	1954–
Economic Section Director (November 1953 Office moves to Treasury)	Sir Robert Hall	–1953

TREASURY

Prime Minister and First Lord of Treasury	Winston Churchill M.P.	28 October 1951
	Anthony Eden M.P.	6 April 1955
Parliamentary Private Secretary to Prime Minister	C. Soames M.P.	1953–5
Principal Private Secretaries to Prime Minister	J. R. Colville	
	D. P. Pitblado	
Private Secretaries to Prime Minister	E. G. Cass	–1952
	D. W. S. Hunt	–1952
	P. G. Oates	–1954
	A. Montague Browne	1952–
Chancellor of Exchequer	R. A. Butler M.P.	28 October 1951
Minister of State for Economic Affairs	Sir Arthur Salter M. P.	31 October 1951– 24 November 1952 (Office abolished)
Financial Secretary	J. A. Boyd-Carpenter M.P.	31 October 1951
	H. Brooke M.P.	28 July 1954
Economic Secretary	R. Maudling M.P.	24 November 1952
	Sir Edward Boyle M.P.	7 April 1955
Parliamentary Private Secretary to Chancellor	Hubert Ashton M.P.	
Parliamentary Private Secretary to Financial Secretary	P. R. L. Newton M.P.	1952–3
Parliamentary Secretary (Chief Whip)	P. G. T. Buchan-Hepburn M.P.	30 October 1951
Junior Lords of Treasury	H. R. Mackeson M.P.	7 November 1951– 28 May 1952
	Sir Herbert Butcher M.P.	7 November 1951– 3 July 1953
	E. R. G. Heath M.P.	7 November 1951

	T. G. D. Galbraith M.P.	7 November 1951– 4 June 1954
	D. F. Vosper M. P.	7 November 1951– 18 October 1954
	H. D. Oakshott M.P.	28 May 1952
	M. Redmayne M.P.	3 July 1953
	R. H. M. Thompson M.P.	28 July 1954
	G. Wills M.P.	26 October 1954
Permanent Secretary	Sir Edward Bridges	
Second Secretaries	Sir Wilfred Eady	–1952
	Sir Bernard Gilbert	
	Sir Leslie Rowan	
	Sir Thomas Padmore	1952–
	Sir Herbert Brittain	1953–
Chief Planning Officer	Sir Edwin Plowden	–1953 (Economic Adviser to H.M.G. takes over November 1953)
Economic Adviser to Her Majesty's Government	Sir Robert Hall (also Director Economic Section)	November 1953
Economic Section (Transfer from Cabinet Office) Deputy Director	I. M. D. Little	1953–5
Senior Economic Adviser	J. C. R. Dow	1953–4
Principal Private Secretary to Chancellor	W. Armstrong L. Petch	–1953 1953–

ADMIRALTY

First Lord	J. P. L. Thomas M.P.	31 October 1951
Parliamentary and Financial Secretary	A. H. P. Noble M.P.	5 November 1951
Civil Lord	K. S. Wingfield Digby M.P	5 November 1951
Parliamentary Private Secretary to First Lord	R. O. Stanley M.P.	
Parliamentary Private Secretary to Parliamentary and Financial Secretary and Civil Lord	R. Speir M.P.	
Permanent Secretary	Sir John Lang	
Deputy Secretary	C. J. Jarrett	
Principal Private Secretary to First Lord	W. Marshall	

447

First Sea Lord	Lord Fraser of North Cape	−1951
	Sir Rhoderick McGrigor	1951–5
	Earl Mountbatten of Burma	1955–

MINISTRY OF AGRICULTURE AND FISHERIES

Minister	Sir Thomas Dugdale M.P.	31 October 1951 −28 July 1954
	D. Heathcoat Amory M.P.	28 July 1954–
Parliamentary Secretaries	Lord Carrington	5 November 1951 −18 October 1954
	G. R. H. Nugent M.P.	5 November 1951
	Earl St. Aldwyn	18 October 1954
	H. Nicholls M.P.	7 April 1955
Parliamentary Private Secretaries	W. M. F. Vane M.P.	−1954
	R. F. Wood M.P.	1954–
Permanent Secretary	Sir Donald Vandepeer	−September 1952
	Sir Alan Hitchman	October 1952–
Deputy Secretaries	Sir George Dunnett	
	Sir Reginald Franklin	−1954
	A. R. Manktelow	1954–

AIR MINISTRY

Secretary of State	Lord De L'Isle and Dudley	31 October 1951
Parliamentary Under-Secretary of State	(E) N. (C) Birch M.P.	3 November 1951
	G. R. Ward M.P.	29 February 1952–
Parliamentary Private Secretary to Parliamentary Under-Secretary of State	Sir Edward Boyle M.P.	−1952
	A. P. L. Barber M.P.	1952–4
Permanent Under-Secretary of State	Sir James Barnes	
Deputy Under-Secretaries of State	Sir Folliott Sandford	
	V. H. Raby	1954–
Principal Private Secretary to Secretary of State	(T) C. (G) James	
Chief of Air Staff	Sir John Slessor	−1952
	Sir William Dickson	1953–

MINISTRY OF CIVIL AVIATION (merges with Ministry of Transport 1 October 1953)

| Minister | J. Maclay M.P. | 31 October 1951– 7 May 1952 |
| | A. T. Lennox-Boyd M.P. | 7 May 1952 |

Parliamentary Secretary	Sir Joseph Gurney Braithwaite M.P.	5 November 1951– 1 November 1953
	R. Maudling M.P.	18 April 1952
	J. Profumo M.P.	24 November 1952
Parliamentary Private Secretary to Minister	B. R. Braine M.P.	
Parliamentary Private Secretary to Parliamentary Secretary	(H) R. Gower M.P.	
Permanent Secretary	Sir Arnold Overton	–1953
Deputy Secretary	Sir George Cribbett	
Private Secretary to Minister	S. M. A. Banister	

COLONIAL OFFICE

Secretary of State	O. Lyttelton M.P.	28 October 1951
	A. T. Lennox-Boyd M.P.	28 July 1954
Minister of State	A. T. Lennox-Boyd M.P.	2 November 1951
	H. L. d'A. Hopkinson M.P.	7 May 1952
Parliamentary Under-Secretary of State	Earl of Munster	5 November 1951
	Lord Lloyd	18 November 1954
Parliamentary Private Secretary to Secretary of State	H. C. P. J. Fraser M.P.	–1954
	A. M. S. Neave M.P.	1954–
Parliamentary Private Secretary to Minister of State	P. H. B. O. Smithers M.P.	1952–
Permanent Under-Secretary of State	Sir Thomas Lloyd	
Deputy Under-Secretaries of State	Sir Charles Jeffries	
	Sir Hilton Poynton	
Educational Adviser	Sir Christopher Cox	
Legal Adviser	Sir Kenneth Roberts-Wray	
Principal Private Secretary to Secretary of State	A. M. Mackintosh	–1953
	J. B. Johnston	1953–

COMMONWEALTH RELATIONS OFFICE

Secretary of State	Lord Ismay	28 October 1951
	Marquess of Salisbury	12 March 1952
	Viscount Swinton	24 November 1952
	Earl of Home	7 April 1955

Parliamentary Under-Secretary of State	J. Foster M.P.	3 November 1951
	A. Dodds-Parker M.P.	18 October 1954
Parliamentary Private Secretary	J. M. Baldock M.P.	
Permanent Under-Secretary of State	Sir Percivale Liesching	–1955
	Sir Gilbert Laithwaite	1955–
Deputy Under-Secretary of State	Sir Stephen Holmes	–1952
	A. C. B. Symon (acting)	1952–3
	Sir Saville Garner	1952–
Private Secretary to Secretary of State	D. J. C. Crawley	1952–3
	R. H. Belcher	1953–4

MINISTRY OF DEFENCE

Minister	Winston Churchill M.P.	28 October 1951
	Earl Alexander of Tunis	1 March 1952
	H. Macmillan M.P.	18 October 1954
	S. Lloyd M.P.	7 April 1955
Parliamentary Secretaries	(E) N. (C) Birch M.P.	28 February 1952
	Lord Carrington	18 October 1954
Parliamentary Private Secretaries to Parliamentary Secretary	Sir Edward Boyle M.P.	1952–3
	J. W. W. Peyton M.P.	1953–4
	H. W. Kerr M.P.	1954–5
Permanent Secretary	Sir Harold Parker	
Deputy Secretaries	Sir Maurice Dean	–1952
	Sir Richard Powell	
Chief Staff Officer	Sir Kenneth McLean	–1952
	Sir Ian Jacob	–November 1952
	Sir Nevil Brownjohn	December 1952–
Scientific Adviser to Minister	Sir Henry Tizard	–1952
	Sir John Cockcroft	1952–4
	Sir Frederick Brundrett	1954–
Principal Private Secretary to Minister	N. G. Morrison	1952–4
	W. N. Hanna	1954–

DUCHY OF LANCASTER (3 September 1953–15 July 1954 also Ministry of Materials)

Chancellor	Viscount Swinton	31 October 1951
	Viscount Woolton	24 November 1952
Private Secretary	G. R. Downes	1951–2
	K. D. Rodgers	1952–3
	J. C. Seddon	1953–

MINISTRY OF EDUCATION

| Minister | Miss F. Horsbrugh M.P. | 2 November 1951 |
| | Sir David Eccles M.P. | 18 October 1954 |

Parliamentary Secretary	K. W. M. Pickthorn M.P.	5 November 1951
	D. F. Vosper M.P.	18 October 1954
Parliamentary Private Secretary to Minister	R. Fort M.P.	1951–4
	J. C. Rodgers M.P.	1954–
Permanent Secretaries	Sir John Maud	–September 1952
	Sir Gilbert Flemming	October 1952–
Deputy Secretaries	Sir Griffith Williams	–1953
	Sir Gilbert Flemming	–1952
	R. N. Heaton	1954–
Senior Chief Inspector	Sir Martin Roseveare	
Principal Private Secretary to Minister	E. B. H. Baker	–1954
	A. Thompson	1954–

MINISTRY OF FOOD (combined with Ministry of Agriculture and Fisheries 18 October 1954)

Minister	G. Lloyd-George M.P.	3 September 1953
	D. Heathcoat Amory M.P	18 October 1954
Parliamentary Secretary	C. Hill M.P.	31 October 1951
Parliamentary Private Secretary	N. T. L. Fisher M.P.	1951–4
Permanent Secretary	Sir Henry Hancock	
Deputy Secretaries	Sir Albert Feaveryear	–1953
	E. Harwood	1953–
	L. N. Helsby	–1954
	R. Herbert	1954–
Principal Private Secretary to Minister	F. Bishop	–1952
	H. Pitchforth	1952–4

FOREIGN OFFICE

Secretary of State	Sir Anthony Eden M.P.	28 October 1951
	H. Macmillan M.P.	7 April 1955
Ministers of State	S. Lloyd M.P.	30 October 1951– 18 October 1954
	Marquess of Reading	11 November 1953
	A. Nutting M.P.	18 October 1954
Parliamentary Under-Secretaries of State	Marquess of Reading	31 October 1951– 11 November 1953
	A. Nutting M.P.	31 October 1951– 18 October 1954
	A. Dodds-Parker M.P.	11 November 1953
	R. H. Turton M.P.	18 October 1954
	Lord John Hope M.P.	18 October 1954
Parliamentary Private Secretary to Secretary of State	(L) R. Carr M.P.	

Parliamentary Private Secretary to Minister of State	W. D. Ormsby-Gore M.P.	1951–4
	R. C. Brooman-White M.P.	1954–
Permanent Under-Secretary of State	Sir William Strang	–1953
	Sir Ivone Kirkpatrick	1953–
Deputy Under-Secretaries of State	Sir Roger Makins	–1952
	Sir (Henry) Ashley Clarke	–1953
	Sir Pierson Dixon	–1954
	Sir Frank Roberts	1951–4
	Sir Roderick Barclay	1953–
	Sir Harold Caccia	1954–
	J. G. Ward	1954–
Principal Private Secretary to Secretary of State	(C. A.) E. Shuckburgh	–1954
	Sir (Horace) Anthony Rumbold	1954–

MINISTRY OF FUEL AND POWER

Minister	G. W. Lloyd M.P.	31 October 1951
Parliamentary Secretary	L. W. Joynson-Hicks M.P.	5 November 1951
Parliamentary Private Secretary	Dr. R. F. B. Bennett M.P.	1954–5
Permanent Secretary	Sir Donald Fergusson	–September 1952
	Sir John Maud	October 1952–
Deputy Secretary	Sir (George) Laurence Watkinson	
Private Secretary to Minister	A. B. Powell	–1951
	M. E. Fletcher	1952–4
	N. E. Martin	1954–

MINISTRY OF HEALTH

Minister	H. F. C. Crookshank M.P.	30 October 1951
	I. N. Macleod M.P.	7 May 1952
Parliamentary Secretary	Miss (M.) P. Hornsby-Smith M.P.	3 November 1951
Parliamentary Private Secretary	Sir Robert Cary M.P.	–May 1952
	G. B. Finlay M.P.	1952–
Permanent Secretary	Sir John Hawton	
Deputy Secretary	Sir (Isaac) Frederick Armer	
Chief Medical Officer	Sir John Charles	
Private Secretary to Minister	A. R. W. Bavin	–1952
	R. Gedling	1952–

452

HOME OFFICE

Home Secretary	Sir David Maxwell Fyfe M.P.	28 October 1951
	G. Lloyd-George M.P.	18 October 1954
Parliamentary Under-Secretaries of State	Sir Hugh Lucas-Tooth M.P.	3 February 1952
	D. T. Llewellyn M.P.	5 November 1951–14 October 1952
	Lord Lloyd	24 November 1952–18 October 1954
	Lord Mancroft	18 October 1954
Parliamentary Private Secretary	Dr. R. F. B. Bennett M.P.	–1954
	N. T. L. Fisher M.P.	1954–
Permanent Under-Secretary of State	Sir Frank Newsam	
Deputy Under-Secretaries of State	Sir William Murrie	–September 1952
	Sir Arthur Hutchinson	
Private Secretary to Home Secretary	R. J. Whittick	1952–3
	R. J. Guppy	1953–

MINISTRY OF HOUSING AND LOCAL GOVERNMENT

Minister	H. Macmillan M.P.	30 October 1951
	D. Sandys M.P.	18 October 1954
Parliamentary Secretary	E. Marples M.P.	3 November 1951
	W. Deedes M.P.	18 October 1954
Parliamentary Private Secretary	J. R. Bevins M.P.	1951–3
	R. S. Russell M.P.	1954–
Permanent Secretary	Sir Thomas Sheepshanks	
Deputy Secretaries	Dame Evelyn Sharp	
	Sir John Wrigley	–1952
Private Secretary to Minister	J. E. Beddoe	–1953
	J. Rogerson	1953–5
Special Adviser	Sir Percy Mills	1951–2

MINISTRY OF LABOUR AND NATIONAL SERVICE

Minister	Sir Walter Monckton M.P.	28 October 1951
Parliamentary Secretary	Sir Peter Bennett M.P.	31 October 1951
	H. A. Watkinson M.P.	28 May 1952
Parliamentary Private Secretary to Minister	C. I. Orr-Ewing M.P.	
Parliamentary Private Secretary to Parliamentary Secretary	J. B. Godber M.P.	1952–

453

Permanent Secretary	Sir Godfrey Ince	
Deputy Secretaries	Sir Guildhaume Myrddin-Evans	
	Sir Harold Wiles	
Chief Industrial Commissioner	Sir Robert Gould	–1952
	H. G. Gee	1952–4
	W. J. Neden	1954–
Private Secretary Minister	A. Sutherland	–1953
	C. Heron	1953–

LAW OFFICERS DEPARTMENT

Attorney-General	Sir Lionel Heald M.P.	3 November 1951
	Sir Reginald Manningham-Buller M.P.	18 October 1954
Solicitor-General	Sir Reginald Manningham-Buller M.P.	3 November 1951
	Sir Harry Hylton-Foster M.P.	18 October 1954
Parliamentary Private Secretary to Attorney General	J. E. S. Simon M.P.	1951–
	F. P. Crowder M.P.	1954–
Parliamentary Private Secretary to Solicitor-General	F. P. Crowder M.P.	1952–4
	P. J. M. Thomas M.P.	1954–

LORD ADVOCATE'S DEPARTMENT

Lord Advocate	J. L. M. Clyde M.P.	2 November 1951
	W. R. Milligan M.P.	30 December 1954
Solicitor-General Scotland	W. R. Milligan M.P.	3 November 1951
	W. Grant	10 January 1955

LORD CHANCELLOR'S DEPARTMENT

Lord Chancellor	Lord Simonds	30 October 1951
	Viscount Kilmuir	18 October 1954
Clerk of the Crown in Chancery and Permanent Secretary to the Lord Chancellor	Sir Albert Napier	–1954
	Sir George Coldstream	1954–
Private Secretary to Lord Chancellor	C. W. B. Rankin	

OFFICE OF THE LORD PRESIDENT OF THE COUNCIL

Lord President	Lord Woolton	30 October 1951
	Marquess of Salisbury	24 November 1952
Permanent Secretary	E. M. Nicholson	–1952
	R. N. Quirk	1952–

454

Adviser on Atomic Energy Organisation	Sir Edwin Plowden	1953–4 (subsequently Chairman, Atomic Energy Authority)
Secretary Atomic Office	F. C. How	1954–
Private Secretary to Lord President	C. H. A. Duke A. H. K. Slater	–1953 1953–

LORD PRIVY SEAL

Lord Privy Seal	Marquess of Salisbury H. F. C. Crookshank	28 October 1951 7 May 1952
Parliamentary Private Secretary	Sir Robert Cary M.P.	1952–
Private Secretary to Lord President	Miss E. A. Hogg	

MINISTRY OF MATERIALS (Ministry of Materials combined with Duchy of Lancaster 1 September 1953– 15 July 1954, wound up 15 July 1954)

Minister	Viscount Swinton Sir Arthur Salter Viscount Woolton	31 October 1951 24 November 1952– 1 September 1953– 15 July 1954
Permanent Secretary	Sir (Edwin) Alan Hitchman Sir James Helmore Sir Eric Bowyer	–1952 1952–3 1953–4
Deputy Secretary	E. F. Muir	–1954
Private Secretary	G. R. Downes	–1952
Private Secretary to Minister	K. D. Rodgers J. K. T. Frost	1952–3 1953–4

MINISTRY OF NATIONAL INSURANCE (office combined with Ministry of Pensions, 3 September 1953)

Minister	O. Peake M.P.	31 October 1951
Parliamentary Secretary	R. H. Turton M.P.	5 November 1951
Permanent Secretary	Sir Geoffrey King	
Deputy Secretary	Sir Nicolas de Villiers	
Private Secretary to Minister	L. Errington	1951–3

MINISTRY OF PENSIONS (AND NATIONAL INSURANCE 3 September 1953–)

Minister	D. Heathcoat Amory M.P. O. Peake M.P.	5 November 1951 3 September 1953

455

Parliamentary Secretaries	J. G. Smyth M.P.	5 November 1951
	R. H. Turton M.P.	3 September 1953–
		18 October 1954
	E. Marples M.P.	18 October 1954
Parliamentary Private Secretary	J. S. W. Arbuthnot M.P.	1952–
Permanent Secretary	Sir Arton Wilson	–1953
	Sir Geoffrey King	1953–
Deputy Secretaries	Dame Marjorie Cox	–1954
	Sir Nicolas de Villiers	1953–
Private Secretary to Minister	R. S. Swift	1953–4

PAYMASTER-GENERAL

Paymaster-General	Lord Cherwell	30 October 1951
	Earl of Selkirk	11 November 1953
Private Secretary	J. R. Madge	–1952
	P. J. Searby	1952–3
	G. A. Gardner	–1954

OFFICE OF THE MINISTER WITHOUT PORTFOLIO

| Minister Without Portfolio | Earl of Munster | 18 October 1954 |
| Private Secretary | M. Lynch | 1954– |

POST OFFICE

Postmaster-General	Earl De La Warr	5 November 1951
	C. Hill M.P.	7 April 1955
Assistant Postmaster-General	(L) D. Gammans M.P.	5 November 1951
Parliamentary Private Secretary to Postmaster-General	Earl of Selkirk	1952–3
Parliamentary Private Secretary to Assistant Postmaster-General	H. Nicholls M.P.	
Director General	Sir (Rudolf) Alexander Little	
Deputy Directors General	B. L. Barnett	
	Sir George Ismay	–1952
	Sir Dudley Lumley	1952–5
	Sir Gordon Radley	1954–5
Private Secretary to Postmaster-General	J. T. Baldry	–1953
	Miss P. Bridger	1953–4
	(A) W. (C) Ryland	1954–5

456

SCOTTISH OFFICE

Secretary of State	J. Stuart M.P.	30 October 1951
Minister of State	Earl of Home	2 November 1951
	T. D. Galbraith M.P.	7 April 1955
Parliamentary Under-Secretaries of State	T. D. Galbraith M.P.	2 November 1951–5 April 1955
	W. M. Snadden M.P.	2 November 1951
	J. H. Stewart M.P.	24 February 1952
Parliamentary Private Secretary	J. N. Browne M.P.	1952–
Permanent Under-Secretary of State	Sir David Milne	
Secretary. Department of Agriculture	Sir Patrick Laird	–1953
	A. Glen	1953–
Secretary. Education Department	Sir John Mackay Thomson	–September 1952
	Sir William Murrie	October 1952–
Secretary. Department of Health	Sir George Henderson	–1953
	H. R. Smith	1953–
Secretary. Home Department	Sir Charles Cunningham	
Private Secretary to Secretary of State	W. G. Pottinger	–1952
	I. M. Robertson	1952–

MINISTRY OF SUPPLY

Minister	D. Sandys M.P.	31 October 1951
	S. Lloyd M.P.	18 October 1954
	R. Maudling M.P.	7 April 1955
Parliamentary Secretary	A. R. W. Low M.P.	3 November 1951
	Sir Edward Boyle M.P.	28 July 1954
	F. J. Erroll M.P.	7 April 1955
Parliamentary Private Secretary	R. S. Russell M.P.	–1954
	Viscount Lambton M.P.	1954
Permanent Secretary	Sir Archibald Rowlands	–1953
	Sir James Helmore	1953–
Deputy Permanent Secretary	Sir Cyril Musgrave	1953–
Deputy Secretaries	Sir Eric Bowyer	–1953
	L. H. Robinson	1953–
	Sir Lewis Hutchinson	
	Sir Cyril Musgrave	–1953
	L. J. Dunnett	1953–
Private Secretary to Minister	R. St. J. Walker	–1953
	E. G. Cass	1954–

BOARD OF TRADE

President	(G. E.) P. Thorneycroft M.P.	30 October 1951
Secretary for Overseas Trade	H. L. d'A. Hopkinson M.P.	3 November 1951
	Sir Harry Mackeson M.P.	28 May 1952– 3 September 1953
Minister of State	D. Heathcoat Amory M.P.	3 September 1953
	T. Low M.P.	28 July 1954
Parliamentary Secretary	H. Strauss M.P.	3 November 1951
	D. Kaberry M.P.	7 April 1955
Parliamentary Private Secretary to President	A. C. M. Spearman M.P.	–1952
	J. A. Hay M.P.	1952–
	A. Cooper M.P.	1951–4
Parliamentary Private Secretary to Secretary Overseas Trade and Minister of State	S. L. C. Maydon M.P.	1952–3
	E. E. Bullus M.P.	1953–5
	R. F. Wood M.P.	1953–4
Permanent Secretary	Sir Frank Lee	
Second Secretaries	Sir James Helmore	–1952
	G. Calder	–1952
	Sir Henry Gregory	
	E. A. Cohen	1952–
	Sir Maurice Dean	1952–
Private Secretary to President	F. W. Glaves-Smith	1952–

MINISTRY OF TRANSPORT (AND CIVIL AVIATION 1 October 1953–)

Minister	J. S. Maclay M.P.	31 October 1951
	A. T. Lennox-Boyd M.P.	7 May 1952
	J. A. Boyd-Carpenter M.P.	28 July 1954
Parliamentary Secretaries	Sir Joseph Gurney Braithwaite M.P.	5 November 1951– 1 November 1953
	R. Maudling M.P.	18 April 1952– 24 November 1952
	J. D. Profumo M.P.	24 November 1952
	(A.) H. (E.) Molson M.P.	11 November 1953
Parliamentary Private Secretary to Minister	H. A. Watkinson M.P.	1951–2
	B. R. Braine M.P.	1952–4
	R. Scott-Miller M.P.	1954–
Parliamentary Private Secretary to Parliamentary Secretaries	(H) R. Gower M.P.	1951–

458

Permanent Secretary	Sir Gilmour Jenkins	
Deputy Secretaries	Sir Cyril Birtchnell	–1953
	Sir Norman Guttery	–1954
	Sir George Cribbett	
	P. D. Proctor	1953–
	G. F. Stedman	1954–
Private Secretary to Minister	O. F. Gingell	
	S. M. A. Banister	

WAR OFFICE

Secretary of State for War	A. H. Head M.P.	31 October 1951
Parliamentary Under-Secretary and Financial Secretary	J. R. H. Hutchinson M.P.	5 November 1951
	F. H. Maclean M.P.	18 October 1954
Parliamentary Private Secretary to Secretary of State	J. D. R. Tilney M.P.	
Parliamentary Private Secretary to	R. C. Brooman-White M.P.	1951–4
Parliamentary Under-Secretary	T. L. Iremonger M.P.	1954–
Permanent Under-Secretary of State	Sir George Turner	
Deputy Under-Secretary	(A) Sir Thomas Cash	–1954
	C. E. Key	1954–
Deputy Under-Secretary	(B) Sir David Roseway	
Private Secretary to Secretary of State	P. F. R. Beards	1951–4
Chief of the Imperial General Staff	Sir William Slim	–1952
	Sir John Harding	1952–

MINISTRY OF WORKS

Minister	Sir David Eccles M.P.	1 November 1951
	(E) N. (C) Birch M.P.	18 October 1954
Parliamentary Secretary	(A) H. (E) Molson M.P.	3 November 1951
	J. R. Bevins M.P.	11 November 1953
Parliamentary Private Secretary	J. Rodgers M.P.	–1954
	J. W. W. Peyton M.P.	1954–
Permanent Secretary	Sir Harold Emmerson	
Deputy Secretaries	Sir Eric de Normann	–1954
	E. A. Seal	1951–
	E. F. Muir	1954–

459

LORDS-IN-WAITING

Earl of Birkenhead	5 November 1951– 28 January 1955
Earl of Selkirk	5 November 1951– 11 November 1953
Lord Lloyd	7 November 1951– 24 November 1952
Lord Mancroft	15 December 1952– 18 October 1954
Lord Hawke	11 November 1953–
Lord Fairfax	18 October 1954–
Lord Chesham	28 January 1955–

H.M. HOUSEHOLD

Treasurer	Sir Cedric Drewe M.P.	7 November 1951
Comptroller	Sir Roger Conant M.P.	7 November 1951
	T. G. D. Galbraith M.P.	7 June 1954
Vice Chamberlain	H. Studholme M.P.	7 November 1951
Captain Gentleman at Arms	Earl Fortescue	5 November 1951
Captain Yeoman of Guard	Earl of Onslow	5 November 1951

Source: Butler and Sloman: *Imperial Calendar*. Dod.

460

Appendix III Election Statistics

Part 1: General Elections

	Electorate	Votes cast	Conservative	Labour	Liberal	Communist	Other
1950	34.269.770	100% 28.772.671	43.5% 12.502.567	46.1% 13.266.592	9.1% 2.621.548	0.3% 91.746	1.0% 290.218
1951	34.645.573	100% 28.595.668	48.0% 13.717.538	48.8% 13.948.605	2.5% 730.556	0.1% 21.640	0.6% 177.329
1955	34.858.263	100% 26.760.493	49.7% 13.286.564	46.4% 12.404.970	2.7% 722.405	0.1% 33.144	1.1% 313.410

	Elec-torate (in '000s)	% Voting	Change in % Voting 1951–1955	Members Elected					Votes (as % of votes cast in constituencies where the party concerned put up candidates)				Swing (Average of Con. % gain and Lab. % loss)		
				Total	Con.	Lab.	Lib.	Other	Con.	Lab.	Lib.	Other	1945–1950	1950–1951	1951–1955
The whole country															
United Kingdom	34.858	76.8	−5.7	630	344	277	6	3	623 50.2	620 47.3	110 15.1	56 15.6	3.3	1.1	1.8
Great Britain															
England	28.795	76.9	−5.8	511	292	216	2	1	508 50.6	510 46.9	95 13.4	21 8.5	3.6	1.3	1.7
Wales	1.801	79.6	−4.8	36	6	27	3	—	32 33.5	36 57.6	10 29.4	13 18.9	0.3	1.2	1.7
Scotland	3.388	75.1	−5.6	71	36	34	1	—	71 50.1	71 46.7	5 31.2	9 9.4	3.1	1.4	0.8
Total	33.984	76.8	−5.8	618	334	277	6	1	611 49.7	617 47.4	110 15.1	43 11.4	3.4	1.3	1.6

Part II: By-Elections 1951–5

Constituency	Date	% Voting	Con. %	Lab. %	Lib. %	Other %	Swing to Cons.
Bournemouth East and Christchurch	6/2/52	63.8	61.8	23.4	10.1	Ind. 4.7	0.2
	1951	80.8	63.3	25.1	11.6	—	
Southport	6/2/52	61.0	62.0	28.5	9.5	—	−1.0
	1951	77.7	60.2	24.8	15.0	—	
Leeds. South-east	7/2/52	55.7	36.8	63.2	—	—	−2.7
	1951	84.4	39.5	60.5	—	—	
Dundee East	17/7/52	71.5	35.6	56.2	—	S. Nat. 7.5 Ind. 0.7	−7.5
	1951	87.2	46.2	53.8	—	—	
Cleveland	23/10/52	71.4	45.9	54.1	—	—	0.7
	1951	85.1	45.2	54.8	—	—	
Belfast South	4/11/52	47.1	75.1	24.9	—	—	−0.7
	1951	73.8	75.8	24.2	—	—	
Wycombe	4/11/52	84.0	52.0	48.0	—	—	0.3
	1951	86.2	51.7	48.3	—	—	
Antrim North	27/10/52	—	Unop.				—
	1951	—	Unop.				
Birmingham, Small Heath	27/11/52	46.6	33.0	67.0	—	—	−0.8
	1951	77.2	30.9	63.4	5.7	—	
Farnworth	27/11/52	70.9	40.1	59.9	—	—	−0.7
	1951	86.8	40.8	59.2	—	—	
Canterbury	12/2/52	49.2	67.1	32.9	—	—	2.1
	1951	80.1	61.1	31.0	7.9	—	
Isle of Thanet	12/3/53	58.7	61.3	38.7	—	—	−0.4
	1951	78.0	61.7	38.3	—	—	
Barnsley	31/3/53	57.9	27.1	72.9	—	—	3.3
	1951	77.2	17.3	69.7	13.0	—	
Stoke-on-Trent, North	31/3/53	50.7	24.5	75.5	—	—	−4.1
	1951	83.8	28.6	71.4	—	—	
Hayes and Harlington	1/4/53	44.9	36.1	63.9	—	—	0.9
	1951	82.2	35.2	64.8	—	—	
North Down	15/4/53	—	Unop.	—	—	—	—
	1951	65.7	81.4	18.6	—	—	
Sunderland. South	13/5/53	72.5	48.6	46.1	5.3	—	2.4
	1951	82.2	49.7	50.3	—	—	

Part II: By-Elections 1951–5—*continued*

Constituency	Date	% Voting	Con. %	Lab. %	Lib. %	Other %	Swing to Cons.
Abingdon	30/6/53	75.4	53.2	39.7	7.1	—	1.3
	1951	*80.0*	*55.5*	*44.5*	—	—	
Birmingham,	2/7/53	50.2	67.6	32.4	—	—	3.3
Edgbaston	*1951*	*76.1*	*64.3*	*35.7*	—	—	
Broxtowe	17/9/53	62.9	25.9	74.1	—	—	−1.4
	1951	*84.1*	*27.3*	*72.7*	—	—	
Crosby	12/11/53	62.0	68.1	27.6	—	Ind. 4.3	−0.6
	1951	*79.8*	*70.9*	*29.1*	—	—	
Ormskirk	12/11/53	54.0	65.4	34.6	—	—	−2.0
	1951	*78.7*	*67.4*	*32.6*	—	—	
Holborn and St.	19/11/53	56.2	45.6	52.1	2.3	—	
Pancras South	*1951*	*73.7*	*45.8*	*50.2*	*4.0*	—	*−1.1*
Paddington, North	3/12/53	58.3	45.3	53.8	—	S.P. of G.B. 0.9	1.0
	1951	*80.8*	*44.3*	*55.7*	—	—	
Ilford, North	3/2/54	45.3	59.8	32.3	7.9	—	5.1
	1951	*84.8*	*55.5*	*38.0*	*6.5*	—	
Harwich	11/2/54	59.0	59.1	40.9	—	—	0.2
	1951	*78.8*	*58.9*	*41.1*	—	—	
Kingston-on-Hull,	11/2/54	45.5	61.8	38.2	—	—	3.7
Haltemprice	*1951*	*82.8*	*58.1*	*41.9*	—	—	
Bournemouth,	18/2/54	45.1	69.7	30.3	—	—	4.2
West	*1951*	*77.7*	*65.5*	*44.5*	—	—	
Arundel and	9/3/54	54.2	68.5	31.5	—	—	1.1
Shoreham	*1951*	*78.0*	*67.4*	*32.6*	—	—	
Harrogate	12/3/54	55.3	70.8	29.2	—	—	0.2
	1951	*78.7*	*70.6*	*29.4*	—	—	
Edinburgh, East	8/4/54	61.8	42.4	57.6	—	—	−3.5
	1951	*83.8*	*45.9*	*54.1*	—	—	
Motherwell	14/4/54	69.9	39.3	56.4	—	Com. 4.3	−1.4
	1951	*84.7*	*42.8*	*57.2*	—	—	
Croydon, East	30/9/54	57.5	56.6	35.4	8.0	—	1.8
	1951	*84.2*	*58.8*	*41.2*	—	—	
Shoreditch and	21/10/54	40.6	21.8	78.2	—	—	−5.6
Finsbury	*1951*	*73.2*	*27.4*	*72.6*	—	—	

Part II: By-Elections 1951–5—*continued*

Constituency	Date	% Voting	Con. %	Lab. %	Lib. %	Other %	Swing to Cons.
Wakefield	21/10/54	68.6	41.9	58.1	—	—	0.2
	1951	*85.6*	*41.7*	*58.3*	—	—	
Aldershot	28/10/54	58.6	60.1	39.9	—	—	−0.2
	1951	*77.8*	*60.3*	*39.7*	—	—	
Aberdare	29/10/54	69.7	14.5	69.5	—	W. Nat. 16.0	—
	1951	*86.2*	*15.4*	*78.5*	—	W. Nat. *6.1*	—
Sutton and Cheam	4/11/54	55.6	66.5	33.5	—	—	3.7
	1951	*81.0*	*62.8*	*37.2*	—	—	
Morpeth	4/11/54	73.0	28.7	71.3	—	—	0.6
	1951	*85.5*	*28.1*	*71.9*	—	—	
Liverpool, West Derby	18/11/54 *1951*	58.9 *80.3*	53.2 *51.6*	46.8 *48.4*	— —	— —	1.6
South Norfolk	14/1/55	66.7	51.4	48.6	—	—	−3.1
	1951	*82.4*	*54.5*	*45.5*	—	—	
Orpington	20/1/55	55.4	65.8	34.2	—	—	3.2
	1951	*82.0*	*62.6*	*37.4*	—	—	
Twickenham	25/1/55	47.3	64.0	36.0	—	—	1.9
	1951	*81.2*	*62.1*	*37.9*	—	—	
Edinburgh, North	27/1/55	46.4	59.4	40.6	—	—	0.6
	1951	*80.0*	*58.8*	*41.2*	—	—	
Stockport, South	3/2/55	64.6	54.3	45.7	—	—	0.1
	1951	*84.2*	*54.2*	*45.8*	—	—	
Wrexham	17/3/55	62.4	30.8	57.9	—	W. Nat. 11.3	−0.3
	1951	*84.8*	*34.9*	*61.5*	—	W. Nat. *3.6*	

Source: Butler: *British General Election of 1955*

Appendix IV Major Acts, White Papers and Reports

A Summary of the Major Acts passed by the Goverment, 1951–5

December 1951
HOME GUARD ACT, 1951
(R.A. 7 December 1951)
Establishes the Home Guard on a
voluntary and limited basis in time of
peace.

MINISTERS OF THE CROWN
(PARLIAMENTARY
UNDER-SECRETARIES) ACT, 1951
(R.A. 7 December 1951)
Enables a third Under-Secretary of State
for Scotland to be appointed and a
second Under-Secretary of State at the
Home Office so that one could deal with
Welsh Affairs.

PNEUMOCONIOSIS AND
BYSSINOSIS BENEFIT ACT, 1951
(R.A. 7 December 1951)
Provides for the payment of benefit out
of the Industrial Injuries Fund to, or in
respect of, certain persons who are
totally disabled or whose death occurs
from pneumoconiosis or byssinosis after
31 December 1949, who were not
insured in respect of these diseases under
the National Insurance (Industrial
Injuries) Act, 1946, or entitled to
workmen's compensation.

March 1952
JUDICIAL OFFICES (SALARIES,
ETC.) ACT, 1952.
(R.A. 13 March 1952)
Increases the salaries of county court
judges, stipendiary magistrates and
certain other holders of judicial offices.

April 1952
MINERS' WELFARE ACT, 1952
(R.A. 30 April 1952)
Dissolves the Miners' Welfare
Commission, which was formed in 1920,
and transfers arrangements for the
welfare of miners to the National Coal
Board, which is now responsible for
pithead baths, colliery canteens, etc, and
to the Coal Industry Social Welfare
Organisations.

May 1952
EMPIRE SETTLEMENT ACT, 1952
(R.A. 22 May 1952)
Extends by five years from 31 May 1952,
the power under the Empire Settlement
Acts, 1922 and 1937, to promote
overseas settlement in the
Commonwealth, and to contribute to
such schemes up to a maximum (since
1937) of £1,500,000 a year.

NATIONAL HEALTH SERVICE
ACT, 1952
(R.A. 22 May 1952)
Extends the existing powers to make and
recover charges for services under the
National Health Service Acts, 1946 to
1951, and the National Health Service
(Scotland) Acts, 1947 to 1951; enables
regulations to be made imposing charges
for supply of drugs, medicines or
appliances under the hospital and
specialist services; gives power to remit
or recover the charge in certain cases,
including grounds of hardship; provides
that a charge of the current authorised

466

fee or £1, whichever is the less, may be made for treatment given under the general dental services (children, those under 21, expectant and nursing mothers, those on national assistance and anybody else who can prove hardship are exempted from the charge, and the initial inspection of teeth is also free of charge).

June 1952
FAMILY ALLOWANCES AND NATIONAL INSURANCE ACT, 1952
(R.A. 26 June 1952)
Provided for a general increase in retirement pensions, unemployment, sickness and widows' benefits, and also in industrial injury insurance benefits and family allowances. It restored the principle of uniformity in the main weekly rates of national insurance benefits at a higher level of 32s.6d. for a single person and 54s. for a married couple; increased the industrial injury pension for 100 per cent disablement to 55s. and improved other benefits under this scheme; and raised family allowances to 8s.

NEW TOWNS ACT, 1952
(R.A. 26 June 1952)
The Act increased from £50m. to £100m. the aggregate amount of advances which may be made to the New Town Development Corporations.

July 1952
FINANCE ACT, 1952
(R.A. 9 July 1952)
Gave effect to the Government's taxation proposals outlined in the 1952 Budget; altered the income tax allowances and graduations of tax to the benefit of all taxpayers, especially in the case of overtime payments; and gave tax relief to help retired people and people living on small fixed incomes. Changes were also made in the entertainment tax, petrol tax, profits tax, stamp duties on sale of small house property, and the excess profits levy was introduced.

Purchase tax on textiles was reduced by 25 per cent.

August 1952
HOUSING ACT, 1952
(R.A. 1 August 1952)
Increased the rates of certain of the Exchequer subsidies and rate fund contributions in the case of houses completed by local authorities after 28 February 1952; and empowered the Minister to give his consent to the sale of houses by local authorities in England and Wales subject to certain conditions.

PENSIONS (INCREASE) ACT, 1952
(R.A. 1 August 1952)
This Act adds to the increases given under the Pensions (Increase) Act 1947. It applies to retired members of the Civil Service, staffs of local authorities, teachers, police and firemen, and some pensioners of the voluntary hospitals who, when they retired, were pensioners of those hospitals, and former employees of some of the friendly and provident societies. The Act allows an increase of up to £26 a year in respect of a married pensioner, or a pensioner with a dependant, and of £20 a year for a pensioner without a dependant. These increases apply only to those whose income (after disregarding the first £104 a year) is less than £550 for married pensioners or £425 a year for the pensioner with no dependants.

TOWN DEVELOPMENT ACT, 1952
(R.A. 1 August 1952)
Empowers local authorities, in rural or small urban areas, to carry out town development (housing and any industrial, or commercial development) to provide accommodation for people from other towns who, because of overcrowding or shortage of land, cannot be housed or rehoused in those areas; and empowers Councils benefiting from such town development, and County Councils and the Minister of Housing and Local Government in certain cases, to contribute to the cost.

467

October 1952
HOUSING (SCOTLAND) ACT 1952
(R.A. 30 October 1952)
Applies similar provisions as in the Housing Act, 1952, to Scotland, except that the rates of subsidy are different, and no provision is made in this Act giving power for the sale of council houses because the Secretary of State for Scotland already has power to ensure that conditions are imposed on intending purchasers.

LICENSED PREMISES IN NEW TOWNS ACT, 1952
(R.A. 30 October 1952)
Repeals that part of the Licensing Act, 1949, which provides for the state management of the liquor trade in New Towns; provides for the granting or removal of justices' licences for or to premises in New Towns in England and Wales, and for the granting and renewal of certificates in respect of premises in New Towns in Scotland.

December 1952
COLONIAL LOANS ACT, 1952
(R.A. 16 December 1952)
Increases from £50m. to £100m. the Treasury guarantee on loans raised by Colonial Governments through the International Bank for Reconstruction and Development.

NEW VALUATION LISTS (POSTPONEMENT) ACT, 1952
(R.A. 16 December 1952)
Confers upon the Minister of Housing and Local Government power to postpone by Order the dates when the new valuation lists for rating under Part III of the Local Government Act, 1948, are to come into force.

March 1953
ROYAL TITLES ACT, 1953
(R.A. 26 March 1953)
Provided for an alteration of the Royal Style and Titles so as to reflect more clearly the existing constitutional relations of the Members of the Commonwealth to one another and their recognition of the Crown as the symbol of their free association and of the Sovereign as the Head of the Commonwealth.

May 1953
PREVENTION OF CRIME ACT, 1953
(R.A. 6 May 1953)
Prohibits the carrying of an offensive weapon (i.e., any article made or adapted for use for causing injury to the person, or intended for such use by the person having it with him) in public places without lawful authority or reasonable excuse.

TRANSPORT ACT, 1953
(R.A. 6 May 1953)
Amends the Transport Act, 1947, by taking away from the British Transport Commission its obligation to integrate the nation's transport services; provides for the decentralisation of British Railways and the abolition of the Railway Executive; gives greater freedom to the railways to vary charges; provides for the return of British Road Services (run by the Road Haulage Executive under the 1947 Act) to private enterprise, but allows the British Transport Commission to retain 5,000 vehicles.

IRON AND STEEL ACT, 1953
(R.A. 14 May 1953)
Winds up the State Iron and Steel Corporation and provides machinery for returning its subsidiary companies to private ownership. It also sets up a new Iron and Steel Board to supervise the iron and steel industry.

COASTAL FLOODING (EMERGENCY PROVISIONS) ACT, 1953
(R.A. 20 May 1953)
Provided for works of defence against sea water in localities affected by the floods of January–February 1953, and

for the rehabilitation of agricultural land damaged by salt water.

TOWN AND COUNTRY PLANNING ACT. 1953
(R.A. 20 May 1953)

Abolishes the Development Charge imposed under the Town and Country Planning Act. 1947. and removes the obligation for immediate payment of 'global compensation' under that Act.

WHITE FISH AND HERRING INDUSTRIES ACT. 1953
(R.A. 20 May 1953)

Makes provision for grants and loans for building and equipping vessels for fishing in inshore waters and for herring fishing vessels. and extends the white fish subsidy.

July 1953

EDUCATION (MISCELLANEOUS PROVISIONS) ACT. 1953
(R.A. 14 July 1953)

Provides better financial help to the voluntary schools in connection with building costs. within the framework of the Education Act. 1944; clarifies the duty of education authorities to make available comprehensive facilities for free dental treatment; and simplifies some aspects of educational administration.

LOCAL GOVERNMENT SUPERANNUATION ACT. 1953
(R.A. 14 July 1953)

Enables improved benefits to be provided for employees of local authorities in Great Britain who are subject to the Superannuation Acts of 1937. without imposing any appreciable extra burden on superannuation funds.

NATIONAL INSURANCE ACT. 1953
(R.A. 14 July 1953)

Amends the National Insurance Acts. 1946 to 1952. in relation to maternity benefits. It improves maternity benefits. provides additional help for home confinements and enables working mothers to stop work earlier in their pregnancy by making benefits available sooner.

RHODESIA AND NYASALAND FEDERATION ACT. 1953
(R.A. 14 July 1953)

Provides for the Federation of Southern Rhodesia. Northern Rhodesia and Nyasaland by Order in Council; and for purposes connected therewith.

FINANCE ACT. 1953
(R.A. 31 JULY 1953)

Gave effect to the Government's taxation proposals outlined in the 1953 Budget. which included a cut of 6d. in all rates of income tax (benefiting 16 million taxpayers); ended the excess profits levy as from 31 December 1953; restored the initial allowances for industrial plant and machinery; raised the income limit up to which old people can claim earned income allowance; made an all-round cut of 25 per cent in purchase tax (except for textiles reduced in 1952). and removed entertainment tax on cricket and amateur sport.

HISTORIC BUILDINGS AND ANCIENT MONUMENTS ACT. 1953
(R.A. 31 July 1953)

Provides for the appointment of Councils for England. Scotland and Wales to advise the Minister of Works on the purchase or maintenance of buildings of architectural or historic interest. whether inhabited or not; makes limited financial provision for this purpose; and strengthens the law for protecting ancient monuments.

NATIONAL INSURANCE (INDUSTRIAL INJURIES) ACT. 1953
(R.A. 31 July 1953)

Makes further provision to the system of insurance established by the National Insurance (Industrial Injuries) Act. 1946. lessens the degree of disablement that must be assessed before benefit is payable. and extends the class of persons to whom certain benefits may be paid under the 1946 Act.

NEW TOWNS ACT, 1953
(R.A. 31 July 1953)
The Act increased from £100m. to £150m., the aggregate amount of advances which may be made to the New Town Development Corporations.

VALUATION FOR RATING ACT, 1953
(R.A. 31 July 1953)
Amends the valuation provisions of the Local Government Act, 1948, and provides that the gross value of dwelling houses, private garages and private storage premises shall be the rental value which would have prevailed at 30 June 1939, had these premises and the circumstances of the locality been what they are at the time of valuation.

October 1953
MONOPOLIES AND RESTRICTIVE PRACTICES COMMISSION ACT 1953
(R.A. 29 October 1953)
Makes the posts of Chairman and Deputy Chairman of the Monopolies Commission pensionable; it speeds the existing machinery by giving the Government power to appoint up to twenty-five members of the Commission. Groups of members with a minimum of five can be formed to deal concurrently with various subjects referred to the Commission; two-thirds of the members of such Groups must agree a report before action under Section 10 of the 1948 Act can be put in hand.

December 1953
ELECTORAL REGISTERS ACT. 1953
(R.A. 18 December 1953)
Alters the qualifying dates and the dates of publication of the registers of parliamentary and local government electors in Great Britain and of the register of United Kingdom parliamentary electors in Northern Ireland. The changes will come into effect for the 1955 and subsequent registers.

March 1954
INDUSTRIAL DISEASES (BENEFIT) ACT. 1954
(R.A. 9 March 1954)
Provides for the payment of benefit at the cost of the Industrial Injuries Insurance Fund to certain persons partially disabled from pneumoconiosis or byssinosis who were not covered by the Workmen's Compensation Acts or the National Insurance (Industrial Injuries) Acts.

HILL FARMING ACT. 1954
(R.A. 26 March 1954)
Amends the Hill Farming Act, 1946, and thereby makes it possible for cottages let on a contract of service ('tied') to qualify for improvement grants under that Act.

April 1954
COTTON ACT. 1954
(R.A. 14 April 1954)
Cleared the way for the reopening of the Liverpool Cotton Exchange by taking away the monopoly powers conferred on the Raw Cotton Commission by the Cotton (Centralised Buying) Act. 1947: and empowering the Board of Trade to provide by order. subject to affirmative resolutions of both Houses of Parliament. for its dissolution if they consider it in the public interest to do so.

JUDGES' REMUNERATION ACT. 1954
(R.A. 14 April 1954)
Increases the salaries of certain high judicial offices in England. Scotland and Northern Ireland.

PENSIONS (INCREASE) ACT. 1954
(R.A. 14 April 1954)
Amends the Pensions (Increase) Acts. 1944 and 1947. so as to bring back

approximately to the 1919 level all pensions or retired pay which were stabilised in 1935.

May 1954
TELEGRAPH ACT. 1954
(R.A. 13 May 1954)
Increases the charges for inland telegrams. while enabling a special overnight service to be provided at the former rates.

June 1954
AGRICULTURE (MISCELLANEOUS PROVISIONS) ACT. 1954
(R.A. 4 June 1954)
Improves the constitution and powers of Agricultural Land Tribunals. clarifying the independence of the tribunals and amending the method of their appointment. The Act amongst other things provides for an appeal to the High Court on points of law; and enables local authorities to collect. process and sell waste food for use as animal feeding-stuffs.

July 1954
BAKING INDUSTRY (HOURS OF WORK) ACT. 1954
(R.A. 30 July 1954)
Restricts night work in the baking industry. and lays down conditions to be complied with in night-bakeries.

FINANCE ACT. 1954
(R.A. 30 July 1954)
Gave effect to the Government's taxation proposals outlined in the 1954 Budget – investment allowances for industry. reduction of entertainments duty. reduction of death duties on small estates and on family businesses. repayment of post-war credits to heirs. Amended the purchase tax valuation so that from 1 January. 1955. sales to ordinary retailers should be taxed on the actual price paid without 'uplift'. Also cleared up death duty and other anomalies and closes certain tax loopholes.

HOUSING REPAIRS AND RENTS ACT. 1954
(R.A. 30 July 1954)
Gives effect to the proposals outlined in the White Paper. 'Houses – the Next Step' (Cmd. 8996). It gives additional powers to local authorities in England and Wales for the clearance or temporary repair of slum houses; provides for Exchequer assistance for certain aspects of that work; amends the provisions of the Housing Act. 1949. making more flexible the grants for the improvement and conversion of houses; abolishes 'cottage certificates'; ends rent control for dwellings completed after the passing of the Act; and enables house owners who bring their rent-controlled property to good general repair and keep it in that condition to obtain a repairs increase of rent.

LANDLORD AND TENANT ACT. 1954
(R.A. 30 July 1954)
Extends the protection of the Rents Acts to residential leaseholders of ground leases of more than 21 years when their leases expire; extinguishes the tenant's obligation to carry out dilapidation repairs himself when he becomes a statutory tenant; gives business and professional tenants the right to apply to the Courts for a renewed tenancy at a fair market rent when their leases expire and enlarges the protection that County Courts can give against excessive claims for dilapidations by extending the Leasehold Property (Repairs) Act. 1938. so as to apply to all classes of premises.

TELEVISION ACT. 1954
(R.A. 30 July 1954)
Sets up. for an initial period of ten years. an Independent Television Authority; makes provision for television broadcasting services. additional to those of the B.B.C.. to be provided by free enterprise companies in contract

with the I.T.A., and so far as possible in competition with one another; gives the I.T.A. reserve powers to ensure proper standards; and lays down rules regarding the broadcasting of advertisements.

November 1954
CIVIL DEFENCE (ARMED FORCES) ACT, 1954
(R.A. 25 November 1954)
Empowers the Home Office and the Ministry of Health to train certain National Service reservists with a view to using them in Civil Defence mobile columns in time of war.

ELECTRICITY REORGANISATION (SCOTLAND) ACT, 1954
(R.A. 25 November 1954)
Transfers the functions of the Minister of Fuel and Power in Scotland in relation to electricity to the Secretary of State for Scotland; establishes the South of Scotland Electricity Board responsible for generating and supplying electricity in Scotland outside the area of the North of Scotland Hydro-Electric Board; transfers the functions of the British Electricity Authority (to be re-named Central Electricity Authority) in the South of Scotland and of the Scottish Area Boards to that Board and amends the Hydro-Electric Development (Scotland) Act, 1943.

FOOD AND DRUGS AMENDMENT ACT, 1954
(R.A. 25 November 1954)
Amends the Food and Drugs Act, 1938, and the Food and Drugs (Milk Dairies and Artificial Cream) Act, 1950. Its main objects are to revise the provisions for protecting the public against the sale of food containing injurious ingredients; and against the misdescription of food and drugs on labels and advertisements; and to provide fuller powers to secure that food is not contaminated in the course of preparation, distribution and sale.

MINES AND QUARRIES ACT, 1954
(R.A. 25 November 1954)
Consolidates and revises the law relating to safety and health in mines and quarries; re-defines the duties and responsibilities of owners (principally the National Coal Board) and managers; maintains in full the power and position of H.M. Inspectors of Mines; makes new requirements concerning ventilation, dust control, transport rules and the prevention of falls of ground in the roadways and workings of a mine; and raises the minimum age for boys employed underground from 15 to 16 (the conditions now applying to boys under 16 working on the surface are extended to all boys under 18).

TOWN AND COUNTRY PLANNING ACT, 1954
(R.A. 25 November 1954)
Provides a new basis for compensating those who are refused permission to develop land or whose land is compulsorily acquired. Provides for payment out of the £300m. fund to landowners only when their land is compulsorily acquired or with certain exceptions if its value is depressed by refusal of planning permission; provides for the compensation of those who suffered hardship in paying the Development Charge between 1948 and 1952, and also for those who sold land cheaply in the same period because they relied on Part VI of the 1947 Act to recoup their loss; and enables the Minister to permit additional payment where public authorities buy land which had development value in 1948, but in respect of which no claim was made on the £300m. fund.

TOWN AND COUNTRY PLANNING (SCOTLAND) ACT, 1954
(R.A. 25 November 1954)
Makes similar provision for Scotland as the Town and Country Planning Act, 1954 (see above).

472

March 1955
COLONIAL DEVELOPMENT AND
WELFARE ACT. 1955
(R.A. 29 March 1955)
Provides further assistance for Colonial
Territories at the expiration of the 10
year period. Provides £80m. of new
money for the period 1955–60. Added to
the £45m. remaining unspent under the
Act of 1945. it puts at the disposal of
Colonial Governments a total of £120m.
for the five year period 1955–60. an
increase of £10m. per annum over the
current rate of expenditure from this
source.

FISHERIES ACT. 1955
(R.A. 29 March 1955)
Designed to raise the statutory limit on
grants to the Herring Industry Board
from £3m. to £3½m.. with a further
£250.000 available by affirmative
resolution.

NEW TOWNS ACT. 1955
(R.A. 29 March 1955)
Increases to £250m. the aggregate
amount of advances which may be made
to the New Town Development
Corporations.

NORTHERN IRELAND ACT. 1955
(R.A. 29 March 1955)
Makes certain alterations found to be
necessary in the method of defraying the
expenses of the office of the Governor of
Northern Ireland. It also transfers to the
Court of Appeal in Northern Ireland the
power of the High Court in Northern
Ireland to hear certain appeals from
courts of summary jurisdiction and
quarter session. Also enlarges the
legislative power of the Parliament of
Northern Ireland in certain respects.

TRANSPORT (BORROWING
POWERS) ACT. 1955
(R.A. 29 March 1955)
Increased the limit imposed by the
Transport Act, 1953 of £275m. out-
standing in respect of borrowings of the
British Transport Commission to £600m.

May 1955
CROFTERS (SCOTLAND) ACT. 1955
(R.A. 6 May 1955)
Set up the Crofters Commission to re-
organise, develop and regulate crofting,
and to look after crofting interests.

FINANCE ACT. 1955
(R.A. 6 May 1955)
Gave effect to the Government's tax-
ation proposals outlined in the 1955 Budget.

NATIONAL INSURANCE ACT. 1955
(R.A. 6 May 1955)
Increases the income limit to which
persons may be excepted from liability to
pay contributions from £104 p.a. to £156
p.a.. etc.

OIL IN NAVIGABLE WATERS ACT.
1955
(R.A. 6 May 1955)
Repealed and substantially re-enacted
the Act of 1922. and was a further
attempt to deal with the oil pollution
problem. The Act arose out of an
International Convention signed in
London in 1954. It prohibited the
discharge of oil in certain sea areas. gave
power to make regulations requiring
British ships to be fitted with equipment
designed to prevent the discharge of oil
in to the sea. and empowered harbour
authorities to provide facilities for
enabling ships to discharge oil residue.

REQUISITIONED HOUSES AND
HOUSING (AMENDMENT) ACT.
1955
(R.A. 6 May 1955)
Took from the Minister of Housing and
Local Government his power under
Defence Regulations to take possession
of. or to retain land for. housing
purposes. The right to possession of
requisitioned houses was vested by the
Act in the appropriate local authority.
who were empowered to retain
possession of a requisitioned house for
housing purposes till 31 March 1960.

Source: *Three Years Work, C.R.D.*

B List of Selected Command Papers (Cited in or used as background to the text).

Session 1951–2

8419
Anglo-Egyptian Conversations on the Defence of the Suez Canal and on the Sudan, December 1950–November 1951.

8452
Purchase Tax/Utility Committee. (W. S. Douglas) Report. December 1951.

8464
United States of America. Agreements on Mutual Assistance and Supply of Steel, Aluminium and Tin. January 1952.

8468
Mr. Churchill's Speech to U.S. Congress. 17 January 1952.

8470
Post Office. Report of the Recognition Committee (Chairman: Lord Terrington).

8474
Air Estimates, 1952–3.

8475
Statement on Defence, 1952.

8476
Navy Estimates, 1952–3.

8477
Army Estimates, 1952–3.

8509
Economic Survey for 1952.

8510
Cotton Import Committee (Chairman: R. V. N. Hopkins) Report. March 1952.

8512
European Defence Community. Relationship between the U.K. and the E.D.C.

8513
Increase in Passenger Fares. Report

on the Transport Commission's Charges Scheme. (Chairman: E. Cadbury)

8538
Transport Policy.

8550
Broadcasting. Memorandum on the Report of the Broadcasting Committee, 1949.

8554
Education in 1951. The Ministry's Report.

8607
Report of a Court of Inquiry into the D. C. Thompson dispute (Chairman: Sir John Forster).

8609
Scottish Financial and Trade Statistics. Report of the Committee (Chairman: Lord Catto).

8629
Staffs Employed in Government Departments, on 1 July 1952.

8635
National Insurance. Ministry's Reports for 1951.

8640
Ministry of Labour and National Service. Annual Report for 1951.

8647
Fuel and Power Resources. Report of the Committee (Chairman: Lord Ridley).

8655
Ministry of Health Report, Part I. The N.H.S. etc.

8678
Wales and Monmouthshire. Report of Government Action, 1951–2.

Session 1952–3
8717
Commonwealth Economic Conference. Final Communiqué, 11 December 1952.

8721
Supply of Teachers in Scotland. Departmental Committee (Chairman: T. Grainger Stewart).

8745
Decontrol of Cereals and Feeding-stuffs.

8753
Southern Rhodesia, Northern Rhodesia and Nyasaland. Report of the London Conference. January 1953.

8768
Statement on Defence, 1953.

8769
Navy Estimates, 1953–4.

8770
Army Estimates, 1953–4.

8771
Air Estimates, 1953–4.

8787
Ministry of Health. Annual Report of Chief Medical Officer for 1951.

8798
Annual Review and Fixing of Farm Prices, 1953.

8800
Economic Survey for 1953.

8835
Education in 1952. Ministry's Report.

8837
West India Federation. Report of the Conference in London, April 1953 (Chairman: O. Lyttelton).

8842
Ministry of Pensions. Proposed Transfer of Functions.

8844
Wales and Monmouthshire. 2nd Memorandum by the Council. February 1953.

8856
Colonial Territories, 1952–3.

8861
Cotton Import (Review). Report of the Committee (Chairman: R. V. N. Hopkins). May 1953.

8882
National Insurance. Annual Report for 1952. (The 4th.)

8883
Amalgamation of Ministry of Transport and Civil Aviation.

8893
Annual Report of the Ministry of Labour and National Service for 1952.

8933
Report of Ministry of Health for 1952. Part I. N.H.S. etc.

8959
Wales and Monmouthshire. Report of Government Action, 1952–3.

8963
Employment of Older Men and Women. First Report of the Advisory Committee (Chairman: H. Watkinson). September 1953.

8980
British Guiana. Suspension of the Constitution.

Session 1953–4
8986
Future Organisation of the U.K. Atomic Energy Project.

8989
Decontrol of Food and Marketing of Agricultural Produce.

8996
Houses. The Next Step.

9004
International Agreement for the Regulation of the Production and Marketing of Sugar. October 1953. London.

9005
Broadcasting. Memorandum on
Television Policy.

9009
Health. Part II. Annual Report of the
Chief Medical Officer for 1952.

9014
Rural Wales.

9015
Housing Summary. 31 October 1953.

9029
Housing Summary. 30 November 1953.

9072
Army Estimates. 1954–5.

9075
Statement on Defence. 1954.

9076
Air Estimates. 1954–5.

9079
Navy Estimates. 1954–5.

9080
Berlin Conference. January–February
1954. Documents relating to the
meeting.

9081
Kenya. Report to Colonial Secretary by
the Parliamentary Delegation. January
1954.

9104
Agriculture. Annual Review and
Determination of Guarantees. 1954.

9108
Economic Survey. 1954.

9155
Education in 1953. Ministry's Report.

9159
Pensions and National Insurance.
Ministry's Report for 1953.

9165
Coastal Flooding. Report of the
Departmental Committee (Chairman:
Lord Waverley). April 1954.

9169
Colonial Territories. 1953–4.

9176
Crichel Down. Public Enquiry. 13 May
1954.

9191
Railways Reorganisation Scheme.

9197
International Conference on Pollution
of the Sea by Oil. London. May 1954.

9199
Criminal Statistics. England and Wales.
1953

9204
Disarmament. Report of Proceedings of
Sub-Committee of U.N. Disarmament
Commission held in London. May–June
1954.

9207
Labour and National Service. Ministry's
Annual Report for 1953.

9212
Scottish Affairs. 1952–4. Report of
Royal Commission (Chairman: Lord
Balfour). July 1954.

9215
Gatwick Airport. Report of Enquiry
into Proposed Development. June
1954.

9222
International Tin Agreement.

9230
Suez Canal. Heads of Agreement.
Signed in Cairo 27 July 1954.

9244
Scottish Valuation and Rating
Committee Report (Chairman: Lord
Sorn) August 1954.

9281
Collective Security. Correspondence
between Governments of U.K. and
Soviet Union. 24 July–10 September
1954.

9282
Collective Defence. South-East Asia
Collective Defence Treaty. Manila,
September 1954.

9287
Wales and Monmouthshire. Report of
Government Action. 1953–4.

9288
Trieste. Memorandum on
Understanding. 5 October 1954.

9289
Nine Power Conference. London. 28
September–3 October 1954.

9296
Gatwick Airport.

9298
Suez Canal Base. Agreement between
Government of U.K. and Egypt.

9304
Paris Conference. 20 October–23
October 1954.

9307
Ministry of Health. Chief Medical
Officer's Report for 1953.

9319
Parliamentary Constituencies.
Statement showing proposed changes.

9322
Air Pollution. Report November 1954
(Chairman: Sir Hugh Beaver).

Session 1954–5
9327
Collective Security. Further
Correspondence Government of U.K.
and Soviet Union. 23 October–29
November 1954.

9332
National Insurance Bill. 1954. Report by
the Government Actuary.

9333
Old Age. Report of the Committee.
November 1954 (Chairman: Sir Thomas
Phillips).

9372
Final Report of a Court of Enquiry into
Railway Dispute. January 1955
(Chairman: Sir John Cameron).

9388
Supply of Military Aircraft.

9389
Nuclear Power. A programme.

9391
Statement on Defence. 1955.

9395
Army Estimates. 1955–6.

9396
Navy Estimates. 1955–6.

9397
Air Estimates. 1955–6.

9406
Annual Price Review and
Determination of Guarantees. 1955.

9412
Economic Survey for 1955.

9413
Review of the General Agreement on
Tariffs and Trade.

9418
Exchange of letters in 1954. Churchill
and Molotov. on a possible Two-Power
Meeting.

9419
Supply of Teachers of Mathematics and
Science in Scotland. March 1955
(Chairman: Sir Edward Appleton).

9439
Report of a Court of Enquiry into the
newspaper dispute. April 1955
(Chairman: Sir John Forster).

9462
Colonial Development and Welfare Act.
1955.

Session 1955–6
9474
Taxation on Profits and Income. Royal

Commission Final Report. May 1955 (Chairman: Lord Radcliffe).

9475
East African Royal Commission Report. May 1955 (Chairman: Sir Hugh Dow).

9489
Colonial Territories. 1954–5.

9495
Pensions and National Insurance. Ministry's Report for 1954.

9504
Monopolies and Restrictive Practices Commission. Report on collective discrimination. May 1955 (Chairman: Sir David Cairns).

9521
Education in 1954. Ministry's Report.

9522
Ministry of Labour and National Service. Annual Report for 1954.

9559
Ministry of Housing and Local Government. Report for the period 1950/1–1954.

9592
Wales and Monmouthshire. Report on Government Action. 1954–5.

9627
Ministry of Health. Chief Medical Officer's Report. 1954.

9663
National Health Service. Report of the Committee of Enquiry. November 1955 (Chairman: C. Guillebaud).

9741
Forth and Forth Road Bridge. Report.

9785
Education in 1955. Ministry's Report.

9791
Labour and National Service. Annual Report of the Ministry for 1955.

9826
Ministry of Pensions and National Insurance. Report for 1955.

9876
Housing and Local Government. Report of the Ministry for 1955.

Source: *Government Publications, 1951–5.* (annual editions).

C List of Selected Major Reports, 1951–5

C1 Royal Commissions

Title	Chairman	Date Appointed	Date of Report	Command Number
Capital Punishment	Sir Ernest Gowers	May 1949	September 1953	8932
Taxation on Profits and Income	Lord Cohen Lord Radcliffe	January 1951	May 1955	9474
Scottish Affairs	Earl of Balfour	July 1952	July 1954	9212
East Africa	Sir Hugh Dow	January 1953	May 1955	9475
The Civil Service	Sir Raymond Priestley	November 1953	November 1955	9613
Law Relating to Mental Illness and Mental Deficiency	Lord Percy of Newcastle	February 1954	May 1957	169

C2   Departmental Committees

Title	Chairman	Date Appointed	Date of Report	Command Number
Broadcasting	Lord Beveridge	January 1949	December 1950	8116
Fuel and Power Resources	Lord Ridley	July 1951	July 1952	8647
National Health Service	Claude Guillebaud	May 1953	November 1955	9663
Air Pollution	Sir Hugh Beaver	July 1953	November 1954	9322
Crichel Down	Andrew Clark	November 1953	May 1954	9176
Electricity Supply Industry	Sir Edward Herbert	July 1954	December 1955	9672
Homosexual Law Reform	Sir John Wolfenden	August 1954	August 1957	247

Source: *Butler and Sloman*

Appendix V Officers of the Conservative Party's Parliamentary Committees

These tables are drawn from the columns of various editions of *The Times*. The lists are incomplete. as it was not possible to trace a comprehensive source of the membership and names of the Committees. Nevertheless, the tables below are of interest primarily as a key to promotion paths. In Opposition, the senior officers were chosen by the Party Leader (except the 1922). After the 1951 Election. all officers were elected annually. The membership remained fairly static until 1955. but changes are not listed, partly because records of membership after 1951 are even more difficult to trace than for those before 1951. An arrow indicates that the officer continued. a gap that records were not traceable.

	April 1950	*Nov. 1950/ Feb. 1951*	*Nov./Dec. 1951*
AGRICULTURE AND FOOD			
(Committees amalgamated Nov. 1951)			
Chairmen	Harry Crookshank (Food) $\longrightarrow$		
	Sir Thomas Dugdale (Agriculture) $\longrightarrow$		Anthony Hurd
Vice Chairmen	Robert Turton (Food) $\longrightarrow$		James Duncan
	William McNair Snadden (Agriculture) $\longrightarrow$		Colin Thornton-Kemsley
Secretaries	Colin Thornton-Kemsley (Food) $\longrightarrow$		John Baker White
	John Baker White (Agriculture) $\longrightarrow$		Sir Austin Hudson
	Anthony Hurd (Agriculture) $\longrightarrow$		Denys Bullard
CIVIL AVIATION			
Chairman	Alan Lennox-Boyd	George Ward	$\longrightarrow$
Vice Chairman	Arthur Harvey $\longrightarrow$		$\longrightarrow$
Secretaries	George Ward	John Grimston	$\longrightarrow$
			Sir Robert Perkins
COMMONWEALTH AFFAIRS			
('Imperial' up until 1951 Election)			
Chairman	Oliver Stanley	Alan Lennox-Boyd	Douglas Dodds-Parker
Vice Chairman	Alan Lennox-Boyd	David Gammans	
	David Gammans		Cuthbert Alport
Secretaries	Douglas Dodds-Parker $\longrightarrow$		Ronald Russell
	Cuthbert Alport $\longrightarrow$		Bernard Braine

480

	April 1950	*Nov. 1950/Feb. 1951*	*Nov./Dec. 1951*
DEFENCE			
Chairman	Winston Churchill $\longrightarrow$		Charles Waterhouse
Deputy Chairman	Anthony Eden $\longrightarrow$		Vacant
Vice Chairman and Chairman of Army Sub-Committee	Antony Head $\longrightarrow$		Otho Prior-Palmer
Vice Chairman and Chairman of Air Sub-Committee	Arthur Harvey $\longrightarrow$		$\longrightarrow$
Vice Chairman and Chairman of Navy Sub-Committee	J. P. L. Thomas $\longrightarrow$		Robert Ryder
Secretary	Henry Legge-Bourke		
EDUCATION			
Chairman		Florence Horsbrugh	Christopher Hollis
Vice Chairman		John Maitland	Angus Maude
Secretaries		Christopher Hollis Angus Maude	Gilbert Longden
FINANCE (merged with Trade and Industry after 1951 Election)			
Chairman		Oliver Lyttelton	Ralph Assheton
Vice Chairmen			Sir Walter Fletcher Reginald Maudling
Secretaries			Geoffrey Stevens Frederick Erroll
FOREIGN AFFAIRS			
Chairman	Anthony Eden $\longrightarrow$		Charles Mott-Radclyffe
Deputy Chairman	R. A. Butler $\longrightarrow$		Vacant
Vice Chairman	Kenneth Pickthorn $\longrightarrow$		Lord John Hope
Secretaries	Charles Mott-Radclyffe $\longrightarrow$ Tufton Beamish $\longrightarrow$		Lord Cranborne $\longrightarrow$

	April 1950	*Nov. 1950/Feb. 1951*	*Nov./Dec. 1951*
FUEL AND POWER			
Chairman			Sir Victor Raikes (in Nov. 1950, he became Chairman of a new Gas Committee)
Vice Chairman			Ralph Clarke
Secretaries			Gerald Nabarro Oliver Crossthwaite-Eyre

HEALTH AND SOCIAL SERVICES
('National Insurance and Pensions' up until 1951 Election)

Chairman		W. S. Morrison	Sir Hugh Lucas-Tooth (until February 1952) Iain Macleod (February–May) John Vaughan-Morgan (May 1952 onwards)
Deputy Chairman		Osbert Peake	Vacant
Vice Chairman			Iain Macleod (until February 1952) John Vaughan-Morgan (February to May) Richard Fort (May 1952 onwards)
Secretaries		Iain Macleod	Mrs. Eveline Hill

HOME AFFAIRS

Chairmen	Osbert Peake		Sir Robert Grimston
Vice Chairmen	Sir Robert Grimston ⟶ Sir Reginald Manningham-Buller ⟶ Sir Edward Keeling ⟶		Otho Prior-Palmer ⟶
Secretaries	Sir Harold Sutcliffe ⟶ John Hay ⟶		

	April 1950	*Nov. 1950/Feb. 1951*	*Nov./Dec. 1951*

HOUSING, LOCAL GOVERNMENT AND WORKS
(Until 1951 Election 'Housing' and also
'Health and Local Government'

Chairman		Harold Macmillan (Housing)	
		Walter Elliot (Health and Local Government)	Henry Brooke
Vice Chairmen		T. D. Galbraith	Geoffrey Hutchinson
			Enoch Powell
Secretaries		Ernest Marples (Housing)	Albert Cooper
			Henry Price

LABOUR

Chairman	Sir David Maxwell Fyfe ⟶		Malcolm McCorquodale
Deputy Chairman	Malcolm McCorquodale ⟶		Vacant
Vice Chairman	John Boyd-Carpenter ⟶		Sir Ian Orr-Ewing
Secretaries	John Langford-Holt ⟶		
	Edwin Leather ⟶		Edwin Leather

LEGAL

Chairman	Sir Reginald Manningham-Buller ⟶	
Vice Chairman	Selwyn Lloyd ⟶	
Secretary	Sir Harold Sutcliffe ⟶	

RADIO AND TELEVISION
(formed July 1953)

Chairman		Walter Elliot
Vice Chairman		Sir Robert Grimston
Secretary		Lord John Hope

SCOTTISH AND UNIONIST MEMBERS' COMMITTEE

Chairman	James Stuart ⟶		Walter Elliot
Vice Chairman	T. D. Galbraith ⟶		Sir Ian Clark Hutchison
Treasurer	Alan Gomme-Duncan ⟶		⟶
Secretaries	Sir Ian Clark Hutchison ⟶		Lord Malcolm Douglas-Hamilton

	April 1950	*Nov. 1950/Feb. 1951*	*Nov./Dec. 1951*

TRADE AND INDUSTRY

Chairman	Oliver Lyttelton	Sir Robert Hudson
Deputy Chairman	Harold Macmillan ⟶	
Vice Chairman	Sir Arnold Gridley ⟶	
	Sir Walter Fletcher ⟶	
Secretaries	Frederick Erroll ⟶	
	William Shepherd ⟶	

TRANSPORT

Chairman	Peter Thorneycroft ⟶	Viscount Hinchingbrooke
Vice Chairman	Viscount Hinchingbrooke ⟶	David Renton
Secretaries	Geoffrey Wilson ⟶	⟶
		Reader Harris

WORKS

Chairman	Duncan Sandys
Vice Chairman	Sir Peter Bennett
Secretary	William Robson-Brown

CONSERVATIVE AND UNIONIST MEMBERS COMMITTEE (the 1922)

Chairman	Sir Arnold Gridley ⟶		Derek Walker-Smith
Vice Chairmen	Sir Peter Bennett ⟶		John Morrison
	Robert Turton ⟶		Alan Gomme-Duncan
Secretaries	Gerald Wills ⟶		
	Allan Noble	John Vaughan-Morgan	Kenneth Thompson
Treasurer	T. G. D. Galbraith ⟶		Charles Mott-Radclyffe

Source: *The Times*

Appendix VI Public Corporations, Authorities, Boards and Commissions

1. ATOMIC ENERGY AUTHORITY

Chairman	Sir Edwin Plowden	1954–60

2. BANK OF ENGLAND

Governor	C. F. Cobbold	1949–61
Deputy Governor	Sir Dallas Bernard	1949–54
	Humphrey Mynors	1954–64

3. BRITISH BROADCASTING CORPORATION

Chairman, Board of Governors	Lord Simon of Wythenshawe	1947–52
	Sir Alexander Cadogan	1952–7
Director-General	Sir William Haley	1944–52
	Sir Ian Jacob	1952–9

4. BRITISH EUROPEAN AIRWAYS

Chairman	Lord Douglas of Kirtleside	1949–64
Deputy Chairman	Sir John Keeling	1947–65

5. BRITISH OVERSEAS AIRWAYS CORPORATION

Chairman	Sir Miles Thomas	1949–56
Deputy Chairman	Whitney Straight	1949–55

6. BRITISH TRANSPORT COMMISSION

Chairman	Lord Hurcomb	1947–53
	Sir Brian Robertson	1953–61
Deputy Chairman	Sir John Benstead	1949–61

7. CABLE AND WIRELESS LTD.

Chairman	Sir Leslie Nicholls	1951–6

8. CENTRAL ELECTRICITY AUTHORITY

Chairman	Lord Citrine	1947–57
Deputy Chairman	Sir Henry Self	1947–57
	Sir John Hacking	1948–53
	Josiah Eccles	1954–7

9. CIVIL SERVICE COMMISSION

First Commissioner	Sir Paul Sinker	1951–4
	Sir Laurence Helsby	1954–9

10. COLONIAL DEVELOPMENT CORPORATION

Chairman	Lord Reith	1950–9

11. CUSTOMS AND EXCISE

Chairman	Sir William Croft	1947–55
	Sir James Crombie	1955–62
Deputy Chairman	Sir William Rhydderch	1949–52
	Douglas Owen	1952–65

12. EXCHEQUER AND AUDIT DEPARTMENT

Comptroller and Auditor General	Sir Frank Tribe	1946–58

13. GAS COUNCIL

Chairman	Sir Edgar Sylvester	1948–51
	Sir Harold Smith	1952–60
Deputy Chairman	Sir Harold Smith	1948–51
	Henry Jones	1952–60

14. INFORMATION, CENTRAL OFFICE OF

Director-General	Sir Robert Fraser	1946–54
	Fife Clark	1954–71

15. INLAND REVENUE, BOARD OF

Chairman	Sir Eric Bamford	1948–55
	Sir Henry Hancock	1955–8
Deputy Chairman	Sir Edward Ritson	1949–57
	Sir Edgar Verity	1951–4
	John Evans	1954–65

16. MONOPOLIES AND RESTRICTIVE PRACTICES COMMISSION

Chairman	Sir Archibald Carter	1949–53
	Sir David Cairns	1954–6

17. NATIONAL ASSISTANCE BOARD

Chairman	George Buchanan	1948–53
	Sir Geoffrey Hutchinson	1954–64
Deputy Chairman	Mrs. Jennie Adamson	1946–53
	William Asbury	1954–61

18. NATIONAL COAL BOARD

Chairman	Sir Hubert Houldsworth	1951–6
Deputy Chairman	Sir Eric Coates	1951–5
	Sir Walter Drummond	1951–5

19. NATIONAL INSURANCE COMMISSIONER, OFFICE OF
Commissioner   Sir David Davies   1947–61

20. NORTH OF SCOTLAND HYDRO-ELECTRICITY BOARD
Chairman   Tom Johnston   1946–59

Deputy Chairman   Sir Hugh Mackenzie   1951–9

21. PRISON COMMISSION
Chairman   Sir Lionel Fox   1942–60

22. SOUTH OF SCOTLAND ELECTRICITY BOARD
Chairman   John Pickles   1954–62

Deputy Chairman   Sir Norman Duke   1954–6

23. UNIVERSITY GRANTS COMMITTEE
Chairman   Sir Arthur Trueman   1949–53
                            Sir Keith Murray   1953–63

Source: Dod, Butler and Sloman

Appendix VII   Party Officers

A.   CONSERVATIVE PARTY

1. Central Office

Chairman of the Party Organisation	Viscount Woolton	1946–55
General Director	Sir Stephen Piersené	1945–57
Treasurers	Lord De L'Isle	1948–52
	Oliver Poole	1952–5
	Christopher Holland-Martin	1947–60

2. Research Department

Directors	Michael Fraser	1951–64
	Percy Cohen	1948–59
Chairman	Rab Butler M.P.	1945–64

3. House of Lords

Leader	Lord Salisbury	1942–57
Chief Whip	Lord Fortescue	1945–58

4. House of Commons

Chairman. 1922 Committee	Derek Walker-Smith M.P.	1951–5

B.   LABOUR PARTY

Leader	Clement Attlee M.P.	1935–55
Deputy Leader	Herbert Morrison M.P.	1945–55
Chief Whip	William Whiteley M.P.	1942–55
	Herbert Bowden M.P.	1955–64
Leader in Lords	Lord Addison	1940–52
	Lord Jowitt	1952–5
Chief Whip	Lord Shepherd	1949–54
	Lord Lucan	1954–64

National Executive Committee

Chairman	Alice Bacon M.P.	1950–1
	Mr. H. Earnshaw	1951–2
	Arthur Greenwood M.P.	1952–3
	Wilfrid Burke M.P.	1953–4
	Edith Summerskill M.P.	1954–5

Secretary	Morgan Phillips	1944–62
National Agent	Leonard Williams	1951–62
Treasurer	Arthur Greenwood M.P.	1943–54
	Hugh Gaitskell M.P.	1954–6

C.   LIBERAL PARTY

Leader	Clement Davies M.P.	1945–56
Chief Whip	Jo Grimond M.P.	1950–6
Leader in Lords	Lord Samuel	1944–55
Chief Whip in Lords	Lord Rea	1950–5

Source: Butler and Sloman: *Labour and Conservative Annual Party Conference Reports*

Appendix VIII   Trade Union Leaders

General Secretary T.U.C.   Sir Vincent Tewson   1949–60

1. AMALGAMATED UNION OF ENGINEERING WORKERS (A.U.E.W)
President   Jack Tanner   1939–54
                           R. Openshaw   1954–6

2. CONFEDERATION OF HEALTH SERVICE EMPLOYEES (C.O.H.S.E.)
Secretary   C. Comer   1948–53
                           J. Waite   1953–9

3. ELECTRICAL TRADES UNION (E.T.U.)
President   Frank Foulkes   1945–63

4. NATIONAL AND LOCAL GOVERNMENT OFFICERS' ASSOCIATION (N.A.L.G.O.)
Secretary   John Warren   1946–57

5. NATIONAL FARMERS' UNION (N.F.U.)
President   Sir James Turner   1945–60

6. NATIONAL UNION OF GENERAL AND MUNICIPAL WORKERS (G.M.W.)
Secretary   Tom Williamson   1946–62

7. NATIONAL UNION OF MINEWORKERS (N.U.M.)
President   Sir William Lawther   1939–54
Secretary   Arthur Horner   1946–59

8. NATIONAL UNION OF PUBLIC EMPLOYEES (N.U.P.E.)
Secretary   Bryn Roberts   1934–62

9. NATIONAL UNION OF RAILWAYMEN (N.U.R.)
Secretary   James Figgins   1948–53
                           James Campbell   1953–7

10. NATIONAL UNION OF TEACHERS (N.U.T.)
Secretary   Sir Ronald Gould   1947–70

11. SOCIETY OF GRAPHICAL AND ALLIED TRADES (S.O.G.A.T.)
Secretary   W. Morrison   1947–59

12. TRANSPORT AND GENERAL WORKERS' UNION (T.G.W.U.)
Secretary   Arthur Deakin   1940–55

13. UNION OF POST OFFICE WORKERS (U.P.W.)
Secretary   Charles Geddes   1941–57

14. UNION OF SHOP, DISTRIBUTIVE AND ALLIED WORKERS
(U.S.D.A.W.)
Secretary   Alan Birch   1949–62

Source: Butler and Sloman: *Dictionary of Labour Biography*

Appendix IX Commonwealth and Colonial Officers

A. THE COMMONWEALTH

1. CANADA

Governor-General	Lord Alexander of Tunis	1946–52
	Vincent Massey	1952–9
U.K. High Commissioner	Sir Alexander Clutterbuck	1946–52
	Sir Archibald Nye	1952–6
Prime Minister	Louis St. Laurent	1948–57
Secretary of State for External Affairs	Lester Pearson	1948–57

2. AUSTRALIA

Governor-General	Sir William McKell	1947–53
	Lord Slim	1953–60
U.K. High Commissioner	Sir Edward Williams	1946–52
	Sir Stephen Holmes	1952–6
Prime Minister	Robert Menzies	1949–66
Minister for External Affairs	Richard Casey	1951–60

3. NEW ZEALAND

Governor-General	Lord Freyberg	1945–52
	Lord Norrie	1952–7
U.K. High Commissioner	Sir Roy Price	1949–53
	Sir Geoffry Scoones	1953–7
Prime Minister	Sidney Holland	1949–57
External Affairs, etc.	Clifton Webb	1951–4
	Thomas Macdonald	1954–7

4. UNION OF SOUTH AFRICA

Governor-General	Dr. Ernest Jansen	1951–9
U.K. High Commissioner	Sir John Le Rougetel	1951–5
Prime Minister	Daniel Malan	1948–54
	Johannes Strijdom	1954–8
External Affairs	Daniel Malan	1948–54
	Eric Louw	1954–63

492

5. INDIA

President	Dr. Rajendra Prasad	1950–62
U.K. High Commissioner	Sir Archibald Nye	1948–52
	Sir Alexander Clutterbuck	1952–5
Prime Minister (also External Affairs)	Jawaharlal Nehru	1947–64

6. PAKISTAN

Governor-General	Ghulam Mohammad	1951–5
U.K. High Commissioner	Sir Gilbert Laithwaite	1951–4
	Sir Alexander Symon	1954–61
Prime Minister	Sir Al-Haj Khwaja Nazimuddin	1951–3
	Mohammad Ali	1953–5
External Affairs	Sir M. Z. Khan	1947–54
	Mohammad Ali	1954–5

7. CEYLON

Governor-General and Commander-in-Chief	Lord Soulbury	1949–54
	Sir Oliver Goonetilleke	1954–62
U.K. High Commissioner	Sir Cecil Syers	1951–7
Prime Minister (also External Affairs)	Stephen Senanayake	1947–52
	Dudley Senanayake	1952–3
	Sir John Kotelawala	1953–6

8. FEDERATION OF RHODESIA AND NYASALAND

Governor-General	Lord Llewellin	1953–7
U.K. High Commissioner	Ian Maclennan	1953–5
Prime Minister (also External Affairs)	Sir Godfrey Huggins	1953–6

B. COLONIES

Governors etc. of Selected Colonies

Barbados	Sir Alfred Savage	1949–53
	Sir Robert Arundell	1953–9
British Guiana	Sir Charles Woolley	1947–53
	Sir Alfred Savage	1953–5
Cyprus	Sir Andrew Wright	1949–54
	Sir Robert Armitage	1954–5
Hong Kong	Sir Alexander Grantham	1947–57
Jamaica	Sir Hugh Foot	1951–7
Kenya	Sir Philip Mitchell	1944–52
	Sir Evelyn Baring	1952–9
Malaya Federation	Sir Gerald Templer	1952–4
	Sir Donald MacGillivray	1954–8

Malta	Sir Gerald Creasy	1949–54
	Sir Robert Laycock	1954–9
Nigeria	Sir John Macpherson	1948–55
Northern Rhodesia	Sir Gilbert Rennie	1948–54
	Sir Arthur Benson	1954–9
Nyasaland	Sir Geoffrey Colby	1948–56
Singapore	Sir Franklin Gimson	1946–52
	Sir John Nicoll	1952–5
Southern Rhodesia	Sir John Kennedy	1946–54
	Sir Peveril William-Powlett	1954–9
Tanganyika	Sir Edward Twining	1949–58
Uganda	Sir John Hall	1944–51
	Sir Andrew Cohen	1952–7
Zanzibar	Sir Vincent Glenday	1946–51
	Sir John Rankine	1952–4
	Henry Potter	1954–60

Source: Dod, Cook and Paxton:
Commonwealth Political Facts

Appendix X   Diplomatic Service: Ambassadors from London to Major Powers and International Organisations

Austria	Sir Harold Caccia	1951–4
	Sir Geoffrey Wallinger	1954–8
France	Sir Oliver Harvey	1948–54
	Sir Gladwyn Jebb	1954–60
Germany (U.K. High Commissioner)	Sir Ivone Kirkpatrick	1950–3
	Sir Frederick Hoyer Millar	1953–5
Italy	Sir Victor Mallet	1947–53
	Sir Ashley Clarke	1953–62
Japan	Sir Esler Dening ('Political Representative' 1951–2)	1952–7
Soviet Union	Sir Alvary Gascoigne	1951–3
	Sir William Hayter	1953–7
Turkey	Sir Knox Helm	1951–4
	Sir James Bowker	1954–8
United States	Sir Oliver Franks	1948–52
	Sir Roger Makins	1952–6
Minister	Sir Christopher Steel	1950–3
	Robert Scott	1953–5
Economic Minister	Denis Rickett	1951–4
	Lord Harcourt	1954–7
NATO	Sir Christopher Steel	1953–7
United Nations	Sir Gladwyn Jebb	1950–4
	Sir Pierson Dixon	1954–60

Source: Butler and Sloman, Dod.

495

Appendix XI 'National' Newspapers (and London Evenings)

Title	General Political Tendency	Owner or Controller	Circulation average January–June (inc.) 1955
Dailies			
The Times	Independent	Times Publishing Co. Ltd.	221,972
Daily Telegraph	Conservative	Lord Camrose and members of his family	1,056,275
Manchester Guardian	Liberal	The Scott Trust	156,154
Daily Express	Independent Conservative. Stresses importance of British Empire.	Beaverbrook Newspapers Ltd.	4,036,137
Daily Mail	Conservative	Associated Newspapers Ltd.	2,068,167
Daily Herald	Labour	Daily Herald Ltd. 51% of shares owned by Odhams Press Ltd., 49% by Trades Union Congress	1,759,098
News Chronicle	Liberal	Daily News Ltd. Two-thirds of trustees members of Cadbury family	1,252,778
Daily Worker	Communist	People's Press Printing Society Ltd. Shares owned by large number of small shareholders. Editorial executives members of Communist Party	83,422

Title	General Political Tendency	Owner or Controller	Circulation average January–June (inc.) 1955
Daily Mirror	Left-wing	Daily Mirror News-papers Ltd.	4.725.122
Daily Sketch	Conservative	Associated Newspapers Ltd.	950.286
London Evenings			
Evening News	As for *Daily Mail*	As for *Daily Mail*	1.312.723
Star	As for *News Chronicle*	As for *News Chronicle*	1.010.809
Evening Standard	As for *Daily Express*	As for *Daily Express*	710.776
Sundays			
Observer	Independent	The Observer Ltd. All shares owned by The Observer Trust	564.307
Sunday Times	Conservative	Kemsley Newspapers Ltd.	606.346
News of the World	General political sympathies Con-servative	News of the World Ltd.	7.971.020
People	Independent	Odhams Press Ltd.	5.075.351
Sunday Express	As for *Daily Express*	As for *Daily Express*	3.235.178
Sunday Dispatch	As for *Daily Mail*	As for *Daily Mail*	2.549.228
Reynolds News	Supports the Co-operative Movement and the Labour Party	Co-operative Press Ltd. Shareholders, co-operative societies	579.180
Sunday Chronicle	Conservative	Kemsley Newspapers Ltd.	830.631
Empire News	Conservative	Kemsley Newspapers Ltd.	2.049.880
Sunday Pictorial	As for *Daily Mirror*	Sunday Pictorial Newspapers Ltd.	5.539.442
Sunday Graphic	Conservative	Kemsley Newspapers Ltd.	1.220.056
Women's Sunday Mirror	As for *Daily Mirror*	Pictorial Publications Ltd.	1.093.513 (started 30th January 1955)

Tables

Table I Combined Public Authorities' Expenditure (Current and Capital) by money

	1950	*1951*	*1952*	*1953*	*1954*	*1955*
			£ million			
Military defence	861	1.179	1.573	1.650	1.625	1.591
Social services:						
Housing	341	368	440	493	467	422
Education and child care	431	487	541	567	608	660
Health services	478	498	510	526	543	585
Social security	674	707	825	914	922	1.016
Total social services	1.924	2.060	2.316	2.500	2.540	2.684
Agriculture and food	384	435	356	321	219	189
Industry and trade	114	195	166	129	139	185
Overseas services	179	85	77	73	75	78
Roads and public lighting	95	104	112	119	129	142
Police and justice	79	87	96	103	109	118
Other services	403	522	486	522	510	488
Debt interest	551	593	654	685	691	771
Total expenditure	4.590	5.260	5.836	6.102	6.037	6.245

Source: *National Income and Expenditure 1961* (Table 43)

Table II   Combined Public Authorities' Expenditure (Current and Capital)* by percentage

			per cent of total			
	1950	1951	1952	1953	1954	1955
Military defence	18.7	22.4	27.0	27.0	26.9	25.5
Social services:						
Housing	7.4	7.0	7.5	8.1	7.7	6.7
Education and child care	9.4	9.3	9.3	9.3	10.1	10.6
Health services	10.4	9.5	8.7	8.6	9.0	9.4
Social security	14.7	13.4	14.1	15.0	15.3	16.3
Total social services	41.9	39.2	39.6	41.0	42.1	43.0
Agriculture and food	8.4	8.3	6.1	5.3	3.6	3.0
Industry and trade	2.5	3.7	2.8	2.1	2.3	3.0
Overseas services	3.9	1.6	1.3	1.2	1.2	1.2
Roads and public lighting	2.1	2.0	1.9	2.0	2.1	2.3
Police and justice	1.7	1.6	1.6	1.7	1.8	1.9
Other services	8.8	9.9	8.3	8.5	8.5	7.8
Debt interest	12.0	11.3	11.2	11.2	11.5	12.3
Total expenditure	100.0	100.0	100.0	100.0	100.0	100.0

*Components may not add to totals due to rounding.
Source: *National Income and Expenditure 1961* (Table 43)

Table III   Public Authorities' Expenditure and Gross Domestic Product

	1950	1951	1952	1953	1954	1955
Total public authorities' expenditure (£ million)	4.590	5.260	5.836	6.102	6.037	6.245
Gross domestic product at market prices (£ million)	12.084	13.364	14.599	15.685	16.639	17.824
Public authorities' expenditure as proportion of GDP (per cent)	38.0	39.4	40.0	38.9	36.3	35.0

Source: *National Income and Expenditure 1961* (Tables 11 and 43)

Table IV Mixed Tables

	1947	1948	1949	1950	1951	1952	1953	1954	1955	1956
Non-Industrial Staff in Civil Service (thousands)	706	693	706	685	675	684	661	655	636	639
Registered unemployed (thousands)	—	—	291	308	215	490	335	269	243	250
Total Working Days lost through industrial stoppages (thousands of days)	2.433	1.944	1.807	1.389	1.694	1.792	2.184	2.457	3.781	2.083
Index of Weekly Wage Rates. Monthly Averages for All Workers. (June 1947 = 100)	—	105.8	108.6	110.7	120.0	129.9	136.0	141.9	151.4	—
Index of Industrial Production. Total all industries (1948 average = 100)	—	—	106.3	113.6	117.2	114.1	121.1	129.6	136.6	136.3
Balance of Payments: Balance of Current Transactions (£ million)	−443	+1	+31	+300	−403	+247	+188	+230	−78	+245
Gross Fixed Capital Formation. At 1948 Prices. (£ million)	—	1.430	1.563	1.641	1.647	1.671	1.849	1.995	2.124	2.234
Consumers' Expenditure. At 1948 prices. (£ million)	—	8.471	8.616	8.825	8.780	8.731	9.009	9.503	9.796	9.847
Index of Retail Prices. All items. June 1947 = 100. Monthly Averages	—	108	111	114	125	136	140	143	149	—

Source: *Annual Abstract of Statistics, 1957*

501

Acknowledgments

I had read in books authors express their indebtedness to those who helped them, but never fully appreciated the significance of this until three and a half years ago I began to write this study. I have received overwhelming help and advice from a large number of people to an extent I had not imagined possible. I shall always be grateful for the kindness shown me. It is not too much to say that whatever value this book has is due largely to their painstaking help. I hope that if they read the book they will feel their efforts were not wholly unworthwhile. This is not to excuse myself from errors and injustices that may remain in the text, for which naturally I claim absolute responsibility.

It seemed clear from the earliest days of research that to write a history of this nature I would need to talk to the principal actors. It would not have been wise, or even possible to progress or to make judgments, without taking into account the perspective and experience of those who helped shape the history of the early 1950s. To my surprise and deep gratitude almost everyone I wrote to agreed to see me for a talk. Many I interviewed more than once, and often further material was supplied in letters. Where I made a direct reference to an interview, I wrote back asking permission and often the points made in interview were elaborated further.

The following amongst others granted me interviews: The Lord Aldington, The Lord Alexander of Potterhill, The Lord Alport, Julian Amery, the late Viscount Amory, Sir John Arbuthnot, Sir Frederick Armer, the late Lord Armstrong of Sanderstead, the late Sir Hubert Ashton, Jack Baldry, Michael Banister, Sir Roderick Barclay, Tom Beagley, Jack Beddoe, Sir Eric Berthoud, Sir Reginald Bennett, The Viscount Boyd of Merton, The Lord Boyd-Carpenter, The Lord Boyle of Handsworth, Ursula Branston, The Viscount Brentford, The Lord Brooke of Cumnor, Sir George Bolton, The Lord Boothby, The Lord Butler of Saffron Walden, The Lord Caccia, Sir David Cairns, The Lord Carr of Hadley, the late Sir Robert Cary, The Lord Carrington, Philip Chantler, Mark Chapman Walker, Sir Fife Clark, Sir Ashley Clarke, David Clarke, The Lord Clitheroe, Percy Cohen, Sir George Coldstream, the late Lord Coleraine, Sir John Colville, The Lord Colyton, Sir Christopher Cox, The Lord Craigton, Desmond Crawley, The Lord Croham, Winifred Crum-Ewing, Sir Charles Cunningham, William Deedes, The Countess De La Warr, Marshal of the Royal Air Force Sir William Dickson, Sir Douglas Dodds-Parker, Sir George Dunnett, Sir James Dunnett, The Viscount Dunrossil, The Viscount Eccles, Sir Harold Emerson, Sir Basil Engholm, Sir Lancelot Errington, Sir Graeme Finlay, Sir Nigel Fisher, Sir Gerald Fitzmaurice, Sir Gilbert Flemming, The Lord Fraser of Kilmorack, Sir Hugh Fraser, Sir John Foster, The Lord Franks, The Lord Garner, Ray Gedling, The Lord Geoffrey-Lloyd, The Lord Gladwyn, Frank Glaves-Smith, The Lord Glendevon, Sir George Godber, Peter Goldman, Sir William Gorell Barnes, Sir Ronald Gould, Admiral Sir Guy Grantham, Sir Douglas Haddow, Field Marshal The Lord Harding of Petherton, The Lord Harlech, The Lord Harmar-Nicholls, Sir Ronald Harris, John Hay, Sir William Hayter, The Viscount Head, Sir Lionel Heald, Neville Heaton, the late Lord Helsby, Sir Conrad Heron, The Lord Hill of Luton, Sir Alan Hitchman, The Lord Holderness, The Lord Home of The Hirsel, The Baroness Hornsby-Smith, Sir Friston How, Graham Hutton, Sir Noël Hutton, The Lord Inchyra, Lieutenant-General Sir Ian Jacob, Sir Clifford Jarrett, Sir Gilmour Jenkins, Sir Alexander Johnston, Sir John Johnston, Sir Donald Kaberry, the late R. Kelf-Cohen, Sir Geoffrey King, The Lord Kings Norton, Sir Sidney Kirkman, Sir Gilbert Laithwaite, Sir John Lang, Sir Joseph Latham, The Lord Lloyd, Sir Gilbert Longden, the late Rt. Hon. Malcolm Macdonald, Sir Donald MacDougall, Sir Fitzroy Maclean, Lieutenant-General Sir Kenneth McLean, Sir Angus Mackintosh, the late Sir George Mallaby, The Lord Mancroft, Sir Robert Marshall, the late Evan Maude, the late Reginald Maudling, Sir Derek Mitchell, The Dowager Viscountess Monckton of Brenchley, Anthony Montague Browne, the late Sir Oscar Morland, Sir Nicholas Morrison, Sir Charles Mott-Radclyffe, Admiral of the Fleet the late Earl Mountbatten of Burma, the late Sir Edward Muir, The Viscount Muirshiel, Sir Hugh Munro-Lucas-Tooth, Sir William Murrie, Sir Cyril Musgrave, Sir Allan Noble, The Lord Nugent of Guildford, Sir Anthony Nutting, Gerald O'Brien, The Lord Orr-Ewing, Sir Thomas Padmore, the late Sir Harold Parker, Sir Antony Part, the late Sir Louis Petch, Sir Arthur Peterson, Sir David Pitblado, Harry Pitchforth, Sir Edward Playfair, George Pottinger, Sir Richard Powell, Sir Hilton Poynton, Sir Neil Pritchard, Sir Dennis Proctor, Sir Victor Raby, The Lord Redcliffe-Maud, The Lord Redmayne, Alfred Richardson, The Lord Robbins, The Lord Robens of Woldingham, The Lord Roberthall, Sir Frank Roberts, Ian Robertson, Sir James Robertson, Sir

Kenneth Roberts-Wray. Sir John Rodgers. John Rogerson. Sir Anthony Rumbold. Sir William Ryland. Sir Folliott Sandford. Sir Donald Sargent. The Earl of Selkirk. the late Lord Selwyn-Lloyd. William Senior. The Lord Shawcross. The Lord Shinwell. Sir Evelyn Shuckburgh. The Lord Simon of Glaisdale. Marshal of the Royal Air Force the late Sir John Slessor, Sir John Smyth, The Lord Soames, Sir Alexander Spearman. Sir Kelvin Spencer. Sir Hugh Stockwell. The Lord Strathclyde. the late Lord Strang. Anthony Sutherland. Field Marshal the late Sir Gerald Templer, the late Sir Vincent Tewson, The Lord Thorneycroft. The Lord Tranmire. Sir Kenneth Thompson. Sir Richard Thompson. the late Henry Walker. Sir John Walley. The Viscount Ward of Witley. Sir John Ward. Sir Richard Way. Sir Toby Weaver. Geoffrey Wheeler. Sydney Wilkinson. the late Sir Arton Wilson. Sir Harold Wilson. Percy Wilson. Simon Wingfield Digby. Sir John Winnifrith.

After I had written the first draft I felt it would be advisable to have the individual sections read over by key figures concerned with the particular field. Again I had not expected such generous help on such a wide scale. and the comments I received proved of enormous value when I wrote the final draft. I must again stress here that I am entirely responsible for the final content; I usually took the advice I was offered. but not always.

The following read over individual sections: The Lord Aldington. Samuel Brittan. Philip Chantler. Sir Fife Clark. Sir George Coldstream. Sir John Colville. Sir Geoffrey Cox. Desmond Crawley. The Lord Croham. Sir Charles Cunningham. Sir Goronwy Daniel. Sir Basil Engholm. Sir Harold Emmerson. The Lord Garner. Frank Glaves-Smith. Sir George Godber. Peter Goldman. Sir William Gorell Barnes. Gordon Grant. Sir Ronald Harris. Sir Conrad Heron. Sir John Johnston. the late R. Kelf-Cohen. Sir John Lang. Sir Robert Marshall. the late Evan Maude. Sir William Murrie. Henry Pelling. the late Sir Louis Petch. Sir Arthur Peterson. Ben Pimlott. Harry Pitchforth. Sir Richard Powell. Sir Dennis Proctor. The Lord Roberthall. Sir Frank Roberts. Ian Robertson. John Rogerson. Sir William Ryland. Sir Folliott Sandford. Sir Evelyn Shuckburgh. the late Henry Walker. Sir John Walley. Sir Richard Way. Sir Toby Weaver. Sydney Wilkinson. Sir John Winnifrith. Geoffrey Wheeler.

The following also looked over the whole manuscript: John Barnes. The Lord Blake. Craig Eadie. The Lord Fraser of Kilmorack. Joanna Pappworth. Naomi Papworth. The Lord Plowden and Ronald Stevens.

I benefited greatly in different ways from listening to the following: Nicholas Aivaliotis. Geoffrey Block. Samuel Brittan. Dr. David

505

Carlton, Dr. Patrick Cosgrave, Dr. Michael Cox, Piers Dixon, Professor John Cross, John Grigg, Lady Hailes, Lord Harris of High Cross, Rex Haymes, Robert Rhodes James, Professor John Jewkes, Michael Lee, Miss Sheila Minto, Dame Margery Perham, Dr. John Ramsden, Bernard Sendall, Diana Spearman, Lady Wills.

For helping enlighten me about the press in the early 1950s, I am indebted to the following for meeting me: Sir Francis Boyd, Sir Harry Boyne, Sir Geoffrey Cox, Sir Trevor Lloyd-Hughes, Andrew Roth, Wilfrid Sendall, Leslie Way, and David Wood. For additional help by telephone or letter my thanks to John Desborough, Mrs. Rona Margach and E. R. Thompson.

For information supplied in letters, for which I am very grateful, my thanks are due to General Alfred Gruenther, W. A. B. Hamilton, Lady Heap (for sending newspaper cuttings), the late Professor John Mackintosh, the late Lord Marples, Pierre Mendès France, Guy Schofield.

For permission to quote from the background tapes of the Thames Television programme, *The Day Before Yesterday*, my thanks are due to Reginald Bevins, The Viscount Chandos, The Lord Crathorne, Donald Cullimore, The Hon. Joanna Lloyd, Michael Marshall, The Lord Stuart, and Phillip Whitehead, M.P. I should also like to thank The Lady Helsby, for permission to quote from my interview with the late Lord Helsby; Lady Mallaby, for permission to quote from my interview with the late Sir George Mallaby; and The Lord Strang, for permission to quote from my interview with the late Lord Strang.

For permission to quote from material by Dean Acheson in the Truman Papers, Truman Library, my thanks are due to David C. Acheson; for permission to quote from interviews in the John Foster Dulles Oral History Archive, Princeton University Library, I am grateful to Mr. Alexander Aldrich, The Hon. Douglas Dillon, Mr. John Eisenhower, and Mr. John W. Hanes.

For permission to quote from private papers in this country, I am grateful to the following: to The Lord Aldington, for permission to quote from a letter of his; to The Lord Alexander of Tunis, for permission to quote from a letter of his father, the first Earl; to the Countess of Avon, for permission to quote from letters of the first Earl; to the Hon. Mark Bonham Carter, for permission to quote from letters of the late Lady Violet Bonham Carter; to The Lord Boothby, for permission to quote from a letter of his; to The Lord Butler of Saffron Walden, for permission to quote from a letter of his; to The Lord Chandos, for permission to quote from material in the *Chandos Papers*; to Mrs. Elizabeth Crookshank, for permission to quote from the diaries of the

ACKNOWLEDGMENTS

late Lord Crookshank; to Mr. Piers Dixon. for permission to quote from material in the Dixon Papers; to The Lady Forres, for permission to quote from the letters and diaries of the late Lord Woolton; to The Lord Hankey. for permission to quote from the *Hankey Papers*; to the Hon. William Lloyd-George. for permission to quote a letter of the late Lord Tenby; to Mr. J. M. O. Mackenzie. for permission to quote from the *Horsbrugh Papers*; to The Rt. Hon. Harold Macmillan. for permission to quote from a letter of his; to The Lord Moran. for permission to quote from a letter of the first Lord Moran; to Mr. Alexander Murray. for permission to quote from the *Murray Papers*; to Mrs. Jane Robinson. for permission to quote from the *Monckton Papers*; to The Lord Simon. for permission to quote from the *Simon Papers*; to A. J. P. Taylor. for permission to quote from the *Beaverbrook Papers*.

I also acknowledge my thanks to the following libraries and institutions. for permission to quote from private papers: to Balliol College. Oxford. for quotations from the *Monckton Papers*; to the Bodleian Library, Oxford, Department of Western Manuscripts, for permission to quote from the *Crookshank. Murray. Simon* and *Woolton Papers*; to the British Library of Political and Economic Science, for quotations from the *Dalton Papers*; to C. & T. Publications. Ltd.. for permission to quote from the letters of Sir Winston Churchill; to the Cabinet Office. Historical Section. for permission to quote from the *Cherwell Papers*; to the Library at Churchill College. Cambridge. for quotations from the *Chandos. Hankey. Horsbrugh* and *Kilmuir Papers*. and to the Masters and Fellows of Churchill College for permission to quote from the letters of Brendan Bracken; to the Trustees of Columbia University in the City of New York. for references to its Oral History Archive; to the Director of the Conservative Research Department. for permission to quote from the Department's Archives; to the Dwight D. Eisenhower Library. for permission to refer to the *Eisenhower, Hagerty* and *Jackson Papers*; to the English-Speaking Union. for permission to quote from the *Cherwell Papers*; to the House of Lords Record Office. for quotations from the *Beaverbrook Papers*; to the Trustees of the *Ismay Papers*. and to the Liddell Hart Centre for Military Archives. King's College. London. for references to the *Ismay Papers*; to Nuffield College. Oxford. for quotations from the *Cherwell Papers*; to Princeton University. Seeley G. Mudd Manuscript Library. for permission to quote from the *Baruch* and *Dulles Papers*; and to the Harry S. Truman Library. for permission to quote from the *Acheson. Connelly* and *Truman Papers*.

The following librarians were of particular help. and I am most grateful to them: Dr. Anthony Alcock. Assistant Librarian. Nuffield

507

College. Oxford; Mrs. Katherine Bligh. House of Lords Record Office; Geoffrey Block. Conservative Research Department; Ms. Nancy Bressler. Curator of Public Affairs Papers. Seeley G. Mudd Manuscript Library. Princeton University; Mrs. Patricia Bradford. former Archivist. Churchill College. Cambridge; Maclyn Burg. of the Dwight D. Eisenhower Library. Abilene. Kansas; Philip D. Lagerquist. Chief Archivist. Harry S. Truman Library. Independence. Missouri; Miss Helen Langley. Archivist. Bodleian Library. Oxford; Miss Patricia Methven. Liddell Hart Centre for Military Archives; Mr. Dennis Porter. Senior Assistant Librarian. Bodleian Library; Ms. Angela Raspin. British Library of Political and Economic Science; Miss Marion M. Stewart. Archivist. Churchill College. Cambridge; John E. Wickman. Director. Dwight D. Eisenhower Library; and the staff of the British Library.

I would like to thank the Information Division of the Treasury for preparing the tables on public expenditure.

David Butler kindly allowed me to use in the Appendix two tables that appeared in his *British General Election of 1955*. Lord Greenhill of Harrow generously allowed me to quote in the Introduction from a letter he wrote to *The Times*. I would like to thank the editors of *The Economist* and *The Times* for permission to quote from back volumes and Constable and Co. Ltd. for permission to quote from *Winston Churchill, The Struggle for Survival, 1940–1965* by Lord Moran.

For taking the lion's share of checking the references. my thanks are due to Rex Haymes. who set about the formidable task with great intelligence and determination.

My thanks are due to the following: to Julia Clarke and Mel Friend. for doing some of the typing; to Simon Lambros. for help in checking the Bibliography; to Nick Friend, for his continual interest, and for his work checking references at Churchill College, Cambridge; to Michael Taylor for trenchant suggestions, especially on style; for checking re-typing accuracy to Gillian Oakley, Sara Pappworth and Pat Pontifex.

The Social Science Research Council provided financial help.

I should like to express my profound gratitude to Mrs. Pauline Oakley, who for three years has handled the major part of my typing. Her patience, skill and good sense were at all times greatly appreciated. Ruth Belkin and Jean Penfold helped much by typing assistance in the closing stages.

To my Uncle Cecil of Harrogate, my thanks are due for financial assistance and encouragement.

At Hodder and Stoughton I was confronted by quite unexpected, but most welcome patience. good humour and incisive judgment. My thanks in particular to Rivers Scott for initial encouragement. and to his successor. Ion Trewin for suggesting substantial improvements; to Morag Robinson. for her careful and sensitive work on editing and to Christine Pye for her copy-editing; finally to Paul Sheldon. for introducing me to the publishing house.

As this is my first book. I feel it appropriate to record very briefly my debt to those who had a formative effect on me: at Tonbridge School. Robert Austin. Dr. Robert Ogilvie. Geoffrey Parker and Colin Reid. and. above all. my great friend Jonathan Smith. At Oxford. G. H. Le May. Gillian Peele and R. G. Smethurst.

This work began as my doctoral thesis at the London School of Economics. I was fortunate indeed to have as my supervisor the distinguished academic, John Barnes. To him I owe a considerable debt, not the least for suggesting the subject of study. for impressing on me the importance of interviewing the key figures from the early 1950s. and for instilling in me some of his extraordinary enthusiasm for political history. I will always be grateful for the encouragement and kindness of John. and of his wife Mary.

My largest debt is due to Joanna. without whose love and ability to work long and late hours beside me. it is no exaggeration to say that this book could never have been completed.

509

Notes

Italic figures in parentheses refer to the Bibliography.

SOURCES pp.xi–xiv

1 For further information see MacKenzie and Grove (*143*) pp.174–5 and 183, and Jennings (*131*) pp.91–2 and 138–9.
2 The rank of the various jobs can often be discovered by the salary. In 1953 a man at Permanent Secretary rank was paid £4,500 per annum, Deputy Secretary rank, £3,250, and Under-Secretary £2,500. Women were paid approximately 10 per cent less. This salary grading is also useful for comparing other jobs: thus, for example, the Cabinet Secretary was paid at Permanent Secretary salary level, the Legal Adviser at the Foreign Office and Chief Scientist at Fuel and Power at the level of a Deputy Secretary. The Head of the Civil Service was paid the top salary, £5,000.
3 There were three ranks below (Assistant) Under-Secretary within the senior grade of the Civil Service, the 'Administrative Class'. They were Assistant Secretaries (£2,000–£1,340), Principals (£1,375–£880) and Assistant Principals (£750–£400). The figures in brackets are annual salaries at 1953 rates.

CHAPTER 1 PART 1 pp.5–18

1 Paul Addison wrote a book published in 1975 entitled *The Road to 1945* in which he argued that: 'The national unity of the war years gave rise to a new consensus at the top which dominated Britain long after the last bomb had fallen.' Addison (*112*) p.13. One of the themes of this study is the continuity during 1951–5 with much of what had gone before. Hence the title of this section, 'The Road to 1951'.
2 *The Annual Register, 1951* p.61. *The Times* 27.10.51.
3 The previous occasions were on 10th May, 1940, at the beginning of the War Coali-

tion, and 23rd May, 1945, at the start of the two-month 'Caretaker Government' in between the end of the war with Germany and the final stages before Japan surrendered (which finally took place three weeks after Labour came to power on 26th July, 1945).
4 Wheeler-Bennett (*103*) p.797.
5 *The Times* 27.7.45.
6 See Bartlett (*118a*) p.44.
7 The *Spectator* 26.10.51 (p.525).
8 Cook and Sked (*115a*) pp.27–8. On the positive side, however, Britain's engineering industry had expanded during the war.
9 The *Spectator*, 26.10.51 (p.525).
10 Dow (*163*) p.6.
11 Brittan (*161*) p.180.
12 Interview with Lord Roberthall, B.O.A.P.A.H.
13 Bartlett (*118a*) p.65.
14 Brittan (*161*) p.181.
15 Dow (*163*) p.66.
16 Cook and Sked (*115a*) p.90.
17 Hoffman (*124*) p.241.
18 Bartlett (*118a*) p.53.
19 Hoffman (*124*) p.245, described it as 'undoubtedly Labour's most hated legislation'.
20 See Barnes and Reid (*177a*) pp.13–19.
21 In 1946 the Government repealed the 1927 Trade Disputes and Trade Union Act which provoked initially strong Conservative opposition. But this did not lead to a lasting improvement in relations with the unions, and trade union criticism led to the abandonment after the February 1950 Election of the policy of voluntary wage restraint, which had been in existence since 1948. Continued opposition from the unions to Order 1305 led to it being replaced in August 1951 by the Industrial Disputes Order 1376. This provided for reference of disputes to an industrial disputes tribunal: an arbitration award by the

511

tribunal continued to be legally binding but there was no restriction on strikes after the award had been made.

22 Labour Ministers had more experience on Cabinet Committees. But only four Labour Ministers headed Departments concerned with these three subjects during the War Coalition: Attlee the Dominions Office (1942–3); Cripps the Ministry of Aircraft Production (1942–5); A. V. Alexander the Admiralty (1940–5); and Herbert Morrison the Ministry of Supply (1940). A similarly small percentage of Labour politicians served as junior Ministers in these fields.

23 *House of Commons* 6.12.51, Vol. 494, Col. 2591.

24 *House of Commons* 6.3.47, Vol. 434, Col. 678.

25 Garner (*202*) p.340.

26 *House of Commons* 28.4.49, Vol. 464, Col. 375.

27 The others were Lord Addison (1945–7) and Philip Noel-Baker (1947–50).

28 Garner (*202*) p.283.

29 India did, however, recognise the King as Head of the Commonwealth.

30 *House of Commons* 9.7.46, Vol. 425, Col. 238. In 1948, the Colonial Office's Annual Report bore a similar message to become a standard text for a decade. Goldsworthy (*203*) p.17.

31 Goldsworthy (*203*) p.15.

32 *House of Commons* 14.11.51, Vol. 493, Col. 984.

33 *House of Commons* 26.1.49.

34 Hoffman (*124*) p.244.

35 Frankel (*214*) pp.185–6.

36 Eden said that during his period as Foreign Secretary, 'There were no differences on any important issue of foreign policy.' *House of Commons*, Vol. 413, Col. 312.

37 *House of Commons* Vol. 494, Col. 54.

38 The Chapters below follow the same order as the topics discussed in this Chapter, from administrative affairs (Chapter 4) to foreign policy (Chapter 10). The Bibliography also follows this pattern.

CHAPTER 1 PART 2 pp.18–21

1 This short section relies heavily on the excellent survey in Butler (*120*) pp.105–36.

2 *The Times* 20.9.51.

3 David Butler notes that the case for television broadcasts was much stronger in 1951 than in 1950: the number of viewers had tripled, and transmission extension meant that most of England was within receiving range. In the event, the broadcasts reached considerably less than ten per cent of the population. Butler (*120*) p.75.

4 Mayhew had been a junior Minister at the Foreign Office, 1946–50.

5 Shawcross, Attorney-General, 1945–51, had been appointed President of the Board of Trade following Wilson's resignation in April 1951.

6 Butler (*120*) p.118.

7 This led Churchill to issue a writ of libel against the paper, settled nearly seven months later, out of court. The paper agreed to make a contribution to a charity nominated by Churchill and printed a retraction on 24th May, 1952.

8 Official Report of 1951 Labour Party Conference at Scarborough.

9 Butler (*120*) p.126.

CHAPTER 1 PART 3 pp.21–27

1 The *Spectator* 26.10.51, p.525.

2 *House of Commons* 13.11.51, Vol. 493, Col. 941.

3 Moran (*169a*) pp.1–2.

4 *The Times* 27.10.51.

5 *House of Commons* 6.11.51, Vol. 493, Cols. 76–7.

6 Butler (*10*) p.157.

7 Macmillan (*36*) p.378.

8 The *Observer* 4.11.51, leading article.

9 *The Times* 7.11.51.

10 The *Sunday Times* 20.1.52, leading article.

11 Several Political Correspondents in the press said they at this stage never saw Harold Wilson as of prime ministerial calibre.

12 Later Editor, *New Statesman*, 1961–5 and British Ambassador in Washington, 1969–71.

13 *The Times* 19.10.51.

14 Garner (*202*) p.334.

15 Ruth Williams survived him when he died in 1980. See Chapter 9 Part 4.

16 *The Times* 3.11.51.

17 The *Observer* 25.11.51.

18 A leader in *The Times* 13.11.51.

19 The *Observer* 20.6.54.

20 *House of Commons* 19.11.51, Vol. 494, Col. 53.

21 *House of Commons* 6.12.51, Vol. 494, Col. 2592

22 *House of Commons* 19.11.51, Vol. 494, Col. 34.

23 See Chapter I Part 2.

24 During the Election campaign, Churchill also called for a lull in Party strife. A leading article in the *Observer* on 28.10.51 endorsed the sentiment, in view of the seriousness of the position the new Government inherited. Three courses it said must be pursued: equality of sacrifice by all classes; undoctrinaire economic policies and a continuation of bipartisan foreign policy.

CHAPTER 2 PART 1 pp.28–38

1 Churchill's close friend from the interwar years. He was Paymaster General, 1942–5, and an *éminence grise* to Churchill throughout the war.

2 Chief Staff Officer to Churchill as Minister of Defence, 1940–5.

3 Minister of War Transport, 1941–5. Churchill was less close to him than the other four but admired his work as Minister.

4 He first got to know Churchill well during the abdication crisis. Solicitor-General, 1945 (in the 'Caretaker Government').

5 He held a number of command posts in the Second World War culminating in the job of Supreme Allied Commander, Mediterranean Theatre, 1944–5.

6 The former Permanent Under-Secretary to the Home Office, 1922–32, Lord President, 1940–3, Chancellor of Exchequer, 1943–5. Created Lord Waverley in 1952.

7 From the family Churchill knew well. Lord Asquith was fourth son of the First Earl and a Lord of Appeal in Ordinary.

8 Minister of Information, 1941–5.

9 Chief of Air Staff, 1940–5. See Chapter 8 Part 1.

10 Head of Civil Service, 1945–56.

11 Colville, Assistant Private Secretary, 1939–41 and 1943–5, had been First Secretary at the British Embassy in Lisbon since 1949.

12 Diary 16.4.57, Moran (*87*) p.758. Mallaby (*37*) pp.36–8. The joint principal private secretaryship to the P.M. was a most exceptional arrangement and has not been repeated since. Colville's appointment was announced on 6th November, 1951.

13 See Chapter 8 Part 1.

14 Churchill's admiration for Brook stemmed from the latter's days serving in the Cabinet Secretariat, 1942–3. See Chapter 4 Part 2.

15 Brook himself was to have gone to the Treasury as deputy to the Permanent Secretary. See Chapter 5 Part 1. Brook had never thought of himself as a 'natural' for the Treasury, so that he had reservations about going. He realised, however, it was an almost necessary step at that time to succeed Bridges as Head of the Civil Service. He was conscious of the danger of growing stale in the very demanding job of Secretary to the Cabinet and had been contemplating the possibility of a change. Brook never expressed disappointment at not going to the Treasury and was undoubtedly excited by the prospect of working again with Churchill. Interviews with Sir Robert Marshall and Sir Alexander Johnston.

16 See Chapter 3 Part 4.

17 See Chapter 4 Part 2.

18 See Chapter 5 Part 1.

19 See Chapter 4 Part 1.

20 See Chapter 6 Part 1. He also told the Minister of Fuel and Power to avoid trouble with the miners. See Chapter 6 Part 6.

21 Diary 15.10.52, *Crookshank Papers*. The party had been for the Turkish mission. The leaders were Sir Vincent Tewson, Tom O'Brien and Sir Lincoln Evans.

22 Interview with Sir John Colville.

23 First Lord of the Admiralty, 1911–15 and 1939–40, Minister of Munitions, 1917–19, Secretary for War and Air, 1919–21.

24 See Chapter 3 Part 2.

25 Interview with Sir Fife Clark.

26 'I tried some propaganda on Winston about cutting out some of these ridiculous Departments which are a burden to the community,' Bracken wrote to Beaverbrook on 7.1.53, but 'Churchill doesn't want to change anything in his Government.' *Beaverbrook Papers*, Box C57.

27 His influence on appointments was felt more when he operated directly on his close friend, Buchan-Hepburn, the Chief Whip.

28 Bracken only marginally exaggerated the position in a letter to Lord Simon of 5.12.52. 'If I were to suggest to W.S.C. that he should do something about [Simon's plan for reforming the House of

Lords]. I should be breaking a command-ment I have given myself, believing as I do that when one is out of office . . . one should not offer any sort of unsought advice to Ministers.' *Simon Papers*, Box F8.

29 For example, Churchill spent some time with Beaverbrook in January 1953 in Jamaica on his return from the U.S., but with the possible exception of Egypt (see Chapter 10 Part 4), Beaverbrook appears to have made little impact on Churchill's views. In particular, Beaverbrook failed during these years to persuade Churchill to oppose either G.A.T.T. or German rearmament. The Beaverbrook press after the first year began to be increasingly critical of the Government, but not of Churchill. See Taylor (*100*) pp.608–9.

30 See letters, Beaverbrook to Bracken, 25.1.55, and Bracken to Beaverbrook, 2.2.55. *Beaverbrook Papers*, Box C58. Swinton was another who was sorry to see him go for personal reasons, although he also believed that it was time Churchill handed over to Eden.

31 See for example Moran's comment in his diary on 14.7.53: '. . . the P.M. has learnt at last that Max is not a reliable counsellor where elections are concerned.' Moran (*87*) p.456.

32 Interview with Sir John Colville.

33 Interview with Sir Fife Clark. Beaverbrook was proprietor of London Express Newspapers Ltd. Bracken was Chairman of the *Financial Times* and managing director of *The Economist*. Camrose was Chairman of the *Daily Telegraph* (he died in 1954). Lord Kemsley, another friend, was Chairman of a large number of provincial newspapers and was Editor-in-Chief of the *Sunday Times*. For information relating to Churchill's dealings with the press, the author is indebted to background papers written by Sir Fife Clark. *Private Papers*.

34 See Lady Soames (*98*), and Colville in Wheeler-Bennett. ed. (*105*) p.65.

35 A consideration of the diary as a historical source appears in the Notes on Sources at the beginning of the book. For a sound analysis of Moran's role, see Colville in Wheeler-Bennett. ed. (*105*) pp.109–12. Sir John Colville said in Interview II that Churchill never trusted Moran so much after he had asked to be Minister of Health. For a good summary of the con-troversy surrounding the publication of Moran's diary, see L'Etang (*117a*) pp.1–5.

36 Colville in Wheeler-Bennett. ed. (*105*) p.111.

37 Mary Soames wrote: 'Lord Moran under-stood Winston thoroughly, and he was indeed fortunate he had as his doctor a man who understood not only the medical considerations and risks to his patient, but one who was also fully aware of the implications, with regard to the office he held, of his condition at any time. Lord Moran moreover understood the relationships between, and with, Winston's colleagues, and where one could expect loyalty, understanding and total discretion – and where one could not.' Soames (*98*) p.431.

38 Moran at one point himself made this comment about their relationship which seems to be a good approximation to the truth. 'It seems, too, to relieve his feelings to go over the difficulties he has to overcome with someone not in the political world, though my part is only to listen; he does not want my views.' Diary 20.6.52, Moran (*87*) p.417. Also Moran quotes himself as saying (22.2.52) p.403: '. . . I maintained that he would listen to me on the medical argument, but that when I began on politics he would switch off.' Not too much weight should be put on incidental remarks like Christopher Soames', quoted in the diary 16.9.53, p.500, where Soames told Moran that he had more influence on Churchill than anyone.

39 Moran (*87*) p.16.

40 To the U.S. in January 1952 and June 1954 and to Bermuda in December 1953. He did not accompany Churchill on his visit to see President-Elect Eisenhower and say 'goodbye' to President Truman in January 1953. This however was only a semi-official trip.

41 Interview I with Anthony Montague Browne.

42 Moran wrote (diary 16.4.57, Moran (*87*) p.758). 'I suppose nobody really understands Winston, but Jock comes as near to it as anyone.' For a brief account of Colville's relationship with Churchill, see Lady Soames' letter to *The Times* 24.10.78.

43 On Churchill's departure in April 1955, Colville left the Civil Service for a career in the City, and also became the author of some notable books and articles, includ-

ing a biography of Field Marshal Lord Gort. Pitblado rose to become Permanent Secretary at Power, 1966–9, and at the Ministry of Technology, 1969–70.

44 Hunt was a young man whose company Churchill found particularly congenial; not only was he extremely erudite, but he had also had the benefit of having been a military assistant to Lord Alexander of Tunis during the war.

45 Beneath Hunt and Montague Browne were two Assistant Private Secretaries, permanent civil servants who had worked at Number Ten since before the war: Miss M. G. Stenhouse, responsible for honours under the Piincipal Private Secretaries, and Miss G. F. Davies, who remained on for one year after her sixtieth birthday in 1954 to take on responsibilities for Parliamentary Questions after Oates' departure. In addition to a number of established and non-established secretaries ('garden room girls'), the complement of secretaries was completed by three personal secretaries, paid for out of Churchill's own purse, Elizabeth Gilliatt, Jane Portal and Jo Sturdee, who dealt with his private affairs. Almost always one was in attendance. Sir Anthony Bevir was engaged on work of a different nature. He was Secretary for Appointments to the Prime Minister from 1947 to February 1956, and responsible for ecclesiastical appointments and patronage. Interviews with Sir John Colville, Anthony Montague Browne and Miss Sheila Minto.

46 Because of Churchill's international standing, it was felt that he should have a private secretary – Montague Browne – to look after his affairs, paid out of public funds. After Churchill's death, Montague Browne was seconded to H.M. Household before entering private commerce in 1967.

47 Interview with Lord Glendevon, formerly Lord John Hope.

48 Interview with Sir Douglas Dodds-Parker. He had just been appointed Chairman of the Commonwealth Affairs Committee and felt he could contribute more in that way.

49 Soames married Cnurchill's youngest daughter, Mary, in 1947. Soames had been M.P. for Bedford since 1950, elected at the age of twenty-nine.

50 See Colville in Wheeler-Bennett, ed. (105) pp.108–9.

51 Diary 17.4.58, Moran (87) p.775.

52 Sir Ian Jacob wrote in some private jottings at the time: 'He no longer read and mastered papers or sent out his scintillating minutes . . . He could still muster his resources for a big occasion but the humdrum slog of daily business bored him.' Private Papers. See also Jacob in (88a) pp.76–7. But there was no widespread feeling amongst Ministers and officials, except perhaps in the Treasury, that Churchill was not up to it until the June 1953 stroke.

53 He had previously suffered a stroke at Monte Carlo in August 1949 and a disturbance of the cerebral circulation in February 1950.

54 Grigg (222) argues both that it was wrong to have covered up the details of Churchill's stroke (pp.10–11), and also that Churchill should have retired in the autumn of 1953 (p.16). I agree that perhaps the full nature of Churchill's illness should have been made public at the time, but disagree that Churchill should have left when Grigg suggests.

55 Brook contributed a piece to Action This Day, Wheeler-Bennett, ed. (105) written, as a riposte to Moran's Diary, shortly before Brook's death in 1967. See, in particular, pp.37–46. For a discussion of the crucial relationship between Brook and Churchill, see Chapter 4 Part 2.

56 Brook does not specifically mention Churchill's desire to serve his country, though he always put this well ahead of saving his life.

57 Commenting on his speech on the Address, House of Commons 3.11.53, a leading article noted: 'His complete authority over the Commons is one of the most important political factors in the new round of the Parliamentary contest that is now beginning . . . It is not the least of his contributions to British politics that he has shown – and to him personally must go much of the credit – that strong and stable government is possible even where there is only a small majority.' The Times 4.11.53.

58 Even then, Lord Amory, who joined the Cabinet for Churchill's last nine months as Prime Minister, said (interview) of Churchill's conduct of Cabinet: 'You realised he was getting older and there were times when he was clearly tired, though he never lost control of the business . . .

Sometimes he got bored with the conversation and he would let his thoughts wander a bit [but] he had a very definite idea that Cabinet business ought to be properly dealt with . . . My general impression is that he was still adequate to preside over a Cabinet though it took longer [than strictly necessary].'

59 This broad pattern of the stages in Churchill's physical decline was also found to be the case by many of those interviewed. Colville also wrote that Churchill was becoming increasingly deaf after his June 1953 stroke. Colville (12) p.253. The Times noted as early as 1.12.54 that to the pressing problems of the previous four months. reduction of inflation, the balance between consumer and agricultural interests, redeployment of the defence programme and the maintenance of exports, Churchill had made little contribution.

60 'It is a most perplexing time, much worse than the war. All talk and no co-operation.' as he said to Moran. Diary 20.6.52. Moran (87) p.417. See also Colville in Wheeler-Bennett, ed. (105) pp.119–20.

61 Churchill in conversation with Eisenhower at the White House on 25.6.54. Ann Whitman Diary. Eisenhower Papers, Box 2.

62 Interview with Sir John Colville.

63 The Times 24.12.51. He repeated the same sentiments in his party political broadcast on 3.5.52. The Times 5.5.52. See also diary 6.3.52. Moran (87). p.406.

64 Ann Whitman Diary 25.6.54. Eisenhower Papers. Box 2.

65 Interview II with Anthony Montague Browne. See also Norman Brook (pp.40–1) and Colville (p.72) in Wheeler-Bennett. ed. (105). But invariably Party speeches were written by George Christ, Parliamentary Liaison Officer of the Conservative Party, June 1946–January 1966. Woolton and Churchill had had to persuade Camrose very hard before he would agree to let Christ leave the Daily Telegraph where he had been Political Correspondent. Christ's main service to Churchill lay in his deep knowledge of Parliamentary minutiae.

66 He spoke on the deterrent on 1.3.55 and on foreign affairs on 14.3.55. House of Commons.

67 These three areas. policy co-ordinator,

Party Leader and leader of the nation, were outlined in an article in The Economist 9.4.55 (p.287).

68 This view is held, for example, by Lord Fraser of Kilmorack (formerly Sir Michael Fraser, Director of the Conservative Research Department, 1951–64). (Interview).

69 After being re-elected in his Woodford constituency, he had said: 'We have all felt that we have a great deal in common and now perhaps there may be a lull in our Party strife which will enable us to understand more what is good in our opponents and not be so very clever finding out all their shortcomings.' The Times 27.10.51.

70 House of Commons 3.11.53, Vol. 520, Col. 22.

71 Sir Henry Channon, M.P. for Southend (Conservative) from 1935 until his death in October 1958.

72 James. ed. (28) p.479.

73 See Chapter 2 Part 2.

74 See diary 28.11.54. Moran (87) pp.641–2.

75 House of Commons 11.5.53, Vol. 515, Cols. 897–8.

76 House of Commons 1.3.55. Vol. 537, Cols. 1896. 1899.

CHAPTER 2 PART 2 pp.38–54

1 Stuart (51) pp. 145–6.

2 Churchill told Eden privately in December 1940 that he must succeed him if for any reason he was incapacitated in the war. Churchill gave more authority to his decision about Eden in June 1942 in a formal submission to George VI. Eden (14) p.266 and Wheeler-Bennett (103) p.544. See also Macmillan (36) pp.46–7. In the event of both Churchill and Eden being killed, Churchill counselled George VI in a letter of 28th January, 1945, to send for Sir John Anderson. Wheeler-Bennett (103) pp.544–6.

3 Interview with Sir John Colville.

4 In the 1945 Election the Conservatives won 213 seats to Labour's 393. At the February 1950 Election that lead was cut considerably. The Conservatives won 298 seats to Labour's 315. Had the Election been lost in 1951, Churchill would have retired. Diary 15.10.51, Moran (87) p.372.

5 Soames (98) p.429.

6 They might lose 2 per cent but they would gain from other Parties. Present Labour

supporters would be more likely to vote for the Conservative Party if Eden were Leader rather than Churchill. *Woolton Papers*, Box 21, Leaf 98. The mutterings against Churchill among the Party were most widespread in 1947 and early in 1949. In particular the South Hammersmith by-election of February 1949 produced the most serious crisis of confidence in Churchill's leadership since the defeat in 1945. On 3.3.49 Churchill attended a meeting of the 1922 Committee and listened to much criticism of the leadership of the Conservative Party, but as Goodhart (*123*) noted on p.148: 'The 1922 Committee had shown that it was prepared to bark at Mr. Churchill in his presence, but the great majority of members had no desire to bite or to seek to force an early retirement of their Leader.' And in the coming months, as the Party's fortunes began to improve, so the unrest became more subdued.

7 See Soames (*98*) p.448. He also originally asked Colville to return for just one year. He didn't want to remain in office long; but he wanted to initiate the recovery of the country under a Conservative Administration. See Colville in Wheeler-Bennett, ed. (*105*) p.120.

8 See pp.29–30.

9 Interview with Sir John Colville. On 21st February, 1952, only fifteen days after King George VI's death, Moran wrote: 'I knew, too, that he had set his heart on seeing the young Queen crowned before he gave up office.' Diary 21.2.52, Moran (*87*) p.399. Churchill's determination to remain until after the Coronation was communicated to Eden by at least April 1952. *Private Papers*.

10 In early January 1953, Butler's Principal Private Secretary informed Eden's that his Minister, though anxious to be Prime Minister, was ready to wait, that he had long-term plans for reforming the Tory Party and was anxious to serve first under Eden. Interview with Sir Evelyn Shuckburgh.

11 See the *Spectator* 23.5.52, p.663. An astute article in the *Scotsman* on 4.4.55 by its Political Correspondent noted that the rivalry that had existed between Eden and Butler for the succession was finally dispelled by Eden's return to work in October 1953 after his six-month illness.

12 Eden had the official title of Deputy Leader of the Opposition, 1945–51.

13 In his book on the British constitution, published in 1954, Herbert Morrison wrote: 'Including and since Mr. Churchill's War Government, the position of Deputy Prime Minister has been publicly announced, though not constitutionally recognised.' Morrison (*133*) p.76.

14 *Private Papers.*

15 He had been Private Secretary to George VI since 1943. He retired as Private Secretary to Queen Elizabeth in 1953.

16 Wheeler-Bennett (*103*) p.797.

17 He used this title for example in his entries in *Who's Who*. An item also appeared in *The Times* on 29.10.51 saying that Eden would act as Deputy Prime Minister.

18 This also occurred in December 1952, September 1953 and September/October 1954. *Private Papers*, and diary 6.8.54, Moran (*87*) p.619. *The Economist* 23.10.54, p.287 and Macmillan (*36*) pp.523, 525 and 541.

19 Interview I with Ian Robertson.

20 Macmillan (*36*) pp.523 and 525.

21 Churchill had initially appointed Eden Leader of the House in October 1951 but he felt the job in addition to the Foreign Office would be too much for him. See Chapter 3 Part 1. Eden had combined the foreign secretaryship with leadership of the House, 1942–5, but with some difficulty. See, for example, Dilks, ed. (*13a*) p.605, or Eden's war memoirs, *The Reckoning*, p.254.

22 Churchill told Colville that Eden was 'Foreign Officissimus'. Interview with Sir John Colville. Indeed Eden's only ministerial experience outside the Foreign Office was as Secretary for Dominions, 1939–40, and Secretary for War, 1940. Lord Ismay, now Secretary-General of NATO, similarly felt that Eden should give up the Foreign Office and become Lord President. Diary 26.5.53. Sulzberger (*51a*) p.736.

23 Diary 13.10.53, Sulzberger (*51a*) p.753.

24 Interview with Sir Anthony Nutting.

25 *Private Papers.*

26 *The Economist* 21.6.52, p.794.

27 *The Times* commented that the change was unlikely to occur, but that it was believed Eden would pay more attention to home affairs. *The Times* 23.6.52.

28 See Chapter 10 Part 1.

29 *Private Papers* and diary 2.9.53, Moran (*87*) p.493.

30 *Private Papers*. In a passage that probably reveals Moran's credulity, he appears to have taken Eden at his word when the latter told him: 'I wanted to give up the F.O. and take some office in the Cabinet which would give me experience of the home front, but [Churchill] . . . was so much against my leaving the F.O. that I gave in.' Diary 2.12.53. Moran (*87*) pp.529–30. But it may be that, with the big swings of attitude that Eden did undoubtedly feel during 1951–5 about his job, he did indeed mean at the time what he told Moran.

31 *The Times* 18.10.54 noted in a leader that plans for Eden to leave the Foreign Office and devote himself to domestic affairs had been 'vigorously canvassed'. It praised Churchill for not acting on the proposal which it never regarded as sensible.

32 Macmillan (*36*) p.545.

33 Interview with Sir Fife Clark.

34 Stuart (*51*) p.178. But Stuart also felt there was no question but that Eden should succeed Churchill.

35 Woolton's note of a conversation with Sir Archibald James on 6.9.46 (Unionist M.P., 1931–45) gives an exaggerated picture of the extent of doubts about the suitability of Eden for Prime Minister, but it still contains some truth. James told Woolton about the very widespread feeling in the Party against Eden but greatly overstates the truth when he says Eden was held in political contempt (although not personal contempt) by most of the people on the Opposition Front Bench (i.e. the Conservative shadow Cabinet). *Woolton Papers*, Box 21, Leaf 42.

36 Eden's stock was at its lowest in February and March 1952. See for example diary 21.2.52. *Dalton Papers*. Dalton wrote 'Bob [Boothby] tells John [Strachey] that Eden's stock is falling very fast. If Winston went, Butler would be P.M. and Macmillan Foreign Office.' This is gossip, but reflects the political position.

37 *The Times* 7.10.54 noted that these achievements put beyond all doubt that he would be the successor to Churchill.

38 Boothby's disappointment went very deep, and coloured his whole attitude to the work of the 1951–5 Government. See Boothby (*7*) pp.83–5 and Boothby (*8*) pp.216–27.

39 The group was led by Charles Waterhouse, and the twenty-seven Conservatives who voted against the Government's policy on withdrawal of the base on 29.7.54 contained senior men such as Ralph Assheton and Sir Robert Grimston. Eden in fact rode the storm very successfully. (It is ironic that when Eden became Prime Minister, due to his desire to prove himself a strong man, he himself decided to adopt many of the attitudes of the Suez Group.) But in 1953–4 he was rather contemptuous of the Suez Group and saw many of their leading men as being men of Munich. Interview with Sir Anthony Nutting. For more on the withdrawal from the Suez base, see Chapter 10 Part 4.

40 Interview with Julian Amery.

41 Even Lyttelton began to feel from about 1953 that Churchill should retire. Other ardent Churchill supporters were to be found amongst the younger backbenchers. *Private Information*. Lyttelton personally liked Eden, but had doubts about his ability to be Prime Minister.

42 Dalton wrote in his diary on 1.4.55 about a conversation with Boothby. 'B. thinks the others will be watching Eden and that he may well be pole-axed in 18 months time.' *Dalton Papers*. (It took 21 months.)

43 Something of Churchill's doubts can be seen in Moran's diary 21.5.54, (pp.578–9), 10.12.54 (p.655) and 26.11.56 (p.743), Moran (*87*).

44 This factor was mentioned in many interviews. A clear expression of it can be seen in September 1951 before Churchill even became Prime Minister again. 'When the struggle for power is at an end and his political life is over, Winston will feel that there is no purpose in his existence. I dread what may happen then . . .' Moran (*87*) p.363.

45 The expression Coleridge gave for Iago's varied justifications for his action in Othello.

46 During the period of Opposition a number of senior men in the Party who were disturbed by the quality of Churchill's peacetime leadership had the meeting at Crookshank's house in Pont Street, described in the text above by James Stuart. There were about eight of them, and they included, besides Crookshank, probably

also Salisbury. Butler. Woolton and Stanley. but definitely not Eden. The unanimous view of those meeting was that Churchill be informed that it was probably in the best interests of the party if he retired. This occurred in 1947. Stuart as Chief Whip was delegated to inform Churchill of his colleagues' views. Churchill did not take it well and showed no inclination to yield to their wishes. Stuart wryly wrote later: '. . . None of the others present at our private meeting repeated to him the views which they had so kindly invited me to convey.' Stuart (51) pp.145–7 and interview·with Lord Stuart, Day Before Yesterday (D.B.Y.). Crookshank does not appear to have kept a diary between October 1947 and October 1951, so it was not possible to ascertain the precise date.

47 Diary 16.6.52, *Crookshank Papers.*
48 See Gallup political barometers in Appendix I.
49 Diary 23.6.52, *Crookshank Papers.*
50 Churchill never had the same close relationship with Buchan-Hepburn when Chief Whip as he had with either Margesson (Chief Whip, 1931–40) or Stuart (1941–8), though this did not damage the efficiency of their working relationship. Earlier in Buchan-Hepburn's career, however, and particularly before the war, he had been close to Churchill.
51 Diary 30.9.52, Moran (87) p.420.
52 *Private Papers.*
53 *Private Papers.*
54 Diary 23.1.53, *Crookshank Papers.*
55 *Private Papers.*
56 *Private Papers.*
57 He learnt about this in a letter from Baruch on 2.8.53, *Baruch Papers.*
58 See Chapter 10 Part 3. It is of interest that although Churchill had said in his Plymouth speech during the 1951 Election campaign that his desire to press for world peace was the 'last prize' he sought to win in politics, it was not until after the death of Stalin that he began to turn his attention seriously to this problem.
59 Colville wrote to Churchill's closest friends, Lord Alexander, Beaverbrook, Bracken, Camrose and Cherwell two days after the stroke, and also to Sir Alan Lascelles. (See letter, Colville to Cherwell, 25.6.53, *Cherwell Papers*, Pers. 12, Pt. VI) and he also told Butler and Salisbury (Col-

ville in Wheeler-Bennett, ed. (105) p. 124. Crookshank guessed that at the Cabinet which Churchill bravely took on 24th June that Churchill had had a small stroke and this was confirmed to him by a phone call from Butler on Saturday, 27th June (diary *Crookshank Papers*, Mallaby (37) pp.47–8 and Macmillan (36) p.516). Ministers as a whole did not hear about it until some time later. News of his incapacity was gradually fed to the press in a modified form. An item in *The Times* 26.6.53 said Churchill had left Number Ten for Chartwell the previous morning to concentrate on work for the forthcoming Bermuda Conference (see Chapter 10 Part 3). A statement announcing the cancellation of the Conference was issued from Number Ten on 27th June, and a medical report was attached to the announcement saying the Prime Minister was in need of a complete rest, and was signed by Sir Russell Brain and Lord Moran. *The Times* 29.6.53. The wording of the communiqué in such mild terms was the result of Butler's and Salisbury's intervention: they removed, *inter alia*, the phrase 'circulatory disturbance'. Moran wrote on 30.7.53 to Beaverbrook: 'When Brain and I drew up the bulletin originally we felt that something must be said to explain his sudden retirement – people like Winston do not suddenly rest on doctor's orders for a month at a critical time without some good reason. The reason I wanted them to give was that he had had a disturbance of the circulation leading to attacks of giddiness. That is a much less damaging admission than to say he had a stroke . . . Anyway it is much too early to say whether what Butler and Salisbury concocted will turn out to be wise or not.' *Beaverbrook Papers*, Box C250. See also Grigg (222) p.15 and diary 26.6.53 and 23.7.53. Moran (87) pp.434 and 465–6. The first public admission of his stroke did not come until two years later. On the second day of the March 1955 defence debate, and the day after his major speech on defence. Churchill was stung into an impromptu speech after a suggestion by Bevan that the failure of Churchill's hopes for a summit meeting was due to U.S. opposition to the plan. Churchill told the House that during Eden's absence from the Foreign Office he had been preparing to go to see Eisenhower preparatory to a three-power meeting: 'However I was struck down by a very sudden illness which paralysed me completely, physically.' *House of Commons* 2.3.55, Vol. 537, Col. 2116. See also Chapter 2 Part 3.

60 See Chapter 3 Part 2.

61 Diary 26.6.53 and 30.5.53, Moran (*87*) pp.437 and 438. Soames (*98*) p.436.

62 On 25th July Churchill told Moran: 'October 10 is the annual Party meeting at Margate and I must make a speech then or get out.' p.468. On 5th August he said: '. . . everything depends on whether I can face October 10th,' p.473. Also diary for 24.8.53. Moran (*87*) p.484. Maxwell Fyfe narrates how 'within a month' of Churchill's stroke, he spent three hours with him discussing Home Office business. Kilmuir (*31*) p.219.

63 Eden was informed of the news of Churchill's stroke by a letter Colville wrote to Clarissa Eden in Boston a few days after the event. Colville asked her to tell her husband as soon as he was well enough. *Private Diary.*

64 *Private Papers.* Eden wrote to Monckton on 3.8.53, that Chequers was pleasant but in no way conclusive, and that Salisbury was aware of the problems and was being as helpful as any man could be expected to be in a situation they all found extremely embarrassing. *Monckton Papers,* Box 3.

65 See Chapter 10 Part 3.

66 On 16th August he told Moran: 'I can do something with the Russians which no one else can do. That is the only reason why I am clinging to office.' Moran (*87*) pp.476–7. He hung on to this theme. On 6th October he told Australian Foreign Secretary, Casey, that the reason he was remaining in office was that he had a unique contribution to make to international politics. Diary 6.10.53, Millar, ed. (*39a*) p.110.

67 Churchill was encouraged by his success at handling his first Cabinet on 18th August. After it Brook told Moran that 'this isn't the moment to make decisions about retiring': Moran (*87*) p.481. Crookshank noted drily that the Cabinet was quite unnecessary, and was merely for Churchill to show he was well enough. Diary 18.8.53, *Crookshank Papers.*

68 When Macmillan saw him on 1st September, Churchill was talking about going on the Queen's return in May, and hinted he

might remain until autumn 1954 or spring 1955 if his health was up to it. Diary 1.9.53, Macmillan (*36*) p.525. Macmillan almost certainly would have communicated this news to his colleagues.

69 Some of the uncertainty of the hour can be gleaned from a letter from Monckton to Watkinson dated 19.8.53; 'I had my talk on Friday [15th August] after dinner with my old master. I think that nothing is decided yet and all too much is fluid. The captain is delaying a decision upon both the principal points, the future of the captaincy and the date of the Test Match until the middle of next month. It is well recognised that thereafter some of the decisions can only wait for a matter of days because of the fixture in early October. In substance all the other things have to wait until then, though there is no doubt that the selectors intend to make considerable changes in the team.' *Monckton Papers,* Box 3.

70 Diary 22.9.53, *Crookshank Papers.* Diary 1.10.53, and 14.4.54, *Woolton Papers.*

71 Diary 21.7.53, Moran (*87*) p.464.

72 Diary 25.8.53, Moran (*87*) p.486.

73 Churchill had been staying at Beaverbrook's villa at Cap d'Ail since 17th September. He had still not decided what to do about his future. He clearly wanted to continue if only he could be sure of his health holding up. On 21.9.53, he wrote to his wife: 'I still ponder on the future and don't want to decide unless I am convinced . . .' Quoted on p.438 of Soames (*98*). Eden had also been holidaying in the Mediterranean since 8th August, also returning to London on 30th September, and arriving at Heathrow two and a half hours after Churchill. *The Times* 1.10.53. He had left London in a relieved state of mind having been informed by Buchan-Hepburn, Lyttelton and Macmillan that he was the undisputed successor to Churchill, and they were convinced that he would retire in October. *Private Papers.*

74 *Private Papers.* Buchan-Hepburn by September felt unequivocally that Churchill should go. Diary 8.9.53, Moran (*87*) p.495. Also Crookshank in his diary on 7.10.53, wrote that Buchan-Hepburn called in for two hours after dinner to 'blow up' about Churchill. *Crookshank Papers.*

75 *Official Report of the 73rd. Conservative Annual Conference* p.116. Hugh Massingham noted in the *Observer* on 11.10.53 that

the Conference's chief importance was to settle the question of the succession.

76 Churchill was also much cheered by his speech in the debate on the address on 3rd November, his first full speech in the House since the 11th May speech.

77 Interviews with Lord Redmayne and Sir Richard Thompson. Both Redmayne and Thompson were junior Whips serving under Buchan-Hepburn. Buchan-Hepburn in the following year felt that the row over teachers' superannuation (see Chapter 7 Part 4) went on far longer than was necessary because of Churchill's indecisiveness on the issue.

78 There were meetings, as on 29.12.53, when Butler and Macmillan invited Eden to join them secretly at Number Eleven where they revealed their anxiety about the state of the Government, the unwillingness of the Prime-Minister to look ahead, and the slowness of Cabinets. It was arranged that Macmillan would sound out Churchill's views at dinner that night about his retirement. At the meal, Churchill made it clear that he would stick to his intention of going before the next General Election, but for the rest gave Macmillan the impression he was in no immediate hurry to give up. Diary 29.12.53, Macmillan (*36*) pp.528–9 and *Private Papers*. But at this period these 'secret meetings' were rare.

79 Colville in Wheeler-Bennett, ed. (*105*) p.125. There were brief periods up until May 1954 when he doubted his ability to be able to stay on, but these were the exception. On his return to London after the Bermuda Conference in December 1963, for example, his will to continue until May temporarily left him, but his spirits soon recovered. Bracken spent the day with him on 30th December and wrote that day to Beaverbrook to say he would be giving up before June. *Beaverbrook Papers*, Box C57. Press criticism, in particular the *Daily Mirror* in January 1954, and an article and cartoon in *Punch* on 3.2.54 wounded him, and caused him in unsurer moments to question his grounds for continuing in office. See Soames (*98*) p.448. For details of the press campaign to get Churchill to retire, especially by the Mirror Group, see Bardens (*58*) pp.336–59.

80 See Chapter 10 Part 3.

81 At certain times he would put forward the need to remain until after the Egyptian troubles had settled down, but once more this was mere 'motive hunting'.

82 Diary 6.4.54, *Woolton Papers*.

83 Butler (*10*) p.173.

84 See, for example, Macmillan (*36*) p.529. Brook told Moran that he felt there would be a row if Churchill didn't retire in July, and that there was a feeling that younger men were required who would be full of energy and drive. Diary 1 4.54, Moran (*87*) p.560.

85 So Brook told Moran. Diary 1.4.54, Moran (*87*) p.560.

86 In particular Macmillan was anxious to see through his Housing Repairs and Rents Bill before the disturbance which would inevitably be caused when Churchill retired. Macmillan (*36*) pp.523 and 525; diary 4.3.54, Moran (*87*) pp.556–7. Macmillan was particularly anxious to avoid the possibility of a dissolution soon after the Bill when its increase in rents became operative, recalling the 1929 Election when rating valuations had risen a week or two before the poll. At the Cabinet meeting on 3.10.53 (the first since early April with both Churchill and Eden in attendance), Macmillan had made it clear that if he went ahead with his plans for tackling substandard dwellings, they should not risk a dissolution for at least eighteen months. Macmillan (*36*) p.526.

87 Churchill had been waiting to make this speech for some weeks because he was deeply disturbed by the effect of the bomb on the general public and by the fact that if the U.S. used it first, Russia might begin by attacking the U.K. because of the U.S. bases on its land. He had led his colleagues to believe that he was not out to gain political capital from the speech, but after Attlee's conciliatory and magnanimous speech, Churchill, to the surprise of almost the entire House, proceeded to attack both Morrison and Attlee. There were many interruptions to his speech and nearly all the press were critical. Lord Plowden later commented that he had not expected to read in an early draft of this book that Churchill's colleagues were surprised by the speech, as those who had worked on the speech with Churchill were fully aware that it would provoke uproar in the House. Salisbury later said to Plowden that in his heyday Churchill would have dominated

the House but that it was beyond him at his present age. Correspondence with Lord Plowden. See also diary 5.4.54. Moran (*87*) pp.562–6.

88 Woolton had been watching from the Gallery. Diary 6.4.54, *Woolton Papers*.

89 *House of Commons* Vol. 526, Col. 60. Boothby walked out of the chamber in disgust at the speech. Boothby in turn was attacked for this act of disloyalty and 'theatrical gesture'. See diary 14.4.54 Moran (*87*) p.570 and letter, Boothby to Beaverbrook, 7.4.54, *Beaverbrook Papers*, Box C47.

90 See Appendix 1.

91 Diary 6.4.54, *Woolton Papers*.

92 Diary 6.4.54, *Woolton Papers*.

93 Diary 14.4.54, *Woolton Papers*. See Chapter 2 Part 4.

94 Mentmore in fact was Lord Rosebery's country home. It is curious why Churchill should have made this slip – unless, of course, it was misreported by Woolton.

95 14.4.54, *Woolton Papers*.

96 He, however, told Colville in private in March that he was thinking of going in September. Colville (*12*) p.259.

97 Regius Professor of Greek, Oxford University, 1908–36.

98 *Murray Papers*, Box 6.

99 Macmillan (*36*) p.530.

100 Macmillan (*36*) p.533, diary 5.6.54.

101 Diary 8.4.54, Moran (*87*) p.568. Malenkov was Chairman of the Council of Ministers of the Soviet Union, 1953–5.

102 The day after the meeting to discuss Election dates, he told Moran he had managed a three-hour Cabinet very well and did not see why he should go. Diary 14.4.54, Moran (*87*) p.571.

103 See Chapter 10 Part 3.

104 So he told Macmillan at dinner on 16th June. Diary 16.6.54, *Crookshank Papers*. He told Moran, 'I shall certainly not retire when any day anything might happen.' Diary 15.6.54, Moran (*87*) p.584. He advanced other reasons for his action, such as Eden's health (p.584) and his wish not to inconvenience his Ministers who had Bills in the House (p.582), diary 4.6.54.

105 Diary 16.6.54, Macmillan (*36*) p.531. Macmillan acted quite courageously and wrote to Churchill on 18.6.54 telling him: '. . . In my view, if a new Administration is to be formed this year, it would be a great advantage for Ministers to be installed in

their new offices before and not after the summer holidays.'

106 Diary 24.8.54 [*sic*], Macmillan (*36*) p.540.

107 Macmillan (*36*) p.533.

108 Diary 4.7.54, Moran (*87*) p.603. Sir John Colville (interview) said he gave the date of 12th September.

109 See Chapter 10 Part 3.

110 See Chapter 2 Part 1.

111 The story of Macmillan's visit is narrated in Soames (*98*) p.449 and Colville (*12*) pp.253–5. Soames gives the date as mid-July. Macmillan does not refer to the incident specifically in his memoirs; indeed, he is inclined to deny it took place. But he does narrate how on 16th July, 'Churchill sent for me and we had a long talk about the situation,' and how he took quite well 'some pretty tough things which I said'. Macmillan (*36*) p.537.

112 Interview with Lord Chandos, D.B.Y.

113 Brook told Moran on 30th July: 'It's really this business of meeting the Russians that keeps him from going. Anthony knows this. He ought to go before Parliament meets. There might be real trouble if he hangs on beyond that. He is trying Anthony and Rab very high.' Diary 30.7.54, Moran (*87*) p.616.

114 On 6th August he told Moran: 'I don't know what to do. For half of the day I am determined to stay and see the business through, and then for the other half my resignation seems inevitable.' Diary 6.8.54, Moran (*87*) p.619.

115 Though Churchill continued to hope for a meeting with the Russians until Malenkov's fall in February 1955, by August 1954 the chances of such a meeting appeared increasingly unlikely. See Chapter 10 Part 3.

116 See Macmillan (*36*) pp.539–40. Butler (*10*) p.174.

117 Woolton had said that if there was a General Election in spring 1955, he advised Churchill to remain as Prime Minister until then. His advice thus related to only one eventuality and was not a blanket endorsement of Churchill's continuation under any circumstances. Churchill either misunderstood or misheard Woolton, unintentionally. See Woolton, note of conversation 28.9.54, and Woolton to Churchill, 28.9.54, *Woolton Papers*, Box 22.

118 Diary 18.8.54, Moran (*87*) p.624.

119 Macmillan (*36*) pp.539–41.

120 Butler (*10*) pp.173–4.

121 The text can be found in Butler (*10*) p.174.

122 Butler (*10*) pp.174–5. Macmillan (*36*) p.541.

123 Diary 28.8.54. Moran (*87*) p.625.

124 Soames (*98*) p.450. After the Cabinet on 27th August, which had pleased Churchill, he told Moran, in an over-confident mood: 'All the members of the Cabinet have accepted my staying on. There won't be any trouble, I think.' Diary 29.8.54. Moran (*87*) p.626.

125 Letter 29.8.54, *Baruch Papers*. On the same day Mary Soames wrote to her mother: 'I'm afraid Papa's decision to stay must in some ways be a blow to you.' Soames (*98*) p.450.

126 Speculation was also damped by a Committee member of Woodford Conservative Association (Churchill's constituency) telling the press on 8th September that despite rumours to the contrary he had it on good authority that Churchill intended to remain as Prime Minister for the foreseeable future. *The Times* 9.9.54.

127 Diary 8.9.54, *Crookshank Papers*. None of them thought seriously of resigning, due to the probable result, which would be splitting the Party. See Macmillan (*36*) p.543.

128 See Chapter 3 Part 1.

129 Macmillan (*36*) pp.544–5.

130 Macmillan (*36*) p.542.

131 *The Times* 11.10.54. Colville recorded in his diary, 'He had a great personal success at Blackpool.' *Private Papers*.

132 Diary 14.10.54. Moran (*87*) p.636.

133 The *Observer* on 24.10.54 discussed Cabinet dismay at the implications of the reshuffle.

134 Churchill talked of continuing until early autumn 1955. Macmillan urged him to retire in early 1955. Macmillan (*36*) p.549.

135 See Broad (*63*) p.615.

136 See Chapter 2 Part 3.

137 *Woolton Papers*, Box 28, Leaves 148–50.

138 See Chapter 2 Part 4.

139 Diary 22.12.54, *Woolton Papers*.

140 Diary 22.12.54, *Woolton Papers*.

141 Diaries for 22.12.54 from *Crookshank* and *Woolton Papers*.

142 Diary 22.12.54, *Crookshank Papers*.

143 Diary 28.12.54, *Crookshank Papers*.

144 Diary 17.1.55, *Crookshank Papers*.

145 Letter, Bracken to Beaverbrook, 17.1.55, *Beaverbrook Papers*, Box C58.

146 Moran asserts (pp.659 and 660) that Macmillan's decision to tell Churchill in early January that he should retire came as a severe shock to Churchill who had come to look on Macmillan as 'Captain of the Praetorian Guard', and on pp.663 and 828 Moran suggests Macmillan's intervention was decisive. Moran (*87*). Macmillan for his part says (Macmillan (*36*) p.552) that he had been expressing this opinion to Churchill, both orally and in writing, over a considerable period, and he goes out of his way in Volume III of his memoirs to describe the number of occasions he suggested to Churchill that he should retire. It is probable that both Moran and Macmillan exaggerated. Macmillan's opinions on this matter counted only little with Churchill, and Macmillan was probably not quite as articulate in his expression to Churchill of the opinion that he should retire (sooner rather than later) than he afterwards remembered. In an interesting comment in his diary on the 22nd December meeting, Woolton wrote that Macmillan said something, the purport of which was unclear – 'He's supposed to be giving Eden strong support, but it doesn't strike me he's going to do anything to offend Churchill.' *Woolton Papers*.

147 See Chapter 10 Part 3. Churchill must also have had doubts about his stamina and relish for leading the Party into another Election.

148 Diary 3.2.55 and 16.2.55. Moran (*87*) pp.663 and 664. Bracken wrote to Beaverbrook on 2.2.55 'I . . . give you worse news, which is that our friend has decided to advance the date . . .' *Beaverbrook Papers*, Box C58.

149 Diary 26.2.55. Macmillan (*36*) p.555. See also Soames (*98*) p.451.

150 The available evidence conflicts slightly on this point. Eden writes that before he left for the Far East at the end of January, he and Churchill had agreed that his return to the U.K. would have to be speeded in view of the spring handover. Eden (*14*) p.269. Moran's diary on 21.2.55 tells of Churchill saying he had given Eden a definite date. Moran (*87*) p.664. Butler told Crookshank and Buchan-Hepburn on 8th February of Churchill's definite decision to go before Easter (in 1955, Easter Sunday was on 10th April) (diary, *Crookshank Papers*), and on 26th February, Churchill told Macmillan he had in mind 5th April as the date he would go (diary 26.2.55, Macmillan (*36*)

p.555). Yet when Crookshank and Macmillan had dinner at Woolton's home on 7th March they were still not at all sure of the date of Churchill's retirement. Diary 7.3.55. *Crookshank Papers*; letter. Woolton to Eden. 8.3.55. *Woolton Papers*. Box 3. Eden told Woolton on 11th March that Churchill told him he would definitely go on 7th April [*sic*] and that if he changed his mind he. along with Salisbury and Butler. would resign (diary 11.3.55. *Woolton Papers*). But at the Cabinet on 14th March. 'most' did not know of Churchill's definite pledge to Eden to go at the beginning of April. Diary 14.3.55. *Woolton Papers*.

151 Diary 25.6.54. Sulzberger (*51a*) p.855.

152 Macmillan (*36*) pp.554–5.

153 See diary 3.2.55 (p.663). 21.2.55 (p.664). 3.3.55 (p.671). 23.3.55 (p.674) Moran (*87*). The argument that Churchill continued for so long because he feared Eden would not be up to the job. an argument repeated in interview by several former close advisers to Churchill and also in such diverse places as Margach (*127*) pp.105–6. is not a wholly convincing one. Churchill certainly repeated this anxiety to those close to him. but it was only a justification. not a reason, for his delayed departure.

154 Brook narrated the whole story to Moran that July. Diary 10.7.55. Moran (*87*) p.708. Maxwell Fyfe makes a rather lazy allusion to the dominance in Churchill's mind of the hope for high-level meetings with the Soviets. Americans and French: 'Even in the last weeks one could see the effect of this in his mind and the reluctance which it created in that great spirit to surrender the reins.' Kilmuir (*31*) p.240.

155 Chancellor. Federal Republic of Germany. 1949–63.

156 Secretary of State. United States. 1953–9.

157 Diary 14.3.55. *Crookshank Papers*.

158 Diary 14.3.55. *Woolton Papers*.

159 U.S. Ambassador at the Court of St. James. 1953–7.

160 The evidence that such an event happened is based on two pieces of information. Brook saying that: '. . . the Party knew all about the date [of the General Election] and Anthony could not have given way even if he had wanted to. So Ike was told privately that the Conservative Party had a General Election in view.' Diary 10.7.55. Moran (*87*) p.709. The second indication is

a note of a telephone call from Eisenhower to Dulles on 15.3.55. Eisenhower who had seen Aldrich's reply to Dulles on the proposed meeting said that a suggestion of a June date should be made instantly, and that they 'can't let that man act indecisively again'. *Eisenhower Papers*. D.D.E. Diary Series. Box 3.

161 Diary 15.3.55. *Woolton Papers*.

162 Diary 23.3.55 and 30.3.55. *Woolton Papers*.

163 Front page stories in the *Manchester Guardian* on the topic of Churchill's future plans in fact appeared on 28.3.55, 31.3.55, 4.4.55 and 5.4.55. See also Chapter 2 Part 3.

164 The *Manchester Guardian* 5.4.55.

165 Diary 5.4.55. *Woolton Papers*.

166 Lord Carr of Hadley (interview) said it was only after Churchill's return to politics in the autumn of 1953 that Eden began to become seriously upset by the delays. Those close to Eden were not so long-suffering. and there was a certain amount of canvassing of support amongst the 1922 Committee of those sympathetic to the view that Churchill should go. This action though was concentrated in the last eighteen months. Randolph Churchill talked of Eden's friends being 'loud-mouthed' in calling for Churchill's resignation. Churchill (*66*) p.192. They were never as noisy as that.

167 There is much truth in Eden's statement that: 'No two men have ever changed guard more smoothly.' Eden (*14*) p.265. And also much in Maxwell Fyfe's: 'His closing months as Prime Minister [were] utterly free from the wretched trivia of personal and political animosities which have been the lot of so many of his predecessors and which was to befall his successor.' Kilmuir (*31*) pp.237–8.

168 Dalton said to Butler that he expected they had to 'push' to persuade Churchill to retire. Butler replied: 'Yes we had . . . You see at the end he couldn't do his business in Cabinet. He spent all his time composing answers to P.Q.s [Parliamentary Questions].' Diary 4.4.55 to 7.4.55. *Dalton Papers*.

CHAPTER 2 PART 3 pp.54–69

1 For details see Chapter 2 Part 4.

2 On 20.3.52. Woolton reported to Churchill

that from all sources it was quite clear that the Party in Parliament and in the country wanted a clear statement of Government policy. *Woolton Papers*, Box 25.

3 There was some feeling in the first months that Churchill's mind was still set on the war and could not adapt to the conditions of 1951. Not only his penchant for old faces in the Cabinet, but also his decision announced in the debate on the Address (*House of Commons* 6.11.51) to hold a secret session for the debate on defence was regarded as regressive. He announced in the House of Commons 21.11.51 that the secret session would not after all take place.

4 *Private Papers* reveal Eden's anxiety here.

5 Churchill announced in the House of Commons 6.11.51 that only minor Bills would be placed before the House by Christmas, and that Parliament would be adjourned from early December to early February to allow Ministers time to study the economic position and to occupy themselves with administration. The announcement was only one of two measures in the 1951 King's Speech to which the Opposition seriously objected in the debate on the Address. (The other was the annulment of the Iron and Steel Act.)

6 Woolton wrote to Churchill on 9.5.52 to say that it was too early yet to say whether Labour gains were due to Conservative apathy, but the likelihood was that a lot of supporters refrained from voting because of displeasure at the Government's performance. *Woolton Papers*, Box 22.

7 The increases in London fares without warning in March 1952 were extremely unpopular, but the Government's decision in April to suspend increases in rail fares outside London was regarded as precipitate and currying favour. A leader in *The Times* 17.4.52 criticised the Government for opportunism.

8 In April 1952, 46 Conservative backbenchers signed an Early Day motion criticising the Government for its delay in setting about denationalisation. Butt (*122*) p.206, and Goodhart (*123*) pp.160–1. See also diary 19.4.52, Moran (*87*) p.412. For evidence of the dilemma the Government was in during early 1952 about whether or not to hold back its programme until the economic position improved, see Kilmuir (*31*) pp.196–7. After all their criticism in

Opposition, the fact that the Conservatives were keeping on many of Labour's innovations meant that the two denationalisations were regarded as having particular political importance. See Kent (*30a*) p.233.

9 See diary 22.5.52, Nicolson (*43*) p.224.

10 David Butler (*121*) p.12. For the position in the polls during 1951–5, see Appendix 1.

11 *The Times* 5.4.52.

12 The *Observer* 1.6.52.

13 The *Observer* 22.6.52. See Part 2 above.

14 The *Sunday Times* 1.6.52.

15 'A Student of Politics' in the *Sunday Times* 29.6.52.

16 A leader in *The Times* 24.6.52 had put the blame for its misfortunes squarely on the shoulders of the Government rather than on poor publicity. The article named three areas where the Government had fared badly from April to June to show that the mistakes it made were its own. Thus the Government had been stampeded by its backbenchers into producing its denationalisation proposals which were premature and ill conceived: its plan in the White Paper on Broadcasting of appointing governors to the B.B.C. was poorly considered and had to be dropped: lastly its sudden and dramatic interference in the procedure for determining fare increases was precipitate and unwise.

17 The *Observer* 3.8.52.

18 Kilmuir (*31*) p.203. This mood of optimism could not have been predicted during the summer. The largest group of prospective motions on any one topic was on the presentation of Government policy, where all the motions received from the constituencies were critical of the Government. *The Times* 25.9.52. But at the actual Conference a motion critical of the Government's presentation was amended by Gilbert Longden welcoming the action taken by the P.M. to improve Government publicity. Delegates were also pleased with a publication prepared by the Research Department 'We Shall Win Through', which was a general statement of the position the Government found in 1951 and the progress that had been made.

19 A leading article in *The Times* 31.10.52 noted that there had been a revival of popular confidence in the Government over the preceding three months, displayed for example in the Cleveland by-election on 23rd October where there was a swing of

0.7 per cent in the Government's favour (the largest swing to the Conservatives during 1952). Two factors in particular were responsible: the protracted divisions within the Labour Party, and the lack of any of the harsh or extreme right-wing measures which Labour had predicted during the 1951 General Election campaign that the Conservatives would enact.

20 'A Student of Politics', *Sunday Times* 2.11.52.

21 A leader in *The Times* 5.12.52 said: 'So far this has been the most unhappy Parliament session since the end of the war.'

22 Attlee in the debate on the censure motion. *House of Commons* 4.12.52.

23 Woolton wrote to Churchill on 2.4.53 to say that the Conservative candidate was an official in the Miners' Union and that they and the Potters' Union regarded him as a traitor, which Woolton reflected was an interesting comment on efforts to get trade union candidates. *Woolton Papers*, Box 22.

24 What made this by-election all the more remarkable was the last-minute intervention of a Liberal candidate. There was much political excitement and press coverage during the run-up to polling day. For a general commentary on this and other by-elections during 1951–5, see Scammon (*234*) p.323.

25 *The Times* 30.9.53. At the by-election at Broxtowe, there was a 1.4 per cent swing to Labour.

26 The *Observer* 9.8.53.

27 A leader in the *Sunday Times* 11.10.53.

28 An annual policy statement had been made for each of the past four years. The aborted 1953 statement was to have been called 'Onward in Freedom'. See Ramsden's book on the Conservative Research Department.

29 See, for example, the leader in *The Times* 2.10.53. Macmillan also wrote: '. . . We felt that in home affairs we were drifting without the formulation of any fixed plan – without a new theme or a new faith. We had almost completed the job of restoration and recovery. We now seemed to need a new programme.' Macmillan (*36*) p.529.

30 The Government, after great pressure from its own Party in and out of the House, overturned the recommendation of an all-Party Select Committee of the House of Commons to increase salary from £1,000 to £1,500 p.a., substituting instead the un-

satisfactory arrangement of a Sessional Allowance. M.P.s' pay had been increased to £600 in 1937 and £1,000 in 1946. (Churchill in *House of Commons* 8.7.54.)

31 Massingham in the *Observer* 6.6.54.

32 See, in particular, Macmillan (*36*) p.541. Eden in a letter to Lyttelton of 10.8.54 complained that the Cabinet hardly took any tough decisions any more. *Chandos Papers*, Box 4/11. For the Party's doubts see diary 10.10.54, Moran (*87*) p.635. The following year, on 11.3.55, Woolton wrote in his diary that he was fed up belonging to a Government which never took any decision on the home front for fear of a bad effect on the General Election. *Woolton Papers*.

33 See Ramsden's book on the Research Department, Ramsden, in Butler, ed. (*115*) pp.417–27, Butler (*10*) pp.126–53 and Egremont (*15*) pp.137–42.

34 Clarke was sole Director, 1945–8, and joint Director after the merger into the enlarged Research Department, 1948–51. He was *de facto* senior Director, the others being Henry Hopkinson, responsible for the Parliamentary Secretariat, and Percy Cohen, responsible for the library and publications.

35 As has been shown: Ramsden, in Butler, ed. (*115*) p.417.

36 Butler talking in 1954, compared the work done in the period of Opposition to Disraeli's achievement. The work that had been done since 1945 'to prepare the mind of the country and to educate our Party' led directly to the Conservatives being 'returned to power in 1951'. Quoted in S. Beer (*112a*) p.309.

37 Thus *The Times* on 15.5.53, noted that Butler in his first two Budgets paid attention to the principles of the Charters that the standard of life should not fall below a minimum and at the same time encouragement and opportunity should be given to those wishing to rise above it.

38 The document was actually drafted by a Committee (Butler Chairman) of senior M.P.s, with the assistance of the Research Department.

39 Butler (*10*) pp.145–7, saw the 'Industrial Charter' as 'serving three purposes: an assurance that modern Conservatism would maintain strong central guidance over the operation of the economy in the interests of efficiency, full employment and social

security, to provide a philosophical alternative to socialism in stressing the importance of the individual in the mixed economy, and thirdly, a charter to the worker offering him employment assurances, incentives and individual status.' (*The Workers' Charter*.)

40 The 'Industrial Charter' talked of the need for 'a system of free enterprise which . . . reconciles the need for central direction with the encouragement of individual effort'.

41 In *House of Commons* 20.5.54 Thorneycroft tabled a Bill to carry out some of the ideas appearing in the 'Industrial Charter', which were mild enough for Labour not to fight them, but this was dropped after right-wing pressure from certain backbenchers. Roth (*94*) p.113.

42 An interesting speculation is what might have happened if Maxwell Fyfe, a member of the Committee, had been appointed Minister of Labour, as was the initial intention. See Chapter 6 Part 1.

43 See Chapter 4 Parts 3 and 4.

44 Though Percy Cohen remained on until 1959 as joint Director, Fraser succeeded Clarke in 1951 as *de facto* senior Director.

45 Head of Home Affairs Section, 1951–5.

46 There was some uncertainty in senior Party circles about the role of the Research Department now the Party was in power. Woolton wrote to Churchill on 15.11.51 that the Research Department must be kept on, and that he had made a successful effort to find the money to provide for this. *Woolton Papers*, Box 21. In particular there was the question about whether the Research Department should continue to continue to service the Backbench Parliamentary Committees, which in the event they did. See letter, Buchan-Hepburn to Michael Fraser, 9.11.51, *C.R.D. Papers*, Box Govt. Correspondence.

47 Interview with Lord Alport. Alport was Director of the Conservative Political Centre, 1945–50.

48 The *Observer* 5.7.53.

49 They published a booklet, *Change is Our Ally*, in May 1954, edited by Maude and Powell, which stressed the need for consumer choice and for a healthy competitive industry. See Roth (*94*) pp.69–70 and 110–11. One particular issue on which the One Nation Group did make its impact felt was in helping Lennox-Boyd, in conjunc-

tion with the Party's Transport Committee, in the passage of the denationalisation of road haulage Bill. See interview with Lord Carr of Hadley, B.O.A.P.A.H.

50 Chairman, November 1951–November 1955. He subsequently became Minister of Health, 1957–60.

51 This was the view expressed repeatedly in interviews with both officers of these Committees and departmental Ministers themselves.

52 See Chapter 4 Part 5.

53 See Kilmuir (*31*) pp.226–7. Diary 21.5.54 and 4.6.54, Moran (*87*) pp.577–78 and 582. Letter, Woolton to Eden, 3.6.54, *Woolton Papers*, Box 22. See also references in diary throughout May and June 1954 in *Crookshank Papers*, also Goodhart (*123*) pp.168–9, Jackson (*125*) pp.109–10 and Roth (*94*) pp.112–13. Dalton wrote in his diary on 24.6.54: 'The class war is here again.' *Dalton Papers*.

54 The opinion of Massingham. The *Observer* 25.7.54. See Chapter 6 Part 3.

55 See Epilogue 2.

56 The most serious backbench difficulty during 1951–5 arose, as is often the case, over an issue in foreign affairs – dislike of the Government's policy towards the Sudan and Egypt in 1953 and 1954. See Chapter 10 Part 4. An interesting development of the early 1950s occurred in the Whip's Office. It had traditionally been the place for the less bright and imaginative of men, and it thus came as a great surprise when Edward Heath was appointed a junior Whip in November 1951 and Deputy Government Chief Whip in the following year. This marked a major change of policy. See interview with Lord Carr of Hadley, B.O.A.P.A.H.

57 The *Sunday Times* 1.6.52.

58 The *Observer* 22.6.52.

59 Scarborough 1952, Margate 1953, Blackpool 1954.

60 See Chapter 7 Part 2.

61 The *Sunday Times* 11.10.53.

62 *House of Commons* 7.5.52.

63 Letter, Davies to Churchill, 4.2.53, *Woolton Papers*, Box 25.

64 Letter, Attlee to Churchill, 18.2.53, *Woolton Papers*, Box 25. According to Moran (*87*) p.422 (diary 18.2.53) Attlee was in favour of joining in the conference but was prevailed against doing so by his colleagues.

65 The first Viscount, former Chancellor of the Exchequer and Lord Chancellor.

66 Letter, Simon to Monckton, 1.5.53, *Monckton Papers*, Box 3.

67 *House of Lords* 25.1.55.

68 *House of Commons* 8.2.55.

69 *House of Lords* 9.3.55 and 10.3.55.

70 *House of Lords* 9.3.55, Vol. 191, Col. 866, after Jowitt had again declared Labour's unwillingness to talk. See also letter, Woolton to Salisbury, 22.6.55, *Woolton Papers*, Box 24.

71 *Private Information*. A major exception, when the standard of debate in the Lords was of the highest quality, was in the debates on the future of the B.B.C. television monopoly. See Chapter 4 Part 5.

72 As was thought probable, Churchill decided not to legislate for the restoration of the University seats in the first year. *The Times* 7.11.51. He again postponed the decision in November 1952.

73 Letter, Monckton to Butler, 18.2.53, *Monckton Papers*, Box 3.

74 'Time has . . . moved on . . . we do not wish to raise all the controversy which this restoration of plural voting would involve.' *House of Commons* 20.10.53, Vol. 518, Col. 1801.

75 *House of Commons* 7.3.50.

76 See letter, Violet Bonham Carter to Gilbert Murray, 6.1.55, *Murray Papers*, Box 6.

77 Later Lord Francis-Williams. He wrote Attlee's memoirs, *A Prime Minister Remembers*, in co-operation with Attlee.

78 See Williams (*236*) pp.260–7.

79 Williams (*236*) p.265. See also Ogilvy-Webb (*128*) pp.87–8.

80 Woolton, writing to Churchill on 9.4.52, stressed that dissatisfaction in the Party was directed against Government publicity, in particular its bad timing and failure to explain the reasons for extra costs and charges recently imposed. The 1922 Committee had made a point of expressing general approval with the Party's propaganda machine. *Woolton Papers*, Box 21.

81 The Committee was set up as a result of the initiatve of John Wyndham (later Lord Egremont), encouraged by Michael Fraser (later Lord Fraser of Kilmorack). Salisbury was approached to be the first Chairman but refused, and Swinton only agreed after much persuasion by Fraser. It was a good choice because Swinton not only had the ear of the Prime Minister but was respected throughout the Party, and under his chairmanship relations between Central Office and the Party in the country were greatly improved. Interview with Lord Fraser of Kilmorack, Egremont (*15*) pp.146–50, and correspondence, Woolton to Churchill, 13.12.51, *Woolton Papers*, Box 21. Swinton was thought a suitable choice because not only had he headed the pre-General Election Tactical Committee, but during the General Election he headed the Policy Committee which provided up-to-date information. See Beichman, *The Conservative Research Department* p.193.

82 See, for example, letter, Orr-Ewing to Woolton, 23.11.51, *Woolton Papers*, Box 21. Also Gammans' memo, 'Government Publicity', 30.5.52. Dep. *Monckton Papers*, Box 2.

83 Interview with Sir Fife Clarke.

84 Swinton had talks in Whitehall and Fleet Street, and Sir Edward Bridges consulted the officers of the Parliamentary Lobby Journalists.

85 Previously a Lobby Correspondent. Principal Press Officer, Ministry of Health, 1939–49.

86 The title: 'Public Relations Adviser to the Prime Minister' that had existed between 1945–51 was adopted again by Eden in 1955 and conferred on Fife Clark, who remained with him until October of that year, when he took over full-time duty as Director-General of the Central Office of Information. He had been appointed to this post in October 1954 pending Churchill's retirement.

87 Churchill to Woolton, 7.4.52, *Woolton Papers*, Box 22.

88 There was always a clear distinction between the Lobby journalists (Political or Lobby Correspondents) and the sketch writers (Parliamentary Correspondents). The former had the task of commenting on events and personalities, and explaining the background to issues: the latter to report and describe events on the floor of the House. Both had a Chairman, Honorary Secretary and Honorary Treasurer, elected annually by their colleagues, along with a small committee. See Baker (*3a*) p.150.

89 It was not until 1949 that provincial evening newspapers were admitted to the Lobby after pressure from some of the bigger ones such as the *Manchester Evening*

News and the *Bristol Evening Post*. See Seymour-Ure (*128a*) p.207 and Boyd-Barnett, etc. (*119a*) p.129.

90 See Sir Harold Evans (Public Relations Adviser to the P.M., 1957–64) in King and Sloman (*126a*) p.74.

91 Interview with Sir Francis Boyd.

92 *Private Information*.

93 Interview with Sir Geoffrey Cox.

94 Interview with Sir Fife Clark.

95 Interview with Sir Fife Clark. A leader in the *Observer* on 28.3.54 however noted that: 'There is a growing tendency . . . for Government Departments . . . to hedge themselves off behind Public Relations Officers . . . it must be remembered that *their* duty is not to the public but to their employers.'

96 Deedes in King and Sloman (*126a*) p.88. Deedes went on to become Editor of the *Daily Telegraph* in 1974.

97 Christ had been one of Wilfrid Sendall's predecessors as Political Correspondent on the *Daily Telegraph*. See Chapter 2 Part 1.

98 Interview with Wilfrid Sendall.

99 Butler (*120*) p.130.

100 For a table of the national newspapers, their political leanings, ownership and circulation, see Appendix II.

101 After his Woodford School blunder on 23rd November, 1954, for example, *The Times* opened a critical leader with the words 'What on earth made him say it?'

102 The *Daily Telegraph* 18.10.54.

103 Boyd also had a good relationship with Butler, of whom he wrote a short life (*61a*) in addition to another book about British politics during 1945–63 (*112b*).

104 Francis Boyd drew together a collection of Boardman's articles after his death, published by Allen and Unwin in 1960 and entitled, *The Glory of Parliament*.

105 Margach (*127*) p.67.

106 Diary 23.3.55, Moran (*87*) p.74.

107 *Private Information*.

108 Einzig, unusually for Lobby Correspondents, published his memoirs, which contained one of the first descriptions of the operation of the Lobby: Einzig (*16*).

109 Einzig (*16*) p.283. On 21.3.55, the *Star* also gave May 26th as the date of the General Election. See Diary 21.3.55, Moran (*87*) p.673.

110 Churchill in his speech to the 1954 annual Party Conference commented, when discussing the British military commitment to Western European Union, that: 'I think Lord Beaverbrook has been rather unfair in doing me out of my share of the blame.' Official Report p.116.

111 A leader in the *Daily Express* 1.10.54.

112 Marks was later Editor of the *Daily Express*, 1965–71.

113 Even during 1951–5 Marks was writing revealing articles about the meetings of the 1922 Committee. In the *Daily Express* on 30.1.53, for example, he wrote of the attempt by Conservative M.P.s to force a show-down with the Government over the British Transport Commission's plan to increase fares.

114 Einzig (*16*) p.277.

115 On 4.2.53 the *Daily Mail* carried a story by Wakeford about the 'Churchill Wall'. He said that Churchill was understood to have raised the question of the wall at the Cabinet meeting the previous day.

116 Butler (*121*) p.102.

117 Cox became Editor and Chief Executive of Independent Television News, 1956–68. Considering the explosion in television and its political coverage, it appears perhaps strange that more did not follow the path of Cox and Trethowan.

118 Interview with Sir Geoffrey Cox.

119 Trethowan had from 1947 to 1955 been Political Correspondent on the *Yorkshire Post*. From 1953 to 1958 he also worked as Political Commentator on *The Economist*. In 1977 he was appointed Director-General of the B.B.C.

120 Hunter wrote a book, *The Road to Brighton Pier*, published in 1959, about the Labour leadership struggles during 1951–7, which damaged his reputation with the Party. See Evans (*122a*) p.94.

121 Muggeridge was Editor of *Punch*, until 1957.

122 The headline in the *Daily Sketch* on 24.5.55 was 'Prime Minister Bevan'. See Butler (*121*) p.104.

123 Seymour-Ure in Boyd-Barrett, etc. (*119a*) p.121.

124 *Private Information*.

125 Randolph Churchill was then working as a freelance journalist, but his abrasiveness discouraged editors from employing him, and he was never regarded as a serious reporter.

126 *Private Information*.

127 *Private Information*.

128 Hutchinson later wrote a biography of Heath, Hutchinson (*81*). Just before he died he wrote a memoir, *The Last Edwardian at No. 10*, about Harold Macmillan.

129 Later appointed Press Secretary to the Prime Minister, 1964–9 and Chief Information Adviser to the Government, 1969–70. As a Lobby Correspondent he had possessed a close relationship with Liverpool M.P. Harold Wilson, who appointed him to the Number Ten job in 1964.

130 Interview with Sir Trevor Lloyd-Hughes. The *Liverpool Daily Post*, 9.7.53. The sub-headline was 'Big Four talks may be off indefinitely. Entirely new Government will be appointed.'

131 See diary 17.8.53, Moran (*87*) pp.479–80.

132 Grigg (*222*) p.11. Churchill later himself disclosed that he had had a stroke to a stunned House of Commons on 2nd March, 1955. See Note 59 to Chapter 2 Part 2.

133 In 1956 Boyne succeeded Wilfrid Sendall as Political Correspondent on the *Daily Telegraph*. Like Hutchinson, Boyne later went to work at Conservative Central Office after his departure from the Lobby in 1976.

134 Interview with Sir Harry Boyne.

135 The *Glasgow Herald* 6.3.55. See also concluding paragraphs of Part 2 above.

136 See Evans (*122a*) p.55.

137 Einzig (*16*) p.381.

138 *Private Information.*

139 Interview with Sir Geoffrey Cox.

140 Margach wrote two books based on his reminiscences (*127*) and (*127a*). These show far more candour than did his active journalism and much insight on the politicians and the working of the Lobby, but could perhaps be criticised for over-subscribing to the 'conspiracy theory' of politics, possibly influenced indirectly by the views of his Editor since 1967 at the *Sunday Times*, Harold Evans.

141 Margach had an advantage over other Sunday paper Political Correspondents in that he had full Lobby membership in his capacity as Political Correspondent for Scottish evening newspapers. He was in fact Chairman of the Lobby, 1952–3. The other Lobby Chairmen during the period were Guy Eden, 1950–1; Geoffrey Cox, 1951–2; W. Harford Thomas, 1953–4, of *Westminster Press*; E. R. Thompson, 1954–5, of

the B.B.C.; Leslie Way, 1955–6, of *Western Morning News*.

142 Interview with Sir Harry Boyne. Mrs. Rona Margach added that a letter from H. V. Hodson (Editor, *Sunday Times*, 1950–61) of 10.5.56 made official Margach's appointment as Political Correspondent.

143 *Private Information.*

144 Margach collaborated with Swinton in producing a book about the latter's recollections of men and events in his long career in politics, Swinton (*52*).

145 *Private Information.*

146 Margach (*127a*) p.146.

147 Gilmour later became the leading philosopher on the pragmatic wing of the Conservative Party, and author of Gilmour (*117*). Entered the House of Commons in 1962. Lord Privy Seal in the Thatcher Government from 1979.

148 The Editor of *The Economist* was Geoffrey Crowther (1938–56). A leading and widely read economic writer since 1949 was Norman Macrae, arguably the most perceptive economic commentator of his day, and author of Macrae (*169*). The Political Commentator, who would write one or two political notes a week, was Geoffrey Cox. In 1953 Ian Trethowan took his place on *The Economist* and a year later also on the *News Chronicle*.

149 Waller became the *Sunday Telegraph*'s Political Correspondent after its inception in 1961.

150 Waller (*222a*) p.75.

151 Interview with Wilfrid Sendall. Sendall wrote three retrospective articles in the *Spectator* in the autumn of 1973 in which he discussed his experience of the Lobby.

152 For a discussion of the problems encountered by the Lobby in approaching Conservative Ministers after 1951, see Epilogue 2.

153 Interview with Sir Geoffrey Cox.

154 For further details, see Epilogue 2.

155 The *Observer* 28.3.54.

156 Interview with Sir Harry Boyne.

157 The *Observer* 21.2.54.

158 *Private Information.*

CHAPTER 2 PART 4 pp.70–75

1 Interviews with Lord Robens of Woldingham and Sir Harold Wilson. The latter said Gaitskell was responsible for persuading

Attlee. For a discussion of Election timing see also diary for 4.9.51, 16.9.51 and 19.9.51, *Dalton Papers*.

2 See diary 21.9.51, Macmillan (*36*) p.355.

3 In particular Morrison, Dalton, Ede, A. V. Alexander and Tom Williams. (Dalton was not a Minister between November 1947 and May 1948.) In addition, through ill health, Bevin had been forced to retire from the Foreign Office in March 1951, and Cripps from the Treasury in October 1950. Bevan, Wilson and Freeman all resigned in April 1951.

4 Interview with David Clarke.

5 Cohen, *A History*, p.491.

6 He held this position jointly with Henry Hopkinson and Percy Cohen, 1948–51.

7 Interview with David Clarke.

8 Hoffman (*124*) p.204 says delay occurred because of disagreement on the contents of the early draft of the statement. Butler began redrafting assisted by the Research Department and Lloyd, who in addition to assisting in formulation of policy, was responsible for integrating the Parliamentary Party with the policy process.

9 *Private Information*.

10 Throughout the period of Opposition, Head assisted Churchill on defence matters. See Chapter 8 Part 2.

11 An M.P. since 1945 and Chairman of the Young Conservatives, 1946.

12 Goldman entered the Research Department in 1946 and was appointed Head of the Home Affairs Section in 1951 in succession to Michael Fraser.

13 Interview with Lord Fraser of Kilmorack.

14 There was in addition a greater emphasis on the need to preserve peace.

15 See Chapter 7 Part 2.

16 Butler (*10*) pp.154–6.

17 Interview I with Peter Goldman.

18 The Election Manifesto of 1935 promised that the defence programme would be carried out without 'unreasonable profit to contractors'. Neville Chamberlain's 1937 Budget therefore proposed a National Defence Contribution which was greeted with a Stock Exchange slump and torrents of criticism and had to be changed to straight tax on profits. So when the draft was read over the phone to Butler, he artfully tacked on a reference to the need to be guided by past experience (and by the recent U.S. prototype). Correspondence with Peter Goldman.

19 Churchill brought this up at the meeting on 22nd September. A Committee of Anderson, Butler and Macmillan was appointed to prepare a draft. Macmillan (*36*) p.355.

20 Lord Fraser's diary for 29.9.51 says that the excess profits levy (E.P.L.) was drafted into 'Britain Strong and Free' by Goldman, Cropper and himself on that day. *Private Papers*.

21 Hoffman (*124*) p.205.

22 D. Butler (*120*) p.44, remarks that the Conservatives were reverting to an earlier practice of presenting their programme in the form of a personal statement from their Leader.

23 Macmillan (*36*) p.354.

24 Diary 19.9.51 and 22.9.51, *Crookshank Papers*. D. Butler (*120*) p.44, refers to Conservative leaders taking part in 'prolonged sessions' at Hyde Park Gate for the first week after Attlee's announcement of the Election date. The Churchills lived at Hyde Park Gate but after the Election moved into Number Ten.

25 For details of the Election, see D. Butler (*120*).

26 See Macmillan (*36*) p.359–60, for example.

27 There was corresponding relief in the Labour camp, somewhat overdone in this extract from Dalton's diary for the 'end of October 1951': 'The Election results are wonderful. We are out just at the right moment, and our casualties are wonderfully light.' *Dalton Papers*.

28 Macmillan (*36*) p.361.

29 See letter, Woolton to Salisbury, 28.9.50, in which Woolton complained that Churchill was being very difficult and was threatening to resign over his pro-Liberal policy. Churchill was determined to bring about some agreement with the Liberals that would ensure victory and had been talking to Violet Bonham Carter about it. *Woolton Papers*, Box 21.

30 Woolton complained that he had made enquiries about the possibility of an electoral agreement with the Liberals, and invited Clement Davies, the Liberal Leader, to lunch in 1951, and they agreed that whilst nothing could be done at H.Q. level, it might be possible to do something in the constituencies. But within forty-eight hours of the talk Davies delivered a speech at Harrogate which made a nonsense of their conversation. Secret Party Report by Woolton 16.6.55, *Woolton Papers*, Box 22.

31 At Bolton East the Liberals did not put up a candidate, permitting the Conservative, Philip Bell, to unseat the Labour member. At Bolton West the Conservatives did not field a candidate, which again resulted in the sitting Labour man being deposed, by the Liberal Arthur Holt.

32 At Huddersfield West the Conservatives, as in 1950, did not oppose the sitting Liberal member, Donald Wade.

33 Secret Party Report by Woolton 16.6.55, *Woolton Papers*, Box 22.

34 See letter 20.11.51, Violet Bonham Carter to Gilbert Murray, *Murray Papers*, Box 6.

35 One of their senior members, Lady Megan Lloyd-George, also lost her seat.

36 *The Times* 29.10.51.

37 The Liberal Party joined Ramsay MacDonald's National Government in 1931, but split over the question of tariff reform. The Free Trade Liberals left the Government in 1932 but Sir John Simon stayed with the Government along with his protectionist followers, known as National Liberals. They became known after the 1947 agreement as the Liberal Unionist Group. For further background, see *Campaign Guide 1955* pp.599–601.

38 Interview with Lord Muirshiel.

39 Diary 26.3.53, *Dalton Papers*.

40 On 10th October at the Margate Party Conference, *Party Conference Reports 1952–5*. See Part 2 above.

41 *House of Commons* 3.11.53.

42 See diary 6.4.54, *Woolton Papers*.

43 Diary 14.4.54, *Woolton Papers*.

44 General Director, Conservative Central Office, October 1945–August 1957.

45 Woolton to Churchill, 1.9.54. *Woolton Papers*, Box 22.

46 Letter, Woolton to Churchill, 23.9.54. *Woolton Papers*, Box 22.

47 Diary 22.9.54, Macmillan (*36*) p.543.

48 Macmillan dined with Churchill on 1st November and discussed *inter alia* Election timing, Macmillan suggesting the closing of the Commonwealth Prime Ministers' Conference on 10th February as a satisfactory time for him to retire. Churchill does not appear to have jumped at this proposal. Macmillan (*36*) p.549.

49 *The Times* 1.12.54.

50 Diaries for 22.12.54 in *Crookshank Papers* and *Woolton Papers*. Macmillan (*36*) p.550.

51 A Woolton Paper of 26.1.55, also letter,

Woolton to Churchill, 23.2.55, *Woolton Papers*, Box 22. See Chapter 5 Part 3.

52 See Chapter 2 Part 2.

53 Apart from his present from members of both Houses of Parliament, the Graham Sutherland portrait in oils, Churchill also received presents from the nation. As well as many thousands of individual gifts, a Winston Churchill Eightieth Birthday Presentation Fund was launched. Over 200,000 contributions had been received for the Fund by the time of his birthday on 30th November, on which day he was handed an interim cheque for £150,000 from the Birthday Fund.

54 Diary 22.12.54, *Woolton Papers*.

55 Letter, Woolton to Eden, 8.3.55, *Woolton Papers*.

56 Interview with Lord Carr of Hadley.

57 Diary 11.3.55, *Woolton Papers*.

58 Diary 14.3.55, *Woolton Papers*.

59 Diary 14.3.55, *Woolton Papers*.

60 Diary 23.4.55 and 30.4.55, *Crookshank Papers*.

61 Dalton noted in his diary on 4.4.55 to 7.4.55 that Butler had told him the day before that he favoured a later Election, but that if this was true it was contrary to all popular guesses. *Dalton Papers*.

62 Diaries in *Woolton Papers* and *Crookshank Papers* for 4.4.55.

63 Diary 5.4.55, *Woolton Papers*.

64 See diary 6.4.55, *Woolton Papers*. Macmillan (*36*) p.583 said nearly all the Ministers whom Eden consulted favoured holding an Election as soon as possible.

65 Eden (*14*) p.270.

66 Crookshank recorded in his diary on 15.4.55, 'I would have preferred to wait, but Cabinet swung much the other way.' *Crookshank Papers*.

67 Interview II with Peter Goldman.

68 Woolton to Eden 29.3.55, *Woolton Papers*, Box 22.

69 In a letter, 3.4.79, to the author, he wrote: 'I remember putting one or two ideas to Anthony Eden, with whom I was on terms of personal friendship in those days, and, if memory does not deceive me, at his suggestion I repeated them to Iain Macleod and one or two Party officials . . . when the Manifesto appeared I could find no trace of my notions in it.'

70 Diary 30.3.55, *Woolton Papers*.

71 *The Times* 30.4.55.

72 The view of Lord Fraser of Kilmorack.

James Griffiths later wrote that Labour were caught unprepared: 'It was a half-hearted fight as it was bound to be after years of internal strife.' Griffiths (20) p.141.

CHAPTER 3 PART 1 pp.76–84

1 Interview with Sir John Colville and with Lord Soames.
2 Interview with Lord Clitheroe.
3 Churchill was always careful not to call it the shadow Cabinet but referred to it as the Consultative Committee. It normally met on a Wednesday evening in the Leader of the Opposition's room to discuss pressing business and to receive tasks. Usually, once a fortnight, Churchill entertained the group to a private lunch in the Savoy Hotel. This sometimes took the place of, and at other times was followed by, the formal Wednesday meeting. Interview with Lord Clitheroe. Macmillan (36) pp.43–4 and Kilmuir (31) p.149. Minutes were not kept. The influential group was the 'inner core' who met to discuss drafts of Manifestoes and general policy statements for the Party Conferences. It consisted of Eden, Butler, Lyttelton, Woolton, Macmillan, Crookshank, Stanley, Maxwell Fyfe and Salisbury. Interview with David Clarke.
4 In dealing with the main Bills on the floor of the House and in Committee, some concentrated on particular issues. In foreign affairs, for example, Eden took the lead in the House of Commons as Salisbury did in the Lords, and economic subjects in the main were taken by Butler, Lyttelton and Salisbury and also Macmillan. But there was no precise designation of someone as shadow Minister. Macmillan (36) pp.43–4.
5 At that time both Beaverbook and Bracken would frequently proffer their views on appointments. See, for example, Colville (12) p.201. No such situation arose again six years later, though it seems Eden was responsible for suggesting Butler for the Treasury and Bracken for suggesting Monckton rather than Maxwell Fyfe for the Ministry of Labour. Also Bracken was very keen on Leathers taking a job in the Government and was responsible for urging him to return. Interview with Bernard Sendall. The conversation

described in Macmillan (36) p.355 shows Bracken must have been present at some stage when Churchill was forming his thoughts about the composition of the Government. Lord Salisbury would also appear to have been consulted on certain senior posts. *Private Information.*
6 See Appendix II for a list of these Committees and officers.
7 The Chairmen of the following Committees and subcommittees in the 1950–1 Parliament became Ministers of the respective Departments in office: Eden (Foreign Office), Sir Thomas Dugdale (Agriculture), Churchill (Defence), Florence Horsbrugh (Education), Harold Macmillan (Housing), James Stuart (Scottish Office), Jim Thomas (Admiralty) and Antony Head (War Office).
8 Namely, the switch from Oliver Lyttelton to Rab Butler (Treasury), Osbert Peake to Sir David Maxwell Fyfe (Home Office), Alan Lennox-Boyd to Lyttelton (Colonial Office) and Lord Ismay (Commonwealth Relations Office), Harry Crookshank to Gwilym Lloyd-George (Food), Walter Elliot to Crookshank (Health), Maxwell Fyfe to Sir Walter Monckton (Labour), Robert Hudson to Peter Thorneycroft (Trade), A. V. Harvey to Lord De L'Isle (Air), W. S. ('Shakes') Morrison to Peake (National Insurance), Thorneycroft and Lennox-Boyd to John Maclay (Transport and Civil Aviation), and Duncan Sandys to Sir David Eccles (Works).
9 Before circumstances changed to make Butler the candidate for the chancellorship, according to reports Butler would have settled for the C.R.O., or better still for a sinecure post with a roving brief over industrial policy. Harris (77) p.140.
10 Sir Norman Brook later said that Churchill envisaged Woolton playing something of the part that Sir John Anderson had done in the war. Kent (30a) p.233. This is one of the few occasions where Brook's words were recorded in a published source.
11 Kilmuir (31) pp.190–1. Whether such a job was indeed the one Churchill envisaged for Leathers could not be confirmed; the job he took on was Secretary of State for the co-ordination of Transport, Fuel and Power.
12 See Chapter 2 Part 2.
13 Chandos (11) pp.342–4.
14 See Chapter 3 Part 4. Anderson, though he

left the House of Commons in February 1950 when University seats were abolished, had continued to attend meetings of the shadow Cabinet. Wheeler-Bennett (*104*) pp.348–9.

15 See Chapter 4 Part 6.

16 See Chapter 8 Part 1.

17 Stanley had held a number of senior posts in Conservative Governments, culminating in his period as Colonial Secretary November 1942–July 1945.

18 See Chapter 5 Part 1. Despite Stanley's intelligence and charm, he was no great decision taker, and might well not have fared as well as Butler.

19 'Alas I cannot accept Winston's invitation to join his Government. I shall be under doctor's orders for months.' Letter, Bracken to Baruch, 5.11.51. *Baruch Papers*. See also Boyle (*62*) pp.312–18. Boyle mentions the Colonial Secretaryship as a job offered to Bracken, and Einzig (*16*) pp.114–5 refers to the same offer. Lysaght (*85*) pp.289–90 says Bracken was tempted to take the Colonial Office but ill health during the Election campaign finally persuaded him that he was not up to it. Bracken formally turned down the offer of a Cabinet job, and a report appeared in *The Times* 31.10.51.

20 Scott Reid had been Front Bench Spokesman on food before he left the House, a particularly effective performer, See Interview with Lord Strathclyde, B.O.A.P.A.H.

21 Leathers was Minister of War Transport May 1941–July 1945. Cherwell in 1951 was also the 'overlord' responsible for co-ordinating scientific research and development, and Churchill visualised his work in the war as *éminence grise* on scientific and statistical matters continuing after 1951.

22 See Chapter 4 Part 6.

23 Sampson (*96*) p.93.

24 See Crookshank's obituary in *The Times* 18.10.61.

25 Diary 30.10.51. *Crookshank Papers*; *The Times* 31.10.51.

26 See Chapter 4 Part 4.

27 See Chapter 5 Part 3.

28 Of the four Departments co-ordinated by the 'overlords', interestingly only one, Agriculture and Fisheries, had its Minister in Cabinet when the Election was called in 1951.

29 There was surprisingly little difference in the overall balance of the Cabinet. One social service job, one 'economic' job and one sinecure were exchanged for the same.

30 He had been Chief Whip of the Conservatives since 1948, in succession to Stuart.

31 Diary 28.10.51, Macmillan (*36*) p.365; diary 28.10.51, *Crookshank Papers*.

32 Bracken noted how a man with a V.C. began with a head start in Churchill's favour, diary 24.7.58, Moran (*87*), p.783. For the same reason, the appointment of Smyth can be traced to Churchill. De L'Isle, in addition to his V.C., was a friend of the Churchill family. See, for example, Lady Soames (*98*) p.521.

33 Crookshank recorded in his diary on 29.10.51: 'endless talk about Sandys for the War Office'. *Crookshank Papers*.

34 Diary 29.10.51, *Crookshank Papers*.

35 Richard Stokes, appointed Minister of Materials on the Ministry's creation by Attlee in July 1951, was already in the Cabinet as Lord Privy Seal.

36 Interview with Sir Robert Marshall. Swinton undoubtedly was upset not to be offered a Cabinet job. Churchill, though, felt that a seventh peer in Cabinet would be too many.

37 Crookshank records how he was at Hyde Park Gate on the evening of 1st November till after midnight working on junior appointments. *Crookshank Papers*. For a short while after the Election, Churchill continued to operate from his London home, 28, Hyde Park Gate. Lady Soames (*98*) pp.430–1.

38 The Ministers of the Crown (Parliamentary Under-Secretaries) Act, 1951. The new Ministers, Lucas-Tooth and Henderson Stewart were accordingly appointed on 3rd and 4th February, 1952.

39 See diary 8.11.51, Moran (*87*) p.373.

40 In a letter from Bracken to Baruch of 5th November, 1951, he tells how Churchill of necessity had to drop former colleagues, writing that, 'this is an inevitable duty but it has been very painful to Winston.' *Baruch Papers*.

41 Amery had been Secretary of State at the India and Burma Office, May 1940–July 1945. A letter he wrote Beaverbrook on 23.11.51 indicates he considered it a possibility that Churchill could have included him in his Government. *Beaverbook Papers*. Box C8. He had, however, lost his seat

in the 1945 General Election and did not wish to go to the Lords.

42 Coote (*68*) says he was offered the Post Office rather than the Scottish Office, p.261. Elliot was given the Companion of Honour in 1952, was elected Chairman of the Scottish Unionist Committee of the Party in November 1951, and Chairman of its Radio and Television Committee in July 1953.

43 Hudson had been Minister of Agriculture and Fisheries May 1940–July 1945 and was very upset not to be included. Interview with Lord Crathorne D.B.Y. Hudson was elevated to the House of Lords in 1952.

44 Morrison had been Minister of a number of Departments, culminating as Minister of Town and Country Planning 1943–5. He was, however, appointed Speaker in 1951, becoming one of the most distinguished figures this century to hold the position.

45 Interview with Lord Clitheroe. Briggs (*136*) says Assheton also was offered the Post Office. See Chapter 4 Part 5. A report in *The Times* 6.11.51 said that Assheton felt he could more usefully serve from the backbenches as he had not been offered an economic job.

46 See Chapter 6 Part 3.

47 Macmillan (*36*) p.365. See Chapter 2 Part 4.

48 In this matter the opinion of Taylor (*100*) p.602 gives a more accurate picture than that of Young (*110*) p.291. Of particular note is the letter, Bracken to Beaverbrook, 24.11.50, in which Bracken remarks that neither of them had any intention of sitting in the Cabinet again. *Beaverbrook Papers*, Box C57.

49 See, for example, Harold Wilson, *House of Commons* 5.11.51.

50 *The Economist* 2.2.52 p.264.

51 He said the Conservatives had six peers in the Cabinet and eighteen in the entire Government, to Labour's three in Cabinet and sixteen in the Government. Churchill in *House of Commons* 6.11.51.

52 Attlee's Cabinet in 1945 had an average age of sixty-two, but Churchill's Cabinet in 1951 still had the highest age of any Cabinet 1950–74. G. W. Jones in Thornhill, ed. (*135*) p.38.

53 Interview with George Pottinger.

54 See Chapter 2 Part 3.

55 See Chapter 7 Part 3.

56 See letter, Churchill to Lady Woolton

November 1952. *Woolton Papers*, Box 22.

57 Diary, 22.11.52, *Private Papers* and *Private Information*.

58 *The Economist* 12.9.53 p.679. See also *The Times* 1.9.53, 2.9.53, 3.9.53 and leader 4.9.53.

59 See letter, Churchill to Woolton 2.9.53, *Woolton Papers*, Box 26. Churchill stressed that because Lloyd-George was winding up the Ministry of Food, the numbers in Cabinet would be permanently increased by only one. Churchill would not have in fact been able to promote the one without the other, though the desire to have the Minister of Agriculture in the Cabinet was the *raison d'être* behind the move.

60 See Chapter 7 Part 4.

61 Margaret Bondfield was Minister of Labour, 1929–31, and Ellen Wilkinson was Minister of Education August 1945–February 1947, both in Cabinet.

62 He spent two days with Churchill at Chequers, from 29th to 31st August. *The Times* 1.9.53.

63 Diary 25.8.53, Moran (*87*) p.485. Crookshank wrote: 'I agreed with them but stressed there must be more Under-Secretary ones before we meet.' Diary 2.9.53, *Crookshank Papers*.

64 Letter, Reading to Cherwell, 15.11.53, *Cherwell Papers*, Pers.101.

65 Interview with Lord Chandos D.B.Y.

66 *The Times* 27.7.54. *The Economist* 31.7.54 p.348 said: 'To a Government needing a blood transfusion, Sir Winston Churchill has given a liver pill.'

67 Note absence of mention of consultation in diary 10.10.54 and 11.10.54, *Crookshank Papers*.

68 Diaries in *Crookshank Papers* and Macmillan (*36*) p.545.

69 *The Economist* 21.7.54 p.348 had suggested that a Minister with supervisory oversight over the domestic front be appointed, commanding respect on both sides of the House, and named three possibles, Eden, Butler and Macmillan, but the first two were unable to be spared. Macmillan was flattered by the suggestion and would have much liked the job.

70 Eden (*14*) p.273 says Ministers were accustomed to their offices and he wanted the Administration to run smoothly in the weeks before the Election. R. Churchill (*66*) p.198, no friend of Eden's, called this

delay of a major reshuffle an 'elementary mistake', missing the opportunity to fashion the Government to his own liking. *The Economist* 16.4.55 p.183 expressed a different view: 'Most people thought Sir Anthony would err on the side of caution. Instead he has produced the most experimental and imaginative list of appointments seen for some time.'

71 Interview with Lord Carr of Hadley and Lord Selwyn Lloyd, D.B.Y. Another factor mentioned in Woolton's diary 22.11.55, was that Mrs. Butler had been very wide in her condemnation of having a divorcee (Eden and his first wife, Beatrice, were divorced in 1950) as Prime Minister, and so if Eden were to have replaced Butler at once it could have produced some acrimony.

72 Diary 11.3.55, *Woolton Papers*.

73 Eden (*14*) pp.273–4. But see note 28 in Chapter 3 Part 2. The *Manchester Guardian* 6.4.55 said that Selwyn Lloyd had a strong chance of promotion to the Foreign Office.

74 Diary 4.4.55, *Woolton Papers*. As early as November 1952, he had favoured Monckton for the Foreign Office, replacing him at Labour by Selwyn Lloyd. Diary 22.11.52, *Private Papers*.

75 Diary 6.4.55, *Woolton Papers*.

76 Diary 6.4.55, *Woolton Papers*.

CHAPTER 3 PART 2 pp.84–97

1 Interview with Sir Ronald Harris and Sir David Pitblado. Woolton (*55*) p.377 remembered incorrectly when he wrote that Churchill rarely sent for men not in the 'inner Cabinet'. It would also be difficult to say of whom the inner Cabinet consisted. Churchill did not have great interest in, for example, education or trade matters, so would rarely see Thorneycroft or Horsbrugh, but it did not follow that such people were 'outs'. It is true to say, however, that Churchill, who liked to deal with a few people he knew, saw much less of Ministers not in Cabinet. Also whether or not he found a man personally sympathetic made little difference to the amount of time he was prepared to give them. Sir John Colville (interview) commented that Churchill respected everyone in the Cabinet, otherwise they would not be there.

Churchill in fact relied less on cronies than almost any other post-war Prime Minister.

2 Interview with Lord Coleraine.

3 Interview I with Sir George Mallaby. Interview with Lord Crathorne, D.B.Y.

4 See entry on 28.4.53, Moran (*87*) p.428.

5 Interview I with Lord Amory. His most frequent way of achieving this would be to tinker with the agenda. He also came near to riding roughshod over Cabinet in early July 1954. See Chapter 10 Part 3. See also Macmillan (*36*) pp.486–8.

6 Crookshank, for example, constantly grumbled about this. On 1.5.52 he noted in his diary that it was 'intolerable' that they were late for lunch. On 14.1.53 he noted that the difference between Eden and Churchill (then on his way back from discussions in the U.S.) was 'wonderful'. On 17.3.53 he thought Churchill 'too woolly for words', on 5.11.53 found him 'hopeless', and he thought the Cabinet on 22.3.54 'quite useless' as Churchill was 'gaga'. *Crookshank Papers*. Eden, too, felt that under Churchill the Cabinet was avoiding taking the tough decisions. Letter, Eden to Lyttelton, 10.8.54. *Chandos Papers*, Box 4.11. Woolton exaggerated again, Woolton (*55*) p.377, when he wrote that Churchill's monologues could mean the whole time was taken up without progressing beyond the first item on the agenda. Woolton's feeling that he was tired of belonging to a Government that never came to any decision on the home front (see Chapter 2 Part 3) was all very well, but Churchill's colleagues were equally to blame for a lack of decisiveness at this stage. Diary 11.3.55, *Woolton Papers*.

7 Lord Normanbrook in Wheeler-Bennett, ed. (*105*) p.42.

8 Maxwell Fyfe wrote, Kilmuir (*31*) p.193: 'Looking back, I am not sure that [Eden's] great authority and knowledge of foreign affairs was not a defect in the Government. Winston was determined not to oppose his successor, and none of the other members had the knowledge or the experience to question or contradict Eden's opinions.' Sir George Mallaby (Interview I) gave a similar view: '. . . Anthony Eden would introduce the subject and would discourse upon it at some length. He had great experience, and many Ministers around the table would feel much too diffident to offer any opinion at all.'

9 See Chapter 4 Part 2.

10 Eden mentions 'consulting' the Cabinet as opposed to discussions there in the final volume of his memoirs, Eden (*14*). A typical reference is on p.61; he says that during the Berlin Conference, Churchill and the Cabinet gave him fullest support.

11 Interview with Sir Anthony Nutting.

12 Interview II with Lord Amory.

13 Diary 17.1.52 and 14.1.53, *Crookshank Papers*.

14 See Eden (*14*) pp.267–9.

15 Interview with Lord Carr of Hadley.

16 See Chapter 5 Part 2.

17 Interview I with Peter Goldman: Carr was a prominent member of the One Nation Group.

18 See for example diary 23.3.55, Moran (*87*) p.674.

19 They quarrelled in particular over the succession, see Chapter 2 Part 2, and issues of foreign policy, see Chapter 10 Part 4. Sir John Colville (interview) said that their clashes became: 'rather more serious than historians will allow or realise. It became really rather a personality conflict at one stage.'

20 Interview I with Sir Evelyn Shuckburgh.

21 *Private Information.*

22 See, for example, Channon diary 5.12.52, James, ed. (*28*) p.470. Eden revealed that he was on very bad terms with Churchill and said he didn't think he could stand it much longer.

23 The 11th Earl of Scarbrough. He had been an M.P., 1922–37, and was Parliamentary Under-Secretary at the India and Burma Office in the 'Caretaker Government' of 1945.

24 He had been Leader of the House of Lords 1942–5 and Secretary of State for Dominion Affairs 1940–2 and 1943–5.

25 At the 1945 General Election the Conservatives won 213 seats to Labour's 393. *The Times* 29.10.51 said that since 1945 in the House of Lords Salisbury had earned the admiration and loyalty of Conservatives and respect of Labour. For a Labour viewpoint of Salisbury's leadership of the Lords, see Longford (*34*) pp.85–7.

26 On 10.1.53 Salisbury wrote to his friend Lord Simon to say that he had worked at full stretch throughout 1952 with very little holiday, and that his doctors were urging him to take a rest. *Simon Papers*, Box F8.

27 Interview II with Lord Plowden.

28 Interview with Sir John Colville, D.B.Y. Eden, however, felt unable to appoint Salisbury Foreign Secretary in April 1955 ostensibly because he was in the House of Lords, but a deeper reason was probably that he wanted to keep foreign affairs in his own hands and this would have been impossible with a man as strong as Salisbury at the Foreign Office.

29 His grandfather (the 3rd Marquis) was Prime Minister three times between 1885 and 1902. His father was Lord Privy Seal November 1924–June 1929 and Conservative Leader in the House of Lords 1925–30.

30 Because he became progressingly out of tune with his colleagues and the Party, there was little surprise when he did resign in March 1957. Salisbury, though on the imperialist right on foreign and Commonwealth questions, had a 'left' streak on domestic policy. For example, he was keen on profit sharing in industry and very much in favour of some reform in the House of Lords.

31 In the Number Ten Private Office it became a matter of some amusement when the news came through that Salisbury was, yet again, threatening to resign.

32 See Chapter 5 Part 4.

33 See Chapter 10 Part 1.

34 He wrote to Churchill in September 1953 to say that younger men ought to come into the Cabinet and that he was quite happy to retire. (Salisbury was then just sixty.) Churchill was angry with him because he obviously regarded it as a hint, and led to a serious deterioration of their relationship for some months. See diary 22.9.53, *Crookshank Papers* and diary 1.10.53 and 14.4.54, *Woolton Papers*.

35 See Young (*110*) p.299.

36 See Chapter 10 Part 3.

37 Salisbury was one of the few men in the Government who still wrote long letters in his own handwriting.

38 Diary 18.2.53, Moran (*87*) p.422.

39 See Chapter 2 Part 2. Moran noted of Salisbury that: 'His complete detachment and single-mindedness, with his lack of personal ambition give me a comfortable sense of security.' Diary 22.2.52, Moran (*87*) p.400.

40 There were two reasons for preferring Salisbury. One was that he was a Peer, and hence could not have been expected to have remained P.M. for long. The other

was that he was a very good friend of both Churchill and Eden and was a man who hence could be totally trusted to resign when Eden was fit to take over. Interview with Sir John Colville.

41 Lord Boyle (interview) thought it most unlikely that the 1922 Committee would have been ready to accept even an acting Prime Minister in the House of Lords. Had Churchill been unable to resume, he said that any rumour that Salisbury might be appointed would have been fiercely resented and contested at a Party meeting, especially as Butler's reputation was then at its height.

42 The view of Brook as narrated by Moran (87) diary 10.7.55, p.709.

43 Sir John Colville (interview) thought Churchill would have been very unlikely to stand down.

44 *The Times* 29.10.51.

45 See Chapter 5 Part 1.

46 Crookshank was initially afforded this honour. Butler, though, took the chair in Cabinet on 18th September, 1952, and on subsequent occasions when Churchill and Eden were away. Crookshank records in his diary on 17th September: 'Very funny interlude on phone. As Anthony is away Winston arranged for Rab to preside at Cabinet instead of me – there was a good deal of uncalled for press publicity unnecessarily hurting me. It now turns out Rab wants to go abroad before Winston returns, so would I be in charge?!! I pointed out it was agreed I was to go to Denmark so he is asking Salisbury to preside . . . I've begged none of this shall be publicised as it will make the Government a laughing stock . . .' *Crookshank Papers.*

47 It was greatly to Butler's credit that he in no way used his position to put down either Churchill or Eden during the months when both were away and when he was in the centre of the stage. *The Times* 3.9.53 said: 'In a period of exceptional difficulty for the Government Mr. Butler unflinchingly shouldered heavy new responsibilities, and much of the credit for the Government's triumph over personal misfortune has been due to his ability and sagacity.' See also Chapter 10 Part 1.

48 See also comment in Kilmuir (*31*) pp.191–2. Maxwell Fyfe's widow explained that her husband felt that it was not always easy to ascertain what Butler

meant. She also said he felt that Butler preferred to argue his case on an individual level rather than in committees. Interview with Lady De La Warr. (Sylvia Maxwell Fyfe married Lord De La Warr in 1968.) Party Vice-Chairman, 1951–4.

49 See, for example, diary 28.5.53 and 6.2.54, Moran (*87*) pp.429 and 552, for remarks by Churchill on Butler.

50 Diary April 1952 and 8.1.53, *Private Papers.*

51 From 1951–5, though, Butler was by no means the regular attender at 24, Old Queen Street, that he had been up to 1951. He never worked from the Research Department after that date but there was no doubt that he still was in control. Interview II with Peter Goldman.

52 This was a reflection of deeper differences. Woolton definitely regarded Butler as 'pink', and temperamentally the men were far apart, Woolton tending to be moved by emotion, Butler by reason. Interview II with Mark Chapman-Walker. It was a curious irony of politics that Woolton, a former member of the Fabian Society, should consider Butler, the life-long supporter of the countryside and the farmers, as 'pink'.

53 Diary 22.12.55, *Woolton Papers.*

54 Diary 5.4.55, *Woolton Papers.*

55 He had been Chairman of Lewis's Investment Trust Ltd. He was Minister of Food April 1940–November 1943 and Minister of Reconstruction November 1943–May 1945. He had been Lord President in the 'Caretaker Government'.

56 See Chapter 3 Part 3.

57 He had also been appointed Chancellor of the Duchy of Lancaster in November 1952.

58 Interview with Lady De La Warr.

59 For example, he was alert to the poverty of Government weapons to ward off unemployment and the need to look in depth at the problem to see what could be done: Paper 30.4.53, 'The Problem of Stable Employment'. *Woolton Papers*, Box 26. See also his Memo to Cabinet on the effects of taxation dated 21.1.54, Box 26, and his words to Churchill on the subject of the balance of payments 21.7.52, Box 25, *Woolton Papers.*

60 See Chapter 4 Part 5.

61 See Chapter 7 Part 4.

62 See Kilmuir (*31*) p.194.

63 See Woolton (*55*) pp.367–70. Woolton had said in a radio broadcast on 13.10.51:

'There's a story that the Conservatives would cut food subsidies. That isn't true.'

64 Letter, Woolton to Churchill, 18.3.52. Salisbury had previously written to him 14.3.52 to counsel against resigning. *Woolton Papers*, Box 25.

65 Woolton stressed that he was not so concerned with the opinions of the socialist leaders or with questions of public and personal integrity. 'Public office to me can have no other attraction than to render such service as my experience makes possible for the welfare of the country.' Letter, Woolton to Churchill, 18.3.52, *Woolton Papers*, Box 25.

66 'Pray dismiss from your mind any idea of resigning from the Government because of malicious debating points . . .' Letter, Churchill to Woolton, March 1952, *Woolton Papers*, Box 25.

67 Viscount Lambton, M.P. for Berwick upon Tweed 1951–1973.

68 See letters, Maxwell Fyfe and Charles Waterhouse to Woolton, 28.3.52, *Woolton Papers*, Box 25.

69 The early fifties was still a time when there was much anti-semitism in the Conservative Party, though not shared by Churchill who was always pro-semitic. See note (presumably from Woolton) to Churchill, 24.4.53, *Woolton Papers*, Box 26. Because of accusations of anti-semitism against a Conservative Club in Lancashire, the Party's General Director was forced to issue a statement that the Party was opposed to all religious discrimination. *The Times* 15.1.54.

70 Interview with Lady De La Warr. Maxwell Fyfe was a Liverpool M.P. 1935–54.

71 Woolton wrote in his diary that he felt Churchill resented the success he had made of the Party chairmanship (diary 25.3.53, *Woolton Papers*), but this is most unlikely. Lady De La Warr said in interview: 'He was never at ease with Churchill and was always slightly apprehensive of him.'

72 Possibly Churchill was irritated by the pompous manner affected by Woolton, or was displaying his disregard for people of the commercial world. Yet one of Churchill's best qualities was that he was very rarely unpleasant about anybody. Woolton recorded in his diary on 11.3.53: 'I asked him if he really wanted my advice

and he seemed a bit surprised at that. I am never sure.' *Woolton Papers*.

73 See Woolton (55) pp.414–5.

74 M.P. since 1931 (except 1945–7). He had been Parliamentary Secretary at the Ministry of Labour 1942–5, where he had done much to gain the confidence of the unions. McCorquodale was not given a job in 1951, but was Chairman of the Party's Labour Committee. His name was to the fore at the end of 1952 because he had been appointed to take charge of 'Operation Doorstep', a recruiting campaign launched at the Party Conference in Scarborough in October 1952. P. Cohen, *A History*. McCorquodale was an exceptionally obliging printer and successful manager of his business, and Churchill thus saw him as a ready-made replacement for Woolton. McCorquodale, though he had been an able junior Minister and was a good businessman, was not by any means a man of the same calibre as Woolton.

75 See letter, Churchill to Lady Woolton, November 1952 (no date) and Woolton's note of 23.3.55 on Prime Minister's paper. *Woolton Papers*, Box 22. See also diary 11.3.55, *Woolton Papers*. Churchill's action should be seen in the context of Woolton's expression of his view to Churchill (letter 15.11.51, Box 21) that he had intended to retire from the Party chairmanship after the General Election in 1951.

76 See Woolton, diary 25.3.53. Also note of meeting with Eden at suggestion of Christopher Holland-Martin (Joint Party Treasurer, 1947–60). Eden saw Heathcoat Amory as a possible successor to Woolton, after the merger of the Ministries of Pensions and National Insurance (which took place in September 1953). *Woolton Papers*.

77 See note, Macmillan to Woolton, 12.4.53, *Woolton Papers*, Box 22.

78 Joint Treasurer, Conservative Party, since 1952.

79 At the time of the 1950 General Election, a leader in *The Times* 14.2.50 quoted in Woolton (55) p.356, said of Woolton that he was 'not merely the maker of the machine; he has also exercised an influence greater than that of any of his predecessors among the Party's organisers on the making of policy'. This gives a misleading impression. Woolton had next to no influence on policy questions 1945–51, but

his predecessors as Party Chairmen had even less.

80 In particular he was responsible for John Hare's appointment as Vice-Chairman in December 1951, Oliver Poole's appointment as Joint Treasurer in March 1952, and Mark Chapman Walker's appointment as Chief Publicity Officer in 1951. All three were figures of major importance in their own fields in Central Office between 1951 and 1955. Woolton, however, was not responsible for the appointment of Sir Stephen Pierssené, General Director (1945–57) who became, on the organisational level, an exceptionally valuable lieutenant.

81 He had been just Solicitor-General, March 1942–May 1945, and Attorney-General, May–July 1945.

82 Moran (87) p.472 wrote in his diary on 30.7.53: 'David has won the solid goodwill – perhaps I might say the affection – of the House of Commons, by his simple straightforward honesty and his kindly nature. They have learnt that when he does a job it is done once and for all.'

83 By the Party Conference in October 1953 the press was talking about the 'triumvirate' under Churchill consisting of Eden, Butler and Macmillan, excluding Maxwell Fyfe. The Times 7.10.54 [sic]. A poll in the Daily Mirror in the summer of 1954 on who its readers would like to see succeed Churchill awarded Eden 52%, Butler 33%, Maxwell Fyfe 13%, others (including Macmillan) 2%. See Kilmuir (31) p.229.

84 Bonar Law became Conservative Leader in 1911. The two leading contestants, Austen Chamberlain and Walter Long, withdrew for fear of splitting the Party.

85 See Chapter 4 Part 6.

86 See, for example, Churchill's comment in Moran (87) 21.5.54, p.578. Contrast this with Maxwell Fyfe's later comment: 'To be part of [Churchill's] unique circle was the greatest privilege and pleasure of my life.' Kilmuir (31) p.167.

87 See Chapter 4 Part 3.

88 Crookshank had none of the qualities Churchill found attractive in a man, except for his excellent record in the First World War in the Grenadier Guards. It is going too far to say that Crookshank 'hated' Churchill, a view attributed to him by Lady Churchill. Diary 12.4.58, Moran (87) p.771. Churchill, for his part, irritated

Crookshank in large degree because of his unmethodical way of dealing with business. Crookshank's diary is full of grumbles about this, and also about Churchill's birthday parties which he found dull (30.11.53 and 1.12.54) Under the circumstances it is surprising that Crookshank should have been 'hurt' at not being invited to Churchill's farewell party at Number Ten on 4th April, 1955 – see his diary of same date, Crookshank Papers. See also Moran (87) diary 1.12.54 (p.650). Crookshank was a 'man of Munich' and not many of them equalled James Stuart who later came to be liked by Churchill. His emphasis on protocol is seen in diary entries on functions, those not invited, etc. He was cross not be to asked to sum up at the 1952 Party Conference after Woolton's illness. Maxwell Fyfe performed the task. Diary 11.10.52, Crookshank Papers.

89 Culminating in Financial Secretary at the Treasury from April 1939 after which he was appointed Postmaster-General in December 1942.

90 Diary 27.1.56, Woolton Papers.

91 Interview with Sir Robert Cary (his P.P.S.).

92 Crookshank said: 'During the Election I remember saying – it was rather an obvious remark – that one could not foreshadow the future exactly for fear of what skeletons there might be in the cupboard. But it was not in the cupboards that the skeletons were; they were hanging like candelabra in every office and Department.' House of Commons 13.11.51, Vol. 493, Col. 939.

93 He noted with great pride in his diary on 1.4.54, that this was the third day when there had been no supplementary Questions on business. It was with obvious regret that he wrote in his diary on 21.4.55 that this was the first time during the Parliament when he would be unable to make the Thursday statement. Crookshank Papers.

94 See Woolton diary 27.1.56, Woolton Papers.

95 Interview with Sir Harold Wilson.

96 Diary 8.12.52, Private Papers.

97 3.1.52, 10.1.52 and 14.1.52 Crookshank recorded in his diary for 30.12.51 that the news broke about his presiding at Cabinet, and how it was played down that he was not No. 3, adding ruefully that they would have said soon enough that it was No. 3

had it been Butler presiding. *Crookshank Papers.* Though Salisbury was regarded as senior to Crookshank, it was felt that the acting Chairman of the Cabinet should be in the Commons, especially as he would answer P.M.'s Questions there.

98 See references in his diary, *Crookshank Papers.*

99 Interview with Sir Robert Cary. Crookshank took over Swinton's work at the C.R.O. when the latter went on a tour to Australia and New Zealand in the autumn of 1953.

100 *Private Interview.*

101 They both married daughters of the 9th Duke of Devonshire.

102 It is of note that Maxwell Fyfe, no great friend of Stuart's, should have written of him that he was one of 'the most consistently underrated of men'. Kilmuir *(31)* p.192.

103 Undated letter, Salisbury to Lyttelton, *Chandos Papers,* Box 4.10.

104 Maxwell Fyfe wrote that Lyttelton didn't care a damn for anyone except Churchill, to whom he was devoted. Kilmuir *(31)* pp.192–3. His widow said her husband felt that Lyttelton would tend to accept what Churchill had to say uncritically but would argue against his colleagues. Interview with Lady De La Warr. Lyttelton wrote to Churchill on 3.12.53: 'I rejoice in the memory of having served the greatest man of his era for seven years and don't really give a damn for anything else.' *Chandos Papers,* Box 4/5.

105 He gives a rather misleading impression in Macmillan *(36)* of having been in on a number of major domestic and foreign matters, whereas, in the first two years of the Government at least, he was invariably on the sidelines.

106 Interview I with Sir George Mallaby. Churchill could be impatient in Cabinet with Macmillan who was apt to be long-winded on housing topics. Mallaby also noted how Macmillan would use his charm to see what Cabinet Office officials would do to help him get round obstructions. Mallaby *(37)* p.62.

107 Woolton in his diary of 5.4.55 noted: 'Very amusingly Harold Macmillan again stopped and posed in the middle of the roadway [Downing St.] before joining me in my car and then waved to the crowds as we passed them. I agree that a public man has

to be something of an actor; I wonder whether it is really necessary to be a showman as well.' *Woolton Papers.*

108 Whenever Churchill had done something notable Macmillan was always seen to be one of the first to rush up to congratulate or have a drink with him. *Private Information.*

109 Churchill, it is worth noting, recommended Macmillan to the Queen rather than Butler for P.M. in January 1957.

110 He was, after all, acting on Churchill's express orders. See Chapter 6 Part 1.

111 See Birkenhead *(60)* p.280.

112 The others being Cherwell, Ismay, Leathers, Lyttelton, Simonds, Stuart and Woolton.

113 He would return to nearby Oxford every night to sleep.

114 For example Moran recites how Churchill sent Cherwell a paper for his comments on how a parachute might be fitted to helicopters. Diary 15.7.53, Moran *(87)* p.460.

115 In particular over the convertibility issue in early 1952, see Chapter 5 Part 2. When he retired Salter wrote to him saying there was now no one in Government with the knowledge and authority to stand up to the Treasury. Letter, Salter to Cherwell, 11.11.53, *Cherwell Papers,* Pers.10.

116 According to Birkenhead *(59)* pp.280–1, Cherwell spent nearly every other weekend until November 1953 with Churchill. He also occupied during the week the top floor of Number Eleven, Downing Street, the Chancellor's official residence. (Butler lived in his house at 3, Smith Square.)

117 Interview with Sir John Colville.

118 Cherwell, for example, was responsible for prompting Churchill's ill-advised attack on Attlee during the debate on the hydrogen bomb on 5.4.54. See diary 5.4.54 and 4.7.57 Moran *(87)* pp.565 and 767.

119 See minute, Cherwell to Churchill. 29.3.54, *Cherwell Papers,* Pers.12A.

120 Letter, Colville to Cherwell, 5.2.54, *Cherwell Papers,* Pers. 63 IV.

121 On 18.8.54 he wrote to inform Churchill he was off on a motoring holiday abroad until the end of September, and that 'I trust you will not need me for anything during this period, but if I were wanted urgently of course I could always fly back.' *Cherwell Papers,* Pers.12A.

122 For example, the one on 7th July, 1954. Letter, Brook to Cherwell, 6.7.54, *Cherwell Papers,* Pers.63 IV. This was the

meeting where Churchill confronted the Cabinet with his proposed trip to the Soviet Union. See Chapter 10 Part 3.

123 He was Chief of Staff to the Minister of Defence, 1940–6.

124 Ismay himself requested his inclusion in the Bermuda party, to gain publicity for NATO. *Ismay Papers*, 111/22/1/1–2.

125 Interview II with Anthony Montague Browne. See also diary 1.12.54, Moran (*87*) p.649.

126 Churchill brought him in from business to become Minister of War Transport, May 1941–July 1945.

127 Simonds was called to the Bar in 1906. He was appointed Lord of Appeal in Ordinary in 1944.

128 Since the war, only one other, Lord Gardiner (1964–70), has held the lord chancellorship without previous ministerial experience.

129 He told one of his senior officials at the Ministry of Defence that he never realised that the Cabinet was a 'sort of soviet'. Interview with Sir Richard Powell.

130 His field commands culminated in his appointment as Supreme Allied Commander, Mediterranean Theatre, 1944–5.

131 He first sat in Cabinet in October 1922, as President of the Board of Trade, and held a number of senior Cabinet positions totalling nearly thirteen years. He thus had far longer and also broader experience than Eden.

132 Churchill later told Moran: 'He always sat opposite me in Cabinet when I was Prime Minister and he impressed me.' Diary 16.4.58, Moran (*87*) p.772.

CHAPTER 3 PART 3 pp.97–102

1 See Chapter 7 Part 4. Also Woolton (*55*) pp.397–401.

2 Woolton (*55*) memoirs pp.402–4 and 414–5.

3 'I have been very ill. – Nearly fatally – and five separate operations have weakened me.' Undated letter, Woolton to Churchill, *Woolton Papers*, Box 22.

4 Letter, Churchill to Woolton, 5.2.53, *Woolton Papers*, Box 25.

5 See Part 2.

6 Diary 13.11.52, Moran (*87*) p.420.

7 'I felt that the Duchy would enable him to do as much or as little as he felt able to during his convalescence.' Letter, Church-

ill to Lady Woolton, November 1952 (no date), *Woolton Papers*, Box 22.

8 See Chapter 8 Part 5.

9 Interview I with Lord Plowden.

10 Interview I with Lord Plowden.

11 '. . . an expansion which but for his insistence and support might well have lost impetus in the face of the economic and political problems of the time.' Todd (*102*) pp.624–7.

12 Now Lord Longford.

13 Diary 11.3.53, *Woolton Papers*.

14 Woolton (*55*) pp.404–5.

15 See Chapter 3 Part 4.

16 September–November 1931: December 1933–June 1935; November 1942–May 1945.

17 August–December 1916; July 1946–March 1947; July 1948–April 1949.

18 See Chapter 3 Part 4.

19 See Chapter 3 Part 2.

20 See Chapter 5 Part 1.

21 Interview with Sir Donald MacDougall.

22 Interview with Lord Selkirk. A notice in *The Times* 12.11.53, said that no special duties were assigned to Selkirk as Paymaster-General, but that he would give general assistance to the Government in the House of Lords.

23 In particular July 1921–June 1935; March 1936–April 1939; September 1947–October 1954.

24 Morrison (*133*) p.42.

25 The announcement from Number Ten said Munster was to assist Salisbury with Government business in the House of Lords. *The Times* 18.10.54.

26 *The Economist* 23.10.54, p.287.

27 See Note on Sources.

28 See Chapter 5 Part 3.

29 'It was thought to be desirable to have a man of [Reading's] age, standing, and also appearance going to these conferences. So he was given a new title of Minister of State, Foreign Office [in November 1953], and Selwyn Lloyd continued as plain Minister of State. Then in 1954 I succeeded Selwyn and was first made plain Minister of State. Reading, who was the nicest of men, though slightly status conscious, came to me and said, "actually, I'm the senior one, so I should be plain Minister of State, and you should be Minister of State, Foreign Office." I then invented the title Minister of State for Foreign Affairs and he agreed to it, and we became the joint

Ministers of State for Foreign Affairs.'
Interview with Sir Anthony Nutting.

30 For more information on Lloyd, Nutting, Home and Reading see Chapter 10 Part 1.

31 See Chapter 9 Part 2.

32 Richard Nugent and Lord Carrington at Agriculture when Sir Thomas Dugdale was Minister (1951–4), Nigel Birch at Defence when Lord Alexander was Minister (1952–4), Charles Hill at Food when Gwilym Lloyd-George was Minister (1951–4) and David Gammans at the Post Office when Lord De La Warr was Minister (1951–5).

33 Anthony Nutting at the Foreign Office (1951–6), Harold Watkinson at Labour (1952–5) and Toby Low at Supply (1951–4).

34 As Robert Cary to Harry Crookshank, Nigel Fisher to Gwilym Lloyd-George, Dr. Reginald Bennett to Maxwell Fyfe, Hubert Ashton to Rab Butler, Jack Nixon Browne to James Stuart, Robert Carr to Eden, John Rodgers to Sir David Eccles, and, above all, Christopher Soames to Churchill.

35 Thus Oliver Lyttelton encouraged Hugh Fraser at the Colonial Office (1951–4); Selwyn Lloyd, David Ormsby-Gore at the Foreign Office (1951–4); and Harold Macmillan, Reginald Bevins at Housing (1951–3).

36 In particular Harmar Nicholls at the Post Office (1951–5) and Harold Watkinson at Transport and Civil Aviation (1951–2).

CHAPTER 3 PART 4 pp.102–106

1 The system of 'co-ordinating Ministers' was taken at the time to be an extension of the system Attlee introduced when he appointed A. V. Alexander Minister of Defence in 1946. See *The Times* 31.10.51. However, the Minister of Defence, a post continued from Attlee's Government, while undoubtedly having a co-ordinating function, will not be treated, for the purposes of this chapter, as a co-ordinating Minister. Some commentators felt that Churchill did not properly test what could have been a valuable exercise in the machinery of government. See *The Economist* 29.11.52 and 12.9.53, p.680.

2 Interview I with Lord Butler and Sir Hubert Ashton.

3 *Private Information.*

4 For a full discussion of the debate in Parliament, see Daalder (*129*) pp.110–20, and Milne (*238*) pp.365–9.

5 Cherwell had been Professor of Experimental Philosophy until he became Churchill's Personal Assistant in 1940. Leathers had had a distinguished career in business, as had Woolton. Anderson, a former Permanent Under-Secretary at the Home Office (1922–32) and Governor of Bengal (1932–7), joined the House of Commons as M.P. for the Scottish Universities in 1938.

6 Wheeler-Bennett (*104*) p.352.

7 Diary 28.10.51, Macmillan (*36*) p.365. Lord Plowden (interview) confirmed, however, that Anderson was certainly offered the overlordship of the Treasury and the Board of Trade.

8 Letter, Bracken to Beaverbrook, 15.1.52, *Beaverbrook Papers.*

9 Wheeler-Bennett (*104*) pp.352–3.

10 Diary 2.6.52, Moran (*87*) p.413.

11 Diary 11.3.53, *Woolton Papers*, Box 3. In his memoirs, however, Woolton says Churchill told him, when forming the Government, that he merited the choice of any office open to him as a peer. Woolton (*55*) p.365.

12 Churchill's valedictory letter to Leathers of 31.8.53 read: 'The office of Secretary of State for the Co-ordination of Transport, Fuel and Power were specially created in order to enable you to apply to the problems of public administration your personal knowledge of these industries and services.' Quoted in *The Times* 4.9.53.

13 *The Times* 6.11.51. Cherwell's precise responsibilities were clarified by Churchill in the *House of Commons* 6.5.52.

14 Letter, Cherwell to Churchill 7.5.50, *Cherwell Papers*, Pers.12A.

15 See Birkenhead (*59*) pp.277–9.

16 *House of Lords* 30.4.52.

17 *House of Commons* 6.5.52. See also Milne (*238*) p.366.

18 Letter, Woolton to Churchill 5.5.52. *Woolton Papers*, Box 25.

19 Woolton described his co-ordinating task as 'indeed a very minor one'. *House of Lords* 30.4.52.

20 Letter, Woolton to Churchill 5.5.52, *Woolton Papers*, Box 25.

21 Diary 11.3.53, *Woolton Papers.*

22 Interview with Lord Hill of Luton.

23 Letter. Churchill to Woolton, 24.3.52, *Woolton Papers*, Box 25.

24 Letter, Minister of Food to Lord Woolton, 27.3.52, *Woolton Papers*, Box 25.

25 Letter, Woolton to Churchill, 28.3.52, *Woolton Papers*, Box 25.

26 Letter, Woolton to Lloyd-George, 12.6.52, *Woolton Papers*, Box 25, and letter, Woolton to Churchill, 6.10.52, *Woolton Papers*, Box 25.

27 *House of Commons* 6.5.52.

28 Leathers' appointment, however, did bear a similarity to the position of regulator over socialised industry that Herbert Morrison had held as Lord President, 1945–51.

29 See, for example, diary 1.6.52, Moran (87) p.12.

30 The official reason for the switch was that Leathers had been advised by his doctors to take a rest. *The Times* 6.3.53.

31 'I foresaw practical and constitutional difficulties in the concept of the appointment of a co-ordinating Minister; a member of the Cabinet but with no departmental responsibilities, not in the House of Commons and hence not subject to the normal political questioning and other contacts.' Interview with Lord Muirshiel.

32 'I knew Lord Leathers from the war when I worked very closely with him. I was delighted to work with him again in 1951 but I realised that he knew nothing about peacetime politics. His great knowledge of shipping would be of less help to him in peacetime and I realised that he would also have difficulties because he was in the House of Lords. We made the arrangement work but it never was really entirely satisfactory.' Interview with Lord Geoffrey-Lloyd.

33 Interview with Lord Redcliffe-Maud.

34 Interview I with Lord Boyd.

35 Interview with Evan Maude.

36 Later Chief Economic Adviser to the Treasury, 1969–73.

37 Later Executive Director of the Bank of England, 1970–.

38 Birkenhead (59) pp.281–2.

39 Interview with Sir Donald MacDougall.

40 See Chapter 8 Part 5.

41 See Chapter 7 Part 4.

42 On Woolton's return to active ministerial life in March 1953, Labour asked Churchill if he would terminate the system of co--ordinators. *House of Commons*, 24.3.53.

Churchill said it was 'a valuable aid to the efficient conduct of Government business'.

43 Letter, Cherwell to Churchill, 19.10.53, *Cherwell Papers*, Pers.10.

44 Letter, Churchill to Woolton, 2.9.53, *Woolton Papers*, Box 26. During Woolton's illness, Churchill refused to make it clear whether Lord Salisbury, the new Lord President, would take over responsibility for overlordship of agriculture and food. *House of Commons* 3.12.52. It was reported in the press that Woolton did not return to his responsibilities as overlord on his resumption of duties in March 1953. *The Times* 4.9.53.

45 Diary 7.3.53 and 2.9.53, Moran (87) pp.427 and 492. In a letter dated 8.8.53, printed in *The Times* 4.9.53, Leathers asked to be released by the end of September at the latest: '. . . I think that I can claim to have done all that I undertook to do.'

46 *The Times* 4.9.53. The previous day an article in *The Times* noted: 'Nobody seems to regard this [overlords system] as having been successful enough to be worth continuing in present circumstances.'

CHAPTER 4 PART 1 pp.107–114

1 Such as Sir Edward Bridges, Sir Norman Brook, Sir Henry Hancock, Sir John Lang, Sir Thomas Lloyd, Sir David Milne, Sir William Strang and Sir George Turner.

2 For example Sir Pierson Dixon, Sir Godfrey Ince, Sir John Lang, Sir Frank Lee, Sir Roger Makins, Sir John Maud, Sir Frank Newsam, Sir Richard Powell, Sir Leslie Rowan, Sir Archibald Rowlands, Dame Evelyn Sharp, and Sir Edwin Plowden, who was never an established civil servant but was always there on a temporary basis.

3 For comments on this side of Bridges' work, see Chapter 5 Part 1.

4 Interview II with Lord Redcliffe-Maud.

5 Strictly speaking, the jobs of Head of the Civil Service and Cabinet Secretary were non-comparable. The Head of the Civil Service's authority was supreme on matters of appointments and Government machinery, as was his position as Permanent Secretary to the Treasury in his advice to the Chancellor. Brook would never have interfered or attempted to overrule Bridges in this. But if one is considering the Cabinet

Secretary's functions as chief official adviser to the Prime Minister, the special relationship between him and Ministers and his key position in the execution of policy, then in these matters Brook was far more influential than Bridges.

6 In later years there has been a reaction in certain quarters of the Treasury to the headship of Bridges: he was thought to be not sufficiently professional or enough of an economist. This was in part a reaction away from the 'generalist' approach at which Bridges excelled.

7 See Lee (*142*) p.147.

8 Interview with Sir John Winnifrith and Winnifrith (*109*) p.47. Bridges was Secretary of the Cabinet, 1938–46.

9 Interview with Sir John Colville.

10 For a well-informed account of Brook's and Bridges' methods, see Kent (*30a*) pp.231–3.

11 It is an interesting if not conclusive observation that whereas Brook wrote at length in his contribution to *Action This Day*, Wheeler-Bennett, ed. (*105*) on Churchill during 1951–5, Bridges confines his essay to the war years. Also in Moran's diary there are frequent references to Brook, but Bridges' name does not occur at all in references to the years 1951–5.

12 See Bridges (*257*) and (*258*).

13 Winnifrith (*109*) p.51.

14 Lee (*142*) p.51.

15 Lee (*142*) p.111.

16 See Chapter 3 Part 4.

17 Louis Petch, then Assistant Secretary in the Machinery of Government Branch, wrote a minute on 7.1.52, suggesting that all machinery of government (M.G.) work was futile unless directed to a specific problem and also if any sense of urgency was removed. He argued that Permanent Secretaries showed little interest in problems which did not affect their own Departments, and had taken an extremely departmental line on those that did. Lee (*142*) p.52.

18 Minute, 28.3.52, quoted in Lee (*142*) p.113.

19 See Chapter 6 Part 5.

20 See Chapter 7 Part 5.

21 See Chapter 6 Part 2.

22 See Chapter 6 Part 4.

23 See Chapter 4 Part 4.

24 Woolton comments, 25.1.54, *Woolton Papers*, Box 3.

25 Lee (*142*) concludes: 'By the time Bridges retired in 1956, the two dominant modes of M.G. exercise – the Ministerial Committee and the Committee of Permanent Secretaries – were generally discredited' p.150.

26 Warden of Nuffield College, Oxford, 1954–78. Writer on aspects of government and administration, and editor of the journal 'Public Administration' from 1943–66. Later Sir Norman Chester.

27 The findings, written up by F. M. G. Willson, were published in 1957. See Chester (*138*).

28 Lee (*142*) p.150.

29 See Bibliography, Newsam (*148*), and following.

30 Lee (*142*) p.148.

31 The explorer and geologist, Principal and Vice-Chancellor, University of Birmingham, 1938–52.

32 *House of Commons* 30.7.53.

33 Cmd. 9613.

34 The report, rather unfairly, had a poor press: it was cramped by inadequate terms of reference, but it did much to bring the problems of the Civil Service into perspective. See Mackenzie (*251*).

35 *The Times* 18.9.52, 28.8.53 and 20.5.54.

36 See File 'Gov't Correspondence' in *C.R.D. Papers*.

37 *House of Commons* 25.1.55.

38 Of the Permanent Secretaries who retired between 1951–6, the majority – Fergusson, Hancock, King, Liesching, Little, Lloyd, Overton, Parker, Rowlands, Sheepshanks, Strang, Turner, Wilson, Vandepeer – retired at or soon after the age of sixty. Only two, apart from Bridges, retired nearer their sixty-fifth birthday, Barnes and Ince. In February 1952, Butler had notified the staff side of the Whitley Council that he had decided to put into operation forthwith new rules for retirement from the Civil Service, and that sixty was in future to be regarded as a minimum retirement age, rather than a normal retirement age, with sixty-five as an upper limit. *The Times* 4.2.52. The effect of this, however, was restricted largely to the clerical grades. *The Times* 26.9.53. Amongst senior officials, the retirement age had gone by the board during the war, but by 1950 eyebrows began to be raised if a man stayed on beyond sixty-five, as was the case with Sir Alan Barlow

and Sir Alexander Maxwell (Home Office).

39 Winnifrith (*109*) p.53; Daalder (*129*) p.110.

40 Bligh later became Private Secretary to the Prime Minister from 1959–64. Bligh had a highly engaging personality, and was a buccaneering type of figure, who in some ways (like Colville) appeared at times rather an anomaly in the Civil Service.

41 *The Times* 3.8.51.

42 See Chapter 5 Part 1.

43 In his last years in office, Bridges would often spend the first half an hour of the day dealing with the affairs of the Box Hill Committee of the National Trust, of which he was the Chairman. At other times, to recharge his mind, he would work for a while preparing the letters of his father, the Poet Laureate, Robert Bridges, O.M. for publication. Interview with Sir Derek Mitchell. (Mitchell was Private Secretary to Bridges in succession to Bligh, 1954–6.)

44 Interview with Sir John Winnifrith.

45 Interview with Sir John Winnifrith. Sir Geoffrey King was another man also on terms of close personal friendship with Bridges.

46 Interview with Sir Derek Mitchell.

47 Interview 1 with Lord Butler. See Chapter 5 Part 1.

48 For an interesting comment on his responsibility over this field see Bridges (*157*) pp.176–7. Bridges wrote that there were three reasons why he felt he did not want to change the system whereby the Permanent Secretary of the Treasury was sole adviser to the P.M. on appointments of top civil servants. He felt one man was quite able to consult all the different people who had specialist knowledge on particular appointments. One-to-one exchanges permitted greater frankness than could be the case if there was a selection board. Thirdly, appointments were a matter of considering the whole field, and one man was needed who would be able to form an overall judgment on the deployment of men in all key posts.

49 Interview with Sir John Winnifrith.

50 *Private Information.*

51 *House of Commons* 10.11.53. Though the numbers of the Civil Service in Government Departments on 1.1.53 was the lowest since 1.4.42, total numbers were still double what they had been on the outbreak of the Second World War. Facts

from a report published on 18.2.53. (Cmd. 8765.) The cuts in the Government information services caused a large amount of resentment. See debate in *House of Commons* 2.4.52. The Government's handling of the economy drive was felt to be rather wooden in this field in particular. They had originally intended to abolish the Central Office of Information in its entirety and the Director-General, Sir Robert Fraser (1946–54), had to fight a hard and successful battle against it. Eventually the Government had to content itself with scrapping the Crown Film Unit.

52 Eccles in a reply to a Question in the House on 3.3.53. Responsibility for official cars was transferred from the Ministry of Supply and other Departments in April 1952 to the Ministry of Works, and in April 1953 the Government car service was amalgamated with the Ministry of Works transport division. *The Times* 18.4.53.

CHAPTER 4 PART 2 pp.114–119

1 Not only had Brook been full Cabinet Secretary since 1947 (and 'Additional Secretary', 1945–6), but he had also served as Deputy Secretary (Civil) to the War Cabinet in 1942 and was Permanent Secretary of the Office of Minister of Reconstruction, 1943–5.

2 Sir Thomas Padmore himself told the author that he does not believe it possible that he could at that stage have won Churchill's confidence to the degree to which Brook already had it.

3 For a good and full account of the working of the Cabinet Office in 1951, and for a formal description of the duties of the officers, see Hewison (*246*) pp.221–5.

4 See Chapter 8 Part 1.

5 Mallaby took over the work of the Civil Deputy, when 'no doubt for economy reasons', Brook decided not to have a second Deputy after Harris' arrival as the second Under-Secretary later in 1952. After that Mallaby and Harris were *de jure* equals, except that Mallaby was senior in the sense of being the older man and having served longer in the office. Interview I with Sir George Mallaby.

6 Mallaby was by no means a typical civil servant. He entered Whitehall in 1942 and served in the Military Secretariat of the War Cabinet until 1945. After a spell out-

side he returned to the Civil Service in 1946 to the Ministry of Defence, and in 1948 became Secretary-General of the Brussels Treaty Defence Organisation before returning to the Cabinet Office in 1950, until 1954. He was a close friend of Brook. Harris had spent his Civil Service career since entering in 1936 in the India Office and Burma Office, and the Treasury, apart from a period as Private Secretary to the Cabinet Secretary, 1939–43. He was Under-Secretary at the Cabinet Office, 1952–5.

7 Interview I with Sir George Mallaby.

8 Mallaby (37) pp.16–17.

9 For Churchill's conduct of Cabinet, see Chapter 3 Part 2.

10 Mallaby (38) p.53.

11 Foreign affairs normally appeared on the agenda of the Cabinet at least once a week 'to be raised orally by the Foreign Secretary'. It provided an opportunity for the Foreign Secretary (and indeed other Ministers) to report on or raise questions on foreign affairs topics.

12 Interview with Sir Friston How.

13 The Defence Committee (formerly the Committee of Imperial Defence, 1903–46) was different to other Committees in that its existence was known publicly. Churchill had had a great deal to do with the Committee in both wars.

14 For a discussion of this see Daalder (129) p.225.

15 It is interesting that Salter (44) p.342 noted that one of the changes in the Civil Service he noticed in 1951 compared to fifty years before was the development of inter-departmental Official Committees. He found that by the time a policy question reached a Minister it might well have been debated by officials from a number of Departments, who in turn would have already presented their conclusions to their own Ministers. Crossman later noted the same.

16 For an account of the informal links between Permanent Secretaries, see Bridges (157) pp.177–9.

17 For example, Morrison *House of Commons* 13.11.51.

18 Chapter 3 Part 4.

19 The view of many; for example, interviews with Sir John Colville and Anthony Montague Browne.

20 Interview with Sir Ronald Harris.

21 Brook's reputed remark to Moran during the Bermuda Conference is interesting: 'Now, of course, he is a lazy Prime Minister; he reads novels after breakfast. But it is much better from the country's point of view that he should stay on.' Diary 6.12.53, Moran (87) p.535.

22 See Brook in Wheeler-Bennett, ed. (105), especially pp.18–36.

23 Brook for example read certain sections in draft of Churchill's war memoirs. See correspondence in *Ismay Papers,* II/3/110/1–2.

24 Interview I with Sir George Mallaby.

25 Colville in Wheeler-Bennett, ed. (105) p.108.

26 Moran's diary is full of interesting insights into their relationship. On 30.6.53 Brook came to dinner and they discussed *inter alia* the last volume of *The Second World War.* Moran says: 'Winston likes him and they talked away for a very long time.' On 25.8.53 Moran says of Brook: 'He is full of good sense, detached and yet friendly to the P.M.', and on 1.4.54, 'Norman Brook is a good friend of the P.M., loyal yet missing nothing.' On 5.12.54 Moran suspects Brook played a part in persuading Churchill to ease his immediate timetable after his birthday celebrations and the furore after his Woodford speech on 23.11.54. Moran (87) pp.439, 485, 560 and 654.

27 Mallaby (38) p.64.

28 Brook was not made an Assistant Secretary until 1938. Another who entered the Home Office as an Assistant Principal in 1928 was told it could be twenty-four years before he was made a Principal because the lack of vacancies in upper echelons.

29 See Woolton (55) p.263

30 Diary 10.7.55, Moran (87) p.708.

31 Interview with Sir Oscar Morland.

32 Interview with Ray Gedling.

33 See for example Garner (202) pp.303–4.

34 Interview with Sir Robert Marshall. (Brook's Private Secretary, 1950–3.)

CHAPTER 4 PART 3 pp.119–129

1 Of Maxwell Fyfe's five predecessors at the Home Office, Sir John Simon, Sir Samuel Hoare, Sir John Anderson, Herbert Morrison and Chuter Ede, the first four were in positions of highest seniority in the Cabinet.

2 Newsam (148) p.26.

3 Interview with Sir William Murrie. See Chapter 7 Part 2.

4 This is the view (in an interview) of Sir Arthur Peterson, Permanent Under-Secretary at the Home Office, 1972–7.

5 See Chapter 4 Part 6.

6 Diary 21.10.54, Moran (87) p.637. Maxwell Fyfe had been a prominent Opposition Front Bench speaker during 1945–51 and had also played an important part in the reform of the Conservative Party Organisation. He entered the House of Commons in 1933. See Kilmuir (31) pp.157–60.

7 Interviews: Lord Shawcross, Sir Arthur Peterson.

8 Diary 10.7.55, Moran (87) p.711.

9 Attlee said that all the House admired Maxwell Fyfe for his ability and untiring courtesy. House of Commons 4.12.52.

10 Diary 10.7.55, Moran (87) p.711.

11 House of Commons 13.2.53.

12 Interview with Lord Lloyd.

13 See article by Sir David Llewellyn in the Observer magazine, 17.10.76, pp.13–15.

14 See Colville (12) pp.250–2.

15 Succeeded to the title in 1941. His first ministerial experience had been as a Lord-in-Waiting since November 1951. His father was High Commissioner for Egypt and Sudan, 1925–9, and Secretary of State for the Colonies, 1940–1.

16 By Woolton and Eden, for example. Diary 21.12.55, Woolton Papers, Box 3.

17 Interview with Lord Mancroft.

18 See letter, Buchan-Hepburn to Michael Fraser, 9.11.51, CRD Papers, Box Gov't Correspondence. In November 1951, Lucas-Tooth had been elected Chairman of the Party's Health and Social Services Committee.

19 He had been an M.P. from 1924–9 but did not rejoin the House until 1945. Also interview with Sir Hugh Munro-Lucas-Tooth.

20 See Chapter 4 Part 6.

21 See Chapter 3 Part 1.

22 Parliamentary Secretary, Ministry of Food 1951–5.

23 Interview with Sir Nigel Fisher.

24 See Eden (14) p.275.

25 Ede was never as happy with Newsam as he had been with Sir Alexander Maxwell. See interview with Sir Arthur Peterson, B.O.A.P.A.H.

26 Maxwell Fyfe thought him 'most distin-

guished', a wise forthright adviser and a great friend. Kilmuir (31) pp.197–8.

27 See Monck (143a) p.179.

28 Newsam 1927–33. Hutchinson 1933–9.

29 Mackenzie and Grove (143) p.230.

30 Newsam (148) pp.216–7.

31 Assistant Under-Secretary of State 1952–5. Allen specialised in police and crime matters and also capital cases. He would report direct to Newsam. Interview with Lord Allen of Abbeydale, B.O.A.P.A.H. Allen became Permanent Under-Secretary at the Home Office 1966–72.

32 Assistant Under-Secretary of State 1943–57. Strutt had been one of the few to enter the Home Office in 1925, as part of the first post-war entry, along with Norman Brook.

33 Assistant Under-Secretary of State 1947–55. He was Head of the Children's Department and had been especially influential under Chuter Ede on children's legislation following the major 1946 Report, Care of Children, Cmd. 6922.

34 Interview with Sir William Murrie.

35 Interview with Sir Hugh Munro-Lucas-Tooth and diary 6.8.54, Moran (87) p.618–9.

36 Macmillan (36) pp.441–3; Kilmuir (31) p.210.

37 Interview with Lord Lloyd.

38 Bresler (61) p.257.

39 Two hundred M.P.s signed a motion urging Maxwell Fyfe to reconsider his decision, but the Speaker, feeling himself bound by rulings of previous Speakers in earlier cases, ordered the motion to be removed from the Order Paper. Kilmuir (31) pp.205–8.

40 The Sunday Times 1.2.53.

41 Leader in The Times 14.2.53 said of Maxwell Fyfe that when the flood dangers decrease he should concentrate 'all his great energies and administrative capacity on the prevention of crime. That is the outstanding duty of a Home Secretary in the months ahead.'

42 House of Commons 26.2.53.

43 Cmd. 4932. Chaired by Sir E. Gowers.

44 House of Commons 28.1.54.

45 For some months The Times had been agitating on this score. See leader 29.1.54.

46 Interview with Sir Sidney Kirkman.

47 Private Information. A further consideration before Maxwell Fyfe and Newsam

was that whereas some authorities were active in carrying out their responsibilities, others appeared to do as little as possible, the chief culprit being Coventry City Council.

48 *The Campaign Guide 1955* p.360.

49 Boothby in *House of Commons* 3.12.53 and letter, Boothby to Maxwell Fyfe, 7.12.53. Monckton Papers, Box 3.

50 Interview with Lord Boothby and Boothby *(8)* pp.211–12. Boothby was made a peer in 1958.

51 *House of Commons* 28.4.54.

52 Interview with Sir Hugh Munro-Lucas-Tooth.

53 'Imperial Policy'. See Chapter 2 Part 3.

54 See *The Campaign Guide 1955* p.149.

55 *House of Commons* 18.2.54 and 18.3.54.

56 Letter, Michael Fraser to Lord Swinton, 3.11.54, Lord Fraser of Kilmorack's *Private Papers*. See also Paul Foot *The Rise of Enoch Powell (1969)* p.31. A letter that Oliver Lyttelton wrote to Sir Alfred Vincent dated 10.4.54 was also illustrative of the mounting concern: 'You are quite right about the colour problem in England. If it is not tackled, which it will be, we may easily get a situation of great proportions in twenty-five years.' *Chandos Papers*, Box 4/10.

57 David Wood wrote two articles in *The Times* in the winter of 1954 entitled 'First Signs of a Colour Problem' and 'Anxiety about the Future if the Inflow Lasts'. David Wood in *The Times* 6.3.78, and letter, Fraser to Swinton, *C.R.D. Papers*. A leader in *The Times* 3.5.54 noted the increasing public unhappiness about the rise in numbers of Commonwealth immigrants and called on the Government to institute a statistical survey so numbers could be assured.

58 *House of Commons* 15.12.54.

59 Philip *(144)* pp.295–7.

60 *House of Commons* 26.1.48.

61 *House of Commons* 13.11.51, Vol. 493, Col. 815.

62 Lee *(142)* pp.132–4. There had been a proposal in October 1943 in the House that a Secretary of State for Wales be appointed, and this was debated the following year. The Machinery of Government Committee under the Coalition Government in 1945 tentatively agreed to the suggestion that the Home Secretary look after Wales in Cabinet, but Churchill declined to make a statement on it during the 'Caretaker Government', May–July 1945.

63 Deputy Secretary at the Ministry of Health. See note 69 below.

64 The first, Cmd. 6938, covered 1.8.45–31.7.46. In December 1953, it was agreed that the Annual Report would in future be supported by a special annual digest of Welsh statistics. *The Times* 7.12.53.

65 This body published its First Memorandum in 1950 (Cmd. 8060) and its Second Memorandum in July 1953 (Cmd. 8844), both of which drew attention to rural depopulation. The Third Memorandum in January 1957 recommended that Wales should have a Secretary of State and a Welsh Office.

66 Ernest Bevin had this responsibility during 1950, and Chuter Ede from 1950–1.

67 Kilmuir *(31)* pp.203–5, 215–18. A leader in the *Sunday Times* on 18.11.51 mentioned Maxwell Fyfe's Scottish background as one of the two reasons why the Welsh were initially disappointed with the Conservatives' gestures in 1951. The other was that there had been some hopes of a separate Ministry for Wales.

68 *The Campaign Guide, 1955*, p. 321.

69 *Private Interview*. The 1951 developments were described by Sir Frederick Armer as 'just a façade to placate the Welsh and make them think that something was really happening'. Interview with Sir Frederick Armer. Armer, Deputy Secretary at Health, had senior responsibility for Welsh affairs. See also interview with Sir Arthur Peterson, B.O.A.P.A.H.

70 Kilmuir *(31)* pp.203–4.

71 *The Times* 21.2.53.

72 See, for example, the leader in *The Times* 9.7.53, which commented that demands for further political separation for Wales were fruitless: 'The root of the matter is that Wales has no economic identity as a nation . . . It is doubtful whether there is any substantial argument for further measures of devolution.' In March 1955 a Private Member's Bill was introduced proposing a Parliament for Wales, but was rejected. See Harrison *(244)* p.270. The decisive rejection of devolution in Wales in the 1978 referendum helped confirm that this judgment was sound.

73 For background pressures behind this, see Randall *(252)* pp.353–72 and

B.O.A.P.A.H. interview with Sir Goronwy Daniel.

74 Newsam (*148*) pp.168–9.

75 Interview with Sir Arthur Peterson.

76 A leader in *The Times* 1.7.53 on the occasion of the Queen's Coronation visit to Northern Ireland told of 'subjects whose loyalty to the crown is inflexible and whose contribution to all sides of British life is historic and abiding.' There was no mention of any problems other than the need to attract more business and industry.

77 This was regained in the 1955 Election, and the minor parties again won only two M.P.s (one Nationalist, Michael O'Neill, one 'Northern Ireland Labour', John Beattie).

78 Woolton to Churchill 24.4.53, *Woolton Papers*. Box 26. A whole series of Acts had been passed since 1951, for example the Re-equipment of Industry Acts of 1951 and 1953, to assist private industry with the cost of new capital equipment. As a result expenditure on all forms of industrial aid to Northern Ireland was running at about £3¼ million p.a. *Campaign Guide 1955* p.332. But these measures were still not felt to be sufficient.

79 Interview with Sir Hugh Munro-Lucas-Tooth.

CHAPTER 4 PART 4 pp.130–140

1 On 25th May, 1951, the Scottish Covenant Association was set up in place of the Scottish Convention.

2 *Annual Register 1951*. See also Kellas (*141*) pp.121–2.

3 'Scottish Control of Scottish Affairs.' A résumé of this appears in the 1950 Party Manifesto. Young (*111*) p.80.

4 Interview with Lord Craigton.

5 *House of Lords* 20.11.51.

6 Lord Catto had been Governor of the Bank of England, 1944–9, Lord Cobbold's immediate predecessor.

7 The 3rd Earl of Balfour. He had been Chairman of the N.C.B.'s Divisional Board for Scotland, 1946–51.

8 Cmd. 9212.

9 *The Economist* 31.7.54 pp.344–5.

10 See Harrison (*243*) p.307.

11 For a further comment on the Royal Commission, see Pottinger (*145*) pp.139–42. Pottinger was Secretary of the Commission.

12 See Chapter 7 Part 2.

13 Interview I with Ian Robertson, Private Secretary to the Scottish Secretary, 1952–5.

14 Lord Stuart interview, D.B.Y. The *Scotsman* on 27.10.51, however, had forecast Stuart for the job, and said his work in Scotland corresponded to the work of Lord Woolton as Party Chairman.

15 Stuart (*51*) pp.160–2.

16 Interview with Lord Strathclyde.

17 Interview with Sir Charles Cunningham.

18 Coote (*68*) p.262.

19 Interview D.B.Y.

20 Interview with Lord Home of The Hirsel. The *Scotsman* on 27.10.51 also tipped Lord Clydesmuir for the job.

21 Stuart (*51*) pp.162–4.

22 In addition Galbraith had been Vice-Chairman of the Party's Scottish Unionist Committee during the period in Opposition, and was also Vice-Chairman of the Party's Housing Committee. See Lord Strathclyde's B.O.A.P.A.H. interview.

23 McNair Snadden was also a Vice-Chairman of the Party's Agriculture and Food Committee in Opposition and the principal spokesman for matters concerned with agriculture in Scotland.

24 Interview with Lord Strathclyde.

25 Interview with Lord Craigton. Lady Tweedsmuir had been M.P. for South Aberdeen since 1946.

26 For interesting comments on Nixon Browne, see Pottinger (*45*) p.135–6.

27 Interviews with Sir Charles Cunningham and Ian Robertson. Stuart regarded Liberals as 'neither one thing nor the other', and oddly enough preferred people on the extreme left, such as John McGovern and James Maxton in earlier days. See Pottinger (*145*) pp.133–4.

28 Interview with George Pottinger.

29 *House of Commons* 21.11.51, Vol. 494, Col. 381.

30 Home (*24*) p.104.

31 Young (*111*) pp.82–3, and Dickie (*69*) pp.89–96.

32 Interview with Lord Home of The Hirsel.

33 Interview with Lord Home of The Hirsel.

34 Interview I with Ian Robertson. See also Macmillan (*36*) pp.449 and 460. The *Scotsman* on 8.8.55 referred to Tom Galbraith as James Stuart's 'Number One' in the House of Commons.

35 Galbraith had been a member of the Corporation of Glasgow, 1933–40. His know-

ledge of housing was responsible for his appointment as a junior Scottish Minister in the 'Caretaker Government' of 1945. He made the major speech on housing at the 1950 Party Conference. See Chapter 7 Part 2.

36 Interview with Sir William Murrie.
37 Interview with Lord Home of The Hirsel.
38 Interview with Lord Craigton. The *Scotsman* on 8.5.55 reported that Stuart's resignation on grounds of health had been thought possible on several occasions.
39 Interview II with Ian Robertson.
40 Interview with Sir Charles Cunningham.
41 Interview with Lord Strathclyde.
42 Interview with Lord Strathclyde.
43 Interview with Sir Douglas Haddow.
44 Stuart *(51)* pp.167–8.
45 Interview with Lord Stuart, D.B.Y.
46 For Stuart's relationship with Churchill, see Chapter 3 Part 2.
47 Stuart *(51)* p.171.
48 See Milne *(152)* pp.64, 101, 142 and 178.
49 Interview with Sir Charles Cunningham.
50 Dickie *(69)* p.95; Young *(111)* p.83.
51 *Annual Register* for 1951 and 1955.
52 The Hon. Lord Sorn was Senator of College of Justice in Scotland, 1944–63.
53 Cmd. 9244. One of the principal recommendations of the Sorn Committee was that owners' rates should be abolished and rents reduced. On 31.10.55 a Bill was introduced to give effect to the Committee's recommendations.
54 Interview with Sir Douglas Haddow.
55 Interview with Lorth Strathclyde.
56 *Annual Abstract of Statistics, 1957* p.61
57 See Macmillan *(36)* pp.398 and 460.
58 *Annual Abstract of Statistics, 1957*, p.63.
59 'I would pay special tribute to Tom Galbraith . . . whom I asked to apply himself particularly to this vitally important matter.' Stuart *(51)* pp.163–4. Galbraith played a key part in tackling one of the greatest of problems for Scottish housing, the continued existence of the Rent Restriction Act, introduced at the beginning of the First World War, which held rents artificially low and prevented repair work being executed.
60 Principal and Vice-Chancellor, University of Edinburgh, 1949–65.
61 It was a typical example of Stuart's concern with all aspects of the Scottish Office's work that his lack of interest in education notwithstanding, he rather than Henderson Stewart went to Edinburgh University to persuade Appleton to take on the chairmanship of the committee.
62 *Annual Abstract of Statistics, 1957*, p.96.
63 *Annual Abstract of Statistics, 1957*, p.97.
64 Clyde was ambitious for further office, and his hopes were realised when he was appointed Lord Justice-General of Scotland in December 1954.
65 For a discussion of Scottish issues before the House, see Burns *(239)* pp.272–96.
66 1955 was the high point of the Conservatives' electoral position in post-war Scotland.
67 Interview with Lord Home of The Hirsel.

CHAPTER 4 PART 5 pp.140–146

1 The Postmaster-General had a seat in Cabinet for most of the early part of the century.
2 The Post Office was also entirely responsible for the B.B.C. and had responsibility for frequency regulation since the 1930s.
3 Interview with Mark Chapman-Walker.
4 Interview with Sir William Ryland.
5 Interview with Sir Donald Sargent.
6 Interview with Mark Chapman-Walker.
7 His obituary in *The Times* 29.1.76, noted that De La Warr's disarming manner in the Lords did much to ease the passage of the Bill. He bore the brunt of the detailed defence of the Bill in Committee, bringing tact and humour to the discussions.
8. Interview with Mark Chapman-Walker. Woolton, so influential in the April 1955 reshuffle, did not have a very high opinion of De La Warr either.
9 Interview with Lord Hill and Hill *(23)* p.164.
10 This was the view, for example, of Lord Harmar-Nicholls (interview).
11 He had been in the Colonial Service in Malaya from 1920 to 1934, since entering the House in 1941 had specialised in colonial affairs, being a member of the Parliamentary Delegation to the West Indies in 1944, Sarawak in 1946 and Ceylon in 1949. He had also been Vice-Chariman of the Party's Imperial Affairs Committee until the 1951 General Election. In a letter, Lyttelton to Lennox-Boyd, 22.4.55, he makes a disparaging reference to Gammans' ambition to become Colonial Secretary. *Chandos Papers*, Box 4.15.
12 His obituary notice in *The Times* 9.2.57

gives a picture of a man who found difficulty in finding his feet in the House of Commons and ne who was never at ease speaking there.

13 One of the 1950 intake of M.P.s he was appointed Parliamentary Secretary at Agriculture in April 1955.

14 Little respected the office of Postmaster-General and he acknowledged De La Warr as the holder of that office and as a man of integrity. The trouble was that both were shy and difficult to know: Little was introverted, cautious but loyal; De La Warr was more outward and spontaneous.

15 Interview with Sir Donald Sargent. Director of Personnel and Accommodation, 1949–53. Director of Postal Services, 1953–5. Sargent became Deputy Director, 1955–9.

16 This experience culminated in a period as Director of Postal Services, 1944–7.

17 Interview with Jack Baldry. He preceded Ryland as Private Secretary to the P.M.G.

18 Engineer-in-Chief, 1951–4, and a third Deputy Director-General, 1954–5.

19 Interview with Sir William Ryland.

20 *The Campaign Guide, 1955* p.305.

21 Interview with Sir Donald Sargent. This meant De La Warr rejected the recommendations of the Terrington Committee. See *The Times* 26.6.52, leader.

22 De La Warr said in a debate in *House of Lords* 21.10.54 that the G.P.O. was now definitely on the offensive.

23 A critical leader in *The Times* 22.10.54 noted that, 'In Britain things have moved too slowly in the past', and that progress on the reduction of waiting lists was slow relative to the U.S.A. and most of Western Europe. It was also critical of the number of shared lines which had risen by 15% to 740.000 from March 1951 to March 1954.

24 *The Times* 15.12.53.

25 The best account is in Briggs (*136*) especially pp.423–44 and 885–936, and in Bernard Sendall's forthcoming first volume on the establishment of independent television. A useful (if not always accurate) account is still Wilson (*147*). See also Butt (*122*) pp.209–10, Goodhart (*123*) pp.161–4 and R. T. McKenzie's review of Wilson's book in the *Observer* 16.7.61.

26 Interview with Anthony Montague Browne.

27 Diary 10.7.55, reports Churchill as saying that Maxwell Fyfe gave him the wrong ad-

vice on television, and on 18.2.56 reports Churchill as saying, 'It was mad of the Tories to bring in commercial television.' Moran (*87*) pp.711 and 724.

28 Diary 3.6.52, Moran (*87*) p.416. Also on 27.11.53, p.528, 'I don't care what happens. The issue does not rouse me at all,' and on 26.3.54, p.559, 'I can't get excited about television. I can't make out what all the fuss is about.' This same attitude can be seen in another source, in a letter, Violet Bonham Carter to Gilbert Murray, 10.12.53, 'I spent a day at Chequers with Winston early in August . . . and he said to me quite frankly: "Well, I don't care tuppence about this business of sponsored television but I am not going to have anyone *forced* to vote for it." When I read De La Warr's declaration at the Conservative Party Conference *against* the free vote I wrote at once to Winston reminding him of his words to me and asking him to repudiate De La Warr, at least in private. He replied, most uncharacteristically, that "casual remarks in the course of an agreeable social conversation with you must not be given the character of an engagement or bargain. I should still prefer a free vote, but if it is the overwhelming view of the Party that the Whips should be on, I should certainly not quarrel with them upon the matter."' *Murray Papers*, Box 6. Despite his declared indifference to television, however, Churchill insisted, apparently against the wishes of almost the entire Cabinet, that the Coronation be televised. See Grigg (*222*) p.13.

29 Eden had been very pleased with his television broadcast during the 1951 Election campaign and after it became far more friendly to television, but remained very cool towards plans for commercial television. Inside Cabinet, Woolton was backed up mainly by Maxwell Fyfe and Stuart. Interview with Mark Chapman-Walker.

30 Diary 26.6.53 and 27.11.53, Moran (*87*) pp.435 and 528.

31 Churchill to Woolton, 14.3.52, *Woolton Papers*, Box 25.

32 Woolton to Churchill, 24.4.52, *Woolton Papers*, Box 25.

33 Cmd. 8550.

34 The details of this incident are recounted by Woolton to Churchill on 12.5.52, *Woolton Papers*, Box 25.

35 Barnett was fortunate to be at the head of a good team. One of the principal men was Alan Wolstencroft, Assistant Secretary, 1949–54. He was seconded to the I.T.A. as its Secretary from 1954–5.

36 *Woolton Papers*, Box 22.

37 Just what is meant by 'intervention' is not clear, but most likely it meant Conservative newspaper interests in I.T.V. The Beaverbrook newspapers had criticised the appointment of Sir Robert Fraser as Director-General because he had stood as a socialist candidate for Parliament in the 1930s. Interview with Bernard Sendall.

38 Diary 22.12.54, *Woolton Papers*, Box 3.

CHAPTER 4 PART 6 pp.146–151

1 Macmillan (*36*) p.356 suggests Churchill wanted to have both an Asquith and a Lloyd-George in his Government. In the event, he secured only Gwilym Lloyd-George, as Minister of Food until 1954, then as Home Secretary. Cys Asquith was the fourth son of the first Earl.

2 Asquith was nine years younger than Simonds. Asquith had been called to the bar in 1920, made a K.C. in 1936 and a Lord Justice of Appeal in 1946. Lord Simonds achieved the first two distinctions in 1906 and 1924, and was made a Judge of the Chancery Division of the High Court in 1937.

3 See Monckton's autobiographical notes, leaf 43, *Monckton Papers*, Box 49.

4 Kilmuir (*31*) p.190. Also Moran diary Churchill talking: 'David always wanted [to be Lord Chancellor]. He wanted it when Simonds got it, but I could not spare him then.' Diary 21.10.54, Moran (*87*) p.637.

5 Lord Shawcross (interview) said, 'I understood from Maxwell Fyfe that it was his understanding that he could become Lord Chancellor when he desired, but how explicit it was made I don't know.'

6 Simon had favoured being appointed to the shadow Cabinet in 1950 as a means of bringing the Liberals into line. Letter, Woolton to Churchill, 9.3.50, *Woolton Papers*, Box 21.

7 Lord Schuster for example (Permanent Secretary to Lord Chancellor, 1915–44). Interview with Sir George Coldstream.

8 He was born in 1873.

9 Neither Maxwell Fyfe nor Monckton possessed the education or intellectual power of Simonds, although Maxwell Fyfe was a far better politician and Monckton had a more varied experience of life than Simonds.

10 Interview with Sir George Coldstream.

11 Interview with Lord Shawcross.

12 Letter, Simonds to Woolton, 8.12.52, *Woolton Papers*, Box 77. See also diary 28.4.54, Moran (*87*) p.572.

13 The Lord Chancellor is in a far stronger position in standing up for the judges if he has the Treasury Ministers' active support, and he is more likely to have this if he has stood the heat and burden as a House of Commons Minister.

14 Interview with Sir John Colville.

15 Lord Gardiner was the same in the Wilson Cabinet.

16 Interview I with Sir George Mallaby.

17 Diary 20.3.53 and 24.3.53, *Crookshank Papers*. The postponement was announced at midnight on 23.3.53.

18 *The Times* 24.3.53. The Bill had proposed that the seventy-nine senior judges received, in addition to their salary, an annual allowance of £1,000 which would not be subject to income tax. No further action, however, was taken before the summer recess, during which Asquith wrote to Monckton asking the Government's intentions on the matter. Monckton replied optimistically: 'I am confident that not only the old man but all of us intend to go ahead on the lines you indicate without further delay.' Letter, Monckton to Asquith, 13.8.53, *Monckton Papers*, Box 3.

19 Jackson (*125*) pp.108–9.

20 He had made a considerable sum at the bar but it would be erroneous to argue that this was the reason for his not claiming his increase.

21 Interview with Sir George Coldstream.

22 For comments on Simonds as a judge, see Gilmour, *The Body Politic*, p.379, and also Robert Stevens, *Law and Politics*, Weidenfeld and Nicolson, 1979.

23 *Private Information*.

24 Diary 21.10.54, Moran (*87*) p.637: diary 10.7.55, p.711. Moran says Churchill 'appeared uncertain how it would be taken'.

25 Letter, Simonds to Cherwell, 22.10.54, *Cherwell Papers*, Pers.101.

26 Kilmuir (*31*) p.233.

27 *Monckton Papers*, Box 4.
28 *Private Information.*
29 Interview with Lord Amory.
30 See Chapter 3 Part 2.
31 Interview I with Sir John Foster.
32 Though not an M.P. until 1951. In his unpublished autobiography, however, Monckton says when Churchill asked him to enter the House in 1951 he made it plain that it was with a view to becoming Attorney-General. *Monckton Papers*, Leaf 43, Box 49.
33 Selwyn Lloyd thought he might have been asked to be a Law Officer, though he did not want to become one. Selwyn Lloyd *(46)* p.3.
34 *The Times* 5.11.51.
35 Interview with Sir Lionel Heald.
36 He was, however, well known in political circles, as M.P. for Daventry 1943–50 and South Northants since 1950. He had been Chairman until the 1951 General Election of the Conservative Party's Legal Committee, with Selwyn Lloyd Vice-Chairman. He had also displayed knowledge of the intricacies of the law and had been of great service to the Opposition from 1945–51. He had been Parliamentary Secretary to the Ministry of Works in the 'Caretaker Government'. The *Sunday Times* on 28.10.51 even thought him a likely Attorney-General in 1951.
37 See, for example, *The Times* 17.11.51.
38 Interview with Sir Lionel Heald.
39 For a contemporary discussion of the job of Attorney-General, see Shawcross *(253)* pp.380–92.
40 In a speech at the annual meeting of the Bar Council on 26th April he referred to the burdens of office and the possibility of his resignation in the following year. This came as no surprise to his colleagues and constituents. *The Times* 28.4.54. There was an unfortunate case in South Wales when he failed to get a conviction for murder, partly on account of his lack of practice at handling criminal cases.
41 Letter, Monckton to Bracken, 12.4.54, *Monckton Papers*, Box 4.
42 The *Economist* 23.10.54 pp.287–8 noted that weakness might develop in the conduct of legal problems in the Commons. Heald was always able to shelter behind Maxwell Fyfe, who had now been promoted to Lord Chancellor and left for the Upper House, and it felt a less gifted

Attorney-General appointed. It continued that there would be a testing initiation for the new and able Solicitor-General.
43 He was Attorney-General until 1962, when he succeeded Kilmuir as Lord Chancellor (as Lord Dilhorne) until the Conservative defeat in 1964.
44 Solicitor-General, 1945–51. Six months before the General Election, Shawcross went to the Board of Trade and Soskice became Attorney-General. Shawcross had been by far the abler of the two.

CHAPTER 4 PART 7 pp.151–153

1 It is difficult to place the Ministry of Works within any category, but perhaps it fits more easily into this chapter than elsewhere.
2 For details of this and other aspects of the Ministry's work, see Emmerson *(151)*, especially pp.19–22 and 115–28.
3 Diary 28.10.51, Macmillan *(36)* p.365.
4 See, for example, Hill *(23)* p.146. Eccles had been heading for high office, according to a profile in the *Observer* on 7.6.53, until he wrote an article in *The Times* at the Election (which I could not trace) which implied that social services would be cut.
5 Interview with Sir John Rodgers.
6 Interview with Sir Edward Muir.
7 See, for example, Bevins *(5)* p.30.
8 '. ... he soon showed his interest in the work of the Department and we found that he had the qualities of a good Minister. He was ready to give clear and firm decisions on matters of policy and then to rely on the Department to see that his decisions were carried out.' Sir Harold Emmerson, 'Masters and Servants' p.95.
9 Interview with Lord Eccles.
10 See Macmillan *(36)* pp.398 and 459–60.
11 See Sir Harold Emmerson's manuscript, 'Masters and Servants' in the Royal Institute of Public Administration.
12 Diary 6.2.53, *Crookshank Papers*.
13 *Private Information.*
14 The job was upgraded to Cabinet on Buchan-Hepburn's appointment, due to his personal qualifications and the position he attained in the Party hierarchy as Chief Whip.
15 Mackenzie and Grove *(143)* p.289.
16 Both junior Ministers were very different types of men. Molson, public school and

Oxford, was an M.P. 1931–5 and again from 1939. He was a barrister and chairman of the Tory Reform Group in 1945. Bevins was educated at state schools and had entered the House in 1950.

17 Interview with Sir Edward Muir.

CHAPTER 5 PART 1 pp.154–169

1 See Macmillan (*36*) p.47 and Chapter 3 Part 1.

2 When Churchill appointed Lyttelton Chairman of the Finance Committee, he said offices were very fluid and he could not rely on being appointed the next Conservative Chancellor. He might very well be, but Churchill would not commit himself. Interview with Lord Chandos, D.B.Y. See also Macmillan (*36*) pp.363 and 497.

3 Anderson was M.P. for the Scottish Universities until University seats were abolished in 1950. See Harris (*77*) p.140.

4 Crookshank had been Financial Secretary at the Treasury May 1940–February 1943.

5 Diary 22.12.55, *Woolton Papers*.

6 Chandos (*11*) pp.342–4.

7 Interview I with Lord Butler.

8 Interview with Lord Chandos, D.B.Y.

9 Interview with Sir Angus Mackintosh.

10 Churchill asked Lyttelton, but had second thoughts, and Anderson was appointed. Chandos (*11*).

11 Letter, Lyttelton to Churchill, 31.7.54, *Chandos Papers*, Box 4/5. A profile on Lyttelton in the *Observer* on 16.11.52 said the appointment of Butler 'must have come as a blow [to Lyttelton]'.

12 Lyttelton had been a successful businessman ever since he first joined the British Metal Corporation in 1920, where he remained for twenty years. He relinquished the chairmanship of Associated Electrical Industries in 1951. Butler had been a fellow of Corpus Christi, Cambridge, until he entered the House in 1929. The *Spectator* (2.11.51) did, however, point out that Butler's own (albeit limited) business experience would equip him well for the job.

13 Butler had been appointed to the Parliamentary under-secretaryship vacated by Salisbury on his resignation from the Foreign Office in February 1938. According to Wilfrid Sendall (interview) Churchill's relationship with Butler had begun to improve as far back as the South Hammer-

smith by-election disaster in 1949, after which Churchill became alerted to the work Butler had been doing in preparing a positive programme for the Party.

14 Interview with Sir Hubert Ashton.

15 He told Piers Dixon in late 1950 that he expected to be made Chancellor. Lyttelton was his only possible rival. *Piers Dixon Diary*. (Son of Sir Pierson Dixon.)

16 Salter was Independent M.P. for Oxford University, 1937–50. Churchill apparently gave Salter this unlikely description. Butler (*10*) p.156.

17 Woolton (*55*) p.374.

18 Wheeler-Bennett (*104*) pp.351–3. This was more a wartime grouping of Departments than one suited to the post-war position. Churchill was thinking of the position Anderson had held during the War Coalition when he had been supervising the home front. It is most unlikely that Anderson could have held such a position in 1951. Certainly the Treasury would have objected most strongly. Interview II with Lord Plowden. See also Chapter 3 Part 4.

19 For example, 'he didn't make the impression of a new broom at all.' Interview with Lord Roberthall.

20 Interview with Lord Armstrong of Sanderstead.

21 Diary 12.5.52, James, ed. (*28*) pp.468–9.

22 His previous ministerial experience had been confined to the India Office (1932–7), Foreign Office (1938–41), Board of Education (1941–4) and Ministry of Labour (1937–8 and 1945). Lord Normanbrook told the historian John Barnes that Butler knew very little about economics, probably as little as any Chancellor he had known, but he had a very good 'feel' for the job. Discussion with John Barnes.

23 'There'd be some issue being carefully debated as to whether he should do this or do that, and he'd have a meeting and thrash it all out, and you'd think he'd agreed with us, and just as you were going out of the door he'd say, "mind you, nothing's been decided."' A senior official in interview.

24 See, for example, diary 8.8.53, Moran (*87*) p.473.

25 'I can never remember on major issues of policy Rab saying either we've got to do this or we've got to do that.' Interview with Lord Roberthall.

26 See Chapter 5 Part 2.

27 Butler (*10*) p.169. Henry Channon wrote

in his diary for 26.7.53: 'He is deeply affected by his mother's death.' James, ed. (*28*) p.478.

28 Butler (*10*) pp.175–6. Lord Butler said (Interview II) of the loss of his mother (and father who died in November 1952): 'It affected my head. I remember having some terrible headaches.' But in neither interview did he volunteer information on the loss of his wife.

29 Woolton (no friend) noted in his diary on 5.4.55: '. . . he will have to take hold of himself before long . . . There's much too much "I" about this gentleman.' *Woolton Papers*.

30 She had been ill for more than a year: in November 1953, she had had a serious operation, and had been unable to accompany Butler to Australia in the New Year. *The Times* 8.12.54. But Butler's confidence was later to return very much after he married Mollie Courtauld in 1959, a particularly happy marriage.

31 Interview with Lord Brooke of Cumnor.

32 Interview with Lord Boyle of Handsworth.

33 Cripps was Minister for Economic Affairs, a far more senior job, with his own Department, from September to November 1947 in the Cabinet. Gaitskell had the job from February to October 1950, not in Cabinet and without his own Department. Butler said in the *House of Commons* on 21.11.51 that the Minister of State for Economic Affairs could advise him on questions of general financial and economic policy and help him within the Treasury itself. In particular his work would be in the field of financial relationships with overseas countries including trade and payments negotiations and exchange control.

34 Churchill said in the *House of Commons* on 2.12.52 that the scope of the Economic Secretary would be 'broadly the same' as the job of Minister of State for Economic Affairs. *The Times* 25.11.52 commented that the position of Economic Secretary was a better one than Minister of State as it made absolutely clear the undivided responsibility of the Chancellor and the subordinate position of the two junior Ministers.

35 'It was not without an inner struggle that I decided to become a Conservative . . . I had no idea myself of ever returning to Parliament, and certainly no wish to do so.

Then this year I felt that I could not say "no" to the only man who could have induced me . . . to enter the fray again.' Letter, Salter to Gilbert Murray 10.4.51, *Murray Papers*, Box 102.

36 Salter (*44*) p.339.

37 Salter (*45*) p.216.

38 Butler (*10*) p.156. Salter (*45*) p.216 says they did work well.

39 Interview I with Lord Butler.

40 Interview with Lord Armstrong of Sanderstead.

41 Interview with Lord Boyd-Carpenter.

42 Maudling (*39*) p.53.

43 'Salter had made some uncautious remarks on cuts.' Diary 23.11.51, *Crookshank Papers*.

44 Interview with Reginald Maudling.

45 Interview with Lord Armstrong of Sanderstead.

46 See Maudling (*39*) p.54.

47 In particular, Woolton, Eden's closest adviser at this time, did not have a high opinion of Thorneycroft. Diary 11.3.55, *Woolton Papers*, Box 3.

48 Interview II with Lord Butler.

49 Butler (*10*) p.156.

50 Lord Selwyn Lloyd (*46*) p.3. He had been a Secretary of the Conservative Party Finance Committee in Opposition.

51 He was a barrister who entered Parliament in 1945. For an account of his period at the Treasury, see Boyd-Carpenter (*8a*) pp.96–106.

52 Interview II with Lord Butler. Butler left a great deal of the discussions on expenditure with Departments to the Financial Secretary of the Treasury and to his officials.

53 Butler gave Brooke various jobs to do in the Research Department after 1951: in January 1954 he invited Brooke to be Chairman of a policy group working on policy statements and draft manifestoes. Butler personally chose Brooke to be Financial Secretary. Interview with Lord Brooke of Cumnor.

54 Harris (*77*) pp.172–3.

55 Chester (*259*) p.21. For details, see Chapter 4 Part 1 where general comments on Bridges in his period as Head of the Civil Service can also be found.

56 There were two main Committees in the Treasury concerned with the Budget. The Budget Committee, presided over by Bridges and composed just of officials; Gil-

bert, Brittain, Hall, Plowden, until his departure, and the Heads of Customs and Excise and Inland Revenue being the main attenders. This began to meet about September and its job was to plan Budget strategy preparatory to making a submission to the Chancellor about what the Budget might contain. About the same time Hall submitted a paper on the state of the economy. The Committee reported in about December, though it continued in existence until the Budget. On receipt of its report, Butler would start his own Committee, on which sat the junior Ministers, also Bridges, Hall, Gilbert, Brittain and the Heads of Inland Revenue and Customs and Excise. For a general discussion on the Budgetary system, see Brittain (*137*). An important book appeared in 1956 written by the American Samuel Beer, which discussed Treasury co-ordination. D. N. Chester wrote: 'Those who wish to understand the Treasury doctrine in the year 1954 or thereabouts cannot find a better guide.' See Chester (*259*) pp.15–18. For another valuable commentary on Beer's book, see Finer (*263*) pp.79–80.

57 Interview II with Lord Butler.
58 *Private Information.*
59 Interview with Lord Armstrong of Sanderstead, who was Joint Permanent Secretary of the Treasury, 1962–8 and Head of the Civil Service, 1968–74.
60 Interview with Lord Croham, who succeeded Armstrong as Permanent Secretary of the Treasury until 1974 and as Head of the Civil Service until 1977.
61 Interview I with Lord Butler.
62 Interview with Sir John Winnifrith.
63 Winnifrith (*109*) pp.48–53.
64 Opinions about tiredness with his job after 1951 varied. Other features that colleagues commented on during his period as Second Secretary were his kindly manner to subordinates and his liking for keeping in touch with all that was going on in Parliament.
65 Interview with Sir Edward Playfair.
66 Winnifrith (*109*) p.53.
67 Interview with Sir Louis Petch.
68 Butler in reply to a question in the *House of Commons* on 7.7.53 said that Gilbert was already acting as deputy to the Permanent Secretary, but when Plowden left the Treasury at the end of October, Gilbert would also take over the duties of the

Chief Planning Officer, aided by a Third Secretary. At Butler's request, Plowden remained a member of the Economic Planning Board. *The Times* 30.6.53.
69 Interview I with Lord Butler.
70 One spending minister, Peake, threatened resignation when Gilbert blocked access to the Chancellor. Interview with Sir Geoffrey King.
71 Butler (*10*) p.157 talks of Brittan and Gilbert as the 'Treasury stalwarts'.
72 In their personal relations, though, Butler tended to be somewhat uncomfortable with Rowan.
73 He had been at the centre of Government during the war as Assistant and later Principal Private Secretary to the Prime Minister from 1941–5. He had been Permanent Secretary of the short-lived office of Minister for Economic Affairs in 1947.
74 A superb sportsman, he had on three occasions captained England at hockey (1937, 1938 and 1947).
75 Interview I with Lord Butler.
76 See Chapter 5 Part 2.
77 Padmore, too, had held a key job during the war, as Principal Private Secretary to the Chancellor of the Exchequer, 1943–5.
78 Interview I with Lord Butler.
79 The Second Secretaries at the Treasury during the 1950s were not as a whole men of the highest calibre as, for example, Sir Frederick Phillips had been, who had died in office in August 1943.
80 *The Times* 3.8.51. Plowden's initial intention had been to stay only one year. Interview I with Lord Plowden. It is worth commenting that it is highly unlikely that Brook's appointment to this economic job would have been a happy one.
81 Attlee told the *House of Commons* on 27.3.47 that Plowden was to be appointed to a new post of Economic Planning Officer under the Lord President of the Council.
82 Interview II with Lord Plowden.
83 Its members were: three representatives of the F.B.I. and the British Employers Association, three representatives of the T.U.C., three members of the Central Economic Planning Staff, the Permanent Secretaries of the Board of Trade, Ministry of Labour and Ministry of Supply, and the Director of the Economic Section.
84 Jennings (*131*) pp.325–6; Daalder (*129*) pp.223–6.

85 Plowden himself felt at the time that Cripps' plan was based on a misconception of what planning involved in peacetime. Cripps thought one could act as one had during the war, when he had been a highly successful planner. Interview II with Lord Plowden. The original plan was that each Department was to have a full-time planning staff under a senior officer, and at the centre was to be a joint staff made up of departmental planning officers with a full-time executive head, Plowden. It was visualised that the new organisation would deal both with the preparation of long-term plans, and the daily adjustment of existing ones in the light of changed circumstances.

86 See Beer (159) p.98.

87 The 1952 Economic Survey, for example, exhibited far less evidence of reliance on planning than earlier Surveys.

88 Strath left the Treasury in 1955 to become a full-time member of the Atomic Energy Authority. What remained of the C.E.P.S. was transferred to the National Resources Group, and for a time was under Otto Clarke. This was in turn absorbed into the National Economy Group in 1962.

89 Correspondence with Lord Roberthall.

90 'I have no doubt that the word planning had a nasty taste to the Conservatives. Though I don't think they had any particular antipathy to what we were trying to do.' Interview II with Lord Plowden.

91 Butler (10) p.157.

92 For an interesting contemporary comparative critique on the position of economists in Government in the U.K. and the Netherlands, see Marris (268) pp.759–83.

93 Butler (10) p.157.

94 Private Secretary, 1953–5; later Head of the Home Civil Service, 1978–

95 Private Secretary, 1954–5; later Secretary to the Cabinet, 1979–

96 Economic Minister at Washington in succession to Rowan until 1954, then Third Secretary 1955–60. He had been Pitblado's predecessor as Principal Private Secretary to the Prime Minister.

97 Butler (10) p.157.

98 Under-Secretary, 1947–55, later Sir Richard Clarke. It was he who helped Butler cut imports in 1952. Interview I with Lord Butler. By the later 1950s, Clarke had become one of the most authoritative and influential officials in the Treasury. He became Permanent Secretary at the Ministry of Technology from 1966–70.

99 Third Secretary, 1949–58; later Comptroller and Auditor General, 1958–66.

100 Economic Section from 1952. Later Deputy Secretary, Central Policy Review Staff, 1971–8.

101 Under-Secretary 1949–55. Formerly Principal Private Secretary to Dalton and Cripps 1945–9. Later Cabinet Secretary, 1963–73.

102 Created Lord Cobbold in 1960.

103 Minutes were not taken at these meetings, which were informal, and Private Secretaries did not attend. Private Information.

104 Interview with Sir George Bolton.

105 Executive Director of the Bank, 1948–57. U.K. Alternate Governor of I.M.F., 1952–7.

106 See Chapter 5 Part 2.

107 Interview with Lord Armstrong of Sanderstead. See Chapter 5 Part 2.

108 There is no evidence, though, that Butler took much note of the views of the Finance Committee en masse.

109 Interview with Sir Hubert Ashton. For more details of the Government's relations with industry, see Chapter 5 Part 3.

110 See Chapter 6 Part 1.

111 Cripps had initiated a 'wage freeze' in 4.2.48.

112 Interview with Lord Roberthall.

113 Woolton to Prime Minister, 24.4.53, Woolton Papers, Box 26.

114 'The Problem of Stable Employment', 30.4.53, Woolton Papers, Box 26.

115 Referring to the T.M.A.C., Butler said: 'Lord Woolton and I never saw eye to eye. He always thought he ought to control things.' Interview I with Lord Butler. Woolton had strong views, which he was wont to express forcibly in the first year, before his illness. Writing to Churchill on 21.7.52, he urged a major change in the Government's economic policy, in the direction of less regulation and also freeing the pound. Woolton Papers, Box 25.

116 The Treasury officials only came before the T.M.A.C. once, on the occasion that they were asked whether or not Gaitskell had followed their advice. Diary 8.1.56, Woolton Papers.

117 Woolton (55) pp.371–4; Mackintosh (132) p.514; Brittan (161) pp.189–90.

118 Diary 6.2.54, Moran (87) p.552.

119 'I cannot tell you how much we shall miss you. There is no one left with your knowledge of the economy as well as our overseas financial policy. I really feel quite bereft.' Letter. Butler to Lyttelton. 10.8.54. *Chandos Papers*. Box 4/11.

120 Interview II with Lord Butler.

121 *House of Commons* 22.11.51.

122 'When you invited me to come back into the Government in November 1951 I felt I could be of little use in the statistical and economic field without MacDougall's help. Very reluctantly he agreed to foresake [*sic*] his family to come back to our assistance and he has proved absolutely invaluable during the time he has been my chief adviser on economic affairs.' Letter. Cherwell to Churchill. 13.3.53. *Cherwell Papers*. OFF 61.1.

123 For a flavour of the Statistical Branch's views on how to tackle the fall in reserves – stricter import controls accompanied by tougher fiscal and monetary controls – see MacDougall (*267*) p.175. MacDougall later became Chief Economic Adviser to the Treasury. 1969–73.

124 Interview with Sir David Pitblado.

125 See Chapter 2 Part 1.

126 Macmillan wrote of Churchill during 1945–51: 'In reality his general views on economic affairs had not substantially changed from those he had absorbed from his Victorian upbringing. While he was always ready to study new ideas . . . he was not capable or desirous of initiating new concepts of financial. monetary or economic policy.' Macmillan (*36*) p.45.

127 Interview with Lord Soames. See also diary 26.10.54. Moran (*87*) p.639.

128 Interview I with Lord Butler. In fact Butler's colleagues felt proud of the record on economic policy, which was a major theme in Conservative publicity during the 1955 Election campaign. It is probable that Butler's recollection is over-coloured by his feelings during his last year at the Treasury (throughout 1955).

129 *Private Information.*

130 *Private Information.* The advice. nevertheless. always presented Butler with a number of policy alternatives. Though an attachment to Keynesianism pervaded almost the whole Treasury. a few were sceptical. one or two Third Secretaries. for example. Clarke, Third Secretary, 1955, and also Playfair and Strath.

131 He was. of course. helped a great deal by exogenous factors. See Chapter 5 Part 2.

CHAPTER 5 PART 2 pp.169–178

1 For bringing attention to these periods. the author is indebted to his interview with Lord Boyle of Handsworth. Details of precise policies and Budgets will be found in several other studies. See. for example. Brittan (*161*), Dow (*163*), Kenen (*167*), Macrae (*169*). Oppenheimer in Bogdanor and Skidelsky. ed. (*114*) and Worswick and Ady (*175*).

2 Interview with Lord Croham.

3 Within a few days of the General Election. a meeting of Ministers took place in the Chancellor's room at the House of Commons. at which Bridges and Plowden represented the Treasury. They stressed to the Ministers the need to increase the Bank rate. and even though the increase was small. they felt that psychologically it would have a marked effect. One Minister in particular was worried about the impact on council house rents. and others expressed general unease at the proposal. Correspondence with Lord Plowden.

4 Thorneycroft and the Board of Trade argued against the Treasury that whereas import controls would lead to an immediate improvement of the balance of payments, inefficiencies would inevitably arise and the policy would thus be counterproductive.

5 See Chapter 2 Part 3.

6 Lord Croham (B.O.A.P.A.H. interview) said the panic with which Labour's rearmament programme was put into force destroyed much of Britain's early post-war reconstruction and in effect made a nonsense of all the planning up until then.

7 See Chapter 8 Part 6.

8 The following section is based on Morgan (*169a*) pp.1–6. As the author on 'official history'. Morgan was given full access to official documents not generally available under the 'thirty year rule'.

9 Interview with Lord Coleraine (R. Law).

10 'You see Butskellism [compounded of the names of both Chancellors after an article in *The Economist* 13.2.54 pp.439–41] really followed upon the demise of "Robot" . . . and after that I reverted to normal Keynesian economics. Not only had my father-in-

law, Samuel Courtauld, been a great friend of Keynes, and also Keynes being in a neighbouring college to mine at King's Cambridge, and I knew Keynes as well, and so my policy in dealing with unemployment was to enlarge the economy when unemployment was getting a little too severe.' Interview with Lord Butler. It is worthy of note that the much cited *Economist* article did not claim Gaitskell and Butler were fundamentally similar, but that they faced similar problems in trying to moderate their less prudent followers. Philip Williams writes in his meticulous biography of Hugh Gaitskell that the supposed area of agreement between Gaitskell and Butler has been much exaggerated. Williams (*106*) pp.312–8. In doing so he himself rather over-states his case.

11 Richard (Otto) Clarke, Under-Secretary at the Treasury, 1947–55. Clarke had been a brilliant planner and a believer in it in the early post-war years, but then switched and became an economic liberal. It would be fair to say that Clarke, though junior to Rowan, was the more influential on this issue. *Private Information*.

12 For published accounts of the episode, see Birkenhead (*59*) pp.283–94, Salter (*45*) pp.215–24, Brittan (*161*) pp.195–200 and MacDougall (*267*) pp.175–6. In particular, these accounts give the arguments on either side, and consequently this aspect of the affair, the economic discussion, will not be dealt with here.

13 Interview with Sir George Bolton.

14 Interview I with Lord Butler. It is not of course accurate to say that floating avoids devaluation – one floats down, instead of taking one jump, though in practice the first day could probably be just the same.

15 Plowden, however, was away from Whitehall during most of the debate. He was busy on NATO work in Paris and Lisbon.

16 The agreed plan at the conference was for sterling area accounts to be restored to balance in the second half of 1952.

17 Diary 20.2.52, *Crookshank Papers*.

18 Interview with Lord Chandos, D.B.Y.

19 *Beaverbrook Papers*, Box C57.

20 Diary 22.2.52, *Crookshank Papers*.

21 Assistant Under-Secretary, Foreign Office, 1948–52. In normal circumstances, Sir Roger Makins would have been dispatched on the errand, but on this occasion

was out of the U.K. on a tour of the Persian Gulf. (Makins was the Deputy Under-Secretary at the Foreign Office responsible for economic affairs.) Berthoud, Makins' deputy, was strongly opposed to the plan, and was convinced that Makins would be as well – which proved to be the case on Makins' return to the U.K.

22 Then a Third Secretary at the Treasury. He became a Second Secretary in 1953.

23 Interview with Sir Eric Berthoud.

24 Swinton was very worried about the likely effect on the Commonwealth and the inflation it was likely to cause. He told Butler that if he introduced it the following year, he would support him. Interview I with Lord Butler. See also the letter from Swinton, quoted in Buter (*10*) p.159.

25 Interview with Lord Robbins. Robbins was formerly Director of the Economic Section of Offices of the war Cabinet, 1941–5.

26 *Private Papers* and also undated Minute, Cherwell to Churchill: 'If you would like an independent view on this matter you might care to see Professor Lionel Robbins, who had, I understand, been consulted by the Treasury . . . I would have suggested your seeing Sir Edwin Plowden . . . but he might find it difficult to speak freely having regard to the views the Chancellor has expressed on the matter.' *Cherwell Papers*, Pers.24 Part III. See also Salter (*45*) pp.219–20.

27 Cherwell and MacDougall had gone to Oxford over the weekend to prepare a paper arguing against 'Robot'. MacDougall played a key role in providing Cherwell with his economic arguments.

28 Diary 26.2.52, 27.2.52, 28.2.52, *Crookshank Papers*. It is indicative that Butler in Butler (*10*) makes no mention of Crookshank or Woolton. Presumably Eccles would have been in favour of 'Robot' (see diary 4.10.51) and also Nicolson (*43*) p.210 who was an influential member of the T.M.A.C., whose members were in favour of freeing the pound.

29 Woolton to Churchill, 21.7.52, *Woolton Papers*, Box 25.

30 Diary 29.2.52, *Crookshank Papers*. Macmillan wrote in his diary for that day: 'It is very likely that we shall come to this in April or May. But that would be after . . . consultation and discussion; not as a panic matter, amounting to default (or 90 per

cent and 80 per cent default).' Quoted in Macmillan (*36*) p.382.

31 The most important of these moves was in February 1955 when the Bank was permitted to support the transferable rate, in fact a *de facto* convertibility. *De jure* convertibility followed in 1958, but at a fixed rate of exchange. Macrae (*169*) pp.43–4, mentions an unfortunate side effect of the protracted discussions over convertibility: the uncertainty generated led to speculation that sterling might go on to a floating rate of exchange after the General Election: there in fact followed a small speculative run against the currency in 1955.

32 The other main features of the 1952 Budget were the imposition of the excess profits levy; reduction in profits tax from 26¼% to 22½% net on distributed profits; a rise in petrol tax of 7½d a gallon; introduction of a flat rate of £12 10s 0d per annum for motor vehicle licences; in May purchase tax on textiles and clothing was reduced by 25%.

33 'The lesson of 1952 was that solvency can only be sought hopefully by admitting and facing fairly the real cost of the claims which compete for the nation's scarce resources. It is a lesson which will always be associated with the name of Mr. Butler.' *The Times* 1.1.53.

34 Dow (*163*) pp.74–5.

35 Butler wrote to Monckton on 7.7.52 before a key Cabinet meeting the following day on Government expenditure. In the letter Butler stressed the importance of giving exports priority over defence, in such a way that the relationship with the United States would not be damaged, neither would they play into Bevan's hands, nor create unemployment. *Monckton Papers*, Box 2.

36 Budget day was 14th April. Principal measures were the reduction in the standard rate of income tax from 9s 6d to 9s; all round reduction of 25% to purchase tax except for textiles and clothing; the announcement of the end of the excess profits levy on 1st January, 1954.

37 *House of Commons* 7.4.54, Vol. 526, Col. 381. It would be an error, however, to see the 1954 Budget merely as a standstill one. Through its introduction of an investment allowance, it superimposed an interest boom on what would, in any case, have been an upsurge in consumer spending.

38 Diary 6.4.54, *Woolton Papers*.

39 Budget day was 6th April, 1954. Other main measures were a reduction of death duties on family businesses; a reduction on entertainments duty (introduced in the previous Budget); post-war credits to be repaid to heirs at a date when the original holder would have reached qualifying age; reduction in purchase tax on certain domestic appliances.

40 *Conservative Party Conference Official Report, 1954,* p.66.

41 Interview II with Lord Butler.

42 Morgan (*169a*) p.6.

43 For example, Brittan (*161*) pp.201–2, called it a 'serious blunder'.

44 For example, Butler's erratic behaviour was noted at a Cabinet meeting by Woolton in his diary on 14.3.55. *Woolton Papers*. Crookshank in his diary for 18.4.55 recorded how during the Budget Cabinet on that day 'Rab got into quite a fret.' *Crookshank Papers*. See Part 1.

45 Eden (*14*) p.278.

46 Lord Boyle of Handsworth (interview) made two further points. First, that, since the early months of 1953, Butler had been carrying with him in his economic policy the great majority of the 1922 Committee and the Party's Finance Committee. Second, that though Butler was able to announce a prospective Budget surplus of nearly £300m., this was an 'above the line' surplus, and a substantial deficit 'below the line' was also forecast.

47 Interview I with Lord Butler.

48 See Butler (*10*) pp.177–9.

49 'One of the physical reasons for this was that I was told there was going to be an Election. I did it . . . to reduce the size of the Finance Bill.' Interview I with Lord Butler.

50 Interview with Lord Brooke of Cumnor.

51 See Bogdanor and Skidelsky, eds. (*114*) p.64.

52 Macrae (*169*) p.42.

53 Interview with Lord Roberthall.

54 Dow makes the point (*163*) pp.79–80 that a faith in monetary policy was widely held in informed circles, e.g. *The Economist*, and that monetary policy measures in late 1951 and early 1952 were praised for making possible the mild 1952 Budget.

55 When he eventually left the Treasury in December 1955, *The Economist* 31.12.55, p.1157 said: 'The essential achievement of

Mr. Butler's chancellorship has been Britain's advance from reliance upon compulsory controls to reliance upon a free market economy.' The previous week, 24.12.55, p.1085, it had said: 'Among foreign observers and holders of sterling, Mr. Butler has built for himself a strong reputation as the guarantor of its value.'

56 As early as 1968, R. C. O. Matthews was writing that the belief that full employment since the war was due to the application by Government of Keynesian theory was open to serious objection. Exogenous factors, he suggested, go part of the way to explain why Britain had had full employment since the war. Matthews (269) pp.55–69.

CHAPTER 5 PART 3 pp.178–186

1 The main industries it was not responsible for were building (Ministry of Works), food, agriculture, fuel and power (the respective Ministries) and engineering and steel (Ministry of Supply).

2 He had been Parliamentary Secretary at War Transport in the 'Caretaker Government', though with the Minister, Leathers, in the Lords, Thorneycroft had more work than the average junior Minister. Churchill had noted Thorneycroft as a good debater from soon after he entered the House in 1938. During the war Churchill would pluck him from the backbenches on occasion to speak on the frontbenches, and was again impressed by Thorneycroft's speaking between 1945–51. Thorneycroft himself thought it likely he would be reappointed junior Minister at Transport. Interview II with Lord Thorneycroft.

3 His appointment was the main concession to the younger men in the Party, Thorneycroft having been one of the leaders of the Tory Reform Group. See Chapter 3 Part 1.

4 O.E.E.C. was set up in 1948 to organise the economic co-operation of Europe and to ensure that the best use was made of Marshall Aid funds.

5 He retired from Foreign Service in 1946. He then headed the Conservative Parliamentary Secretariat until it became part of the enlarged Conservative Research Department in 1948, of which he became a Joint Director until entering the House in 1950.

6 He was appointed a Conservative Whip in 1947 and Deputy Chief Conservative Whip in 1950, jobs he had executed with some credit. But some felt him a poor Whip.

7 Mackeson joined the army in 1925 after Sandhurst and remained in it until becoming an M.P. in 1945. He had, however, a good knowledge of domestic industry and was a director of Mackeson and Co. Ltd.

8 It was obvious that Mackeson was not suitable and that a replacement had to be found. Heathcoat Amory, who had been Minister of Pensions, was about to be out of a job after the merger with the Ministry of National Insurance. The job was upgraded to the title of Minister of State largely to provide a suitable position for him. The *Economist* on 12.9.53 (p.679) called the upgrading an imaginative move, as the Secretary of Overseas Trade had of late become little more than a second Parliamentary Secretary.

9 *The Times* 4.9.53. Butler had made an important speech to the National Joint Advisory Committee on 22.7.53 stressing the importance of exports. See Chapter 6 Part 1.

10 Interview II with Lord Amory.

11 For an exposition of Heathcoat Amory's time at the Board of Trade, see Allen (56) pp.127–40.

12 He served as Parliamentary Secretary at the Ministry of Works and Planning 1942–3, and Town and Country Planning, 1943–5.

13 Interview with Sir Alexander Spearman.

14 Interview with John Hay.

15 Lord Thorneycroft (Interview I) thought Lee 'brilliant', 'superb' and a 'wonderful man to work with'.

16 Woods retired unexpectedly from the Civil Service four years before his sixtieth birthday, and went into private industry. Lee came from Permanent Secretary at Food to succeed him.

17 It was not until the period of the D.T.I. (1970–4) that the Department again became as prominent in general economic discussions as it had been under Lee.·

18 It is interesting that Lee, like Brook, had a fairly pedestrian career in the Civil Service until the war, when both forged ahead. From 1926–40 Lee had been in the Colonial Office, whence he joined the Treasury. For a particularly good obituary, see *The Times* 29.4.71.

19 Interview I with Lord Thorneycroft.
20 At the Conservative Party Conferences in 1948–50. the leadership had been called on to denounce the no new Preference clauses in G.A.T.T.. and this policy appeared in the 1950 and 1951 Election statements.
21 For a partisan background. see Amery (*56a*) pp.1046–7.
22 *Private Information.* Thorneycroft was particularly influenced by Sir Edgar Cohen. Second Secretary in charge of the Overseas Divisions. an ardent free trader. MacDougall and Hutt (*267a*) found that there had been a large reduction in Imperial Preference since 1938 due to tariff changes. including those of G.A.T.T.. and large price rises, reducing the *ad valorem* value of specific margins.
23 Interview with Frank Glaves-Smith.
24 The Board of Trade had traditionally been in favour of Imperial Preference. In the 1950s the Board, however, began to feel that the advantages to Britain of the system were being eroded by the actions. particularly of the Canadian Government (in their arrangement with the United States), and also of the Australian Government, whereas for a variety of reasons the British were retaining in full their preferences to Commonwealth imports (many of them still duty free). Lee felt that reciprocal preferences were getting out of balance and that Britain was entitled to further concessions in Commonwealth markets in return for what we gave them. Interview with Lord Garner.
25 Salisbury in particular was opposed to the move away from Imperial Preference.
26 E.D.M. No. 75 of May 1952.
27 Leo Amery. champion of the Imperial Preference faction and the former Secretary of State for the Dominions, 1925–9, and for India and Burma, 1940–5.
28 Morgan (*169a*) p.5.
29 President of Empire Industries Association. 1956–60.
30 Morgan (*169a*) pp.5–6.
31 'The advice tendered to [Mr. Butler] by our partners in the Commonwealth is clear and overwhelming. It is that we should remain members of the General Agreement on Tariffs and Trade.' Thorneycroft, Blackpool, 7.10.54.
32 So certain was Butler that Thorneycroft would be defeated that he prepared his own speech in the expectation that this

would occur. He then had to adjust it at the last minute. Interview with Lord Fraser of Kilmorack.
33 See Goldsworthy (*203*) pp.289–93.
34 *House of Commons* 12.11.46. Vol. 430. Cols. 21–2. Quoted in Gardner (*163a*) pp.351–2.
35 *Personal interview.*
36 Morgan (*169a*) p.5.
37 Talking about the Sydney Conference. Butler noted that it 'had a considerable success in the field of moving towards a system of freer trade'. *House of Commons* 4.2.54. Vol. 523. Col. 594.
38 See telephone call. Eisenhower to Dulles, 7.7.54. *Eisenhower Papers.* Box D.D.E. Diary Series. Number 4.
39 See Thorneycroft. *House of Commons* 9.3.55. 'No measure taken to limit imports is likely to help [the loss of exports]. though some measures might well hamper the export situation.'
40 Woolton wrote a paper on 26.1.55. in which he argued that Lancashire was bound to play an important part in any close contest. In the marginals cotton was the main industry, and there were widespread fears of unemployment due to competition from Japan and India. *Woolton Papers.* Box 22.
41 When Woolton saw Eden to discuss Cabinet changes on 11.3.55. he told Eden that with Thorneycroft at the Board of Trade they had no hope of winning Lancashire, and that he had completely failed to get the confidence of the business community. On 6.4.55. again in private with Eden. Woolton repeated the same message. He said, however, that Lancashire and Thorneycroft could be carried if a quota was put on Indian goods. which Thorneycroft was against. and relief on purchase tax on higher grades of cotton goods, which Butler was against. Diary, *Woolton Papers.* Heathcoat Amory. Selwyn Lloyd and Maudling were all considered by Eden and Woolton as possible replacements.
42 Letter. Woolton to Churchill. 23.2.55. *Woolton Papers.* Box 22.
43 For example. in an article published in 1956, Wiseman and Yamey (*277a*) found that the deficiencies of the Commission from 1948–52 stemmed largely from its position as a statutory monopolist and sole seller. and that the provision of cover facilities was the only way that the Commission

provided services superior to those of the free market.

44 The Hopkins Committee, which reported in March 1952. It said that until some form of cover not using public funds became available, the Raw Cotton Commission should continue in existence. Cmd. 8510. Sir Richard Hopkins was Chairman, Head of the Civil Service, 1942–5.

45 This was just one facet of backbenchers' anxiety to press for greater freedom. Interview with Lord Orr-Ewing. Thorneycroft was not the only one under pressure: there were also constant demands on Butler to reduce purchase tax on textiles. D. Butler (*121*) p.11.

46 Interview with Sir Harold Wilson. Wilson led the Opposition on this, on the floor and in Committees, and at one point almost killed the Bill.

47 Interview with Sir Edward Muir.

48 The Committee appointed in July, reported in December 1951. Cmd. 8452.

49 The old utility schemes had contained over one hundred orders and laid down 300 pages of specifications.

50 *House of Commons* 25.2.54.

51 *House of Commons* 26.7.54.

52 For example, the system of guarantees by the Export Credit Guarantees Department was extended to the banks. See Thorneycroft in *House of Commons* 12.4.54.

53 Interview II with Lord Thorneycroft.

54 The E.P.U. was set up after the war to facilitate payments, and thereby trade, between European countries.

55 The I.M.F. was set up at the end of the war with the primary object of preventing the kind of competitive exchange depreciation which occurred in the 1930s, and of encouraging the expansion of world trade by ensuring stable exchange rates.

56 In accordance with agreements reached between all the O.E.E.C. countries. Thorneycroft would argue against the Treasury that import controls led to inefficiencies and should only be applied in the short term.

57 Cairns had stood as a Liberal in the Epsom division by-election in 1947 and since 1951 had been a member of the Liberal Party Committee (in effect, their shadow Cabinet).

58 Interview with Sir David Cairns. See his interesting article on monopolies and res-

trictive practices in *Law and Opinion in the Twentieth Century*, ed. Morris Ginsberg.

59 It reported in May 1955 (Cmd. 9504). Cairns was Chairman of the committee which made the report.

60 See Richardson (*274*) pp.350–74.

61 *House of Commons* 25.2.53. Thorneycroft noted that in July 1951 development areas accounted for 45% of total unemployment, by 1953, it had fallen to 30%.

62 See G. McCrone (*168*) pp.115–16. Moore and Rhodes (*271*) p.96, found a slightly more 'active' regional policy in Northern Ireland, as a result of investment incentives under the Capital Grants to Industry Act, 1954.

63 For a full account of the F.B.I. and its relations with the Government, see Finer (*262*) pp.61–84. Finer notes that the F.B.I. was instrumental in substantially amending important legislation such as the Transport and Iron and Steel Bill of 1952–3, and the Town and Country Planning Bill of 1953–4. S. Blank (*160*) pp.119–27 goes so far as to suggest that due to their anxiety to establish good relations with the unions, association with industry representatives was regarded as not only unnecessary but a damaging encumbrance. See also Kipping (*32*) p.89. Of relations between the Government and the F.B.I. in 1952, he wrote: 'Disenchantment was mutual. Genuine consultation and any question of mutual involvement or shared policy-making waned and ceased.' On p.90 Kipping wrote 'The Government's policy was obviously to placate the trade unions rather than us.'

64 'This from a new Government to which industry had been looking for incentive and encouragement.' Kipping (*32*) p.89.

65 The *Observer*, 17.1.54.

66 Lord Thorneycroft (interview II) said how greatly he had been assisted by him.

CHAPTER 5 PART 4 pp.186–195

1 The Heyworth Committee, set up by the Coalition Government in June 1944, reported in November 1945 (Cmd. 6699) in favour of all existing gas undertakings being compulsorily purchased.

2 Both Gridley and Swinton had connections with the power industries. Gridley was Chairman of the 1922 Committee, August 1945–November 1951.

3 A background paper prepared in the Conservative Research Department in February 1955 also noted that there was no eagerness on the part of private enterprise to come forward in the gas and electricity industries. *CRD Papers*, Box 'RSG-Gen. Corresp'.

4 Interview with Lord Muirshiel. It is an interesting comment that it took nearly twenty years for private operators, for example British Caledonian and Laker Airways, to become viable competitors to the established corporations.

5 See Chapter 6 Part 5.

6 *The Times* 10.4.52.

7 See Butt (*122*) pp.206–7 and Jackson (*125*) pp.104–5.

8 *House of Commons* 3.11.53, Vol. 520, Col. 23.

9 Woolton wrote that Churchill was not primarily interested in the denationalisations though gave every encouragement to his ministerial colleagues. Woolton also noted that the public showed little interest in the denationalisation of road haulage, and even less in steel. Woolton (*55*) p.379.

10 Interview with Lord Muirshiel (J. Maclay).

11 Diary 22.4.52, *Crookshank Papers*.

12 Transport Policy Cmd. 8538. *The Times* thought it ill considered and premature: 'It is the sketch for a picture rather than the picture itself of policy: still less is it the material for a Bill.' *The Times* 9.5.52. For the (surprising) lack of public interest in these issues, see also Hollis (*247*) p.168.

13 *The Times* 10.7.52.

14 *House of Commons* 10.7.52.

15 Diary 29.10.52, *Crookshank Papers*.

16 This was published on 5.11.52. *The Times* 6.11.52 commented, 'It is rare, if not unprecedented, for a Government to present a proposed Bill in three widely differing forms before the second reading is reached.'

17 The modification of the levy owed a great deal to Lennox-Boyd's power of persuasion. The senior officials in the Ministry wanted the levy, and Churchill had also been sold the idea. Lennox-Boyd felt it would be a recipe for continued friction between road and rail, and managed to get the levy considerably modified.

18 *House of Commons* 20.11.52.

19 See diary for 31.3.53 and 22.4.53, *Crookshank Papers*.

20 For a discussion of the Act, see Grunfeld (*264*) pp.43–54 and *Public Administration* (*273*) pp.399–406.

21 See Gwilliam (*179*) pp.100–3.

22 Later Lord Silsoe. He held a large number of administrative positions. In 1954 he was appointed First Crown Estate Commissioner and First Church Estates Commissioner.

23 Interview I with Lord Boyd of Merton.

24 The backbenchers favoured breaking up the road-haulage network and selling it in parts. Boyd-Carpenter, by then Minister, was opposed to that policy. He took the issue to Cabinet and won the argument. Sir Malcolm Trustram Eve and the Disposal Board also felt it wrong to break up the road-haulage network and Trustram Eve made it clear that if the Government insisted on breaking it up he would resign.

25 Interview I with Lord Boyd of Merton.

26 The Iron and Steel Act had become law in November 1949 and the vesting day had not been until 15th February, 1951. The 1948–9 Session of Parliament had been dominated by the Iron and Steel Bill.

27 The first sentence of a leader in *The Times* 23.10.52 was, 'Steel nationalisation was in no way addressed to the needs of the industry and never aroused popular interest or support.'

28 *House of Commons* 6.11.51.

29 *House of Commons* 12.11.51.

30 Diary 24.4.52, *Crookshank Papers*.

31 Blank (*160*) p.121.

32 See Kent (*30a*) p.234. Kent writes (on p.237) that the Bill might have been introduced in the first year as intended were it not for the delay caused by the considerations of the Steel Committee.

33 Interview with Lord Chandos, D.B.Y.

34 Sandys was determined to produce an Act in the long-term interests of the industry, and one which corrected existing defects. As he said: 'I am convinced that even if nationalisation were to continue, a radical change in the present organisation would be necessary.' *House of Commons* 23.10.52. Vol. 505, Col. 1276.

35 Interview with Lord Boyle of Handsworth.

36 Interview with Lord Chandos, D.B.Y.

37 Diary 15.7.52, *Crookshank Papers*.

38 *Beaverbrook Papers*, Box C89.

39 For an account of Sandys' painstaking work on the preparation of the Bill, see Kent (*30a*) pp.234–7.

40 See Burn (*162*) pp.152–3.

41 Burn (*162*) commented (p.153) that the main effect of the 1953 Act was to preserve the continuity which the 1949 Act had failed to break. See also Public Administration (*272*) pp.55–62.

42 Iron and Steel Industry, Cmd. 8619. This set out the detailed proposals of the Government, the main provision being the establishment of a Board to supervise the industry, including capital development and distribution of raw materials, and it was also to have the power to fix maximum selling prices. *The Times* criticised the White Paper for delegating too much policy-making function to the Board. *The Times* 29.7.52. Wilson (*107*) pp.33–5 argues that the strong positive powers of the Board owed much to pressure from Sir Ellis Hunter (President Iron and Steel Federation, 1945–53).

43 The chief weakness of the White Paper was felt to be its failure to show whether the Board would be given any 'guiding principles' to apply in fixing maximum prices and approving investment projects. The Bill of November 1952 was clearer on this point, but there was still some ambiguity. See *The Times* 7.11.52.

44 Harris (*164*) p.187. Both Ministers considered the absence of a guillotine a major achievement. Instead of the resort to a guillotine, a voluntary timetable was agreed with the Opposition.

45 Crookshank recorded in his diary that he had always thought that too much had been offered. Diary 24.2.53, *Crookshank Papers*. Careful tactics were displayed for the count out which took place in the early hours of the morning.

46 *House of Commons* 17.3.53.

47 For the differences between the Board and Labour's earlier Board, see Ross (*171*) p.152.

48 'The attempt to return the nationalised companies to private ownership has foundered and the resulting state of affairs is becoming deplorable.' *Manchester Guardian* 27.4.54. For anxiety in the Conservative Party at the slow rate at which denationalisation was being effected, see note, Woolton to Churchill, 22.3.54, *Woolton Papers*.

49 Keeling and Wright (*165*) p.179.

50 He had been Chairman of the first Iron and Steel Board 1946–9. Between 1951–3 he had been President of the F.B.I.

51 Some of those connected with the steel industry after denationalisation felt that it was only after 1959 that the blight of renationalisation affected investment decisions. They felt in the first few years after the Act that there were safeguards against renationalisation, and Hugh Gaitskell was not making any threats at that time.

52 Vaizey (*174*) pp.150–79.

53 Butt (*122*) p.207 traces the origin of the proposal to set up such a committee to a letter written to *The Times* 8.9.49, by Hugh Molson. Also interview with Lord Clitheroe.

54 Butt also argues that the creation of the Committee was as a direct result of backbench pressure, mainly from Conservative members. Butt (*122*) pp.207–8. Discussion of the establishment of the Select Committee can also be found in Thornhill, ed. pp. 155–7, Chester (*260*) pp. 93–5, Hanson (*265*) pp. 328–40, Harrison (*243*) pp. 310–1 and Chester (*162a*) pp.999–1001.

55 *The Times* 3.3.53.

56 Chester (*162a*) pp.1058–9.

57 *Private Information.*

58 See Chapter 6 Part 6.

59 *Report on the Advisory Committee on Organisation (N.C.B.)* p.15, and Davies (*261*) p.106. For a most interesting commentary on the nationalised industries, 1951–5, see Davies pp.104–16.

60 See Chapter 6 Part 5.

61 Davies (*261*) p.108.

62 The Conservatives also pledged themselves in their 1951 Manifesto to bring nationalised industries within the scope of the Monopolies Commission, but this plan was stillborn.

63 'This is a natural corrective to the disadvantages of monopoly and we should make full use of it.' Geoffrey Lloyd in *House of Commons* 9.11.54, Vol. 532, Col. 1046. In a speech four months earlier, he had said: 'We believe in freedom of consumer choice, and we believe that the nationalised industries are most likely to avoid stagnation . . . if, within broad limits of national policy, they are left free – and, indeed, encouraged – to compete with one another.' *House of Commons* 9.7.54, Vol. 529, Col. 2512.

64 Interview with Sir Kelvin Spencer.

65 Kilmuir (*31*) p.191.

66 It is of note that a 'Padmore Committee' in

1953 considered amalgamating both Ministries. Lee (*142*) p.107.

67 See Chapter 8 Part 5.

CHAPTER 6 PART 1 pp.196–207

1 As the Ministry of Labour. It was renamed the Ministry of Labour and National Service in September 1939 because of its new responsibilities in the manpower field. It reverted to plain Ministry of Labour in November 1959. The system of 'national service' was eventually brought to an end in 1962. The Ministry called up those eligible; the actual organisation and employment thereafter was the responsibility of the Service Departments.

2 Robertson (*146*) pp.63–4.

3 Autobiographical fragments, *Monckton Papers*, Box 49. Geoffrey Cox wrote in the *News Chronicle* on 27.10.51 that Monckton would 'almost certainly' be Attorney-General.

4 In his autobiographical notes Monckton explains what happened when he was summoned to Hyde Park Gate before lunch on 27th October. Churchill, quite possibly acting on the advice of Brendan Bracken (the suggestion in interview of the Dowager Viscountess Monckton of Brenchley), said, 'he had got a job for me, did I know what it was, and I said I was very much hoping it was Law Office . . .[*sic*]. "Oh my dear, I cannot spare you for that, I have the worst job in the Cabinet for you." I was pretty sure that that must be the Ministry of Labour . . . I protested that I had no political experience and should find that a great handicap in such a difficult post. Mr. Churchill said on the contrary my great strength would be that I had no political past; I said you are making it pretty sure that I shall have no political future.' *Monckton Papers*, Box 49.

5 Barnes and Reid (*177a*) p.21.

6 Interview with Lord Orr-Ewing. (Monckton's Parliamentary Private Secretary November 1951–May 1955). Orr-Ewing was one of the bright young men to enter the House in 1950.

7 Maxwell Fyfe had said that the trade unions' political levy should not be automatically paid by members. He had made a study in Opposition of trade union legislation in different countries. He had been Chairman of the Party's Labour Committee up until the 1951 Election. Rab Butler considered it possible Churchill would appoint himself Minister of Labour in 1951. Interview I with Lord Butler.

8 Birkenhead (*60*) p.280.

9 Interview with the Dowager Viscountess Monckton of Brenchley.

10 He was ill in December 1953 with flu and took a two-week holiday, but was ill again in January, necessitating a spell in hospital. See *The Times* 1.1.54.

11 'Monckton agrees to stay, at least through the winter.' Diary 11.10.54, Macmillan (*36*) p.546.

12 *The Times* 17.12.54. But as early as the October 1954 reshuffle, the *News Chronicle* had commented (18.10.54) that it was a 'surprise' that Monckton had decided to remain at Labour.

13 It was announced from Number 10 on 13th January, 1955, that Monckton had been ordered by his doctors to take a complete rest, and that Watkinson was to be in charge under the general supervision of Churchill. *The Times* 14.1.55. He returned to work in mid-March 1955, and attended his first Cabinet since his illness on 23rd March. *The Times* 24.3.55.

14 Letter, Monckton to Churchill, 11.1.55, *Monckton Papers*, Box 5.

15 Interview with Anthony Sutherland. Goddard was Lord Chief Justice from 1946–58.

16 Birkenhead (*60*) p.301.

17 Letter, Monckton to Watkinson, 19.8.53. *Monckton Papers*, Box 3.

18 Letter, Monckton to Bracken, 12.4.54, *Monckton Papers*, Box 4.

19 See letter, Bracken to Monckton, 22.4.54, *Monckton Papers*, Box 4.

20 Letter, Bracken to Monckton, 22.4.54, *Monckton Papers*, Box 4.

21 As above.

22 Birkenhead (*60*) p.279. Neden was Chief Industrial Commissioner, 1954–8.

23 An example of the way Monckton viewed his remit was that when in 1952 Butler said he was going to remove bread rationing, which would have involved an increase in the price of bread, Monckton said that if this was done, it would undermine trade union confidence in him and he must resign. (In fact bread rationing came off with scarcely a ripple of protest from the unions.) Interview with Lord Orr-Ewing.

24 Even comparatively harmless items of re-

form, like legislation to improve conditions of work which had been included in the 'Industrial Charter', were dropped after the unions' cool response. Barnes and Reid (*177a*) p.22.

25 Conrad Heron quoted in Birkenhead (*60*) p.279. Heron felt that when dealing with departmental matters, Monckton proved himself a better civil servant than any of his officials. Correspondence with Sir Conrad Heron.

26 His great experience of human affairs was also felt to be a major advantage. He was Attorney-General to the Duchy of Cornwall, 1932–6, and had been a prominent figure in the abdication crisis. He had held a number of senior posts in the war, including being an additional Deputy Under-Secretary of State for Foreign Affairs in 1940.

27 Interview with Sir Conrad Heron.

28 Monckton later wrote, 'I was always told that he [Ernest Bevin, Minister of Labour, 1940–5] thought Godfrey Ince the most able civil servant he ever came across. I certainly never met anyone abler nor a better or more loyal friend and supporter.' *Monckton Papers*, Box 49.

29 From 1941–4 he had been Director-General of Manpower at the Ministry.

30 Ince did not find it easy in general to adjust to the reduced role the Ministry was called on to play in a peacetime economy.

31 In 1949. He was also Chairman, 1945–7 and 1956–7.

32 Later Sir Conrad Heron, Permanent Secretary at the Department of Employment, 1973–6.

33 See, for example, Maudling (*39*) pp.142–3. Bennett had been a Vice-Chairman of the 1922 Committee and on the Party's Works Committee up until the Election in 1951. He was joint managing director of Lucas Industries and a past President of the F.B.I.

34 See debate in *House of Commons* 13.5.52, Vol. 500, Cols. 1403–6.

35 Watkinson had first-hand industrial experience which Monckton had not, and was at pains to know what Conservative opinion in the House was. In both areas he was able to provide Monckton with the benefit of his knowledge. Watkinson had previously made a name for himself as Parliamentary Private Secretary to Maclay, Minister of Transport and Civil Aviation, 1951–2.

36 The *Economist* 24.12.55 (p.1092) noted that the Opposition, scenting the possibility of his succession some months ago, had been making a dead set at him in Parliament.

37 Interview with Sir Conrad Heron.

38 Details of strikes and disputes are discussed in Birkenhead (*60*) pp.290–301, Butler (*121*) p.12, Clegg (*280*) pp.31–43 and Barnes and Reid (*177a*) pp.23–5.

39 For a breakdown of the responsibilities of Ministry, see Ince (*155*) pp.13–30.

40 This laid down conditions to be complied with in night-bakeries.

41 Interview with Sir Conrad Heron.

42 Interview II with Lord Butler.

43 See Chapter 2 Part 1. Just before Churchill left for his trip to the United States at the end of December 1951, he wrote to Sir Vincent Tewson, General Secretary of the T.U.C., about the school-leaving age. Churchill stressed at the end of the letter that on his return to Britain he looked forward to a talk with Tewson and some of his colleagues, whose opinion and advice Churchill valued. Letter, Churchill to Tewson, 24.12.51, *Monckton Papers*, Box 2. Churchill took the precaution of sending a draft of the letter to Monckton for his comments.

44 Diary 2.9.53, Moran (*87*) p.491.

45 See Allen (*177*) pp.97–8.

46 Birkenhead (*60*) p.299.

47 For example, when Tom O'Brien M.P., Chairman of the General Council of the T.U.C., sent a goodwill message to Churchill when he visited the United States in January 1953, there were immediate protests from many trade union branches. See George Isaacs' contribution, in Eade (*73*) pp.386–7. There was also considerable furore amongst trade unionists in January 1953 at Lincoln Evans' acceptance of a knighthood, illustrating again the ambivalent attitude of the unions to the Government.

48 Two such occasions were in 1952, when Churchill received a deputation from the T.U.C. on the Government's policy towards wage councils, and later in the year when another deputation met Churchill over the D. C. Thomson printing dispute, where he was asked to help reach a satisfactory settlement. *The Times* 9.9.52. In the first case, the unions had greatly resented the Government's intervention into

wage negotiation. See *The Times* 22.7.52.

49 Bracken. as ever with his ear to the ground, wrote: 'A large number of Monckton's colleagues are alarmed lest he should give way to the engineers, the builders and the many other trade unionists who want sharp increases in pay.' Letter, Bracken to Beaverbrook, 30.12.53, *Beaverbrook Papers*, Box C57.

50 Diary 29.10.54, *Crookshank Papers.*

51 It was rare for Monckton to put up to Cabinet a paper for full discussion about the handling of a dispute, although in order to minimise difficulties with Cabinet colleagues, he made it a set practice to warn them at the end of Cabinet meetings of difficulties and disputes looming ahead.

52 A number of Ministry officials, however, recall Robertson saying to Monckton in the 1953 rail dispute that he thought his people underpaid. Monckton took this as the signal that Robertson wanted to reach a settlement by increasing the offer, even though, for public purposes, he might have to appear resistant. *Private Information.*

53 Diary 13.12.54, *Woolton Papers.* A leader in *The Times* 19.12.53 drily commented on the December 1953 rail dispute: 'Relief that the railway strike was averted in time for Christmas has tended to overshadow the fact that, once again, the normal machinery for determining wages on the railways was set aside under the threat of a strike and after ministerial intervention.'

54 Diary 13.12.54, *Woolton Papers.*

55 Diary 13.12.54, *Woolton Papers.*

56 Diary 6.1.55, *Crookshank Papers.*

57 Diary 7.1.55, Moran (*87*) p.658. Lord Butler, in interview, said that Churchill was 'so sensible in a way' because he said railway strikes dislocate the country, and that Cabinet should be grateful to him for helping prevent one.

58 Autobiographical fragments, *Monckton Papers*, Box 49.

59 See leader in *The Times* 9.1.54. It concluded by asking 'But if arbitration is to lose its authority, what is to take its place?' This trend provoked Sir Godfrey Ince to make a speech in February 1954 in which he expressed anxiety to extend the arbitration system to all industries. Reported in *The Times* 25.2.54. The unions were far from keen on this proposal.

60 V. L. Allen noted that the Conservative Government after 1951 had been even more willing to appoint trade unionists to its consultative committees than Labour had been. See Allen (*177*) p.34 and p.304.

61 It merged with the F.B.I. (see Chapter 5 Part 3) in 1965 to form the C.B.I.

62 He had been Director since 1921. Sir Norman Kipping wrote that when George Pollock became Director in 1954 there was an easing of relations with the F.B.I. The B.E.C. originally was set up to provide a means for organisations of employers to exchange information to endeavour to concert their policy on labour matters, primarily on wages and working conditions, though they increasingly became involved in broader economic matters. Kipping (*32*) pp.48–9.

63 'It is our long standing practice to work with whatever Government is in power, and through consultations jointly with the Ministers and with the other side of industry to find practical solutions to the social and economic problems facing this country. There need be no doubt, therefore. of the attitude of the T.U.C. towards the new Government.' Reported in *The Times* 1.11.51. Before the Election Churchill had given trade unionists an assurance that Conservatives had no intention of penal action or sanctions against trade unions. Deakin told the Post Office Engineering Union this. reported in *The Times* 26.6.52. Labour candidates had made widespread predictions during the 1951 General Election campaign that there would be strikes of political nature if the Conservatives won. See also diary 15.10.51, Moran (*87*) p.372.

64 Interview. Tewson was General Secretary, 1946–60.

65 General Secretary, Transport and General Workers Union from 1940 until his death at a May Day gathering in 1955.

66 Monckton was closest to Deakin and would lunch with him on a regular basis. (See Allen (*176*) pp.114 and 150.) He liked Tom Williamson (General Secretary, National Union of General and Municipal Workers, 1946–61, who was Chairman of the T.U.C. side of the N.J.A.C. when Monckton was Minister) and respected his judgment though saw less of him. Sir William Lawther (President, National Union of Mineworkers, 1939–54) he knew very well, though there was not a great deal of business to discuss with the miners. The

Ministry of Fuel and Power was responsible for relations here. (See Chapter 6 Part 6.) Moreover, because the coal industry had a completely self-contained procedure, culminating in binding arbitration, the Government took no part in mining disputes. The accepted doctrine at the time required the Government to refuse all contact with unofficial movements, on the ground that to do so could have weakened the position of the established union leaders. This made it possible for Lawther in a sense to comment on trade union affairs at large, and Monckton encouraged him to do this, as he had no conceivable N.U.M. axe to grind. Others with whom he came into frequent contact were Tom O'Brien (Labour M.P., 1945–59, General Secretary, National Association of Theatrical and Kine Employees, 1932–70) whom he thought inclined to be volatile, Alan Birch (General Secretary, Union of Shop, Distributive and Allied Workers, 1949–61), Charles Geddes (General Secretary, Union of Post Office Workers), 'a very good man' (letter, Monckton to De L'Isle, March 1953, *Monckton Papers*, Box 3), Sir Alfred Roberts (General Secretary, Amalgamated Association of Card, Blowing and Ring Room Operatives, 1935–62), 'extremely able and intelligent' (letter, Monckton to De L'Isle, March 1953, *Monckton Papers*, Box 3), and Sir Lincoln Evans (General Secretary, Iron and Steel Trades Confederation, 1946–53). He was under obligation to see Sir Vincent Tewson regularly but was not as close to him as to some other union leaders. Tewson was not as formidable a figure as his predecessor, Lord Citrine (1926–46); senior union leaders didn't wish to see a powerful General Secretary succeed Citrine.

67 See Chapter 2 Part 3.
68 In a written reply in *House of Commons* 2.12.52.
69 *The Times* 18.8.53. A background paper 'Points of Vulnerability' prepared by the Research Department in February 1955 noted that there had been no pressure in the country to introduce the 'Workers' Charter'. *C.R.D. Papers*, Box R.S.G. Gen. Corresp.
70 Also a number of pamphlets were published by the C.P.C., from September 1953 in a new 'Trade Union Series'. See Cohen, *A History* p.499.

71 During the 1951 General Election campaign, Churchill said the Conservatives did not intend to introduce legislation affecting the unions, but expressed concern on the question of the closed shop, raised in particular by the actions of the Labour-controlled Durham County Council which insisted all its workers belonged to an appropriate union. At a speech at Woodford on 9.10.51, Churchill said that in the Party's view Durham County Council was wrong, but the matter would be left to the working of common sense. (In fact in this case the position deteriorated so much that the intervention of Monckton was sought in June 1952.) The background paper in preparation for the 1955 General Election, 'Points of Vulnerability', noted that though the closed shop had been spreading over the last few years the Government was reluctant to upset the unions about it. *C.R.D. Papers*, Box R.S.G. Gen. Corresp.
72 In a letter to Michael Fraser of 14.1.54, Harold Watkinson wrote that the official line was that this was a matter for individual trade unions and not one for Government, and that at the moment Watkinson was quite sure they would not get agreement even amongst right-wing union leaders. *C.R.D. Papers*, Box R.S.G. Gen. Corresp.
73 Autobiographical fragments, *Monckton Papers*, Box 49.
74 Interview with Sir Vincent Tewson.
75 See, for example, Brittan (*161*) pp.193–5.
76 Correspondence with Sir Conrad Heron.
77 Diary 13.12.54, *Woolton Papers*.
78 Macmillan (*36*) p.490.
79 Woolton (*55*) p.380.
80 Interview I with Lord Butler.
81 Interview I with Lord Butler.
82 For example, Deakin, Sir Vincent Tewson and Tom Williamson.
83 Arthur Tiffin was appointed General Secretary after Deakin in 1955 but died before the end of the year. See Dorfman (*178*) pp.81–2.
84 Interview with Lord Robens of Woldingham.
85 Interview with Sir Harold Wilson.
86 Interview with Anthony Sutherland.
87 This measure was in effect a continuation of the wartime Control of Engagement Order.
88 For background, see Barnes and Reid

(*177a*) p.23. For figures of the increase in wage rates relative to the retail price index, see tables at end of book.

89 Pelling (*180*) p.239.

90 Reported in *The Times* 23.7.53. Butler had made a speech on similar lines to the N.J.A.C. on 15th May, 1952. The misgivings that had encouraged Butler to deliver these speeches had found an earlier voice in the Cripps White Paper of 1947, which had mentioned the idea of a wages policy.

91 Woolton noted in his memoirs that the inflationary spiral caused by the Government's wages policy (or lack of it), coupled with the heavy spending on the building programme 'greatly disturbed some of us in the Cabinet'. Woolton (*55*) p.380. This is borne out by entries in Woolton's diary. However, those in Cabinet worried about inflation were no more successful than Treasury officials in ameliorating the position.

92 The impact of arbitration since the war, however, had been to produce, without intentional design, something akin to a 'wages policy'. There had grown up since the war the assumption that an award in one industry would serve as a standard in others. A suggestion was in fact put forward for some form of permanent machinery for the settlement of industrial disputes. This was suggested in the reports of the Courts of Enquiry into the engineering and ship-building wage claims, presided over by Lord Justice Morris, and entailed the establishment of permanent bodies to consider the complex economic arguments arising in disputes. Monckton welcomed the idea and passed it on to the N.J.A.C. for their consideration, but the unions were unenthusiastic and the plans came to nothing. Pelling (*180*) p.242.

93 The Chairman was the influential Malcolm McCorquodale. He told an officer of the Research Department on 13th April, 1954 that the Committee held the viewpoint that the Government should soft pedal on industrial relations, and aim to remove them from politics altogether rather than to woo trade unionists over to the Conservative side. McCorquodale felt the Government should not formulate a wages policy, but only go as far as advocating the acceptance of arbitration rather than resorting to the strike weapon. *C.R.D. Papers*, Box R.S.G., Notes of Meetings.

CHAPTER 6 PART 2 pp.207–213

1 Interview with Lord Helsby.

2 Hill (*23*) pp.149–50.

3 Interview with Lord Helsby.

4 Interview II with Lord Amory.

5 Hill (*23*) pp.147–8.

6 See Hill (*23*) p.149.

7 Many other officials made major contributions to the success of the Ministry's programme, in particular, Frederick Bishop, the Principal Private Secretary, and Under-Secretaries George Bishop, Eric Roll and John Wall.

8 Helsby was later Head of the Home Civil Service, 1963–8.

9 Recalled one former civil servant in interview: 'It [bulk purchase] strained the doctrine of collective responsibility worse than anything I've ever known.' This was because the Minister for Food would press for low prices, the Colonial Secretary for high, and when a compromise was reached both were supposed to defend the decision publicly e.g. in Parliament. Thus he continued, 'I'm very glad the markets opened up again.' Interview with Sir Hilton Poynton. (Deputy Under-Secretary at the Colonial Office responsible for economic affairs.)

10 Lloyd-George wrote: 'As far as other sources of supply are concerned, there is virtually no additional fresh meat available other than from our principal suppliers which we can afford to buy in our present economic circumstances . . . any increase . . . is virtually ruled out by our present currency difficulties.' Minister of Food to Lord President, 27.3.52, *Woolton Papers*, Box 25.

11 Woolton to Churchill, 28.3.52, *Woolton Papers*, Box 25.

12 *Private Papers* and Minister of Food to Lord President, 18.6.52, *Woolton Papers*, Box 25.

13 Hill (*23*) p.159. See also article in *The Times* 27.1.54. A leader in *The Times* on 9.10.53 said that the main reason for the continuation of rationing was the inability of the Government to decide how some of the food trades would be organised after derationing.

14 Interview with William Senior (an Assistant Secretary in Scottish Agriculture Department).
15 Letter, Salisbury to Woolton, 14.3.52, *Woolton Papers*, Box 25.
16 See Chapter 3 Part 2.
17 Interview with Lord Helsby.
18 Interview with Sir John Colville. See also Macmillan (*36*) pp.490–1 and Woolton (*55*) p.376.
19 See Churchill to Woolton and Lloyd-George, 24.3.52, *Woolton Papers*, Box 25.
20 See Churchill to Woolton and Lloyd-George, 25.3.52, *Woolton Papers*, Box 25.
21 Interview with Lord Crathorne, D.B.Y.
22 See, for example, conversation on a Cabinet paper on meat. Diary 27.10.53, Moran (*87*) pp.513–4.
23 Interview with Sir John Colville.
24 See Lloyd-George to Woolton, 1.5.52, *Woolton Papers*, Box 25.
25 Hill (*23*) p.161.
26 Interview with Lord Hill of Luton.
27 Interview with Lord Crathorne, D.B.Y.
28 Woolton (*55*) pp.367–71.
29 See Churchill to Woolton and Lloyd-George, 24.3.52, *Woolton Papers*, Box 25.
30 Hill (*23*) p.160.
31 The day before the Cabinet meeting where the issue was to be settled, Lloyd-George was still unaware of how exactly deficiency payments would work. *Private Information*.
32 Hill (*23*) p.162.
33 Interview with Harry Pitchforth. The merger of Agriculture and Food had been proposed by a group of senior officials, Brook, Lee and Emmerson, in 1951. Lee (*142*) p.113.
34 The prevailing orthodoxy in the Ministry of Agriculture before the war was that the salvation of the agricultural industry lay in increased efficiency in the marketing of its produce. Many felt during 1952–3 in the Ministry of Agriculture that the industry's best interests would not be served if Food was amalgamated with their own Department, and wanted to return to the pre-war position and have the Board of Trade looking after the consumer interest. Others considered, however, that the merger of Food and Agriculture was in the best national interest and would help to reconcile the conflicting interests of the consumer and the farmer. Interview with Sir Basil Engholm (an Agriculture official).

35 As late as January 1955 Sir Cleveland Fyfe, a prominent figure in agricultural circles (he had been General Secretary of the N.F.U. from 1932–44), was urging the Government to change its mind and adopt the Board of Trade option. Letter, Sir Cleveland Fyfe to Lord Kilmuir, 11.1.55, *Kilmuir Papers*, File 6.8. The N.F.U. generally were frightened that their interest would become submerged if the amalgamation with Food went ahead.
36 Interview with Sir Basil Engholm.
37 Interview with Lord Hill of Luton.
38 *Labour Gazette 1956*.
39 In particular the movement of world food prices and improvements to the balance of payments.

CHAPTER 6 PART 3 pp.213–221

1 Daalder (*129*) pp.217–8.
2 Winnifrith (*156*) pp.30–2.
3 Interview with Sir George Dunnett. For the economic background to these developments, see Hallett (*281*) pp.522–40.
4 Winnifrith (*156*) p.31.
5 Though he had done very well as the Minister in the war, there is some doubt as to how well Hudson would have performed in the conditions of peacetime. Hudson was a member of the shadow Cabinet and was appointed Chairman of the Party's Trade and Industry Committee in February 1951.
6 Dugdale was also a member of the committee that produced the Agricultural Charter. See Chapter 2 Part 3. The fact that Dugdale was one of Eden's close friends also made him a strong candidate for high office.
7 For four years previously he had been Parliamentary Private Secretary to Swinton, 1931–5, a close friend and neighbour. He was a Whip from 1937–42.
8 Labour imagined Dugdale to be responsible for opposing the move away from guaranteed prices, and that underlying differences with Cabinet rather than Crichel Down were responsible for his resignation in July 1954. See the Labour pamphlet 'Record of the Tory Government: Three Wasted Years' (1955) p.66.
9 Interview with Sir George Dunnett.
10 Interview I with Lord Amory.
11 Self and Storing (*181*) pp.118–19 and

121–2. argue that the change from Dugdale to Heathcoat Amory symbolised the change from a paternalistic to a more liberal view on direct state controls. Thus Dugdale had been as ready as Williams to apply the disciplinary provisions of the 1947 Act, whereas, in the autumn of 1954, Heathcoat Amory reaffirmed that farmers were under obligation to make the most efficient use of land, but emphasised that sanctions of the 1947 Act would only be used in the last resort.

12 Interview with Lord Holderness (R. Wood).
13 Winnifrith (156) p.233.
14 Interview with Lord Carrington.
15 Hurd had been a farmer in Wiltshire since 1926 and a member of the Council of the N.F.U., 1936–40. Father of Douglas Hurd, M.P. for mid-Oxfordshire since February 1974.
16 Diary 5.12.51, *Piers Dixon Papers.*
17 Interview with Lord Carrington.
18 Winnifrith (156) pp.234–5.
19 Ronald Wall, 1952–9.
20 *The Campaign Guide, 1955* pp.141–2.
21 Cmd. 6447.
22 Interview with Lord Nugent of Guildford.
23 *Annual Abstract of Statistics, 1957.*
24 Cmd. 8556.
25 The 1953 Annual Review was exceptional in that 1953 was the first year when exports depended not on what could be spared but on what could be sold.
26 Figures from the 1955 Annual Review (Cmd. 9406).
27 Cmd. 9104.
28 The possibility of moving in this direction was in fact envisaged in Part 1 of the 1947 Act, which consequently did not have to be changed fundamentally. Interview with Sir Basil Engholm.
29 Cmd. 8989. There had been widespread anxiety in the Conservative Party throughout 1953 at the Government's unwillingness to make its intentions clear on agriculture. It reached a height at the October 1953 Party Conference when there were demands for a clear lead from Dugdale. *The Times* 12.10.53 commented that anxieties over agricultural policy was the most unsettled part of the Conference.
30 The Conservatives' Agricultural Charter of 1948 had promised guaranteed prices and markets to British farmers.
31 As a result of anxiety amongst farmers in

January 1953, Dugdale reassured them in a speech at Northallerton of the Government's adherence to the 1947 Act's commitment to guaranteed prices and assured markets. Reported in *The Times* 12.1.53.
32 Interview with Sir Basil Engholm.
33 It is probable that Labour themselves would have gone for deficiency payments, though not perhaps setting them as high.
34 Later Lord Netherthorpe.
35 See Chapter 5 Part I.
36 After the 1955 General Election, 95 of the 110 seats, where agricultural employment exceeded 15% of total male employment, were Conservative. Self and Storing (181) p.194. Pennock discusses the feeling that in the 1955 Annual Price Review the farmers received a very good 'deal' because of the Government's desire to have an agreement before the Election. Pennock (283) p.292.
37 Lord Nugent of Guildford (in interview), however, stressed the patriotism of the N.F.U. during these years and their loyalty to the Government, but some other Conservatives felt that Turner rather took advantage of Dugdale.
38 The impact of Crichel Down was greater than it might have been. It followed in the wake of the celebrated case of Mr. Pilgrim, who took his life after he was notified of a compulsory purchase order. It left a feeling of unfair behaviour by the Administration. See Garner in Thornhill, ed. (135) p.120. In 1955 a book was published about Crichel Down, Douglas Brown (139). For contemporary accounts see also Chester (240) pp.389–401 and Harrison (244) pp.383–7. For a retrospective analysis see Wheare (254) pp.390–408.
39 Interview with Lord Crathorne, D.B.Y. (the former Sir Thomas Dugdale).
40 Public Enquiry Ordered by the Minister of Agriculture into the Disposal of Land at Crichel Down. Cmd. 9176.
41 *Annual Register, 1957* p.180.
42 Records of the meeting amongst the Conservative Party Archives at Newcastle University.
43 See diary 28.6.54 *Crookshank Papers.* Woolton was also a member and felt strongly that the episode had been mishandled by the officials. *Private Information.*

44 Interview with Lord Crathorne, D.B.Y.
45 Diary 10.7.55. Moran (*87*) p.711.
46 Diary 30.12.53. Moran (*87*) pp.545–6.
47 Interview with Lord Crathorne, D.B.Y.
48 *Private Information.*
49 'It is 24 years since Sir Thomas Dugdale resigned over Crichel Down. Since then, officials have become subject to a greater degree of personal and public accountability not only by Select Committees but before tribunals . . .' Leader in *The Times* 16.3.78.
50 'I would not say it reduced morale generally because it came definitely in one department . . . It had no repercussions outside that department . . . I never found any difficulties coming on to me as a result of [it] at all.' Interview I with Lord Amory.

CHAPTER 6 PART 4 pp.221–226

1 There were other factors at play which led to the setting up of the Ministry. There was felt to be a need to have more effective machinery to guard against other nations grabbing all available raw materials. The Board of Trade was not in very good odour at the time. Finally, there was an element of the Government merely changing administrative arrangements in the face of an intractable problem in the faith that this would somehow ameliorate the position.
2 Interview with Sir Edward Muir.
3 Previously Chairman B.O.A.C., 1943–7 and Governor of Bermuda, 1941–3. He was also Minister at the British Embassy in Washington, 1951–2, responsible for raw materials, where he had the benefit of a good British team.
4 Woolton (*55*) p.406.
5 Chester and Willson (*138*) pp.111–13.
6 Interview with Sir Edward Muir.
7 Hitchman had served in the Ministry of Labour before being transferred to the Treasury in 1947. His work there was concentrated on planning and on international payments (from 1948–9 he was deputy to the Chief Planning Officer). This work equipped him ideally for his post at Materials.
8 Letter, Bowyer to Woolton, 13.8.54. *Woolton Papers*, Box 28. Also Woolton (*55*) pp.409 and 414.
9 See Chapter 3 Part 4.
10 See Chapter 3 Part 1.
11 Interview with Sir Alan Hitchman.

12 *The Times* noted how the Conservatives in Opposition attacked the idea of a Ministry of Materials, but in office found it both sensible and workable. *The Times* 25.11.52.
13 Interview with Sir Edward Muir.
14 Diary 2.9.53. Moran (*87*) p.493.
15 See, for example, Salter (*44*) p.343.
16 Letter, Salter to Woolton, 4.9.53, *Woolton Papers*, Box 28. Salter wrote in his resignation letter of 2nd September published in *The Times* 4.9.53 that he had drafted a letter of resignation at the end of June but had not sent it due to Churchill's illness.
17 *The Times*, 4.9.53.
18 Woolton (*55*) pp.405–7.
19 Woolton (*55*) pp.405–7.
20 Interview with Sir Alan Hitchman.
21 Woolton (*55*) p.409.
22 For details see Chapter 5 Part 3.
23 See the note, the Ministry to Woolton, September 1953, *Woolton Papers*, Box 26, Leaf 169–70.
24 Woolton (*55*) pp.408–10, and material in *Woolton Papers*.
25 See Woolton (*55*) p.407 and letter, Butler to Woolton, 13.3.54, *Woolton Papers*, Box 28.
26 Letter, Woolton to Churchill, 19.3.54, *Woolton Papers*, Box 26.
27 Woolton (*55*) p.407.
28 Letter, Woolton to Churchill, 19.3.54, *Woolton Papers*, Box 26.
29 Note, Woolton to Churchill, 10.2.54 and letter, Woolton to Butler, 13.2.54, *Woolton Papers*, Boxes 3 and 26.
30 Letter, Woolton to Churchill, 19.3.54, *Woolton Papers*, Box 26.
31 Letter, Butler to Woolton, 7.4.54, *Woolton Papers*, Box 28.
32 Letter, Woolton to Butler, 8.4.54, *Woolton Papers*, Box 28.
33 Churchill to Woolton, 7.6.54, *Woolton Papers*, Box 28.
34 Interview with Sir Edward Muir.
35 Woolton (*55*) p.407.

CHAPTER 6 PART 5 pp.226–234

1 Lee (*142*) pp.101–2. The Machinery of Government Committee met in December 1949 and the possibility of a merger was considered. However, after the Election in February 1950, Attlee reappointed a separate Minister of Civil Aviation, Lord Pakenham. Neither Ministry advocated

the merger. Chester and Willson (*138*) pp.112–13.

2 Interview with Lord Muirshiel (the former John Maclay).

3 Interview with Michael Banister. Banister from 1950 to 1956 was Private Secretary to successive Ministers.

4 Interview II with Lord Boyd of Merton.

5 Sir Gilmour Jenkins (interview) said certain officials in the Ministry of Transport would have preferred to have remained as a separate Ministry. Sir James Dunnett (interview) said various officials at Civil Aviation felt that their Department had not been merged but submerged. Dunnett was Permanent Secretary of the Ministry. 1959–63. The appointment of a separate Parliamentary Secretary for Civil Aviation, announced by Churchill in *House of Commons* 26.2.53, was partly to counteract the feeling that Civil Aviation was being demoted. Jenkins (*154*) p.202 described the merger as a 'painful process', which 'could not be expected to take place without a good deal of thought and planning and without some degree of heart burning.'

6 The merger had been announced in February and a White Paper (Cmd. 8883) published in June contained detailed plans.

7 He had been Parliamentary Secretary at the Ministry of Production in the 'Caretaker Government'. He was a shipowner himself, and headed the British Merchant Shipping Mission to Washington in 1944.

8 See Chapter 3 Part 4. It was a potential 'dropped catch' between Leathers and Maclay, due to the unsatisfactory working of the 'overlord' arrangement, that led Swinton finally to agree to become Chairman of the Liaison Committee. See Chapter 2 Part 3. Correspondence with Lord Fraser of Kilmorack.

9 'I got overtired and did too much work . . .' Interview with Lord Muirshiel. (He wrote to Churchill on 3rd May who accepted his resignation two days later.) *The Times* 7.5.52. Some felt Maclay almost 'too nice' to be a strong Minister. He however proved his considerable ability when he came back to ministerial life in 1956, initially as Minister of State, Colonial Office, October 1956–January 1957, and then as Secretary of State for Scotland, 1957–62.

10 A number of additional problems arose. Proposals urged on Maclay by Lord Hurcomb who. as Chairman of the British Transport Commission, 1947–53, was a powerful centraliser, caused unease between Maclay and Churchill. These entailed the abolition of certain special rates for the less fortunate on British Railways which Churchill was in favour of maintaining. The fuss in April about the Government's prevention of fare increases outside London was a further source of friction. See Chapter 2 Part 3.

11 For a peculiar constitutional reason the Minister of Transport's functions could not be carried out by another Minister.

12 Interview II with Lord Boyd of Merton.

13 A profile in the *Sunday Times* 26.4.53.

14 Lennox-Boyd told his officials at the Ministry of Civil Aviation very early on that he was afraid the road and rail problems had to take first priority until the legislation was passed. Interview II with Lord Boyd of Merton.

15 *Private Information.*

16 *The Times* 29.7.54 noted that Lennox-Boyd had been 'outstandingly successful' as Minister of Transport.

17 Churchill originally asked Macmillan to succeed Lennox-Boyd. Diary 16.6.54, *Crookshank Papers.*

18 *The Times* 2.11.53 noted that though only fifty-eight. he had been feeling strain for some months.

19 Interview with Sir Dennis Proctor. From 1953 to 1958 Proctor was Deputy Secretary at the Ministry.

20 This was another factor mentioned by Lord Muirshiel (interview) as contributing to his difficulties.

21 Maudling (*39*) p.52.

22 Profumo had been an M.P. for Kettering, 1940–5 and was returned for Stratford in 1950. During the interval, he had acted as an adviser on broadcasting at Conservative Central Office.

23 Interview with Sir James Dunnett.

24 Although not a full Deputy Secretary, the position of Controller was nevertheless senior to Under-Secretary.

25 For an account of the organisation of the Ministry after the merger, see Hampden (*282*) pp.95–101.

26 Except the Civil Aviation Ground Services, headed by the Controller of Ground Services (Le Maitre).

27 Jenkins became Permanent Secretary at the Ministry of Transport and Civil Aviation, a post he held until 1959, the year he was sixty-five.

28 He had specialised in shipping throughout his Whitehall career, having been appointed Second Secretary at the Ministry of Shipping in 1939 and Deputy Director-General of the Ministry of War Transport, 1941–6.

29 *House of Commons* 27.5.52, Vol. 501, Col. 1152.

30 See Chapter 5 Part 4.

31 Labour were, however, not entirely convinced by his assurances, and in the debate in the *House of Commons* 8.3.54 argued that recent Government decisions on freight services and cheap flights to the Commonwealth were damaging the position of the corporations. See Davis (*261*) pp.111–12.

32 A leader in *The Times* 27.10.53, for example, noted that the annual reports of both corporations were disappointing.

33 *The Campaign Guide, 1955*, pp.103–4.

34 'London Airports, 1952–3', Cmd. 8902.

35 A Public Enquiry was appointed in January 1954 under the chairmanship of C. Campbell. It reported in June that the site was suitable, but due to the limitations of the Enquiry it was unable to express an opinion as to whether it was the most suitable of various options.

36 Amongst the thirty-five lost in the crash was Chester Wilmot, the former war correspondent and B.B.C. journalist. Originally from Australia, his influential book, *Struggle for Europe*, had been published in 1952.

37 Ship-building itself was the departmental responsibility of the Admiralty, not the Ministry of Transport.

38 One politician, in particular, however, made a significant contribution to the anti-pollution campaign, James Callaghan, junior Minister at Transport, 1947–50 and at the Admiralty, 1950–1, who made the subject very much his own when a back-bencher after 1951.

39 Faulkner was Chairman of the British Oil Pollution Committee, 1953–7, and a Deputy Secretary at the Ministry, 1957–61.

40 Jenkins (*154*) pp.76–7. These international conferences and conventions about oil pollution at sea were the embryo out of which the Intergovernmental Maritime Consultative Organisation (I.M.C.O.) grew, the only specialist agency of the United Nations to have its headquarters in London. Interview with Sir Dennis Proctor.

41 See Chapter 5 Part 4 for a discussion of the denationalisation of road transport.

42 *House of Commons* 8.12.53, Vol. 521, Col. 1813.

43 Interview II with Lord Boyd of Merton.

44 *House of Commons* 2.2.55.

45 Interview with Lord Boyd-Carpenter.

46 Interview with Lord Boyd-Carpenter. Boyd-Carpenter called Hyde Park Corner the most congested area of London, and said in his statement in the *House of Commons* on 2.2.55 that the Government were considering a 'boulevard' scheme. The M1, Britain's first full length motorway, was eventually opened in 1959 on a seventy-mile stretch between Birmingham and London.

47 Boyd-Carpenter (*8a*) pp.107–21.

48 'Britain Strong and Free', 1951.

49 Watkinson (*181a*) p.64. Harold Watkinson continued to write that as a former Permanent Secretary at Transport (1927–37), Hurcomb knew how to make these relations as difficult as possible. Problems were also caused by the narrowness of the Minister's responsibilities: he had to represent 'the public interest', and to defend the Commission in Parliament.

50 See Watkinson (*181a*) pp.62–7.

51 'Railways Reorganisation Scheme', Cmd. 9191.

52 Modernisation and replacement of stock had virtually ceased during the war and early post-war years. This was in contrast to the United States and most of Europe's progress post-1945, where there had been far more investment to convert their railways to either electric or diesel electric. *The Times* 13.9.54 noted that the two 'spasms of politically induced reorganisation' since the war had done little to promote technical progress.

53 The modernisation plan, aided by substantial financial help authorised in 1957 and supplemented in 1959, failed, however, to achieve the long hoped-for goal of financial viability.

54 The Permanent Secretary, Sir Gilmour Jenkins, had been instrumental in securing Robertson's appointment. Jenkins, who

576

had met Robertson early on after the war (when the former had been Permanent Secretary of the Control Office for Germany and Austria and Robertson Deputy Military Governor), had a high regard for him. Since 1950 Robertson had been Commander-in-Chief of the Middle East Land Forces.

55 The story is recounted also in Boyd-Carpenter (*8a*) p.92.

56 Interview II with Lord Boyd of Merton.

57 The *Observer* 12.7.53.

58 A leader in the *Sunday Times* 6.2.55.

59 See Chapter 4 Part 4. Boyd-Carpenter announced that, 'The Government have in mind that tolls should be charged in suitable cases.' *House of Commons* 2.2.55, Vol. 536, Col. 1099. But Boyd-Carpenter refused to be tied down about quite what the Government intended.

60 The *Sunday Times* 6.2.55.

61 See Chapter 8 Part 5. This was the V1000.

62 The *Sunday Times* 23.1.55.

CHAPTER 6 PART 6 pp.234–243

1 Gwilym Lloyd-George was the first Minister, June 1942–July 1945. The Ministry was formed from parts of the Board of Trade, which had responsibility for coal, gas, electricity (since 1941) and oil. Coal and petroleum were the business of special sub-Departments with their own political heads (The Mines Department and Petroleum Department). See Chester (*138*) pp.99–103.

2 Some officials felt that the Ministry of Fuel and Power as it existed after the war remained an inherently unsatisfactory Department until its upgrading and clarification of responsibility in 1957.

3 Macmillan, having just become Prime Minister, wanted to bring his old friend Sir Percy Mills into Government, and felt the addition of iron and steel would upgrade the job to utilise to the full his considerable talents. See p.225.

4 Mackenzie and Grove (*143*) p.431.

5 Ridley had been appointed in 1942 Regional Controller for the North, Ministry of Production.

6 Cmd 8647, *The Report of the Committee on National Policy for the Use of Fuel and Power Resources*. The title came after an intervention by Fergusson, who felt the original title, which mentioned 'National Fuel Policy', was inappropriate, as fuel policy was the responsibility solely of the Government.

7 *The Times* 11.9.52.

8 Pressure for a national fuel policy did not fade away, however, and periodically reasserted itself. In the House of Lords, (former miner and socialist Minister) Lord Lawson drew attention to the British Productivity Council's Report of September 1953, on fuel policy, and called for the three nationalised fuel industries to be co-ordinated under a Fuel and Power Board and for a national fuel policy. Lord Selkirk, replying for the Government, said it would not do this, partly because it would undermine the position of the individual Boards. *The Times* 2.12.53.

9 Citrine had previously been the General Secretary of the T.U.C., 1926–46. Ministers of both Parties after the war were always especially anxious to hear his views. *Private Information*. Citrine for his part felt he always received as fair treatment from Conservative as from Labour Ministers. Citrine (*11a*) p.348.

10 *House of Commons* 7.7.52.

11 Nabarro had been M.P. for the Kidderminster Division of Worcestershire since 1950. For a flavour of his views, see Nabarro (*42*) pp.208–21.

12 A Lancashire M.P. since 1938.

13 An Essex M.P. from 1931–45 and a Liverpool M.P. from 1945, he was one of the longer serving backbenchers in the Party who never became a Minister.

14 *The Times* 1.4.53.

15 Goodhart (*123*) pp.165–6.

16 Demands had moved away from pressing for denationalisation to urging for enquiries into the nationalised fuel industries. Conservative Party Research Department Papers: Note of discussions with Raikes 13.4.54, Box R.S.G., Notes of Meetings.

17 Citrine comments of Lloyd that he provided a 'striking tribute to the fairness and sense of ministerial responsibility in disposing of hostile backbench criticism'. Citrine (*11a*) p.348.

18 Lloyd had been Secretary for Mines, 1939–40, Secretary for Petroleum, 1940–2, Chairman of the Oil Control Board, 1939–45, Minister in Charge of the Petroleum Warfare Department, 1940–5, and Parliamentary Secretary (Petroleum)

at the Ministry of Fuel and Power, 1942–5. Lloyd was thus in the centre of wartime discussions on fuel, playing almost as important a part as the Minister, Gwilym Lloyd-George. But some felt Lloyd never fully recovered from having been out of the House from 1945–50.

19 See Chapter 3 Part 4.

20 Interview with Lord Brentford (the former Lancelot Joynson-Hicks).

21 William Joynson-Hicks, Home Secretary, 1924–9. Created Viscount Brentford in 1929.

22 Interview with Lord Robens of Woldingham. (Parliamentary Secretary, 1947–51.)

23 Maud was an academic who entered Whitehall in 1941. Many others followed the same route, including Sir Oliver Franks and Sir Laurence Helsby.

24 After he left the Ministry in 1955, Kelf-Cohen went on to become one of the leading experts on the nationalised industries, publishing a number of authoritative studies, of which Kelf-Cohen (*166*) was the first. He was assisted on the coal side by a particularly able junior official, the Chief Statistician, Goronwy Daniel, later knighted and Permanent Secretary at the Welsh Office, 1964–9.

25 He had been Deputy Director of Scientific Research at the Ministry of Aircraft Production, 1940–3, and Director of Special Projects there from 1943–4.

26 He described the work in progress in the Hawksley Memorial Lecture for 1951, a paper he gave to the Institute of Mechanical Engineers.

27 Interview with Sir Kelvin Spencer.

28 Interview with Lord Kings Norton (formerly Sir Harold Roxbee Cox).

29 Fergusson was reputed to dislike economists and confessed a lack of understanding of the subject – this from a man who had spent sixteen years (1920–36) as Private Secretary to successive Chancellors. Fergusson was, however, courteous and helpful to the economists, as he was to all who served under him.

30 Interview with Philip Chantler.

31 By the Coal Industry Nationalisation Act, 1946.

32 See 'Britain Strong and Free'. It is also of interest that it said that, in line with the N.U.M.'s long-term desire to fix wages on a national, rather than a coalfield basis, 'wage negotiations will remain on a national basis'. Chester (*162a*) p.1029.

33 Houldsworth had previously had the good fortune to be the Chairman of the East Midlands Division, the most prosperous and harmonious coalfield. But his barrister's training did not equip him with the qualities needed to provide the continuity of policy and planning required in a large industrial undertaking. Interview with Sir Joseph Latham. (Latham was the N.C.B.'s Director-General of Finance, 1946–55).

34 *Private Information.*

35 Letter, Bracken to Beaverbrook, 7.1.53, *Beaverbrook Papers*, Box C57.

36 *The Campaign Guide, 1955* pp.88–9. Output of deep-mined coal rose circa eleven per cent, 1947–51, but from 1951–7 output was almost static. See also Kelf-Cohen (*166*) pp.46–7.

37 Clegg (*279*) p.269 called it 'a clear, incisive, interesting and well-constructed report'. See also Roberts (*275*) pp.1–14. The main contributor to the report was in fact the distinguished accountant Henry Benson. Interview with Sir Joseph Latham.

38 The post of Deputy Chairman was potentially a very powerful one. The first holder of the post after nationalisation had been Sir Arthur Street, the former official head of the Air Ministry. With his outstanding ability he carried the major responsibility in those difficult years, more even than the first Chairman, Lord Hyndley. *Private Information.*

39 A leader in *The Times* 14.5.53.

40 *Safety in Coal Mines*, Chairman Lord Rockley. Appointed December, 1935, reported December 1938. Cmd. 5890.

41 *House of Commons* 2.7.54, Vol. 529, Cols. 1663–4.

42 See Horner (*25*) pp.205–6.

43 Interview with Sir Joseph Latham.

44 Interview with Lord Geoffrey-Lloyd.

45 Interview with Lord Redcliffe-Maud.

46 Roberts and Sallis (*276*) p.116.

47 The Conservatives in 1951 pledged themselves to reorganising the Central Electricity Board, but as there was no pressure to implement this, it was quietly dropped. 'Points of Vulnerability', February 1955, *C.R.D. Papers*, Box R.S.G., Gen. Corresp.

48 See Citrine (*11a*) pp.306–7.

49 See Macmillan (*36*) pp.431–2.

50 See letter, Hugh Molson to Lord

Cherwell, 13.11.53, *Cherwell Papers*, Pers. 63 1V.

51 The Chairman, Sir Hugh Beaver, managing director of Arthur Guinness, had been Director General and Controller General, Ministry of Works, 1940–5.

52 A. N. Braithwaite and Hinchingbrooke, for example, moved an amendment to reject a Bill introduced by Lloyd in 1954 to extend the industry's borrowing powers. *House of Commons* 9.7.54. See Harris (*164*) pp.195–6.

53 Cmd. 9672. Hanson (*266*) pp.211–14 described it as an 'excellent' report, 'very thoughtful' and 'acute'.

54 See debate, *House of Commons* 17.12.55.

55 Cmd 9389. For further background see Citrine (*11a*) pp.302–5.

56 See Kelf-Cohen (*166*) p.100.

57 Interview with Sir Kelvin Spencer. Sir Kelvin recalls that to the best of his memory he never at any time came across discussion of the adverse biological and radioactive hazards inherent in the nuclear programme. Pierre (*195*) p. 78 records that in the early post-war years there was little discussion in Britain – in contrast to the position in the United States – of uses for atomic energy, and that the press were discouraged from visiting the Research Establishment at Harwell.

58 A leader in *The Times* 16.2.55 said, 'To Britain, nearing the point where coal output can no longer be easily expanded to cover the increasing demands of industry, the advent of nuclear power comes as a relief.'

59 Those meetings would usually take place fortnightly, and outstanding problems would be talked over, usually quite informally. Relations were more intimate with gas than with the electricity industry. Gas was a good deal smaller and thus facilitating personal contacts. Interview with Lord Brentford.

60 Appointed June 1944, signed November 1945, Cmd. 6699.

61 But by halfway through the seven-year period, domestic consumption had actually fallen. Kelf-Cohen (*166*) p.117.

62 Kelf-Cohen (*166*) p.112.

63 Interview with R. Kelf-Cohen.

64 *The Campaign Guide, 1955* p.92.

65 *Personal interview.*

66 Interview with Lord Geoffrey-Lloyd.

67 Interview II with Lord Redcliffe-Maud.

68 *The Campaign Guide, 1955* p.92. There were always very close links between the Petroleum Division and the Treasury, especially as oil was then bought and sold in sterling.

69 See draft Minute to Churchill, undated, in *Cherwell Papers*, Pers.24, Pt.111.

CHAPTER 7 PART 1 pp.244–247

1 The Report was published in November 1942 (Cmd. 6404).

2 *A National Health Service*, Cmd. 6502.

3 Churchill speaking on 27th May, 1954, at the Conservative Women's Meeting in the Royal Albert Hall, London.

4 See Table 1.

5 Ramsden notes in his forthcoming book on the Conservative Research Department that Iain Macleod felt the Conservatives should first formulate a policy of their own towards the N.H.S. before criticising Labour's.

6 See Part 3 and Epilogue I below.

7 The *Sunday Times* 20.1.52.

8 Expounded, for example, on p.211 of *The Campaign Guide, 1955*.

9 See this Chapter, Part 3.

10 *The Times* 17.1.52. In his book Ramsden notes that there were increasing Conservative anxieties at the shape the N.H.S. was taking under Bevan (Minister of Health, 1945–51), and that the Party produced some plans for cuts and charging, which were not broadcast due to Labour's electioneering prophecies of Conservative intentions to cut social services.

11 In housing, Labour's 1955 Election Manifesto said Labour would ask local authorities to submit schemes for gradually taking over and modernising rent-controlled private property. In health: 'We have come to the decision that when we are returned to power, pay-beds in hospitals will no longer be provided.' (Margaret Herbison, speaking for the Labour's National Executive Committee at Scarborough on 30.9.54.) On education: '. . . our aim will be to take over the best of the "public" and independent day schools'. (Labour's 'Challenge to Britain, 1953'.) Labour's policy on pensions, as on many other social service topics, was far from settled: nevertheless, an indication of their

future thinking is seen in this excerpt from the *Sunday Pictorial* of 28.11.54, (quoted in *The Campaign Guide, 1955* p.226): 'The biggest battle . . . will be for a National Pensions Service financed not by flat-rate contributions, which fall heaviest on the poorest, but by taxation, which hits the richest hardest.' (Written by Richard Crossman on the eve of a new Session of Parliament.)

12 Some officials at the Ministry of Education saw a deliberate policy on the part of the Government of favouring housing at the expense of education.

13 See Chapter 5 Part 2. Marwick noted that the term Butskellism could be applied to social policy as well as to economic policy; not only had Gaitskell first introduced charges for the N.H.S. in 1951, but Butler played a leading part in ensuring Conservative acceptance of the welfare state. Marwick (*187*) p.374.

CHAPTER 7 PART 2 pp.247–261

1 Chester and Willson (*138*) p.179. Sharp (*158a*) pp.15–16 makes the point that though the staff of Town and Country Planning were happy about the merger, those from Health were less so. They felt like victims of a takeover and regarded planning with some impatience, but by the mid-1950s the new Ministry had settled down.

2 Churchill in *House of Commons* 12.11.51, Vol. 493, Col. 643.

3 Interview with Sir Robert Marshall.

4 Harmar Nicholls became P.P.S. to Gammans at the Post Office. Robson-Brown, the older man, was one of the authorities in the Party on the steel industry. He had been M.P. for Esher since 1950.

5 Interview with Lord Harmar-Nicholls.

6 Interview with Lord Strathclyde (the former Tom Galbraith). He wound up for the Government in the debate.

7 Interview with Mark Chapman Walker.

8 *Report of the 71st Annual Party Conference* p.112.

9 For a full account of the way the commitment came to be accepted, see the *Manchester Guardian* 13.10.50, Cohen: *A History* p.488 and the Conference Report pp.56–65.

10 Woolton (*55*) pp.364–5.

11 Interview with Mark Chapman Walker. At the conclusion of the housing debate at Blackpool, Woolton had said: 'This is magnificent. You want a figure of 300,000 put in. (*Cries of "Yes".*) Madam Chairman, I am sure that those of us on the platform here would be very glad indeed to have such a figure put in.' Conference Report p.65.

12 Bevins (*5*) p.28.

13 A leader in the *News Chronicle* 31.10.51.

14 Diary 21.2.52 *Dalton Papers*.

15 Macmillan (*36*) pp.375 and 460.

16 Of the four post-war posts he held (except the premiership), Housing was the only position he held for a sufficient period to make much mark (just under three years). The other three (Defence, Foreign Office, Exchequer) he held for one year or less.

17 On 7.1.53, Bracken wrote to Beaverbrook that Macmillan was 'desperately anxious' to get out of Housing, and mentioned the Foreign Office as the job he most desired. In February 1953 Bracken wrote that the Ministry of Agriculture was now beginning to attract him. *Beaverbrook Papers*. By 1953 or 54, Macmillan was widely regarded as the likely successor to Eden at the Foreign Office. Lord Ismay favoured the move, and the American Ambassador in London thought it a strong possibility. See diary 26.5.53 and 3.6.53, Sulzberger (*51a*) pp.736 and 738. Some officials thought Macmillan was 'constantly eager' for a chance to leave, but were less emphatic about his urgency. *Private Information*.

18 Macmillan served at Supply from May 1940–February 1942.

19 Interview with Sydney Wilkinson, the Under-Secretary responsible for housing 1951–4.

20 His ministerial experience had been confined to Ministries responsible for defence, colonial and foreign policy.

21 Interview with Sir Noël Hutton (First Parliamentary Counsel, 1956–68). Sir Noël added that the draftsmen much enjoyed working on Bills with Macmillan, and further that he would give a party at the completion of the passage of a Bill for the officials who had worked on it.

22 Interview with Jack Beddoe. Ramsden, in his book on the Conservative Research Department, also notes how much Macmillan after 1951 employed the detailed

preparatory work carried out at the Research Department to great effect.

23 See Macmillan (*36*) pp.439–40. Macmillan was also fortunate to possess in A. P. G. Brown one of the few departmental P.R.O.s who saw it as his job to promote his Minister.

24 Interview with Lord Harmar-Nicholls.

25 See letter, Macmillan to Fraser, 2.4.54, about the Housing Repairs and Rents Bill. *C.R.D. Papers*, Box Govt. Corresp.

26 Interview with Sydney Wilkinson. Macmillan's business connection was with the publishing house of the same name.

27 Macmillan (*36*) pp.397–8.

28 Interview with Reginald Bevins, D.B.Y.

29 *Private Information.*

30 For the building programme in Scotland, see Chapter 4 Part 4.

31 Macmillan (*36*) p.398.

32 Macmillan (*36*) pp.395–9. Interview with Jack Beddoe.

33 Sampson (*96*) p.94.

34 'Sir P. Mills is very anxious to set up Regional Housing Production Boards . . . This frightens the Department; but I have decided in favour of Sir Percy's plan.' Diary 1.2.52, 2.2.52, 3.2.52 and 4.2.52, Macmillan (*36*) p.399. See also Sharp (*158a*) pp.214–16. A major part in the establishment of the Ministry's regional offices had been played by another 'outsider', Henry Benson. He had been Special Adviser to the Minister of Health on housing production in 1945.

35 Macmillan (*36*) p.399.

36 Memo by Macmillan, April 1952. Quoted in Macmillan (*36*) pp.400–1.

37 Sharp (*158a*) p.216.

38 Macmillan (*36*) pp.402 and 460.

39 Diary 29.3.52, Macmillan (*36*) p.410.

40 Macmillan (*36*) pp.459–60.

41 Macmillan wrote on 15.4.55 to Wilkinson: 'I shall always look back on those three years with pleasure, and I am deeply grateful for the part you played. You were the man who really made it possible to achieve the success which we undoubtedly did.' *Private Papers.*

42 Macmillan (*36*) p.364.

43 Macmillan (*36*) pp.457–8.

44 Macmillan had married into the aristocracy – a daughter of the 9th Duke of Devonshire.

45 Macmillan (*36*) p.410.

46 Interview II with John Rogerson.

47 Interview with Jack Beddoe.

48 Bevins (*5*) p.29.

49 The effects of ill health were not however all that apparent during 1951–5. Interview with Sydney Wilkinson.

50 Interview with William Deedes, who succeeded Marples as Parliamentary Secretary in 1954.

51 See for example Dalton (*13*) p.351.

52 Macmillan described her as 'the pillar of the Ministry'. Macmillan (*36*) p.460.

53 As a result of the smog, the Air Pollution Committee was set up under the chairmanship of Sir Hugh Beaver. Its Report, published in November 1954, urged the strengthening of the law on the control of air pollution. The Fuel and Power scientist, Kelvin Spencer, thought Beaver a highly competent and intelligent Chairman of the Committee. Very early on both he and the Committee realised that there was no way that impurities like sulphur dioxide could be controlled economically, and therefore, guided by Beaver, the Committee decided to clean up the atmosphere by using permitted fuels without controlling sulphur dioxide. Interview with Sir Kelvin Spencer.

54 Macmillan (*36*) pp.432 and 439. For the background of this work see Murphy (*289*) pp.410–27.

55 Macmillan (*36*) pp.404 and 411.

56 Macmillan (*36*) pp.376 and 430–2.

57 Swinton (*52*) p.179.

58 Macmillan (*36*) p.417.

59 Circular No. 93/52.

60 Circular No. 69/53.

61 This, however, helped to produce overexpansion in the economy. The decision to abolish building controls had not been taken in consultation with the Treasury's Economic Section. See Lord Boyle of Handsworth's article 'The Economist in Government', p.8. See Bibliography.

62

	Houses for local authorities	Houses for private owners	Total
1951	166,000	25,000	202,000
1952	199,000	37,000	248,000
1953	245,000	65,000	327,000
1954	239,000	92,000	354,000
1955	196,000	116,000	324,000

Source: *Annual Abstract of Statistics*, 1957 p.63

These figures covered the whole of the U.K., whereas responsibility for house-building in Scotland belonged to the Scottish Office. The 'Total' figure includes houses for families of policemen, armed forces, etc. It was noted at the time that Macmillan benefited considerably in 1952 from the houses already begun by Labour and that only bad bungling could have prevented less than 230,000 houses being built that year.

63 Macmillan (*36*) pp.444–58.

64 'Houses – The Next Step' Cmd. 8996, published in November 1953. The plans were outlined in the Queen's speech on 3.11.53. Churchill said in his speech in *House of Commons* 3.11.53, Vol. 520, Col. 25, that the Government would give 'earnest attention' to any constructive proposal put forward by Labour.

65 Reported in Sampson (*96*) p.97. Bevan was Minister of Health, July 1945–January 1951.

66 *Private Information.*

67 These twelve were all in England and Wales, of which eight, like Stevenage and Bracknell, were designed to absorb excess population from the Greater London area. Two towns were initially designated in Scotland – East Kilbride and Glenrothes. These came within the jurisdiction of the Department of Health of the Scottish Office.

68 For a discussion of planning in the first post-war decade see Wright (*291*) pp.73–91.

69 *Private Information.* Macmillan does not refer to these initial doubts in his memoirs – for example: 'As soon as I came into Office I determined to give all possible assistance to the [new towns'] progress.' Macmillan (*36*) p.418.

70 Interview I with John Rogerson.

71 *The Times* 24.6.53. It went on to criticise the new towns for not having enough amenities or a sufficient variety of industry. It continued: 'Most of the new towns differ but little from housing estates.' It singled out Crawley as an example of one that did work well, with a balanced development of houses, amenities and industry.

72 This Act owed much to the initiative of the people of Worsley in Lancashire who, before the passage of the Act, started building houses for Salford people. Wolverhampton and Walsall also made similar arrangements before the Act. See also Macmillan (*36*) pp.419–20.

73 Interview with George Pottinger. See also Pottinger (*145*) p.137.

74 See Kilmuir (*31*) pp.197, 200–1.

75 *House of Commons* 21.7.52, Vol. 504, Col. 67.

76 Woolton was Chairman of a Cabinet subcommittee on Housing set up to consider the question of the development charge, and its Report in June 1952 formed the basis of Macmillan's proposals. Woolton to Churchill, 17.6.52, *Woolton Papers*, Box 25.

77 Receiving the Royal Assent in May 1953 as the Town and Country Planning Act, 1953.

78 Town and Country Planning Act, 1947 – Amendment of Financial Provisions (Cmd. 8699).

79 Those officials in the Department who had been involved with the 1947 Act, and who believed that it had settled the vexed problem of land ownership once and for all, were very upset to see it go. Despite their qualms, however, they co-operated fully with Macmillan.

80 Her letter is quoted in Macmillan (*36*) p.429.

81 Macmillan (*36*) pp.413–16.

82 Macmillan said in 1953 that a Bill to reform local government could not be introduced before 1955. Harrison (*242*) p.202. In a written reply on 22.3.55 Sandys said meetings had taken place with the Association of Local Government Authorities but more time was needed before proposals would be submitted. Harrison (*244*) pp.272–3. A contemporary discussion on the need for local government reform can be found in Maddick (*288*) pp.246–57.

83 This postponed the dates when the new valuation lists under the Local Government Act, 1948 would come into force. These had been originally a plan of the Inland Revenue Department, which by 1952 decided they would not work. The matter was settled in the Valuation for Rating Act, 1953, which restored the valuation basis that Bevan, Minister of Health, 1945–51, had dispensed with in the 1948 Act and returned instead to the 1939 rental value.

84 'I was destined during the first months and even years to wage a continual battle with the Treasury.' Macmillan (*36*) p.375.

85 Macmillan (*36*) p.498.

86 See Chapter 5 Part 1.

87 Interview I with Lord Butler.

88 See, for example, diary 25.8.53, Moran (*87*) p.487.

89 *Official Report of the 71st Annual Party Conference*, p.112.

90 'He didn't interfere in my housing, just left it all to me.' Macmillan to Moran, diary 9.1.55, Moran (*87*) p.659.

91 In his memoirs, Maxwell Fyfe praised the economic sense of the housing drive, Kilmuir (*31*) p.201.

92 *The Times* 6.2.54.

93 See, for example, Pinto-Duschinsky in Bogdanor and Skidelsky, eds. (*114*) pp.58–63.

94 *Dalton Papers.*

95 *House of Commons* 18.5.53, Vol. 515, Col. 1712.

96 *House of Commons* 1.7.53, Vol. 517, Col. 515. See also Chapter 7 Part 4.

97 Same speech, Col. 518.

98 Macmillan (*36*) p.544.

99 Macmillan (*36*) p.545.

100 Diary 11.10.54, *Crookshank Papers.*

101 Macmillan (*36*) p.356. Also Piers Dixon's diary in 1950 mentions Butler seeing Macmillan as a possible Minister of Defence in the next Conservative Government. *Private Papers.*

102 Interview with William Deedes.

103 Sandys had been Financial Secretary at the War Office (1941–3) under David Margesson and Sir James Grigg and Parliamentary Secretary at Supply when Sir Andrew Duncan was Minister.

104 Interview with William Deedes.

105 In the event, the high-point of Deedes' career was not to be in politics (although he did reach the job of Minister without Portfolio from 1962–4) but in journalism, and he was appointed editor of the *Daily Telegraph* in December 1974.

CHAPTER 7 PART 3 pp.262–270

1 Interview with Sir George Godber.

2 Diary 7.12.51 and 10.1.52, *Crookshank Papers.*

3 The Government had to introduce the Guillotine after twenty-one hours had been spent in Committee disposing of only five lines. *The Times* 25.4.52. Herbert Morrison later wrote, 'The fight over the Health Service charges was to my mind, something of a sham.' Morrison (*40*) p.291.

4 It was thought that Macleod chose Guillebaud (Senior Tutor, St. John's College, Cambridge, 1952–6) as he had been a former pupil of his at Cambridge. (Macleod himself had been at Gonville and Caius.)

5 *House of Commons* 1.4.53, Vol. 513, Col. 1230.

6 This was the view expressed in interview with several senior Ministry officials.

7 For a commentary on Guillebaud, see Chester (*286*) pp.199–210.

8 Titmuss had been Professor of Social Administration at London University since 1950 and was the author with Abel-Smith of *The Cost of the National Health Service in England and Wales* (1956). Abel-Smith was later a Professor of Social Administration at London University.

9 There is still the Crookshank Lecture in the Royal College of Radiologists.

10 Interview with Sir Robert Cary.

11 See Chapter 3 Part 1.

12 Interview with Sir Robert Cary.

13 Diary 9.11.51, *Crookshank Papers.*

14 Diary 20.2.52, *Crookshank Papers.*

15 *Private Papers.*

16 *House of Commons* 24.4.52.

17 Diary 9.5.52, *Crookshank Papers.*

18 Interview with Sir George Godber.

19 Interview with Baroness Hornsby-Smith.

20 Interview with Baroness Hornsby-Smith.

21 See Fisher (*74*) pp.80–5 and also Roth (*94*) p.92.

22 *House of Commons* 27.3.52, Vol. 498, Col. 886.

23 Interview with Ray Gedling. Gedling was Principal Private Secretary to the Minister of Health from 1952–5. Later Deputy Secretary of D.H.S.S., 1971–7.

24 *Private Information.*

25 *The Economist* 24.12.55 (p.1092).

26 Ramsden notes in his book on the Conservative Research Department that Macleod had been reluctant, while serving as an officer there until 1950, to engage in the Conservative pastime of spotting flaws in the N.H.S., and argued that it was essential to give the Service time to settle down.

27 *Private Information.*

28 Interview with Ray Gedling. Officials would of course visit Macleod in his small room in the House to discuss Ministry work.

29 The annual Report of the Ministry for 1952

said: 'The slow increase of health centres must be disappointing to those who had thought of these centres as the answer to such problems as professional isolation, inadequate premises and lack of ancillary help.' It concluded: 'Group practice may be found to be an easier development of the present structure of general practice.' The report in fact found only three health centres provided by local authorities in the way prescribed by the original N.H.S. Act. *The Times* 21.9.53. In January 1954 Macleod decided to set aside £100,000 for the encouragement of group practice. *The Times* 29.1.54.

30 See Chapter 7 Part 4.

31 The other, Florence Horsbrugh, was Minister of Education, 1951–4.

32 Interview with Baroness Hornsby-Smith. She also discusses her relationship with Crookshank in King and Sloman (*126a*).

33 A young M.P., entering the House in 1951 for Epping.

34 Because of this factor senior officials played an especially important part. Sir Frederick Armer, the single Deputy Secretary, concentrated on the mental health side and performed a key role in holding the Department together. Of the five Under-Secretaries Macleod worked closely with two in particular, Dame Enid Russell-Smith on G.P. and local Government matters and John Pater, one of the ablest of men not to reach the top two levels of the Service, on hospitals.

35 *Annual Abstract of Statistics, 1957*, p.60. The need, however, was less for more beds than for better beds. As the provision of supporting resources improved, the turnover increased and the numbers of beds could be reduced. In 1979 there were about twelve per cent fewer beds than in 1949.

36 *House of Commons* 9.2.55.

37 'Britain Strong and Free', p.30.

38 *Annual Abstract of Statistics, 1957*, p.60.

39 A Bill designed to permit experiments of dental auxiliaries had to be withdrawn in 1952 due to short-sighted professional opposition.

40 A new dental hospital had been begun under the Labour Government at Sheffield in 1951. opened in October 1953.

41 Fisher (*74*) p.100. The Law Relating to Mental Illness and Mental Deficiency, Cmnd. 169.

42 *Annual Abstract of Statistics, 1957*, p.60.

43 *Annual Abstract of Statistics, 1957*, p.60.

44 *The Times* 25.9.53.

45 See Part 2 above.

46 'Social Services: Needs and Means' (C.P.C. January 1952).

47 *The Times* 29.3.54. See also Abel-Smith and Titmuss (*188*) pp.58–9.

CHAPTER 7 PART 4 pp.270–282

1 The invitation was one of the leading news stories in most London newspapers in the early days after the Election. See also diaries for 28.10.51 in *Crookshank Papers* and Macmillan (*36*) p.365.

2 Coote (*68*) p.261.

3 Four women who have sat in British Cabinets (almost half the total) have had the Education portfolio: Ellen Wilkinson 1945–7, Florence Horsbrugh, Margaret Thatcher, 1970–4, and Shirley Williams, 1976–9. Churchill might have considered appointing the Vice-Chairman, Christopher Hollis (M.P. for Devizes, 1945–55, an author and publisher) to the job of Minister of Education (or even Parliamentary Secretary) were it not for Hollis' Catholic faith. Interview I with Peter Goldman.

4 The usual mechanism for Departments hearing who was their new boss was a communication to either the Permanent Secretary or the Principal Private Secretary. Interview with Sir Antony Part, B.O.A.P.A.H.

5 She was also Parliamentary Secretary at the Ministry of Food for the two months of the 'Caretaker Government', 1945. She was out of the House between 1945–50, and from 1950–9 was M.P. for the Moss Side division of Manchester.

6 The *Sunday Times*, in a profile on 3.2.52.

7 The local education authorities understood that Horsbrugh was under pressure to economise but still felt that she could have fought harder for education. Interview with Lord Alexander of Potterhill.

8 Interview with Sir Ronald Gould, then General Secretary of the N.U.T. He later wrote: 'I wish I could say something good of Miss Florence Horsbrugh . . . but I can think of nothing.' Gould (*19a*) p.150.

9 The Ministry contained one of the brightest collections of young men in any

Department in Whitehall. Some of them like Derek Morrell and David Nenk died before they were fifty. Others rose to the highest jobs in the Civil Service – like Antony Part who was a Permanent Secretary of Industry and Trade Departments from 1968–76; Toby Weaver, Deputy Secretary at the Ministry from 1960–73, and William Pile, Permanent Secretary there from 1970–6.

10 *The Times* 5.11.51 noted that the only previous occasions were in 1931 and during the War Coalition Government. The article continued that it was bound to be taken as a sign of the times and the value set by the new Government on education. It thought it an unfortunate omission.

11 *House of Commons* 6.11.51, Vol. 493, Col. 75.

12 *House of Commons* 24.6.53, Vol. 516, Col. 1904. Later Lord Maybray-King, Speaker of the Commons, 1965–70.

13 See, for example, diary 24.2.53, Moran (*87*) p.426. The N.U.T. certainly felt that Churchill was partly to blame for the low priority the Conservatives gave to education. Interview with Sir Ronald Gould.

14 Woolton (*55*) p.373.

15 Letter, Macmillan to Horsbrugh, 25.6.53, *Horsbrugh Papers*, Box 1/5

16 Letter, Eden to Horsbrugh, 15.10.54, *Horsbrugh Papers*, Box 1/5.

17 Interview with Lord Brooke of Cumnor.

18 *The Economist* 23.10.54.

19 *The Times* 18.10.54.

20 Letter, Bracken to Beaverbrook, 16.2.54, *Beaverbrook Papers*, Box C58.

21 Letter, Horsbrugh to Woolton, 23.10.54, *Woolton Papers*, Box 78.

22 One of his best known works was his *Early Tudor Government*, published in 1934.

23 Interview with R. N. Heaton.

24 The *News Chronicle* recorded on 18.10.54 that Pickthorn was – along with Horsbrugh – one of those who 'failed to come up to expectations'.

25 Holmes had spent his entire Civil Service career in the Department. He was an especially knowledgeable and respected Secretary, and the author of much of the 1944 Education Act.

26 The appointment, which would have meant unseating Sheepshanks, was not pursued because it was felt that in preceding years he had suffered from a number of moves of job. *Private Information.*

27 Letter, Maud to Horsbrugh, 5.8.52, *Horsbrugh Papers*, Box 1.5.

28 Dame Mary Smieton (1959–63) had a Ministry of Labour background; Sir Herbert Andrew (1963–70) came from the Board of Trade.

29 Maud was a keen supporter of maintaining international education contacts, as at UNESCO. Tomlinson had warmly applauded Maud's interntional work.

30 After Flemming's promotion there was just one Deputy Secretary, Sir Griffith Williams. A sympathetic and popular figure, and a representative of the 'old guard' in the Ministry, his chief interest lay in the schools side, especially the grammar and independent sectors. When he retired in December 1953, he was succeeded by Neville Heaton, who became an exceptional Deputy, and who was one of the first of the younger men in the Ministry to be advanced to a top position. The job of Senior Chief Inspector was of an equivalent status to Deputy Secretary. Sir Martin Roseveare held the job (1944–57), but some felt that as years passed he became increasingly less approachable and proficient. *Private Information.*

31 By Circular 242, on 7th December. The Opposition were immediately critical as the Circular went out when Parliament was not sitting.

32 Circular 245 of 4th February, 1952, affecting school building.

33 *The Times* 4.2.52.

34 *The Campaign Guide, 1955*, p.254.

35 *Annual Abstract of Statistics, 1957* p.88.

36 School-building was the responsibility of the Schools Branch, which was throughout 1951–5 still by far the most important of the several branches of the Ministry. Other branches, however, had been increasing in importance since the end of the war, in particular the Teachers Branch, because of the emergency training scheme, and the Architects and Building Branch, formed after the war at the instigation of the Permanent Secretary, Sir John Maud.

37 *The Times* 18.12.53. The leader was commenting on two P.E.P. broadsheets, published the same day, on overcrowding in schools. The broadsheets said that for some time the chief reason for large classes was thought to be slowness in building, but

the broadsheets suggested the real problem was shortage of teachers.

38 *Annual Abstract of Statistics, 1957* p.91.

39 *The Campaign Guide, 1955* p.266.

40 *Official Report, 72nd Annual Party Conference* p.95.

41 The meeting was held on 30th December, 1954.

42 'Challenge to Britain' p.23.

43 This Circular thus confirmed policy in a direction which had already been laid down. As Lord Boyle told Maurice Kogan: 'One of the historical myths is that comprehensive reorganisation all started with Circular 10/65. It didn't. It started a number of years before.' Kogan (*186*) p.78.

44 As expressed, for example, in these two letters: 'May I also say . . . how much I appreciate all that you have done and tried to do for religious education as a whole? I know something of the difficulties with which you have had to contend.' Emphasis was laid on the Church's 'indebtedness' to her. Letter, Bishop of London to Horsbrugh. 18.10.54. *Horsbrugh Papers*, Box1.5.; and 'I know . . . the courage needed to introduce any measure which might even indirectly inflame religious controversy.' Letter, Bishop of Brentwood to Horsbrugh. 17.7.54. *Horsbrugh Papers*, Box 1.5.

45 Horsbrugh, for example, on one occasion took Gould's advice on not dismissing a secondary school teacher for Communist inclinations. See Gould (*19a*) pp.150–1.

46 See Lord Boyle's Mays Lecture of May 1976. 'Parliament's Views on Responsibility for Education Policy since 1944', delivered at Birmingham University. Not all informed opinion regarded the Bill as a bad one. for example, a leader in *The Times* called it an 'eminently reasonable measure'. *The Times* 17.3.54.

47 *Private Information.*

48 Diary 5.5.54 and 12.5.54. *Crookshank Papers.*

49 Interview with Lord Boyle of Handsworth. *The Economist* 23.10.54 wrote that Horsbrugh's downfall was largely due to her inability to go and make peace in smoking rooms while revolt was brewing over the Pensions Bill.

50 Crookshank announced the postponement in the *House of Commons* on 20.5.54, and declared the Government's determination

to pass the Bill by the end of March 1955.

51 The Queen's Speech, delivered in *House of Commons* 30.11.54. contained a passage about the Government's determination to have a sound financial basis for their new scheme of teachers' pensions.

52 Vosper was M.P. for Runcorn, 1950–64. Appointed Minister of Health in 1957, he had to resign due to ill health which was to plague his ministerial career. (Later Lord Runcorn.) He died in 1968 aged fifty-two.

53 A leader in the *News Chronicle* on 18.10.54. It continued that Eccles had been 'working hard' for Cabinet rank.

54 Eccles announced this reorganisation in the debate on the Queen's Speech on 30th November, 1954.

55 Lord Eccles (interview) mentioned these as his two priorities in his early months at the Ministry.

56 Cmd. 9703.

57 See Kogan (*186*) p.20. The Ministry's annual Report for 1955 (Cmd. 9785) said that plans had been in progress throughout the year for major developments in technical education. Head of Schools Branch was traditionally regarded as the most prestigious of the six Under-Secretaries' jobs. So to have moved Part away from this to the Further Education Branch was an important indication of a reorientation within the Ministry.

58 *Ministry of Education Annual Report, 1954.*

59 Lord Boyle of Handsworth's 1976 Mays Lecture. Local education authorities themselves felt that without such reorganisation, full meaning could not be given to the 1944 Education Act. Interview with Lord Alexander of Potterhill.

60 Clarke in Thornhill, ed. (*135*) p.93.

61 Cmnd. 2154. In the early 1950s the issue of the freedom of universities from the normal process of Parliamentary accountability was fought by the Treasury against the Public Accounts Committee, a stubborn and a successful fight for the Treasury. But it became clear that with the expansion of higher education in the later 1950s the position of non-Parliamentary accountability could not continue. For an interesting contemporary discussion of the relationship between the U.G.C. and Parliament, see Wiseman (*290*) pp.75–92.

62 'Higher Technological Education', Cmd. 8357.

63 Master of Gonville and Caius College, Cambridge, 1948–58.
64 Woolton (*55*) pp.397–402.
65 Salisbury wrote to Butler on 27.4.53 to say that he had always had an open mind on the question. *Cherwell Papers*, Pers. 82A.
66 See, for example *Times Educational Supplement* 27.1.50.
67 Letter, Cherwell to Woolton, 6.12.51, *Cherwell Papers*, Pers. 82A.
68 Woolton to Bridges, 7.12.51, *Woolton Papers*, Box 25.
69 Interview I with Lord Redcliffe-Maud.
70 See Woolton to Butler, 22.4.53, *Woolton Papers*, Box 26.
71 Letter, Stuart to Butler, 3.12.52, *Cherwell Papers*, Pers. 82A.
72 Letter, Salisbury to Butler, 12.5.53, *Cherwell Papers*, Pers. 82A.
73 Colville (*12*) p.256.
74 *The Times* 23.9.53.
75 *House of Commons* 1.7.53. Macmillan (*36*) pp.433–5 and *The Times* 2.7.53. See also Chapter 7 Part 4.
76 *The Times* 18.7.53.

CHAPTER 7 PART 5 pp.282–286

1 Interview with Sir John Walley.
2 *Social Insurance and Allied Services*. Cmd. 6404.
3 It should be pointed out, however, that Beveridge did not suggest the Ministry of Health be in the proposed Ministry of Social Security, nor Local Government. The decision that the Ministry of Labour should keep the running of employment exchanges in its own hands when in March 1945 responsibility for unemployment insurance was transferred to National Insurance was a definite rejection of Beveridge. The Ministry of Pensions and National Insurance did, however, have a very close relationship with the National Assistance Board, a most important welfare organisation.
4 Interview I with Lord Amory.
5 Allen (*56*) pp.119–20.
6 Allen (*56*) pp.119–20.
7 Heasman (*237*) p.323.
8 Smyth (*49*) pp.282–3.
9 Smyth (*49*) pp.280–1 and 283.
10 Interview with Lord Holderness, the former Richard Wood.
11 Interview II with Lord Amory.

12 Interview with Lord Shinwell.
13 Monckton had served as Solicitor-General in the 'Caretaker Government', although he was not an M.P.
14 Interview II with Lord Amory.
15 Interview with Sir John Walley.
16 He had first been elected an M.P. in 1924 and remained a member apart from 1929–31 and 1936–40.
17 These improvements took place from May and affected nearly 800,000 war disabled and war widows, at a cost to the Treasury of about £10m. per annum.
18 *House of Commons* 26.2.53.
19 Interview with Sir John Smyth.
20 Lee (*142*) p.49.
21 Interview I with Lord Amory.
22 Interview with Sir John Smyth.
23 A White Paper (Cmd. 8842) had been presented to Parliament on 13th May explaining the background to the merger.

CHAPTER 7 PART 6 pp.286–294

1 Chester and Willson (*138*) pp.180–2; Mackenzie and Grove (*143*) pp.239–43.
2 *Private Information.*
3 Peake had been Chairman of the Party's Home Affairs Committee and Deputy Chairman of the National Insurance and Pensions Committee until the Election in 1951.
4 Interview with Sir Geoffrey King. Sir Lancelot Errington (interview), too, felt that the prime need was for a period of consolidation leading up to the first Quinquennial Review. Peake had, however, displayed initiative in talks on the pension age and was very interested in moving to it by improving the 'increments' for staying longer at work and in the possibility of earnings-related pensions and benefits. Errington was Principal Private Secretary to Peake from 1951–3. (From 1973–6 he was Second Permanent Secretary at the D.H.S.S.)
5 'He was not entirely happy staying on at the Ministry of Pensions and National Insurance.' Interview with Sir John Smyth.
6 Interview with Sir Geoffrey King.
7 *Private Information.*
8 Interview with Sir Geoffrey King.
9 M.P. for Thirsk and Malton Division, 1929–74. Father of the House, 1965–74. Later Lord Tranmire. Geoffrey Cox in the

News Chronicle 27.10.51 saw Turton as a possible Minister of Food in 1951.

10 Interview with Lord Tranmire.

11 'One of the most experienced men in the House on national insurance and had an extremely good brain.' Smyth (*49*) p.292. Lord Tranmire (interview) said: 'I admired [him] very much. I knew I would enjoy working with him. And I did.'

12 Macmillan (*36*) pp.546–7.

13 When Macmillan became Prime Minister, he brought Marples back, as Postmaster-General, in January 1957. The dismissal of Marples was particularly awkward. It meant that the incoming Minister in December 1955, Boyd-Carpenter, came in from Transport without the benefit of the continuity of a Parliamentary Secretary.

14 Interview with Sir John Arbuthnot.

15 Interview with Sir John Walley.

16 Macmillan (*36*) p.548.

17 In 1925. See also diary 10.9.54, Moran (*87*) pp.628–9.

18 King had come over from the Assistance Board in 1946 to take charge of the arrangements for starting the payment of family allowances in that year, working later on the implementation of the Industrial Injuries Act and the National Assistance Act. He played no part in the creation of the main scheme of national insurance.

19 Sir John Woods' surprise departure to private enterprise from Permanent Secretary at the Board of Trade meant Lee moved from Food to take his job, and Hancock left National Insurance to become Permanent Secretary at Food. See Chapter 5 Part 3.

20 Interview with Sir Geoffrey King.

21 An interesting factor mentioned in interview which perhaps explains why King never became as fully 'integrated' as he might have done at National Insurance was that since the Ministry's inception in 1944, many of its senior officials belonged to the Oxford and Cambridge Club, but King was an Athenaeum man.

22 De Villiers was a product of the Ministry of Labour with a background in pre-war unemployment insurance. He was in charge of the first Conscription Act and later of all military recruitment, and with John Walley he was responsible for the Ministry's war planning. He was posted to the Ministry of Works in 1945 after attract-

ing the attention of its Ministers. As military work slackened off he took on, at Ernest Bevin's initiative, responsibility for a scheme for building industry development, and thereafter it was in this industry that he concentrated much of his time.

23 Later Sir John Walley, Deputy Secretary, 1958–66, and well-known authority and author on social security matters.

24 'It [the Ministry] was completely in the hands of the Treasury, because of the large sums involved and the Exchequer contribution.' Interview with Sir Geoffrey King.

25 The national insurance fund and the separate fund for industrial injuries was under the control of the Ministry, which was responsible for collecting the weekly insurance contributions payable by the 23 million insured (in 1955) under national insurance schemes. (War pensions and family allowance funds came solely from money voted annually by Parliament.) However, the fact that the cost to the Treasury would increase more than contribution income was inherent in the financial structure of contributory pensions laid down by Churchill in 1925. Interview with Sir John Walley.

26 Interview with Sir John Walley. The National Insurance Advisory Committee was a valuable adjunct to responsible government in containing political pressure and acting as a safety valve for disposing of awkward problems. The Chairman since 1947, the influential Sir Will Spens, was a distinguished academic and public administrator, Master of Corpus Christi College, Cambridge, 1927–52, its most effective members being Sir Richard Snedden, general manager of the Shipping Federation, and a trade unionist, Sir Alfred Roberts, General Secretary of the Amalgamated Association of Card, Blowing and Ring Room Operatives since 1935. Both this body and the less significant Industrial Injuries Advisory Council would have matters referred to them by Ministers.

27 *Official Reports of the 72nd–74th Conservative Party Annual Conference* (1952–4).

28 Thirty-six M.P.s in 1951 were sponsored by the N.U.M. See Chapter 6 Part 6.

29 The Conservatives, not surprisingly, made much of Labour's record on benefits. In fact there was little Parliamentary pressure

588

for increases until 1950, and it was anyway impossible to suggest improvement in rates until the administrative machine had settled down. Labour had elected to rely on national assistance rather than force the pace by increasing national insurance benefits.

30 For a commentary on these and subsequent changes to benefit rates, see Marwick (*187*) pp.376–8. Public service pensions were also increased, by the Pensions (Increase) Act, 1952. This cost £6m. per annum. (£2m. from rates, £4m. from the Treasury) and benefited over 300,000 retired civil servants, teachers and policemen, etc.

31 *House of Commons* 11.3 52, Vol. 497, Cols. 1299–1300.

32 *Private Information.*

33 Under-Secretary, Ministry of Labour, 1946–55. Permanent Secretary, Ministry of Education, 1959–63.

34 The latter was a Ministry of Labour Committee set up under the chairmanship of Harold Watkinson, the Parliamentary Secretary, which presented one Report in October 1953 (Cmd. 8963) and another in December 1955 (Cmd. 9628). The Reports, which were both authoritative, recommended people being encouraged to stay on at work, but had less impact than they deserved since the political climate was no longer so favourable to their proposals.

35 *Private Information.*

36 Peake had been quite clear from 1951 about the need, and the political advantage, to go on from where the Attlee Government had left off on the question of retirement pensions.

37 See *House of Commons* 6.4.54, 7.4.54 and 8.4.54 and *The Times* 12.7.54.

38 This was the Quinquennial Review of the National Insurance Act of 1946, referred to above in note 4.

39 See leader in *The Times* on 8.4.54.

40 Cmd. 9333.

41 *House of Commons* 21.7.54.

42 The broadcast took place on Saturday, 18th September. Macmillan indicated that preliminary decisions on increases had been taken already by the Cabinet.

43 *House of Commons* 1.11.54.

44 A Labour Party propaganda document, 'Record of the Tory Government: Three Wasted Years,' wryly noted that for all the notice the Government took of the

Actuary's Review and the Phillips Report, the increases could have come about long ago. For a further account of the whole issue of retirement pensions, see George (*183*) pp.148–69.

45 Interview with Sir Lancelot Errington.

46 Interview with Lord Tranmire.

47 Sir Geoffrey King was a particularly strong supporter of national assistance and would tend to favour increasing assistance rather than national insurance benefits. The Labour Party, however, were always suspicious of anything that appeared to be 'public assistance'.

48 Interview with Sir John Walley.

CHAPTER 8 PART 1 pp.295–306

1 There were only two such Ministers, Sir Thomas Inskip, 1936–9, and Lord Chatfield, 1939–40.

2 'Central Organisation for Defence.' Cmd. 6923.

3 These Committees were the Standing Committee of Service Ministers, over which the Minister of Defence presided, responsible for co-ordinating the demands and operations of the Service Ministers; the Consultative Committee of Principal Personnel Officers and Principal Supply Officers to assist it. Both these Committees were linked with the Chiefs of Staff Committee, responsible for preparing strategic military plans; the Defence Production Committee, consisting of the Service Ministers, Ministers of Supply and Labour, with the Minister of Defence as Chairman responsible for production; the Joint War Production Staff under it, composed of serving officers and officials, and responsible for studying all aspects of war potential; finally there was a Defence Research Policy Committee, a Committee of the Ministry of Defence, responsible for research and development, chaired by an independent scientist on the staff of the Ministry of Defence.

4 Jennings (*131*) pp.313–16; Daalder (*129*) pp.184–8; Chester and Willson (*138*) pp.236–9.

5 The only evidence in print that this took place is three references in Moran's diary, on pp.369, 393 and 710, Moran (*87*). Portal's biographer, Richards (*92*) on p.371 finds no further substantiation, and Portal did not mention that event either to

his wife or family. Both Sir John Colville and Sir Richard Powell in interview, two men likely to know, felt it highly improbable that a formal approach would have been made to Portal. Sir John Colville added that Churchill had as high an opinion of Portal as any other wartime Chief of Staff.

6 The *Spectator* in an article on 2.11.51 (p.559) thought Ismay 'booked' for the job of Minister of Defence.

7 Churchill had been Chairman of the Party's Defence Committee in Opposition.

8 *House of Commons* 6.11.51. Vol. 493, Col. 74.

9 Alexander of Tunis' official biographer, as well as several of those interviewed, said Churchill originally intended to be Minister for an unspecified period, but quickly found it unfeasible. Nicolson (*88*) pp.302 and 313. On the other hand Lord Head (interview) was 'almost certain' at his meeting with Churchill just after the Election that Churchill said he would appoint Alexander Minister of Defence when he was available from Canada. Diary 11.10.51, Moran (*87*), pp.369–70, said Churchill originally wanted Alexander but he was not free. Churchill said in the opening day of the defence debate in *House of Commons* 5.3.52 that on the day he had accepted George VI's commission to form a Government, he had proposed the appointment of Alexander of Tunis, but that a delay was inevitable while arrangements were made. If this was the case. Churchill must have made the proposal without Alexander's prior endorsement. for it would not appear that he heard of the plan until Churchill visited him in Ottawa in January 1952. Alexander's appointment was announced from Downing Street on 28th January. Churchill told the House of Commons he would remain as Minister of Defence himself until Alexander of Tunis could take over. *The Times* 29.1.52.

10 This is a widely held view amongst those interviewed. See also diary 1.3.55 Moran (*87*) p.667 where he expresses the same view: 'He appointed Alex Minister of Defence. partly because he liked having him about the place. but more because he was of a mind to be his own Minister of Defence. as he had been in the war.' Sir

David Hunt, who had worked for Alexander, wrote that Churchill chose him because he thought Alexander by far the best British General of the war, and also because he thought he excelled in personal gallantry and military chivalry. Hunt (*26*) p.75.

11 Interview with Sir Richard Powell and Geoffrey Wheeler.

12 Interview with Sir Harold Parker.

13 See Chapter 8 Part 6.

14 For example. interview with Sir John Slessor: 'He didn't know how to run the thing in peacetime.' Eden (*14*) p.274: 'Sir Winston, whatever his head ordained, never accepted in his heart the position of a Minister of Defence divorced from his own authority. In impatient moments he would sometimes murmur that the post did not exist.'

15 For example, diary 16.1.52, Moran (*87*) pp.390–1: 'He is obsessed with the precarious existence of Britain.'

16 See Chapter 8 Part 2.

17 *Private Information*.

18 Interview with Sir John Slessor.

19 Interview with Lord Harding of Petherton.

20 Correspondence with Sir William Dickson.

21 Ismay (*27*) pp.454–5.

22 See Chapter 9 Part 1. The Commonwealth was also of course an integral part of defence.

23 See Chapter 10 Part 2 and Part 3 of this Chapter.

24 Paper on Approach and Objectives for Talks. *Truman Papers*. The Combined Chiefs of Staff consisted of the British and U.S. Chiefs of Staff of the three Services. Under President Roosevelt and Prime Minister Churchill it had initiated strategy, drafted plans, allocated forces and directed the war.

25 Churchill in *House of Commons* 2.7.52. Alexander had been speaking at a Dominion Day Dinner in London. Nicolson (*88*) p.310. 'A Student of Politics' in the *Sunday Times* on 29.6.52 noted that: 'Lord Alexander's *faux pas* – and it certainly was one – surprised and irritated many [Conservatives].'

26 Labour had criticised Alexander's appointment, questioning whether a Field Marshal could really be free of the Chiefs of Staff and his own Service in particular.

27 Interview with Sir Harold Parker. Parker

accompanied Alexander on his trip to the United States in July 1954. The shrewd United States journalist, C. L. Sulzberger, had an 'extremely good long talk' with Alexander (and also Sir Kenneth Strong, Head of British Intelligence) in March 1953. Sulzberger was quick to notice weakness but appeared impressed by Alexander's conversation. Diary 3.3.53, Sulzberger (*51a*) p.716.

28 Of his speech at the 1952 Party Conference, Charles Gayton wrote: 'He spoke on defence like a man who knows what he is talking about.' *Sunday Times* 12.10.52.

29 Interview with Sir Harold Parker.

30 Churchill said: 'It was decided to ask Alex to talk to the Foreign Affairs Committee. I didn't want that. He isn't good at this kind of thing.' Diary 17.12.53, Moran (*87*) p.542. The question of Service pensions was of continuing interest to the 1922 Committee. On 26.11.53 Butler and Eden went to the Committee to head off a plea that cuts imposed in 1935 on retired officers' pensions would have to be restored. The Government's line was not popular and Eden had to assure the backbenchers that the Cabinet had considered the matter in great detail and that the decision was a unanimous one. Goodhart (*123*) p.166.

31 *Private Papers.*

32 'As Winston puts it in his kindly way, Alex is a soldier and he knows nothing of politics.' Diary 1.3.55, Moran (*87*) p.667.

33 Interview with Sir John Colville.

34 Interview with Sir William Dickson.

35 After only five months in office, he confessed to Moran: 'He said he would be glad to be done with it all. "I would never have taken this job on if I had known what the House of Commons was like."' Diary 30.7.52, Moran (*87*) pp.418–19. *The Times* 18.10.54 also tells of how Alexander made it known for some time that he wished to give up being Minister of Defence.

36 Nicolson (*88*) p.308. Nicolson's book gives an entirely fair picture of Alexander as Minister of Defence. He mildly exaggerates Alexander's contribution to policy on the Korean trip in June 1952 (pp.307–9) and to the Egyptian problems (pp.306 and 312). It is also not quite accurate to say (p.312) that Alexander never tried very hard to be a great success as Minister of Defence. He did try, but he realised he was

not having much success. The verdict of *The Economist* 23.10.54 (p.287) was that under Alexander the Ministry of Defence had become little more than a technical link between the Prime Minister and the Chiefs of Staff.

37 Letter, Alexander to Cherwell, 21.10.54, *Cherwell Papers*, Pers.101.

38 It is interesting that when Macmillan was Minister of Defence he actually resisted the downgrading of the Service Ministers on the grounds that as the Forces belonged to the Crown, the Service Ministers were the Crown's Secretaries of State. See letter, Colin Coote to Lord Ismay, 7.7.58, *Ismay Papers* 111.4.64.

39 Diary 9.1.55, Moran (*87*) p.659. Macmillan himself wrote that his observation of Churchill discussing defence topics 'confirmed my opinion of his failing powers', and that 'now I saw him at much closer quarters and was saddened by signs of increasing fatigue'. Macmillan (*36*) pp.548–9.

40 *The Economist* 16.4.55 (p.183).

41 For Macmillan's own account of his time at the Ministry, see Macmillan (*36*) pp.560–81. Macmillan had himself gained valuable ministerial experience of Defence during the war when he had been Parliamentary Secretary at Supply (1940–2) and Secretary of State for Air in the 'Caretaker Government' of 1945.

42 See Chapter 8 Part 6.

43 Interview with Geoffrey Wheeler.

44 Interview with Sir Richard Powell.

45 Interview with Lord Selwyn-Lloyd, D.B.Y. See note 16, p.596.

46 Minister of Defence, 1970–4, Foreign Secretary, 1979–.

47 Wilson Smith remained at the Treasury till 1951, retiring at the age of forty-six to enter private industry.

48 At the Treasury he had been responsible for a while for Service estimates.

49 Macmillan (*36*) p.562.

50 Interview with Sir Harold Parker.

51 For example, Macmillan (*36*) p.562 '. . . [Powell] was a man of exceptional ability.' He went on to become Permanent Secretary at Defence, 1956–9 and subsequently at the Board of Trade, 1960–8. See interview with Sir Richard Powell, B.O.A.P.A.H.

52 A second Deputy Secretary, however, was again appointed in 1957.

53 It had a large and flexible membership where the Prime Minister acted as Chairman, the Minister of Defence as Vice-Chairman, with the Lord President, Foreign Secretary, Chancellor, Service Ministers, and Ministers of Labour and Supply in regular attendance.

54 1943–5. He had also been a Secretary to the Committee of Imperial Defence, 1940–1.

55 Jennings (131) p.314. It had apparently been contemplated in 1946 that in event of war, the Prime Minister would assume the chairmanship.

56 Interview II with Anthony Montague Browne.

57 Correspondence with Sir William Dickson.

58 Interview with Sir Kenneth McLean.

59 '. . . He spoke scornfully of the First Sea Lord's ineffectiveness. He had no grasp of things.' Diary 9.1.52, Moran (87) p.384.

60 Churchill retained his high opinion of Slim. After his formal appointment as C.I.G.S. had been terminated, and before he went to take up his new job as Governor-General of Australia in early 1953, Churchill thought of Slim as the most suitable man to take part in joint Anglo-American talks with Neguib in Egypt on the British base on the Canal. The talks did not in the end take place, but it seemed for a while that Slim's departure would be delayed. See Lewin (84) pp.282–3, Carver (65) pp.186–7 and diary 24.2.53, Moran (87) p.425.

61 Interview with Sir John Slessor. See Chapter 8 Part 4.

62 Interview II with Anthony Montague Browne.

63 Slessor was responsible for representing the three Chiefs at the numerous NATO meetings between 1950–2, indicative of his primacy in matters of broad strategy. See Slessor (48) p.14.

64 Private Information. An unimportant feature of the Harding, Dickson, McGrigor team, much commented on at the time, was their diminutive size. McGrigor was popularly known as 'wee Mac'.

65 Interview with Sir Ian Jacob.

66 Shinwell (47) p.201.

67 Interview with Sir Kenneth McLean.

68 Interview with Sir Kenneth McLean.

69 Jacob was Military Assistant Secretary to the War Cabinet, 1939–46. He was a contributor to Wheeler-Bennett, ed. (105).

70 Mallaby (37) pp.37–8.

71 See Chapter 8 Part 6.

72 Brownjohn according to Macmillan (36) p.562 was 'a universal favourite and a skilled negotiator'.

73 Interview with Tom Beagley. (Beagley served in the Cabinet Office, 1951–2 and in the Ministry of Defence, 1952–4.)

74 Jennings (131) p.314.

75 Until Cockcroft took over from Tizard in 1952, the job was known just as Chairman of the Defence Research Policy Committee.

76 See Clark (67) p.401. A further minor factor in Tizard's decision to retire may have been his poor relations with Cherwell, which never entirely healed. See Clark p.416.

77 Daalder (129) p.195.

CHAPTER 8 PART 2 pp.306–311

1 Mackenzie and Grove (143) p.171.

2 There was also a two-month period in 1931 when he was out of the Cabinet.

3 Assistant Secretary, C.I.D., 1940–1 and representative with Directors of Plans for Amphibious Operations, 1943–5.

4 Head had also been Chairman of the Party's Army Committee in Opposition.

5 Interview with Lord Head.

6 Diary 29.10.51, Crookshank Papers.

7 See, for example, diary 7.3.53, Moran (87) p.427; '[Churchill] has just made a speech on defence which has taken him a week to prepare, though Head could have done the donkey work for him.' See also Part 1.

8 Head went on to become Minister of Defence in October 1956, at the height of the Suez crisis, but this gifted Minister's career was cut tragically short when he resigned in January 1957 after a disagreement with Macmillan over defence expenditure. Subsequently he took on a number of official jobs, including the (first) U.K. High Commissioner in the Federation of Nigeria, 1960–3.

9 The full title of the new job was Parliamentary Under-Secretary of State for War and Financial Secretary of the War Office.

10 See Hutchison (26a).

11 See article by Maclean in 'Forum', University of Houston pp.2–7, for Maclean's relations with Churchill.

12 Interview with Sir Fitzroy Maclean.
13 On this side were three Assistant Under-Secretaries, Wilfred Curtis (1952–8), John Wade (Director of Establishments, 1939–53) and Charles Fife (Comptroller of Lands and Claims, 1948–55). In addition a special assistant under-secretaryship was created for William Gardner (1952–5) for a limited period, a job created by Turner *ad hominem* for a man at the end of his career with a roving brief on occupation costs in Germany.
14 Beneath him also three Assistant Under-Secretaries, known as Director of Finance, Henry Care (1945–54), James McGregor (1945–58) and, until he succeeded Cash, Charles Key (1951–4). Key was in turn succeeded by Richard Way.
15 Playfair had been a Third Secretary at the Treasury since 1950. Way went on to become Permanent Under-Secretary, in succession to Playfair, from 1960–3, and subsequently Permanent Secretary at Aviation until his decision to retire early in 1966. See interview with Sir Richard Way, B.O.A.P.A.H.
16 Interview with Sir Richard Way.
17 An account of Slim's period as C.I.G.S. can be found in Lewin (*84*) pp.266–81.
18 Some who knew him well, however, felt he excelled more as a Commander-in-Chief in the war than as C.I.G.S.
19 The *Sunday Times* 26.7.53. An account of Harding's period as C.I.G.S. can be found in Carver (*65*) pp.177–94.
20 *The Times* 23.4.55, announcing the change, said Templer had been the obvious candidate for some time to succeed Harding. Sir Gerald said when he became C.I.G.S. in 1955 the strengthening of the contribution of forces to Europe was the number one priority. Interview with Sir Gerald Templer.
21 See Chapter 10 Part 4.
22 Malaya, however, despite absorbing the greater part of Britain's defence effort, was not a problem to which the War Office had to devote a great deal of attention. See Carver (*65*) p.179 and Chapter 9 Part 3.
23 See Chapter 9 Part 4. It is clear that Harding, who also visited Kenya in February 1953, did much personally to strengthen the position of the anti-terrorist forces. See Carver (*65*) pp.181–3.

24 A full-scale Army base on the lines of the Canal base was not envisaged for Cyprus (where the Suez base was transferred to), but a smaller base with about half a division stationed permanently with facilities for activation to a larger base if the need arose.
25 Bartlett (*190*) pp.88–92.
26 Eden (*14*) pp.166–8. This was the Western European Union, referred to above. See Chapter 10 Part 4.
27 Although the Army had a total size of over 400,000 through 1951–5, more than half this number consisted of national servicemen on a two-year engagement.
28 See Chapter 10 Part 4. See also Carver (*65*) pp.184–9.
29 White Paper. Cmd. 9230.
30 Macmillan (*36*) p.504.
31 Eden (*14*) p.234.
32 Bartlett (*190*) p.83.
33 Interview with Lord Harding of Petherton. In the spring of 1955 the 'Enosis' unrest erupted in Cyprus and it was felt a top British Officer was required to replace the Colonial Service Governor: Harding was the man chosen on his retirement as C.I.G.S.
34 Head in *House of Commons* 8.3.55.
35 *Private Information.*
36 Interview with Sir John Slessor. See Part 1 above.
37 Bartlett (*190*) p.79.
38 House of Commons, 12.11.52, Vol. 507, Col. 947.

CHAPTER 8 PART 3 pp.311–316

1 See Chapter 8 Part 6.
2 This was a subcommittee of the Party's Defence Committee.
3 Interview with Sir Allan Noble.
4 Interview with Sir Guy Grantham. Grantham was a Vice-Chief of Naval Staff, 1951–4, and a highly respected voice on the Admiralty Board. He almost became First Sea Lord in 1959 but Sir Charles Lambe was chosen instead to succeed Mountbatten. *Private Information.*
5 Kent (*30a*) p.246.
6 From 1942–5 there were three junior Ministers at the Admiralty.
7 Interview with Sir Clifford Jarrett.
8 When Churchill had his hernia operation in 1947, it was announced in the press on

12th June: 'During this time Mr. Eden will lead the Opposition. Commander Noble will assist Mr. Eden in carrying out his additional duties, and in maintaining contact with backbench M.P.s.' Interview with Sir Allan Noble.

9 It was Wingfield Digby's only ministerial job. Noble went on to become Parliamentary Under-Secretary of State at the Commonwealth Relations Office, 1955–6, and Minister of State for Foreign Affairs, 1956–9.

10 Interview with Sir Allan Noble.

11 Lang came to the job due to the premature death in December 1946 of his predecessor, Sir Henry Markham, aged forty-nine.

12 Unlike the Army and Air Councils, the Board of Admiralty had no subordinate committee to discuss more routine affairs.

13 Mountbatten's fortunes had risen dramatically during the war. He become Chief of Combined Operations, 1942–3; Supreme Allied Commander, South East Asia, 1943–6, and Viceroy of India, March–August 1947. He was the younger son of Prince Louis Francis of Battenberg (later Marquess of Milford Haven) who had been First Sea Lord, 1912–14.

14 Interview with Sir Clifford Jarrett.

15 Interview with Lord Mountbatten of Burma.

16 *Private Information.*

17 Fraser was not Churchill's favourite sailor and his agreement to give the job of Supreme Allied Commander of the Atlantic to a United States officer (see Chapter 10 Part 2) could not have helped. Interview with Sir Harold Parker.

18 Interview with Sir John Lang.

19 He had been Assistant C.N.S., 1941–3 and Vice C.N.S., 1945–7.

20 Interview with Sir Clifford Jarrett.

21 So Bracken (First Lord of the Admiralty in the 'Caretaker Government' of 1945) wrote to Beaverbrook, 30.12.53, *Beaverbrook Papers*, Box C57.

22 In that year Sir John Cunningham retired as First Sea Lord.

23 When McGrigor became First Sea Lord one of the first items before him was to argue the case for a U.S. officer against Churchill. Interview with Sir Kenneth McLean.

24 See Gretton (76) pp.315 and 318–19. On p.318 Gretton cites Churchill's speech in a debate on Naval estimates as illustrating how out of touch Churchill had become with reality on technical matters in the Navy.

25 Interview with Lord Mountbatten of Burma.

26 Interview with Sir John Lang.

27 There was a general feeling after the war that the Navy's officer structure did need a fresh examination. Thomas set up a Committee under Sir Aubrey Mansergh (President, Royal Naval College, Greenwich, 1952–4). When Mountbatten became First Sea Lord he took a great interest in the work of the Committee and helped ensure that its proposals went easily through the Board. It was the first major review of officer structure since the Great War. Interview with Bernard Sendall.

28 Interview with Bernard Sendall.

29 *Annual Abstract of Statistics, 1957*, p.111.

30 Cmd. 9396.

31 Thomas, *House of Commons* 3.3.55.

32 Thomas, *House of Commons* 16.3.53.

33 Cmd. 9396. The previous year, the 1954–5 Navy estimates had been a dispiriting document, forecasting no major developments for the Navy. In the debate in the *House of Commons* 9.3.54 Thomas had talked about the difficult period the Navy had been through in the past years.

34 See Chapter 8 Part 6.

35 Not only had Sir John Slessor (Chief of Air Staff, 1950–2) since 1953 been arguing that nuclear weapons and guided missiles had led to a greatly reduced role for the Navy, but Lord Montgomery of Alamein (Deputy Supreme Allied Commander, Europe, 1951–8) in particular in a speech in the United States on 21.10.54, was saying the same thing. A long article had appeared in *The Economist* 25.12.54 entitled, 'Do We Need a Navy?'

36 *Ark Royal* was commissioned at Birkenhead at the end of February 1955, amidst some criticism which felt that the need for heavy carriers had passed.

37 A good and well-informed critique of Navy policy during 1951–5 can be found in Gretton (76) pp.315–17.

CHAPTER 8 PART 4 pp.316–321

1 In 1956 he was created a Viscount under the title of plain Viscount De L'Isle, and

will be referred to henceforth by his shorter name. He had a most varied career, in the Army, politics and financial world, and from 1961–5 was Governor-General of Australia. De L'Isle (as a member of the House of Lords), was the only one of the three Service Ministers not to have been Chairman of the Party's respective House of Commons Committee until the 1951 Election. The Chairman had been Air Commodore A. V. Harvey, who continued in this position after 1951.

2 The scope of the Secretary of State for Air, however, was not large. In practice his authority was decisive only in his own professional sphere, that of Parliamentary politics, and in matters where the Air Staff disagreed amongst themselves, thus affording scope for a layman's judgment. Mackenzie and Grove (*143*) p.233.

3 Both these junior Ministers went on to become Secretary of State; Birch, December 1955–January 1957; Ward, January 1957–October 1960.

4 Decisions on matters of appointment of Chiefs of Staff were taken by the political head of the Ministry in consultation with the Prime Minister.

5 Interview with Sir Ian Jacob. For an assessment of Slessor in the war, see Dean (*191a*) p.313.

6 Letter, Cherwell to the Registrar of Oxford University, 31.1.53, *Cherwell Papers*, Pers.51.

7 See Chapter 8 Part 6.

8 Developments in helicopters occurred later. Ward said in the *House of Commons* on 10.3.55 that, 'We are developing new anti-submarine helicopters and a suitable technique for operating them.' Vol. 538, Col. 634.

9 Interview with Sir John Slessor. Slessor also wrote: '. . . Churchill . . . was not the easiest of men to work under and did not particularly care for me – so it was with some relief that I handed over . . .' Slessor (*48*) p.14.

10 The Air Ministry had been fortunate in the 1930s in having recruited a number of exceptionally able young men, including, Maurice Dean, James Dunnett, Michael Cary, Folliott Sandford and Ronald Melville, although after the war new demands meant the first three were absorbed into other Departments. Dean went on to become Permanent Under-Secretary at the Air Ministry (1955–63), Dunnett at Defence (1966–74), Cary also at Defence (1974–6). Sandford was Deputy Under-Secretary at Air from 1947 until he left Whitehall in 1958. Melville culminated his Civil Service career as the senior civil servant responsible for Aviation, 1966–71.

11 For the origins of the V-bomber fighting force, see Goldberg (*293*) pp.606–18.

12 For background to these developments, see the comprehensive survey in Pierre (*195*) pp.151–7.

13 Goldberg (*293*) p.612.

14 *House of Commons* 5.3.53, Vol. 512, Col. 686.

15 See Chapter 8 Part 6 and Pierre (*195*) p.154. Churchill in *House of Commons* 5.3.53, said that as a 'result of the Government's strategic Review, the types and quantities of weapons and ammunition to be produced have been more precisely related to the kind of war or wars which we might have to fight . . .' Vol. 512, Col. 579.

16 Slessor after his retirement in 1952 wrote and lectured about the importance of the nuclear bombing force as the best guarantor of peace. See, for example, Slessor (*197*) and Slessor (*297*).

17 *House of Commons* 10.3.55, Vol. 538, Col. 645.

18 Interview with Lord Ward of Witley. See also Pierre (*195*) pp.148–9.

19 'The Supply of Military Aircraft' Cmd. 9388. Maxwell Fyfe wrote that this was part of 'one of the most important trilogies of White Papers ever published by any Government' (the other two being the defence and the nuclear energy White Papers). Kilmuir (*31*) p.239.

20 Macmillan (*36*) p.575.

21 See interview with Sir Cyril Musgrave, B.O.A.P.A.H.

22 Selwyn Lloyd in *House of Commons* 2.3.55.

23 *House of Commons* 10.3.55, Vol. 538, Col. 634.

CHAPTER 8 PART 5 pp.321–327

1 Daalder (*129*) p.194. In August 1945, Attlee had appointed one man, John Wilmot, Minister of Supply and of Aircraft Production.

2 Shortly after the Government was formed in 1951, there was a proposal (which was

defeated) to separate aircraft production and give it to the Air Ministry.

3 The transition of responsibility for atomic energy away from the Ministry came in two stages. On 1st January, 1954 the statutory powers of the Minister of Supply were transferred to the Lord President. On 1st August, 1954 the Atomic Energy Authority Act came into force. This set up the new Authority, which took away most of the powers entrusted to the Lord President the previous January, but leaving him with considerable jurisdiction. See Chester and Willson (*138*) pp.272–3.

4 Chester and Willson (*138*) pp.236–9.

5 Sandys had benefited earlier from his methodical training in the Diplomatic Service, which he had entered in 1930 prior to becoming an M.P. in 1935. His entry into the Diplomatic Service, in the face of stiff competition, also speaks of his intellectual qualities.

6 Interview with Henry Walker.

7 See Chapter 4 Part 1.

8 See Chapter 5 Part 4.

9 For Sandys' performance in Defence Committee and in other defence policy dealings, see Chapter 8 Part 1.

10 Interview with Lord Aldington.

11 *Private Information.*

12 So successful had Sandys been at Supply that few, if any, disputed his right to be promoted to Minister of Housing in October 1954. Interview with William Deedes.

13 Colonel Post, who had been attached to the War Office, 1941–2, and the Ministry of Supply, 1943–4, was brought back by Sandys to the Ministry of Housing, 1956–7 and Ministry of Defence, 1957–9.

14 The job had been offered first to Frederick Erroll, who since entering the House in 1945 had shown himself as a promising backbencher. He turned it down, but accepted the post on Boyle's departure in April 1955. *Private Information.*

15 Interview with Lord Boyle of Handsworth.

16 During the war he served as General Staff Officer at H.Q. Second Army from its formation to the surrender of Germany.

17 Interview with Sir James Dunnett. Dunnett succeeded Musgrave as a Deputy Secretary in 1953, appointed at the very young age of thirty-nine.

18 Interview with Lord Boyle of Handsworth, B.O.A.P.A.H. For a discussion of the

Swift and the Hunter, see end of Chapter 8 Part 4.

19 Interview with Reginald Maulding.

20 Interview with Sir James Dunnett. Rowlands had previously been Permanent Secretary at M.A.P., 1940–3.

21 Interview with Sir Cyril Musgrave.

22 He retired at the age of sixty and died that August.

23 He had been in the Board of Trade all his career until his appointment as Permanent Secretary at the Ministry of Materials in 1952.

24 Interview with Reginald Maudling.

25 Interview with Sir James Dunnett.

26 Interview with Sir Cyril Musgrave.

27 See Chapter 8 Part 6.

28 See Chapter 5 Part 4.

29 Sandys was one of those Ministers who had a wide range of interests outside his own specialist work, extending, for example, to the Civic Trust and to European policy.

30 The devolution of responsibility for atomic energy has been recorded thoroughly elsewhere, so only a few remarks will be made here. See in particular Gowing (*192*) Vol. I pp.405–50, and Birkenhead (*59*) pp. 297–316. For an early account of the Atomic Energy Authority itself, see Best (*292*) pp.1–16.

31 Immediately after the Election in 1951 there had been much jockeying for authority between Cherwell and Sandys, the matter being far from resolved when Churchill announced in the *House of Commons* 14.11.51 that the Paymaster-General (i.e. Cherwell) should advise him on atomic energy questions. For these early developments in particular, see Oliphant and Penney (*89*) p.168.

32 Interview with Sir Friston How.

33 Sir John Anderson became Viscount Waverley in 1952. The Report (Cmd. 8986) suggested the establishment of a non-departmental authority.

34 In his diary on 8.4.54, Moran (*87*) p.568 says Churchill was bored by Sandys. This should be contrasted with the opinion expressed by Mary Soames (*98*) p.412, that 'Winston esteemed and liked Duncan very much.' The latter is the more balanced view.

35 Eccles insisted that a good constitutional Bill should be presented, rather than a complex one which some peers such as Lords Adrian and Waverley favoured.

Cherwell thought the Bill excellent. Interview with Lord Eccles.

36 Cherwell suggested Plowden's name to Churchill for Chairman. Cherwell had got to know Plowden during the 1952 convertibility discussions. Interview II with Lord Plowden.

CHAPTER 8 PART 6 pp.327–335

1 Almost all the surviving senior figures connected with defence during the years 1951–5 were interviewed by the author in 1977 and 1978. The unattributed views below came from those interviews.

2 See B.O.A.P.A.H. interviews with Sir Richard Way, Sir Robert Scott, Sir Edward Playfair and Sir Ian Jacob.

3 Jones (29) pp.526–7.

4 See Clarke in Thornhill, ed. (135) p.75. The subject is also discussed in Johnson (194a). See in particular pp.35–53. Lord Mountbatten of Burma was very favourable to the views expressed in this book. He not only wrote a foreword, but also strongly commended the forthcoming book to me when I interviewed him in June 1978. The Sunday Times said in a leader as early as 20th February, 1955 that: 'If the ultimate integration of the three Services is to be effective [which it felt a necessary step] one man and one Ministry should be responsible for the overall plan.'

5 Interview with Sir Harold Parker. Two other Ministers of Defence apart from Sandys were particularly powerful during the 1946–64 period: Emanuel Shinwell (1950–1) and Peter Thorneycroft (1962–4). Lord Shinwell (in interview) said he found the defence arrangements in his period as Secretary for War (1947–50) and as Minister of Defence ambiguous and unsatisfactory.

6 See the final section of Sir Richard Powell's paper, 'Evolution of British Defence Policy, 1945–59'.

7 Interview with Sir Ian Jacob, B.O.A.-P.A.H. Even in 1956 the size of the Ministry of Defence was still very small in contrast to the other four defence departments. Its non-industrial staff was only 835 – in contrast to the Admiralty's 33,765, the War Offices 38,870, the Air Ministry's 27,150 and Supply's 34,650. Chester and Willson (138) p.238.

8 See rough draft of the Jacob/Ismay Report in Ismay Papers 111.4.85.2.

9 Interview with Sir Ian Jacob, B.O.A.-P.A.H.

10 See letter, Slessor to Thorneycroft, 15.12.62, Ismay Papers 111.4.74.3.

11 Letter, Selwyn Lloyd to Lord Ismay, 21.11.55, Ismay Papers, 111.4.41.

12 Mountbatten expressed these views in his letter to Ismay, 30.1.63, Ismay Papers, 111.4.82.1.

13 See letter, Jacob to Ismay, 18.1.63, Ismay Papers, 111.4.78.1. As a result of the re-organisation which became effective on 1st April, 1964, the three separate Service Departments were regrouped under a single Ministry of Defence.

14 Defence policy in the early years after the war is perhaps the area which has been written up most widely and successfully of all aspects of Government policy. See in particular Bartlett (190) pp.78–104, Darby (191) pp.46–93, Groom (193) pp.92–108, Pierre (195) pp.86–94, Rosecrance (196) pp.152–218, Snyder (198) pp.9–42, William Wallace's contribution in Bogdanor and Skidelsky ed. (114) pp.192–202, Goldberg (293) pp.600–18, Goldberg (294) pp.409–29 and Gott (295) pp.238–52.

15 Pierre (195) p.73.

16 House of Commons 26.2.52, Vol. 496, Col. 964.

17 The first test of an atomic bomb had been conducted by the United States at Alamogordo, New Mexico, in 1945. The first Soviet atomic test had taken place in 1949.

18 Later Chairman of the Atomic Energy Authority and, along with Cockcroft, one of Britain's atomic pioneers.

19 For a discussion of post-war U.S./U.K. nuclear collaboration, see Pierre (195) pp.112–20 and 136–44.

20 See House of Commons 23.10.52.

21 See Chapter 10 Part 2.

22 See Chapter 8 Part 2.

23 Chapter 2 Part 2.

24 House of Commons 5.4.54, Vol. 526, Col. 51.

25 See Sir Richard Powell's Southampton Lecture, listed in the Bibliography.

26 Interview with Sir John Slessor.

27 The most authoritative account of the 1952 Defence Review can be found in Lewin (84) pp.278–83. Churchill admitted in the

House of Commons on 1.12.54 that the advance of the hydrogen bomb had rendered considerations founded on the atom bomb 'almost old fashioned'. Vol. 535, Col. 176.

28 Sir Ian Jacob (interview) described his contribution in this way: 'The Chiefs of Staff had all drafted it in bits and tried to amend it in Committee and . . . they had produced this frightful document. I told them: "I don't think this needs a great deal of re-doing but if you could go over it again and tell me exactly what it is [you want me to draft], and we will write it with the hand of one man and it will be a much better paper."' Sir John Slessor said (in interview) that he thought Jacob had a brilliant mind and that his contribution to the paper was far more significant than Sir Ian himself modestly allows.

29 If it is indeed the case that the 1952 paper on Global Strategy had the key significance in evolution of post-war thought that Pierre (*195*) p.87 and Rosecrance (*196*) p.159 imply, then it is strange that none of the senior officials from the Ministry of Defence or Service Ministries could recall a paper in 1952 that was of especial significance.

30 Statement on Defence, 1952, Cmd. 8475.

31 For example, Slessor was dispatched to Washington by Churchill to argue the case for a reduction of NATO force goals. Slessor's visit in particular and the views that were expressed in the Global Strategy Paper of 1952 in general are alleged to have played an important part in influencing the U.S. 'New Look' in their defence strategy of 1953, in which they moved over to a reliance on the new concept of deterrence, 'massive retaliation'. See, for example, Rosecrance (*196*) pp.171–2.

32 'The Government . . . decided that in the interests of true economy as well as of the vitally needed increase in exports, any substantial rise above the high level of expenditure on defence production in 1952–3 was not possible.' Statement on Defence, 1953, Cmd. 8768.

33 Lord Alexander of Tunis told the Party's Defence Committee in the Lords that the major points from the Chief's Review had been incorporated into paragraphs 9–14 of the 1954 White Paper. He added that not all their recommendations could be accepted and that he had set in train a further

Defence Review. Minutes 10.3.54, *Conservative Party Archives*, Newcastle, Box 1502.

34 Statement of Defence, 1954, Cmd. 9075.

35 See Chapter 8 Part 4.

36 The Cabinet discussed the question of whether to build the hydrogen bomb at a meeting on 8th July, but discussion of the issue does not appear to have been protracted. See diary 8.7.54, *Crookshank Papers*. Nigel Birch appeared to be the only defence Minister who questioned the wisdom of building the hydrogen bomb. See Pierre (*195*) p.91. The first British thermonuclear test was carried out at Christmas Island in 1957.

37 Churchill was told about the impact of the bomb in a letter from Bernard Baruch of 2.8.53, *Baruch Papers*.

38 Details of America's first thermonuclear explosion were released in February 1954 by Sterling Cole (Chairman of the Joint Congressional Committee on Atomic Energy) in February 1954. Churchill was clearly vexed not to have had access at once to full information about the American bomb, and in the *House of Commons* on 12th July, 1954 said he had been 'astounded' by the revelations. Vol. 530, Col. 34. See Chapter 10 Part 2.

39 Statement on Defence, 1955, Cmd. 9391.

40 *House of Commons* 1.3.55, Vol. 537, Col. 1897.

41 See diary 1.3.55, Moran (*87*) p.665.

42 See Chapter 9 Part 1.

43 Macmillan discusses how as Minister of Defence he and the Chiefs of Staff opposed the American thesis that a clear distinction be drawn between the major thermonuclear bombs and small tactical nuclear arms. Macmillan (*36*) pp.571–2.

44 Source: *Annual Abstract of Statistics, 1957*, table 133.

45 See Statement on Defence, 1955, Cmd. 9391.

46 Source: *Annual Abstract of Statistics, 1957*, table 294.

47 See Table 2 at the end of the study.

CHAPTER 9 PART 1 pp.336–347

1 The main function of the Dominions Office had been to act as the channel of communication between the British

Government and the Governments of the Dominions, Canada, Australia, New Zealand and the Union of South Africa. The India Office had been responsible for relations with India and Pakistan.

2 Ismay (27) p.459.

3 The Times 17.11.51.

4 Ismay (27) p.453.

5 Ismay, for example, had played a major role in the establishment of the new Ministry of Defence in 1946. See Chapter 8 Part 1.

6 Interview with Lord Dunrossil. Dunrossil, the son of the Speaker 'Shakes' Morrison, was an Assistant Private Secretary to the Commonwealth Secretary, 1952–4. He succeeded his father as Lord Dunrossil on the latter's death in 1961.

7 Wingate (108) pp.187–8.

8 Interview I with Sir George Mallaby.

9 He in fact spent very little time actually at the Office. In his first two months he was busy settling in and spending much time with Churchill and working on defence affairs. Then there was Christmas. He was away from 30th December, 1951 to 17th January, 1952, on the trip to the United States. In early February he was much preoccupied with the death of George VI. He was at the Lisbon Conference of NATO from 19th to 25th February. On 10th March Churchill offered him the secretary-generalship of NATO and on 24th March he surrendered the seals of the office. See Ismay Papers, 1.9.4–1.9.5.1.

10 Interview with Sir Neil Pritchard. Pritchard was an Assistant Under-Secretary at the C.R.O., 1951–4.

11 The British, after Franks' refusal, offered Sir Ivone Kirkpatrick, but Dean Acheson was anxious to have someone of Cabinet status, and specifically mentioned Ismay. See message, Eden to Pearson, 10.3.52, Ismay Papers, III.II.I. Also Acheson's comments at the Princeton Seminars on 14.2.54. Acheson Papers. The Americans felt the British had rather mishandled the episode, as indeed they had. See diary 5.3.52. Sulzberger (51a) p.629 and Sunday Times 2.3.52.

12 Most of Salisbury's ministerial experience had been in non-domestic Departments. He had been Parliamentary Under-Secretary at the Foreign Office, 1935–8, Secretary of State at the Dominions Office, 1940–2, and again, 1943–5. He had

also been Secretary of State at the Colonial Office, February–November 1942.

13 Interview with Lord Dunrossil.

14 The Times 25.11.52, announcing the changes, said that Salisbury, who was much concerned with the opening of the Commonwealth Economic Conference at the end of the month, would continue to act as Secretary of State until 15th December. Swinton (his successor at the C.R.O.), however, would attend the Conference in the place of Thorneycroft, President of the Board of Trade, in hospital with a slipped disc.

15 So poor was Swinton's reputation at handling his officials that the Private Office received various private letters of consolation when the appointment was announced. Private Information.

16 Interview with Lord Chandos, D.B.Y. Kilmuir (31) p.191 says, however, that Salisbury was the first choice for Colonial Secretary. See Chapter 3 Part 1.

17 Interview with Sir John Foster.

18 Private Information. One issue which caused bad feeling in private and which was also expressed by the press followed a speech Nehru made in Delhi on 13th April, 1953, criticising British policy towards Kenya. Swinton protested so strongly that Nehru sent a telegram to the Indian High Commissioner in London, saying: 'Our Government is not used to being addressed in this way by any Government and I can only conclude that he [Swinton] has for the moment forgotten that he is addressing the independent Republic of India.' Quoted in Gopal (75a) p.168.

19 He returned to London on 4th December, having visited New Zealand, Australia, Ceylon, India and Pakistan. The Times 5.12.53.

20 See later in this section where Australia is discussed (p.344).

21 See Chapter 8 Part 2.

22 Swinton's trip had some administrative significance as he made some changes in High Commission posts and in operations by the British Council.

23 It was announced that Swinton would continue after his appointment to be Deputy Leader of the House of Lords. The Times 25.11.52. Swinton, however, was not nearly as popular a figure with the Opposition in the House of Lords.

24 For an account of Swinton's responsibili-

ties during 1951–5, see Chapter 3 Part 2.

25 Interview with Lord Garner.

26 Swinton (*52*) pp.164 and 168. Churchill thought Eden's not using Swinton was his one mistake in the April 1955 reshuffle.

27 Interview with Lord Home of The Hirsel. Home had – as Lord Dunglass – been Parliamentary Private Secretary to Neville Chamberlain during the Munich crisis when Eden resigned as Foreign Secretary.

28 Stuart (*51*) p.162. Home was later – after a storm in the Commons at the appointment of a Lord – made Foreign Secretary by Macmillan in 1960.

29 See Garner (*202*) pp.284–5.

30 Interview with Sir Gilbert Laithwaite.

31 Interview with Sir John Foster.

32 He was not sacked, but he came to feel increasingly that his future did not lie on the ministerial ladder. A report in the *News Chronicle* on 18.10.54 said Foster had retired of his own volition. Foster had in fact made a promising start in his first months in the job: 'A Student of Politics' in the *Sunday Times* on 3.8.52 said he was one of those Ministers who had done well since the Election.

33 Dodds-Parker proceeded from the Sudan Political Service to join the Grenadier Guards, where throughout the war he was occupied on 'special duties'. Like Foster, he entered the House in 1945.

34 See Garner (*202*) pp.289–94, Cross (*201*) p.59. Mackenzie and Grove (*143*) pp.224–8.

35 For a general assessment of Liesching see Lord Garner's appreciation in *The Times* 8.11.73, as well as Garner (*202*) pp.291–2.

36 For a different view on the reorganisation to Garner's see Sir Algernon Rumbold's review of Lord Garner's book in *Round Table*, April 1979.

37 He had been U.K. representative there from 1949 before diplomatic relations were elevated to Embassy status, and Ambassador to the Republic, 1950–1.

38 As was natural for a former India Office man, he had little experience of the Commonwealth outside the sub-continent. He had been Private Secretary to the Viceroy of India, 1936–43.

39 Interview with Sir Neil Pritchard.

40 Interview with Lord Garner.

41 Garner served under Sir Alexander Clutterbuck, the Commissioner, 1952–5,

who succeeded Laithwaite as Permanent Under-Secretary in 1959.

42 Garner became Permanent Under-Secretary of the Office, 1962–5, and of the new Commonwealth Office, 1965–8, after the merger with the Colonial Office. Garner was another with a Dominions Office background. After his retirement, he wrote the authoritative study of the Office, Garner (*202*).

43 A Question in the *House of Commons* 2.4.54 raised the issue of whether the time was right to reorganise both Offices. Hopkinson replying for the Government agreed that this should be considered when some of the colonial territories had actually achieved higher status, but that for the present both Secretaries of State still had large and very distinct spheres of work. See Harrison (*243*) p.306 and also Tierney (*299*) pp.221–2. The merger was also put forward by the Padmore Committee in 1956. Lee (*142*) p.51. The merger in 1966 was preparatory to the amalgamation with the Foreign Office in 1968.

44 Garner (*202*) p.303. Problems arose over their joint responsibility for the conduct of affairs of the Central African Federation. It was not just Colonial Office/C.R.O. divergence that produced adverse comment at the time. There was also a feeling that the Colonial Office needed to have closer relations with the Foreign Office. See, for example, the leader in *The Times* on 11.5.54.

45 Known officially as Legal Adviser, Commonwealth Relations Office and Colonial Office. Roberts-Wray held the job, 1945–60.

46 Interview with Sir Kenneth Roberts-Wray. This greater emphasis on Colonial Office work was a natural consequence of the substantial governmental authority exercised by the Office over the colonies, in contrast to the far looser relations the C.R.O. had with the Commonwealth countries.

47 Two Assistant Legal Advisers, four Senior Legal Assistants and three Legal Assistants.

48 A deputy Legal Adviser and Senior Legal Assistant.

49 Interview with Sir Kenneth Roberts-Wray.

50 The communiqués and other detail of these conferences can be studied in more

detail in the Commonwealth Relations Office List for 1955 (pp.82–5) and for 1956 (pp.34–5) and in Mansergh (*208*).

51 Some in the Office felt, for example, that without these regular contacts Nehru might have become as alien as Nasser.

52 The communiqué (Cmd. 8717) reaffirmed 'the achievement of convertibility' and stated three requisite conditions: the curbing of inflation, the general adoption of unrestrictive trade practices and the availability of adequate international credit.

53 These talks were felt to have been of little value. Interview with Sir John Foster (an attender along with Butler).

54 Macmillan (*36*) p.575.

55 Swinton (*52*) pp.205–6. The communiqué referred to the resolve of the Commonwealth Governments to do their utmost to relieve international strain, and in the economic field the Conference reaffirmed existing policies, including the progressive approach towards the widest practicable system of trade and payments.

56 See diary 3.2.55, Moran (*87*) pp.662–3.

57 Nehru to Indira Gandhi, 1.2.55. Quoted in Gopal (*75a*) p.234.

58 Macmillan (*36*) p.575.

59 Diary 2.2.55, Pearson (*43b*) pp.79–80.

60 Interview with Sir Neil Pritchard. For a good portrait of Commonwealth Prime Ministers' conferences by one who served in the Cabinet Office's Secretariat in the early 1950s, see Mallaby (*37*) pp.136–49.

61 Pearson (*43b*) p.106.

62 Talk with Ismay on 6.1.52, *Acheson Papers*, Memoirs of Conversations.

63 Swinton notes how valuable he found consultations with them. Swinton (*52*) pp.221–2. See also Pearson (*43b*) p.4.

64 Diary 8.10.52, Millar, ed. (*39a*) p.90. See also diary 28.9.52 (p.90), 6.10.53 (p.110) and Chapter 10 Part 2.

65 *House of Commons* 14.10.52.

66 Richard Casey, quoted from one of his recent speeches in a letter he wrote to Ismay: 'Membership of the Commonwealth is of supreme importance for a country like Australia, which is geographically remote and is not a member of the North Atlantic Treaty Organisation.' Letter, Casey to Ismay, 13.3.52, *Ismay Papers*, IV/CAS/18.

67 Sir George Mallaby wrote: 'I think he did more than any man in these years to reconcile the divergent views of the old and

new Commonwealth on international affairs.' Mallaby (*37*) p.147. Swinton described Menzies as 'a statesman who exerted over the years a consistent and sometimes a commanding influence in Commonwealth unity'. Swinton (*52*) p.207.

68 Casey also had reservations about Nehru. See diary 18.4.54, Millar, ed. (*39a*) p.133.

69 Menzies (*39aa*) p.188.

70 Created Viscount Malvern in 1955.

71 *Private Information* from a former C.R.O. senior official. Malan had been well known for some time for his anti-British views. Malan was six months older than Churchill, having his eightieth birthday in May 1954.

72 See diary 3.1.53, Sulzberger (*51a*) pp.699–700. See also Sulzberger's interview with Malan on pp.703–5.

73 Swinton found these talks 'most friendly and co-operative'. Swinton (*52*) p.212. See also Macmillan (*36*) pp.574–5.

74 See Mallaby (*37*) p.145. Don Senanayake died in March 1952. He was succeeded for a year by his son, Dudley, who later also became Prime Minister in 1960 and 1965–70.

75 See Garner (*202*) pp.322–5.

76 Diary 27.10.51 and 29.10.51, Millar, ed. (*39a*) pp.47 and 48.

77 Nehru to B. G. Kher, 9.8.52. Quoted in Gopal (*75a*) p.167.

78 Gopal (*75a*) p.169. After Churchill's retirement he wrote to Nehru: 'One of the most agreeable memories of my last years in office is our association. At our conferences your contribution was a leading and a constructive one.' Letter, Churchill to Nehru, 30.6.55. Quoted in Gopal (*75a*) p.237.

79 'Governments change in democratic countries; in other countries, too, other forces may come up. Therefore it is not a question of my trusting any of these big or small countries.' Nehru in the Lok Sabha on 29.9.54. Quoted in Mansergh (*208*) p.465.

80 Gordon Walker (*204*) pp.316–18.

81 See Frankel (*214*) p.158. For a contemporary discussion of British attitudes to the Commonwealth, see Tierney (*299*) pp.220–33. Tierney discusses the comparative lack of attention given in Britain to Commonwealth problems, 1951–8. He cites *The Economist* 29.11.52, which noted

'a widespread lack of genuine interest in the Commonwealth idea'.

82 Quoted in *The Campaign Guide, 1955* p.35.

CHAPTER 9 PART 2 pp.347–355

1 This involved an expansion from nine departments in 1925 to thirty in 1955, including nine geographical departments (East and Central Africa (2), West Africa (2), West Indies (2), Far Eastern, Pacific and Mediterranean). The area which expanded most was the economic field, and after the war a separate division was created, which from 1947 had its own Deputy Under-Secretary, supervising seven departments. Jeffries *(150)* pp.105–15.

2 If anything, he had expected the Ministry of Defence. Chandos *(11)* pp.431–2. Lyttelton became Lord Chandos in 1954.

3 Salisbury did not want the post. Kilmuir *(31)* p.191.

4 Diary 4.10.51, Macmillan *(36)* p.356.

5 See Chapter 3 Part 1.

6 Chandos *(11)* pp.342–4. When Hilton Poynton was his Private Secretary at the Ministry of Production, 1942–3, Lyttelton once confided in him that the colonial secretaryship was a job he thought he would always rather like, thus following in the footsteps of his father, Alfred Lyttelton. Interview with Sir Hilton Poynton. For speculation about how Lyttelton at the Treasury might have fared in contrast to Butler, see Brittan *(161)* p.189.

7 Interview with Sir John Johnston.

8 He had also been Minister of State, June 1941–February 1942 and Minister Resident in the Middle East, February–March 1942. He had been in private industry until becoming an M.P. in 1940.

9 *The Times* 30.7.54. See also Goldsworthy *(203)* p.25. Sir William Gorell Barnes, however, commented (in interview) that Lyttelton played a much larger part on the economic front than popularly given credit for, partly because much of the work, being routine, did not catch the public eye.

10 He was greatly respected there. Salisbury wrote him a letter (undated) on his retirement saying it must have been nice to feel it recognised, as they all did, how supremely well he was doing his job. Letter, Salisbury to Lyttelton. *Chandos Papers*, Box 4.10.

11 George Hall, August 1945–October 1946; Arthur Creech Jones, October 1946–February 1950; James Griffiths, February 1950–1.

12 Interview with Sir Angus Mackintosh. Lyttelton took great pleasure in finding in 1951 that there was a really tough job to do.

13 Letter, Eden to Lyttelton, 10.8.54, *Chandos Papers*, Box 4.11.

14 A leader in *The Times* 16.12.53, for example, noted 'Mr. Lyttelton, no doubt, is an inviting target. He does not have a good Parliamentary manner. Too often his choice of words leaves the impression that he has not grasped how important mere words and gestures can be . . .'

15 Lyttelton did, however, manage to go down well with his own backbenchers. Toby Low, the one time Vice-Chairman of the Commonwealth Affairs Committee, wrote to Lyttelton on his retirement: 'The disappearance of your strong hand from the controls revives all sorts of anxieties and fears. You may find it difficult to realise how greatly we respect you for what you have done.' Letter, Low to Lyttelton, 29.7.54, *Chandos Papers*.

16 There were, however, some excellent performances, for example his speech in the debate on the crisis in British Guiana, *House of Commons* 22.10.53, and on the Uganda crisis on 2.12.53.

17 Letter, Lyttelton to Churchill, 3.12.53, *Chandos Papers*, Box 4.5.

18 Diary 25.4.54, *Private Papers*. Also letter, Eden to Lyttelton, 10.8.54: 'I am afraid that I plagued you with those repeated appeals to stay.' *Chandos Papers*, Box 4.11.

19 Letter, Lyttelton to Churchill, 18.5.54: '. . . I have undertaken to return to the company before May 31st . . . However, Patrick [Buchan-Hepburn], in view of the tenuous majority on which our fortunes depend, pressed me to stay until July 31st . . .: this I would willingly do if you could arrange it with the company . . . If you can tell them categorically I shall be free on July 31 . . .' *Chandos Papers*, Box 4.5.

20 Chandos *(11)* pp.431–2.

21 Letter, Lyttelton to Massigli, 19.8.54, *Chandos Papers*, Box 4.11.

22 Letter. Lyttelton to Michael Berry, 26.7.54. *Chandos Papers*, Box 4.10.

23 This was in harness with his chairmanship of the Party's Imperial Affairs Committee from February 1950 in succession to Oliver Stanley. Stanley had once told Churchill that Lennox-Boyd would make a good Colonial Secretary, but at that time he was still hoping for the job himself. Interview I with Lord Boyd of Merton. Stanley had been Colonial Secretary, November 1942–July 1945, and until his premature death in December 1950 was the major authority in the Conservative Party on colonial affairs.

24 Jeffries (*150*) p.118.

25 Interview I with Lord Boyd of Merton.

26 A keen European, he was a member of the Consultative Assembly of the Council of Europe, 1950–2, and a delegate to the General Assembly of the United Nations, 1952–5. Later Lord Colyton.

27 Interview with Lord Colyton. Hopkinson spent August 1952 visiting the three territories in an effort to reassure the Africans of their safeguards under Federation.

28 *House of Commons* 28.7.54, Vol. 531, Col. 504. Hopkinson said, the Government 'cannot contemplate a change of sovereignty in Cyprus'.

29 Lord Boyd of Merton (interview II) said this: 'What he really meant, I think it is fair to say, is that the geographical position would make it always difficult for us to surrender all powers of defence or rights to have ships in the harbour . . . and the size of the island was so small that they could hardly sustain an independent economy. It was a widely held view at the time.' Lyttelton wrote that Hopkinson meant Britain would 'never' abandon her responsibilities until a stable life could be assured for minorities, and this was the argument which he used at the time to pacify the Opposition. Chandos (*11*) p.43. Hopkinson himself wrote to Lyttelton to say he was sorry that the latter's last day in office should have been marred by what Hopkinson feared was his 'misunderstanding' of the Cyprus statement. Hopkinson felt a rather lighter touch might have made what had to be said a bit more acceptable. Letter. Hopkinson to Lyttelton, 31.7.54. *Chandos Papers*, Box 4.10.

30 He had been a Lord-in-Waiting, 1932–8 and Paymaster-General, 1938–9. He then held junior ministerial posts at the War Office, February–September 1939, India and Burma Office, January 1943–October 1944, and Home Office until July 1945.

31 Interview with Hugh Fraser.

32 Lord Lloyd had previously been Parliamentary Under-Secretary at the Home Office. See Chapter 4 Part 3.

33 Interview with Hugh Fraser.

34 See Chapter 3 Part 3. Fraser had been a Stafford M.P. since 1945. He was only thirty-three when appointed Lyttelton's Parliamentary Private Secretary.

35 Interview with Sir William Gorell Barnes.

36 Chandos (*11*) p.374.

37 Chandos (*11*) p.403.

38 Interview with Sir John Johnston.

39 Lennox-Boyd did not come to the Office with as much experience of holding responsible senior positions in either industry or Government.

40 Interview with Lord Lloyd.

41 Dawe was the single Deputy Under-Secretary from 1945. He retired in 1947, though he was still four years off sixty, the usual retirement age. Lloyd was promoted from Assistant Under-Secretary, a job he had held since 1943.

42 Lloyd excelled in organising everything without apparent effort, delegating successfully, yet missing nothing. Interview with Sir Christopher Cox (the Educational Adviser to the Colonial Secretary, 1940–61).

43 Chandos (*11*) pp.346–7. Lloyd was not, however, completely passive, and did argue his points in a highly articulate manner.

44 Jeffries (*150*) p.141. Jeffries was the only non former Permanent Secretary to be the author of a Volume in the New Whitehall Series, suggesting the high regard in which he was held as an administrator.

45 Cmd. 9768.

46 Caine left Government service in 1952 to become Vice-Chancellor of the University of Malaya. He was Director of the London School of Economics, 1957–67.

47 Interview with Hugh Fraser and Chandos (*11*) p.347.

48 When Minister of Production, 1942–3. See Sir Hilton Poynton's B.O.A.P.A.H. talk.

49 Interview. Poynton himself became Permanent Under-Secretary of the Office. 1959–66 (the last holder of the job).

50 The field of colonial development has been

exhaustively explored by D. J. Morgan. See in particular Morgan (*169a*).

51 Munster announced in the *House of Lords* 28.5.52, that the C.D.C. had been set up to deal with commercial-type projects and that it should only undertake such new projects in the future. There are some grounds for believing that Lyttelton was over-suspicious of the C.D.C.

52 See Rendell (*212*) pp.26–7.

53 See Chapter 6 Part 2.

54 Interview with Sir Hilton Poynton.

55 'I am sure it was right to get back to the free market.' Interview with Sir Hilton Poynton.

56 Thus came about the Tin Agreement, which never worked well. Indeed, Lyttelton always expressed scepticism about the value of such agreements. Interview with Sir Hilton Poynton. The Commonwealth Sugar Agreement was an exception to the move towards free markets and was designed to protect the Commonwealth sugar producers.

57 Morgan (*210b*) p.56. The author of the book, an official history, was given full access to official documents.

58 Morgan (*210b*) pp.57–8.

59 Interview II with Lord Boyd of Merton.

60 See Gopal (*75a*) p.167.

61 For example, Colville to Moran on the question of possible self-government in the Gold Coast: 'I am afraid the P.M. will not be interested in the inhabitants of those parts.' Diary 14.7.53, Moran (*87*) p.457.

62 Interview with Lord Soames.

63 Interview with Lord Chandos, D.B.Y. Churchill, unfortunately, did not feel a great deal of sympathy for the coloured people of the colonies. See, for example, diary 8.4.55, Moran (*87*) p.682.

64 See Ronald Hyam: *Elgin and Churchill at the Colonial Office, 1905–8* p.499, Macmillan, London, 1968.

65 Morgan (*210b*) p.58 and diary 7.12.54, *Crookshank Papers*.

66 *Private Information*. Eleven Mau Mau prisoners had died in a detention camp at Hola in March 1959.

CHAPTER 9 PART 3 pp.355–359

1 Interview with Sir Gerald Templer.

2 Chandos (*11*) p.362.

3 Interview with Hugh Fraser.

4 In a speech at the Imperial Defence College on 21st January, 1952, he said of Malaya: 'something to which I have given almost continuous attention both in London and on the spot since I took office, and on which I feel extremely strongly'. *Chandos Papers*.

5 This is an impossible statement to verify, but many interviewed felt that without Lyttelton's decisive action in November–December 1951 the position might well have deteriorated beyond repair.

6 Interview with Sir Angus Mackintosh, and Chandos (*11*) p.362. Mackintosh was Principal Private Secretary until 1953. He was succeeded by John Johnston, both high calibre staff who worked closely with their masters. See Chandos (*11*) pp.348 and 403–4.

7 Chandos (*11*) p.362.

8 The idea of appointing one man responsible for both was very much Lyttelton's own. Interview with Hugh Fraser.

9 Interview with Malcolm MacDonald. See also Chandos (*11*) p.380. After Templer's appointment, MacDonald later admitted that his judgment had been wrong.

10 Chandos (*11*) pp.378–80.

11 Chandos (*11*) pp.379–80.

12 He was C.-in-C. Middle East Land Forces, 1950–3. Robertson himself preferred not to have another overseas posting. See Chapter 8 Part 2. The *Sunday Times* on 23.12.51 mentioned either Lord Montgomery of Alamein or his successor as C.I.G.S., Sir William Slim, as likely for the Malaya job.

13 Templer's appointment was first suggested by Lord Munster. Interview II with Lord Boyd of Merton.

14 Interview with Sir Gerald Templer.

15 *Private Papers*.

16 Interview with Sir John Johnston.

17 Interview with Sir Gerald Templer.

18 Diary 11.1.52, Moran (*87*) p.388.

19 Interview with Lord Harding of Petherton.

20 Interview with Sir Angus Mackintosh.

21 Interview with Sir Gerald Templer. Templer did, however, send a large number of telegrams back to London.

22 Chandos (*11*) pp.382–3.

23 Director of Operations, Federation of Malaya, 1950–1.

24 Interview with Sir Gerald Templer.

25 Sir Gerald Templer (in interview) stressed the crucial role that teamwork played

during his period in Malaya. Three others gave him particularly effective support: Lockhart, Deputy Director of Operations, 1952–3; Oliver, Principal Staff Officer, 1953–4; and Morton, Director of Intelligence, 1952–4.

26 Interview with Sir Hugh Stockwell. He also praised Templer's foresight in seeing the need to train native Malayan politicians and officials in preparation for independence. Templer obviously formed a similarly high opinion of Stockwell; in 1956 he chose him to command the land forces in the Suez expedition.

27 MacGillivray held the job until 1958. He subsequently became Chairman of Kenya's Council of State.

28 Interview with Malcolm MacDonald. From 1946 MacDonald urged that Britain's policy in Malaya be one of progress towards eventual independence for a multi-racial nation.

29 In February 1952 the Government issued a directive to Templer which stressed that the Government's policy was that Malaya in due course should become a fully self-governing nation. Quoted in *The Campaign Guide, 1955* p.437.

30 MacDonald's official duties were primarily concerned with South-East Asian regional matters, but at Templer's prompting he privately continued to exert influence with the Malayan leaders on some of Malaya's internal developments.

31 Interview with Malcolm MacDonald. Lord Gore-Booth later wrote, in an obituary, notice in *The Times* after MacDonald's death in January 1981: 'The conferences over which he presided in Singapore were outstanding.' This is not to belittle the contribution of the Governor, Sir John Nicoll (1952–5), which was a decisive one in steering Singapore towards self-government.

32 Lennox-Boyd also visited Hong Kong for a week in August 1955.

33 Chandos (*11*) pp.374–7.

34 MacDonald had been, June 1935–May 1940, Secretary of State at either the Colonial or the Dominion Office, and at one period held both these posts at once (1938–9). He was the son of Ramsay MacDonald, Labour Prime Minister, 1924 and 1929–31. Partly because of antipathy towards his father, Malcolm MacDonald never had many friends amongst Labour

politicians, and neither was he particularly popular with senior Conservatives. According to David Bruce, the U.S. Ambassador to France, Churchill 'detested' MacDonald. Diary 5.3.52, Sulzberger (*51a*) p.629. Both Eden and Lyttelton also had reservations about MacDonald.

35 Interview with Malcolm MacDonald.

36 The organisation included a Colonial and Foreign Office side, each with its own staff. Jeffries (*150*) pp.84–5.

37 'Pendennis' in the *Observer* on 29.6.52.

CHAPTER 9 PART 4 pp.359–375

1 Neither the Cameroons nor the Somaliland Protectorate are discussed below. They became independent in 1961 and 1960 respectively. The Anglo-Egyptian Condominium of the Sudan was the responsibility of the Foreign Office, and is discussed briefly in Chapter 10 Part 4. The Sudan was untypical of emerging African nations in that its inhabitants displayed notably little anti-colonialist feeling in their struggle for independence: not just gratitude to Britain for training its well-organised Civil Service and for providing development projects, but also the country's lack of religious, social and economic unity – with a quarter of the population Negroes in the South, the remainder predominantly Moslem Arabs in the North – being mainly responsible. A further difference with the Government's policy towards other territories in Africa was that the rate of progress to independence in the Sudan, achieved in 1956, was inextricably bound up with British foreign policy in a wider context, above all Britain's relations with Egypt.

2 The detailed history behind the discussions can be found in a number of sources. See, in particular, Blake (*199*) pp.243–69. Also Garner (*202*) pp.383–5, Goldsworthy (*203*) pp.214–30 and Hatch (*204b*) pp.108–12 and 268–82.

3 Baxter had been Chairman of the original Officials' Conference in March 1951. He was an Assistant Under-Secretary at the C.R.O., 1947–55.

4 W. A. W. Clark was Chief Secretary to the High Commissioner for Basutoland, Swaziland and Bechuanaland, 1940–50. He returned to the C.R.O. in 1950 and was

appointed Assistant Under-Secretary in 1954–6 and 1958–60.

5 Sir Gilbert Rennie was Governor of Northern Rhodesia, 1948–54. Sir Geoffrey Colby was Governor of Nyasaland 1948–56. Huggins (as Viscount Malvern from 1955), became Prime Minister of the Federation, 1953–6.

6 Ismay had, however, served for six years, 1914–20, in operations in Somaliland.

7 'Neither Lord Salisbury nor Lord Chandos [formerly Oliver Lyttelton] ever wavered in faith in the Federation, nor in the staunchness of their friendship to us who strove to prove, by our work, that the faith was justified.' Welensky (54) p.52.

8 *Private Information.*

9 Cohen had a profound influence on the shape of early post-war colonial policy of the Labour Government. He had deep, progressive and liberal-minded views on African advance (becoming known as 'Emperor of Africa' in the Office), and had Labour won the General Elections in 1951 or 1955 might well have made Permanent Under-Secretary in succession to Lloyd. Goldsworthy (203) p.52. For an assessment of Cohen's career, see Robinson in Gann and Duignan, eds. (201b) pp.253–63. More popular with Labour than Conservatives, he was promoted by the new Labour Government to Permanent Secretary to the new Ministry of Overseas Development, the job he held on his premature death in 1968. John Hatch felt he 'lacked any real understanding of the harsh facts basic to the racial struggle'. Hatch (204a) p.269.

10 Cohen had persuaded Griffiths to hold a conference of officials in London in 1950. Goldsworthy (203) p.216. The Federation proposals emerged from this Officials' Conference.

11 Gorell Barnes was the most important of the eight Assistant Under-Secretaries in the Colonial Office, with responsibility for the African departments. He had a progressive outlook, sharp mind, and was devoted to his work, although perhaps less passionately interested than Cohen in Africa. Sir Hilton Poynton (B.O.A.-P.A.H. interview) commented that Gorell Barnes was as responsible as anybody in the Department for changing attitudes that the Colonial Office was not just running a little backwater lobby of its own, but that

its work was very much in the mainstream of the responsibilities of the British Government. When Lyttelton retired, he wrote to Gorell Barnes: 'No one lives and breathes Africa more than you do,' and paid him the exaggerated compliment (they were not always in agreement): 'I have the happiest recollections of being run by you in these affairs.' Letter, 10.8.54. *Chandos Papers*, Box 4.10.

12 *Private Information.*

13 Blake (*199*) p.258. Goldsworthy (*203*) p.26.

14 *Private Information.* This contrasts with Hatch (*204a*) who wrote (p.271) that Lyttelton: 'Immediately took a more positive line than his predecessors'. Hatch was a stern critic of the Federation and would in all probability have been basing his evidence on the views of his Labour friends.

15 Interview with Lord Colyton.

16 Chandos (*11*) pp.386–7.

17 Blake (*199*) p.285.

18 Interview II with Lord Boyd of Merton.

19 Morgan (*210b*) p.98, summarising the conclusions of a 1957 Cabinet Paper (Colonial Policy Committee (57) 27, 26.7.57) on the political and constitutional outlook in the colonies.

20 For the detailed background of Kenya in these years, see in particular Douglas-Home (*72*) pp.216–86, Blundell (*6*) pp.88–201 and Carver (*65*) pp.180–3.

21 Lyttelton (Chandos (*11*) p.394) says he regrets not asking Baring to curtail his leave by two to three months, but it is doubtful if this would have made much difference. Carver (*65*) p.180 says that there had been a 'serious deterioration' of the position between Mitchell's departure and Baring's arrival.

22 Chandos (*11*) p.397.

23 Commander-in-Chief, Middle East Land Forces, 1950–3.

24 Senior Army officers in the War Office up to that point had no clear idea of what was going on in Kenya as all information went direct to H.Q., Middle East. Blundell (*6*) pp.138–9.

25 Douglas-Home (*72*) p.238.

26 Letter, 11.8.54. *Chandos Papers*, Box 4.10.

27 Lathbury had previously been Commandant, Staff College, Camberley, be-

fore his appointment as C.-in-C., East Africa, a job he held until 1957.

28 Kenyatta's imprisonment and detention lasted until 1961. He later became a widely respected President of Kenya from 1964 until his death in August 1978. In Baring's defence it should be stated that few in 1953 foresaw the responsible leadership qualities Kenyatta was later to develop.

29 Cmd. 9081.

30 See Douglas-Home (72) pp.251–6.

31 Douglas-Home (72) p.251.

32 Letter, Baring to Lyttelton, 30.7.54, *Chandos Papers*, Box 4.10.

33 Interview II with Sir George Mallaby.

34 Douglas Home (72) pp.270–4. Lyttelton, himself says proposals were much framed on Baring's advice. Chandos (11) pp.406–7.

35 Interview with Sir John Johnston.

36 Letter, 12.8.54, *Chandos Papers*, Box 4.11.

37 Cmd. 9103.

38 Hatch (*204a*) p.334. He wrote: 'The British Government now recognised that to hand over political power to the white settlers would be to provoke further outbreaks . . . with continuing demands on British money and military aid.'

39 The Kabaka held the job until deposed in June 1966, when he came to England for the last years of his life, dying, aged forty-five, in November 1969. He published his memoirs in 1967, Mutesa (*41a*). His own account on pp.113–41 of the years should be read, not the least because of the picture it gives of his relations with Cohen. The first Prime Minister, appointed in 1962, was Milton Obote.

40 A major plank of Lyttelton's policy was the building up of smaller groups of territories into larger ones, and Lyttelton in his London speech was no doubt testing the ground. However, the Government did not expect the question of federation in East Africa to arise for a long time, and their decision to appoint a Royal Commission on East African living standards can be seen as a preliminary step to viewing the area as a whole. The Commission was suggested by Sir Philip Mitchell and the Cabinet agreed to the proposal on 20.5.52. The underlying purpose was to show that the Government had positive plans for economic and social development and were not just concerned to send in troops.

The Commission, chaired by Sir Hugh Dow, reported in May 1955 (Cmd. 9475) and made clear the vast potential of agriculture. The possibility of federation was discussed again in 1960. Morgan (*210b*) pp.66 and 193.

41 Hatch (*204a*) p.315.

42 Mutesa had spent two years at Magdalene College, Cambridge (1945–7), and held an honorary commission in the Grenadier Guards, of which he was always proud. (Lyttelton himself had served in the Grenadiers.)

43 Chandos (*11*) pp.418–20.

44 Chandos (*11*) p.420. Uganda was the main item on the agenda at Cabinet on 23rd and 25th November, 1953. Diary. *Crookshank Papers*.

45 *House of Commons* 2.12.53, Chandos (*11*) pp.420–1. *The Annual Register, 1953* establishes a clear causal link between Lyttelton's summer speech and the subsequent problems in Uganda, as does, for example, John Hatch (*204a*) p.315.

46 Chandos (*11*) p.423.

47 Chandos (*11*) p.418.

48 Letter, Lyttelton to Cohen, 10.8.54, *Chandos Papers*, Box 4.10.

49 See Bates (*58a*) pp.202–81.

50 See Morgan (*210b*) pp.123–30 and Cohen (*200*) pp.48–9.

51 Until 1945 she had been married to the Earl of Listowel (who in 1947 had been Secretary of State for India). Her book is perhaps over-critical of Twining.

52 Listowel (*205c*) p.163.

53 The former Head of the Commonwealth Department at Labour's Transport House said Nyerere had more influence on his country in the 1950s than any other African leader outside the Gold Coast (where Nkrumah was). Hatch (*204a*) p.301.

54 Morgan (*210b*) p.123.

55 Listowel (*205c*) p.164.

56 The Legislative Council was enlarged to sixty-one members, the unofficial Bench consisting of ten Africans, ten Asians and ten Europeans, with thirty-one on the official side.

57 Garner (*202*) p.335 cites two former High Commissioners arguing the case on different sides in 1951.

58 *House of Commons* 22.11.51.

59 *House of Lords* 13.4.54. On 12th April a resolution had been introduced into the House of Assembly in Capetown urging

the transfer of the territories to the South African Government.

60 Bechuanaland (as Botswana) and Basutoland (as Lesotho) both received their independence in 1966. Swaziland followed in 1968.

61 Hatch (*204a*) pp.94 and 233–4.

62 Interview with Sir John Foster.

63 *House of Commons* 27.3.52.

64 He became Prime Minister of Bechuanaland in 1965, and on its independence in 1966. President of the Republic of Botswana. He was knighted in that year.

65 Nkrumah was Prime Minister of the Gold Coast until 1960 (of Ghana, 1957–60). After Ghana became a Republic in 1960, Nkrumah became its first President until his fall from power in February 1966. He was a popular and respected Prime Minister, but from at least 1957 began to show increasing signs of tyrannical behaviour, the key-note of his years as President.

66 For contacts between the colony and London, see Jeffries (*205*) p.82.

67 In order to investigate violent riots in Accra in 1948, the Labour Government had appointed a Commission of Enquiry under the chairmanship of Aiken Watson, a barrister. The Commission found that the Government must become more representative of the people.

68 He joined the Colonial Service in 1920 and served in Nigeria, 1920–36, Bechuanaland, 1936–42 and Basutoland, 1942–6.

69 Diary 30.1.53, Sulzberger (*51a*) p.710.

70 Cohen (*200*) p.44.

71 Colonial Policy Committee of the Cabinet (57) 27, 26th July, 1957. Reported in Morgan (*210b*) pp.97–8.

72 Morgan (*210b*) pp.82–3.

73 *House of Commons* 28.4.54, Vol. 526, Col. 1625.

74 See Jeffries (*205*) pp.70–81.

75 Morgan (*210b*) pp.84–5.

76 Morgan (*210b*) p.85.

77 In his autobiography Nkrumah acknowledged his debt to Arden-Clarke, without whose co-operation and help he might not have emerged as Prime Minister of Ghana. Autobiography of Kwame Nkrumah (*43a*) p.282.

78 This is not to say that Lyttelton's role was of no importance in the Gold Coast. The importance was in backing up the Governor and providing confidence. This

is recognised in a letter from the Chief Regional Officer of Ashanti (W. H. Beeton) to Lyttelton on 28.7.54. He assured him that it meant much to people in the Service to know that he was at the Colonial Office, and it meant much to the Gold Coast; he was sure its leaders felt this deeply. *Chandos Papers*, Box 4.10.

79 Morgan (*210b*) p.97.

80 After the Governor of Nigeria, 1943–7, Sir Arthur Richards.

81 *House of Commons* 21.5.53.

82 Morgan (*210b*) p.85.

83 Lyttelton gives his own account in Chandos (*11*) pp.409–15.

84 Sir Charles Jeffries in (*83*) p.11 says the two men who led their countries out of colonial status who made the biggest impression on him were Akubakar and Sir Oliver Goonetilleke of Ceylon.

85 *Private Information.*

86 In the event it met at Lancaster House in London in May 1957.

87 For full details see the official Report of the London Conference, Cmd. 8934.

88 Chandos (*11*) p.409.

89 'The considerable differences which still exist between the Regions are recognised by giving increased functions to the Regional Governments . . .' Lyttelton, *House of Commons* 10.2.54, Vol. 523, Col. 1625.

90 Colonial Office practice at this time was to use 'oversea' as an adjective, 'overseas' as an adverb: Lennox-Boyd later decreed that the 's' be included in both cases. Jeffries (*205*) p.101.

91 Cmd. 9059.

92 Lennox-Boyd did, however, make an extensive tour of Nigeria, visiting all three Regions and the Cameroons, after the Election in 1955. The new Governor in 1955 said he was never precisely told that he had to move on towards the goal of self-government when he was appointed, but that the policy had in fact been laid down by the 1953 and 1954 Conferences. Interview with Sir James Robertson and Robertson (*43c*) p.179.

93 This is omitting the British Cameroons, mentioned briefly in Note 1 above.

94 John Hatch expressed the feeling of many when he wrote: 'A few leading personalities made considerable fortunes from their new offices, but the mass of the people were unaffected, except that the admini-

stration was rather less efficient and more corrupt. Perhaps self-government and independence came too easily.' Hatch (*204a*) p.183.

CHAPTER 9 PART 5 pp.375–378

1 Much has been written on colonial policy largely centring on the process of decolonisation. Three sources in particular are recommended. Sir Leslie Monson's contribution to Thornhill, ed. (*135*) pp.261–87, Kirk-Greene, ed. (*205a*), which contains a number of invaluable contributions from those connected with the colonial administration, and Goldsworthy (*203*), especially pp.205–316. For interesting earlier discussion see Young in Gann and Duignan, ed. (*201a*) pp.450–502. For an excellent general survey of the British Governor in Africa, see Anthony Kirk-Greene in Gann and Duignan, eds. (*201b*) pp.209–57.

2 The *Observer*, 28.3.54. A good analysis of Parliament's concern with the colonies can be found in Goldsworthy (*203*) pp.65–99.

3 Two Fleet Street journalists in particular provided authoritative reports on colonial affairs from very different points of view: Oliver Woods of *The Times* and the more anti-establishment Colin Legum of the *Observer*. Some of those who worked as colonial administrators in the field always felt however, perhaps not surprisingly, that there was insufficient Fleet Street coverage of their colonies. Sir James Robertson (interview) mentioned the existence of this feeling.

4 Margery Perham, for example, felt that the Governments and administrators were slow to react to the changes in the balance of power wrought by the Second World War, and also that insufficient lessons were learnt from the experience of the colonies which could have been applied to other colonies. See her introduction to Perham (*211*) for a discussion of her views. Margery Perham for many years was one of the foremost authorities on colonial policy.

5 Lyttelton discussed the opening consciousness of Africa to outside influences in one of his major speeches as Colonial Secretary. *House of Commons* 16.12.53.

6 See Chapter 5 Part 3. Critical voices were, however, increasingly raised in the Cabinet from 1954 onwards about progress to independence, considered by some to be too swift. See conclusion of Chapter 9 Part 2.

7 Butler (*121*) p.9.

8 The Labour Party's 1955 Manifesto, 'Forward with Labour', however, merely maintained: 'We shall continue the transformation from Empire to Commonwealth as each colonial people becomes ready for independence.' A forceful statement of the need for orderly progress towards independence can be found in Chandos (*11*) pp.388–9.

9 Lyttelton announced in the *House of Commons* 14.11.51 that 'I should like to make it plain at the outset that H.M.G. intend no change in [the late Labour Government's] aims.' (Vol. 493, Cols. 983–4). These aims, announced by Lyttelton, were twofold: orderly progress to self-government within the Commonwealth, and the pursuance of economic and social development in line with political development.

10 There was always a major difference in the mind of the Colonial Office between the West Indian and Central African federations. In the former all parties were prepared to give the Federation a chance to see if it would work out: there was no sense in which it was imposed. The form of federation visualised for the West Indies was only loose. The proposals had their origin in the work of both Conservative and Labour Governments, and Parliament accepted them with little fuss. Lord Lloyd played an active part in touring the West Indies and egging on federation talks. Interview with Lord Lloyd.

11 Cmd. 8980.

12 Cmd. 9274.

13 One of the most persistent of Labour critics on colonial policy was Fenner Brockway, then M.P. for Eton and Slough. See Brockway (*9*) pp.188–96. But not all Brockway's fellow M.P.s possessed his degree of sincerity. The Kabaka of Buganda was unimpressed by the sincerity of Labour's defence of his deportation from Uganda. See Mutesa (*41a*) p.125.

14 A leader in *The Times* 16.12.53, discussing Labour's censure motion on colonial policy. It commented further: 'The shifts to which the Opposition have resorted in recent months in their criticisms of

[Lyttelton] and his policy have been equalled only by their reluctance to face him squarely on any of the several issues which they have raised.' The article criticised Labour's left-wing backbenchers thus: 'They have scant knowledge and even less experience of the colonies and colonial peoples,' and were impelled by little other than instinct. A leader on 19.1.54 said: '. . . The Opposition, having been badly defeated in its campaign against Mr. Lyttelton, has yet to find a policy that is concerned with the colonies and not with personalities.'

15 See the leader in *The Times* 16.12.53.

16 Morgan (*210b*) p.22, narrates how Lord Boyd of Merton told him that the Opposition in Parliament were privy to these understandings. He further comments that both Lyttelton and Lennox-Boyd believed they possessed the authority to influence the rate of political evolution.

17 The creation of the Colonial Development Corporation was announced by the Colonial Secretary in the *House of Commons* on 25.6.47. Borrowing powers of approximately £100m. were to be made available on competitive lines to assist any enterprise in the colonies designed to increase their general productive capacity.

18 *The Times* 30.7.54.

19 Morgan (*210b*) pp.59–60. Morgan comments that 'the Committee failed to fulfil its purpose.'

CHAPTER 10 PART 1 pp.379–387

1 The *News Chronicle* 31.10.51. The names of Eden and Selwyn Lloyd were mentioned, and also Lord Salisbury, who, according to a report in the paper two days before, was to manage foreign affairs alongside Eden. This plan, however, appears to have lapsed when Eden himself dispensed with the idea of being Leader of the House a few days after the Election. See Chapter 3 Part 1.

2 Herbert Morrison took over the last few months of the Government (March to October) but Eden was not so close to Morrison, and this 'special relationship' was not continued. Though Eden would not as a rule discuss matters in private with Morrison, his Parliamentary Private Secretary (1947–51) Allan Noble, did have occasional talks with Edward Shackleton, Morrison's Parliamentary Private Secretary. But Shackleton himself had no direct recollection of these talks. Interview with Lord Shackleton, B.O.A.P.A.H. When Eden became Foreign Secretary, informal talks continued with Morrison and Attlee, and Eden found them utterly reliable in respecting confidence. Diary 2.5.54, Millar, ed. (*39a*) p.146.

3 Eden (*14*) p.5. Also Dixon (*70*) pp.179 and 183–4.

4 Interview with Sir Evelyn Shuckburgh. Morrison had been a distinguished Home Secretary, 1940–5. He had been Lord President throughout the Labour Government until his appointment to the Foreign Office.

5 The Sixth Assembly met exceptionally at Paris while the United Nations building in New York was being completed.

6 The most recent unfavourable accounts appear in McDermott (*215*) (a former Foreign Office official, 1935–62, not wholly impartial in his judgments) and in Shlaim, ed. (*97*) pp.81–109. McDermott's contribution in particular makes Eden out on occasion to be little more than a Colonel Blimp figure. Three main reasons explain this antipathy to Eden. The Suez crisis of 1956 and his poor performance as Prime Minister has made it difficult for some to view his performance during 1951–5 in isolation. His stonewall attitude to the suggestion of closer economic links with Europe undoubtedly coloured the judgment of many, such as Maxwell Fyfe, (Kilmuir (*31*) pp.186–9). Finally there was Eden's manner, with his use of phrases like 'my dear' which made him appear (unjustly) to some to be a pre-war relic unhappily washed up on the shores of the post-war world. A further factor that could be mentioned is the negative personal feelings that Eden could excite, which caused some at a later date to write unfavourably about him. See, for example, Swinton (*52*) p.164. It is quite possible that the unfavourable picture of Eden given in Lord Bethell's and Count Nikolai Tolstoy's books on the forcible repatriations of former prisoners of war from 1944–7 to Russia will also make it harder for historians to reach a fair assessment of his achievement during 1951–5. An excellently balanced survey of Eden's career

can be found in the appreciation (by Lord Blake) in the *Sunday Times* 16.1.77.

7 Interview with Sir Frank Roberts. Bevin had been a more popular figure in the Office, and, some felt, despite his eccentricities, even more competent. From 1947–9 Roberts had been Bevin's Principal Private Secretary.

8 Moran quotes Macmillan extolling the virtues of Eden's skill in negotiation and provides a good example of it in his discussions with John Foster Dulles. Diary 9.1.55, Moran (*87*) p.659.

9 Acheson narrates how Franks (British Ambassador at Washington, 1948–52) came to see him one day in early January 1952 during the Churchill/Eden visit to Washington. There had been a disagreement at dinner the previous night between Acheson and Eden. Franks made some observations about the working of Eden's mind which Acheson thought very illuminating: that Eden had one great asset, political instinct, but was not trained in any kind of rational process. He knew he was now at point A, which he did not like and wanted to be at point B, but was not capable of saying how to get there, or indeed why he preferred it to point C. He just had a 'feel' that he did not want to be 'here' and wanted to be 'there'. Princeton Seminar 13.12.53, *Acheson Papers*.

10 Interview with Sir Evelyn Shuckburgh.

11 Moran quotes Churchill as saying: 'Anthony is very good with other people. His voice is so smooth and his manner so quiet, so persuasive.' Diary 8.12.53, Moran (*87*) p.538.

12 In the Office he quickly decided whom he cared for and whom he would disregard, but he was equally loyal to all his colleagues *vis-à-vis* the outside world. Interview with Sir Eric Berthoud. Berthoud was an Assistant Under-Secretary, 1948–52.

13 Western European Union, for example, despite Eden's claim (Eden (*14*) p.151) was not his own idea. See Chapter 10 Part 4.

14 Eden's inability to reach a decision on whether to agree to the Dulles-Radford Plan for joint military action in South-East Asia and his return to England to consult with Churchill on the night of 24th April is an example. Iverach McDonald wrote that Eden did stand up forthrightly to Dulles at

Geneva, 22nd–24th April (McDonald (*35*) p.137), but his evidence is based on personal conversations with Eden.

15 Grimond (*21*) p.193. *The Times* reported during his illness in 1953 that 'The House likes him, respects him and misses him.' *The Times* 8.3.53. See also Chandos (*11*) pp.291–2.

16 Interview with Sir Anthony Rumbold. Rumbold succeeded Shuckburgh as Eden's Principal Private Secretary in the spring of 1954.

17 Lord Strang (interview) thought Eden was never really himself even after 1952.

18 He had also been away from the Office for a few days in March 1952 with influenza and laryngitis.

19 Their engagement was announced on 11th August and they were married three days later.

20 Diary 24.3.53. Sulzberger (*51a*) p.718. Sulzberger had drinks with Eden on that day.

21 *The Times* 6.4.53. For details of his illness, see Eden (*14*) pp.51–2.

22 Diary 24.4.53. Moran (*87*) p.427 and *The Times* 20.5.52. A communiqué issued on 30th May said a bile duct had been cut and a further operation was necessary.

23 Interview with Lord Sherfield (formerly Sir Roger Makins).

24 Letter, Eden to Eisenhower, 30.6.53. International Series, Box 18. *Eisenhower Papers*.

25 Macmillan (*36*) p.520.

26 Diary 8.8.53. *Private Papers*.

27 There was some considerable uncertainty in the late summer of 1953 as to whether Eden would ever again resume active duty at the Foreign Office. *The Times* 3.10.53 said the announcement from Number Ten the day before that Eden would continue as Foreign Secretary ended the speculation about his future. See Chapter 2 Part 2.

28 Interview with Lord Carr of Hadley. Others, for example, Sir Ashley Clarke (interview) felt that Churchill's delayed retirement as Prime Minister seriously aggravated his health.

29 Officials noted the great vitality he produced during the Geneva Conference and at the Nine Power Conference in London in September 1954. At the Bermuda Conference in December 1953 Moran however records how 'thin and drawn' he had been looking. Diary 7.12.53 Moran (*87*) p.537.

But he was found to be in 'pretty good form' by Hoyer Millar, the British High Commissioner in Germany with whom Eden stayed during the Berlin Conference, January–February 1954. Interview with Lord Inchyra (the former Sir Frederick Hoyer Millar). Eden confessed to Churchill and Moran that he found the six-hour sessions at Geneva 'very fatiguing', especially when he was Chairman. Diary 24.6.54, Moran (*87*) p.587. Channon (diary 26.10.53, James, ed. (*28*) p.479) thought Eden looked 'extremely old and tired' on his return to the Foreign Office in October 1953.

30 *Private Papers.*
31 Interview with Lord Strang. See Chapter 2 Part 1.
32 Moran recorded in his diary how great a struggle Churchill was finding keeping up with his job (diary 28.5.53, Moran (*87*) p.429), and a month later how he was finding coping with the Foreign Office very hard work (diary 23.6.53, Moran (*87*) p.430).
33 *House of Commons* 11.5.53, Vol. 515, Col. 897. See Chapter 10 Part 3.
34 Diary 29.6.53, *Crookshank Papers.* Butler had announced earlier, on 29th June, that Churchill was merely to be 'assisted' by Salisbury during his illness. Attlee felt a Cabinet Minister should be directly responsible. See *The Times* 30.6.53.
35 Lord Strang (interview) thought Salisbury had a 'feel' for foreign policy.
36 There was a Cabinet on 6th July to brief Salisbury, and a further one on 13th July about the Washington talks, for example. Diary. *Crookshank Papers.*
37 Interview with Roderic O'Connor. *Dulles Papers.*
38 Nutting (*219*) pp.53–4; Colville (*12*) p.239.
39 *House of Commons* 22.7.53, Vol. 518, Col. 392.
40 Diary 12.7.53, 13.7.53 and 16.7.53, Moran (*87*) pp.454–60.
41 *The Times* 21.7.53.
42 After the talks Salisbury wrote to Dulles on 15th July to say how very pleased he had been by the talks. *Dulles Papers*, Box 75.
43 *Private Papers.*
44 See, for example, Gore-Booth (*19*) p.195.
45 *Private Papers.*
46 Diary 26.7.53, James, ed. (*28*) p.478. See also diary 22.7.53, Moran (*87*) p.465 and diary 21.7.53, *Crookshank Papers.*

47 *House of Commons* 21.7.53, Vol. 518, Col. 215
48 Interview with Sir Hubert Ashton. See letter, Stuart to Butler, quoted in Butler (*10*) p.170. For a contemporary account of Butler in action at this time, see diary 8.8.53, Moran (*87*) pp.473–4.
49 Interview with Lord Caccia.
50 Interview with Lord Harlech (formerly David Ormsby-Gore.)
51 Interview with Lord Glendevon (formerly Lord John Hope.)
52 Lloyd (*46*) pp.3–4.
53 Butler (*10*) pp.156–7.
54 Interview with Sir Anthony Nutting.
55 Hopkinson, though a newcomer to politics (he entered the House of Commons in 1950), had served in the Foreign Service, 1924–46. Instead he was appointed in 1951 Secretary for Overseas Trade at the Board of Trade and in May 1952 became Minister of State at the Colonial Office. Randolph Churchill wrote that while still in Opposition Eden had promised to make Hopkinson Minister of State for European Affairs. Churchill (*66*) p.199.
56 Interview with Lord Harlech. Lloyd had been Secretary of the Conservative Party's Finance Committee for a while in Opposition.
57 Interview with Lord Selwyn-Lloyd, D.B.Y.
58 It was in the months of Eden's absence during 1953 that British approval was given to a C.I.A. plot to overthrow Moussadeq. See Grigg (*222*) p.15.
59 The State Department, however, did not have a high opinion of Lloyd. See Acheson (*1*) pp.583 and 656. This unfavourable U.S. opinion of him continued, so Macmillan informed Woolton on 24.10.55. Diary, *Woolton Papers.*
60 Interview with Sir Douglas Dodds-Parker.
61 Interview with Sir Roderick Barclay. Barclay was Principal Private Secretary to the Foreign Secretary, 1949–51. In 1953 he was appointed a Deputy Under-Secretary.
62 For a discussion of the titles of the Ministers of State, see Chapter 3 Part 3.
63 He had been Chairman of the Young Conservatives since 1946. He was Chairman of the National Union in 1950, and Chairman of its Executive Committee, April 1951–April 1952.
64 Because of their disagreement over Suez in 1956, it is easy to underestimate the close-

ness of Eden's relationship with Nutting during these earlier years. There were, however, increasing tensions as Nutting became more and more successful and independent-minded. Nutting resigned in November 1956, the end to his exceptionally promising ministerial career.

65 Interview with Sir Anthony Nutting.

66 There was a hope amongst the Conservative M.P.s' Suez Group that Dodds-Parker's appointment would stiffen the ranks of those who were against evacuating the Suez base. Letter, Julian Amery to Hankey, 18.11.53, *Hankey Papers*, Box 14.25.

67 Interview with Lord Tranmire (formerly Robert Turton).

68 Interview with Lord Glendevon.

69 Interview with Lord Carr of Hadley.

70 Eden obviously liked having Carr close to him and took him to Number Ten with him as his Parliamentary Private Secretary in April 1955.

71 Ormsby-Gore was the third member of the team who had a distinguished figure connected with international affairs. His father, Lord Harlech, had been Colonial Secretary, 1936–8, and U.K. High Commissioner in South Africa, 1941–4. Ormsby-Gore went on to become Minister of State for Foreign Affairs, 1957–61, and British Ambassador to the U.S., 1961–5. Hope's father, Lord Linlithgow, was Viceroy of India, 1936–43. Reading's father had been Viceroy of India, 1921–6, and Foreign Secretary in 1931.

72 Interview with Lord Harlech.

73 Moran records that Norman Brook said that he '. . . thought well of Shuckburgh, and said he was intelligent, exceptionally tough and thoughtful'. Diary 10.7.55, Moran (87) p.709.

74 Interview with Sir Ashley Clarke.

75 Montgomery, when Deputy Supreme Allied Commander, Europe, was over-harsh when he said of Strang '. . . He is a routine fellow. Prudent no doubt, but without vision.' Diary 5.7.53, Moran (87) p.445.

76 Gladwyn (18) p.269. See also Barclay (4) pp.19–20. Lord Gladwyn, however, added in interview that Kirkpatrick was in fact rather European minded before his day.

77 Makins subsequently in fact became Joint Permanent Secretary to the Treasury, 1956–9, a unique appointment for a

Foreign Office official. Later Lord Sherfield.

78 For an insight into Eden's high opinion of Dixon, see diary 3.12.53, Moran (87) p.532.

79 Eden was almost certainly disappointed after 1951 not to be able to form a similar close relationship with the senior Legal Adviser as he had had with Sir William Malkin (1929–45). He did not find Malkin's successor, Sir Eric Beckett, so sympathetic personally, and Sir Gerald Fitzmaurice, who took over in 1953, he subsequently disagreed with on the use of force during the Suez crisis. Interview with Sir Gerald Fitzmaurice.

80 *The Times* 24.11.53.

81 *Private Papers*.

82 Gladwyn (18) p.266.

83 Princeton Seminars 14.2.54, *Acheson Papers*. On Franks' departure from the United States at the end of November 1952, he received many notable tributes in the American Press. The *Washington Post* on 28th November spoke of his unremitting search 'to find bases of agreement when a different approach on common problems has appeared', and how the State Department officials 'will testify to his fertility in coming up with formulas and acceptable compromises'. Quoted in *The Times* 29.11.52. 'Pendennis' in the *Observer* 5.10.52 said that in addition to the secretary-generalship of NATO, Franks had also been invited to become Editor of *The Times* and Director-General of the B.B.C. Judged by the glittering promise of Franks in his forties and the prospects before him, his subsequent career as, *inter alia*, a banker (Chairman of Lloyds, 1954–62) and academic administrator (Provost of Worcester College, Oxford, 1962–76) appears somewhat subdued.

84 Interview with Lord Franks and the *Observer* 2.3.52.

85 Salisbury was at one time one of those considered as a successor to Franks. Diary 5.3.52, Sulzberger (51a) p.629.

CHAPTER 10 PART 2 pp.387–396

1 As noted in the Introduction, details of all foreign policy matters will not be discussed. This study will instead confine

itself to just two areas, relations with the United States and with the Soviet Union. On neither topic has much been written, and both were of major concern to Churchill. Those seeking information or details of other aspects of foreign policy should consult Frankel (*214*), Northedge (*217*), David Carlton's forthcoming biography of Eden (Allen Lane), and above all Eden's own (dull but full) account, Eden (*14*).

2 *House of Commons*, 14.3.55. Vol. 538, Col. 968.

3 See closing passages in Part 3. Churchill had been concerned earlier lest the Americans take offence at the last Volume of his history of the war, which contained criticism of the U.S. policy at Yalta.

4 Frankel (*214*) p.209. The United States were disturbed because they felt Burgess and Maclean had been allowed to operate undetected, and were anxious lest other spies had taken their place. Britain had no big investigative committee to rival those in the U.S., but it did have a Cabinet Committee on Subversive Activities, set up in May 1947 and chaired by Attlee. Few civil servants were actually dismissed, but a number were moved to less sensitive work. See *The Times* 6.1.81.

5 Interview with Lord Strang. Dean Acheson said at a meeting of the U.S. Cabinet on 19th October 1951, on the eve of the General Election, that if the Conservatives were victorious there would not be much change in British foreign policy. A Conservative Government, however, would be more united on foreign policy and more responsible. *Papers of Matthew J. Connelly*. Notes of Cabinet Meetings.

6 Colville (*12*) p.233.

7 Paper on Approach and Objectives for Talks, *Truman Papers*.

8 After he left office Truman referred to the 'distinct pleasure' of again seeing an 'old friend' (Churchill) in January 1952: Truman (*53*) p.259. (In fact, Churchill had never ever met Truman before the latter succeeded Roosevelt as President in April 1945. Neither did they meet before the Potsdam Conference, a fact that Churchill later much regretted.) Dean Acheson went even further: 'We were personally fond of one another . . . All the time I was there I would have five or six people spend a week in the Foreign Office to find out

what they thought about subjects, and they would come over here. There were no mysteries . . . The British, I think, are our closest allies.' Acheson 18.2.55., Post Presidential Memoirs File, *Truman Papers*.

9 Letter, Bernard Baruch to Churchill, 22.12.52, *Baruch Papers*. (Baruch, already over eighty in 1952, was an important New York figure, with many friends in high places in Washington. He was a close friend of Churchill.)

10 Paper on Approach and Objectives for Talks, *Truman Papers*.

11 Averell Harriman at the Princeton Seminar 13.12.53, *Acheson Papers*. See Chapter 8 Part 3.

12 Churchill said after the January 1952 meeting 'I like Truman fearfully.' Diary 19.1.52, Moran (*87*) p.393. And in a letter from Acheson to Lester Pearson in Canada 23.1.52, he wrote: '. . . the President made it very clear that he not only respected Mr. Churchill greatly, but also that he was very fond of him.' *Acheson Papers*.

13 Acheson recorded in a memorandum on 8.1.53 that Truman had been very anxious to see Churchill and thought it would be their last chance to meet for some years. *Acheson Papers*.

14 Interview with Sir Evelyn Shuckburgh.

15 Acheson at Princeton Seminar 13.12.53, *Acheson Papers*.

16 Acheson talking at the Princeton Seminar on 13.12.53. *Acheson Papers*. Acheson had had an audience with the young Queen after diplomatic talks in London. She asked him how they went and Acheson decided to tell her in detail the points of disagreement. Eden became quite annoyed, feeling that the audience should have been restricted to small talk, and told Acheson at the Lisbon Conference later in the month that he had behaved badly. Eden makes no reference to the incident when he discusses the London talks. Eden (*14*) p.40.

17 *Newsweek* 14.4.52 (p.17). Amongst other points, the article said that relations were not helped by Acheson's conviction that Bevin was the greatest British Foreign Secretary, and Eden's that Cordell Hull was the most distinguished American Secretary of State.

18 Acheson referred to the 'most happy

comradeship we have had in some great constructive work together', quoted at the Princeton Seminar on 13.12.53, *Acheson Papers.*

19 *Private Papers.*

20 See Eden (*14*) pp.21 and 63. See also Manderson-Jones (*216*) pp.108–17.

21 Letter. Baruch to Churchill, 2.8.53, *Baruch Papers.*

22 Diary 21.12.51, *Eisenhower Papers.*

23 Diary 13.2.53, *Eisenhower Papers.*

24 Colville in Wheeler-Bennett, ed. (*105*) pp.129–30.

25 6.1.53, *Eisenhower Papers.*

26 Diary, 13.2.52, *Eisenhower Papers.*

27 Diary 6.1.53, *Eisenhower Papers.*

28 See, for example, diary 19.8.53, Macmillan (*36*) pp.522–3.

29 During war relief work Aldrich became acquainted with Eden and Churchill. He was a more sociable figure than Gifford but was not on a basis of intellectual ease with either officials or Ministers in London, and neither was he confided in on important matters by Dulles. Interview with Walton Butterworth. *Dulles Papers.* Butterworth was American Minister in London when Aldrich was Ambassador. Aldrich himself said: 'The real trouble with my relations with Dulles was that . . . he kept having private conversations with the British without my being there. I never knew exactly what he was saying to Eden . . .' Interview with Winthrop Aldrich, *Eisenhower Papers.* Officials at the British Embassy in Washington also were never quite sure what had been discussed when Dulles had talks with Eden and others whilst on his travels. See also Sulzberger's diary for 3.6.53 (*51a*) p.737. In it Aldrich complains that Eisenhower would set out American foreign policy in one speech, but Dulles would modify it in another.

30 Colville refers to Churchill's attempt to persuade Eisenhowever to break the American precedent of political appointments to important foreign Embassies and leave the intelligent and much respected Gifford in the job. Colville (*12*) p.236. Eden told Acheson that Gifford was the best Ambassador in London in his lifetime. Acheson 18.2.55 at the Princeton Seminar. *Acheson Papers.* Gifford, however, was not himself anxious to remain in London, and wrote to Truman to say he wished to retire, whatever the outcome of

the Presidential Election. Letter Gifford to Truman 29.9.52. *Truman Papers.* The British were unaware of Gifford's anxiety to go. *Private Papers.*

31 Interview with Winthrop Aldrich. *Eisenhower Papers.*

32 Colville (*12*) p.235. For Churchill's attitude to Dulles see also diary 19.7.53 and 4.5.54, Moran (*87*) pp.462 and 573.

33 Interview with Winthrop Aldrich. *Eisenhower Papers.*

34 Eisenhower (*17*) p.142. Eisenhower repeated this claim in his interview for the Dulles Oral History Archive, *Dulles Papers.*

35 Eden himself denied this to his friend and one-time prospective biographer. Sir John Wheeler-Bennett. See Wheeler-Bennett (*220*) pp.619–20.

36 *Private Papers.*

37 This arose from the period 1950–1 when Dulles was special representative of the President. The British felt that Dulles had given them certain reassurances but had then misled them. After only a month of Dulles' period as Secretary of State. Bracken wrote to Beaverbrook (11.2.53) that Whitehall was already mourning the departure of Truman and Acheson, and that Dulles was already upsetting many people there. *Beaverbrook Papers.* Box C57.

38 Interview with Walter Judd. *Dulles Papers.*

39 *Private Papers.*

40 Diary 13.11.52. *Private Papers.*

41 Letter. Dulles to Eisenhower. 14.11.52. *Dulles Papers.* Box 60.

42 Eden (*14*) pp.63–4.

43 Interview with Livingston Merchant. *Eisenhower Papers.*

44 Diary 9.12.53. Sulzberger (*51a*) p.781.

45 Diary 27.6.54. *Hagerty Papers.* Box 1.

46 Some of those in the State Department attach great importance to a disagreement between Eden and Dulles on the question of how far Britain should support possible joint intervention on behalf of the French in Indo-China. This occurred in late April 1954, in the run-up to the Geneva Conference. See, for example, interview with Douglas Dillon. *Dulles Papers.* Churchill felt a need to mention to Eisenhower on 26.6.54 that Dulles had said a couple of things to Eden which need not have been said. Eisenhower telephoned Dulles and

said that by purely personal little things, matters could be helped. *Eisenhower Papers*. D.D.E. Diary Series, Box 4. See also diary 26.6.54. Moran (*87*) p.592. It would appear that the April episode did indeed cause severe strains, and in particular anger from Dulles, but these wounds seem to have been patched up during the June 1954 talks. See also diary 16.6.54, Sulzberger (*51a*) p.852.

47 *Dulles Papers*, Box 79. Eden earlier had told Iverach McDonald that during the Bermuda Conference the previous December he had got on very well with Dulles, particularly over talks on the Middle East. 'I came to like him more and more.' Eden said. McDonald (*35*) p.135.

48 Interview with Winthrop Aldrich. *Dulles Papers*.

49 Diary 9.12.53. Sulzberger (*51a*) p.781.

50 Diary 9.12.53. Sulzberger (*51a*) p.781.

51 In addition to being Assistant Secretary for European Affairs, Merchant was senior adviser or delegate at the Bermuda, Berlin, Geneva and London Conferences.

52 Letter. Eden to Bedell Smith, 21.9.54. *Walter B. Smith Papers*, Box 28. There was no evidence of any corresponding antipathy towards the U.S. as a whole in the Foreign Office, though there was no love for certain individuals, in particular Dulles.

53 Chandos (*11*) p.355. The State Department can be justifiably criticised for giving very little thought to what might happen if Britain abrogated her responsibilities to her colonies and left prematurely, as some U.S. officials wanted.

54 Aldrich (interview in *Dulles Papers*) thought the general anti-colonial attitude of the U.S. Government the principal cause of disagreement between both countries.

55 Correspondence with Sir Frank Roberts.

56 Interview with Lord Robens of Woldingham.

57 Sir Leslie Rowan (Head of the Treasury's Overseas Finance Division, 1951–8), Sir Donald Fergusson (Permanent Secretary at Fuel and Power, 1954–52) and Martin Flett (Under-Secretary, Treasury, 1949–56).

58 Acheson, Harriman *et al.* at the Princeton Seminar 15.5.54. *Acheson Papers*. See also Acheson (*1*) p.511.

59 See Chapter 8 Part 2.

60 Churchill appealed in his Congressional address (Cmd. 8468, 1952), for U.S. forces to support British troops in Egypt. See also diary 10.1.52 and 17.1.52, Moran (*87*) pp.386–7 and 391. Churchill saw Eisenhower's election as facilitating 'one last attempt' to persuade U.S. troops to go to Egypt. *Private Papers*.

61 The British felt that American officials responsible for Egypt were more sympathetic to the Egyptian Government than to British interests. Interview with Winthrop Aldrich, *Dulles Papers*. Aldrich isolated an episode that helped foster this belief amongst the British, Dulles' gift of a pistol to General Neguib on behalf of Eisenhower, a trivial incident but for its exaggerated treatment by the British press.

62 The 'Northern Tier' was originally a U.S. idea, which Britain later became eager to join, partly as it provided an opportunity of continuing her alliance with Iraq. Dulles, when he became Secretary of State, did not wish to take part as he felt the U.S. was not in a position to have a standing army in the Middle East. Interview with Loy Henderson, *Dulles Papers*. Eden apparently had a 'great respect and liking' for the American Ambassador to Persia, Loy Henderson. Diary 9.12.53, Sulzberger (*51a*) p.781. A senior British Minister said there was a feeling 'all the time' that the U.S. just wanted Britain to get out of the Middle East, and that they did not care whether or not a vacuum was left.

63 The Foreign Office were surprised by the vehemence of Churchill's dislike of the A.N.Z.U.S. Pact. Eden disliked it also but felt far less strongly than Churchill. The Foreign Office, however, were in the main quite happy for the U.K. not to be in the Pact, feeling that it would have become merely a U.S./U.K. discussion body if Britain were to have joined. Even more important, they feared that if Britain was a member, it would have entailed an obligation to join in any military entanglements occurring in either Indo-China or Taiwan. See interview with Sir Robert Scott, B.O.A.P.A.H. (Scott was Assistant Under-Secretary of State at the Foreign Office responsible for Far Eastern Affairs, 1950–3). See Chapter 9 Part 1.

64 For example, Dulles complained on one

occasion that Churchill and Eden were continually trying to wean Menzies from a friendly close relationship with the U.S. Jim Hagerty's diary 24.6.54, *Hagerty Papers*, Box 1. Official British attempts to get observer status at the Honolulu meeting of the A.N.Z.U.S. Council in 1952, were a failure. Churchill declared in the *House of Commons* on 17.6.53: 'I did not like the A.N.Z.U.S. Pact at all,' Vol. 516, Col. 973.

65 Sir Gladwyn Jebb, for example, thought American policy towards China 'idiotic'; Humphrey Trevelyan (British Chargé d'Affaires in Peking, 1953–5) thought it 'insane'. Diary 17.4.54 and 28.4.54, Sulzberger (*51a*) pp.835 and 841.

66 Letter, Eisenhower to Churchill, 29.3.55. Eisenhower went on to refer specifically to troubles over Formosa, Quemoy and Matsu, the application of the Manila Pact to Laos, and the most recurrent problem of all, the existence of the Chinese Nationalist Government. *Eisenhower Papers*, D.D.E. Diary Series, Box 6.

67 See Chapter 5 Part 3 and Northedge (*217*) pp.179–85.

68 See interview with Lord Sherfield, B.O.A.P.A.H.

69 See Gowing (*192*) Vol. 1, pp.405–421, Pierre (*195*) pp.136–40 and Northedge (*217*) pp.175–9.

70 Letter, Dixon to Sir Ivone Kirkpatrick, 20.8.54, *Dixon Papers*.

71 Interview with Lord Selwyn-Lloyd, D.B.Y.

CHAPTER 10 PART 3 pp.396–409

1 Frankel (*214*) p.199 notes how impressed Churchill was by the explosion of the first Soviet atomic bomb in September 1949, and how in the following year Churchill called for fresh Western diplomatic approaches to the Soviet Union.

2 *House of Commons* 10.12.48, Edinburgh, during the Election campaign, on 14.2.50, *House of Commons* 6.11.51 and 11.5.53.

3 Churchill at the Usher Hall, Edinburgh, 14th February, 1950. David Butler noted how during the course of the 1950 campaign Churchill had implied that the return of a Government headed by himself might lead to a significant reduction in world tension. Butler (*120*) p.119.

4 Stalin was General Secretary of the Soviet Communist Party from 1922, during the war and continued until his death in March 1953.

5 Sir Oliver Harvey, the British Ambassador in Paris, reported this information back to Sir William Strang in a secret letter. Churchill asked to see the record of this correspondence in November 1951. *Private Papers*.

6 U.S. Cabinet Meeting Minutes, 19.10.51, *Matthew J. Connelly Papers*.

7 Paper on Approach and Objectives for Talks for the January 1952 meeting, *Truman Papers*.

8 *House of Commons* 6.11.51, Vol. 493, Col. 79.

9 In February 1953 Emrys Hughes, Victor Yates and ten other Labour M.P.s tabled a motion calling on the Prime Minister to reconsider talks with Stalin. *The Times* 14.2.53.

10 Colville narrates how in the early summer of 1952, Churchill mentioned his intention, if Eisenhower was elected, of attempting to make peace by a meeting of the 'Big Three', Colville (*12*) p.235. He confided to Colville that with Eisenhower at the White House he had every hope of a joint approach to Stalin, proceeding perhaps to a Congress at Vienna, where the Potsdam Conference would be reopened and concluded. Colville in Wheeler-Bennett, ed. (*105*) p.129. Eisenhower's notes after their talk in January 1953 (diary 6.1.53, *Eisenhower Papers*) do not refer to Churchill bringing up the specific topic of summits. Colville says during Churchill's visit there was little reference to Russia made in his talks with the Republicans. Colville (*12*) p.235. Moran in his diary, however, has an entry, the veracity of which I have been unable to confirm. Churchill is talking: 'Dulles lied when he said Ike did not want to do detail: when I saw him six months ago [one assumes at the January 1953 meeting] it was Ike himself who suggested a conference at Stockholm. Of course the Russians may refuse to attend a conference on these terms . . .' Diary 19.7.53, Moran (*87*) p.462.

11 Interview with Lord Soames,

12 Diary 7.3.53, Moran (*87*) p.427.

13 Diary 20.3.53, *Private Papers*.

14 Lord Gladwyn in his memoirs speculates that the more constructive attitude of the

Soviet leader Malenkov might conceivably have been inspired by the ex-Foreign Office diplomats. Donald Maclean and Guy Burgess. who defected to Moscow in 1951. Gladwyn (*18*) p.277.

15 See leader in *The Times* 11.4.53 and Hayter (*22*) pp.105–7. The Minister at the Moscow Embassy from 1954. Cecil Parrott. also talked of a more favourable climate in diplomatic relations following the death of Stalin. Parrott (*43aa*) p.62.

16 Eden returned to London for a few days before going off to an O.E.E.C. Council meeting. *The Times* 26.3.53. While in London he took part in several discussions on the possibility of a fresh advance to the Soviet Union.

17 Churchill was asked by Norman Dodds (Labour M.P.) in *House of Commons* 26.3.53 why he appeared so negative in public about the question of summit talks for which he was once the main advocate. Churchill. however. did not see this as an opportunity for divulging his plans.

18 Interview with Sir Evelyn Shuckburgh.

19 Gascoigne was in London from 1st–9th April. 1953. *The Times* 10.4.53.

20 Eden excelled at one-to-one meetings and greatly liked them. He also had no objection to proposing personal talks to the Soviets himself: at the United Nations in Paris in November 1951 and again in Paris on 20th January. 1952. he had hopes of a private talk with Vyshinsky. though this failed to transpire. *Private Papers*. It would appear that there had been some discussion between Churchill and Eden before the 1951 Election in which they had agreed on the prime need to bridge the gap between East and West. This is apparent from Churchill's words at the close of his speech in *House of Commons* 6.11.51. In *Full Circle* Eden does not mention his initial enthusiasm for a meeting with Molotov after the death of Stalin. and wrote instead: 'I did not share the optimism of those who saw in this event [Stalin's death] an easement of the world's problems.' Eden (*14*) p.49. He was not opposed to the idea of summit meetings *per se*. Merchant noted the irony that Eden was the most resistant to what he regarded as Churchill's folly over summits. but it was Eden who was really responsible for finally changing Eisenhower's attitude to summits in July 1955. Interview with

Livingston Merchant. *Eisenhower Papers*. See also diary 11.5.55. Moran (*87*) p.685.

21 Interview with Sir Frank Roberts.

22 *Private Papers*. For a discussion of Dixon's and Roberts' views on talks with the Soviet Union. see also McDonald (*35*) p.133.

23 Diary 4.7.54. Moran (*87*) p.604. (This is assuming the 'last year' referred to by Moran means April 1953 rather than April 1954. Either date would be possible.)

24 Eden also had a second meeting with Gascoigne on 6th April. *The Times* 8.4.53. Eden's operation was to be on 9th April. but it was delayed three days and he spent the day working at the Foreign Office. See Chapter 10 Part 1.

25 House of Commons. Vol. 514. Col. 650.

26 Colville said he lunched at the Soviet Embassy just once. Correspondence with Sir John Colville.

27 Interview with Lord Soames. See also diary 8.4.54. Moran (*87*) p.568.

28 Interview with Sir William Hayter. Hayter himself was disinclined to believe that there were any changes in basic Soviet policy. although there was a change in method and external appearances. Diary 1.2.54. Sulzberger (*51a*) p.801.

29 *Private Papers*.

30 A source close to Churchill denied any knowledge of Amery's and Boothby's talks. *Private Information*. But the *ad hoc* talks in fact continued right up until Malenkov's fall in February 1955.

31 Reported in *The Times* 27.4.53.

32 Interview with Lord Selwyn-Lloyd. D.B.Y.

33 *House of Commons* 11.5.53. Vol. 515. Col. 897.

34 Interview with Lord Selwyn-Lloyd. D.B.Y.

35 Colville (*12*) p.238 and interview with Sir John Colville.

36 Nutting (*219*) p.50.

37 So Boothby told Dalton. diary 17.6.53. *Dalton Papers*. William Hayter. whose appointment to Moscow had recently been announced. apparently thought the speech 'a disaster'. Diary 15.5.53. Sulzberger (*51a*) p.735. Boothby also told Dalton that the Cabinet was never consulted on foreign affairs. and that Churchill wanted to spend the next three months at the Foreign Office working at the pursuit of summit meetings. and that if Churchill pulled it off he would win the Nobel Peace

Prize. Ironically, Churchill's health (because of his stroke) only allowed him to stay at the Foreign Office another six days.

38 Nutting (*219*) pp.51–2. Winthrop Aldrich, however, was in almost complete agreement with Churchill's speech. Macmillan (*36*) p.511. The State Department gave its first official reaction to the speech on 13th May, saying that they were in complete agreement on the desirability of a high-level conference but felt that timing would be crucial. Reported in *The Times* 14.5.53. On 14th May Eisenhower said in a speech that he had no objection to Churchill's proposal but first wanted to see evidence of good faith before committing the U.S. Government.

39 Macmillan (*36*) p.511.

40 Nutting (*219*) p.51.

41 The Cabinet had discussed the proposed Bermuda trip at noon that very day. Diary 21.5.53. *Crookshank Papers.*

42 Colville (*12*) p.239.

43 Letter, Baruch to Churchill, 24.6.53, *Baruch Papers.*

44 Diary 1.5.55, Moran (*87*) p.666.

45 Nutting (*219*) p.50.

46 Colville (*12*) p.239.

47 *Private Papers.*

48 Labour were furious because they felt that Salisbury in his trip to Washington had damaged the cause of a summit meeting. Desmond Donnelly said it was well known that Salisbury was opposed to the whole concept of Big Four talks. *House of Commons* 22.7.53. Other Labour speakers in the debate said Churchill's initiative had been thrown away.

49 Colville (*12*) p.239.

50 Quoted in diary 21.7.53, Moran (*87*) pp.463–4. This would have been in reply to a message Churchill sent Eisenhower on 17.7.53 in which he asked Eisenhower to consider whether it might not be better for a Four-power meeting to begin as Salisbury urged (or as he assumed Salisbury urged) with a preliminary survey by Heads of Governments of all problem areas in an informal spirit. This, Churchill continued, would be better than coming in after a vast network of detail had been erected. International Files in *Eisenhower Papers.*

51 Not only did such a conference imply a precise agenda, but also it was to be between Foreign Ministers, not Heads of Governments. See Eden (*14*) pp.53–4.

From 15th July until the end of November there followed a long period of tripartite notes between Britain, U.S. and France, and Soviet replies. This phase lasted until the Bermuda Conference in December 1953.

52 Diary 21.7.53, Moran (*87*) p.452.

53 Diary 4.8.53, *Private Papers.*

54 Diary 16.8.53, Moran (*87*) pp.476–8.

55 Apparently Eisenhower told Churchill in May 1952, that if elected President he would pay only one visit outside the U.S., to the U.K. Colville in Wheeler-Bennett, ed. (*105*) p.128. Churchill told Moran this on 9th July (Moran (*87*) p.451) but in his letter of 21st July Eisenhower appeared to rule out this possibility. Aldrich kept the idea alive by passing on to Churchill that Eisenhower might be willing to come to England, and on 3rd August Churchill sent an enthusiastic invitation note, but received a very damp reply on 10th August. Aldrich denied that he expressed any such opinion on Eisenhower's possible movements to Churchill. Memorandum, Aldrich to Eisenhower, 7.8.53, Box 18. International Files, *Eisenhower Papers.*

56 Message, Eisenhower to Churchill, 7.10.53. International Files, Box 18. *Eisenhower Papers.* Diary 10.10.53, Moran (*87*) p.507. Colville in Wheeler-Bennett, ed. (*105*) pp.130–1. Colville (*12*) p.239 and *Private Papers.*

57 Reported in *The Times* 29.9.53.

58 Diary 3.11.53, Moran (*87*) p.515.

59 *Private Papers.*

60 Diary 5.10.53, *Private Papers.*

61 *Eisenhower Papers*, International Files, Box 18. Eden also apparently told C. L. Sulzberger at the Bermuda Conference that it was 'Winston's Conference', and that 'it had no real use.' Diary 9.12.53, Sulzberger (*51a*) p.781.

62 Diary 10.11.53, Moran (*87*) p.525.

63 Diary 6.11.53 and 7.11.53, *Eisenhower Papers*, D.D.E. Diary Series, Box 3.

64 Diary 3.12.53, Sulzberger (*51a*) p.777.

65 See Nutting (*219*) p.60. At the first plenary meeting on 4th December, Churchill discussed the change of heart in the Soviet Union since Stalin. He urged a twofold policy, of strength yet maintaining an open mind towards signs of change in Russia. Russians feared infiltration behind the Iron Curtain more than we, he said, and for this reason the West had nothing to fear

from increasing trade and contact with them. Notes of Bermuda meetings, *Dixon Papers*. Livingston Merchant described Bermuda as a rather claustrophobic conference. with E.D.C. and Germany being the common problem, but the British being preoccupied with Suez and the Middle East, the French with Indo-China, and Eisenhower with atomic matters, which were dealt with mainly in bilateral U.S./U.K. talks, Interview with Livingston Merchant. *Eisenhower Papers*. (On 8th December Eisenhower delivered his 'Atoms for Peace' proposal to the U.N.)

66 See diary 3.12.53, 4.12.53, 5.12.53, 6.12.53, 7.12.53. Moran (*87*) pp.531–6. Macmillan, however, recorded that Churchill was 'much encouraged' by the Russian final agreement to the proposed Foreign Secretaries Conference to be held at Berlin, on which the allies had agreed at Bermuda. Macmillan (*36*) p.528.

67 Churchill said he would not relinquish office until he met Malenkov, though would 'pop over' to the U.S. first to make it all right with them. Diary 8.4.54, Moran (*87*) p.568.

68 The motion was passed unanimously. A month later Churchill said in reply to a Parliamentary Question that his determination to press for a summit meeting was unabated, but it must await the right time. *House of Commons* 11.5.54.

69 Message. Eisenhower to Churchill, 26.4.54, *Eisenhower Papers*, International Files, Box 18.

70 Diary 15.5.54, Moran (*87*) p.576.

71 Diary 2.6.54, Moran (*87*) p.581.

72 Eden (*14*) p.131.

73 Macmillan (*36*) p.530.

74 Macmillan (*36*) p.532.

75 Diary 14.6.54, *Hagerty Papers*, Box 1.

76 Colville (*12*) p.242, and Colville in Wheeler-Bennett, ed. (*105*) p.131.

77 Diary 25.6.54, Moran (*87*) p.589.

78 *Eisenhower Papers*. International Files, Box 18.

79 Diary 27.6.54, *Hagerty Papers*.

80 Diary 29.6.54, *Hagerty Papers*.

81 Ann Whitman diary, 25.6.54, *Eisenhower Papers*, Box 2.

82 Colville (*12*) p.242.

83 Churchill was most anxious for the Declaration to be submitted to Cabinet for their views before it was released. Diary 28.6.54, 29.6.54, *Hagerty Papers*. Crook-

shank narrates how the Cabinet discussed amendments which they wanted to make to the Declaration. Diary 29.6.54.

84 Diary 2.7.54, Moran (*87*) pp.601–2.

85 Moran wrote that Churchill was glad he took Eden's advice and consulted the Cabinet. Diary 4.7.54, Moran (*87*) p.604. Colville records that Eden succeeded in persuading Churchill to send the telegram to the Cabinet for approval, and discusses the row there on 7–8th July. Colville (*12*) p.242. According to Macmillan, Eden agreed on the boat to the message being sent to Molotov, but, 'Owing to some confusion on the ship and to the position not being fully understood in London, the important telegram was sent off without the Cabinet being consulted or informed.' Macmillan (*36*) p.534. The distinct impression given by Crookshank's diary is that the Cabinet had no prior knowledge of the telegram being sent. Diary 7.7.54 and 8.7.54, *Crookshank Papers*. See also Colville in Wheeler-Bennett, ed. (*105*) pp.135–6. Here Colville states that Eden so disliked the proposal of the telegram being sent without the Cabinet being consulted that Churchill finally agreed to send the telegram to the Cabinet provided he could tell them Eden accepted it in principle. Eden in despair agreed. According to correspondence with Sir John Colville Butler then sent the telegram to Moscow with one or two minor amendments.

86 Churchill divulged information about the Soviet reply and the content of his note to Molotov in his speech to *House of Commons* 14.3.55.

87 See Macmillan (*36*) p.535. See also telephone call. Eisenhower to Dulles, 7.7.54, *Eisenhower Papers*, D.D.E. Diary Series, Box 4.

88 Interview with Sir John Colville and Colville (*12*) p.242.

89 See diary 6.8.54, 12.8.54 and 11.5.55, Moran (*87*) pp.620, 621 and 685.

90 *Chandos Papers*, Box 4.6. (This quotation is from a handwritten draft letter, on which the writing is not always clear.)

91 Diary 23.7.54, *Crookshank Papers*.

92 *Woolton Papers*, Box 28, Leaves 235–8.

93 Interview with Sir John Colville, D.B.Y.

94 Macmillan (*36*) p.536.

95 Diary 26.7.54, *Crookshank Papers*.

96 Two days after the Soviet note was received, Churchill sent Molotov a message

on 26th July. He said that he had been on the verge of sending a message suggesting a meeting at a 'halfway house' like Berne, Stockholm or Vienna, but that the Soviet note of 24th July had changed the whole picture, and that the big formal conference proposed in the note had obviously superseded for the time being the small informal meeting he had himself proposed. Molotov replied that he did not agree; that the major set-piece conference had no bearing on the question of a personal visit from Churchill, to which he was not unfriendly. Churchill's reply at the beginning of August repeated that he did not see the personal informal conference as a practical policy as long as there was a large international conference in the offing. Churchill in *House of Commons* 14.3.55 and Macmillan (*36*) pp.537–8. See *House of Commons*, Vol. 538, especially Col. 963.

97 Both his Cabinet colleagues and the Foreign Office managed to convince Churchill that it would not be practicable to have a conference on Europe going on at the same time as Churchill's informal top-level meeting.

98 Diary 12.8.54, Moran (*87*) p.621.

99 In a letter to Baruch in late August 1954 Churchill was still talking of a meeting as a likelihood (letter, Churchill to Baruch, 29.8.54, *Baruch Papers*), as he was to Moran (diary 7.9.54, Moran (*87*) p.628. He was also most anxious lest his bad error in his speech at Woodford on 23rd November (see Chapter 2 Part 1) should damage his standing in Moscow and hence the likelihood of the meeting taking place. Diary 28.11.54 and 29.11.54, Moran (*87*) pp.641–5 and McDonald (*35*) p.140.

100 Labour members, for example, put forward Questions in *House of Commons* 26.10.54 about Churchill's failure to take up the Russians on their willingness to talk. David Butler noted that the Opposition over the last two years of the Government became increasingly impatient in their demand for a high-level meeting. Butler (*121*) pp.7–8.

101 A report in the press on 9th February said that Malenkov had resigned as Prime Minister and would be replaced by Bulganin.

102 Diary 1.3.55, Moran (*87*) p.666.

103 *House of Commons* 14.3.55.

104 See, for example, Churchill's speech in *House of Commons* 3.11.53 and 1.3.55.

105 See Churchill's concluding remarks in his speech, *House of Commons* 11.5.53, Vol. 515, Cols. 897–8.

106 Letter, Churchill to Eisenhower, 18.7.55, *Eisenhower Papers*, International Files, Box 18.

CHAPTER 10 PART 4 pp.409–415

1 McDonald (*35*) p.132.

2 Interview with Sir Evelyn Shuckburgh.

3 For example, at the 1948 Party Conference, Eden had said: 'Our foreign policy should pursue three immediate objectives, which we can call the three unities. First, unity within the British Commonwealth and Empire. Second, unity within Western Europe. Third, unity across the Atlantic.' See Shlaim (*97*) p.91. Frankel (*214*) p.157 says an example of the importance attached by the new Government in 1951 to the notion of three circles was that they instructed diplomatic missions to use it in their publicity. The King's Speech in 1951 envisaged how Britain 'in concert with the other members of the Commonwealth, the United States of America and our European partners, will share in a supreme effort to build a more tranquil and prosperous world'. *House of Commons* 6.11.51, Vol. 493, Col. 50.

4 Interview with Sir Anthony Nutting.

5 McDonald (*35*) p.137.

6 Millar, ed. (*39a*) p.163.

7 Whether the idea of adopting the Brussels Treaty as an alternative to E.D.C. originated with Eden (Eden (*14*) pp.149–51, Macmillan (*36*) p.481) or in the Western European departments of the Foreign Office is immaterial here. Informed opinion has generally agreed that W.E.U. was a far apter and better conceived proposal than E.D.C. See, for example, Wheeler-Bennett (*220*) p.624.

8 Letter, 13.10.54, *Ismay Papers*, Box 111.12.

9 Letter, Eden to Hankey, 25.2.53, *Hankey Papers*, Box 15.11.

10 See Eden (*14*) pp.189–233. On p.219 he records a note of 17.12.54 in which he said Iran was the toughest of all the problems solved in 1954.

11 Sir Ashley Clark (interview) felt that, apart from the outstanding ability of the

officials who conducted the secret discussions in London to reach agreement over Trieste. the successful outcome was in large measure due to the fact that they had behind them a Foreign Secretary who understood the problem and who was prepared to back them up. The main officials working on the problem were Geoffrey Harrison of the Foreign Office (Assistant Under-Secretary. 1951–6) and L. E. Thompson. U.S. Ambassador in Vienna. See Eden (*14*) pp.175–88.

12 *Report of the 74th annual Conference* p.34.

13 Diary 9.1.55. Moran (*87*) p.659. See also 10.7.55. Moran (*87*) p.709.

14 Interview with Lord Soames.

15 This can be seen by a brief glance at Eden (*14*). where Churchill's two main enthusiasms. the special relationship and the pursuit of a summit receive only passing mention.

16 See diary 10.5.54 (p.574). 18.5.54 (p.577) and 2.6.54 (pp.581–2) Moran (*87*).

17 *Report of the 74th Annual Conference* p.118.

18 See also Eden (*14*) pp.104 and 247. and diary 26.6.53 (p.433) and 17.12.53 (p.542) Moran (*87*).

19 See diary 24.6.54. Moran (*87*) p.587. See also Colville in Wheeler-Bennett. ed. (*105*) p.107 and Macmillan (*36*) pp.498–500.

20 See Chapter 2 Part 2.

21 See Lord Normanbrook's contribution to Wheeler-Bennett. ed. (*105*) pp.41–2 for a discussion of Churchill's general interest in international affairs.

22 Eden (*14*) p.247. Eden once told his colleague Charles Mott-Radclyffe. the influential Chairman from 1951 of the Party's Foreign Affairs Committee. that the Sudan problem was worrying him almost more than any other issue since he became Foreign Secretary. Interview with Sir Charles Mott-Radclyffe and also see Mott-Radclyffe (*41*) pp.204–26. Churchill. largely for reasons of sentiment. disliked giving the Sudan independence. fearing that it would fall into Egypt's hands. See diary 8.2.54. Moran (*87*) pp.554–5. Churchill eventually yielded. and told Eden that if he could sell it to the Party. he would back it. Eden. in one of his most impressive speaking performances during the life of the Government. addressed the Foreign Affairs Committee and won over the audience. Interview with Sir Anthony Nutting. There was originally far stronger feeling in the Party about the Sudan than about Egypt. and the group who opposed Eden's policy in the Sudan were the embryonic Suez Group who came to the fore in 1954. led by Charles Waterhouse and supported by men such as Julian Amery and Viscount Hinchingbrooke. Interview with Julian Amery.

23 Note of conversation 6.1.52. *Acheson Papers*. Throughout he wanted to maintain a more unyielding attitude than Eden. See. for example. note of conversation at lunch. Beaverbrook and Churchill. 8.9.52. *Beaverbrook Papers*. Box C89.

24 Lord Strang (interview) thought Egypt the only major issue on which they disagreed.

25 Interview I with Anthony Montague Browne.

26 Letter. Churchill to Eisenhower. 16.4.56. *Eisenhower Papers*. International Files. Box 18.

27 Diary 5.3.53. *Dalton Papers*.

28 Interview with Sir John Colville.

29 Diary 11.10.53. Moran (*87*) p.509. See also diary 9.12.53. Sulzberger (*51a*) p.782.

30 On 2.8.53 Baruch wrote to Churchill to inform him of the effects of the explosion of the U.S. hydrogen bomb at Bikini: '. . . With H. bomb it was total [destruction] for a radius ten times or more than atom B.' He told him that '. . . We would have them in production in 8 months in quantity.' *Baruch Papers*. Churchill would thus appear to have been informed of the effect of the H. bomb at an earlier date than allowed for by Colville. See Colville in Wheeler-Bennett. ed. (*105*) pp.121–2. Churchill had said in the *House of Commons* on 12th July. 1954 (Vol. 530. Col. 34) that he was 'absolutely astounded' by the hydrogen bomb revelations recently made in the U.S.. especially 'considering the immense differences the facts disclosed made to our whole outlook for defence'. See Chapter 8 Part 6.

31 Interview with Sir Anthony Nutting.

32 *Private Information*.

33 Diary 7.3.58. Moran (*87*) p.769.

34 Grigg (*222*) p.769.

35 See. for example. Kilmuir (*31*) pp.186–9. These few pages appear to be almost an afterthought tacked on at the end of a far better reasoned chapter. 'A Gleam in Alsace'. Some excellent material on this

subject. including valuable eye-witness reports, appeared in a series on B.B.C.'s Radio 4. presented by Michael Charlton in the spring of 1981.

36 From a personal Minute. Eden to Churchill. 1.12.51. Quoted in Eden (*14*) pp.33–4. Sulzberger reports Eisenhower and David Bruce as saying that Eden supported the E.D.C. plan. Eden certainly wanted a settlement on the European front. and that is perhaps why Eden gave the Americans the impression he favoured E.D.C. See Diary 13.12.51, Sulzberger (*51a*) pp.614–16.

37 Wheeler-Bennett, ed. (*105*) pp.41 and 98.

38 Eisenhower thought the European Army plan 'absolutely necessary from a military point of view'. But he also disapproved of divisions containing soldiers from different nations. Diary 13.12.51. Sulzberger (*51a*) p.615.

39 Diary 21.12.51, *Eisenhower Papers*.

40 Kilmuir (*31*) p.174. Macmillan (*36*) p.154.

41 See Lord Normanbrook in Wheeler-Bennett, ed. (*105*) p.41.

42 For the views held at the time by Sir William Hayter, typical of the outlook of many of his colleagues, see Hayter (*22*) pp.94–5. (Hayter was Minister at the British Embassy in Paris, 1949–53.) One of the principal Foreign Office sceptics of closer integration with Europe, Sir Roger Makins, explains his views in a B.O.A.-P.A.H. interview (Lord Sherfield).

43 See Kilmuir (*31*) pp.186–7 and Boothby (*7*) pp.83–5.

44 Both Macmillan and Maxwell Fyfe were apt to be wise after the event. See Kilmuir (*31*) pp.186–9 and Macmillan (*36*) pp.461–83. Macmillan after 1951 was the more determined supporter of Europe and at one time seriously considered resigning on the issue. *Private Information*. He wrote two Cabinet memoranda, 'European Integration' of 16.1.52 and 'Future of the Council of Europe', 29.2.52. *Private Papers*.

45 *Private Information*.

46 Both Sandys and Eccles joined the Cabinet towards the end of the Government's life in October 1954. Colville wrote that Churchill was to a considerable extent carried along by Sandys into agreeing to sponsor the European Movement. Wheeler-Bennett, ed. (*105*) p.98. This exaggerates the picture. Sandys was primarily responsible for the success of the United Europe Movement. and he had a close family relationship to Churchill. But the old man was not 'carried along' by him.

47 Boothby has written frequently since about the 'missed opportunity' of the Conservative Government after 1951 in not taking on the leadership of Europe. not the least in the correspondence columns of *The Times*.

48 See Frankel (*214*) pp.43–5.

49 The *Spectator*. 26.10.51. p.525.

50 *Report of the 74th annual Conference*. p.35.

51 House of Commons 12.5.53. Vol. 515. Col. 1062.

52 The *Tribune* 21.5.54.

53 See Chapter 2 Part 2.

EPILOGUE I pp. 416–418

1 See, for example. 'A Student of Politics' in the *Sunday Times*. 9.11.52.

2 The *Sunday Times* 31.1.54. Churchill had said in a statement on 19th January. which passed almost unnoticed except for a few Opposition cheers. that the Government had no intention of departing from the principle that trade unions should. to the fullest extent. be left to manage their own affairs free of Government interference.

3 The *Observer* 8.5.55.

4 This is the *Spectator* article of 26.10.51 referred to at the opening of Chapter 1. Part 3.

EPILOGUE II pp.419–435

1 First published in 1967 (Macmillan). Skidelsky argues that the real issue in interwar domestic politics was not the struggle between supporters of socialism and of capitalism. but between the economic radicals and the economic Conservatives.

2 A discussion of Massingham's writing can be found in Chapter 2 Part 3.

3 The *Observer* 1.8.54.

4 The *Observer* 5.12.54.

5 Diary 25.11.51. Millar. ed. (*39a*) p.61.

6 The *Observer* 6.6.54.

7 The *Observer* 20.6.54.

8 See Chapter 2 Part 1.

9 The *Sunday Times* 6.3.55.

10 Samuel Beer reached the same conclusion in (*112a*) about convergence of policies. He found the welfare state to be a valuable area for examining the continuity theory and concluded that. '. . . Throughout the 1950s Conservative Governments maintained very much the same priorities in social policy that had been established by Labour.'

11 See Tables on pp.499–501.

12 Woolton to Churchill. 28.12.51, *Woolton Papers*. Box 25.

13 For an account of how the War Coalition Government. containing a majority of Conservatives. helped pave the way for the Labour reforms of 1945–51. see Addison (*112*).

14 Macmillan (*36*) p.311.

15 Sir Charles Taylor (Conservative M.P. for Eastbourne. 1935–74) characterised the difference between the pre- and post-war membership of the Party in Parliament by saying that the predominant atmosphere changed from being officers' mess to public school. *Private Correspondence*.

16 A leader in *The Times* on 15.6.54.

17 Waterhouse had been appointed a junior Whip in 1935. From 1941 to 1945 he had been Parliamentary Secretary at the Board of Trade.

18 Assheton was the far abler man. Financial Secretary to the Treasury, 1943–4. he was Party Chairman. 1944–6. In 1951 he became Chairman of the Party's Finance Committee. Created Lord Clitheroe in 1955.

19 Kilmuir (*31*) pp.157–9.

20 See the article by Michael Pinto-Duschinsky on the Central Office in *Political Studies* of 1972. pp.1–16.

21 The distinguished Oxford economist. He had served in Churchill's office. 1940–2. Also close to Cherwell. of whom he wrote a personal memoir. Harrod (*78*).

22 Kilmuir (*31*) p.159. Randolph Churchill had been Conservative M.P. for Preston, 1940–5. In 1951 he had stood at Plymouth, Devonport. and was beaten by Michael Foot.

23 Leader in *The Times* 15.6.54.

24 'A Student of Politics' in the *Sunday Times* 29.6.52. Hugh Massingham in the *Observer* (13.4.52) went further; having said Assheton was the only 'real threat' to Churchill on the backbenches. Massingham continued: '. . . And one could as

soon think of a lamb turning to cannibalism as Mr. Assheton becoming a Conservative Jacobin.' The following year. Massingham wrote of Assheton (the *Observer* 15.2.53): 'No one has greater influence with the rank and file, for ever since he refused office when this Government was formed. he had become keeper of the Party's conscience in times of difficulty and moral stress.'

25 M.P. for Bury (and Radcliffe). 1945–55.

26 Hugh Massingham in the *Observer*. 13.4.52.

27 See Chapter 2 Part 3.

28 For a discussion of this. see also Chapter 2 Part 3.

29 Margach (*127*) p.85.

30 *Private Information*.

31 The *Observer* 28.3.54.

32 *Private Information*.

33 Einzig (*16*) p.280.

34 *Private Information*.

35 The views expressed in interview with Andrew Roth.

36 Interview with Sir Geoffrey Cox.

37 See Chapter 1 Part 2.

38 Interview with Sir Geoffrey Cox.

39 Laski was Professor of Political Science at the University of London. 1926–50.

40 The *Manchester Guardian* 18.10.54.

41 *Private Information*.

42 Diary 28.4.53. Moran (*87*) p.428.

43 See Brittan (*161*) p.195.

44 Following the Government's acceptance of the Fleck Report on coal, and its agreement to the appointment of the socialist, James Bowman. as heir apparent to the N.C.B.. the *Observer* (20.2.55) talked about a 'significant milestone' being passed in the evolution of democratic society. and said that industry had not proved to be (as some predicted under the Conservatives) a 'major battleground' of the class war.

45 *The Times* 11.1.50.

46 A leader in *The Times* on 13.10.53 commenting on the first two years of the Government. The article felt that Labour was regrouping in the autumn of 1953. but during 1954. reports in the newspaper continued to criticise Labour for its inability to be a good Opposition Party. principally due to internal disagreements over German rearmament.

47 A discussion of the Labour Party during 1951–5 will not be found in these pages.

48 McKenzie (228) pp.178–9.
49 Beer (112a) p.318.
50 Beer (112a) p.222. Beer says (p.221) that Bevan could count on a solid core of about a quarter of the Parliamentary Party which when the issue was favourable could be raised to about a half.
51 See article by Sir Edward Boyle in the *Sunday Times*, 12.7.53. The problem of the heavy work-load on M.P.s is also discussed by Herbert Morrison in (133) p.160.
52 See 'A Student of Politics' in the *Sunday Times* 23.11.52.
53 The *Sunday Times* 23.11.52.
54 The M.P. for the Isle of Ely. He had resigned the Conservative Whip in protest at the proposed withdrawal from the Suez base. See Jackson (125) pp.111–12.
55 The *Observer* 28.3.54. The tendency was also, for example, noted by 'A Student of Politics' in the *Sunday Times* 20.12.53. He discussed the inability of Parliament to act as a deliberative body and the fact it was increasingly taken up by Party and personal conflicts. This, he continued, gave increased importance to the Cabinet and to intra-party discussions. Party meetings of backbench Committees may have produced interesting discussion but in fact seldom led to changes of policy. See Chapter 2 Part 3.
56 The most important discussions took place when the senior Minister was in the Lords, as Swinton, when Commonwealth Secretary, Woolton on food matters, 1951–2, and Salisbury when acting Foreign Secretary in 1953. Important and protracted debates took place in the Lords on the Transport Bill in 1953. Morrison (133) p.197.
57 As noted in Chapter 4 Part 5.
58 See for example, Robert Skidelsky's thoughtful contribution to Bogdonor and Skidelsky, ed, (114), pp.168–90.
59 'The Tories' concept of their post-imperial responsibilities rested upon the illusion of power. Once that illusion was shattered [by Suez], little remained of that concept; the way was opened to joining Europe.' Skidelsky in (114) p.189. A far more balanced assessment of the impact of Suez

is to be found in Northedge (217) pp.140–1.
60 Quoted by Wallace in (114) p.207.
61 Cosgrave (221a) pp.98–9. See also Gilmour (117), especially pp.11–21.
62 See the Tables.

EPILOGUE III pp.436–439

1 The London newspapers were on strike when Churchill retired so could not print the appreciation of his last years in office. The press comments that did appear, as in the *Scotsman* (6.4.55) and the *New Statesman* (9.4.55) were complimentary without being highly enthusiastic. *The Economist* did, however, have some high praise for Churchill's last years in power. The memoirs that appeared between his retirement and death tended to be non-committal about Churchill's last period at Number Ten. For example, Chandos (11), Eden (14), Kilmuir (31) and Woolton (55). Press reports when Churchill died in January 1965 commented almost exclusively on his pre-1951 career. The publication of Wheeler-Bennett, ed. (105), intended as a riposte to Moran, went some way to restoring Churchill's post-war reputation. Macmillan's memoirs covering the period, published in 1969, also helped in the same direction. Macmillan mentions that some felt Churchill's last years were barren and that he should have retired in 1945, but expresses his own opinion that the period 1945–55 were amongst the most fruitful of Churchill's life, and that his 'last service' was to set the Western powers in the direction of detente with Russia. Macmillan (36) pp.558–9. But the view that Churchill was not effective in his last years had already begun to creep into the text-books. One of the first to cover the post-war years says that the Government was a highly successful one – but, in contrast, Churchill was handicapped by age and deafness, and an insensitivity to new domestic problems. Medlicott (117b) p.536.
2 Graham Sutherland painted the portrait of Churchill for his eightieth birthday on 30th November, 1954, presented to him by M.P.s. He disliked it and it was later destroyed by his wife, Lady Churchill, a

fact only made public after her death in December 1977. See Soames (*98*) pp.501–4 and Moran (*87*) p.652.

3 Regan says at the end of Act 1 Scene 1 of *King Lear* that her father does 'but slenderly know himself'.

4 *House of Commons* 6.11.51. Vol. 495. Cols. 68–9.

5 Election Address. 16.10.51. Newcastle upon Tyne.

6 *House of Commons* 1.3.55. Vol. 537. Col. 1905.

Bibliography: In Outline

I *PRIMARY SOURCES*

A Official Publications A1 Cmd. Papers
           A2 Parliamentary Debates and
               Papers

B Publications of Political B1 Conservative Party
  Parties   B2 Labour Party
           B3 Other Groups

C Newspapers and Periodicals C1 Dailies
           C2 Weeklies
           C3 Monthlies
           C4 Others

D Unofficial Annuals, Almanacs and Guides

E Private Papers

F Interviews   F1 Interviews conducted by A. F. Seldon
           F2 Interviews from *The Day Before
               Yesterday*
           F3 Interview for the British Oral Archive of
               Political and Administrative History
           F4 Interviews from John Foster Dulles –
               Oral History Project: Princeton
               University
           F5 Interviews from Harry S. Truman – Oral
               History Project, Independence, Missouri
           F6 Interviews from Dwight D. Eisenhower –
               Oral History Project: Abilene, Kansas

G Other Unpublished   G1 Theses
  Sources   G2 Lectures
           G3 Other

H Memoirs

II SECONDARY SOURCES

A Biography

B Monographs   B1 Introduction and Argument
             B2 Prime Minister and Government I
             B3 Prime Minister and Government II
             B4 Administrative Affairs
             B5 Economic Policy I
             B6 Economic Policy II
             B7 Social Policy
             B8 Defence Policy
             B9 Commonwealth and Colonial Policy
            B10 Foreign Policy

C Articles, etc.   C1 Introduction and Argument
             C2 Prime Minister and Government I
             C3 Prime Minister and Government II
             C4 Administrative Affairs
             C5 Economic Policy I
             C6 Economic Policy II
             C7 Social Policy
             C8 Defence Policy
             C9 Commonwealth and Colonial Policy
            C10 Foreign Policy

I PRIMARY SOURCES

A. *Official Publications*
 A1 Command Papers

 A2 Parliamentary Debates and Papers
  Parliamentary Debates, House of Commons, 5th Series, Official Report
  Parliamentary Debates, House of Lords, 5th Series, Official Report
  Parliamentary Papers

B. *Publications of Political Parties*
 B1 Conservative Party
  I Published Material
  a C.P.C. Pamphlets
   'Social Services – Needs and Means' by I. Macleod & E. Powell (C.P.C. No. 115, January 1952)
   'Commonwealth and Empire' by Lord Salisbury (C.P.C. for Commonwealth Council April 1951)
   'Change is our Ally' Ed. by E. Powell & A. Maude (May 1954)
   'The New Conservativism: an Anthology of Postwar Thought' (C.P.C. No. 150, October 1955)

   b Other Pamphlets
     'Manifesto of the Conservative and Unionist Party. General Election 1951'
     'Britain Strong and Free: A Statement of Conservative and Unionist Party
        Policy'
     'United for Peace and Progress: 1955 General Election Manifesto'
     'Three Years Work: Achievements of the Conservative Government'
        (C.R.D. December 1954)
     'Agriculture and Politics' by P. Brembridge and E. Briggs (3rd ed. 1955)

   c Bound Volumes
     Campaign Guide and Supplement, 1951
     The Campaign Guide, 1955
     Notes on Current Politics, 5 Volumes, 1951–55
     Official Report of the 72nd Annual Conference, Scarborough, 1952
     Official Report of the 73rd Annual Conference, Margate, 1953
     Official Report of the 74th Annual Conference, Blackpool, 1954

  II Unpublished Material
     Minutes of Backbench Committee Meetings, 1951–55
     Conservative Party Archives at Newcastle University
     Conservative Party Archives at Conservative Research Dept.

B2 Labour Party
    Reports of Labour Party Annual Conference, 1952–4
    Various other material, including pamphlets and leaflets at Transport House

C. *Newspapers and Periodicals*
  C1 Dailies
     Daily Telegraph   *Daily Express*
     The Times   *Daily Mail*
     Manchester Guardian   *News Chronicle*
     Scotsman

  C2 Weeklies
     The Economist   *Observer*
     New Statesman and Nation *Sunday Times*
     Spectator

  C3 Monthlies – various (referred to under 'Articles')

  C4 Other – various journals (referred to under 'Articles')

D. *Almanacs, Annuals and Guides*
  Annual Abstract of Statistics, 1957
  Annual Register, Vols. 1951–5
  Breviate of Parliamentary Papers 1940–54, by P. & G. Ford
  Commonwealth Relations Office Lists, Vols. 1951–5
  Dod's Parliamentary Companion
  Foreign Office Lists, Vols. 1951–5
  Guide to Papers of British Cabinet Ministers, 1900–51, compiled by C. Hazlehurst
    and C. Woodland
  Imperial Calendar and Civil Service List, Vols. 1951–5
  Modern Britain, 1901–70. Bibliographical Handbook compiled by A. Havighurst
  Public General Acts and Measures, Vols. 1951–5
  Source Book on Conservatism by G. Block (64).

Sources in British Political History, *Vols. I–II*, compiled by C. Cook
The Times House of Commons, 1951 & 1955
Obituaries from *The Times*, Vols. 1951–60, 61–70, 71–75
Whitaker's Almanack. Various editions
Who Was Who 1951–60, 1961–70 and *Who's Who* annually

E. *Private Papers:* amongst others, the following were consulted
ACHESON – Harry S. Truman Library, Independence, Missouri
BEAVERBROOK – House of Lords
BARUCH – University Library, Princeton
CHANDOS – Churchill College, Cambridge
CHERWELL – Nuffield College, Oxford
CONNELLY – Harry S. Truman Library, Independence, Missouri
CROOKSHANK – Bodleian Library, Oxford
DALTON – British Library of Political and Economic Science
DIXON – Private possession
DULLES – University Library, Princeton
EISENHOWER – Dwight D. Eisenhower Library, Abilene, Kansas
HAGERTY – Dwight D. Eisenhower Library, Abilene, Kansas
HANKEY – Churchill College, Cambridge
HORSBRUGH – Churchill College, Cambridge
ISMAY – Liddell Hart Centre for Military Archives, King's College, London
JACKSON – Dwight D. Eisenhower Library, Abilene, Kansas
KILMUIR – Churchill College, Cambridge
LIDDELL HART – Liddell Hart Centre for Military Archives
MONCKTON – Bodleian Library, Oxford
MURRAY – Bodleian Library, Oxford
SELBORNE – Bodleian Library, Oxford
SIMON – Bodleian Library, Oxford
SLESSOR – R.A.F. Museum, Hendon
SMITH – Dwight D. Eisenhower Library, Abilene, Kansas
TRUMAN – Harry S. Truman Library, Independence, Missouri
WOOLTON – Bodleian Library, Oxford

F. *Interviews*
F1 Interviews conducted by Anthony Seldon from 1977–80.
Two hundred and twenty-five interviews. Most of these interviewed have their names in the Acknowledgments.

F2 Interviews for *The Day Before Yesterday* (D.B.Y.). Background interviews conducted in 1970 for Thames Television Programme.

Lord Allan of Kilmahew	Lord Boyle of Handsworth
Lord Chandos	Sir John Colville
Lord Crathorne	Sir Robert Menzies
Sir Anthony Nutting	Lord Orr-Ewing
Lord Poole	Lord Stuart of Findhorn

F3 Interviews for the British Oral Archive of Political and Administrative History (B.O.A.P.A.H.)

Lord Allen of Abbeydale	Sir Charles Cunningham	Sir Cyril Musgrave	Sir Hilton Poynton
			Lord Roberthall
Lord Amory	Sir Goronwy Daniel	Sir Antony Part	Sir Robert Scott

Lord Brooke of Cumnor	Sir George Godber	Sir Arthur Peterson	Lord Shackleton
Lord Butler of Saffron Walden	Lord Harlech	Sir Edward Playfair	Sir John Walley
Lord Carr of Hadley	Lord Inchyra		Sir Richard Way
	Sir Ian Jacob		

F4   Interviews for John Foster Dulles Oral History Project

Sherman Adams	Winthrop W. Aldrich
Stewart Alsop	Andrew H. Berding
David Bruce	Robert R. Bowie
Richard Casey	Walton Butterworth
James B. Conant	General Mark Clark
Dwight D. Eisenhower	Douglas Dillon
Walter Hallstein	Sir Oliver Franks
Loy Henderson	John Hanes, Jr.
Walter Judd	Julius Holmes
Sir Thomas MacDonald	Henry Cabot Lodge
Sir Leslie Munro	Livingston Merchant
Richard M. Nixon	Sir Walter Nash
Admiral Arthur Radford	Roderic O'Connor
Paul-Henri Spaak	Sir Roger Makins
Sir Percy Spencer	

F5   Interviews for the Harry S. Truman Oral History Project

Theodore C. Achilles	J. Wesley Adams
Sir Edmund Hall-Patch	Loy Henderson
Roman L. Horne	Benjamin M. Hulley
Sir Edwin Plowden	Dirk Stikker

F6   Interviews for the Dwight D. Eisenhower Oral History Project

Winthrop Aldrich	George V. Allen
James Hagerty	Robert R. Bowie
Livingston Merchant	Andrew Goodpaster
Loy Henderson	Robert D. Murphy

G. *Other Unpublished Sources*

G1 Theses

DEACON, D.: *Change and the Conservative Party in the Postwar Era*, Ph.D., London

PINTO-DUSCHINSKY, M.: *Constituency Leadership in the Conservative Party, 1945–72*, D. Phil.

G2 Lectures

BOYLE OF HANDSWORTH, Lord: 'Parliament's Views on Responsibility for Education Policy Since 1944': Mays Lecture delivered at Birmingham University, May 1976

POWELL, Sir Richard: Paper on 'Evolution of British Defence Policy 1945–59': delivered at Southampton University, May 1975

G3 Other Unpublished Material

BEICHMANN, A.: *The Conservative Party Research Department* (73) Copy at the C.R.D.

COHEN, P.: *A History of the Conservative and Unionist Party Organisation*, Vol. 2 (64) Copy at the C.R.D.

EMMERSON, Sir Harold: *Masters and Servants*. Copy at the R.I.P.A. Library
FRASER, Lord: *A History of the Conservative Research Department*, private
possession
RAMSDEN, John: *History of the Conservative Research Department*
(published in 1980)

H. *Memoirs*

(*1*)   ACHESON, Dean: *Present at the Creation*, Hamish Hamilton, London,
1970

(*2*)   ADENAUER, Konrad: *Memoirs, 1945–1953*, Weidenfeld and Nicolson,
London, 1966

(*3*)   ATTLEE, C. R.: *As It Happened*, William Heinemann, London, 1954

(*3a*) BAKER, Arthur: *The House is Sitting*, Blandford Press, London, 1958

(*4*)   BARCLAY, Sir Roderick: *Ernest Bevin and the Foreign Office, 1932–1969*,
Latimer, London, 1975

(*4a*) BERKELEY, Humphry: *Crossing the Floor*, George Allen and Unwin,
London, 1972

(*5*)   BEVINS, Reginald: *The Greasy Pole*, Hodder and Stoughton, London,
1965

(*6*)   BLUNDELL, Sir Michael: *So Rough a Wind*, Weidenfeld and Nicolson,
London, 1964

(*7*)   BOOTHBY, Lord: *My Yesterday, Your Tomorrow*, Hutchinson, London,
1962

(*8*)   BOOTHBY, Lord: *Recollections of a Rebel*, Hutchinson, London, 1978

(*8a*) BOYD-CARPENTER, John: *Memoirs*, Sidgwick and Jackson, London,
1980

(*9*)   BROCKWAY, Fenner: *Towards Tomorrow*, Hart-Davis MacGibbon,
London, 1977

(*10*) BUTLER, Lord: *The Art of the Possible*, Hamish Hamilton, London, 1971

(*11*) CHANDOS, Lord: *The Memories of Lord Chandos*, Bodley Head, London,
1962

(*11a*) CITRINE, Lord: *Two Careers*, Hutchinson, London, 1967

(*12*) COLVILLE, Sir John: *Footprints in Time*, Collins, London, 1976

(*13*) DALTON, Hugh: *High Tide and After*, Frederick Muller, London, 1962

(*13a*) DILKS, David, ed.: *The Diaries of Sir Alexander Cadogan, 1938–45*,
Cassell, London, 1971

(*14*) EDEN, Anthony: *The Memoirs of Sir Anthony Eden: Full Circle*, Cassell,
London, 1960

(*15*) EGREMONT, Lord: *Wyndham and Children First*, Macmillan, London,
1968

(*16*) EINZIG, P.: *In the Centre of Things*, Hutchinson, London, 1960

(*17*) EISENHOWER, Dwight D.: *The White House Years: Mandate for Change,
1953–1956*, Heinemann, London, 1963

(*17a*) EVANS, Sir Harold: *Downing Street Diary*, Hodder and Stoughton,
London, 1981

(*18*) GLADWYN, Lord: *Memoirs of Lord Gladwyn*, Weidenfeld and Nicolson,
London, 1972

(*19*) GORE-BOOTH, Paul: *With Great Truth and Respect*, Constable, London,
1974

(*19a*) GOULD, Sir Ronald: *Chalk Up the Memory*, George Philip Alexander,
Birmingham, 1976

(20)   GRIFFITHS, James: *Pages from Memory*, Dent, London, 1969

(21)   GRIMOND, Jo: *Memoirs*, Heinemann, London, 1979

(21a) HAILSHAM, Lord: *The Door Wherein I Went*, Collins, London, 1975

(22)   HAYTER, Sir William: *A Double Life*, Hamish Hamilton, London, 1974

(23)   HILL, Baron: *Both Sides of the Hill*, Heinemann, London, 1964

(24)   HOME, Lord: *The Way the Wind Blows*, Collins, London, 1976

(25)   HORNER, A. L.: *Incorrigible Rebel*, MacGibbon and Kee, London, 1960

(26)   HUNT, Sir David: *On the Spot*, Peter Davies, London, 1975

(26a) HUTCHISON, Sir James: *That Drug Danger*, Standard Press, Montrose, 1977

(27)   ISMAY, Lord: *The Memoirs of General Lord Ismay*, Heinemann, London, 1960

(28)   JAMES, R. R., ed. *'Chips', The Diaries of Sir Henry Channon*, Weidenfeld and Nicolson, London, 1967

(29)   JONES, R. V.: *Most Secret War*, Hamish Hamilton, London, 1978

(30)   KEIR, Thelma Cazalet: *From the Wings*, Bodley Head, London, 1967

(30a) KENT, Sir Harold: *In on the Act: Memoirs of a Lawmaker*, Macmillan, London, 1979

(31)   KILMUIR, Lord: *Political Adventure*, Weidenfeld and Nicolson, London, 1964

(32)   KIPPING, Sir Norman: *Summing Up*, Hutchinson, London, 1972

(33)   KIRKPATRICK, Ivone: *The Inner Circle*, Macmillan, London, 1959

(34)   LONGFORD, Lord: *Five Lives*, Hutchinson, London, 1964

(35)   McDONALD, Iverach: A Man of 'The Times', Hamilton, London, 1976

(36)   MACMILLAN, Harold: *Tides of Fortune, 1945–55*, Macmillan, London, 1969

(37)   MALLABY, Sir George: *From My Level*, Hutchinson, London, 1965

(38)   MALLABY, Sir George: *Each in His Office*, Leo Cooper, London, 1972

(39)   MAUDLING, Reginald: *Memoirs*, Sidgwick and Jackson, London, 1978

(39a) MILLAR, T. B., ed.: *Australian Foreign Minister, The Diaries of R. G. Casey, 1951–60*, Collins, London, 1972

(39aa) MENZIES, Sir Robert: *Afternoon Light*, Cassell, London, 1967

(39b) MONNET, Jean: *Memoirs*, Collins, London, 1978

(39c) MORGAN, Janet, ed.: *The Backbench Diaries of Richard Crossman*, Hamish Hamilton and Cape, London, 1981

(40)   MORRISON, Herbert: *An Autobiography*, Odhams, London, 1960

(41)   MOTT-RADCLYFFE, Sir Charles: *Foreign Body in the Eye*, Leo Cooper, London, 1975

(41a) MUTESA, Sir Edward: *Desecration of My Kingdom*, Constable, London, 1967

(42)   NABARRO, Sir Gerald: *NAB 1: Portrait of a Politician*, Maxwell, London, 1969

(43)   NICOLSON, Nigel, ed.: *Harold Nicolson: The Diaries and Letters, 1945–62*, Collins, London, 1968

(43a) NKRUMAH, Kwame: *Autobiography*, Thomas Nelson and Sons, Edinburgh, 1957

(43aa) PARROTT, Cecil: *The Serpent and the Nightingale*, Faber and Faber, London, 1977

(43b) PEARSON, Lester: *Memoirs 1948–57*, Victor Gollancz, London, 1974

(43c) ROBERTSON, Sir James: *Transition in Africa*, C. Hurst, London, 1974

(44) SALTER, James Arthur: *Memoirs of a Public Servant*, Faber and Faber, London, 1961
(45) SALTER, James Arthur: *Slave of the Lamp*, Weidenfeld and Nicolson, London, 1967
(46) SELWYN-LLOYD, Lord: *Suez 1956*, Cape, London, 1978
(47) SHINWELL, E.: *Conflict Without Malice*, Odhams, London, 1955
(48) SLESSOR, Sir John: *These Remain*, Michael Joseph, London, 1969
(49) SMYTH, Sir John: *Only Enemy*, Hutchinson, London, 1959
(50) STRANG, Lord: *Home and Abroad*, André Deutsch, London, 1956
(51) STUART, Lord: *Within the Fringe*, Bodley Head, London, 1967
(51a) SULZBERGER, C. L.: *A Long Row of Candles, Memoirs and Diaries 1934–54*, Macdonald and Co. Ltd., London, 1969
(52) SWINTON, Lord: *Sixty Years of Power*, Hutchinson, London, 1966
(52a) TEELING, Sir William: *Corridors of Frustration*, Johnson, London, 1970
(53) TRUMAN, Harry S.: *Memoirs, II: Years of Trial and Hope*, New American Library of World Literature, New York, 1965
(54) WELENSKY, Sir Roy: *Welensky's 4000 Days*, Collins, London, 1964
(55) WOOLTON, Lord: *Memoirs*, Cassell, London, 1959

II SECONDARY SOURCES

A. BIOGRAPHY

(56) ALLEN, W. Gore: *The Reluctant Politician: Derick Heathcoat Amory*, Christopher Johnson, London, 1958
(56a) AMERY, Julian: *Joseph Chamberlain and the Tariff Reform Campaign*, Macmillan, London, 1969
(57) ASTER, Sidney: *Eden*, Weidenfeld and Nicolson, London, 1976
(58) BARDENS, D.: *Churchill in Parliament*, Hale, London, 1967
(58a) BATES, Darrell: *A Gust of Plumes, A Biography of Lord Twining*, Hodder and Stoughton, London, 1972
(59) BIRKENHEAD, Lord: *The Prof in Two Worlds*, Collins, 1961
(60) BIRKENHEAD, Lord: *Life of Viscount Monckton of Brenchley*, Weidenfeld and Nicolson, London, 1969
(61) BRESLER, Fenton: *Lord Goddard*, Harrap, London, 1977
(61a) BOYD, Francis: *Richard Austen Butler*, Rockliff, London, 1956
(62) BOYLE, Andrew: *Poor Dear Brendan*, Hutchinson, London, 1974
(63) BROAD, Lewis: *Winston Churchill* (revised ed.), Hutchinson, London, 1956
(64) CAMPBELL-JOHNSON, Alan: *Sir Anthony Eden*, Robert Hale, London, 1955
(65) CARVER, Michael: *Harding of Petherton*, Weidenfeld and Nicolson, London, 1978
(66) CHURCHILL, Randolph: *The Rise and Fall of Sir Anthony Eden*, MacGibbon and Kee, London, 1959
(67) CLARK, R. W.: *Tizard*, Methuen and Company, London, 1965
(68) COOTE, Sir Colin: *A Companion of Honour: The Story of Walter Elliot*, Collins, London, 1965
(69) DICKIE, John: *The Uncommon Commoner: A Study in Sir Alec Douglas-Home*, Pall Mall Press, London, 1964
(70) DIXON, Piers: *Double Diploma*, Hutchinson, London, 1968

(71) DONOUGHUE. B. and JONES. G. W.: *Herbert Morrison.* Weidenfeld and Nicolson. London. 1973

(72) DOUGLAS-HOME. Charles: *Evelyn Baring.* Collins, London. 1978

(73) EADE. C.. ed.: *Churchill by his Contemporaries,* Hutchinson. London. 1953

(74) FISHER. Nigel: *Iain Macleod.* André Deutsch. London. 1973

(75) FOOT. Michael: *Aneurin Bevan, II, 1945–60.* MacGibbon and Kee. London. 1973

(75a) GOPAL. S.: *Jawaharlal Nehru, Volume 2, 1947–56.* Jonathan Cape. London. 1979

(76) GRETTON. Peter: *Former Naval Person.* Cassell and Company. London. 1968

(77) HARRIS. Ralph: *Politics Without Prejudice: A Political Appreciation of the Right Hon. Richard Austen Butler.* Staples Press. London. 1956

(78) HARROD. Roy: *The Prof: A Personal Memoir of Lord Cherwell.* Macmillan. London. 1959

(79) HUGHES. Emrys: *Sir Alec Douglas-Home.* Housman's Publishers. London. 1964

(80) HUGHES. Emrys: *Macmillan: Portrait of a Politician.* George Allen and Unwin. London. 1962

(81) HUTCHINSON. George: *Edward Heath: A Personal and Political Biography.* Longmans. London. 1970

(82) JONES. R. V.: *W. L. S. Churchill,* in Biog. Memoirs of F.R.S.. Vol. 12. London. 1966

(83) JEFFRIES. Sir Charles: *'O.E.G.' A Biography of Sir Oliver E. Goonetilleke,* Pall Mall Press. London. 1969

(83a) JENKINS. Robert: *Tony Benn,* Writers and Readers Publishing Cooperative. London. 1980

(84) LEWIN. Ronald: *Slim, the Standardbearer: a biography of Field Marshal the Viscount Slim,* Cooper. London. 1976

(85) LYSAGHT. C. E.: *Brendan Bracken,* Allen Lane. London. 1979

(85a) MACDONALD. Malcolm: *Titans and Others,* Collins, London. 1972

(86) McLELLAN. David: *Dean Acheson,* Dodd. Mead and Company. New York. 1976

(87) MORAN. Lord: *Winston Churchill: The Struggle for Survival, 1940–65.* Sphere Books (paperback edition). London. 1968

(88) NICOLSON. Nigel: *Alex: The Life of Field Marshal Earl Alexander of Tunis.* Weidenfeld and Nicolson. London. 1973

(88a) AN OBSERVER APPRECIATION: *Churchill by his Contemporaries.* Hodder and Stoughton. London. 1965

(89) OLIPHANT. Sir Mark and PENNEY. Lord: *J. D. Cockroft,* in Biog. Memoirs of F.R.S. Vol. 14. London. 1968

(90) PELLING. Henry: *Winston Churchill,* Macmillan. London. 1974

(91) REES-MOGG. William: *Sir Anthony Eden,* Rockliff, London. 1956

(92) RICHARDS. Denis: *Portal of Hungerford,* Heinemann. London. 1977

(93) ROSKILL. Stephen: *Hankey, Man of Secrets,* Vol. III, Collins, London. 1974

(94) ROTH. Andrew: *Enoch Powell.* Macdonald and Company. London. 1970

(95) ROTH. Andrew: *Heath and the Heathmen,* Routledge and Kegan Paul. London. 1972

(96)   SAMPSON, Anthony: *Macmillan: A Study in Ambiguity*, Allen Lane, London, 1967
(97)   SHLAIM, Avi etc.: *British Foreign Secretaries since 1945*, David and Charles, Newton Abbot, 1977
(98)   SOAMES, Mary: *Clementine Churchill*, Cassell, London, 1979
(99)   SPARROW, Gerald: *'R.A.B.' Study of a Statesman*, Odhams, London, 1965
(100) TAYLOR, A. J. P.: *Beaverbrook*, Hamish Hamilton, London, 1972
(101) TERRAINE, John: *The Life and Times of Lord Mountbatten*, Hutchinson, London, 1968
(102) TODD, Lord: *5th Marquess of Salisbury*, in Biog. Memoirs of F.R.S. Vol. 19. London, 1973
(103) WHEELER-BENNETT, John W.: *King George VI*, Macmillan, London, 1958
(104) WHEELER-BENNETT, John W.: *John Anderson, Viscount Waverley*, Macmillan, London, 1962
(105) WHEELER-BENNETT, John W., ed.: *Action this Day, Working with Churchill*, Macmillan, London, 1968
(106) WILLIAMS, Philip: *Hugh Gaitskell*, Cape, London, 1979
(107) WILSON, Charles H.: *A Man and His Times: A Memoir of Sir Ellis Hunter*, Newman Neame, London, 1962
(108) WINGATE, Sir Ronald: *Lord Ismay*, Hutchinson, London, 1970
(109) WINNIFRITH, Sir John: *E. E. Bridges*, in Biog. Memoirs of F.R.S. Vol. 16. London, 1970
(110) YOUNG, Kenneth: *Churchill and Beaverbrook*, Eyre and Spottiswoode, London, 1966
(111) YOUNG, Kenneth: *Sir Alec Douglas-Home*, Dent, London, 1970

B. *MONOGRAPHS*

B1 INTRODUCTION AND ARGUMENT

(112)   ADDISON, Paul: *The Road to 1945*, Cape, London, 1975
(112a) BEER, S. H.: *Modern British Politics*, Faber and Faber, London, 1965
(112b) BOYD, Francis: *British Politics in Transition, 1945–63*, Pall Mall Press, London and Dunmow, 1964
(113)   BLAKE, Robert: *The Conservative Party from Peel to Churchill*, Eyre and Spottiswoode, London, 1970
(114)   BOGDANOR, V. and SKIDELSKY, R., eds.: *The Age of Affluence, 1951–1964*, Macmillan, London, 1970
(115)   BUTLER, Lord, ed.: *The Conservatives, A History from their Origins to 1965*, Allen and Unwin, London, 1977
(115a) COOK, C. and SKED, A.: *Post-War Britain*, Penguin, London, 1979
(115b) CHILDS, David: *Britain Since 1945*, Ernest Benn Ltd., London, 1979
(115c) COLERAINE, Lord: *For Conservatives Only*, Tom Stacey Ltd., London, 1970
(116)   GAMBLE, A.: *The Conservative Nation*, Routledge and Kegan Paul, London, 1974
(117)   GILMOUR, Ian: *Inside Right*, Hutchinson, London, 1977
(117a) L'ETANG, Hugh: *The Pathology of Leadership*, William Heinemann Medical Books Ltd., London, 1969
(117b) MEDLICOTT, W. N.: *Contemporary England, 1914–64*, Longmans, London, 1967

(118) THOMPSON, Alan, ed.: *The Day Before Yesterday*, Sidgwick and Jackson, 1971

B2 PRIME MINISTER AND GOVERNMENT I
(118a) BARTLETT, C. J.: *A History of Postwar Britain, 1945–74*, Longman, London, 1977
(119) BERRINGTON, Hugh: *Backbench Opinion in the House of Commons, 1945–55*, Pergamon, Oxford, 1973
(119a) BOYD-BARRETT, Oliver, SEYMOUR-URE, Colin and TUNSTALL, Jeremy: *Studies on the Press*, H.M.S.O., London, 1977
(120) BUTLER, D. E.: *British General Election of 1951*, Macmillan, London, 1952
(121) BUTLER, D. E.: *British General Election of 1955*, Macmillan, London, 1955
(122) BUTT, R.: *Power of Parliament*, Constable, London, 1967
(122a) EVANS, Harold, *Downing Street Diary*, Hodder and Stoughton, London, 1981
(123) GOODHART, P.: *The 1922*, Macmillan, London, 1973
(124) HOFFMAN, J. D.: *Conservative Party in Opposition, 1945–51*, MacGibbon and Kee, London, 1964
(125) JACKSON, Robert J.: *Rebels and Whips*, Macmillan, London, 1968
(126) JAMES, Robert Rhodes, ed.: *Complete Speeches of Sir Winston Churchill, Vol. VIII, 1950–1963*, Chelsea House Publishers in association with R. R. Bowles, London, 1974
(126a) KING, Anthony and SLOMAN, Anne: *Westminster and Beyond*, Macmillan, London, 1973
(127) MARGACH, J.: *The Abuse of Power*, W. H. Allen, London, 1978
(127a) MARGACH, J.: *The Anatomy of Power: An Enquiry into the Personality of Leadership*, W. H. Allen, London, 1979
(128) OGILVY-WEBB, M.: *The Government Explains*, Royal Institute of Public Administration, London, 1965
(128a) SEYMOUR-URE, Colin: *The Press, Politics and the Public*, Methuen, London, 1968
(128b) TUNSTALL, Jeremy: *The Westminster Lobby Correspondents*, Routledge and Kegan Paul, London, 1970
(128c) WHALE, John: *Journalism and Government*, Macmillan, London, 1972

B3 PRIME MINISTER AND GOVERNMENT II
(129) DAALDER, H.: *Cabinet Reform in Britain, 1914–1963*, Oxford University Press, London, 1964
(130) GORDON WALKER, P.: *The Cabinet*, Cape, London, 1970
(131) JENNINGS, Sir W. Ivor: *Cabinet Government* (3rd ed.), University Press, Cambridge, 1959
(132) MACKINTOSH, John: *British Cabinet* (2nd ed.), Stevens and Sons, London, 1968
(133) MORRISON, H.: *Government and Parliament*, Oxford University Press, London, 1954
(134) PUNNETT, R. M.: *Front-Bench Opposition*, Heinemann, London, 1973
(135) THORNHILL, W., ed.: *Modernisation of British Government*, Pitman, London, 1975

B4 ADMINISTRATIVE AFFAIRS
(*136*)   BRIGGS, Lord: *The History of Broadcasting in the United Kingdom, IV: Sound and Vision*, Oxford University Press, Oxford, 1979
(*136a*) BRITAIN: *An Official Handbook*, H.M.S.O., London, 1956
(*137*)   BRITTAIN, Sir Herbert: *The British Budgetary System*, Allen and Unwin, London, 1959
(*138*)   CHESTER, D. N. and WILLSON, F. M. G.: *The Organisation of British Central Government, 1914–1956*, Royal Institute of Public Administration, London, 1957
(*139*)   DOUGLAS BROWN, R.: *Battle of Crichel Down*, Bodley Head, London, 1955
(*140*)   ECKSTEIN, H.: *Pressure Group Politics*, George Allen and Unwin, London, 1960
(*141*)   KELLAS, James G.: *The Scottish Political System*, University Press, Cambridge 2nd. ed. 1975
(*142*)   LEE. J. M.: *Reviewing the Machinery of Government, 1942–1952: An Essay on the Anderson Committee and its Successors*, 1977
(*143*)   MACKENZIE, J. M. W. and GROVE J. W.: *Central Administration*, Longmans, London, 1973
(*143a*) MONCK, Bosworth: *How the Civil Service Works*, Phoenix House, London, 1952
(*144*)   PHILIP, Alan Butt: *The Welsh Question*, University of Wales Press, Cardiff, 1975
(*145*)   POTTINGER, George: *The Secretaries of State for Scotland, 1926–76*, Scottish Academic Press, Edinburgh, 1979
(*146*)   ROBERTSON, James H.: *Reform of British Central Government*, Chatto and Windus, London, 1971
(*147*)   WILSON, H. H.: *Pressure Group*, Secker and Warburg, London, 1961

NEW WHITEHALL SERIES:
(*148*)   *Home Office* – Sir Frank Newsam, George Allen and Unwin, London, 1954
(*149*)   *Foreign Office* – Lord Strang, George Allen and Unwin, London, 1955
(*150*)   *Colonial Office* – Sir Charles Jeffries, George Allen and Unwin, London, 1956
(*151*)   *Ministry of Works* – Sir Harold Emmerson, George Allen and Unwin, London, 1956
(*152*)   *Scottish Office* – Sir David Milne, George Allen and Unwin, London, 1957
(*153*)   *Ministry of Pensions and National Insurance* – Sir Geoffrey King, George Allen and Unwin, London, 1958
(*154*)   *Ministry of Transport and Civial Aviation* – Sir Gilmour Jenkins, George Allen and Unwin, London, 1959
(*155*)   *Ministry of Labour and National Service* – Sir Godfrey Ince, George Allen and Unwin, London, 1960
(*156*)   *Ministry of Agriculture, Fisheries and Food* – Sir John Winnifrith, George Allen and Unwin, London, 1962
(*157*)   *Treasury* – Lord Bridges, George Allen and Unwin, London, 1964
(*158a*) *Ministry of Housing and Local Government* – Dame Evelyn Sharp, George Allen and Unwin, London, 1969
(*158b*) *Central Office of Information* – Sir Fife Clark, George Allen and Unwin, London, 1970

(*158c*) *Department of Education and Science* – Sir Wiliam Pile, George Allen and Unwin, London, 1979

B5 ECONOMIC POLICY I
(*159*) BEER, S. H.: *Treasury Control* (2nd ed.), Clarendon Press, Oxford, 1957
(*160*) BLANK, S.: *Industry and Government in Britain*, Saxon House, Farnborough, 1973
(*161*) BRITTAN, Samuel: *Steering the Economy*, Penguin, London, 2nd ed., 1971
(*162*) BURN, D.: *The Steel Industry, 1939–1959*, University Press, Cambridge, 1961
(*162a*) CHESTER, Sir Norman: *The Nationalisation of British Industry, 1945–51*, H.M.S.O., London, 1975
(*163*) DOW, J.: *The Management of the British Economy, 1945–60*, University Press, Cambridge, 1970
(*163a*) GARDNER, R. N.: *Sterling-Dollar Diplomacy*, Oxford University Press, London, 1956
(*164*) HARRIS, N.: *Competition and the Corporate Society*, Methuen, London, 1972
(*165*) KEELING, B. and WRIGHT, A.: *The Development of the Modern British Steel Industry*, Longmans, London, 1965
(*166*) KELF-COHEN, R.: *Nationalisation in Britain*, Macmillan, London, 1958
(*167*) KENEN, P. B.: *British Monetary Policy and the Balance of Payments in 1951–57*, Harvard University Press, Cambridge, Mass., 1960
(*168*) McCRONE, G.: *Regional Policy in Britain*, Longmans, London, 1964
(*169*) MACRAE, Norman: *Sunshades in October*, George Allen and Unwin, London, 1963
(*169a*) MORGAN, D. J.: *The Official History of Colonial Development, Volume 3*, Macmillan, London, 1980
(*170*) PEACOCK, A. and WISEMAN, J.: *The Growth of Public Expenditure in the U.K.*, Oxford University Press, London, 1961
(*171*) ROSS, G.: *The Nationalisation of Steel*, MacGibbon and Kee, London, 1965
(*172*) SHONFIELD, A.: *British Economic Policy Since the War*, Penguin, Harmondsworth, 1958
(*173*) THOMSON, A. W. J. and HUNTER, L. C.: *The Nationalized Transport Industries*, Heinemann, London, 1973
(*174*) VAIZEY, J.: *The History of British Steel*, Weidenfeld and Nicolson, London, 1974
(*175*) WORSWICK, G. D. N. and ADY, P. H.: *The British Economy in the Nineteen-Fifties*, Clarendon Press, Oxford, 1962

B6 ECONOMIC POLICY II
(*176*) ALLEN, V. L.: *Trade Union Leadership*, Longmans, Green and Company, London, 1957
(*177*) ALLEN, V. L.: *Trade Unions and Government*, Longmans, London, 1960
(*177a*) BARNES, Denis and REID, Eileen: *Governments and Trade Unions, The British Experience 1964–79*, Heinemann Educational Books, London, 1980
(*178*) DORFMAN, G.: *Wage Politics in Britain, 1945–1967*, Charles Knight and Company, London, 1974
(*179*) GWILLIAM, K. M.: *Transport and Public Policy*, George Allen and Unwin, London, 1964

(*180*) PELLING, H.: *A History of British Trade Unionism*, Penguin,
Harmondsworth, 1963

(*180a*) ROBSON, W. A.: *Nationalised Industry and Public Ownership*, Allen and
Unwin, London, 1960

(*181*) SELF, P. and STORING, H. J.: *The State and the Farmer*, George Allen and
Unwin, London, 1962

(*181a*) WATKINSON, Viscount: *Blueprint for Industrial Survival*, George Allen
and Unwin, London, 1976

B7 SOCIAL POLICY

(*182*) DENT, H. C.: *The Educational System of England and Wales*, University of
London Press, London, 1961

(*183*) GEORGE, V.: *Social Security: Beveridge and After*, Routledge and Kegan
Paul, London, 1968

(*184*) GREGG, P.: *The Welfare State: An Economic and Social History of Great
Britain from 1945*, Harrap, London, 1967

(*185*) HALL, M. Penelope: *The Social Services of Modern England* (4th ed.),
Routledge and Kegan Paul, London, 1959

(*186*) KOGAN, M.: *The Politics of Education*, Penguin, Harmondsworth, 1971

(*187*) MARWICK, Arthur J. B.: *Britain in the Century of Total War, 1900–67*,
Bodley Head, London, 1968

(*188*) SMITH, Brian Abel, and TITMUSS, R. M.: *The Cost of the National Health
Service in England and Wales*, University Press, Cambridge, 1956

(*189*) SMITH, William Owen Lester: *Education in Great Britain* (5th ed.), Oxford
University Press, London, 1965

B8 DEFENCE POLICY

(*190*) BARTLETT, C. J.: *The Long Retreat: A Short History of British Defence
Policy, 1945–70*, Macmillan, London, 1972

(*191*) DARBY, P. P.: *British Defence Policy East of Suez, 1947–1968*, Oxford
University Press, London, 1973

(*191a*) DEAN, Sir Maurice: *The Royal Air Force and two World Wars*, Cassell,
London, 1979

(*192*) GOWING, M.: *Independence and Deterrence, Vols. I and II*, Macmillan,
London, 1974

(*193*) GROOM, A. J. R.: *British Thinking About Nuclear Weapons*, Frances
Pinter, London, 1974

(*194*) JOHNSON, Franklyn: *Defence by Committee*, Oxford University Press,
London, 1960

(*194a*) JOHNSON, Franklyn: *Defence by Ministry, The British Ministry of Defence,
1944–74*, Duckworth, London, 1980

(*195*) PIERRE, A. J.: *Nuclear Politics: The British Experience, 1939–70*, Oxford
University Press, London, 1972

(*196*) ROSECRANCE, R. N.: *Defence of the Realm: British Strategy in the
Nuclear Epoch*, Columbia University Press, London and New York, 1968

(*197*) SLESSOR, Sir John: *Strategy for the West*, Cassell and Company, London,
1954

(*198*) SNYDER, W. P.: *The Politics of British Defence Policy, 1945–1962*, Ernest
Benn, London, 1965

B9 COMMONWEALTH AND COLONIAL POLICY

(198a) ALLEN, Charles, ed.: *Tales from the Dark Continent*, André Deutsch and B.B.C., London, 1979

(199) BLAKE, Robert: *A History of Rhodesia*, Eyre Methuen, London, 1977

(200) COHEN, Sir Andrew: *British Policy in Changing Africa*, Routledge and Kegan Paul, London, 1959

(201) CROSS, John A.: *Whitehall and the Commonwealth*, Routledge and Kegan Paul, London, 1967

(201a) GANN, L. H. and DUIGNAN, P., eds.: *Colonialism in Africa, 1870–1960*, *Vol. 2*, Cambridge University Press, London, 1970

(201b) GANN, L. H. and DUIGNAN, P., eds.: *African Proconsuls, European Governors in Africa*, Collier, Macmillan, London, 1978

(202) GARNER, Joe: *The Commonwealth Office, 1925–68*, Heinemann, London, 1978

(203) GOLDSWORTHY, David: *Colonial Issues in British Politics, 1945–61*, Clarendon Press, Oxford, 1971

(204) GORDON WALKER, P.: *The Commonwealth*, Secker and Warburg, 1962

(204a) HATCH, John: *A History of Post-War Africa*, André Deutsch, London, 1965

(205) JEFFRIES, Sir Charles: *Transfer of Power*, Pall Mall Press, London, 1960

(205a) KIRK-GREENE, A. H. M., ed.: *The Transfer of Power*, University of Oxford, Inter-Faculty Committee for African Studies, Oxford, 1979

(205b) LEE, J. M.: *Colonial Development and Good Government*, Oxford University Press, London, 1967

(205c) LISTOWEL, Judith: *The Making of Tanganyika*, Chatto and Windus, London, 1968

(206) MANSERGH, Nicholas: *The Commonwealth Experience*, Weidenfeld and Nicolson, London, 1969

(207) MANSERGH, Nicholas: *Survey of British Commonwealth Affairs 1939–52*, Oxford University Press, London, 1958

(208) MANSERGH, Nicholas: *Documents and Speeches on Commonwealth Affairs 1952–62*, Oxford University Press, London, 1963

(209) MILLER, John D. B.: *The Commonwealth in the World*, Gerald Duckworth and Company, London, 1958

(210) MILLER, John D. B.: *Britain and the Old Dominions*, Johns Hopkins Press, Baltimore, 1966

(210a) MILLER, J. D. B.: *Sir Winston Churchill and the Commonwealth of Nations*, University of Queensland Press, Australia, 1967

(210b) MORGAN, D. J.: *Official History of Colonial Development, Vol. 5*, Macmillan, London, 1980

(211) PERHAM, Dame Margery: *Colonial Sequence, 1949–1969*, Methuen and Company, London, 1970

(212) RENDELL, Sir William: *The History of the Commonwealth Development Corporation, 1948–1972*, Heinemann, London, 1976

(212a) TAYLOR, Don: *The Years of Challenge, The Commonwealth and the British Empire, 1945–59*, Robert Hale, London, 1959

B10 FOREIGN POLICY

(213) ACHESON, Dean: *Sketches from Life, of Men I Have Known* (New York and London), Hamish Hamilton, London, 1961

(214) FRANKEL, J.: *British Foreign Policy, 1945–1973*, Oxford University Press, London, 1975

(215) McDERMOTT, Geoffrey: *The Eden Legacy and Decline of British Diplomacy*, Frewin, London, 1969

(216) MANDERSON-JONES, R. B.: *The Special Relationship: Anglo-American Relations and Western European Unity 1947–56*, Weidenfeld and Nicolson, London, 1972

(217) NORTHEDGE, F. S.: *Descent from Power*, George Allen and Unwin, London, 1974

(218) NUTTING, Sir Anthony: *Disarmament*, Oxford University Press, London, 1959

(219) NUTTING, Sir Anthony: *Europe Will Not Wait*, Hollis and Carter, London, 1960

(220) WHEELER-BENNETT, Sir John (with Anthony Nicholls): *Semblance of Peace*, Macmillan, London, 1974

C. *ARTICLES*

C1 INTRODUCTION AND ARGUMENT

(221) COSGRAVE, Patrick: 'The Failure of the Conservative Party 1945–75', in the *Future That Doesn't Work*: ed. R. Emmett Tyrrell, Jr., Doubleday and Company Inc., New York, 1977

(222) GRIGG, John: 'Churchill, Troubled Giant' (*Encounter*: April 1977)

(222a) WALLER, Ian: 'The "Lobby" and Beyond' (*Encounter*: June 1965).

C2 PRIME MINISTER AND GOVERNMENT I

(223) BIRCH, A. H., etc.: 'The Popular Press in the British General Election of 1955' (*P.S.*, 4: 1956)

(224) CLARK, T. Fife: 'Do we need Government Information Services?' (*Pub. Admin.* 35: 1957)

(225) JONES, C. O.: 'Inter-Party Competition in Britain 1950–59' (*Parl. Aff.*, 17; 1963–64)

(226) LIPSON, L.: 'Common Ground and Emerging Conflicts Between the British Parties' (*P.Q.*, 27: 1956)

(227) McKENZIE, R. T.: 'Power in British Parties' (B.J.S., 6: 1955)

(228) McKENZIE, R. T.: 'Policy Decision in Opposition: A Rejoinder' (*P.S.*, 5: 1957)

(229) PARLIAMENTARY AFFAIRS: 'The Trade Unions and Parliament' (*Parl. Aff.*, 9: 1955–56).

(230) PINTO-DUSCHINSKY, M.: 'Central Office and "Power" in the Conservative Party' (*P.S.*, 20: 1972)

(231) POTTER, A.: 'British Pressure Groups' (*Parl. Aff.*, 9: 1955–56).

(232) POWELL, J. E.: '1951–59, Labour in Opposition' (*P.Q.*, 30: 1959).

(233) PUNNETT, R. M.: 'The House of Lords and Conservative Governments 1951–64' (*P.S.*, 13: 1965)

(234) SCAMMON, R. M.: 'British By-Elections, 1951–55' (*J. of P.*, 18:1956)

(235) SPECIAL NO.: 'The Conservative Party' (*P.Q.*, 24: 1953)

(236) WILLIAMS, F.: 'The Office of Public Relations Adviser to the Prime Minister' (*Parl. Aff.*, 9: 1955–56)

C3 PRIME MINISTER AND GOVERNMENT II

(237) HEASMAN, D. J.: 'Parliamentary Paths to High Office' (*Parl. Aff.*, 15: 1961–62)

(*238*) MILNE. R. S.: 'The Experiment with "Coordinating Ministers" in the British Cabinet 1951–53' (C.J.E.P.S.. 1955)

C4 ADMINISTRATIVE QUESTIONS

(*239*) BURNS. J. H.: 'The Scottish Committees of the House of Commons. 1948–59' (*P.S.*. 8: 1960)

(*240*) CHESTER. D. N.: 'The Crichel Down Case' (*Pub. Admin.*. 32: 1954)

(*241*) HAMSON. C. J.: 'The Real Lesson of Crichel Down' (*Pub. Admin.*. 32: 1954)

(*242*) HARRISON. W.: 'The British Constitution in 1953' (*Parl. Aff.*. 7: 1953–54)

(*243*) HARRISON. W.: 'The British Constitution in 1954' (*Parl. Aff.*. 8: 1954–55)

(*244*) HARRISON. W.: 'The British Constitution in 1955' (*Parl. Aff.*. 9: 1955–56)

(*245*) HELSBY, L. N.: 'Recruitment to the Civil Service' (*P.Q.*, 25: 1954)

(*246*) HEWISON. R. J. P.: 'The Organisation of the Cabinet Secretariat' (*Pub. Admin.*, 30: 1952)

(*247*) HOLLIS. C.: 'The British Constitution in 1952' (*Parl. Aff.*, 6: 1952–53).

(*248*) KEIR. D. Lindsay: 'The British Constitution in 1951' (*Parl. Aff.*. 5: 1951–52)

(*249*) KILMUIR. Lord: 'The Office of Lord Chancellor' (*Parl. Aff.*. 9: 1955–56)

(*250*) MACKENZIE. W. J. M.: 'Pressure Groups in British Government' (*B.J.S.*. 6: 1955)

(*251*) MACKENZIE. W. J. M.: 'The Royal Commission on the Civil Service' (*P.Q.*. 27: 1956)

(*252*) RANDALL. P. J.: 'Wales in the Structure of Central Government' (*Pub. Admin.*. 50: 1972)

(*253*) SHAWCROSS. Sir H.: 'The Office of the Attorney-General' (*Parl. Aff.*. 7: 1953–54)

(*254*) WHEARE. K. C.: 'Crichel Down Revisited' (*P.S.*. 23. 1975)

C5 ECONOMIC POLICY I

(*255*) ABEL. D.: 'British Conservatives and State Ownership' (*J. of P.*. 19: 1957)

(*256*) BEER. S. H.: 'Treasury Control: The Coordination of Financial Policy in Great Britain' (*A.P.S.R.*. 49: 1955)

(*257*) BRIDGES. E. E.: 'Treasury Control' (*The Stamp Memorial Lecture*: 2nd ed. 1956)

(*258*) BRIDGES. E. E.: 'The Treasury as the Most Political of Departments' (*Pollak Lecture*. Harvard. 1961)

(*259*) CHESTER. D. N.: 'The Treasury. 1956' (*Pub. Admin.* 35: 1957)

(*260*) CHESTER. D. N.: 'The Select Committee on the Nationalised Industries' (*Pub. Admin.*. 34: 1956)

(*261*) DAVIES. E.: 'Government Policy and the Public Corporation' (*P.Q.*. 26: 1955)

(*262*) FINER. S. E.: 'The Federation of British Industries' (*P.S.*. 4: 1956)

(*263*) FINER. S. E.: 'Treasury Control' (*P.S.*, 5: 1957)

(*264*) GRUNFELD. C.: 'The Transport Act' (*P.Q.*, 25: 1954)

(*265*) HANSON. A. H.: 'Parliamentary Control of Nationalised Industries' (*Parl. Aff.*. 11: 1957–58)

(*266*) HANSON. A. H.: 'Electricity Reviewed: The Herbert Report' (*Pub. Admin.*. 34: 1956)

(*266a*) LITTLE. I. M. D.: 'The Economist in Whitehall' (*Lloyds Bank Review*, April 1957)

(*267*) MacDOUGALL. Sir Donald: 'The Machinery of Economic Government:

Some Personal Reflections' (in ed. David E. Butler and A. H. Halsey: *Policy and Politics* 1978)

(267a) MacDOUGALL, Sir Donald and HUTT, R.: 'Imperial Defence: A Quantitative Analysis' (*E.J.*, 66: 1956)

(268) MARRIS, R. L.: 'The Position of Economics, and Economists in the Government Machine' (*E.J.*, 64: 1954)

(269) MATTHEWS, R. C. O.: 'Why has Britain had full Employment since the War?' (*E.J.*, 78: 1968)

(270) MILNE, R. S.: 'Britain's Economic Planning Machinery' (*A.P.S.R.*, 46: 1952)

(271) MOORE, B. and RHODES, J.: 'Evaluating the Effects of British Regional Economic Policy' (*E.J.*, 83: 1973)

(272) PUBLIC ADMINISTRATION: 'Denationalisation of Iron and Steel' (*Pub. Admin.*, 31: 1953)

(273) PUBLIC ADMINISTRATION: 'The Transport Act, 1953' (*Pub. Admin.*, 31: 1953)

(274) RICHARDSON, J. J.: 'The Making of the Restrictive Trade Practices Act, 1956' (*Parl. Aff.*, 20: 1966–67)

(275) ROBERTS, C. A.: 'The N.C.B. and The Fleck Report' (*Pub. Admin.*, 35: 1957)

(276) ROBERTS, R. D. V. and SALLIS, H.: 'Joint Consultation in the Electricity Supply Industry, 1945–59' (*Pub. Admin.*, 37: 1959)

(277) TREND, B. S.: 'The Formation of Economic and Financial Policy, Great Britain' (*I.S.S.B.*, 8: 1956)

(277a) WISEMAN, J. and YAMEY, B.: 'The Raw Cotton Commission, 1948–52' (*Oxf. Econ. Papers*, 1956)

(278) WOODS, Sir John: 'Treasury Control' (*P.Q.*, 25: 1954).

C6 ECONOMIC POLICY II

(279) CLEGG, H. A.: 'The Fleck Report' (*Pub. Admin.*, 33: 1955).

(280) CLEGG, H. A.: 'Strikes' (*P.Q.*, 27: 1956)

(281) HALLETT, G.: 'The Economic Position of British Agriculture' (*E.J.*, 69: 1959)

(282) HAMPDEN, F. C.: 'The Organisation of the Ministry of Transport and Civil Aviation' (*Pub. Admin.*, 33: 1955)

(283) PENNOCK, J. R.: 'The Political Power of British Agriculture' (*P.S.*, 7: 1959)

(284) SELF, P. and STORING, H.: 'The Farmers and the State' (*P.Q.*, 29: 1958)

(285) WHETHAM, E. H.: 'A Record of Agricultural Policy, 1947–52, 1952–54, 1954–56' (*Occasional Papers*, Cambridge University Department of Agriculture)

C7 SOCIAL POLICY

(286) CHESTER, T. E.: 'The Guillebaud Report' (*Pub. Admin.*, 34: 1956)

(287) ECKSTEIN, H.: 'The Politics of the B.M.A.' (*P.Q.*, 26: 1955)

(288) MADDICK, Henry: 'Local Government: Reorganisation or Reform (*P.Q.*, 25: 1954)

(289) MURPHY, L. R.: 'Rebuilding Britain: The Government's Role in Housing and Town Planning 1945–57' (*Historian*, 1970)

(290) WISEMAN, H. V.: 'Parliament and the University Grants Committee' (*Pub. Admin.*, 34: 1956)

(291) WRIGHT. H. M.: 'The First Ten Years: Postwar Planning and Development in England' (*Town Planning Review*. 26: 1955–56)

C8 DEFENCE POLICY

(292) BEST. R. Darcy: 'The United Kingdom Atomic Energy Authority' (*Pub. Admin.*. 34: 1956).

(293) GOLDBERG. A.: 'The Minatory Origins of British Nuclear Deterrent' (*I.A.*. 40: 1964)

(294) GOLDBERG. A.: 'The Atomic Origins of the British Nuclear Deterrent' (*I.A.*. 40: 1964)

(295) GOTT. R.: 'The Evolution of the Independent British Deterrent' (*I.A.*. 39: 1963)

(296) HUMPHREY-DAVIES. B.: 'Internal Administrative Services in the Air Ministry' (*Pub. Admin.*. 33: 1955)

(297) SLESSOR, Sir John: 'Air Power and the Future of War' (*J.R.U.S.I.*, 99: 1954)

(298) WILLSON. F. M. G.: 'Defence Organisation – 1958 Style' (*Pub. Admin.*. 36: 1958)

C9 COMMONWEALTH AND COLONIAL POLICY

(299) TIERNEY. James: 'Britain and the Commonwealth: Attitudes in Parliament and Press in the United Kingdom since 1951' (*P.S.*. 6: 1958)

C10 FOREIGN POLICY

(300) EDEN. A.: 'Britain in World Strategy' (*F.A.*. 29: 1950–51)

Index

651